If only we could learn to preach like P solid reality in Dennis Johnson's wo Jesus Christ in the twenty-first cen first. Under Johnson's tutelage, preac redemptive-historical, missiological sermons that are grace driven becomes a dream within reach.

Bryan Chapell
President and Professor of Practical Theology
Covenant Theological Seminary
Author, *Christ-Centered Preaching: Redeeming the Expository Sermon*

Him We Proclaim is a masterful work that should help preachers to understand the necessary interplay between hermeneutics and homiletics that results from a comprehensive biblical theology and a deep commitment to preaching the Word of God. This book holds the promise of the recovery of biblical preaching for those who will give themselves to the demanding and glorious task of setting each text within the context of God's redemptive plan. This is a book that belongs on every preacher's bookshelf.

R. Albert Mohler, Jr.
President
The Southern Baptist Theological Seminary

Him We Proclaim is by far the most comprehensive study of what the Bible says about preaching. Through a very wide-angle lens, Johnson is able to show that none of the popular theories of preaching says everything that should be said; but each has some insights and can be seen as an aspect of the biblical picture. The book also gives a clear and full account of the hermeneutical questions that preachers must deal with. Johnson's arguments are cogent, his evaluations sound. If I could have only one book on preaching, this would be the one.

John M. Frame
J. D. Trimble Chair of Systematic Theology and Philosophy
Reformed Theological Seminary, Orlando

Every once in a while, a book comes along that is truly worth reading, and Dennis Johnson's meaty volume, *Him We Proclaim*, is one of them. Although this work is indeed about preaching, it is no mere homiletics manual, for Johnson provides rich exegetical fare and incisive theological reflection in an understandable, literate style.

In an area where considerable disagreement exists, the author's commitments are clear, but he refuses to be drawn to extreme positions, and his irenic treatment of competing views can only affect the discussion in a positive way. Even those who may not be fully persuaded by Johnson's arguments will be deeply grateful by what they have learned.

Moisés Silva
Formerly Professor of New Testament
Westminster Theological Seminary
Gordon-Conwell Theological Seminary

Dennis Johnson has written a magnificent book that magnifies Christ in all of Scripture. Every preacher and teacher of the Scriptures should read this gem of a book.

Johnson convincingly explains and defends the thesis that Christ should be proclaimed from all of Scripture. But he also illustrates with specific examples what it looks like to proclaim Christ in both the Old Testament and the New Testament.

This book is exegetically faithful, theologically profound, and practically helpful. I wish I had read a book like this when I started my theological education thirty years ago.

Thomas R. Schreiner
James Buchanan Harrison Professor of
New Testament Interpretation
The Southern Baptist Theological Seminary

Apostolic hermeneutics? Dare we read the Scripture backward as well as forward? Dennis Johnson's answer is a marvelously informed, and convincing "yes!" Yes, we can read and interpret and teach as the apostles did. *Him We Proclaim* is sure to be widely read and discussed both in the academy and by groups of serious-minded preachers of the Word. Sure to become a staple in the homiletical discussion of the twenty-first century.

R. Kent Hughes
Senior Pastor Emeritus
College Church, Wheaton, Illinois

This book is dedicated to the memory of Edmund Clowney, who inspired many of us to find and preach Christ in all the Scriptures. Clowney was a brilliant practitioner of Christocentric preaching. The question for the rest of us is how to do it well. In a wide-ranging discussion, Dennis Johnson brings his deep knowledge of the Bible and hermeneutics together with his experience and teaching of preaching to reflect on just this question.

One need not agree with all his arguments or assumptions to appreciate the value and importance of what Johnson offers as the fruit of years of wise reflection and practice. The first part of his work defends the whole enterprise of Christological interpretation and preaching in the light of issues in present-day biblical scholarship and homiletical debates. Not content simply to theorize, he provides extended expositions of apostolic preaching and teaching, samples of Christological readings of OT and NT passages, and an appendix proposing basic procedures for moving from text to Christological proclamation.

There is much, then, to stimulate thought and to give practical help in this major contribution. Not the least part of that contribution is Johnson's persuasive argument that preaching that makes Christ its primary focus should at the same time be preaching that addresses the needs of its hearers in their particular cultural setting.

Andrew T. Lincoln
Portland Professor of New Testament
University of Gloucestershire

This is an important book, a timely book much in need of being written and one that will be read with the greatest profit. This is especially so for those who, committed to a redemptive- or covenant-historical reading of the Bible, recognize and seek to honor and proclaim as its central theme, Old Testament as well New, Christ in his person and work as the consummate revelation of the triune God.

This magnum opus, written out of the author's many years' experience of wrestling with and teaching seminarians how to preach Christ from all of Scripture, is at the same time as much a book about sound biblical interpretation. His key contention is "that the apostolic preachers through whom God gave us the New Testament normatively define not only the content that twenty-first century preachers are to proclaim, but also the hermeneutic method by which we interpret the Scriptures and the homiletic method by which we communicate God's message to our contemporaries."

This dual hermeneutical-homiletic program is articulated at considerable length and worked out with many examples, always with an eye to the ultimate goal of preaching. In particular, concerning the use of the Old Testament in the New, about which currently among evangelicals there is considerable confusion or uncertainty that threatens, however inadvertently but nonetheless inevitably, to obscure the clarity of the Bible and undermine its full authority as God's word, Johnson takes us a good distance along the only constructive way forward. For this we are greatly in his debt.

Richard B. Gaffin Jr.
Charles Krahe Professor of Biblical and Systematic Theology
Westminster Theological Seminary, Philadelphia

DENNIS E. JOHNSON

Him We Proclaim

PREACHING CHRIST FROM ALL THE SCRIPTURES

P&R PUBLISHING

P.O. BOX 817 • PHILLIPSBURG • NEW JERSEY 08865-0817

In Memory of
Edmund Prosper Clowney
(1917–2005)
Pastor, Preacher, Professor, Leader, Mentor,
Who showed us what it means to

Preach Christ from All the Scriptures,
To Marvel at the Savior's Grace,
To Love His Church

Contents

Abbreviations

AB	Anchor Bible
BD	Bauer, Arndt, Danker, *Greek-English Lexicon*
dej	Dennis E. Johnson (author's translation)
ESV	English Standard Version
ET	English translation
HNTC	Harper's New Testament Commentaries
JETS	*Journal of the Evangelical Theological Society*
LXX	Septuagint
NAC	New American Commentary
NASB	New American Standard Bible
NIGTC	New International Greek Testament Commentary
NIV	New International Version
NKJV	New King James Version
NT	New Testament
OT	Old Testament
SNTS	Society for New Testament Studies
TNTC	Tyndale New Testament Commentary
WBC	Word Biblical Commentary
WCF	Westminster Confession of Faith
WLC	Westminster Larger Catechism
WSC	Westminster Shorter Catechism
WTJ	*Westminster Theological Journal*

Preface

This book has been over thirty years in the making. In the summer of 1970, my wife, Jane, and I drove from California to Philadelphia for one purpose: I would take a year or two of courses in Bible, theology, and apologetics at Westminster Theological Seminary before applying to grad school and becoming a college English professor—or so I thought. It is no understatement to say I did not know what I was getting us into. I knew that Westminster was Reformed in its theology and presuppositional in its apologetics, and I had an inkling of what these terms meant.

What I did not appreciate until I arrived—entering the Reformed community as I did from the broader evangelical "neighborhood"—was Westminster's way of reading Scripture as a single Story with a single Hero. Without ignoring the obvious fact that the Bible contains many stories, spanning thousands of years, with many participants, my professors in biblical studies patiently pointed out that the individual stories were threads woven into the pattern of a single tapestry: the Big Story of the Creator-King whose inscrutable wisdom, justice, and love devised and enacted a unified, multifaceted plan to redeem, reconcile, reconquer, and recreate his rebel creatures, transforming them into his trusting children, his glad and grateful servants, his beautiful bride. And Edmund Clowney, Westminster's president and professor of practical theology, challenged, coaxed, coached, and critiqued us as we made our first feeble, stumbling efforts to preach the wonder of this Story and the glories of its Hero, Jesus.

For me this holistic way of reading Scripture (which is not unique to Westminster or to its Reformed heritage, as we will see) was like finding a hidden treasure that had been waiting for an unsuspecting plowman to unearth it. I still enjoyed English literature, but I could

xiv   Preface

not bring myself to cut short my study of the Story for the sake of devoting my time and strength to other stories, poems, and essays, however beautiful and true they might be. Needless to say, my path led not to graduate school in English literature and a college classroom but to pulpits in New Jersey and California, where I tried to learn, as I am still learning, to preach "the whole counsel of God" (Acts 20:27), which is to say, to preach "nothing . . . except Christ, and him crucified" (1 Cor. 2:2).

By the mid-1980s, I was teaching New Testament at Westminster's "daughter" institution, Westminster Seminary California. Dr. Jay Adams, then director of advanced studies, asked me to teach an intensive Doctor of Ministry course on "apostolic hermeneutics for preaching" to accompany and complement a series of modular courses in which Dr. Clowney challenged, coaxed, and coached experienced pastors to preach Christ from all the Scriptures—Genesis through Revelation. Twice a year, Dr. Clowney would fly to California to take a group of shepherds on a week-long, whirlwind tour of Christ in the Pentateuch, or Christ in Psalms, or Christ in the Wisdom Literature, or Christ in the Prophets, or Christ in the Gospels, or Christ in the Epistles of Paul. These classes, usually taught in the morning hours, were heady trips; and one pastor, at least, was touched so profoundly by the glory of Christ radiating from the Bible's every page that he proposed to his fellow leaders that their church be renamed, from a nondescript reference to its locale to "*Christ* Community Church." Although these D.Min. students were mature men who had received their basic pastoral preparation in a variety of theological venues and had subsequently preached the Word for some time, some found the claim that the entire Bible, in all its diversity of eras, circumstances, authors, and genres, focuses on a single theme—on Christ, the divine agent of creation and the divine and human mediator of redemption—unfamiliar and somewhat suspect. They wondered whether this hermeneutic, built on the assumption that all redemptive history and the whole Bible were designed to drive hearts toward Jesus, might obscure important distinctions or open the door to unbridled subjectivism and wild allegorical imagination, untethered to the specifics of the biblical text. It was not that they heard such flights of fancy from Dr. Clowney; but where, they wondered, were the "guardrails" to keep evangelical preaching "on the straight and narrow" and away from "drop offs" of medieval allegory or postmodern reader-response subjectivism?

That was where my afternoon course came in. As one charged to teach New Testament interpretation, my task was to help my fellow pastors see "the sub-structure of New Testament theology," as C. H. Dodd aptly characterized the convictions that found expression in the apostles' appeals to the Old Testament Scriptures as fulfilled in Jesus the Messiah.[1] Frankly, while admitting that this approach meant "swimming against the current" of the guild of academic biblical scholarship—both critical and evangelical, I tried to defend the revolutionary, somewhat countercultural concept of "reading the Bible like Peter and Paul."[2] After all, Jesus was *their* instructor in biblical hermeneutics, and as evangelicals we confess that his Holy Spirit breathed out through these original witnesses his own divine, flawless testimony in the New Testament Scriptures. If loyalty to Jesus entails eager submission of our thoughts to the *theology* revealed in these apostolic writings, should we not also learn from them our *way of reading* Scripture? I have no way of gauging the influence of those courses on the preaching of all the pastors who passed through our D.Min. program, but the assignment to define and defend what *hermeneutically responsible*, Christ-centered preaching entails certainly did me good, drawing me further along a path that I had begun to follow a decade and a half earlier.

Over the last decade, two further surprising twists of providence have contributed to the writing of this book. First, in 1997 I was invited to redirect the focus of my study and instruction from the New Testament to homiletics. I gather that in some institutions such a shift of focus would be akin to leaping the Grand Canyon; but happily at the school in which I serve, the boundaries between biblical studies, theology, and the practice of ministry, although clear, are not so high or wide as to be impassable. Despite the diversity of our academic specialties, it is my privilege to serve on a team of pastors, preachers, and practical theologians, each of whom cares deeply about the communication of Christ's gospel and the growth and health of his church. (Colleagues on the faculty of Westminster

---

1 C. H. Dodd, *According to the Scriptures: The Sub-structure of New Testament Theology* (London: Nisbet, 1952).

2 The title of an unpublished essay distributed to Westminster Seminary California's D.Min. students in those years, much of which has found its way into this book.

Seminary California have contributed to this book by their careful reading and critique, by their example as preachers of the Word, and through hallway and lunch table conversations too numerous to recount—thank you, brothers!)

Second, not long after my reassignment to practical theology, the congregation on whose session of elders I serve needed my services as interim pastor for a period of twenty months. To my ordinary seminary responsibilities, this assignment added the privilege of opening the Word almost weekly to the family of God with whom our lives have been interwoven for over two decades and precipitated a profound awareness of my need for prayer. If my memories of the weekly pains and joys of sermon preparation had faded since 1982, when I was called from the pulpit to the seminary lectern, the Lord had designed for me a remarkably effective "refresher course" on the realities of pastoral life in the trenches!

Although the thoughts offered below have been "brewing" slowly for over three decades, the prospect of publishing them is of more recent vintage. Preliminary discussions with P&R Publishing Company's editorial director several years ago were encouraging, but other duties delayed my completion of the project. My hope had been to present this work to Dr. Clowney, whose example and instruction had been so instrumental in opening my eyes to Scripture's multifaceted witness to Christ, for his loving and no doubt rigorous critique. God's timing, however, was different and better than mine. While some of these chapters were beginning to take their present shape, in March 2005, the Christ whom Ed preached and served for a lifetime called him home to heaven. Although *Him We Proclaim* would no doubt have been a better book had it passed under Dr. Clowney's editorial and theological scrutiny, it is offered to readers in his memory, with the prayer that it will encourage you to read the Bible with the apostles and, if you are called, to preach it as they did.

Acknowledgements

As I explain in the preface, this book has been brewing for decades. It would be futile to attempt to trace the influence of all who have contributed to it in some way and to give credit in all the places that credit is due, but I do wish to thank some whose influence and help must not go unrecognized.

I am thankful to pastors who participated in Westminster Seminary California's Doctor of Ministry program in preaching, whose pulpit experience and pastoral wisdom sharpened my thinking regarding the full-orbed nature of Christ-centered preaching as practiced by the apostles. I also thank recent classes of Master of Divinity students whose insightful questions have helped focus the book's argument and whose sharp eyes have caught many typos before the typescript reached the editors.

I thank my faculty colleagues at Westminster Seminary California, who have read portions of the typescript and made suggestions that have improved the book.

Thanks to Allan Fisher, former director of publications of P&R Publishing, who first expressed interest in an essay that would grow into *Him We Proclaim*; to P&R's president, Bryce Craig, and Marvin Padgett, P&R's present editorial director, who eventually welcomed the finished product with enthusiasm; and to Eric Anest, P&R's associate director of editorial, who guided it through the editorial process with both dispatch and accuracy.

Special thanks to John J. Hughes, president of Bits & Bytes, Inc., who has brought to this project not only his editorial expertise and knowledge of biblical studies but also his love for the Christ-centered, redemptive-historical exposition of Scripture, as he and I together learned it from Edmund Clowney and others in the classrooms of Westminster Theological Seminary in the 1970s.

I also thank Stephen Fix, soon to graduate from Westminster Seminary California, for conscientiously checking the accuracy of biblical references and of citations from the English Standard Version.

Finally, I thank my bride of almost thirty-seven years, Jane: loving encourager, precise proofreader, incisive editor, and the loveliest "Grammy" I know.

1

Introduction
Preaching the Bible Like Peter and Paul

Now when they heard this they were cut to the heart, and said to Peter and the rest of the apostles, "Brothers, what shall we do?" And Peter said to them, "Repent and be baptized every one of you in the name of Jesus Christ for the forgiveness of your sins, and you will receive the gift of the Holy Spirit . . . ." So those who received his word were baptized, and there were added that day about three thousand souls. (Acts 2:37–38, 41)[1]

And Paul went in [to the synagogue], as was his custom, and on three Sabbath days he reasoned with them from the Scriptures, explaining and proving that it was necessary for the Christ to suffer and to rise from the dead, and saying, "This Jesus, whom I proclaim to you, is the Christ." And some of them were persuaded and joined Paul and Silas, as did a great many of the devout Greeks and not a few of the leading women. (Acts 17:2–4)

What preacher can read passages like these and not long to be able to preach the Bible like Peter and Paul? What an inestimable privilege to see God's almighty Holy Spirit change people's lives before your eyes through the message of the cross and resurrection of Jesus! We read the biblical accounts of sermons that gave spiritual birth to thousands and similar stories from the later history of the church, and we long for God to move in such power and mercy in our time and through us.

We are aware that the early record reports apparent defeat as well as glowing victories: "Now when they heard these things they

---

1   Unless otherwise noted, Scripture citations are from the English Standard Version—ESV (Wheaton, IL: Crossway, 2001). Citations marked "dej" are the author's translation.

were enraged, and they ground their teeth at him [Stephen]" (Acts 7:54). "Now when they heard of the resurrection of the dead, some mocked. But others said, 'We will hear you again about this.' So Paul went out from their midst. But some men joined him and believed, among whom also were Dionysius the Areopagite and a woman named Damaris and others with them" (Acts 17:32–34).

We know that it is ours simply to plant and to water and that God alone can give growth and fruitfulness to the seed of his Word (1 Cor. 3:6; Col. 1:5–6; Acts 6:7). In our best moments, therefore, it is not merely the bountiful results of apostolic preaching that we seek but the apostles' rich insights into Scripture's multifaceted witness to the person and work of Christ. We long to preach "the *whole* Bible as *Christian* Scripture," that is, to preach "*Christ* in *all* of Scripture."[2] Perhaps we have heard such preaching done well and found our hearts stirred and surprised to behold the glory of the Savior in a text where we least expected to meet him, or we have heard such preaching attempted badly (even, perhaps, by ourselves) and come away feeling that the text itself was abused or ignored and its connection to Christ drawn in strained and implausible ways. You may even wonder whether it is legitimate to learn biblical hermeneutics and homiletics from the apostolic exemplars of the New Testament, because their inspiration by the Spirit of God gave them privileged access to revelatory resources not available to ordinary Christians and preachers.

Yet, the apostolic affirmation rings true: in Christ "are hidden all the treasures of wisdom and knowledge" (Col. 2:3). Therefore, the apostolic resolve makes perfect sense: "I decided to know nothing among you except Jesus Christ and him crucified" (1 Cor. 2:2). Whatever our biblical text and theme, if we want to impart God's life-giving wisdom in its exposition, we can do nothing other than proclaim Christ, "the power of God and the wisdom of God . . . our righteousness and sanctification and redemption" (1 Cor. 1:24, 30).

But how? This book tries to answer that question, first by arguing in favor of reuniting insights and disciplines the apostles displayed in harmonious unity but that sadly have become disconnected since

---

2   Graeme Goldsworthy, *Preaching the Whole Bible as Christian Scripture: The Application of Bible Theology to Expository Preaching* (Grand Rapids: Eerdmans, 2000); Edmund P. Clowney, *Preaching Christ in All of Scripture* (Wheaton: Crossway, 2003). Emphases added.

then. Then it suggests perspectives and strategies to help ordinary Christians discover their Savior throughout Scripture and to equip ordinary preachers to proclaim this Savior convincingly and powerfully from the diverse panorama of Scripture's genres and eras.

Tragic Divorces

"What therefore God has joined together, let not man separate" (Mark 10:9). Jesus was speaking, of course, of the inviolable union of husband and wife in marriage as designed by God. Nevertheless, these words can be applied aptly to the major thrust of this book, which makes a case for imitating the interpretive and communicative methods employed by the apostles to proclaim Christ to the first-century Greco-Roman world as we minister in the twenty-first century. It advocates reuniting things wrongly separated between the apostles' day and ours to the impoverishment of biblical hermeneutics and pastoral homiletics. Reforging these divinely established bonds will refocus biblical interpretation on Christ, the center of gravity who holds the Bible together and the key who unlocks Scripture's meaning from Genesis to Revelation. Furthermore, the three reunions we will advocate will empower the proclamation of the gospel in a global postmodern culture that increasingly resembles the pluralism and relativism of the first-century Hellenistic environment into which the apostles first announced God's good news.[3]

---

3 Postmodernity and postmodernism are notoriously slippery concepts. Generally speaking, postmodernism perceives itself as a reaction against the Enlightenment's confidence in reason and it harbors deep suspicion toward any and all claims to be able to articulate absolute and universal truth or to provide a culture-transcending "metanarrative." "In *The Condition of Postmodernity*, [David] Harvey observes that modernity rejected tradition and religious authority but held on to the hope that reason alone would lead us to truth. Postmoderns have given up on the illusion that reason alone will lead us to truth, but they have not recovered tradition and authority. Instead, they courageously celebrate and play amid our limitations and finitude, in a sort of cheerful nihilism" (Craig G. Bartholomew, "Postmodernity and Biblical Interpretation," in Kevin J. Vanhoozer, gen. ed., *Dictionary for Theological Interpretation of the Bible* [Grand Rapids: Baker, 2005], 601). Bartholomew also cites J.-F. Lyotard's definition of postmodernity as "incredulity towards metanarratives" (Ibid., citing J.-F. Lyotard, *The Postmodern Condition* [Minneapolis: University of Minnesota Press, 1984], xxiv). As in the religious and philosophical pluralism of the ancient Greco-Roman world, so also today increasing exposure to diverse cultures, each confident of its own metanarrative, fosters postmodern thinkers' skepticism toward claims of objectivity or

To testify faithfully and effectively about Jesus the Christ in the twenty-first century, as the apostles did in the first, we need to reconcile three divorced "couples" whose "marriages" were made in heaven: we need to reunite *Old* Testament and *New* Testament, apostolic *doctrine* and apostolic *hermeneutics*, biblical *interpretation* and biblical *proclamation*.

Reuniting Old and New Testaments

We need to rediscover and appreciate with deeper levels of insight the bond between God's partial and preparatory words of promise spoken through Israel's prophets and his final word spoken in Jesus, the Son who is the Word (Heb. 1:1–2; John 1:1, 14). The contemporary sense of estrangement of the Old Testament from the New Testament is an anomaly in the history of the church. From the apostolic period through the Church Fathers, the Middle Ages, the Renaissance, and the Reformation, the church maintained a hearty confidence that God's role as the primary author of Scripture, speaking his message infallibly through distinctive human voices, secures the harmony and unity of the Bible's message from Genesis to Revelation. Admittedly, some like Marcion denied that the Lord who addressed Moses on Sinai is the Father of our Lord Jesus. The church, however, condemned such aberrant repudiation of the Old Testament as contradictory to the teaching of Jesus himself. Others failed to recognize the diversity within the Bible's unity, especially the fact that the Messiah, in bringing Old Testament promises and institutions to fulfillment, also has transformed God's covenantal modes of relating to his people. Nevertheless, despite such anomalies in relating the Old Testament to the New Testament, the heartbeat of the church as a whole has coincided with Augustine's pithy maxim: "The old is in the new revealed, the new is in the old concealed."[4]

The eighteenth century "Enlightenment" (as its proponents viewed it) and its resulting historical critical hermeneutic began to

---

universally valid perceptions of reality (see Robert L. Wilken, *Remembering the Christian Past* [Grand Rapids: Eerdmans, 1995], especially ch. 2, "Religious Pluralism and Early Christian Thought").

4   Cf. Christopher Hall, *Reading Scripture with the Church Fathers* (Downers Grove: InterVarsity, 1998); John J. O'Keefe and R. R. Reno, *Sanctified Vision: An Introduction to Early Christian Interpretation of the Bible* (Baltimore: Johns Hopkins University Press, 2005).

drive a wedge between the Old Testament and the New—a division that continues to infect much biblical scholarship today. Enlightenment scholarship's ostensible concerns were to liberate biblical exegesis from dogmatic tradition and to impose rational controls on interpreters' imaginative creativity, of which patristic and medieval allegorism offered many extreme examples. Underlying the Enlightenment's critique of its predecessors' "dogmatic" and "unscientific" interpretation, however, lay a more insidious denial of the divine authorship that earlier Christian interpreters had assumed as grounds for expecting to discover a single, God-given purpose and message in biblical documents written and received over a time span of well over a millennium.[5]

Subsequently, dispensational theologians, for different reasons and offering different arguments, adopted a hermeneutic that drove another wedge between Old Testament and New. Reacting to historical criticism's dismissal of the church's pre-critical reading of its Scriptures as subjective and imprecise, dispensationalism believed that it could establish the objectivity of its reading of Scripture by treating symbolism with suspicion and preoccupying itself with establishing the text's "literal" sense. Thus over the last three centuries, the theological substructure of apostolic hermeneutics and homiletics has been assaulted both by the "hostile fire" of Enlightenment criticism and by the "friendly fire" of Bible-believing students who sought to develop an objective hermeneutic sufficient to withstand the acidic rigors of Enlightenment doubt.[6]

Even more recently, the atrocities inflicted on the Jewish people under Nazism, before and during World War II, and the West's reaction in a salutary repudiation of anti-Semitism, together with new emphases on toleration amid religious pluralism have driven a third wedge between the Hebrew Scriptures and the New Testament. This wedge is visible in a growing discomfort with the New Testament authors' many assertions and implications that the church, now composed of believing Jews and Gentiles, is the legitimate heir to the benefits (now magnified to eschatological dimensions) once promised to ancient Israel. Although the original apostles, Paul,

---

5   See chapter 4 below.

6   These assaults and their legacy in contemporary hermeneutic and homiletic discussion, especially among evangelicals and confessional Protestants, will be analyzed more fully in chapter 4.

were themselves Jewish (as was Jesus, from whom they learned to interpret the Old Testament), the "supercessionism"[7] articulated in their New Testament writings (for example, Matt. 21:43; Gal. 3:27–29; Phil. 3:2–3; Rev. 3:9) offends many today as insensitive, arrogant, and disrespectful of the religious tradition that gave birth to the church. The problem is further compounded by the church's abuse of the Jewish people in the centuries between the apostles and Adolf Hitler,[8] a shameful record that seems to prove that the New Testament's theological "supercessionism" naturally breeds virulent and violent anti-Semitic behavior. The only remedy would seem to be for the church to avoid co-opting what it has traditionally called "the Old Testament," as though it were the church's book, and instead to allow the Hebrew Scriptures to remain thoroughly Jewish.

Anti-Semitic prejudice and religious pride should have no credibility for Christians who *listen carefully* to the apostles' proclamation of Jesus as the fulfillment of God's promises to Israel and the bestower of unmerited grace to Jew and Gentile alike. The same apostle who announces that Gentiles are now Abraham's descendents through faith in Israel's Messiah also puts Gentiles in their place in his great apostolic discourse on God's mysterious ways with Israel and the nations (Romans 9–11):

> But if some of the branches were broken off, and you, although a wild olive shoot, were grafted in among the others and now share in the nourishing root of the olive tree, do not be arrogant toward the branches. If you are, remember it is not you who support the root, but the root that supports you. (Rom. 11:17–18)

The same apostle laments with great pathos over the unbelief of his many kinfolk in Israel (9:1–3; 10:1) and expresses confidence that the sovereign mercy that could engraft pagan Gentiles can likewise reattach "natural branches" to the olive tree through which divine blessing flows (11:22–24). If, in fact, the insistence of Jesus and his apostles is true—that Israel's ancient Scriptures are eschatologically directed to draw her hope forward to the arrival of her Divine

---

7   "Supercessionism" refers to the New Testament's assertions and implications that the church is the legitimate heir to the benefits once promised ancient Israel.

8   For one shameful example, cf. Martin Luther, "On the Jews and Their Lies" (1543), trans. by Martin H. Bertram, *Luther's Works*, vol. 47, The Christian in Society IV (Philadelphia: Fortress Press, 1971), 268–93.

Rescuer as a Suffering Servant—to suppress such insight for fear of seeming impolite or proud would be selfish cruelty toward the Jewish people, not compassionate respect! Despite these formidable trends working against an appreciation of the unity of Old Testament and New, the church's historic conviction—that the two testaments (two covenants,[9] described in the Hebrew Scriptures, e.g., Jer. 31:31–34) are two chapters in one grand, true story in which the triune God is the protagonist—still has articulate defenders. In fact, some recent trends in biblical studies even encourage greater attention to the unity of Scripture as the divine-human record of a single, consistent, progressive plan for the redemption and re-creation of the cosmos.

At the risk of omitting deserving names and titles, I mention here a sampling of twentieth and twenty-first century biblical scholars whose work deepens our understanding of the Christ-focused marriage of Old Testament promise and New Testament fulfillment: Geerhardus Vos,[10] Herman N. Ridderbos,[11] R. T. France,[12] Meredith G. Kline,[13] O. Palmer

---

9   English versions have traditionally been influenced by Jerome's translation of the Greek *diathēkē* into the Latin *testamentum*, and Western theology has likewise understood the New Testament's references to the new *diathēkē* as drawing the analogy to a last will and testament, with its stipulations enacted subsequent to the testator's death. More recently increased understanding of covenant arrangements between living parties suggests that in all (or almost all) uses of *diathēkē* in the New Testament, its meaning is "covenant," consistent with the use of *diathēkē* in the LXX to translate the Hebrew *berit*, e.g., John J. Hughes, "Hebrews ix 15ff. and Galatians iii 15ff. A Study in Covenant Practice and Procedure," *Novum Testamentum* 21 (1979): 27-96.

10   Geerhardus Vos, *Biblical Theology: Old and New Testaments* (Grand Rapids: Eerdmans, 1948); *The Self-Disclosure of Jesus: The Modern Debate about the Messianic Consciousness* (Phillipsburg: P & R, 1953); *The Teaching of Jesus concerning the Kingdom of God and the Church* (New York: American Tract Society, 1903); *The Pauline Eschatology* (Princeton: Princeton University Press, 1930); *Redemptive History and Biblical Interpretation: The Shorter Writings of Geerhardus Vos* (R. B. Gaffin, Jr., ed. Phillipsburg: P & R, 1980); *The Eschatology of the Old Testament* (J. T. Dennison, Jr. ed. Phillipsburg: P & R, 2001).

11   Herman Ridderbos, *The Coming of the Kingdom* (Philadelphia: Presbyterian & Reformed, 1962); *Paul: An Outline of his Theology* (Grand Rapids: Eerdmans, 1975).

12   R. T. France, *Jesus and the Old Testament: His Application of Old Testament Passages to Himself and His Mission* (Downers Grove: InterVarsity, 1971); *Matthew: Evangelist and Teacher* (Grand Rapids: Zondervan, 1989).

13   Meredith G. Kline, *Kingdom Prologue* (South Hamilton, Massachusetts: self published, 1991); *Images of the Spirit* (Grand Rapids: Baker, 1980); *Glory in our Midst: A Biblical-Theological Reading of Zechariah's Night Visions* (Overland Park, Kansas: Two Age Press, 2001).

Robertson,[14] Raymond B. Dillard,[15] Tremper Longman III,[16] Iain M. Duguid,[17] Willem VanGemeren,[18] S. Lewis Johnson,[19] Moisés Silva,[20] Vern S. Poythress,[21] Gregory K. Beale,[22] Christopher J. H. Wright,[23] Hans K. LaRondelle,[24] and Graeme Goldsworthy.[25]

---

14   O. Palmer Robertson, *The Christ of the Covenants* (Phillipsburg: P & R, 1980); *The Christ of the Prophets* (Phillipsburg: P & R, 2004).

15   Raymond B. Dillard, *Faith in the Face of Apostasy: The Gospel according to Elijah and Elisha* (Phillipsburg: P & R, 1999); with Tremper Longman III, *An Introduction to the Old Testament* (Grand Rapids: Zondervan, 1994).

16   Tremper Longman III, *An Introduction to the Old Testament* (with Raymond B. Dillard); *Immanuel in Our Place: Seeing Christ in Israel's Worship* (Phillipsburg: P & R, 2001); with Daniel G. Reid, *God is a Warrior* (Grand Rapids: Zondervan, 1995); *How to Read Genesis* (Downers Grove: InterVarsity, 2005); *How to Read the Psalms* (Downers Grove: InterVarsity, 1988); *How to Read Proverbs* (Downers Grove: InterVarsity, 2002).

17   Iain M. Duguid, *Living in the Gap between Promise and Reality: The Gospel according to Abraham* (Phillipsburg: P & R, 1999); *Living in the Grip of Relentless Grace: The Gospel according to Isaac and Jacob* (Phillipsburg: P & R, 2002).

18   Willem VanGemeren, *The Progress of Redemption: The Story of Salvation from Creation to New Jerusalem* (Grand Rapids: Baker, 1988).

19   S. Lewis Johnson, *The Old Testament in the New: An Argument for Biblical Inspiration* (Grand Rapids: Zondervan, 1980).

20   Moisés Silva, *Has the Church Misread the Bible? The History of Interpretation in the Light of Current Issues* (Grand Rapids: Zondervan, 1987); with Walter Kaiser, *An Introduction to Biblical Hermeneutics: The Search for Meaning* (Grand Rapids: Zondervan, 1994).

21   Vern S. Poythress, *The Shadow of Christ in the Law of Moses* (Brentwood, Tennessee: Wolgemuth & Hyatt, 1991); *God-Centered Biblical Interpretation* (Phillipsburg: P & R, 1999). See also Dan McCartney and Charles Clayton *Let the Reader Understand: A Guide to Interpreting and Applying the Bible* (Wheaton: Victor, 1994).

22   G. K. Beale, ed. *The Right Doctrine from the Wrong Texts? Essays on the Use of the Old Testament in the New* (Grand Rapids: Baker, 1994); *The Temple and the Church's Mission: A Biblical Theology of the Dwelling Place of God* (Downers Grove: InterVarsity, 2004). See also other volumes in the InterVarsity Press series, New Studies in Biblical Theology, as well as the stimulating older Studies in Biblical Theology series published in the U.S. by Alec R. Allenson and authored by scholars representing a broader theological spectrum. (e.g., Joachim Jeremias, Oscar Cullmann, Werner G. Kümmel, Eduard Schweizer).

23   Christopher J. H. Wright, *Knowing Jesus through the Old Testament* (Downers Grove: InterVarsity, 1992).

24   Hans K. LaRondelle, *The Israel of God in Prophecy: Principles of Prophetic Interpretation* (Berrien Springs: Andrews University Press, 1983).

25   Graeme Goldsworthy, *According to Plan: The Unfolding Revelation of God in the Bible* (Leicester: InterVarsity, 1991); *The Goldworthy Trilogy—Gospel and Kingdom, Gospel in Revelation, Gospel and Wisdom* (Exeter: Paternoster, 2000);

In addition to the works of these scholars, who recognize Scripture's divine authorship and therefore expect its message to exhibit theological coherence, fruitful insights into the connections between Old Testament and New Testament texts are emerging in critical circles as a result of interest in the biblical authors' literary artistry in drawing intertextual allusions[26] to earlier Scriptures.[27] Although many participants in these discussions do not affirm the divine inspiration of Scripture, they often make insightful observations about the allusive employment of Old Testament wording or imagery by New Testament authors. Their studies therefore offer stimulating starting points for reflection on the hermeneutic substructure and rationale for the New Testament's use of the Old Testament.

One major theme, to which this book will return repeatedly, therefore, is the unity of the Old Testament and the New in the person and redemptive work of Jesus Christ and consequently, also, in the community composed of believing Jews and Gentiles that his Spirit is now assembling. This unity, I am persuaded, unlocks the whole of the Scriptures to the twenty-first century preacher and his hearers.

Preaching the Whole Bible as Christian Scripture: The Application of Biblical Theology to Expository Preaching (Grand Rapids: Eerdmans, 2000).

26   An "intertextual allusion" is a deliberate allusion (not a direct quotation) by the author of one text to a passage in another text that has significance for interpreting the author's statement. For example, the reference in John 3:16 to "only Son" is a clear allusion to Isaac in Genesis 22:2, 12, and 16 (cf. Heb. 11:17) who, like Jesus, was offered to God as a sacrifice. (Likewise, "did not spare his own Son" in Romans 8:32 alludes to Genesis 22:16.) The interpretative importance of this is manifold. (1) Isaac is a type of Christ. (2) Like Christ, Isaac is a son of promise. (3) Like Christ, Isaac's birth is supernatural. (4) Like Christ, Isaac is the only and beloved son. (5) Both Isaac and Jesus were "suffering sons." Isaac suffered as a type of the Redeemer; Jesus was the Suffering Son who redeems. (6) Just as Abraham showed his love for and fear of God by his willingness to offer his beloved, only son, so God the Father shows his love for a fallen world by offering his beloved, only Son as an offering for sin. (7) Just as Abraham reasoned that God would raise Isaac from the dead (Heb. 11:19), so God raised his Son, Jesus, from the dead.

27   Note, however, Kevin J. VanHoozer's critique that "intertextuality" in a postmodern frame of reference displaces authorial intention and definite textual meaning with subjective and politically controlled reader-centered interpretation. *Is There a Meaning in This Text? The Bible, the Reader, and the Morality of Literary Knowledge* (Grand Rapids: Zondervan, 1998), 121–22, 132–33.

Reuniting Apostolic Doctrine and Apostolic Hermeneutics

A second "couple" that has been sadly estranged consists in the *theological truths* articulated by the apostles, on the one hand, and the *interpretive methods* by which they grounded those truths in Scripture, on the other. This issue is posed provocatively in the question that New Testament scholar G. K. Beale selected as the title for his collection of essays debating the normativeness of the New Testament's interpretation of the Old Testament: *The Right Doctrine from the Wrong Texts?*[28] The authors of some essays in this collection would answer this question affirmatively: the apostles did indeed teach right doctrine, but they supported their doctrine by appeal to inappropriate Old Testament texts interpreted by illegitimate (or no longer plausible) methods.[29] Other contributors argue that the flaws in the apostles' hermeneutic also taint their theological conclusions. Beale himself, however, responds to his own question with a careful affirmation that the apostles not only taught true doctrine but also developed and supported their message from appropriate Old Testament passages that they interpreted through a credible hermeneutic that is worthy of our emulation today.[30]

As we shall see in chapters 4 and 5, Beale's conclusions are not universally endorsed even by evangelical biblical scholars who affirm the theological authority of the Scriptures. As additional resources and research have exposed similarities between the New Testament's interpretation of Old Testament texts and hermeneutic methods employed widely in Second Temple Judaism[31] (both mainstream rabbinism and fringe sects such as the Qumran community), some scholars have argued that the apostolic hermeneutic was rhetorically

---

28   Beale, *Right Doctrine*, cited in note 22 above.

29   E.g., Richard N. Longenecker, " 'Who Is the Prophet Talking About?' Some Reflections on the New Testament's Use of the Old" (Beale, *Right Doctrine*, 385): "It is my contention that . . . Christians today are committed to the apostolic faith and doctrine of the New Testament, but not necessarily to the apostolic exegetical practices as detailed for us in the New Testament."

30   Beale, "Did Jesus and His Followers Preach the Right Doctrine from the Wrong Texts? An Examination of the Presuppositions of Jesus' and the Apostles' Exegetical Method" (*Right Doctrine*, 387–404).

31   Second Temple Judaism (STJ) refers to the period between the construction of the second Jewish temple in Jerusalem in 515 B.C. and its destruction by the Romans in 70 A.D. STJ was a time of theological development (e.g., angelology), literary production (e.g., Dead Sea Scrolls), and the growth of various movements and sects (e.g., Pharisees) in Judaism.

and persuasively effective in its ancient time and place but is not to be emulated in our intellectual milieu.[32] Interpretive devices that were credible to first-century audiences no longer are seen as cogent or persuasive today, at least in the Academy and its biblical studies guilds. To convey the gospel in our time as effectively as the apostles did in theirs requires not that we reproduce their exegetical strategies but that our reading of the Old Testament be controlled by presuppositions and methods widely recognized across the spectrum of contemporary Old and New Testament studies.

Others who embrace apostolic doctrine are reluctant to emulate apostolic hermeneutics for another reason. They point to the history of unbridled embellishment exemplified in the allegorical excesses of the patristic School of Alexandria and the medieval church, and they applaud the Protestant Reformation's efforts to bring sanity and restraint to biblical interpretation through its insistence that each passage has a "single sense" that is discovered through attention to linguistic features.[33] In view of the church's embarrassing track record of outlandishly and imaginatively twisting Scripture, the fact that Jesus, the Divine Son, and the apostles, speaking and writing under the inspiration of the Holy Spirit, sometimes made surprising typological connections between Old Testament events and the Messiah[34] cannot justify attempts of later, non-inspired preachers to make similar links.

---

32   See, e.g., Richard N. Longenecker's negative answer to the question, "Can We Reproduce the Exegesis of the New Testament?" *Tyndale Bulletin* 21 (1970): 3–38; and an affirmative answer by Scott A. Swanson, "Can We Reproduce the Exegesis of the New Testament? Why Are We Still Asking?" *Trinity Journal* 17 (1996): 67–76. Accessed online: http.//www.bible-researcher.com/swanson.html. See examples of Longenecker's and other evangelical NT scholars' misgivings about the contemporary credibility of exegesis that emulates the apostles' methodology.

33   Westminster Confession of Faith (1646) 1:9: "The infallible rule of interpretation of Scripture is the Scripture itself: and therefore, when there is a question about the true and full sense of any Scripture (which is not manifold, but one), it must be searched and known by other places that speak more clearly." The Second Helvetic Confession (1566), ch. 2) identifies the factors to be considered in deriving Scripture's meaning from Scripture itself as: its language, the circumstances in which it was set down, comparison with like and unlike passages, and conformity with Scripture's over-arching purposes, namely God's glory and human salvation. See chapter 4.

34   For example, the bronze serpent raised by Moses in the desert as a prefigurement of the crucified Son of Man (John 3:14), or the water-supplying rock in the wilderness as "Christ" (1 Cor. 10:4).

Both of these objections to the argument that allegiance to apostolic doctrine should entail humble imitation of apostolic hermeneutics are weighty and worthy of serious answers.[35] For the present, be "forewarned" that I shall try to make a persuasive case that preachers who believe in the gospel revealed through the apostles should proclaim that gospel in the light of Christ's fulfillment of the Law, the Prophets, and the Writings (Luke 24:44–47).

Reuniting Biblical Interpretation and Biblical Proclamation

A third breach in what was once an intimate alliance concerns the relationship between the disciplines of *biblical scholarship* on the one hand and the churchly task of *gospel preaching* on the other. The roots of this estrangement are diverse, complex, and difficult to identify exhaustively.

The Reformation challenged the hegemony of church tradition over biblical interpretation and formulated a concept of vocation that legitimized and dignified occupations outside of ecclesiastical structures, including scholarship and education. Thus the long-standing legacy of ecclesiastically controlled biblical scholarship, which included patristic catechetical schools, medieval cathedral schools, the preservation of learning in monasteries, and the early European universities, could in principle receive competition from educational institutions that initially were no less committed to Christian convictions but were not directly under church authority nor aimed exclusively at ministerial preparation.

The rise of the Enlightenment, with its suspicion and contempt for the distorting influences of church dogma, coincided with the rise of the modern research university. As the objective pursuit of truth through experimentation unbiased by presupposition came to be viewed as the apex of intellectual certainty, the usefulness of biblical research to the church came to be treated, at least tacitly, as incidental, and sometimes as a distraction from the aims of "pure" scholarship. Meanwhile, the explosion of knowledge seemed to demand that scholars direct their energies into increasingly narrow specializations.

Even within the narrower parameters of the university divinity school and the theological seminary, institutions originally founded

---

35   See chapter 6.

to place scholarship in service to the church, specialization and the Academy's expectations often divide biblical research from its practical and personal applications. One result of such this sharp "division of labor" in theological scholarship is exegesis that stops short of biblical interpretation's ultimate aim, proclamation.[36] In his introduction to the flagship volume that launched the New International Greek Testament Commentary, for example, I. Howard Marshall called attention to an intentional omission:

> In order not to expand the commentary beyond measure I have deliberately refrained from offering an exposition of the text as Holy Scripture with a message for the contemporary world, although I believe that exegesis must lead to exposition.[37]

This is a legitimate strategic decision in a finite world, but one hopes that readers—especially preachers—will notice Marshall's disclaimer and recognize the implications of his frank acknowledgement that this commentary has left the interpretive task unfinished. Just as the interpretation of an ancient document in its original historical context would be aborted prematurely without consideration of the occasion that evoked it and the effect that its author sought to achieve in its first readers, so the interpretation of a biblical text is incomplete unless carried through to the purposes that Scripture's divine author intends it to accomplish in every generation of his church, including ours. Exegesis itself is impoverished when specialization and professional pressures in the academy inculcate into faculty and students a model of biblical interpretation that aborts the process short of *application*, depriving it of its sweetest fruit.

Meanwhile, pressures on pastors to market and manage church growth as entrepreneurs and CEOs produce pragmatism in the pulpit that is revealed in sermons ungrounded in biblical interpretation. Pastors' linguistic and exegetical skills atrophy in the flurry of activity to keep institutional operations functioning smoothly. Disciplined grammatical, lexical, rhetorical, and theological analysis of Old Testament texts requires more time and effort than many feel they can

---

36 By *proclamation* I mean the application-focused communication of the meaning and transformative purpose of the text, by means of preaching, counseling, the written word, and in other ways.

37 I. Howard Marshall, *The Gospel of Luke: A Commentary on the Greek Text* (NIGTC; Grand Rapids: Eerdmans, 1978), 16.

afford, especially when lessons of obvious practical relevance to the daily stresses of twenty-first-century life seem to lie on the surface of any English translation. Of course, a hermeneutic of some sort is always operative, at least behind the scenes, when pastors preach and people read Scripture. The question is whether this pragmatic hermeneutic, which portrays Scripture as a newspaper advice column, fits the real character and purpose of the Bible and therefore whether it actually meets its hearers' deepest, truest need. Application that does not emerge from the purpose for which God himself gave his Word will, in the end, lack credibility and power to motivate hearers who hunger for the truth and mercy that is found nowhere but in Jesus. Just as interpretation without proclamation in the Academy is fruitless, so proclamation without sound interpretation in the pulpit is rootless. We need to rediscover the church's older insight, drawn from the Bible itself, that the purpose of understanding Scripture is nothing less than to believe and obey its Author, and the purpose of preaching Scripture is to ground hearers' faith and life in the depths of wisdom, justice, and grace hidden in Christ and unveiled in infinite variety on every page.

Why "Apostolic" Preaching?

One might ask why the homiletic approach presented in this book is called "apostolic" rather than "Christ-centered" or "Reformational" or "redemptive-historical" or or "covenantal" or "Reformed." In fact, the homiletic presented here fits all of those labels as well. Above all, apostolic preaching must be *Christ-centered*. The title, *Him We Proclaim*, is drawn from Colossians 1:28, in which the apostle Paul sums up the message he preaches as, simply, Christ (1 Cor. 2:2; cf. 1:18, 23–24, 30; 15:1–5; Eph. 3:4, 8; 4:21; Gal. 6:14). Between his resurrection and his ascension to God's right hand, the Lord Jesus taught the original apostles that the Law of Moses, the Prophets, and the Psalms all predicted the Messiah's suffering, rejection, death, resurrection, outpouring of the Spirit, and worldwide reign through the servants of his Word (Luke 24:44–49; Acts 1:3-8; cf. John 5:45–47).[38]

---

38   The canon of the Hebrew Scriptures, unlike our English versions (which derive their order from the Greek Septuagint (LXX), is divided into three sections: Law (Torah, meaning "instruction"), Prophets, and Writings. The Prophets section includes the "former prophets" (Joshua-Kings), who narrated and interpreted Israel's covenant history, and the "latter prophets" (Isaiah, Jeremiah, Ezekiel, twelve

The fruit of this intensive forty-day hermeneutics course is heard in the apostolic sermons preserved in the book of Acts, as well as in the Gospels themselves[39] and the other New Testament books.

Apostolic preaching, therefore, must be Christ-centered. But there are various ways that preaching might be conceived to be "Christ-centered." Charles M. Sheldon's classic, *In His Steps* (1896), presented Jesus as the exemplar of selfless love in service to others and portrayed the unsettling effects among an affluent congregation when members took up the challenge to be guided by the question, "What would Jesus do?" (About a century later bracelets, T-shirts, and other accessories emblazoned "WWJD" posed the same question for a younger generation of earnest disciples.) Sheldon's title alludes to 1 Peter 2:21, which speaks of Christ's "leaving you an example, so that you might follow in his steps," so the imitation of Christ is a biblical theme. Yet, Christ centeredness in preaching must not be reduced to portraying Jesus as example, to the neglect of the good news in which Peter's exhortation is embedded: "Christ also suffered for you . . . . He himself bore our sins in his body on the tree, so that we might die to sin and live to righteousness. By his wounds you have been healed" (1 Peter 2:21, 24). To focus on Jesus as example is to reduce him from sovereign Savior to ethical coach, and to transform his gospel into law.

The preaching of Sheldon's older contemporary Charles Spurgeon was Christ-centered in a more grace-focused and apostolic way than *In His Steps*. In his sermon on 1 Peter 2:7, "Christ Precious to Believers," Spurgeon attributed to a Welsh preacher a story that resonated with Spurgeon's priority in preaching. A young preacher, having preached in the presence of a "venerable divine" and asking his evaluation of the message, was perplexed to hear it judged "a very poor sermon." His lack was not in the research, selection of text, or use of argument and metaphor, but in that fact that "there was no Christ in it." When the young man defended himself by contending,

---

Minor Prophets), who pressed the Lord's lawsuit against his wayward servant but also promised restoration after judgment. The Psalms lead the Writings section, and Luke may intend to refer to the whole section by mentioning its first book.

39   The prologue of the third gospel, which traces its contents back to "those who from the beginning were eyewitnesses and ministers of the word," implies that not only the sermons in Acts but also the Gospel's narratives of Jesus' earthly ministry of word and deed are included in the deposit entrusted to the church through the apostles (Luke 1:1–4).

"Christ was not in the text; we are not to be preaching Christ always, we must preach what is in the text," his mentor replied:

> Don't you know, young man, that from every town, and every village, and every little hamlet in England, wherever it may be, there is a road to London?" "Yes," said the young man. "Ah!" said the old divine, "and so from every text in Scripture, there is a road to the metropolis of the Scriptures, that is Christ. And my dear brother, your business is when you get to a text, to say, 'Now what is the road to Christ?' and then preach a sermon, running along the road towards the great metropolis—Christ. And," said he, "I have never yet found a text that had not got a road to Christ in it, and if I ever do find one that has not a road to Christ in it, I will make one; I will go over hedge and ditch but I would get at my Master, for the sermon cannot do any good unless there be a savour of Christ in it."[40]

While concurring wholeheartedly with Spurgeon, the Welsh preacher, and the old divine that every text of Scripture is on a road that leads to Christ, I must confess that on occasion brother Spurgeon's sermons (admittedly more eloquent and passionate than mine) strike me as involving much hedge climbing and ditch fording, when the Spirit of God has already blazed a clearer and more convincing trail by means of the apostolic writings of the New Testament.

There is a distinctively apostolic way of being Christ-centered, and it is this hermeneutic that places appropriate checks on the preacher's hyperactive imagination, thereby assuring listeners that the message is revealed by God, not merely generated by human creativity. This *apostolic* approach to Christ centeredness has three additional features that will be developed more fully in later chapters: Apostolic preaching of Christ is redemptive-historically structured, missiologically communicated, and grace-driven.

Apostolic preaching is *redemptive-historical* in its presentation of the substructure of Christ's person and saving work. As chapter 3 will show with reference to a pivotal Pauline text (Col. 1:25–2:7), and as chapters 6 and 7 will illustrate more fully, the apostles were conscious of standing at the consummation of the ages and were vividly aware that the events that precipitated this watershed in history were the incarnation, obedience, death, resurrection, and exaltation of

---

40   Charles H. Spurgeon, "Christ Precious to Believers" (March 13, 1859). Accessed online: http://spurgeon.org/sermons/0242.htm.

Jesus of Nazareth. The coming of the Messiah fulfilled ancient promises and age-old longings for deep redemption and an eternal Ruler who would reign in holy justice and in mercy. It filled up and filled in previous patterns and shadows in Israel's communion with her covenant Lord, and this filling process also entailed a transformation of ancient institutions into new forms better suited to more intimate interactions between the King and his joyful subjects. Reading and preaching the Bible redemptive historically is more than drawing lines to connect Old Testament types in "Promise Column A" with New Testament antitypes in "Fulfillment Column B." It is recognizing that Adam's, Abraham's, and Israel's entire experience was designed from the beginning to foreshadow the end, and that ancient believers experienced true but limited foretastes of sweet grace because in the fullness of the times, Jesus, the beloved Son, would keep the covenant and bear the curse on their behalf and ours.

"Redemptive-historical preaching," however, connotes various things in confessionally Reformed circles today. Some associate the label with sermons that are literary masterpieces, works of art that exhibit the preacher's scholarship and ingenuity in "connecting the dots" and discerning subtle patterns that link abstruse passages to Christ but fail to address the messy particulars of hearers' struggles. Or young preachers enamored with the ways that biblical theology exhibits the variegated unity of Scripture fail to translate the theological jargon of their sources into the language of their listeners. In their zeal, they lace their lecture-sermons with "semi-eschatological," "protology," "intrusion," and other meaning-packed terms that are, sadly, unintelligible to the uninitiated. Sometimes the redemptive-historical preacher's eagerness to paint the pattern of redemption obscures his hearers' view of the person who redeems. Some who eagerly trace Scripture's covenantal character fail to note that God's address to his servants is always for the purpose of eliciting a faith-filled and faithful response to his sovereign, saving initiative.

The apostles' proclamation of Christ as the fulfiller of prophetic promise and redemptive history avoids these imbalances and omissions. The promise-fulfillment pattern remained a semi-visible substructure[41] for their proclamation of Christ himself. Although Jesus' original apostles watched in wonder as he welcomed sinners into his

---

41   C. H. Dodd, *According to the Scriptures: The Sub-Structure of New Testament Theology* (London: Nisbet, 1952). As a semi-visible substructure, the prom-

fellowship, despite their unworthiness, and Paul found his own self-made righteousness by law-observance worthless (and worse) when compared to God's gracious gift of righteousness in Christ (Phil. 3:6-9), none of them denied, ignored, or failed to guide the trusting, grateful, obedient response that such amazing grace evokes in those who receive it by faith. It is this apostolic sort of redemptive-historical preaching that this study advocates.

Apostolic preaching also is *missiologically communicated.* Edmund P. Clowney has observed that among the four classic attributes of the church, "apostolicity" refers not only to the divinely revealed norm that defines the church (Matt. 16:13-19; Eph. 2:20; Gal. 6:16) but also to the church's commission to disseminate the gospel among the nations.[42] Apostles (Greek: *apostoloi*) not only bore divine authority delegated to them by the Lord Jesus (Luke 10:16) but also were *sent* (*apostellō*) by Jesus to exercise that authority in witness to Israel and to the Gentiles to the ends of the earth (John 20:21; Acts 1:8; 13:46). Jesus' parable of the ten minas dramatically illustrates that merely preserving the Master's treasure unrisked and returning it to him unchanged would not be commended as faithful stewardship. Those who respond in that manner to the gospel are rebuked as wicked, faithless, and slothful (Luke 19:22-23). Consequently, the book of Acts shows us Jesus' authorized missionaries moving out with the treasure to Judea, Samaria, an Ethiopian dignitary, a Roman centurion, Antioch, Cyprus, Asia, Macedonia and Achaia, and even Rome, the ancient world's "Big Apple."

To fulfill their commission from the King, these missionary-ambassadors mixed with pagans and spoke their language. It might have seemed safer theologically to keep the good news of Jesus safely stored in the Hebrew language in which God had spoken in times past and in a Jewish culture that the exile had purged from the temptations of pagan idolatry. Paul's correspondence with Gentile churches at Corinth, Colossae, and elsewhere illustrates the potential for misunderstanding and distorting the gospel that the pagan pluralism of the Hellenistic world posed. Yet, one consequence of the redemptive-historical epoch in which the apostles—and we—

---

ise-fulfillment pattern is more visible in some parts of the New Testament than others but underlays the entire New Testament.

42   Edmund P. Clowney, *The Church* (Contours of Contemporary Theology; Downers Grove: InterVarsity, 1995), 77-78.

minister the good news of God's kingdom is that God now speaks the languages of the world's unreached peoples (Acts 2:4–11), summoning those at earth's end to turn to him for salvation. Apostolic preaching refuses to veil its world-changing truth behind dialects intelligible only to the initiated (2 Cor. 4:2–6) or to lock its life-giving power away from spiritual aliens who most need it. This missiological dimension of apostolic preaching has enormous implications for our choice of vocabulary and illustration and for our engagement with the cultures and worldviews that have molded our hearers, as we preach in the same redemptive-historical epoch as the apostles, despite the passing of two millennia.

Finally, *apostolic* Christ-centered, redemptive-historical, missiological preaching is *grace-driven*. Like their Master, the apostles frankly labeled sin for the evil it is and loved their hearers enough to warn them bluntly of sin's dire consequences. For that very reason—*because* they exposed the ugliness of human rebellion and guilt—their proclamation of the grace of God in the cross of Christ rings out with heart-captivating power. We glimpsed one example of this in the mercy-saturated context in which Peter embedded the summons to follow in Jesus' steps. In the following chapters, we will observe other illustrations of ways in which the gospel entrusted to the apostles is "the power of God for salvation to everyone who believes" (Rom. 1:16)—a salvation abundantly adequate to remedy every aspect of human depravity and misery: removing guilt and bestowing righteousness and replacing death with life, alienation with reconciliation, slavery with liberty, and self-absorbed ingratitude with God glorifying thanksgiving.

The Plan of the Book

This book has two parts.

Part 1 (chapters 2–5) makes the case for apostolic hermeneutics and homiletics exegetically, historically, and polemically. In a sense, the argument for the reunion of Old and New Testaments, of apostolic doctrine and apostolic hermeneutics, and of Scripture's interpretation and its proclamation is simply a call for a return to insights and practices that have borne fruit in previous generations but more recently have fallen into disfavor or forgetfulness. In view of those unhappy contemporary separations profiled above, some readers may find strange and not immediately persuasive a simple assertion that today's exegetes and preachers should imitate interpretive and communicative techniques that functioned effectively twenty centuries ago.

Therefore, after surveying contemporary homiletic "schools" or trends that tend toward polarization around one or another of the biblical priorities for preaching (ch. 2), chapter 3 offers an exegetical argument for apostolic preaching grounded in a Pauline text that draws together in brief compass a comprehensive description of what the apostle understood when he asserted, "Him we proclaim." Chapter 4 goes on to sketch in broad overview the ebb and flow of apostolic preaching in the history of the church, from the apostles' day to ours. Objections to or reservations about imitating apostolic hermeneutic and homiletic practice, some of which were mentioned above, receive answers in chapter 5.

Part 2 (chapters 6–10) is constructive more than defensive. It provides both a theoretical framework and concrete strategies for preachers who desire to reflect the Christ-centered confluence of apostolic hermeneutics and apostolic homiletics in their own pulpit ministries. Chapter 6 first presents arguments for regarding the epistle to the Hebrews as an apostolic sermon in written form—the only such sermon delivered to a regular congregation of Jesus' followers after Pentecost that the New Testament records.[43] Then the Old Testament interpretation and congregational application in the epistle to the Hebrews are analyzed for the principles and reproducible methods they offer to guide our preaching.

Starting from those patterns of typological correspondence between Old Testament and New Testament that are generally recognized, chapters 7 and 8 probe the theological foundations of this typology and explore two pervasive biblical paradigms, covenant and (new) creation, that help us map the network of "roads" (to use the metaphor of Spurgeon's Welsh colaborer) that connect Old Testament texts, persons, and events not overtly identified in Scripture as types to their appropriate fulfillment in Christ, his redemptive mission, and its results in the new covenant church.

Finally, chapters 9 and 10 sketch suggestive proposals for the application of apostolic hermeneutic and homiletic principles to the

---

43   All the sermons in Acts are addressed to those who at the time did not believe in Jesus as the Messiah. Paul's address to the Ephesian elders in Acts 20:17-35 is not a sermon as such but his parting pastoral instructions.

Bible's various narrative and non-narrative genres, in both the Old Testament and the New Testament. A concluding appendix proposes a step-by-step procedure for moving "from text to sermon" in a way that, pursued prayerfully, will help readers do justice both to the passage's immediate context and to its wider context in the history of redemption and Scripture's overarching purpose, to bear witness to Christ and elicit faith in him.

Part 1

The Case for Apostolic, Christocentric Preaching

2

Priorities and Polarities in Preaching

One of the classics of American homiletic thought is the Lyman Beecher Lectures delivered by Episcopal Bishop Phillips Brooks at Yale College in 1877. Toward the conclusion of his first lecture Bishop Brooks observed:

> The purpose of preaching must always be the first condition that decrees its character. The final cause is that which really shapes everything's life. And what is preaching for? The answer comes without hesitation. It is for men's salvation. But the idea of what salvation is has never been entirely uniform or certain. . . . If to be saved was to be saved from sin, preaching became spiritual. If to be saved was to be saved from punishment, preaching became forensic and economical. If salvation was the elevation of society, preaching became a lecture upon social science. The first thing for you to do is to see clearly what you are going to preach for, what you mean to try to save men from.[1]

Three aspects of this observation are as timely today as they were over a century ago. First, if the preacher has a clear conception of preaching's purpose, that purpose will control the whole process of his study, composition, delivery, and follow-up. Contemporary Presbyterian homiletician Jay Adams reinforces Brooks's point about the all-controlling role of *purpose* in preaching: "I am convinced that purpose is of such vital importance to all a preacher does that it ought to control his thinking and actions from start to finish in the preparation and delivery of sermons."[2]

---

1 Phillips Brooks, *Lectures on Preaching delivered before the Divinity School of Yale College* (New York: E. P. Dutton, 1877, repr. 1894), 32–33.
2 Jay Adams, *Preaching with Purpose: The Urgent Task of Homiletics* (Grand Rapids: Zondervan, 1982), 1.

Second, one's understanding of the purpose of preaching is controlled by one's theology proper, theological anthropology, and soteriology—that is, by one's conceptions of the nature of the God who defined our purpose by creating us in his image, of the nature of our need as those who have turned away from him, and of the remedy God has provided for our problem. A particular diagnosis of our human malady and corresponding prescription of divine cure will produce one sort of sermon rather than another, and will seek one sort of response from the hearers rather than another.

Third, different diagnoses and cures—radical or moderate, individual or corporate—have in fact been proposed throughout the history of the church, and these variations have influenced homiletic content and practice. Brooks assigns no labels to the conceptions of salvation that he surveys, but those familiar with nineteenth-century American Protestantism have little trouble recognizing the movements. Pietists give priority to salvation from the control of sin by focusing their preaching on spiritual experience. Confessional Lutherans (and some Reformed) proclaimed a "forensic and economical" gospel (focusing on the "economy" by which Christ accomplished redemption), so that their hearers might be saved from punishment. Liberal advocates of the social gospel sought to elevate society by discourses on the social sciences.

As we shall see, Adams goes on to distinguish sharply between preaching for an evangelistic purpose, which belongs in "the marketplace" *outside* the corporate worship of the church, and preaching designed to edify Christians, which he considers appropriate to the pastor's ordinary proclamation of the Word in worship on the Lord's Day. In Brooks's categories, Adams sees non-Christians and Christians as needing to be "saved" from different threats or problems, and therefore as needing to be addressing with different types of sermons, with different objectives.[3] Other homileticians are equally adamant that preaching in the church's worship *must* address non-Christians and Christians together, intelligibly calling unbelievers to faith as it calls believers to the obedience that flows from faith. Still others concur with Adams's insistence that worship service preaching is for

---

3   The threat confronting the non-Christian—namely condemnation under God's wrath and spiritual death in trespasses and sins—must be remedied by the Holy Spirit's sovereign grace, drawing the person to trust in Jesus, before the Christian's ongoing war against indwelling sin (that is, sanctification) can begin.

the covenant community, not those outside; but they believe that he overemphasizes sanctification and Christian living and would insist instead that preaching's primary purpose is to teach the congregation the systematic theology of Scripture or to capture their imaginations with the drama of redemptive history.

In other words, the homiletic diversity in the early twenty-first century, even among evangelical pastors committed to Scripture and the gospel, is no less than it was when Phillips Brooks lectured in the late nineteenth century. Because human nature is prone to oversimplification and imbalance, differences of opinion on priorities to be pursued in preaching easily degenerate into polarization. A single homiletic purpose and approach are elevated and absolutized as the only biblical, theologically correct, pastorally sensitive, or missiologically effective (depending on one's preferred criterion) homiletic alternative, and all its rivals are dismissed as inferior at best and harmful at worst.

This chapter provides a sympathetic but critical hearing to rival homiletic approaches that vie for the preacher's allegiance in the twenty-first century, noting both the strengths and potential weaknesses of each. In subsequent chapters, apostolic preaching—that is, preaching that interprets Scripture christologically and presents the gospel intelligibly to diverse hearers, as the apostles did—will be shown to capture the valid priorities of all the competing visions surveyed here. Let us consider the cases that are made for preaching (1) to convert, (2) to edify, and (3) to instruct.[4]

Two qualifications must be stated before we begin. First, all three emphases seek to transform listeners as whole persons, so it would oversimplify matters to claim that each appeals only to one

---

4 These categories overlap with a taxonomy that appears in various forms in Dutch Reformed circles as a way of categorizing contrasting perceptions of what it means to be a "Reformed" Christian. I heard the three categories in that taxonomy first from Derke Bergsma, my colleague and predecessor as chairman of the practical theology department at Westminster Seminary California: pietists (emphasizing personal devotion and the Great Commission), doctrinalists (emphasizing theological orthodoxy), and Kuyperians (emphasizing cultural transformation and the cultural mandate). For descriptions of each, see George M. Marsden, "Reformed and American," in David F. Wells, *Reformed Theology in America: A History of its Modern Development* (Grand Rapids: Eerdmans, 1985), 1–12. My focus, however, is narrower, concerning itself with the way each of the three approaches described below conceives the purpose (and consequently form and content) of preaching specifically.

aspect of human personality. Yet, as a generalization, it would not be unfair to say that: (1) at least some who see their preaching mission as evangelizing non-Christians focus on affective (emotional) needs, (2) many who aim at edification seek volitional change, and (3) those who see preaching as instruction attend primarily to cognitive growth.

Second, each of these three broad categories includes preachers who differ among themselves. Some evangelizing preachers may stress God's tender mercy; others emphasize his holy wrath. Some argue that the gospel fulfills human longings; others stress the offense of the cross to human pride and prejudice. Some edifying preachers concentrate on the struggle against personal sin; others summon believers to fulfill their corporate responsibility within the church or their kingdom calling in the culture. Some instructional preachers seek systematic theological orthodoxy in their hearers; others seek to paint the sweeping panorama of redemptive history on the canvas of the listeners' minds and imaginations; still others seek to instill a biblical worldview that engages the challenges of alternative religions and philosophies.

Preaching to Convert

In one sense, of course, no Christian preacher would deny that a primary purpose of preaching—at least in some venues—is to proclaim the gospel of Jesus' death and resurrection for sinners (1 Cor. 15:3–4) and on this basis to summon people alienated from their Creator to trust in his Son and receive his reconciling mercy (2 Cor. 5:11–21). The Shorter Catechism constructed by the Westminster Assembly (1646) wisely comments, "The Spirit of God maketh the reading, but *especially the preaching* of the Word, an effectual means of *convincing and converting sinners* . . . ."[5] The history of preaching to local congregations abounds with instances of pastors whose preaching called non-Christians to repentance and faith and bore abundant fruit in the conversion of the lost: Martin Luther and John Calvin in the sixteenth century, the Puritans in the seventeenth, Jonathan Edwards in the eighteenth, Charles Spurgeon in the nineteenth, and D. Martyn-Lloyd Jones in the twentieth century are noteworthy

---

5   Westminster Shorter Catechism, Answer 89 (emphasis added). See, in ch. 3 below, the full, expanded statement of the Westminster Larger Catechism, A. 155, concerning the purposes that God's Spirit achieves through the preaching of the Word.

exemplars of evangelistic pastoral preaching, among many others. Even Jay Adams, who states that evangelistic preaching addressed to unbelievers does not belong in the church's corporate worship,[6] nevertheless asserts that pastors should follow the apostolic model visible in Acts and take their gospel preaching out of the church's "territory" and into venues of public discourse, rather than waiting for non-Christians to venture through church doors.

Evangelism (or outreach or church growth) has become the *dominant* purpose for preachers who, having noticed that the church in North America and Europe has become a marginalized minority, desire to reverse negative trends rather than retreating in self-protective retrenchment. The increasing secularization of Western cultures and societies, in combination with increasing immigration and ethnic diversity, is creating an environment in which Christian preachers can no longer assume that even simple theological terms and formerly familiar biblical allusions are intelligible to vast numbers of the church's neighbors. Although external factors and complex intellectual and cultural currents have contributed to the decline of the church's societal influence, many pastors suspect that the church's complacency with its *status quo*, its insularity, and its loss of spiritual vitality and missiological passion for the unreached within its own community have also played their role.

Yet, churches in the West still have liberty to worship publicly and even maintain a degree of visibility in most communities, from small towns to large cities. Many pastors, mindful of the fact that Jesus' Great Commission has been neither repealed nor outsourced to the developing nations overseas, refuse to settle for maintaining a dwindling and ingrown remnant. The Church Growth Movement, armed with anthropological observations about the causes of evangelistic effectiveness in the developing world, called pastors of established congregations in North America and Europe to rethink, in missiological terms, their congregation's relationship to the "hidden peoples" within their own cities, suburbs, and even rural towns. Megachurches in major urban centers have made it their aim to reach out and enfold those who have dropped out of traditional church backgrounds, or who have never been engaged at all, particularly by using as a bridge those personal inadequacies and relational difficulties of which non-Christians are painfully aware, such

---

6   See Adams, *Preaching with Purpose*, 70, cited below.

as stress, alienation, dysfunctional family relationships, materialism, fear, worry, and violence.

The "felt needs" approach to preaching espoused by seeker-sensitive megachurches, such as Willow Creek Community Church and the Willow Creek Association, is by no means the only contemporary expression of preaching intended to evangelize the unreached in the context of the church's worship service.[7] It is, however, a highly visible expression of the conviction that the preaching that occurs in public worship on Sunday should have as its primary purpose the evangelization and conversion of the unsaved. Moreover, the same essential philosophy of ministry that governs megachurches' outreach to the Baby Boomer generation finds expression in niche-marketed congregations that target younger generations: Busters, Gen-X, Millennials, and beyond. The predominant concern is to minimize the cultural distance that non-Christians must traverse in order to be engaged by the gospel. To this end, virtually everything that can be adapted, both in worship style and in preaching, is adjusted to the comfort zone of the unchurched.

Stated this baldly, the driving principles behind the megachurches' "felt needs" preaching and "seeker sensitive" ministry raises theological eyebrows (as well as, perhaps, a touch of secret envy).[8] Nevertheless, pastors who are grounded in the apostolic gospel and driven by apostolic mission to reach all peoples with that gospel will seek ways to break down stereotypes of the church (fire-and-brimstone condemnation, uptight regulations, somber and archaic music, money-grubbing manipulation, "frozen chosen"), and they may conclude that the way to reach out is to preach sermons that address the personal and family needs that non-Christians experience. After all, stress, alienation, dysfunctional family relationships, materialism,

---

7   The homiletic stance of Timothy Keller, who formerly taught preaching and ministry at Westminster Theological Seminary (Philadelphia) and pastors Redeemer Presbyterian Church in New York City, is analyzed later in this chapter. Keller insists that the same gospel that converts unbelievers also sanctifies believers. He intends his preaching to be both intelligible to unchurched New Yorkers and counter-cultural, challenging their idolatries and strategies of self-defense against the gospel of grace. His and Redeemer's engagement with the city is influencing church planters in other urban centers, not only in North America but internationally.

8   For a fair and thorough critique of seeker-sensitive services, see G. A. Pritchard, *Willow Creek Seeker Services: Evaluating a New Way of Doing Church* (Grand Rapids: Baker, 1996).

fear, worry, violence, and other evils with which unbelievers struggle are the symptoms of our fall into sin.[9] Is it not consistent with God's accommodation[10] to our limitations and weakness in revealing himself in Scripture and the Incarnation to take as our starting point some element of human experience that painfully exposes our neediness, then to trace the problem to its root in our alienation from the Creator, and finally to apply the cure in the gospel of Christ?

Seeker-sensitive churches can appeal to the example of audience adaptation in the book of Acts and the New Testament epistles. The apostles adjusted the presentation of their message not only to the language of their hearers but also to the issues raised by the hearers' worldviews and experience, yet without compromising the central message of Christ and his saving work.[11] The gospel does have solutions to human problems, because at their root all human problems are attributable to the fall into sin. "The fall brought mankind into an estate of *sin* and *misery*. . . . The *sinfulness* of that estate whereinto man fell, consists in the guilt of Adam's first sin, the want of original righteousness, and the corruption of his whole nature, which is commonly called original sin; together with all actual transgressions which proceed from it. . . . All mankind by their fall *lost communion with God*, are under his *wrath and curse*, and so made *liable to all the miseries of this life*, to death itself, and to the pains of hell forever."[12]

To be sure, the grace of Christ does not immediately remove all the miseries of our fallen estate the instant we come to Christ, or even in this life, prior to Christ's return and our final resurrection. Instead, Jesus and his apostles prepared new disciples for the harsh reality that following him often increases life's difficulties: "If anyone would come after me, let him deny himself and take up his cross daily and follow me" (Luke 9:23). "Through many tribulations we

9   Lynne and Bill Hybels, *Rediscovering Church: The Story and Vision of Willow Creek Community Church* (Grand Rapids: Zondervan, 1995), 173–75.

10   John Calvin, *Institutes of the Christian Religion* (trans. F. L. Battles, ed. J. T. McNeill; Philadelphia: Westminster, 1960), 1.17.13: "What, therefore, does the word 'repentance' [God's 'repentance'] mean? Surely its meaning is like that of all other modes of speaking that describe God for us in human terms. For because our weakness does not attain to [God's] exalted state, the description of him that is given to us must be accommodated to our capacity so that we may understand it."

11   Jay E. Adams, *Audience Adaptations in the Sermons and Speeches of Paul* (Phillipsburg: P & R, 1976).

12   Westminster Shorter Catechism, Answers 17, 18, 19 (emphasis added).

must enter the kingdom of God" (Acts 14:22). "Everyone who wants to live a godly life in Christ Jesus will be persecuted" (2 Tim. 3:12).

On the other hand, just as the Samaritan woman was drawn by Jesus through a dialogue about water and husbands (felt needs) into a recognition of her deep need (John 4:7–26), and just as Peter led the crowd in Solomon's colonnade through the "restoration" of a lame man's feet into a recognition of Jesus, who will bring the "restoration of all things" (Acts 3:12–26), so also the contemporary preacher may lead people from the pains that they feel—sin's symptoms and toxic waste—into a recognition of the ultimate source of their distress— our rebellion, enslavement, and defilement by sin—and finally to the only solution, the one provided by the Lord whom we defied, namely, the reconciling sacrifice of Jesus and his life-renewing resurrection. Rather than playing into the culture's stereotypes of the church as an irrelevant, archaic institution that concentrates on condemnation, felt-needs preachers emphasize the attractiveness of the gospel—the fact the joy for which our hearts hunger is found in Christ alone.

Felt-needs preachers especially seek to distance themselves from approaches to preaching that assume, explicitly or tacitly, that the only hearers who need to understand the sermon are the cov- enant people of God. They avoid theological jargon that is unin- telligible to the non-Christian, in the spirit of Paul's counsel to the Corinthians (1 Cor. 14:23–25).[13] They may also feel that the public worship service (sometimes called a "seeker service") is not the time or place to address issues of doctrine or responsibility that would appear irrelevant to unchurched people or needlessly alienate them by feeding their negative stereotypes of the church as arrogant or exclusive. They definitely seek to apply the message of the text in a way that all their hearers, Christian and non-Christian alike, can sense its relevance to the problems people face in daily life. Their desire is that the non-Christian will experience the church as a place of warm acceptance populated by people who are honest about their struggles but whose lives manifest "something more" than is present

---

13   Calvin Miller, *Marketplace Preaching: How to Return the Sermon to Where It Belongs* (Grand Rapids: Baker, 1995), 33: ". . . it is inexcusable that sermons should ever become so congregationally-specific that they have lost their ambas- sadorial status. They have talked about Jesus in-house without representing him to those outside the church." But Miller also warns, ". . . we must interest our audience without syncretizing what the Bible teaches with other multicultural values" (44).

in other groups: the grace of God. Through the preaching and other aspects of worship, and through friendships and small groups the unchurched come to understand what it means to trust in Christ and commit their lives to him.

Yet, despite the laudable motives and even biblical rationales that can be offered by practitioners of the felt-needs, seeker-sensitive variety of "preaching to convert," when this approach dictates a congregation's spiritual diet as it gathers for corporate worship on the Lord's Day, dangers of anemia and even toxemia present themselves. Such questions and reservations as the following can legitimately be raised.

1) Is this approach to the selection of sermon topics fundamentally man centered rather than God centered? Does it make non-Christians' perception of their need primary and the Word of God secondary? If among our profoundest needs is to recognize that God is God and we are not, and if we cannot appreciate the wonder of grace without having glimpsed the terrifying holiness of the Creator whom we have offended, are preachers committing a disservice not only to the Lord who commissioned them but also to their hearers if they tacitly portray God as the solution to our problems rather than the Sovereign whose will is supreme over his creatures?

2) Does the "felt needs" approach run the risk of failing to proclaim the "whole counsel of God,"[14] including those things we need to hear but do not feel we need, either because we are oblivious to our deep needs or because we suppress truth when it challenges us to repentance and radical change?[15] Does making an evangelistic purpose (to call non-Christians to faith) primary, whether through seeker-sensitive, felt-needs preaching, or in some other form, require the pastor to avoid preaching on certain biblical texts and themes?

---

14   Miller, *Marketplace Preaching*, 127: "A real danger of the marketplace sermon arises at this point. So many of the megachurch pastors have begun seeker services to attract seekers. Theology has been seen as a kind of 'white' demon that destroys the secular draw. In tiptoeing around their worldview, an impression might be left that the preacher's real worldview is too offensive to speak about openly. A caution must be sounded. Worldviews are so essential that preachers must not try to give seekers any reinforcement that their own worldview is OK as it is."

15   On the other hand, Hybels, *Rediscovering*, 76, 98–99, reports having preached on the holiness of God (because of the influence of R. C. Sproul), on the centrality of God's glory in worship, on the ten commandments, and an expository series on 1 Corinthians (because of influence of John MacArthur).

3) Do manifestly "relevant" sermons, addressed to everyday needs (stress, parenting, marriage, money, time management, self-image) for the sake of connecting with non-Christians, run the risk of replacing the gospel of sovereign grace for the helpless with moralistic advice on how to help oneself by prescribing "seven habits" for highly effective child rearing (from Proverbs or Ephesians 6, of course) or "twelve steps to worry-free finances"? In 1990 Doug Murren argued in *Baby Boomerang* that, in order to hold Boomers' attention, within the first two minutes sermons must establish their relevance to everyday problems: "How can I have a happier marriage? How can I handle my money better? I don't like my job. What can I do about it? . . . Will I be caught in an ACOA (adult children of alcoholics) pattern all my life? . . . How can I be a better parent? How can I get more time for myself? How can I feel better about my self?"[16] Even if we grant the possibility that an answer to the last question could discuss guilt before the holy God and then Christ's reconciling death, the this-worldly, temporal focus of this list, as well as its preoccupation with coping strategies that *hearers* may attempt (rather than the saving work that God has achieved in his Son), suggests that at least some preaching that intends to be evangelistic—that is, to draw unbelievers to faith in Christ—may, ironically, obscure the good news on which non-Christians' eternal destiny depends by deflecting attention from God's grace and eternal outcomes to our actions and temporary difficulties. This result would be both tragic and ironic, because the felt-needs preacher wants non-Christians to be gripped and transformed by God's grace in the gospel. That transformation begins with an utter abandonment of self-reliance on our own attempts to follow principles or take steps. Yet, the sermons sometimes preached to show non-Christians that the Bible speaks relevantly to their issues may sound more like a *Reader's Digest* "tips for living" article than a summons to abandon self reliance and rest on Christ alone for all his saving benefits, lavished freely on helpless paupers.

4) Does the desire to avoid reinforcing non-Christians' mental stereotypes of churches and preachers as condemnatory and self-

---

16   Doug Murren, *Baby Boomerang* (Ventura: Regal, 1990), 103, as summarized in Douglas D. Webster, *Selling Jesus: What's Wrong with Marketing the Church* (Downers Grove: InterVarsity, 1992), 82–83. Murren does also include one theological question (an important one) in his list: "How did we get the Bible? How do I know it's God's Word?"

righteous tempt felt-needs preachers to avoid frank talk about human sin and guilt—thus obstructing the wholesome path of true humiliation, which leads to the discovery of Christ's grace?[17] Since "God opposes the proud but gives grace to the humble" (1 Peter 5:5–6), do preachers push their hearers away from grace when they shy away from Scripture's heart searching challenges to our sinful pride?

5) Does the laudable desire to communicate the gospel intelligibly to people unfamiliar with the biblical story and worldview run the risk of "translating" the Christian message in such a way that the message itself is distorted and its offensive challenge to pagan and secularized conceptions of reality is muted? Some early church fathers tried to "translate" the Bible's personal, covenantal, and historical message of redemption into the abstract categories of Hellenistic thought (for example, neo-Platonism), sometimes inadvertently distorting the message to force it to "fit" an alien worldview. Twenty-first century preachers are not immune to this danger. William Willimon, who is committed to communicating the gospel to our unchurched contemporaries, issues a sober caution about the dangers of translation:

> Biblical illiteracy, cultural pluralism, all of the linguistic and theological compromises we have made in our church's interface with the world suggest that the best hope for Christian preachers is to find some sort of religious Esperanto, a culturally approved common mode of discourse.... For most sermons I hear, and too many that I have preached, this is exactly what we have done. Biblical apocalyptic is existentialized, biblical prophecy is moralized, biblical narrative is psychologized, all in the interest of enabling our worldly hearers to take us seriously.[18]

Willimon later cites Missiologist Leslie Newbigin's identification of the tightrope that the evangelistic preacher must walk:

> On the one hand, he may simply fail to communicate: he uses the words of the language, but in such a way that he sounds like a foreigner; his

---

17   Lynne Hybels acknowledges the struggle her husband has had to maintain balance between the justice/holiness of God and the grace of God in his preaching (*Rediscovering*, 89). Don't we all?

18   William H. Willimon, *Peculiar Speech: Preaching to the Baptized* (Grand Rapids: Eerdmans, 1992), 75–76. This quote is from the chapter "Preaching to Pagans."

message is heard as the babblings of a man who really has nothing to say. Or, on the other hand, he may so far succeed in talking the language of his hearers that he is accepted all too easily as a familiar character—a moralist calling for greater purity of conduct or a guru offering a path to the salvation that all human beings want. His message is simply absorbed into the existing worldview . . . .[19]

Admittedly, too many preachers, forgetting their evangelistic calling when they step into the pulpit, fall into the former error, speaking as unintelligible foreigners to their own neighbors; but we must not underestimate the opposite danger of so accommodating the biblical message into the thought categories of secularized and re-paganized cultures that the message that Greeks once scorned as folly and Jews rejected as offensive sounds palatable and unexceptional.[20]

6) We must ask further: Is "felt needs," or other variations of preaching designed for the unchurched, adequate to meet the nourishment and maturation needs of Christian believers? With an exclusive stress on keeping everything "within reach" of the unchurched person's horizon of intelligibility, both in terminology and in topics, what has become of preaching's role in "building [converted sinners] up in comfort and holiness"?[21] Will not believers who long for maturity eventually want to move beyond the "milk" that the non-Christian or new Christian can digest? But if mature Christians, desiring meat, move on to churches with "doctrinal" or "edifying" or "worldview transforming" or "redemptive-historical" preaching, who will be left behind to care for spiritual newborns in the "seeker-sensitive" church? Or must mature believers who bear the load of service in such churches get their "protein" elsewhere than in worship, and through

19   Lesslie Newbigin, *Foolishness to the Greeks: The Gospel and Western Culture* (Grand Rapids: Eerdmans, 1986), 7, cited in Willimon, *Peculiar Speech*, 88.
20   See also Barbara Brown Taylor, *Speaking of Sin: The Lost Language of Salvation* (Cambridge, Massachusetts: Cowley, 2000), who first notes, "One of the more interesting effects of secularism on the language of sin and salvation has been the replacement of that language with the languages of medicine and law" (p. 31), but later notes how both of these other languages fall short of the full reality named by the biblical concept of sin: "Contrary to the medical model, we are not entirely at the mercy of our maladies. . . . Contrary to the legal model, sin is not simply a set of behaviors to be avoided" (p. 58). She insists that sin (in its biblical depth) is "our only hope," for its diagnosis of our problem opens the possibility of repentance and real pardon (pp. 40–96).
21   Westminster Shorter Catechism, A. 89.

means other than the proclamation of the Word, means such as small groups, personal Bible study, or private reading?[22]

Not all preaching that places priority on presenting the gospel clearly and persuasively to those who find the church's life and language foreign raises these troubling questions in the way that some expressions of "felt-needs" preaching raise them. Nevertheless the final question and the Shorter Catechism's wise and biblical insistence that the preaching of Scripture is designed by God for a bigger purpose than only the initial conversion of sinners caution us against absolutizing this (valid) evangelistic priority, as if it were the only purpose to be pursued in our preaching.

Preaching to Edify

This second category, like the first, includes a collection of approaches to preaching that differ from each other in many respects. They share, however, a consensus that emphasizes the use of Scripture in preaching to *edify hearers*, who are assumed to be professing believers in Christ, in the context of a corporate worship service. The English word "edify" reflects, via Latin, Paul's mixed architectural-physiological metaphor, in which the church is portrayed as a body that is being "built" (Greek: *oikodomeō*) toward maturity as its members serve each other (e.g., Eph. 4:12, 16, 29; 1 Cor. 14:3, 5, 12, 26). Advocates of this priority insist that regular preaching to a gathered congregation on a Lord's Day should aim to motivate and guide believers to pursue changes that bring their patterns of behavior and relationships into growing conformity to God's Word. Whether the focus is on personal holiness, corporate responsibility within the church, or cultural engagement, the objective of "preaching to edify" is to engage Christians in the intentional pursuit of transformation in both behavior and relationships.

This focus on the application[23] or implementation of God's Word to further Christians' sanctification creates strange bedfellows,

22   At Willow Creek the edification needs of maturing believers are met through the evening "New Community" meeting and through the small group structure. "By January 1976 it had become evident that the core believers, who were working so hard and giving out so much, desperately needed deeper Bible teaching and corporate worship. So we started the New Community, our midweek believers service." Hybels and Hybels, *Rediscovering*, 63–64 (cf. p. 130 on small groups).

23   Although some would characterize this approach as concentrating on "application," Adams denies that it is the preacher's task to "apply" the text to the

uniting counselor-homiletician Jay Adams, for example, with some strands of Puritan preaching, even though Adams sharply critiques the adverse influence of Puritan rhetorical forms on later Reformed homiletics. It also includes the "exemplaristic" homiletic tradition in the Netherlands in the early twentieth century, although Adams rejects the use of Old Testament narrative as exemplary or illustrative of general principles, whether psychological or interpersonal.[24] This "edifying" emphasis fits the distinctive emphases of the theonomists, who advocate enforcement of Mosaic judicial laws by modern states and embrace postmillennial eschatology. It is also practiced by preachers who do not share theonomic distinctives but want to motivate church members to lead holy lives amid a paganizing culture, or to bring their Christian faith to bear on their vocations in marketplace, community, and state.[25]

The core conviction of this priority (as developed by Adams, whom I will use as exemplary) is that preaching must aim to elicit change in the lives of hearers by proclaiming the *telos* (purpose) of the text. The *telos* is not merely the text's theme, which could be stated as an abstract proposition; the *telos* is the effect that God intends the text to produce in those who hear the sermon. This purpose is never merely to reveal information but always to bring hearers into greater conformity to Christ and his commands, especially in the establishment of new, godly patterns of behavior.[26] Thus Adams concludes,

> The purpose of preaching, then, is to effect *changes* among the members of God's church that build them up individually and that build up the body as a whole. *Individually*, good pastoral preaching helps each person in the congregation to grow in his faith, conforming his life more and more to biblical standards. *Corporately*, such preaching builds up the

congregation. In Adams's view, when we are thinking biblically, we assume that the text is addressed as much to our present hearers as to its first readers and is therefore *already applied* to our situation. The preacher's task is merely to "find the *equivalent* to the original circumstance and situation to which God then (and now) applied the warning, the promise, the principle, or the command" (*Preaching with Purpose*, 133), and then to offer guidance on how to *implement* the application of the text in hearers' behavior (pp. 138–45).

24   Jay E. Adams, *Preaching with Purpose: the Urgent Task of Homiletics* (Grand Rapids: Zondervan, 1982), x, 103.

25   Marsden's "culturalists" ("Reformed and American," 2, 9–10).

26   See the discussion of Col. 1:28 in the next chapter, particularly the comments of Geerhardus Vos cited there regarding the practical purpose of Scripture.

church as a body in the relationship of the parts to the whole, and the whole to God and to the world.[27]

This purpose means that the preacher must not only expound the doctrinal content of the text but also help the congregation to see how the spiritual situation and spiritual needs of the text's first recipients parallel their own situation and need for change through repentance and growth in sanctification.

Moreover, preaching must offer guidance in strategies for the implementation of biblical change. The preacher not only diagnoses the symptoms of evil behavior patterns that must be "put off" and describes godly patterns must be "put on," he also offers practical suggestions about *how* to effect the change.[28] Guidance on how to implement change is often found in the biblical text itself, and the preacher needs to sensitize himself and his congregation to recognize these normative directions. Where the text does not command steps for implementation, the preacher can suggest approaches, making clear that his suggestions do not have equal authority with scriptural commands.

Adams asserts that regular, week-in, week-out, pastoral preaching in a congregation has the purpose of edification, *not evangelism*. Of course edification presupposes evangelism, since only those who have been reborn by the Spirit and who have trusted Christ will have the power to change their patterns of behavior for the good. Adams therefore encourages evangelistic preaching; but he also insists that such preaching "is done 'out there,' where the unbelieving are, not primarily in the services of the church."[29] On the other hand, Adams also insists that the distinctive characteristic of "truly Christian" preaching to edify believers

> . . . is the all-pervading presence of a saving and sanctifying Christ. Jesus Christ must be at the heart of every sermon you preach. That is just as true of edificational preaching as it is of evangelistic preaching. But, while edificational preaching always must be evangelical, it must not become simply evangelistic. . . in which the major thrust is to proclaim the gospel with the intent of calling unbelievers to faith in Christ.[30]

27   *Preaching with Purpose*, 13 (emphases original).
28   Adams, *Preaching with Purpose*, 138–45.
29   Adams, *Preaching with Purpose*, 70. This is in sharp contrast, as we will see, to the assumptions and model developed in the New Life churches under Jack Miller's influence, and by Tim Keller at Redeemer Presbyterian in Manhattan.
30   Adams, *Preaching with Purpose*, 147.

Thus, although much preaching that aims to edify tends to concentrate on Christians' duties and strategies for fulfilling them, Adams (for one) would insist that the presupposition of the gospel of Christ's grace must distinguish this hortatory emphasis from moral admonition in other religious traditions.

Adams is representative of preachers who aim to edify when he opposes "preaching" that consists in an objective doctrinal or redemptive-historical lecture rather than a personal address of the Word of God to contemporary hearers that summons them to respond.[31] Believing that "the Spirit of God maketh . . . especially the preaching, of the Word, an effectual means of convincing and converting sinners, and of *building them up in holiness and comfort,* through faith, unto salvation,"[32] edification-oriented preachers aim their sermons toward effecting character and behavioral change in their hearers by the power of the Spirit. New Christians and old need to be taught how to put off the old man and put on the new and all the more so in a culture that has abandoned Christian morality and offers few models of the Christlike lifestyle. Preaching, like counseling, concerns the "cure of souls," so it must touch down into people's experience and point the way to maturity in Christ.[33] Its aim is more than the transfer of information.

Edificatory preachers also repudiate preaching that aims to elicit only an emotional response, without bringing a concrete challenge to pursue biblical change. Adams believes that when a Christian's struggle against sin seems stalled, typically the short circuit is found

---

31   Hence Adams's insistence that the "preaching stance" (in contrast to a "lecture stance") will be exhibited in a sermon outline having points expressed in the second person "you" rather than in the third person, or in impersonal topics or propositions ("God delivered the Israelites," "The Greatness of God's Love," etc.). *Preaching with Purpose,* 42–56.

32   *Westminster Shorter Catechism,* Answer 89 (emphasis added).

33   Hendrik Krabbendam, a winsome latter-day Puritan, critiques a certain extreme in the redemptive-historical homiletical tradition (see further below): "Indeed, preaching in the redemptive-historical tradition is often comparable to a ride in a Boeing 747 high above the landscape with its hot deserts, its snowpeaked mountains, its wide rivers, its dense forests, its open prairies, its craggy hills and its deep lakes. The view is panoramic, majestic, impressive, breathtaking, and always comfortable. But there is one problem. The Christian is not 'above' things. He is in the middle of things. He is trekking through the landscape." "Hermeneutics and Preaching," in Samuel T. Logan, Jr., ed. *The Preacher and Preaching: Reviving the Art in the Twentieth Century* (Phillipsburg: P & R, 1986), 235.

not in a lack of motivation but in ignorance of practical steps by which old habits are broken and new ones forged. On this point, however, many preachers who aim to edify Christians would demur, affirming instead that preaching must impress upon believers' hearts both the "why" and the "how" of sanctification, since coaching about strategies for implementing God's commands remains powerless apart from the stirring of the heart to gratitude through new vistas of the grace of Christ.[34]

As we will hear Paul assert in Colossians 1, and as we will later see illustrated in the "word of exhortation" that we now call the epistle to the Hebrews (Heb. 13:22), apostolic preaching has as one of its primary purposes the ongoing transformation of believers into the image of Christ. Paul proclaims Christ with the objective of "present[ing] everyone mature in Christ" (Col. 1:28). Therefore the aim to *edify* must be a priority in the pastor's purpose for his weekly sermons. Nevertheless, questions can be raised about the appropriateness of elevating of this purpose to primacy or exclusivity as the norm that controls the pastor's pulpit ministry.

1) Despite Adams's insistence that the gospel is foundational because spiritual growth cannot begin until one has trusted in Christ alone for salvation, does not his emphasis on concrete steps for pursuing behavioral change have the potential of drifting over into a moralism that draws attention so overwhelmingly to believers' duties that Christ's grace is obscured, at least in the impression left on his listeners? If the preacher attributes "stalling" in sanctification to faulty methods rather than to feeble faith and failing motivation, might he not emphasize self-discipline at the expense of grace, and make duty displace grateful love as the engine that drives the pursuit of holiness?

2) Although many preachers who aim to edify Christians might not concur *theoretically* with Adams's banishment of evangelistic preaching from corporate worship, yet *in practice* many pastors approach their weekly preaching with the assumptions that few unbelievers will be present, and therefore Sunday preaching's task is to summon the faithful to greater faithfulness in daily living. But does

---

34 C. John Miller, *Outgrowing the Ingrown Church* (Grand Rapids: Zondervan, 1986), 120–34.

not this separation between evangelistic and edificatory preaching convey the impression that the gospel of grace and the gratitude it evokes can be left in the background as Christians go on to deal with the nitty-gritty issues of sanctification? As we will see in Part 2, the apostolic model of *parenesis* (exhortation) in the New Testament grounds believers' obligations in the gospel itself, showing how the indicatives describing Christ's saving work precede and entail the imperatives that define our believing response to his mercy. When Christ's redemptive work is treated as an implicit backdrop to the sermon rather than an active character in the drama, three categories of listeners in the congregation may be misled. First, the unchurched who may be present (whether or not the preacher expects them) have their stereotypes of Christianity reinforced, and come away more firmly persuaded that Christian faith is a system of duties comparable to Buddhism, Hinduism, Judaism, Islam, Scientology, Marxism, or some secular self-improvement program. Second, even if the pastor's (pessimistic) assumption that unconverted adults are not present is correct, covenant children growing up the congregation may pick up the signal that being a Christian is really "about" what one does and refrains from doing, with trusting Jesus as merely a prelude to the main event.[35] Finally, Christian believers, who should (and probably do, in their "heart of hearts") know better, may find their joy in Christ and assurance of God's love clouded by a vague sense that the Father's delight over them (though not their eternal destiny) hangs contingent on their progress in the struggle against sin and for love and justice.[36]

3) Could a focus on transformation of observable behavioral patterns (which does not characterize all edificatory preaching, but probably fits much of it) fail to challenge hearers to see deeper dimensions of sanctification? Scripture warns that external conformity of action or speech apart from internal allegiance and affection of

---

35   God took care to avoid this inference by instructing Israelite parents to answer their children's question, "What is the meaning of the testimonies and the statutes and the rules that the LORD our God has commanded you?" by retelling the gospel of the exodus, highlighting the Lord's sovereign and gracious initiative as the very framework in which the commandments' meaning is found (Deut. 6:20–25).

36   See Jerry Bridges, *The Discipline of Grace: God's Role and Our Role in the Pursuit of Holiness* (Colorado Springs: NavPress, 1994), 13–27.

heart fails to please God (Matt. 23:25–28; Mark 7:6–7; Ps. 51:16–17). The transformation that the Holy Spirit produces not only restrains and compels actions but also reaches deeply into motives. Sanctification can be viewed as a progressive weaning of the heart from its idols, those hollow "authorities" whose approval we crave and from whom we seek security. Often, perhaps always, Christians' behavioral failures can be traced to misplaced trust and worship, to misgivings about the mercy and power of the triune God that tempt us to look elsewhere for acceptance and safety.[37] Preaching that aims to edify can and must delve down into the deep, invisible fountains of motivation, from which our actions spring (Prov. 4:23). To do so, it must overtly and consistently exhibit the transforming insight of apostolic preaching, namely that *the same gospel of grace* that reconciles alienated rebels continues to direct and drive their growth as reconciled children of God.

4) As we asked whether limiting the purpose of preaching to evangelizing unbelievers could result in the omission of biblical texts and topics from the pulpit ministry, so we may ask whether the edificatory approach can adequately address the diversity of biblical genres, texts, and topics. Apostolic preaching recognizes that no doctrine revealed in Scripture is given merely for information. Every revealed truth in some way transforms God's people in our covenantal relation to our Sovereign Savior. Changing our beliefs about God, ourselves, or our circumstances is as edifying an application of the Word as is reforming our behavior and habits. Yet, if preachers define edification more narrowly than Scripture does, limiting their purview to behavioral changes, they may neglect biblical texts, sections, or books that seem more cognitive rather than life transforming.

The edification of believers—our growth into Christlikeness internally and externally in thought, word, and deed, in motive and in action—is unquestionably one of the purposes of preaching exemplified in the ministry of the apostles. If, however, edification is exalted to the exclusion of evangelism or narrowed to address behavior but not belief, it falls short of the comprehensive aim that is exemplified in apostolic preaching.

---

37 David Powlison, "Idols of the Heart and Vanity Fair," *Journal of Biblical Counseling* 13.2 (Winter 1995): 35–50.

Preaching to Instruct

A third collection of approaches gives priority to the cognitive purpose of preaching. Preaching's aim is to turn hearers from error to truth, to "renew the mind" and "take every thought captive" to Christ, to replace erroneous worldviews with a true perception of reality and to refurbish the mind with biblical categories of thought. This emphasis on the cognitive is reflected in several distinct approaches to sermon content.

Theological Preaching. A thematic or systematic theological approach to instructional preaching focuses on the pastor's responsibility to preach *doctrine*—that is, "the whole counsel of God" (Acts 20:27). This approach is often implemented through topical sermons based on several biblical texts that address a single theme. It could also be embodied in a series of single-text expository sermons, in which the organization of the *series* is systematic or topical, rather than following the canonical order of texts in a particular biblical book (the latter being referred to historically as *lectio continua*). Whether worked out in a topical series of expository sermons, each explaining one biblical text, or in topical sermons that enlist various passages to illumine a revealed truth, the purpose is to impart to listeners various aspects of the Bible's system of truth about the triune God, creation, humanity, sin, redemption, and consummation.

The topical, thematic, or theological approach to instructional preaching is exemplified in the catechetical preaching required in the Christian Reformed Church and United Reformed Churches.[38] It also appears in preaching that explores the cardinal doctrines of the Christian faith (Trinity, creation, incarnation, atonement, second coming, etc.), the *solas* of the Reformation, and such distinctives of Reformed theology as divine sovereignty in history and the *ordo salutis*, the "five points," covenant theology, common grace, and the cultural mandate. Thematic preaching is sometimes overtly

---

38   Church Order of the Synod of Dort, Art. 68, in David W. Hall and Joseph H. Hall, eds. *Paradigms in Polity: Classic Readings in Reformed and Presbyterian Church Government* (Grand Rapids: Eerdmans, 1994), 182; Christian Reformed Church Order, Art. 54, in Richard R. DeRidder and Leonard J. Hofman, *Manual of Christian Reformed Church Government*, 1994 revision (Grand Rapids: CRC Publications, 1994), 290–91; *Church Order of the United Reformed Churches in North America.* 2nd ed. (1997), Art. 40 Available online: http://www.covenant-urc.org/urcna/co.html.

polemical, setting biblical truth in contrast to errors all around: Arminianism, dispensationalism, Catholicism, Eastern Orthodoxy, cults, individualism, anti-intellectualism, emotionalism, charismatic theology, secular humanism, New Age pagan spirituality, or major world religions.

In reaction to the theological malaise of Protestantism generally and evangelicalism in particular, articulate voices are emphasizing the need for a renewed emphasis on preaching the meat of confessional Reformation theology.[39] Preaching needs to fortify and deepen the covenant community, the church, in its apprehension of the biblical worldview, its awareness of the antithesis between it and all others, and its ability to discern truth from error. The theological homiletic is especially alarmed at the emotional manipulation and thinness of content in the preaching of the American church. No wonder the evangelical churches in North America, despite their reported large numbers of attendees, are being swept along by the culture rather than transforming the culture biblically. The contemporary church is "a mile wide and an inch deep"! Solid doctrinal teaching is the only remedy for "the scandal of the Evangelical mind."[40] The evangelical's mind needs to be renovated with biblical truth—the system of truth revealed in Scripture and summarized in Reformation confessions—if it is to be a truly Christian mind, able to withstand error's onslaughts. When Christians have a firmer and fuller grasp of the great doctrines of the faith, the church may again exert the vibrant influence on the culture that it did in Europe during the Reformation.

There are, therefore, strong reasons to applaud the resurgence of preaching that provides clear, deep theological instruction to congregations. Nevertheless, some questions or cautions could be raised concerning this emphasis on doctrinal preaching.

---

39   The Alliance of Confessing Evangelicals, organized through the leadership of the late Dr. James Montgomery Boice and now chaired by Dr. Ligon Duncan, is recalling evangelicalism to its Reformational-confessional roots, Calvinistic and Lutheran, as is White Horse Media (Dr. Michael Horton, president) through its magazine, *Modern Reformation*, and its radio talk show, *White Horse Inn*.

40   Mark A. Noll, *The Scandal of the Evangelical Mind* (Grand Rapids: Eerdmans, 1994), was more concerned over Evangelicals' non-participation or ineffective participation in the Academy and the intellectual issues affecting the direction of North American culture, than over the loss of the theological depth exemplified in the confessionalism of the Reformation churches, Lutheran and Calvinist, but the two symptoms of intellectual decline are not unrelated.

1) The selection and collocation of appropriate passages from diverse biblical books is as justified in homiletics as it is in the whole enterprise of systematic theology.[41] Nevertheless, we can ask, Are thematic-theological-topical preachers sufficiently sensitive to the suspicions that some hearers harbor toward pastors or theologians who seem to impose their own system on the biblical text rather than listening submissively to what the text itself, in its context, has to teach? When the preacher thematically pre-selects a group of biblical texts (whether for use in a single sermon or as the basis for a series), the skeptical and the unconvinced may suspect that he is avoiding the scriptural passages that pose difficulties for his theological tradition, or that texts are being wrenched out of their literary and historical contexts in order to prove a point. Suspicions deepen when catechetical preaching is practiced as an exposition of the catechism's statements themselves rather than as an exposition of Scripture with the assistance of the catechism's structure and summaries. Doctrinal preaching is not necessarily guilty of inappropriate "prooftexting," but it is suspect to postmodern Christians who resist what they perceive as unreflectively rigid and "foundationalist" systems of human theological thought.[42] In particular, topical preaching that appears to replace Scripture itself with documents derived from the church's history runs the risk of returning, or seeming to return, to the medieval hegemony of ecclesiastical tradition over the Word of God.

2) Does an emphasis on enriching Christians' intellectual growth and theological precision run the risk of encouraging imbalance in their spiritual growth? Can the objective, forensic, representative work of Christ on behalf of believers—absolutely vital as the ground of justification and basis for assurance—be so strongly emphasized that the subjective, transforming work of the Spirit in sanctification, which flows from justification, becomes eclipsed from

41   John M. Frame, *The Doctrine of the Knowledge of God* (Phillipsburg: P & R, 1987), 212: "While exegetical theology focuses on specific passages and biblical theology focuses on the historical features of Scripture, systematic theology seeks to bring all the aspects of Scripture together, to synthesize them . . . . the systematic theologian asks, What does the *whole* Bible teach about faith?—or about anything else."

42   E.g., Brian D. McLaren, *A Generous Orthodoxy: Why I am a Missional, Evangelical, Post/Protestant, Liberal/Conservative, Mystical/Poetic, Biblical, Charismatic/Contemplative, Fundamentalist/Calvinist, Anabaptist/Anglican, Methodist, Catholic, Green, Incarnational, Depressed-Yet-Hopeful, Emergent, Unfinished Christian* (Grand Rapids: Zondervan, 2004).

the congregation's view? Is it even possible that preaching intended to instruct the mind in the humbling truths of sovereign grace may tempt hearers to take pride in their superior understanding of such mysteries, puffing them up rather than building them up (1 Cor. 8:1)? Might such instructional preaching, contrary to the preacher's intention or expectation, tacitly lead hearers to identify spiritual maturity with the acquisition of orthodox concepts, forgetting the stress that Scripture places on one's whole-life response to revealed truth in sacrificial love and Christlike purity?

3) In seeking to deepen Christians' theological understanding and maturity, do preachers who delight in expounding to believers the depths of glorious gospel truths such as *sola gratia*, *sola fidei*, and *solus Christus* risk losing sight of preaching's complementary (and prior) purpose to communicate this good news to the unsaved, including the unchurched to whom theological jargon (in English, let alone Latin) means little?

Redemptive-Historical Preaching. The redemptive-historical approach to biblical interpretation in confessionally Reformed circles can be traced to the seminal thought of Geerhardus Vos, who served as the first professor of biblical theology at Princeton Theological Seminary from 1894 to 1932. Vos's redemptive-historical hermeneutic was transplanted through his writings and former students to the newly formed Westminster Theological Seminary in 1929. Its implications for homiletics were developed by Edmund P. Clowney, the seminary's president and professor of practical theology, through his example as a preacher, his classroom instruction, and his publications.[43] Through the influence of Clowney (under whose presidency Westminster Seminary California was founded in 1980) and of Derke Bergsma, the California school's first professor of practical theology, this approach has become a hallmark of the Westminster Seminary California homiletics curriculum.[44] It receives reinforcement from the biblical-theological emphasis of the biblical studies department,

---

43   *Preaching and Biblical Theology*; "Preaching Christ from All the Scriptures," in Logan, ed., *The Preacher and Preaching*, 163–91; *The Unfolding Mystery: Discovering Christ in the Old Testament* (Phillipsburg: P & R, 1988); and *Preaching Christ in All of Scripture* (Wheaton: Crossway, 2003).

44   Derke P. Bergsma, *Redemption: The Triumph of God's Great Plan* (Lansing, IL: Redeemer Books, 1989).

reflecting the influence of Geerhardus Vos, Herman Ridderbos, Richard Gaffin, Meredith G. Kline, and others. Similar emphasis can be seen in the homiletic publications of Sidney Greidanus of Calvin Theological Seminary, Bryan Chapell of Covenant Theological Seminary, and Graeme Goldsworthy of Moore Theological College.[45] A distinctive form of redemptive-historical preaching has been advocated by James Dennison, formerly librarian at Westminster Seminary California and now affiliated with Northwest Theological Seminary, particularly through the journal *Kerux*, of which he is editor. Some proponents of redemptive-historical homiletics have placed it in stark contrast to the pastoral aims and interpretive strategies of the "preaching to edify" approach. In the Netherlands prior to World War II, for example, K. Schilder, B. Holwerda, and M. B. Van't Veer advocated a redemptive-historical approach to the Bible's historical narratives in sharp critique of those who practiced "exemplaristic" preaching by drawing ethical applications from the obedient or wicked behavior of the human participants in the biblical account..[46] The issues in this debate have been communicated in North America through the writings of Sidney Greidanus and C. Trimp.[47]

Redemptive-historical preaching ties homiletics closely to hermeneutic considerations. It emphasizes the organic unity of the history of redemption—the enactment of God's plan for the rescue, reconciliation, and re-creation of his people, climaxing in the person,

---

45   Sidney Greidanus, *The Modern Preacher and the Ancient Text: Interpreting and Preaching Biblical Literature* (Grand Rapids: Eerdmans, 1988); *Preaching Christ from the Old Testament: A Contemporary Hermeneutical Method* (Grand Rapids: Eerdmans, 1999); Bryan Chapell, *Christ-Centered Preaching: Redeeming the Expository Sermon* (2nd ed; Grand Rapids: Baker, 2005); Graeme Goldsworthy, *Preaching the Whole Bible as Christian Scripture: The Application of Biblical Theology to Expository Preaching* (Grand Rapids: Eerdmans, 2000).

46   In English translation, note M. B. Van't Veer, "Christological Preaching of Historical Materials of the Old Testament," Parts 1 and 2. Available online at http://www.spindleworks.com/library/veer/veer.html and http://www.spindleworks.com/library/veer/veer2.html. B. Holwerda, "The History of Redemption in the Preaching of the Gospel." Available online: http://www.spindleworks.com/library/holwerda/holwerda.htm. See also S. G. de Graaf, *Promise and Deliverance*, 4 volumes. H. E. Runner and E. W. Runner, trans. (St. Catherine's, Ontario: Paideia, 1977–1981).

47   Sidney Greidanus, *Sola Scriptura: Problems and Principles in Preaching Historical Texts* (Toronto: Wedge, 1970); C. Trimp, *Preaching and the History of Salvation: Continuing an Unfinished Discussion*. N. D. Kloosterman, trans. (Scarsdale, NY: Westminster Book Service, 1996).

obedience, sacrifice, resurrection, and exaltation of Jesus Christ, and reaching consummation at his return in glory. Progress in the history of special revelation, conveyed to us now in the Scriptures of the Old Testament and New Testament, coincided with development in the history of redemption. Therefore, the feature that defines each discrete epoch, thereby delineating the primary historical context of any biblical passage, is the progressive advance of God's plan of redemption through the period of promise from the fall to the ministry of John the Baptist, preparatory to the ministry of Jesus the Messiah. Major advances in God's redemptive plan—the establishment of his kingdom and new creation—are linked to the Lord's inauguration of covenants with his servant-people (Adam, Noah, Abraham, Moses/ Old Covenant Israel, David, Jesus/New Covenant Israel).

Christians need to be shown how to read each Scripture, first in the context of its original redemptive-historical epoch, and then in terms of the focal point and climactic "horizon" toward which the particulars of God's plan always pointed, namely Jesus the Messiah, who is the second and last Adam, seed of Abraham, true Israel, royal descendent of David, and obedient and suffering Servant of the Lord.[48] Redemptive-historical hermeneutics, therefore, offer a framework for preaching Christ from all the Scriptures (cf. Luke 24:44–49) in a way that treats each text's and epoch's distinctiveness with integrity and at the same time does justice to the progressively unfolding clarity by which God sustained his people's hopes for the redemption that has now arrived in Jesus.[49] Integral to this approach

---

48   Clowney, *Preaching and Biblical Theology*, 88–112.

49   This concern that every *Christian* sermon expound its text in relation to Christ and his saving work is solidly rooted in the Reformation and the Protestant heritage that is its legacy. Note these remarks from a nineteenth-century Reformed pastor in New Jersey, Henry C. Fish, *Power in the Pulpit* (London: Banner of Truth, n.d.; reprint of an article that appeared in the *British and Foreign Evangelical Review*, 1862), 5–6: "[The preacher] who would have power must dwell much upon two great, all-comprehensive doctrines of the Scriptures—man a *sinner*, and Christ a *Saviour*. Hence, the law will be used as an effective instrument, for 'by the law is the knowledge of sin.' . . . The law must therefore be preached—it is indispensable to the authority and cogency of the pulpit—but not so much the law as the *gospel*—chiefly the *cross* of *Christ*. It was unto 'the *gospel* of God' that Paul was 'separated.' . . . The heart will yield to the power of the cross, when it will yield to nothing else. . . . Chalmers was not the only preacher who had spent years in laboriously describing vice and virtue, and urging men to be better, and all to no effect, simply because there was no 'cross' in his preaching. And it is undoubtedly a chief defect in the sermons even of evangelical pulpits, that there is not enough

is careful attention to biblical typology and an openness to seeing typological connections between Old Testament persons, events, and institutions not only where a New Testament author explicitly ties Old Testament foreshadow to New Testament fulfillment but also where other intertextual bridges (such as verbal allusion or striking situational correspondence) can be seen to connect Old Testament events with New Testament Christological fulfillment.[50] (The apostolic practice of typological interpretation will be discussed in more depth in chapter 7.)

Redemptive-historical preachers oppose the moralistic, particularly the exemplaristic, preaching of biblical historical narratives.[51] They find it a serious misunderstanding of the purpose of biblical history to focus on the human participants in the narrative either as positive moral examples to be emulated, or as negative examples whose experiences warn against unbelief and evil.[52] The Christian

---

of *Christ* in them. . . " On the other side of the Atlantic a few years later, Patrick Fairbairn of Scotland wrote: "And as in the gospel itself everything is found linked on one side or another to the mediation of Christ, so in [the pastor's] public ministrations he will never want opportunities, whatever may be the particular theme or passage handled, to point the attention of his audience to the central object, and press on *their* regard what is uppermost in *his own*, namely, the surpassing love and beauty and preciousness of the Crucified One, and the alone sufficiency of His great salvation. . . . The Apostle to the Gentiles, in this respect pre-eminently the model of a Christian teacher, amid manifold diversities of subject and object, things present and things to come, never lost sight of his calling to preach the unsearchable riches of Christ, and made the crucified Redeemer the Alpha and the Omega of his testimony to men." Fairbairn, *Pastoral Theology: a Treatise on the Office and Duties of the Christian Pastor* (1875; repr. Audubon, NJ: Old Paths Publications, 1992), 150.

50   See note 26 in chapter 1's discussion of "intertextual allusion," where John 3:16 was used as an example.

51   Sidney Greidanus, *Sola Scriptura: Problems and Principles in Preaching Historical Texts* (Toronto: Wedge, 1970), 78–83.

52   B. Holwerda, *The History of Redemption in the Preaching of the Gospel* (ET Orange City: Mid-America Reformed Seminary, n.d.), 26: "It is of great importance to determine exactly what God does in a certain section. Often we begin immediately by looking at the persons and are busy identifying them with people of today. Of course we may not forget the human aspect since each detail asks for attention. But we should always see those human deeds as reaction in [sic] God's action. Abraham and Abimelech for example: this is not the sin of a white lie in general but an attempt to secure in this way the promise of the seen, the heir. . . . The same is true of Israel's grumbling; we are not dealing here with the sin of rebellion, but with the rejection of God's redemption as they had seen by the water from the rock; 'the rock was Christ.' "

preacher must never preach an Old Testament text (narrative or other genre) in such a way that his sermon could have been acceptable in a synagogue whose members do not recognize that Jesus is the Messiah.[53] The purpose of Old Testament historical narrative is not to teach moral lessons, but to trace the work of God, the Savior of his people, whose redeeming presence among them reaches its climactic expression in Christ's incarnation. The indicative mood—Scripture's declaration of God's redemptive action in history—*precedes* the imperative, which specifies the appropriate response on our part. In some redemptive-historical circles, the reaction against perceived moralism is carried further, with a motto, "The indicative *implies* or *entails* the imperative," understood to mean that the preacher need not and should not make specific applications, calling for changed attitudes or behavior, lest he trespass into the Holy Spirit's territory or distract his listeners from Scripture's primary summons to adore the Redeemer.

The dedication of this book to the memory of Dr. Clowney and the apostolic hermeneutic-homiletic method laid out in Part 2 make clear that I try to preach and to teach preaching in light of the insights and emphases of the redemptive-historical approach. Nevertheless, outside observers have objections, suspicions, concerns, or questions about this model of preaching, and these deserve answers. Many of these will be addressed in chapter 5 and in the exposition of "apostolic preaching," in Part 2.

1) Many conservative biblical scholars, mindful of patristic and medieval allegorical interpretations that appear implausible when assessed by the criteria of post-Enlightenment historical criticism, are reluctant to give credence to any typological treatment of Old Testament events, institutions, or persons for which explicit New Testament warrant cannot be cited. Their question is legitimate: Does the loosening of strictures on identifying typological connections between Old Testament shadows and New Testament substance give

---

53   Fish, *Power*, 6: "The criticism of a certain theological professor upon the trial sermon of a student in the Seminary, would apply to a multitude of the *moral essays* read from our pulpits: 'Young man, an educated *heathen* could write just as good a sermon as that!' It is a historical fact that the most successful ministers, in any age or country, have been those who determined, with Paul, to know nothing 'save Christ and him crucified.' Beyond question, Flavel was right: 'The excellency of a sermon lies in the plainest discoveries and liveliest applications of Jesus Christ.'"

too much rein to the preacher's imagination, allowing him to substitute "eisegesis" for exegesis? Does expanding the parameters of possible typology tempt the preacher to draw forced and unconvincing lines of contact between Old Testament texts and Christ, sometimes on the basis of incidental and external details rather than in terms of the passage's central spiritual thrust in its literary and historical contexts?

2) Does the insistence on relating each historical text to the flow of redemptive history climaxing in Christ obscure the distinctiveness and particularity of each text and, consequently, of each sermon? We recall Krabbendam's critique that redemptive-historical preaching often seems like a transcontinental air flight at cruising altitude, high above both the particularities of the biblical text and the messy daily obstacles confronting hearers in their pilgrimage of faith.[54] At ground level the sharp contrasts between mountains, plains, and valleys are easily visible, but they tend to disappear when observed at high altitudes. Do all redemptive-historical sermons sound essentially alike?

3) Can the redemptive-historical, Christocentric model of preaching do justice to other genres of biblical literature besides historical narrative: for example, to wisdom literature, Old Testament legal material, or New Testament ethical instruction? How should these other genres of biblical literature be preached in such a way that they are properly related to their place in the history of revelation (rather than treating Old Testament wisdom literature, for example, simply as timeless truths) and, more importantly, to relate them to the centrality of Christ and his redemptive work? To avoid moralism, must the redemptive-historical preacher not only show hearers how Scripture's indicatives precede its imperatives but also strive mightily to transform imperatives into indicatives?[55]

4) Can redemptive-historical preaching consistently offer any more specific application of Scripture than, "Trust Christ and give

---

54   See note 33 above.

55   For example, student preachers, thinking they are being faithful to Vos's insights, have asserted, appearances notwithstanding, that in Ephesians 5:22–33 Paul had *no intention* to instruct Christian wives and husbands how to relate to each other but sought only to extol the bond of Christ with his church.

thanks to God for his gracious redemption"?[56] Krabbendam charges that some redemptive-historical preaching seems, by design, to effect in its hearers nothing more than "aesthetic contemplation" of the beauties of God's redemptive plan.[57] As we observe the diverse ways in which the New Testament actually interprets and employs the Old Testament, does apostolic practice actually sustain the absolute claim made by some advocates of redemptive-historical homiletics that Old Testament historical narrative is *never* given for the purpose (even a secondary purpose) of providing ethical guidance? Do not the actions that the divine and human narrators approve or disapprove show us *something* instructive about what a faithful response to God's covenant grace would be? And do not the New Testament authors' commendation of past saints' faith and faithfulness (Heb. 11; James 5:10, 17–18) and warnings drawn from past infidelity (1 Cor. 10:1–14; Heb. 3–4) imply that such ancient examples, positive and negative, are ethically instructive for us, who inhabit a more privileged epoch of redemptive history?[58]

One indispensable purpose of preaching is to instruct its hearers, both to provide a matrix for interrelating Scripture's teachings about God, creation, humanity, sin, salvation, and so on (systematic theology) and to map the historical drama by which God worked out the redemption of his people through Jesus his Son (biblical theology). Non-Christian listeners need instruction in the truths of Scripture, particularly concerning Christ and his redeeming work, if the

---

56 Greidanus, *Sola Scriptura*, 187–89 identifies this problem pointedly among the Dutch redemptive-historical advocates in the early twentieth century: "Schilder calls for sermons 'which open the treasures of the Word and disclose the glories of Reformed dogma and of redemptive history,' in a word, sermons which are 'masterpieces.' The question arises whether Schilder wants sermons which are *theological* masterpieces. His ideal is to preach the facts in their significance for the course of redemptive history. The danger in trying to attain this goal is that the congregation will not hear a *sermon* but a *lecture* on redemptive history. . . . We wonder, in other words, whether such sermons describing the beauty of the redemptive-historical building do not lack precisely that character which makes a sermon a sermon: the Word of God addressed to this particular congregation."

57 Krabbendam, "Hermeneutics and Preaching," 235.

58 For the apostolic authors through whom God gave us the New Testament, the contrast between ancient Israel's era and "the end of the ages" (1 Cor. 10:11) in which Christian believers live *heightens* (rather than eliminates) our responsibility to draw ethical inferences from Israel's experience and to modify our behavior accordingly. See chapter 6 below, on Hebrews as a paradigm of apostolic preaching of the Old Testament.

preacher's call to "believe" is to be meaningful to them. Christians likewise need instruction in the truths of Scripture, if preaching is to achieve its objective to edify them. Apart from the truths of the gospel of grace, preaching to edify sinks into moralism, for imperatives ungrounded in the indicative of God's gracious initiative breed in hearers either self-righteous hypocrisy or self-condemning despair.

On the other hand, preaching intended *only* to instruct—seeking only cognitive outcomes, on the assumption that other responses are less essential or will follow inevitably when listeners' thinking is straightened out—falls short of the homiletic norm laid out for us in the apostolic preaching of the New Testament.

In the next chapter we will hear the apostle Paul's articulation (in a single, super-rich portion of his epistle to Colossae) of the purpose, content, and method of his own preaching ministry. Before concluding this survey of contemporary priorities and polarities in preaching, however, we take note of an approach that seems to capture (no doubt imperfectly, but faithfully and effectively) the balance and integration of homiletic purposes that we will observe in the apostolic model.

"The Gospel Changes Everything": An Approach to Evangelistic, Edificatory Redemptive-Historical Preaching

In one way or another, this approach to preaching and its purpose agrees with all the other approaches: preaching must be *Christ centered*, must interpret biblical texts in their *redemptive-historical contexts*, must aim for *change*, must proclaim the *doctrinal center* of the Reformation (grace alone, faith alone, Christ alone, God's glory alone) with passion and personal application, and must speak in a language that connects with the *unchurched* in our culture, shattering their stereotypes of Christianity and bringing them face to face with Christ, who meets sinners' real needs—felt and unfelt.

Yet this approach, which I have encountered in the pastoral ministries of Timothy Keller and Jack Miller, differs somewhat from each of the others. Its difference lies partly in its blend of the Reformed heritage of preaching, evangelism, and pastoral care, with a concern to enflesh the biblical aspects of our heritage in the midst of contemporary post-Christian and postmodern culture. Keller and Miller are certainly indebted to earlier preachers, particularly the Puritans in Great Britain and America. Keller credits a foundational insight that molds his approach to preaching in New York City to the influence of

George Whitefield's sermon "The Method of Grace," but he also cites other Puritan preachers, particularly Jonathan Edwards, with deep appreciation. Miller's doctoral studies in English literature focused on the American Puritans and their literary heirs; his teaching on sonship and sanctification cites Martin Luther, Walter Marshall, and others. Keller also emphasizes that the most formative influence on his approach to Scripture is the Christocentric, redemptive-historical homiletic of Edmund Clowney—so much so, that Keller believes his own approach should not be viewed as completely distinct from the redemptive-historical approach but as a subcategory of redemptive-historical preaching in the mold of Clowney.[59]

I will take Tim Keller as typical of this approach, since I have had opportunity (1) to listen to tapes of his lectures on "Preaching to the Secular Mind," delivered in summer 1997 in London under the auspices of World Harvest Mission; (2) to observe his approach in action during my visit to Redeemer Presbyterian Church in New York in October 1997; and (3) to receive from him an extensive and very helpful response to an earlier draft of this chapter (July 1999).[60] Among the central emphases of Keller's homiletic approach are the following.

1) What both the unbeliever and the believer need to hear in preaching is the gospel, with its implications for a life lived in confident gratitude in response to amazing grace.[61] Christians are constantly

---

59   Timothy Keller, *email* to Dennis Johnson, July 13, 1999: "I don't really think my approach can be classified by one of my favorite Bible themes ("idolatry"). [DEJ: An earlier version of this chapter, sent to Keller for review, had characterized his approach as combating the idols of the heart with the gospel of Christ's grace.] It really is just the Christo-centric method, I think. That fact that my sermons 'feel' so different than Clowney's probably comes from the fact that he is a professor who forged much of his thinking in an academic environment, and I didn't. I owe more to him by far than to Adams (approach #2) . . ., Sproul . . . (approach #3) or Hybels and ilk (approach #1) . . . though I love and benefit from them all. . . . So it feels odd to be set out as #4. It's probably, therefore, not accurate to pair me with Miller rather than Clowney. I even feel much, much more like I'm following in Clowney's footsteps. . . ."

60   See also Timothy Keller, "A Model for Preaching," parts 1, 2, 3, *The Journal of Biblical Counseling*, 12.3 (Spring 1994): 36–42; 13.1 (Fall 1994): 39–48; 13.2 (Winter 1995): 51–60. Tim Keller's sermons are available online from http://www.redeemer3.com/store/ in MP3, CD, and tape formats.

61   In his *email* response to an earlier draft of this chapter, Keller wrote: "You yourself say that this is a hard approach to give a title to. . . . I believe the key to it has to do with sanctification by faith-alone—that believers and non-believers need

tempted to relapse into legalistic attitudes in their pursuit of sanctification, so we never outgrow our need to hear the good news of God's free and sovereign grace in Christ.[62] Sanctification, no less than justification, must come by grace alone, through faith alone—we grow more like Christ only by growing more consistent in trusting Christ alone, thinking, feeling, acting "in line with the truth of the gospel" (Gal. 2:14). From this grace alone can flow true sanctification, motivated by gratitude and empowered by the Spirit.[63] We need to repent not only of our *sins* but also of our *righteousness*—our efforts at self-atonement in lieu of surrender to the all-sufficient grace of Christ.[64] Keller traces his

---

the same thing—that the gospel is not just the way to be justified, but to be sanctified. That is what sets it apart from all the other approaches (#1, #2, #3) except Clowney's."

62   In this connection note the comments of Hughes Oliphant Old on 2 Clement (ca. 125), which Old identifies as perhaps the earliest preserved post-apostolic Christian sermon: "This sermon is also interesting because of what it tells us about how the second-century Church approached evangelism. It is preached to a Christian congregation and yet it is also a witness to non-Christians. That the sermon is to be understood as having an evangelistic purpose is clear from the auxiliary text chosen from the Gospels, 'I came not to call the righteous, but sinners' (Matt. 9:13 and par.). We see here that the church of the second century did its evangelistic preaching in the midst of the worshiping congregation, and it was the worshiping congregation which did the evangelism. This is not an evangelism based on some sort of theology of decisional regeneration, nor one based on a theology of baptismal regeneration. It is rather an evangelism based solidly on justification by faith, on the confidence that faith comes by hearing and hearing by the Word of God. But this evangelism also puts a strong emphasis on sanctification. The Christian life is lived out of gratitude to God for the gracious gift of salvation. Non-Christians are present in the service of worship, both Jews and Gentiles, and non-Christians as well as Christians need repentance. The preacher begs his listeners to repent from the bottom of their hearts that they might be saved. Evangelism did not require a special message preached for the unconverted, different from the one for the converted, nor did it mandate that the faithful hear and enthusiastically support again and again evangelistic sermons that were not really directed to them. Rather, when Christ is proclaimed as Lord and Savior, when God's promises are proclaimed and a witness is given that God is faithful and that in Christ those promises have been fulfilled, and will yet be fulfilled, then evangelism is done." Hughes Oliphant Old, *The Reading and Preaching of the Scriptures in the Worship of the Christian Church*, vol. 1, *The Biblical Period* (Grand Rapids: Eerdmans, 1998), 283.

63   Timothy Keller, "The Centrality of the Gospel." Available online at: http://www.redeemer2.com/resources/papers/centrality.pdf.

64   Keller cites the late Southern writer Flannery O'Conner's observation that religious people think "that the way to avoid Jesus was to avoid sin . . . ." He finds in both the irreligious person who appeals to relativism to evade repentance and in the religious person who tries to establish his or her own righteousness by fol-

discovery of this need of two-fold repentance to George Whitefield's sermon, "The Method of Grace."[65]

2) The root of the unbeliever's sin and misery is his worship (recognized or, often, unrecognized) of a false god, an idol.[66] Likewise the believer's frustration, resentment, lack of joy, anger, worry, fear, etc., are symptoms of lingering allegiance to various idols of the heart that persistently reassert themselves as rivals with Jesus for our trust, devotion, and service. Our idols are whatever (other than the triune God) we trust in to gain "salvation," however we define it—whatever we believe that we cannot live without. Keller cites Calvin as calling our hearts "idol factories," constantly manufacturing rivals to the living God.[67] Idols may include financial success, career achievement, parental approval, spousal love, sexual fulfillment, academic or artistic achievement or recognition, parenthood and grateful admiration by well-behaved children, or other things that are not in themselves evil. The god we serve defines for us what, in practice, we mean by "sin or righteousness" and "curse or blessing." "Sin" is behavior on our part that hinders our receiving our god's "blessing." "Righteousness" is the behavior that we expect to bring us

---

lowing Jesus' example the desire to avoid, at all costs, the humiliating experience of utter dependence upon Jesus as Savior. "Centrality of the Gospel."

65   *Select Sermons of George Whitefield* (London: Banner of Truth, 1958), 75–95. See especially pp. 81–83: "When a poor soul is somewhat awakened by the terrors of the Lord, then the poor creature, being born under the covenant of works, flies directly to a covenant of works again. And as Adam and Eve hid themselves . . . and sewed fig leaves . . . so the poor sinner, when awakened, flies to his duties and to his performances, to hide himself from God, and goes to patch up a righteousness of his own. Says he, I will be mighty good now—I will reform—I will do all I can; and then certainly Jesus Christ will have mercy on me."

66   In an earlier draft, I had labeled Keller's approach, "Grace vs. the Idols of the Heart," but Keller clarified (July 13, 1999, e-mail) that this "focus is really just a key theme for an 'existential' perspective on the gospel. The theme is especially helpful for counseling people with the gospel. The new-creation and the kingdom vs. the old world and kingdom of Satan motifs are more 'situational' perspective on the gospel. That theme is very helpful for directing people to live a life of justice and mercy toward the poor and excluded on the basis of the gospel. Many of the other themes you mention later in your paper seem more 'normative' to me."

67   Calvin, *Institutes* 1.11.8 (McNeill/Battles, p. 108): "From this we may gather that man's nature, so to speak, is a perpetual factory of idols . . . . Man's mind, full as it is of pride and boldness, dares to imagine a god according to its own capacity; as it sluggishly plods, indeed is overwhelmed with the crassest ignorance, it conceives an unreality and an empty appearance as God."

"blessing." For the worshiper of Career, hard work and long hours on the job are "righteousness," for which we expect our god to reward us with the "blessings" of recognition, promotion, sense of accomplishment, and salary increases. For the worshiper of Family, on the other hand, excessively hard work and long hours are "sin," threatening the "blessing" of domestic tranquillity in which our emotional needs are met. People need to see that every idol will fail them for two reasons: unlike the triune God who came to save his people in Jesus, (a) no idol will forgive the "sin" committed against it; and (b) every idol will be torn away from its worshiper sooner or later—no idol can promise, "Never will I leave you, never will I forsake you."[68] The idols of our hearts are unforgiving because they always belong to a system of works-righteousness: Fulfill expectations, you will live; fail, and you die. Moreover, because every idol is a specific expression of our propensity to worship and serve the creature rather than the Creator (Rom. 1:25) and no creature lasts forever, no idol can sustain its worshiper through life and through death.

3) The preacher and his congregation assume the presence of unbelievers in their midst, people to whom the "language of Zion" is a foreign tongue and to whom biblical truths (including the very concept of absolute truth) are alien. Preaching must take account of the fact that the truths of the gospel are counter-intuitive to the unregenerate mind, and this reality is becoming more overt as western culture abandons even the shell of a biblical worldview. Therefore, preaching must incorporate apologetics—"sidebars" addressed to unbelievers where the preacher frankly acknowledges the alienness of the gospel to prevailing cultural assumptions but also respectfully challenges non-Christians to recognize the coherence of biblical truth and its superior adequacy to address the dilemmas of human life and thought.

This approach rejects moralistic attempts to attract and hold non-Christians' attention by offering practical lists of "helpful" tips for self-remedy. While intentionally adjusting its language to make the gospel's beauty and offensiveness intelligible to postmodern

---

68   In Heb. 13:5 the promise of God, "Never will I leave you" (NIV), provides the sufficient alternative and antidote to the love of money as a source of security from threat and insulation from fear (vs. 5). Certainly money can make no such promise to its worshiper, as Jesus' parable of the rich fool shows (Luke 12:16–21).

unchurched urbanites,[69] it challenges the assumption (shared by seeker-sensitive "preachers to convert" and those who believe that edifying believers is the sole purpose of congregational preaching) that preaching addressed to the church should differ significantly from preaching addressed to the unbelieving and uncommitted. Keller insists that the same gospel that introduces people into the family of God is the power that transforms them as children of God. He therefore implicitly challenges Adams's view that committed Christians need preaching that, only *presupposing* justifying grace, concentrates on establishing godly patterns of behavior through self-discipline aided by the Holy Spirit. He also rejects the seeker-sensitive assumption that certain biblical topics should be avoided in the presence of "seekers" lest they cause offense.[70] Rather, the whole counsel of God can and must be preached to all sorts of people, whatever their level (or lack) of commitment to Christ, because the whole counsel of God finds its integrative center and meaning in God's sovereign grace in Christ.[71] This also means that it is the preacher's challenge to cross the chasms of misunderstanding and alienation that separate his hearers, including secularized, relativized postmoderns, from the biblical revelation of the living God. The preacher cannot lazily wait for his unchurched hearers to do the difficult, cross-cultural work of translation: learning church lingo in order to hear Christ's word of life to them. Instead, the preacher himself must be the cross-cultural traveler and translator, bringing the Bible's alien message into the indigenous language and thought-forms of those to whom God has sent him.

---

69 Timothy Keller, "The Missional Church" (June 2001). Available online: http://www.redeemer2.com/resources/papers/missional.pdf.

70 Seeker-sensitive models that avoid the very topics on which the Bible is most radically and offensively counter-cultural cast a cloud of suspicion over the integrity and authenticity of the church and its message—and, even more seriously, deflect the gospel's sharp cutting edge from its purpose of shattering our culture's most treasured idols. On the other hand, Keller says: "The sermons at Redeemer regularly tackle doctrines that are very offensive to post-modern people. . . . A) that Jesus is the only way to God (a defense of Christian 'exclusivism'), B) the inerrancy of Scripture, C) the reality of hell, D) the sovereignty of God over every circumstance including trouble and suffering, E) the sinfulness of any sex outside of marriage, F) total depravity, G) propitiation and the anger of God, H) last-day judgment, and I) the reality of transcendent moral absolutes. . . . Now this is highly offensive" (July 13, 1999, *email*).

71 "The gospel is not just the A-B-C's but the A to Z of Christianity. The gospel is not just the minimum required doctrine necessary to enter the kingdom, but the way we make all progress in the kingdom" ("Centrality of the Gospel").

Keller's is an ambitious and daring homiletic enterprise that runs counter to the prevailing American cultural and ecclesiastical practice of finely sliced demographic subdivision and niche marketing. Redeemer's approach to urban ministry rubs against the grain of the church-growth movement's homogeneous unit principle[72] by cultivating a worship environment accessible both to Christians and pagans, as well as to people of diverse ages, races, and educational and economic backgrounds. Keller's preaching, likewise, resists pressures to customize his message and style to target one audience subgroup instead of others. The task is daunting, and concerns have been raised about this effort to address Christian and non-Christian together: Will preaching that remains intelligible to the non-Christian in both verbal and conceptual "vocabulary" be adequate to deepen the spiritual and theological maturity of Christians over the long run? Can one sermon consistently provide a call to repentant faith for the uncommitted, milk for spiritual infants, and meat for the mature?[73] From another perspective, can preaching that always takes into account the interpretive horizon of secularized, postmodern listeners encompass the breadth and diversity of themes, genres, and texts that fill the Scriptures? Can this approach preach "the whole counsel of God," making appropriate use of all the Scriptures, since the *whole* Bible is breathed by God and therefore useful for some aspect or other—teaching, rebuking, correcting, training in righteousness—of the Spirit's grand new creation project in the individual and the church (2 Tim. 3:16–17)?[74]

---

72   Donald McGavran, *Understanding Church Growth* (Grand Rapids: Eerdmans, 1970), 85–87, 285–91.

73   At InterVarsity Christian Fellowship's Urbana '93, before I had firsthand knowledge of Redeemer, I met a young woman who lived in New York, who had worshipped at Redeemer for a while, who appreciated its ministry as a gateway into God's kingdom for many, but who had moved on to another church, seeking what she considered to be deeper, meatier teaching. On the other hand, a colleague on the Westminster in California faculty affirms that he regularly listens to recordings of Keller's sermons and finds them stimulating, challenging, and edifying; this has generally been my experience, as well.

74   Keller has talked with Christians who have attended Redeemer for some time and expressed a desire for "deeper, meatier" teaching than they have found in his public preaching ministry. He has found they typically want one of three things: (1) "More theological distinctives spelled out" (different views of baptism, charismatic gifts, etc.). Keller's response is that a large number of those present in Redeemer worship services need *first* to be taught *even meatier* and *more offensive* truths of Scripture (such as those listed in footnote 70, uniqueness of Christ,

These are serious questions, and Keller's extensive email response indicates that he has given significant thought to these issues. His intention is to hold together the evangelistic and edificatory purposes of preaching, anchoring both directly in a Christ-centered, grace-grounded proclamation of God's Word in words that engage the postmodern mission field confronting the church in the West. Those who appreciate the attempt, as I do, must not underestimate the difficulty of maintaining this unity and balance. Here is where the hermeneutic and homiletic strategies of the apostles, learned from Jesus himself and applied in diverse venues, ranging from biblically literate Judaism to backwater paganism to urbane intellectualism, have much to teach us.

---

divine justice and wrath, etc.) before considering, for example, the case for infant baptism (which is addressed elsewhere in Redeemer's ministry, in classes or small groups). (2) "More doctrinal and ethical details spelled out" (divorce and remarriage, Christian schools, how to do family devotions or church discipline, politics, end times). Keller responds: "Every Christian will need to get eventually into biblical and theological details that are inappropriate for a sermon . . . during a worship service. Therefore every preacher draws a line somewhere and says, 'If you want the details of biblical knowledge you need to know to grow mature, you will have to get into classes or groups where they can be covered.' This means that almost every preacher will have someone who draws the line between 'sermon' and a 'lecture' further toward the 'lecture' than the preacher does, and who therefore will say 'I want more meat.' . . . All the old Puritans (especially Edwards) knew better the difference between a lecture and a sermon. The sermon was more 'edifying'—more oriented to the affections and less oriented to detailed cognitive arguments." (3) ". . . more talk about 'hot' topics" (abortion, homosexuality, etc.). Keller responds: "I absolutely believe in preaching the whole counsel of God, but in an order that makes sense of it. If doctrine D, E, and F are completely premised on doctrines A, B, and C—you have to persuade people of ABC first. It's silly to tell someone 'abortion is a sin' if they don't understand the meaning of the word sin. . . . Therefore, we never at Redeemer avoid a subject because it is offensive, but we may postpone a subject and put it into classes or small group material which people work through after they've been brought toward Christ by the preaching" (*email*).

3
Paul's Theology of Preaching

W hich of the homiletic emphases described in the previous chapter is the "right" one? To which should the preacher commit himself as devoted apprentice, shunning all others? Wrong questions! Each view has valid, biblical insights, which can be illustrated in the apostolic preaching that we find in the New Testament. These insights will be lost to our detriment if we repudiate altogether the emphasis of any of the views. Moreover, if genuinely biblical, apostolic insights are to be found in all the approaches, in principle these insights can be reconciled and incorporated into a more complex and richer homiletic that will enable us, by the grace, wisdom, and power of the Spirit, to preach the rich diversity of Scripture's witness to Christ.

A helpful starting point, as Phillips Brooks and Jay Adams have observed, is to define the purposes of preaching, which are determined by the purposes of the Scriptures that we preach. Paul indicts self-appointed teachers of God's law who misunderstand "the things about which they make confident assertions," thereby failing to use the law "lawfully," in accord with its divinely ordained purpose (1 Tim. 1:7-8). Likewise, Peter speaks of the twisting of Paul's epistles and "the other Scriptures" by those who are ignorant and unstable, warning that such abuse of Scripture leads to one's own destruction (2 Peter 3:16). Our preaching of any and every Scripture must go "with the grain" of the purpose or purposes for which God gave that particular text The moment we begin to reflect on the challenge of becoming more effective preachers, we are confronted with the question: "What is *effective* preaching?" This question, in turn, can only be answered when we understand the *effect* that preaching is supposed to have. We cannot evaluate our own strengths and weaknesses in preaching, nor our progress in strengthening strengths and minimizing weaknesses, unless we know what preaching is supposed to *do*, what *purpose* it is to accomplish.

Since God commissions and sends preachers (Rom. 10:15; Matt. 28:18–20), the right to define the purpose of preaching is his. The Scriptures have much to say about preaching and its purpose, but one text that encapsulates in brief compass[1] much of the Bible's teaching on the purpose of preaching (and many other dimensions of apostolic proclamation) is Paul's comment on his own ministry in Colossians 1:24–2:7:

> Now I rejoice in my sufferings for your sake, and in my flesh I am filling up what is lacking in Christ's afflictions for the sake of his body, that is, the church, of which I became a minister according to the stewardship from God that was given to me for you, to make the word of God fully known, the mystery hidden for ages and generations but now revealed to his saints. To them God chose to make known how great among the Gentiles are the riches of the glory of this mystery, which is Christ in you, the hope of glory. Him we proclaim, warning everyone and teaching everyone with all wisdom, that we may present everyone mature in Christ. For this I toil, struggling with all his energy that he powerfully works within me.
>
> For I want you to know how great a struggle I have for you and for those at Laodicea and for all who have not seen me face to face, that their hearts may be encouraged, being knit together in love, to reach all the riches of full assurance of understanding and the knowledge of God's mystery, which is Christ, in whom are hidden all the treasures of wisdom and knowledge. I say this in order that no one may delude you with plausible arguments. For though I am absent in body, yet I am with

---

1   Of course, Paul's epistles overflow with descriptions of the content and purpose of his preaching and of the written Scriptures. Scripture's aim is to instruct, encourage, and give hope (Rom. 15:4) and to equip the man of God for teaching, reproof, correction, and training in righteousness (2 Tim. 3:16; see 4:2). Timothy's pastoral aim in opposing false teachers at Ephesus must be "love that issues from a pure heart and a good conscience and a sincere faith" (1 Tim. 1:3-5). In his farewell charge to the elders of Ephesus, Paul summed up his aims in preaching in several ways: he declared everything that would be spiritually profitable to his hearers (Acts 20:20), testifying of "repentance toward God and faith in our Lord Jesus Christ" (vs. 21) and imparting "the gospel of the grace of God" (vs. 24), indeed "the whole counsel of God" (vs. 27). As we will see, these purposes and motifs as well as others (e.g., Matt. 28:20; Luke 1:3-4; John 20:30-31; 1 John 5:13) are elaborations of themes introduced in Col. 1:27-2:7.

you in spirit, rejoicing to see your good order and the firmness of your
faith in Christ. Therefore, as you received Christ Jesus the Lord, so walk
in him, rooted and built up in him and established in the faith, just as you
were taught, abounding in thanksgiving.

It is evident that Paul is reflecting on his task as a preacher. He
speaks of his responsibility before God to "make the word of God
fully known," to disclose among the Gentiles the once-hidden-but-
now-revealed mystery of Christ, in short, to "proclaim" Christ. His
rich description of the high honor and responsibility of proclaiming
the Savior in the gospel of God interweaves seven themes that conve-
niently summarize the apostle's theology of apostolic preaching.

1) Paul defines the *purpose* of his proclamation: to "present
everyone mature [or 'perfect'] in Christ." His aim is not merely to
convey information but to be instrumental in God's effecting transformation of the most radical and comprehensive sort in the hearts,
lives, and relationships of those who hear his preaching.

2) That purpose brings into consideration the identity and need
of the *listeners* to whom Paul refers: the "everyone" includes Gentiles,
once excluded from God's presence, but now incorporated into the
community in which the riches of God's glory are unveiled in Christ.
They need the word that Paul proclaims precisely because they are
now far from "perfect in Christ," although that is the destiny that
God has for them.

3) Paul knows that he has good news from God that is fully
adequate to meet his listeners' spiritual needs in all their depths and
diversity. His message has *content* to be communicated authoritatively and persuasively, and Paul encapsulates the entire content of
his message in a single word—or, more precisely, a single person:
"*Him* we proclaim"—the Christ who now indwells even Gentiles.

4) The twofold character of his listeners' need is implied in the
participles that identify the concrete *communication tasks* that Paul's
preaching accomplishes: "teaching and admonishing . . . in all wisdom." His hearers need, and Paul delivers, not only the declaration
of Jesus' redemptive achievement but also direction regarding the
response appropriate to this glad news.

5) Paul mentions the *price* to be paid by the preachers of his gospel—sufferings, afflictions, toil, and struggle—just as elsewhere he exposes the great cost borne by Christ to accomplish the redemption that displays his glory among Gentiles. The bearers of Christ's gospel—a message of life imparted through sacrificial death, of strength imparted through weakness—must themselves be illustrations of their message, sacrificing themselves, out of gratitude for mercy received and eager longing that others share that mercy.

6) Paul also refers to the divine *power* that operates through the frailty and travails of the gospel's human preachers: "struggling with all *his energy* that he powerfully works within me." Although preachers bear responsibility both to interpret God's Word accurately and to convey its message clearly, apostolic preaching cannot be reduced to exegetical techniques and communication skills. The preaching of the apostles and their successors is a ministry that imparts life and achieves its purpose only because it is "the ministry of the Spirit" of the sovereign and gracious God (2 Cor. 3:7–9).

7) Finally, this text introduces the motif of the preacher's *office*, entailing authority and accountability, through the imagery of stewardship. As the servant of Another, entrusted with a most precious treasure, the apostolic preacher must be prepared to answer to his Master as one found faithful in administering his stewardship, both preserving and propagating the message of life without modifying its content.

Let us explore each of these in greater depth.

The Purpose We Pursue: "To Present Everyone Mature in Christ"

The purpose of preaching is not only to inform or even to elicit assent to its truths. Preaching God's Word produces change in those who hear it, and the change is not merely intellectual or academic. To be sure, God's truth in Christ exposes and refutes false ideas about the nature of the divine, the nature of humanity, and the purpose of the universe, for example. But Paul preaches Christ not merely to produce theologically correct thinkers. Through preaching Christ Paul seeks to recreate people into the image of God, so they enjoy

God's presence in unashamed purity, serve his will in unreserved love, express God's justice and mercy in relationships with other.

Preaching progressively conforms hearers of the Word to the image of Christ by the power of the Holy Spirit. In fact, preaching's mission is nothing less than the *complete spiritual maturity* of those who hear the apostle. This goal of maturity is defined by the absolute perfection of Christ himself. The Greek adjective used here (*teleios*) and translated "mature" in the ESV occasionally refers to less-than-perfect maturity, as when Paul challenges the "mature" (*teleios*) at Philippi to share his recognition that he has not yet been "perfected" (*teleioō*, Phil. 3:15; cf. vv. 12–14). In Colossians 1, however, Paul has in view the final day on which the Holy Spirit's sanctifying work in the church will have been completed and Paul will "present" believers to Christ as the perfectly mature fruit of his apostolic labors (2 Cor. 11:2)—as on that wedding day Christ will "present" the church to himself as his blemish-free bride (Eph. 5:27; cf. Col. 1:22).

Paul's letter to the Ephesians, written concurrently with Colossians, confirms that Paul's purpose in preaching is nothing less than his hearers' complete perfection at the consummation. The ascended Christ bestows ministers of the Word (apostles, prophets, evangelists, pastors, teachers) to serve the saints and build the body "until we all attain to the unity of the faith and of the knowledge of the Son of God, to mature (*teleios*) manhood, to the measure of the stature of the fullness of Christ (Eph. 4:13)." When maturity is measured by Christ's fullness, plainly it entails nothing less than sinless perfection, the consummation of the Spirit's purifying process in glory.

Paul's aim in preaching included, but was not limited to, his hearers' initial conversion. Paul was sent particularly to those who had not heard of Christ (Rom. 15:20). He knew that no one would be presented "perfect in Christ" at the Last Day who had not been reconciled to God through the blood of the beloved Son (Col. 1:20–22) and that this reconciliation takes effect when a person believes the promises of the gospel and trusts the Savior who sealed those promises with his blood. His preaching therefore included what we often call "evangelism," the announcement of the good news of Christ's redemptive achievement to people who had not submitted themselves to his loving Lordship. Yet, the goal of preaching is not fully achieved when a rebel becomes a child of God. Christian preaching has as its purpose nothing less than the complete conformity of every child of

God to the perfect image of Christ the Son (Rom. 8:29; Col. 3:10–11; Eph. 4:24).

It would be easy to read Paul's "everyone" in individualistic terms, as if his only aims were the conversion and sanctification of solitary believers. This would be a serious misunderstanding. Ephesians 4:13–16 shows that growth toward Christlike perfection is not an individualistic pursuit but a corporate, cooperative, community endeavor to reach a goal that none will reach until all have reached it: "until *we all* attain . . . to mature manhood, to the measure of the stature of the fullness of Christ. . . . *the whole body*, joined and held together by every joint with which it is equipped, when each part is working properly, makes the body grow so that it builds itself up in love." Paul's "everyone" is intentionally inclusive of the Gentiles, who had previously been excluded from the Lord's covenant community (Col. 1:27; Eph. 2:11–22). The goal of God's redemptive plan is not merely the rescue of individual sinners from their justly deserved eternal condemnation but also the gathering of a redeemed people, a community that together worships its Creator-Redeemer and that exhibits in the loving and trustworthy interrelationships of its members a reflection of the image of the Triune God himself. Paul emphasizes the corporate dimension of the new humanity in Colossians 3:10–11, first echoing the creation language of Genesis 1 ("having put on the new man who is being renewed into complete knowledge *in the image* of the One who *created* him," dej) and then emphasizing that in this new man social barriers are broken down in the unity of Christ ("not one Greek and another Jew, circumcision and uncircumcision, barbarian, Scythian, slave, free, but Christ is all and in all," dej). Preaching is God's instrument to elicit faith, thereby uniting us to Christ and to his community, the body that is growing together toward perfection and the bride who is being beautified for presentation to her groom.

Does the comprehensiveness of Paul's ultimate objective mean that apostolic preaching moves beyond the gospel, outside the Pauline preoccupation with Christ, in order to address other, "practical" topics concerning the nitty-gritty of the Christian life, struggle against sinful habits, resolving interpersonal conflict, financial management, responsible citizenship, social justice, and the other themes that fill modern pulpits? No, the logic of Paul's interlinking clauses implies that preaching prods us toward the goal of perfection not by moving our gaze away from Jesus to other issues but by driving our exploration deeper into Christ, who is the manifold wisdom of God.

Paul knows that it is only "*in Christ*" that he can hope to present his hearers perfect before God's judgment seat on the Last Day. On the one hand, the fact that perfection is "in Christ" means that Christ's completeness (holiness, truth, love, justice) as the image of God, in whom the divine fullness dwells and in whom we are filled (Col. 2:9–10), is the goal and measure of our growth, the destination of Paul's preaching. On the other hand, Christ is also the Savior who imparts life to people who are dead (Col. 2:13), draws us to faith, assures us of forgiveness and the Father's favor, and sustains struggling believers throughout their stumbling pilgrimage in this life. Spiritual maturity is derived only from living union with Christ, by faith and through the Spirit. Only in Christ and our union with him in his death and resurrection do believers find the motive and the power to pursue growth in godliness and love.

Therefore, the same gospel that initially called us to faith is the means that perfects us in faith. As surely as Christ's obedience, death, and resurrection constitute the all-sufficient, once-for-all ground of our justification by faith, so also Christ's righteous life, sacrificial death, and vindication in resurrection power are the fount from which flows our sanctification by faith as we grow in grace.[2] The preaching that matures and edifies, no less than the preaching that evangelizes and converts, calls believers not "beyond" the gospel to "deeper mysteries" (as some were promising the Colossian Christians[3]) but more deeply into the gospel and its implications for our attitudes, affections, motivations, and actions.

In Colossians the overarching exhortation that marks the transition from theological exposition to ethical application falls at the end of our text: "Therefore, as you received Christ Jesus the Lord, so walk in him, rooted and built up in him and established in the faith,

---

2   This point is developed more fully in Dennis E. Johnson, "*Simul iustus et peccator*: The Role of Justification in Pastoral Counseling," in R. Scott Clark, ed. *Covenant, Justification and Pastoral Ministry: Essays by the Faculty of Westminster Seminary California* (Phillipsburg: P & R, 2007), 399–429.

3   Cf. Col. 2:16–23. The seductive teachers at Colossae apparently promised that those sufficiently committed to ascetic self-denial could achieve mystical visionary experiences of a "fullness" of superior realities beyond and behind the mundane material world. Paul, however, insists that the "fullness of deity" dwells *in bodily form* in Jesus. See Peter T. O'Brien, *Colossians, Philemon* (WBC 44; Waco: Word, 1982), xxx–xxxviii.

just as you were taught, abounding in thanksgiving" (Col. 2:6–7). The Christian "walk" follows the path already laid out in the gospel by which Christ was first received, namely the path of faith, with thanksgiving for amazing grace. Paul goes on to explain that "walking in" Christ means living out the implications of the reality that we have died with Christ (2:20), both to the conscience-controlling authority of human regulations and to conscience-staining sins (3:5–9). It is also living out the implications of our having been raised with Christ and seated with him in heaven (3:1–2), setting our minds on things above: compassion, kindness, humility, gentleness, patient forgiveness toward those who give us grief, and above all love, the bond of unity (3:12–14).

The same gospel, faithfully preached, accomplishes both evangelism leading to conversion and edification leading to sanctification—both individual and corporate renewal together! The comprehensive purpose of preaching is captured in the Westminster Larger Catechism, 155:

> The Spirit of God maketh the reading, but *especially the preaching of the word*, an effectual means of *enlightening, convincing, and humbling sinners*; of *driving them out of themselves, and drawing them unto Christ*; of *conforming them to his image, and subduing them to his will*; of *strengthening* them against temptations and corruptions; of *building* them up in grace, and *establishing* their hearts in holiness and comfort through faith unto salvation. [Emphases added]

The same preached word that turns sinners away from themselves and their sin toward Christ also sanctifies and strengthens them to offer thankful obedience pleasing to God through the grace of his Son.

The Listeners We Address: "To Make Known . . . among the Gentiles"

Apostolic preaching is addressed to people in need. The very fact that preaching's purpose is to "present everyone perfect in Christ" implies that our hearers are not now perfect. They need change.

Scripture is always addressing people in need. If people were not needy, there would be no need for a gospel or for preaching. Although evangelical preaching is dominated by much misguided thinking regarding "relevance" and "felt needs," the remedy to this confusion is not to swing the pendulum to the opposite extreme and imagine that we can make our preaching more God-centered by ig-noring the human needs to which Scripture is addressed. We are ad-dressing guilty, broken sinners who live in a world put out of joint by sin and its toxic by-products, sinners who must not be left as they are but can be changed by the Spirit through the instrument of the preached Word.

In 1894 Geerhardus Vos's inaugural lecture as professor of bib-lical theology at Princeton Seminary showed that Scripture's change-producing purpose helps to explain why God embedded his revela-tion in the process of history. Vos argued that one ground of

> . . . the historical character of revelation may be found in its eminently practical aspect. The knowledge of God communicated by it is nowhere for a purely intellectual purpose. From beginning to end it is a knowledge intended to enter into the actual life of man, to be worked out by him in all its practical bearings. . . . God has interwoven the supernaturally communicated knowledge of himself with the historic life of the chosen race, so as to secure for it a practical form from the beginning. Revelation is connected throughout with the fate of Israel. Its disclosures arise from the necessities of that nation, and are adjusted to its capacities. . . . God has not revealed himself in a school, but in the covenant; and the covenant as a communion of life is all-comprehensive, embracing all the conditions and interests of those contracting it.[4]

When Vos asserts that the "disclosures" of the Bible "arise from the *necessities* of [Israel], and are *adjusted* to its *capacities,*" he makes God sound so seeker-sensitive! But of course Vos is simply developing more concretely Calvin's observation that God accommodates his revelation to humanity in our finitude and fallenness. Calvin and Vos are right: if Israel had not committed the sins they did, had not fallen into the slaveries they experienced, had not capitulated to doubt, flirted with apostasy, and lost heart when confronted by obstacles and opponents, or if the Corinthian church hadn't been confused over sexuality and meat offered to idols and the resurrection, or if the Galatians had clearly understood justification by faith alone, we would not have the Bible that God gave us. The Scriptures we have are addressed and adjusted to needy people: guilty, defiled,

4   Geerhardus Vos, "The Idea of Biblical Theology as a Science and as a Theo-logical Discipline" (May 4, 1894), in R. B. Gaffin Jr., ed. *Redemptive History and Biblical Interpretation; the Shorter Writings of Geerhardus Vos* (Phillipsburg: P & R, 1980), 10.

spiritually dead, broken, enslaved, tyrannized by fear, self-deceived, alienated and alone. So our preaching of these Scriptures must be formed and informed by the complex needs—spiritual, intellectual, social, moral, physical—that evokes them.

The dimensions of our guilt and brokenness are so diverse that nothing less than the manifold grace and wisdom of God in Christ can bring us to perfection. Colossians 1 offers a glimpse of some aspects of our need, as God defines it: We need liberation from the domain of darkness (1:13–14), as well as forgiveness of sins and redemption from the liability to judgment that our sins have incurred (1:14). Christ's identity as "firstborn from the dead" brings into view death, the last enemy that threatens us (1:18). His work of reconciliation addresses our problem of alienation and hostility toward God, as well as his just indignation toward us (1:20–22). Paul knows that his Christian hearers are not immune from the danger of "shifting from the hope of the gospel" (1:23), and that deceptive and erroneous teaching can undermine confidence, with ruinous results.

Apostolic preaching addresses human needs in all their diversity and depth. It does not just apply bandages to "felt needs," which are symptoms of secret infection. When God does the diagnosis through his whole Word, he pierces through the surface symptoms all the way to the heart, with the radical cure of God's holy truth exposing our infection in all its ugliness and applying Christ's amazing grace in all its sweetness and strength.[5]

---

5   As will be discussed more fully below, this recognition that every Scripture is addressed to some dimension of human fallenness and designed to lead its hearers toward the goal of perfection in Christ has far-reaching hermeneutic as well as homiletic implications. Hermeneutically, the interpretation of any text of Scripture must take into account the occasion into which it was written and the circumstances of its first readers. Identifying the *particular problem* that evoked the text in the first place, the need of the first recipients, is essential to our discovery of its *God-given purpose* in creating the holy community whose members grow together toward perfection in Christ. Homiletically, recognizing how the first recipients' spiritual problem manifests itself in our hearers' experience—despite all the differences in time and place and culture and surface appearances—provides the surest guide to the application of the text's message to our contemporaries. Because such application can be seen to arise directly from the text, it carries both credibility and conviction. The link between the first recipients' need that occasioned the Scripture and the forms that this need takes in our hearers' experience is what Bryan Chapell calls the text's "Fallen Condition Focus," defined as "*the mutual human condition that contemporary believers share with those to or about whom the text was written that requires the grace of the passage for God's people to glorify and enjoy*

Paul emphasizes another characteristic of his and our hearers that profoundly influences apostolic preaching: he and we preach in the era in which God is calling people from all nationalities to repent and believe the gospel. "God chose to make known how great among the Gentiles are the riches of the glory of this mystery, which is Christ *in you,* the hope of glory" (Col. 1:27). Christ *among the Gentiles* is the new phase in God's covenant and kingdom. The mystery is Christ—specifically that Christ has come among the Gentiles (to people outside God's law and covenant) to draw them to the Father through his redemptive death and resurrection. Our "location" in redemptive history, which we share with the apostles, sets our preaching apart from the preaching of Israel's ancient prophets and the Torah instruction of her faithful priests. Preaching Christ at *this* point in redemptive history is preaching *to the Gentile nations* to bring them under the sway of Christ's reign. New Covenant preaching is necessarily missiological, addressed not only to those with long heritage and pedigree in the covenant community but also to unchurched pagans, whom God *now* calls to turn from idols to his Son, in whom alone salvation is found (1 Thess. 1:9–10; cf. Acts 17:30–31; 4:12; Isa. 45:22–25).[6]

One significant aspect of the newness of the new covenant, therefore, is the extension of the boundaries of the people of God to embrace all the peoples and nations of the earth, not merely the physical descendants of Abraham, Isaac, and Jacob. This was the promise that God made to Abraham when he first called him out from the nations: "in you all the families of the earth shall be blessed" (Gen. 12:3; 22:18; cf. Acts 3:25). Earlier we noted that God's "mystery," his secret plan that centers in Christ, includes not only the salvation of individuals but also the establishment of a redeemed community, a people in covenant with God. Now the insight is added that this new-creation community is composed not of one ethnic or language group, one race or economic class or culture, but of the wide diversity of the human family. Now that Christ has come, a purpose of gospel

---

him." Bryan Chapell, *Christ-Centered Preaching: Redeeming the Expository Sermon* (2nd ed. Grand Rapids: Baker, 2005), 50 [emphasis original]. Consistent with Vos's observation, such attention to the recipients' needs is intrinsic to preaching that is *rooted in the history* in which God spoke his redemptive words.

6   See Dennis E. Johnson, "Jesus against the Idols: The Use of Isaianic Servant Songs in the Missiology of Acts," *WTJ* 52 (1990): 343–53; and Dennis E. Johnson, *The Message of Acts in the History of Redemption* (Phillipsburg: P & R, 1997), 44–50.

preaching is to announce among unreached peoples everywhere the inauguration of the Creator's reign of grace in Jesus the Messiah.[7]

This multiethnic, international, and religiously diverse identity of those who now hear apostolic preaching has profound implications for the preacher's mode of communication. At the most basic level, it influenced the language in which Paul spoke and wrote. Though a "Hebrew of Hebrews," raised in a home in which he learned and spoke the ancient language of the Holy Scriptures (Phil. 3:5), as a preacher Paul spoke and wrote Greek, the *lingua franca* of the Roman empire, to reach the Gentiles to whom God had sent him. The framers of the Westminster Confession recognized the implications of our place in redemptive history for the way the Word of God has been imparted this side of the cross, the resurrection, and Pentecost:

> The Old Testament in Hebrew (which was the native language of the people of God of old), and the New Testament in Greek (which, at the time of the writing of it, was most generally known to the nations), being immediately inspired by God, and, by His singular care and providence, kept pure in all ages, are therefore authentical. . . . Because these original tongues are not known to all the people of God, who have right unto, and interest in the Scriptures, and are commanded, in the fear of God, to read and search them, therefore they are to be translated into the vulgar language of every nation unto which they come. . . .[8]

Their point is cogent, although some pastors, fearful of "dumbing down" their preaching, resist it: God adjusts his language to his audience, and *now* God's audience is *all nations*. Because this is the age in which God's grace brings outsiders in, now God speaks his Scriptures in Greek.

---

7   Paul's unique calling as *apostle to the Gentiles* was to announce the good news to non-covenant peoples—to pagans who formerly were alienated from citizenship in Israel, who were "not a people" from the perspective of God's covenantal dealings with Abraham, Isaac, and Jacob—as particularly characteristic of this age of redemptive history in which we live. He marvels at this privilege in Eph. 3:1–7: "For this reason I, Paul, a prisoner for Christ Jesus *on behalf of you Gentiles*—assuming that you have heard of the stewardship of God's grace that was given to me *for you*, how the mystery was made known to me by revelation . . . the mystery of Christ, which was not made known to the sons of men in other generations as it has now been revealed to his holy apostles and prophets by the Spirit. This mystery is that *the Gentiles are fellow heirs, members of the same body, and partakers of the promise in Christ Jesus* through the gospel" (emphasis added).

8   Westminster Confession of Faith 1.8.

Not only are Paul's nouns and verbs those used by Greek speakers all over the Roman Empire, his illustrations and figures of speech are drawn from biblical sources (Abraham and Sarah, redemption, seed, etc.) *and* from extrabiblical sources, from the culture and experience of his intended audience: slavery, commerce, Greek athletics, Roman legal arrangements, agriculture and manufacturing, warfare, and public pageants.[9] Although Paul shunned the self-glorifying ornamentation of Greek rhetoric, he exhibited great sensitivity to his obligation to communicate God's message in a form that would communicate meaningfully to his hearers—exposing their rebellion and unbelief, showing the sharp contrast between the living God and the dead idols in which they had trusted, and calling them to repentance and faith.

Unlike the practitioners of the mystery cults, who magnified the importance of their beliefs and rituals by covering them in a veil of secrecy, Paul stressed that God's gospel was so important that it had to be communicated with complete plainness of speech, not veiled behind insider jargon (2 Cor. 3:12–4:6).

Like Paul, we are called to preach in the redemptive-historical epoch in which God speaks his gospel in the languages of all the peoples. We face the same challenge: to show how every Scripture proclaims Christ in ways that make the message clear and vivid to diverse audiences. We dare not be content simply to *preserve* the message; we must *propagate* it boldly. New Covenant preaching cannot remain comfortably inside the New Covenant community, speaking that community's special dialect! We live and preach in the redemptive era when the crucified and risen Christ sits enthroned in heaven as the Lord who announces: "All authority in heaven and on earth has been given to me. Go therefore and make disciples of all nations" (Matt. 28:18). In view of our place in the unfolding of God's plan, the preacher's calling is not merely to put the finishing touches on Christians who are already biblically literate and theologically sophisticated. Nor is it only setting straight Christians from other churches and traditions who need correction. If pastors ever had the luxury of assuming that they were ministering in Christendom—that is, in a community and culture dominated by Christian conviction—those

---

9   Herbert M. Gale, *The Use of Analogy in the Letters of Paul* (Philadelphia: Westminster, 1964); David J. Williams, *Paul's Metaphors: Their Context and Character* (Peabody, Massachusetts: Hendrickson, 1999).

days are over. We need to recapture the apostolic sense of gospel mission to the pagans, not only in far away pre-Christian cultures but also in post-Christian America and Europe.

The Content We Preach: "Him We Proclaim" (1:28)

Paul summed up the content of his preaching by naming a person, Christ. Christ's saving presence among the Gentiles is the secret formerly hidden but now revealed. Christ is the one in whom *all* the treasures of God's wisdom and knowledge are hidden (Col. 2:3). Paul had told the Corinthians that he had resolved in coming to them to preach nothing but Jesus Christ, and him crucified (1 Cor. 2:2). Yet, this "monotone message" was adequate to meet all their needs, for God's apparently foolish, weak, cross-centered message is wiser than human wisdom and stronger than human strength (1:21–25). Christ is the wisdom of God: our righteousness, holiness, and redemption (1:30). In Acts 20:20, 26–27 we overhear Paul assuring the elders of the Ephesian church that his conscience before God was clear because he had not refrained from declaring anything that would benefit them but had fully disclosed "the whole counsel of God." Yet, Paul adamantly insists more than once that the theme of his preaching ministry was always and only Jesus Christ. Paul's single-minded focus on one motif—Jesus Christ—raises questions when we consider the breadth of life issues that confront those to whom we preach and the diversity of topics addressed in the Scriptures. How can contemporary preachers preach "nothing but Christ" and at the same time preach *the whole Bible* as it addresses *the whole spectrum of spiritual and ethical issues* that confronts our hearers?

We will explore this question more deeply in Part 2. For the moment, we can observe *why* the apostle Paul saw in Christ's person and work a depth and complexity ("all the treasures of wisdom and knowledge") that encompassed the whole of his message, with all of its variety of topics and implications, and thereby addressed the whole spectrum of human need. Paul preached nothing but Christ because he knew Jesus to be the supreme revealer of God the Creator and the only reconciler of God's people.

Christ reveals God the Creator with a fullness and clarity unmatched by any other mode of revelation. This supremacy of Christ in revelation is relevant to the false teaching that threatened the

Colossian Christians' faith. The "Colossian heresy," as New Testament scholars now call it, apparently claimed to offer superior insight into the "fullness" (*plērōma*)—the succession of spiritual emanations from the highest level of deity down to the mundane, material cosmos—and mystical visions of angelic worship evoked by fasting and harsh treatment of the body (Col. 2:8, 16–19, 23). From what we can piece together from Paul's descriptions, this heresy was a syncretistic blending of Jewish elements (2:16—food, drink, feast, new moon, Sabbaths), ascetic practices, and pagan preoccupation with mystical experience, apparently bound together by contempt for the material world and physical existence. Paul insists, by contrast, that the "fullness" of deity dwelt in Christ in *bodily* form (2:9). It is not the *physical* that is unworthy of contact with the divine but those who are sinful, morally defiled, and therefore alienated from God. This moral alienation is the great chasm that needs to be crossed, not from the immaterial to the material, but from the holy God to morally defiled humans. Therefore, immediately before our text in Colossians 1:23, Paul urges the Colossian believers to remain in the gospel and its hope, not allowing anyone to shake them loose from that gospel.

Christ is uniquely qualified to disclose the Creator because he is God's beloved Son (1:13). Paul here echoes the Father's words at Jesus' baptism and (especially) on the Mount of Transfiguration: "This is my beloved Son; listen to him" (Mark 1:11; 9:7). Jesus had affirmed his unique authority as Son to reveal the Father: "All things have been handed over to me by my Father, and no one knows the Son except the Father, and no one knows the Father except the Son and anyone to whom the Son chooses to reveal him" (Matt. 11:27). Jesus reveals God not only from the intimacy of his filial communion with the Father but also from his essential identity as the visible disclosure of the Creator, "the image of the invisible God" (Col. 1:15). The background is Adam's and Eve's creation in the image of God (Gen. 1:26), both resembling God in a creaturely way and representing God's rule as they exercised dominion over their fellow-creatures (1:28). Christ transcends Adam's role as *imago Dei* in both respects. He reveals the invisible God not merely as the preeminent creature on earth (as Adam was) but because by him all things, visible and invisible, were created and are sustained in an orderly cosmos (Col. 1:16–17).

In Colossians 1:19, moreover, using language drawn from the Old Testament sanctuary, Paul emphasizes that in Christ we see the God whom we cannot see: "in him all the fullness of God was pleased to dwell." Although Paul is probably using the terminology of his proto-Gnostic opponents, he gives it an Old Testament turn by alluding to Psalm 68:16, which describes Zion and the mount in which the Lord "was pleased to dwell."[10] The glory of God's presence had "filled" first the tabernacle, and later the temple, in such overwhelming intensity that Moses could not enter the tabernacle, nor later priests the temple, until the fullness of glory began to dispel (Ex. 40:34–35; 1 Kings 8:10–11; cf. Rev. 15:8). Yet, Solomon himself confessed that the "house" that he had built could not contain God himself (1 Kings 8:27). Christ is the new and better sanctuary, in whom the divine fullness now dwells and the divine glory shines.[11]

As the image of God and last Adam, Jesus also represents God's rule as the perfect man, which Adam failed to be. "Firstborn of all creation" alludes to the role of the firstborn son in ancient Israel as the preeminent ruler, as reflected in the metaphorical description of David as the Lord's "firstborn" among the kings of the earth (Ps. 89:27). Christ is not only the agent *through* whom all things were created, but also the heir *for* whom all things were created (Col. 1:16). Whereas Adam abused his authority, disobeyed, and plunged us all into condemnation and death, Christ exercised his authority in complete obedience, bringing all who belong to him into justification and life (Rom. 5:12–21; cf. 1 Cor. 15:21–22, 45–49). Consequently, as we saw above, Christ defines the goal of *perfection* toward which Paul's preaching ministry aims, and union with Christ is the invincible means to this goal: "to present everyone mature *in Christ*." Elsewhere Paul explains the mysterious relationship that he often simply refers to as "in Christ" by using the metaphor of clothing (Gal. 3:27–29; Rom. 13:12, 14), and in Colossians and Ephesians the "take off/put on" clothing metaphor for spiritual and ethical transformation is presented using the imagery of creation in the image of God. Believers have removed the old man (Adam) and his deceitful and corrupt practices, and have clothed themselves with the new man (Christ), for they are newly created in the image of God, in knowledge (Col. 3:10) and in the righteousness and holiness that flow from truth (Eph. 4:24).

---

10   O'Brien, *Colossians*, 52–53.

11   Edmund P. Clowney, "The Final Temple" *WTJ* 35 (1973): 156–89; Tremper Longman III, *Immanuel in Our Place: Seeing Christ in Israel's Worship* (Phillipsburg: P & R, 2001); G. K. Beale, *The Temple and the Church's Mission: A Biblical Theology of the Temple* (Downers Grove: InterVarsity, 2004).

Christ's supremacy as the *reconciler* of God's people is the other great reason that Paul's whole preaching ministry can be summed up as "proclaiming Christ." In fact, Jesus' redemptive achievement addresses every aspect and, ultimately, every effect of our fallen condition as guilty, twisted, self-deceived and condemned rebels on whom the divine image is nevertheless still indelibly imprinted. Christ's reign by grace in human hearts brings liberation from the lethal domain of darkness (Col. 1:13–14). The redemption that he bestows also includes forgiveness of sins (1:14). This addresses the problem of our guilt before God's justice and holy wrath. Against the background of Israel's exodus from Egypt, "redemption" is not only to be liberated from slavery but also to be exonerated from liability to death as punishment for sin.[12] By removing our guilt, Christ's death effects reconciliation with God (Col. 1:20–22). This addresses the issue of our alienation from God, the enmity and distance between us and the Creator whose presence we were created to glorify and enjoy. In verse 20 Paul says that the purpose of the Son's incarnation was to reconcile "all things," to make peace so that *everything* in earth and the heavens is returned to its right relationship with the Creator. Two verses later he personalizes and particularizes this theme: "*You* were alienated and enemies, but now he reconciled *you*." The means of this reconciliation is embedded in history, and worked out through suffering and death: "by the blood of his cross" (1:20), "in his body of flesh by his death" (1:22).

Paul's preaching, centered as it is on Jesus Christ, is unified but not monotonous. This single message is as manifold as the manifestations of human sin and suffering, as manifold as the wisdom of God, now displayed in the church to which the gospel has given birth (Eph. 3:10). In Part 2 we will explore more fully the rich diversity of the Scripture's single testimony to Christ, but at this point we must note in Colossians 1:27–2:7 two sub-motifs that are integral to the rich "texture" of Paul's single, Christocentric message: redemptive history and grace.

Preaching Christ is preaching *the fulfillment of God's redemptive plan for history*. According to Colossians 1:27, Christ (specifically

---

12   In the exodus, Israel was redeemed not only from Egyptian slavery but also from the angel of death who slaughtered the firstborn. Only lamb's blood could shield Israelite households from the capital punishment that Egyptian and Israelite alike deserved. The atoning sacrifice that achieved our redemption is made explicit in Paul's insertion to Ephesians 1:7, which otherwise parallels Col. 1:14: "in him we have redemption *through his blood*, the forgiveness of our trespasses."

Christ indwelling Gentiles) is the mystery of God. This mystery had been "hidden for ages and generations" but is "now revealed to his saints" (1:26). This is not a "mystery" in the sense that we sometimes use the term in theology. That is, it is not a combination of truths that our reason cannot reconcile, such as the Trinity, the union of divine and human natures in the incarnate Son of God, or the interaction of divine sovereignty and uncoerced and responsible human decision. This mystery is a secret once hidden but now unveiled for the whole world to see. So Paul draws a contrast in the history of revelation between the previous era in which the mystery was hidden and the present in which it is revealed.

This contrast between the age of promise and the age of fulfillment appears throughout the New Testament, and Jesus the Christ is always the watershed between the ages. The apostolic witnesses emphasize that the mystery was "hidden" in one respect but not in another. It was *not* hidden, as though no previous revelation or Scripture contained a hint of the Savior who was to come or his inclusion of the Gentiles in his redemptive work. Rather, through apostolic preaching the mystery is now made known to all nations *through the prophetic writings* that God had given to Israel during the period of hiddenness (Rom. 16:25–27). "But now the righteousness of God has been manifested apart from the law, although *the Law and the Prophets bear witness to it*" (Rom. 3:21). On the other hand, the way in which God would fulfill his promise to redeem and gather his people, drawing them not only from Israel but also from all nations, was a "hidden" mystery, its full meaning not disclosed until its enactment by Christ in history. Paul points out in Ephesians 2:14–3:6, for example, that God includes the Gentiles in his redemptive plan not simply by incorporating them into ancient Israel (as might have been anticipated from a reading of Isaiah 56:6–8) but by creating both believing Jews and believing Gentiles into "one new man in place of the two," so that in the new covenant community Gentile believers stand on equal footing with Jewish believers as "fellow heirs, members of the same body, and partakers of the promise in Christ Jesus through the gospel."

The epistle to the Hebrews, which opens with a sharp distinction between the former era in which God spoke through prophets and "these last days" in which he has spoken in a Son (Heb. 1:1–2), nonetheless demonstrates repeatedly that the ancient prophetic

Scriptures foreshadowed and foretold the better covenant secured by Jesus. As a faithful servant, Moses testified to things that would be spoken in the future (Heb. 3:5; cf. John 5:39–47). The redemptive institutions of the age of anticipation functioned as "shadows of the good things to come," now realized through Jesus' redemptive work (Heb. 10:1). Likewise, Peter observes that ancient prophets, speaking by the Spirit of Christ, foretold Christ's sufferings and subsequent glories, understanding that their words referred to a future generation (1 Peter 1:10–12; cf. Dan. 12:4–9).

Samples of apostolic evangelistic preaching in Acts demonstrate a profound awareness that the life, death, resurrection, and exaltation of the Messiah mark the watershed in the history of revelation because it is the watershed of all history, a "Continental Divide" that divides time into two ages, before and after, times past and "these last days." Whether addressing biblically literate listeners in temple or synagogue or pagan Gentiles, apostolic preachers alert their audiences to the epochal shift that Jesus has brought about. To the former Peter declares, "But what God foretold by the mouth of all the prophets, that his Christ would suffer, he thus fulfilled. . . . All the prophets who have spoken . . . proclaimed these days" (Acts 3:18, 24). To the latter Paul announces that the age of Gentile ignorance is over, as God's good news and summons to repentance now goes out to all nations (14:15–16; 17:30–31).

Paul's proclamation of Christ comes at the pivotal time in the history of God's self-disclosure to his covenant people and to the whole human race. We stand with Paul in that same time period, subsequent to Christ's incarnation, cross, resurrection, exaltation, enthronement, and pouring out of the Spirit. This privileged vantage point illumines our reading and preaching of Scriptures spoken by prophets in past eras, as well as our exposition of the Word spoken at last in the Son and confirmed to us by his apostolic witnesses (Heb. 1:1–4). The division of our Bibles into two sections, "Old Testament" and "New Testament," reflects the Latin rendering of a twofold subdivision of the history of redemption that is embedded in Scripture itself, in the promise of a "new covenant" vastly superior to the covenant God made with Israel at Sinai (Jer. 31:31–34; Heb. 8:6–12). Jesus' death is the sacrifice that establishes the promised "new covenant," of which he is mediator and guarantor (1 Cor. 11:25; Heb. 7:22; 9:15). That promise made the Sinaitic covenant "old" and obsolescent (Heb. 8:13), and the Scriptures associated with it are appropriately called "the old covenant" (2 Cor. 3:14). Although God's words spoken to "the fathers" in the age of anticipation still address his people in this age of fulfillment, the arrival and achievement of Christ have transformed the way in which the new covenant people of God understand and implement the message of the old covenant shadows and Scriptures.

Preaching Christ is preaching *grace*. This may seem obvious, but it is not obvious to all. It is, after all, true that Jesus spoke more words about hell than about heaven. The book of Revelation speaks of the wrath of the Lamb and assures us that history's end will be anything but gracious for those who receive his judgment. Many preachers have thought they were preaching Christ when, like Charles Sheldon, they pointed to him as a stellar example to be followed. It is possible to preach about Jesus, and even mention grace in the process, and yet be preaching law, calling people to reform themselves with a little help from their heavenly Friend. Such a message breeds either self-deluded complacency or self-contemptuous despair.

Preaching Christ as Paul preached Christ, however, is preaching grace as the sole source and rationale of salvation and transformation from start to finish: grace that imparts life to the spiritually dead, grace that imputes Christ's righteousness to the guilty, grace that instills the Spirit's power in those otherwise impotent to want or to do good, grace that holds fast the feeble and fainting, securing pilgrims' arrival at their destination in glory. Grace points hearers to the sovereign, saving initiative and intervention of God to do for guilty and paralyzed sinners what we could never do for ourselves, not even with heavenly help. Paul reminds the Colossians of "the day you heard [the gospel] and understood the grace of God in truth" (Col. 1:6). This grace is manifested in the Father's rescuing them from darkness and qualifying them for a holy, light-filled inheritance in the peaceable kingdom of his Son (1:12–14). It is shown in the reconciling work of the Son, replacing hostility with peace and shameful evil with blameless purity through his death (1:21–22).

In Ephesians, composed almost simultaneously with Colossians and sharing many themes with it, Paul elaborates on our desperate need and God's amazing grace. We were dead in trespasses and sins, guilty, lifeless, helpless, yet also culpably active in pursuing further evil, still "walking" the path of disobedience and passionate desire for pleasures of mind and body that paralyze and corrode (Eph. 2:1–3). But God intervened in Christ to create life for the dead, and Paul ransacks the Greek lexicon to underscore the utterly gracious motive that moved the Sovereign, so abused by his subjects, to come to their rescue. God is "rich in *mercy*," prompted by "the great *love* with which he *loved* us" (2:4). Not once but twice, the apostle exults, "By *grace* you have been saved" (2:5, 8). Indeed, all the coming ages will be required fully to display and explore "the immeasurable riches of his grace in *kindness* toward us in Christ Jesus" (2:7). Far from being "your own doing" or "a result of [our] works," salvation is "the *gift* of God" from start to finish (2:8–9).

Of course the only divine grace that Paul can preach is the grace imparted by *union with Christ*, through faith. God makes the spiritually dead alive "together with Christ," raises them "with him," and seats them "with him in the heavenly places in Christ Jesus." For those who are "in Christ," what happened to Jesus has happened to them—condemned to death and punished for sin, vindicated and raised to life as a reward for righteousness (see 2 Cor. 5:14–15, 21). God's grace in Christ, received by faith, is the fountain from which everything good flows into believers' lives: forgiveness of sin and freedom from guilt, liberation from tyranny of sinful habits and desires, reconciliation in place of alienation, hope amid suffering, and finally vindication and glory in resurrection life. Just as preaching Christ necessarily entails preaching grace, so also there is no faithful preaching of saving grace that is not a preaching of Christ, in whom and through whom alone God's reconciling favor and re-creative power flow to human beings.

The Communication Tasks We Perform: "Warning and Teaching . . . with All Wisdom"

Paul uses two participles to make explicit the specific modes of communication that are involved in proclaiming Christ: "warning" (or "admonishing" NIV; *noutheteō*) and "teaching" (*didaskō*). "Teaching" focuses on imparting truth and directs our attention to the fact that the gospel communicates truth about the nature of God, our nature as the creatures in his image and our need as rebels against him, and the drama of redemption worked out in history, climaxing in Christ's death and resurrection. Christian preaching is not merely words that manipulate emotions, offering empty comfort to sufferers or haranguing and harassing the complacent into action through threats or pathos. Included in Paul's calling as apostle and preacher is the office of "teacher of the Gentiles in faith and truth" (1 Tim. 2:7; cf. 2 Tim. 1:10–11). Christian preaching communicates a message that hearers must first understand and then embrace in faith.

"Admonishing" implies that the truth taught in the gospel demands a response. Moreover, the response that preaching elicits is not mere acquiescence to truth claims. Rather, genuinely to embrace what the gospel *teaches* is to heed its *admonitions* to change; and this change affects not only external behavior but also unseen convictions, allegiance, values, affections, and attitudes. Admonition is an urgent, passionate appeal to hearers to respond appropriately to God's truth, as Paul reminds the Ephesian elders of his own ministry of the Word among them: "For three years I did not cease night or day to admonish (*noutheteō*) everyone with tears" (Acts 20:31). Paul was not content just to lay out the facts of the gospel and let people take it or leave it; nor did he leave it to his hearers to figure out how to respond.[13]

Paul affirms that his warning/admonishing and teaching activities as a preacher are performed "with *all* wisdom." This is a bold claim to make in the Hellenistic world and to people preoccupied with "wisdom." Paul claims that there is a comprehensive wisdom to be found in his gospel proclamation—in the message that he elsewhere acknowledges seems sheer foolishness to the intellectually sophisticated (1 Cor. 1:18–25). Scripture describes wisdom as blending insightful perception into reality with the skill to respond effectively

---

13 In 2 Tim. 3:16–4:2 the apostle likewise defines the preacher's task as one that combines instruction in the truth with an urgent summons to respond appropriately to the truth through repentance and faith. Because Scripture is profitable "for teaching (*didaskalia*), for reproof (*elegmos*), for correction (*epanorthōsis*), and for training (*paideia*) in righteousness" (3:16), equipping the man of God (an Old Testament title applied to God's spokesmen, e.g., 1 Sam. 2:27) for his ministry as Christ's herald, Timothy must therefore "preach (*keryssō*) the word . . . reprove (*elegchō*), rebuke (*epitimaō*), and exhort (*parakaleō*), with complete patience and all teaching (*didachē*)" (4:2). "Teaching" entails the communication of truth. "Reproving" is closely related to teaching since it includes exposing error for what it is, but it also entails calling people to abandon falsehood and embrace God's truth (see Titus 1:9, where the ESV translates *elegchō* as "rebuke"). "Correction," "training," "rebuke," and "exhort" all focus, with varying nuances, on calling the whole person—allegiance, affections, and actions—to respond appropriately to the truth proclaimed in and from the Word.

and appropriately to that reality. The wisdom of artisans is their skill at working with materials to create objects of beauty (Ex. 35:30–35).[14] The wisdom of judges is their skill at discerning the facts and applying appropriate principles of justice to a dispute (1 Kings 3:16–28). Paul dares to claim that his preaching exposes deep reality ("teaching") and guides skillful, faithful response ("admonishing") because he knows that his theme, Christ, is the One in whom all the treasures of divine wisdom are hidden (Col. 2:2–3). His proclamation of that theme contains comprehensive insight into the nature of things, the meaning of life, and the way to discern appropriate courses of action in various circumstances. The seamless unity of preaching's instructional and transformational objectives is shown in Paul's report of his prayer that God would fill the Colossian believers "with the knowledge of his will in all spiritual wisdom and understanding, so as to walk in a manner worthy of the Lord" (Col. 1:9–10). Truth proclaimed is both to be embraced in faith and translated into a worthy "walk" (the biblical metaphor for conduct of life: Gen. 17:1; Deut. 10:12; Ps. 1:1; Eph. 4:1; Col. 2:6). Paul prays that the gospel, which is "bearing fruit and growing" throughout the world, may enable the Colossians to bear fruit in good deeds and a growing knowledge of God—again illustrating wisdom's blend of insight and integrity (Col. 1:5–6, 10).[15] As Paul preaches to Gentiles "the unsearchable riches of Christ," God's sovereign Spirit draws them by faith into union with the Savior as members of one household, one body, one church (Eph. 2:19; 3:6-9). Through this church, a surprising community of Jewish "insiders" and Gentile "outsiders," both reconciled to God in the sacrificed body of Jesus (2:13–16), "the manifold wisdom of God" is displayed to rulers and authorities in heavenly places (3:10). The

---

14   The Hebrew noun rendered "skill" in the ESV is *hokmah*, "wisdom" (LXX *sophia*).

15   In Col. 1:10 Paul repeats the two agricultural verbs that he used metaphorically in 1:6 to convey the gospel's global impact: "bearing fruit" (*karpophoreō*) and "growing" (*auxanō*). G. K. Beale, "The Old Testament Background of Paul's Reference to 'the Fruit of the Spirit' in Galatians 5:22," *Bulletin for Biblical Research* 15 (2005): 1–38, recently argued persuasively that behind Paul's discussion of the fruit (*karpos*) of the Spirit in Gal. 5:22–23 lies Isaiah's imagery of the Spirit's descent as rainfall to impart fruitfulness to Israel's barrenness (Isa. 32:15–18; 57:16–18; cf. 44:3–4). Both Isaiah (55:10–11) and Jesus (Mark 4:1–20) attributed the same fruit-producing power to the word of God, as Paul does in Col. 1:6—not surprisingly, since Isaiah links the Spirit and the Word of God in the closest possible way (Isa. 59:21).

entire range of human need finds its answer in the comprehensive provision of God in Jesus Christ. The entire range of divine glory and grace is displayed in Jesus Christ. No wonder Paul resolved to preach nothing but Christ!

The comprehensive wisdom of Paul's gospel reflects the comprehensive sufficiency of God's Word written, as is testified elsewhere in Scripture:

> Ps. 119:96: I have seen a limit to all perfection, but your commandment is exceedingly broad.

> 2 Tim. 3:16–17: All Scripture is breathed out by God and profitable for teaching, for reproof, for correction, and for training in righteousness, that the man of God may be competent, equipped for every good work.

The spheres of the Scripture's profitability show the breadth of Scripture's purpose and of the preaching task for which the Word equips the man of God.[16] Scripture's purpose is not merely intellectual ("teaching"); it also includes reproving, correcting, and training. Since the fall into sin not only has brought intellectual delusion but also includes volitional, affective, and relational distortion as a result, Scripture as an instrument of God's Spirit is designed to apply Christ's saving accomplishment to the whole syndrome of human sinfulness.

This purpose of preaching has implications for what we say and do in preaching: Preaching not only informs the mind but also employs truth to appeal to emotions and to challenge the will to respond in ways appropriate to the truth revealed in the gospel. In fact, in the Bible's psychology "mind," "heart," and "will" are not distinct faculties of our personality but different ways of viewing the "inner person," the unseen conscious center from which flow "the springs of life": our thoughts, affections, priorities, decisions, words, and ultimately actions (Prov. 4:23; Rom. 12:2; Eph. 4:23; 2 Cor. 4:16).

It should be noted that Paul expected his preaching methods to be reproduced in ordinary believers' ministry of the Word to one another as "general officers" who have a share in Christ's offices of

---

16   The title "man of God," which Paul applies to Timothy in relation to his ministerial office of proclaiming the Word and shepherding the church (1 Tim. 6:11; 2 Tim. 3:17), belonged to prophets as God's spokesmen in the Old Testament (1 Sam. 2:27; 1 Kings 13:1).

prophet, priest, and king.[17] In Colossians 3:16 Paul repeats the three components that we are presently considering—namely, "admonishing," "teaching," and "in all wisdom"—in his exhortation to the whole church: "Let the word of Christ dwell in you richly, *in all wisdom teaching and admonishing* each other" (dej). The tasks that Paul performs with apostolic authority as servant (*diakonos*) of the gospel (1:23) and of the church (1:24) and as God's steward (*oikonomos*, 1:25) are also tasks that all church members, each according to ability and opportunity, are to do for one another.

The Price We Pay: "Sufferings . . . Christ's Afflictions . . . Toil, Struggling"

The first four motifs—purpose, listeners, content, communication tasks—are the heart of this book. The last three motifs that emerge from Colossians 1:28–2:7, however, are essential to a full-orbed understanding of apostolic preaching. These final three—the price we pay, the power that produces preaching's fruit, and our responsibility as stewards—demonstrate that more is entailed in apostolic preaching than hermeneutic procedures or communication strategies. Apostolic preaching is no nine-to-five job at which employees put in the required hours and then leave workplace worries behind at day's end, paychecks in hand, to pursue their "real" lives. To be entrusted with the treasure of God's gospel is not a responsibility that can be switched "off" and "on" at will.[18] In a profound way, this calling consumes those

---

17   On the "general (or universal) office" in which every Christian serves, see Clowney, *The Church*, 199–214; R. B. Kuiper, *The Glorious Body of Christ: A Scriptural Appreciation of the One Holy Church* (London: Banner of Truth, 1966), 126–32. The Heidelberg Catechism elaborates on the theme that every believer, by virtue of union with Christ, shares in his messianic anointing (cf. 1 John 2:27) to fulfill our calling "to confess his name" (prophetic ministry), "to present myself to him as a living sacrifice of thanks" (priestly ministry), "to strive with a good conscience against sin and the devil in this life, and afterward to reign with Christ over all creation for all eternity" (kingly ministry, A. 32, Lord's Day 12).

18   This caution should not be understood, however, to justify the too-frequent idolatry of workaholism among pastors, to the neglect of family needs and friendships. Too many pastors, driven by insecurities, guilt, and fear of failure, sacrifice marriage and children on the altar of "effective and sacrificial ministry," turning success and sacrifice into the false gods from whom they seek validation, rather than resting in Jesus' righteousness and serving gladly and strenuously (and yes, sacrificially) out of assurance of the Father's love. Gospel-grounded gospel ministry sets the pastor free to love and serve his wife and children, as well

who receive it, and its faithful fulfillment demands not only readiness to suffer but also a humble dependence on God's sovereign Spirit to convey his life-giving good news through our weak words.

The price we are called to pay can be summed up in the words *struggle*, *suffering*, and *toil*. There is good reason to view struggle (*agōnizomai*, 1:29; *agōn*, 2:1) as inclusive of both suffering and toil, and of more besides. Paul borrows the noun and its cognate verb from the realms of military conflict and athletic competition, which in the Greek world were intimately linked (as shown in Olympic events such as javelin and wrestling). As a metaphor for gospel ministry, "struggle" calls attention to formidable opponents who stand against the gospel, and who therefore harass the bearers of God's good news.

Sometimes the opposition expresses itself in overt persecution by human enemies: "For it has been granted to you that for the sake of Christ you should not only believe in him but also suffer for his sake, engaged in the same conflict (*agōn*) that you saw I had and now hear that I still have" (Phil. 1:29–30). More profoundly, however, "we do not wrestle against flesh and blood, but against . . . the cosmic powers over this present darkness, against the spiritual forces of evil in the heavenly places" (Eph. 6:12). For this reason the apostolic preacher's struggle is not only against external enemies, but also against Satan's exploitation of one's own sin, timidity, and laziness. The preacher struggles to maintain credibility through the purity of his life. Paul applies the military-athletic metaphor not only to his own ruthless self-discipline in rooting out his own sin (1 Cor. 9:26–27) but also in his counsel to his ministerial apprentice Timothy:

> Train (*gymnazō*)[19] yourself for godliness; for while bodily training (*gymnasia*) is of some value, godliness is of value in every way. . . . For to this end we toil (*kopiaō*) and strive (*agōnizomai*), because we have our hope set on the living God, who is Savior of all people, especially of those who believe. (1 Tim. 4:7–8, 10)

The apostolic preacher's struggle, therefore, is at its root a spiritual wrestling match with evil spiritual forces whose strength outmatches our own—were it not for the victorious power of our Champion Jesus.

---

as his congregation and community, out of rested joy, not a feverish pursuit of self-justification.

19   This verb referred specifically to athletic training, since Greek athletes often trained and competed naked (*gymnos*).

Paul's focus of attention in Colossians 1:29–2:1, however, is not on the preacher's personal struggle against sin, but on the "toil," the hard labor (*kopiaō*) entailed in his imparting the gospel to others. This toil includes, first of all, the strenuous effort involved in studying the Scriptures in order to understand accurately and express clearly God's once-hidden, now-revealed mystery, Christ. Paul would later urge Timothy to strive to present himself to God as an approved craftsman, who handles the word of truth accurately (2 Tim. 2:15). Paul may be invoking an image from his own original craft, tent making, when he refers to "cutting straightly" (*orthotomeō*; ESV: "rightly handling") the word of truth.[20] The one who explores and expounds God's Word of truth should be no less rigorous in attending to his "materials" than the most skillful tentmaker is in cutting leather or canvas. He does not want to be ashamed when craftsmanship is inspected by the Author of the word himself on the last day. Even now God is present and listening in as the preacher conveys his message (2 Cor. 2:17).

Paul's tent-making trade brings into view another dimension of the "toil" that is entailed in apostolic preaching. The preacher is called to sacrifice his own leisure, comfort, and safety for the purpose of delivering his message and removing obstacles to faith for his hearers. Although Paul insisted that gospel preachers have a divinely mandated right to financial support from those to whom they serve the Word (1 Cor. 9:3–14; Gal. 6:6), in pioneer missions and church-planting venues he supported himself by his own labor. His purpose was to match his medium to his message, to offer his gospel about God's free grace, free of charge, counting it his greatest "reward" to forego his rights for the sake of showing in person the sacrificial servanthood of the Savior whom he proclaimed (1 Cor. 9:18).

Preeminently, however, the apostolic preacher's struggle entails suffering in the course of fulfilling his commission. When Corinthian Christians, under the influence of "super-apostles" (2 Cor. 11:5; 12:11) who flaunted their power and polish while demanding others' subservience, challenged Paul's apostolic credentials, he defended himself with a résumé not of "successes" but of sufferings: imprisonments, beatings, stoning, shipwreck, hunger, thirst, exposure, long hours and

---

20   This verb does not appear elsewhere in the Greek New Testament, but is used of cutting a straight road in LXX Prov. 3:6; cf. 11:5. How apt it would be for Paul to use a metaphor from the trade that Timothy had observed the apostle practice to provide for himself and his team (Acts 18:1–5; cf. 20:34)!

sleepless nights, travel dangers on land and sea, from pagans, Jewish kinsmen, and even false brothers bearing Jesus' name (2 Cor. 11:23–28). This catalogue of shameful (to Corinthian eyes) weaknesses is, in Paul's eyes, the hallmark of his genuineness as a "servant of Christ." Paul's message is about a death that brings life, the death of Jesus; and Paul himself, in his weakness and suffering, is a walking illustration of the message he proclaims. He and his colleagues are "always carrying in the body the death of Jesus, so that the life of Jesus may also be manifested in our bodies" (2 Cor. 4:10). As death works in the preacher, life works in his hearers, and grace reaches more people, magnifying expressions of gratitude, to the glory of God (vs. 15). The super-apostles' philosophy of ministry—that representatives of the Almighty display his power and share his glory in the present—is pleasant for the preacher but deadly for his hearers!

Therefore, to the Colossians Paul writes, "I rejoice in my sufferings for your sake, and in my flesh I am filling up what is lacking in Christ's afflictions for the sake of his body, that is, the church" (Col. 1:24). This statement contains two surprises. First, it is unnatural to rejoice in sufferings. Yet, Paul repeatedly rejoices to see Christ's strength shining most brightly in the apostle's frailty and pain (2 Cor. 4:7; 12:7–10; 1 Cor. 2:1–4; Phil. 1:12–14; 2:17–18; cf. Acts 5:41; 1 Peter 4:13).

The second surprise is more shocking: Paul claims that his woes are "filling up *what is lacking* in Christ's afflictions." Can we seriously believe that the apostolic preacher who would boast in nothing but Christ's cross (Gal. 6:14) and shunned his own righteousness in order to receive the gift of God's righteousness through faith in Christ (Phil. 3:9) could conceive the possibility that Jesus had left *anything* unfinished in his redemptive suffering for his own? Certainly not! Yet, as he was suddenly transformed from one who inflicted suffering to one endured suffering for Jesus' name (Acts 9:16), Paul learned how intimately Jesus identifies himself with his suffering witnesses. "Saul, Saul, why are you persecuting me?" said the voice of the Lord Jesus from the radiance of his heavenly glory (Acts 9:4). Long before the apostle expounded the truth of our union with Christ, through which the curse that we sinners deserve was imputed to Jesus in his death (Gal. 3:13) and the vindication that he received as the righteous and resurrected Servant is imputed to us (Rom. 4:25), Paul had heard Jesus reckon his followers' sufferings as inflicted on himself. In this sense the suffering of Paul and other apostolic preachers "fills up what is lacking in Christ's afflictions." Christ's suffering, which accomplished redemption is completed once for all (John 19:30; Heb. 10:10). But suffering is also entailed in the *communication* of the good news of Christ's finished work, for it is through preaching that the Holy Spirit evokes faith, applying Christ's blood-bought redemption to God's elect from every nation.

Occasionally, Christians pursue pastoral ministry because they are burned out in the cutthroat competition of the business world and imagine that they will find a tranquil (and even restful) life in the church, especially as a pastor who preaches on Sunday and enjoys a flexible schedule the rest of the week. Some starry-eyed ministerial aspirants imagine that people always admire, respect, and appreciate pastors. Such adulation can be a great boost to shaky self-esteem! Paul, however, awakens us from fantasyland and introduces us to the real world: those who would practice apostolic preaching must be prepared for both toil and suffering.

The Power on Which We Rely: "All His Energy . . . Within Me"

Paul rejoices in suffering and boasts in weakness because both show that in apostolic preaching more is at work than human intelligence or articulateness. Nothing can explain the life-changing effects of the message of the Cross except the almighty operation of God's sovereign Spirit. Therefore, Paul's toil and struggle are sustained by "all [Christ's] energy that he powerfully works within me" (Col. 1:29).

In 2 Corinthians 10:4–5, Paul compares the preacher's task to the siege and conquest of forbidding fortresses: "For the weapons of our warfare are not of the flesh but have divine power to destroy strongholds. We destroy arguments and every lofty opinion raised against the knowledge of God, and take every thought captive to obey Christ." The strongholds are cleverly defended, deep-seated error that arrogantly opposes God's truth in Christ. These defenses of the human heart are harder fortifications to breach than the massive walls of unscaleable stone that encircled ancient Jericho. Yet, the apostolic preacher has in his arsenal the very weapons that can pierce stone-hard hearts and invade spiritual death with new life: the gospel of Christ, carried forward by the invincible Spirit of Christ.

Paul often emphasizes that the task of the apostolic preacher far outstrips his own capacities. Yet, because God magnifies his own power through his messengers' weakness, Paul expects Christ's Spirit to achieve mighty victories through the weak preaching of a "weak" cross. He reminds the Corinthians: "And I was with you in weakness and in fear and much trembling, and my speech and my message were not in plausible words of wisdom, but in demonstration of the Spirit and of power, that your faith might not rest in the wisdom of men but in the power of God" (1 Cor. 2:3–5). Faith grounded in human wisdom can be dislodged by the next smooth-talking spiritual salesperson who comes along. Faith rooted in God's power, exerted improbably through unpolished heralds, will stand fast. The basis of the preacher's confidence lies not in his intelligence or eloquence but in the sovereign God who makes him sufficient for the task as a gift of sheer grace:

> Such is the confidence that we have through Christ toward God. Not that we are sufficient in ourselves to claim anything as coming from us, but our sufficiency is from God, who has made us competent to be ministers of a new covenant, not of the letter but of the Spirit. For the letter kills, but the Spirit gives life. (2 Cor. 3:4–6)

This is not to say that Paul was indifferent to those factors that produce effective communication. His sermons recorded in Acts and his epistles show him to be a master of persuasion, ably interpreting Israel's ancient Scriptures as fulfilled in Jesus to audiences in temple and synagogue and teasing out God's revelatory clues embedded in the universe and human nature to build his case that Gentiles must turn from dead idols to the living God.[21] Apostolic preaching puts no premium on obscurity, disorganization, or indifference to the hearers' level of understanding. The worthiness of the Lord who commissioned him and the desperate need of those to whom he is sent placed upon Paul, as he preached, the obligation to engage the full arsenal of resources providentially entrusted to him through creation, Jewish upbringing, rabbinical training, and exposure to Hellenistic and Roman cultures. Paul used every legitimate resource at his disposal to pierce the darkness of his hearers' minds; but he would not, could not trust in technique or argument to effect the change that none but God's Spirit could produce.

---

21   Jay Adams, *Audience Adaptations in the Sermons and Speeches of Paul* (Nutley: P & R, 1976); Roger Wagner, *Tongues Aflame: Learning to Preach from the Apostles* (Fearn: Mentor, 2004); Johnson, *Message of Acts*, 141–65.

Because Paul was so aware that the power that made his ministry effective was not his own, Paul saturated his ministry in prayer. The openings of his epistles give us a glimpse of his constancy and urgency in prayer for the churches he planted, and for those whom he had never met (e.g., Eph. 1:15–19; 3:14–19; Col. 1:9–12).[22] He knew that his Spirit-given words, true and precious as they were, could be carried into hearers' hearts only by the Spirit of God himself. Aware of his own temptations to timidity, Paul also begged his Christian brothers and sisters to pray for him, both for opportunity to speak and for the boldness to seize the opportunities as God opens them.

> Continue steadfastly in prayer, being watchful in it with thanksgiving. At the same time, pray also for us, that God may open to us a door for the word, to declare the mystery of Christ, on account of which I am in prison—that I may make it clear, which is how I ought to speak. (Col. 4:2–4)

> . . . and also [pray] for me, that words may be given to me in opening my mouth boldly to proclaim the mystery of the gospel, for which I am an ambassador in chains, that I may declare it boldly, as I ought to speak. (Eph. 6:19–20)

Paul, who seems so fearless as we view him in action in the book of Acts,[23] knows what it is to be intimidated, tempted to fearful silence rather than energized in bold confidence.

Preachers like Paul, who realize their own desperate need and the Spirit's almighty power, will saturate their ministry of the Word with prayer—for their hearers, themselves, and each other—and will urgently seek the support of others' prayers.

The Office We Fulfill: "Minister according to the Stewardship from God"

Paul is invested with authority, and his ministry is accompanied by life-changing power. But neither the authority nor the power is his own. Paul is profoundly aware of the fact that he is not called to

---

22   The other apostles likewise saw prayer as integral to their ministry of the Word. Other leaders were appointed to oversee mercy ministry so that the apostles would not have to "give up preaching the word of God" but would be free to "devote ourselves to prayer and to the ministry of the word" (Acts 6:2, 4).

23   Note, however, the Lord's encouragement to Paul at Corinth: "Do not be afraid, but go on speaking and do not be silent, for I am with you . . . ." (Acts 18:9).

lord it over others, to make them do his bidding or meet his needs. Rather, as Jesus taught his competitive, self-serving disciples, in his kingdom leadership is servanthood. It is to be slave of all, caring for others' interests above one's own (cf. Phil. 2:1–11). In Colossians 1–2, this motif appears in the terms "minister" and "stewardship."

Paul is a minister or servant (*diakonos*), both of the gospel and of the church (Col. 1:23, 25). Although the English word "minister" today carries connotations of dignity and authority in both the ecclesiastical and the political spheres, its Greek antecedent typically referred to a household servant who waited on the master, his family, and their guests at meals. The mindset appropriate to a servant's place was concern for others and their needs, not preoccupation with one's personal fulfillment, rights, or recognition. In other cultures and communities, the perks of religious leadership may be wealth, honor, and influence. The power to guide others' lives, to have others listen to you, respect you, follow your advice, and do your bidding is very alluring. In the community ruled by Jesus, however, accepted assumptions about leaders and followers are reversed: "Whoever would be great among you must be your servant (*diakonos*), and whoever would be first among you must be slave (*doulos*) of all" (Mark 10:43–44). Contrasting his own ministry to the approach of the "super-apostles," Paul uses an even more abject title, "slave" (*doulos*), to convey his relationship to those who receive his preaching and his leadership in Jesus' name: "For it is not ourselves that we proclaim [as lords] but [we proclaim] Jesus Christ as Lord, and ourselves as your slaves for Jesus' sake" (2 Cor. 4:5 dej).

In service to the gospel, Paul freely foregoes his rights, making himself a slave to all, that he might "win" more people, enlisting them as glad and grateful followers of Jesus (1 Cor. 9:19). He goes so far as to say, "I try to please everyone in everything I do, not seeking my own advantage, but that of many, that they may be saved" (1 Cor. 10:33). Of course, the apostle is not slavishly trying to keep everyone happy. To do so would deny his accountability as a steward of God, and Paul elsewhere repudiates the suggestion that he is trying to "please" people (Gal. 1:10). He seeks to "please everyone" only in the sense that his preeminent consideration is what will benefit the many—bringing them salvation—rather than his personal comfort, convenience, fame, or affirmation. Paul calls attention to his servant-heart in order to call the Corinthians to imitate himself, as he himself reflects the Christ whose servanthood in self-sacrifice is the heart of Paul's gospel (1 Cor. 11:1). Ultimately, both Paul's freedom from others' opinions and his enslavement to others' needs arise from the fact that he is a servant of the Lord, entrusted with the Lord's treasure, the gospel, as a stewardship.

The steward (*oikonomos*) in a Greco-Roman household was a slave invested with great authority, combining the powers of a British butler and a ranch foreman in the American West. The steward owned nothing but controlled virtually everything in the household and on the estate, and always with the understanding that he was accountable to the master for how he administered the master's properties and personnel. The positions of unparalleled power to which Joseph rose in Egypt, first in Potiphar's house and then in the court of Pharaoh, aptly illustrate the authority and accountability of the ancient steward (Gen. 39:4; 41:40–45).

Paul employs stewardship as a metaphor to describe his ministry of the gospel not only in our text (Col. 1:25) but also elsewhere in his epistles (Eph. 3:2, 9; 1 Tim. 1:4). In fact, all overseers or elders fulfill the role of "steward of God" (Titus 1:7). Paul's most detailed elaboration of the implication of this imagery for preachers is 1 Corinthians 4:1–5:

> This is how one should regard us, as servants of Christ and stewards of the mysteries of God. Moreover, it is required of stewards that they be found trustworthy. But with me it is a very small thing that I should be judged by you or by any human court. In fact, I do not even judge myself. I am not aware of anything against myself, but I am not thereby acquitted. It is the Lord who judges me. Therefore do not pronounce judgment before the time, before the Lord comes, who will bring to light the things now hidden in darkness and will disclose the purposes of the heart. Then each one will receive his commendation from God.

Having been entrusted with his Master's richest treasure, "the mysteries of God" (the gospel of grace once hidden but now revealed), and having been charged to use it for the Master's purposes, Paul the steward is answerable for the conduct of his trusteeship when the Master "audits the books."[24]

---

24   Paul uses another metaphor with similar import in the Pastoral Epistles, describing the gospel as a "deposit" (*parathēkē*) entrusted (*paratithēmi*) by Paul to Timothy, who in turn must place it, undiminished and unaltered, into the faithful care of other trustees (1 Tim. 6:20; 2 Tim. 1:14; 2:2).

Unlike the situation portrayed in Jesus' parables (Luke 12:41; 19:12–27; and perhaps 16:1–8), Paul's Master is not an absentee landlord. Rather he is present in power and glory (though invisibly) in the person of the Holy Spirit. Therefore, it is not only at an "audit" at history's end, when Christ returns bodily from heaven, but at every moment that the Master knows and evaluates the faithfulness of his stewards. The apostolic preacher's consciousness of the unseen presence of God himself in every venue in which he brings the Word sets him apart from those religious hucksters who had no qualms about reshaping the content of their message to suit the tastes of their audience: "For we are not, like so many, peddlers of God's word, but as men of sincerity, as commissioned by God, *in the sight of God* we speak in Christ" (2 Cor. 2:17, emphasis added). "But we have renounced disgraceful, underhanded ways. We refuse to practice cunning or to tamper with God's word, but by the open statement of the truth we would commend ourselves to everyone's conscience in the sight of God" (2 Cor. 4:2).

The apostolic preacher has a vivid sense of his accountability to the God who gave him his message and expects him to deliver it accurately to others. The preacher speaks in God's name, and he does so not only as one who will *some day* give an account for his handling of the divine Word (2 Tim. 2:15) but also as one who stands *today* in the very presence of the God whose word he proclaims.

Conclusion

To draw together Paul's rich theology of preaching as revealed in Colossians 1:24–2:7 (and other Pauline texts), we can conclude that apostolic preaching is:

1. The proclamation, explanation and application (communication tasks)
2. of the Word of God written, in relation to its integrating center—Christ, the only Mediator between God and man—(content)
3. by a man called by God, gifted by the Holy Spirit, and growing in Christlikeness, (office)
4. to people made in God's image but alienated and marred by sin and its toxic by-products (listeners)

5. in the presence of God (office)
6. to serve as the Spirit's means of grace by which he replaces unbelieving hearts of stone with believing hearts of flesh, and then brings immature children of God into conformity to Christ, (purpose)
7. to the glory of God in his church (purpose).

Through the proclamation of God's good news about Christ, in dependence on the power of God's Spirit, the preacher seeks to change people's "inner" life and, as a result, their "outer" life, so that both in the hidden recesses of the heart and in the behavior that others observe they increasingly conform to Christ's perfect maturity. This entails a radical recreation of every aspect of our personality through the Word of God.

1. *Cognitive*: so that we perceive reality as the God of truth defines it.
2. *Moral/Volitional*: so that we approve what God approves as right and are repelled by what God condemns as evil.
3. *Affective* (desires, emotions): so that we define delight as God does and so that we grieve, rejoice, love, and hate as God defines the circumstances in which each is an appropriate response.
4. *Behavioral*: so that we do what God commands in the Spirit's strength, out of love for God and others, for the sake of God's glory.
5. *Communal, interpersonal*: so that we participate in the growth of a community of love, holiness, mutual service, and witness—the body of Christ, the church.

Since this comprehensive new creation project is wholly the work of God's sovereign grace, preachers who would follow the apostles' lead must proclaim Christ in all the depth and richness of his person and saving work—in his justice and his mercy—from every passage of Scripture. In order for people to be brought into a reconciled relation to God and into increasing conformity to the image of God (Christ himself), preachers must labor with integrity to display each biblical text's distinctive testimony to the Savior and then to broadcast in humble boldness both God's achievement in Jesus and the believing, grateful, obedient response that this redemption evokes in all who receive it.

The history of preaching since the apostles' day presents a checkered picture of their successors' efforts to fulfill their high calling as heralds of the King's gospel. The mixed success of past preachers over the last twenty centuries shows that it is no easy task to proclaim a passage of Scripture in a way that respects its original context, displays its unique message and purpose, relates it rightly to the grand flow of Scripture's witness to Jesus, and applies it with life-changing relevance to a diverse audience. The next chapter surveys our predecessors' uneven efforts and draws humbling lessons, as well as encouragement, from this history.

4

The Complication, Chastening, Rejection, and Recovery of Apostolic Preaching in the History of the Church

T he purpose of this chapter is not to survey the Christ-centered interpretation and proclamation of Scripture over the twenty centuries that separate us from the apostolic age of the apostles. Other resources survey more deeply the history of the church's attempts to proclaim Christ in the footsteps of the apostles.[1] Our purpose here is more modest: to sample several pivotal hermeneutic controversies that have influenced preaching through the ages, specifically from the perspective of the role of *context* in biblical interpretation and proclamation. Our hypothesis is that much of the debate throughout the history of the church over the question of whether and how the Old Testament, in particular, bears witness to

---

1   For example, Sidney Greidanus's *Preaching Christ from the Old Testament*, takes two chapters (pp. 69–176) to survey, selectively, patristic, medieval, Reformation, and modern approaches to christocentric homiletics. Greidanus analyzes the tension between allegorical and typological preaching in the patristic period, the fourfold method of the medieval period, two Reformation preachers (Luther and Calvin), and two post-Reformation preachers (Charles Spurgeon and Wilhelm Visscher). Although Hughes Oliphant Old's magisterial (six volumes, 3,662 pages) series, *The Reading and Preaching of the Scriptures in the Worship of the Christian Church*, covers a wider range of homiletic and liturgical issues than is our focus, his comments on particular preachers and on broader historical trends take note of the extent to which Christ and his gospel remained central to the church's pulpit in various ages. Vol. 1 *The Biblical Period*, vol. 2 *The Patristic Age*, vol. 3 *The Medieval Church*, vol. 4 *The Reformation*, vol. 5 *Moderatism, Pietism, and Awakening*, vol. 6 *The Modern Age 1789–1989* (Grand Rapids: Eerdmans, 1998–2007).

Christ turns on disagreement over the weight to be accorded to various concentric circles of context in which a biblical text can be read.

In a compact and insightful statement of sound hermeneutic principle, the Second Helvetic Confession of 1566, cited below, identified the issues of context and purpose as intrinsic to the Reformation's insistence on hearing Scripture interpret itself. Having challenged the infallible authority of ecclesiastical tradition as interpreter of the Bible, Reformed theologians confronted the question of what constitutes credible warrant for the interpretation of a biblical passage. The Church of Rome alleged that independence from the authority of fathers, councils, and tradition would open the door to radical subjectivity, and the mystical directions taken by some sections of the Radical Reformation seemed to bear out this charge. The Swiss Confessors and others, however, answered that "Scripture its own interpreter" was no mere slogan to justify exegesis cut loose from constraints but instead entailed a sober and disciplined procedure and criterion for discerning the meaning of the biblical texts— in their relevant contexts.

In fact, Christian preachers and theologians, as well as Jewish rabbis before them, had always justified their readings of Scripture by (at least implicit) appeal to context. Different hermeneutic schools in the patristic, medieval, Reformation, and Enlightenment periods have been distinguished by their disagreement over which context or contexts are appropriate or most relevant to validate a particular reading of Scripture. In particular, the role of the original historical context in which a biblical book was given has been pitted against the theological context supplied by later revelation and the church's dogmatic reflection on the completed canon. Conflicts over context, and the related issue of genre, provide a helpful perspective through which to view the history of the complication, chastening, rejection, and recovery of apostolic, Christ-centered preaching in the church.

Complication: From the Church Fathers through the Middle Ages

"Complication" is perhaps simplistic as a one-word description of patristic and medieval preaching and reading of Scripture. Others might choose harsher terms, portraying the second through fifteenth centuries as a period of the "loss," "decline," "corruption," or "metastasis" (as in spreading cancer) of apostolic hermeneutics and homiletics in various fanciful, imaginative, and unscientific directions. Having exposed the unjustified bias against patristic and medieval interpretation, shown by both critical and evangelical scholars in the wake of the Enlightenment, Moisés Silva has recommended that today's students of Scripture adopt a humbler, more teachable attitude toward those who have gone before us, respecting both the intelligence and the theological integrity of giants such as Origen, even when some of their hermeneutic strategies fail to persuade us.[2] Other voices are joining Silva's in contending that the Fathers and their medieval successors have much to teach modern interpreters and preachers, had we humility and patience enough to learn from such ancient sources. Thomas Oden and his editorial colleagues are producing the multi-volume *Ancient Christian Commentary on Scripture* to summon modern students of Scripture back into conversation with expositors from the first Christian millennium, whose historical proximity to Jesus and his apostles suggests that they deserve a respectful hearing.[3]

Nevertheless, although the patristic and medieval periods offer many wise students and preachers of Scripture to instruct us in the path of apostolic, Christ-centered proclamation of the whole Bible, by the late Middle Ages well-meant hermeneutic principles and practices had developed in directions that undermined the clarity of Scripture and damaged the credibility of the church's interpretation. A process of "complication" had set in, both in the sense of an increase in complexity of method and of meanings and, metaphorically, in the medical sense of an adverse development that threatened the health of the "patient." The process was gradual and no doubt largely imperceptible as it happened, although at points voices, such as those of the school of Antioch, were raised in alarm and protest.

At the outset, however, it should be noted that underlying whatever hermeneutic disagreements Antioch had with Alexandria, or the Reformers with medieval practitioners of fourfold interpretation, lay common convictions that set the consensus of classical Christian interpretation and preaching from the first through seventeenth centuries apart from the Enlightenment and its historical critical legacy.

---

2   Moisés Silva, *Has the Church Misread the Bible? The History of Interpretation in the Light of Current Issues* (Foundations of Contemporary Interpretation, vol. 1. Grand Rapids: Zondervan, 1987).

3   Downers Grove: InterVarsity, 1998—.

Classical preachers, whether patristic, medieval, or Reformational, shared the beliefs that all of Scripture is ultimately the Word of one divine Author and therefore that the primary context in which any passage should be interpreted is the entire, completed canon of the Old and New Testaments, which has its integrating center in the person and work of Jesus Christ.

In *Reading Scripture with the Church Fathers*, an introductory orientation to the *Ancient Christian Commentary*, Christopher Hall makes the summary statement that to read Scripture with the Fathers means to "read the Bible christologically. All the fathers read Scripture through the prism of Christ's incarnation, crucifixion, resurrection, and ascension."[4] John J. O'Keefe and R. R. Reno likewise find that for the church fathers Jesus and his redemptive work constitute the structure that unifies the canon of Holy Scripture, despite its wide diversity in age, genre, and situation.

> Irenaeus provides a sketch of what proved to be the dominant patristic theory of the unified truth of scripture. It is an approach that vindicates Ignatius' assertion that Jesus Christ is the sacred text and provides us with insight into the structuring principles that guided the interpretation of other patristic figures. . . . For Irenaeus, the coming of Jesus Christ is the decisive event that clarifies the divine economy. . . . [Irenaeus] shows in countless digressions into the details of biblical history that Jesus Christ is the key to all the inconclusive patterns and open questions raised by scripture . . . . The scriptures remain the vast body of heterogeneous material, retaining its reality as a text that speaks about a vast array of events and people, and records law, parables, proverbs, prayer, and poems. However, for Irenaeus and the patristic tradition as a whole, Jesus Christ is the hypothesis [unifying literary motif]. He reveals the logic and architecture by which a total reading of that great diversity may be confidently pursued.[5]

Hall cites, as representative of the Fathers' consensus on the unity of the entire biblical canon in Christ, Irenaeus' statement in *Against Heresies*, 4.26.1:

> If one carefully reads the Scriptures, he will find there the word on the subject of Christ—*de Christo sermonem*—and the prefiguration of the

---

4   Christopher A. Hall, *Reading Scripture with the Church Fathers* (Downers Grove: InterVarsity, 1998), 192.

5   John J. O'Keefe and R. R. Reno, *Sanctified Vision: An Introduction to Early Christian Interpretation of the Bible* (Baltimore: Johns Hopkins, 2005), 34, 38, 39, 41.

new calling. He is indeed the hidden treasure in the field—the field in fact is the world—but in truth, the hidden treasure in the Scriptures is Christ. Because he is designed by types and words that humanly are not possible to understand before the accomplishment of all things, that is, Christ's parousia.[6]

In a similar vein, O'Keefe and Reno begin their chapter entitled "Christ Is the End of the Law and the Prophets" with the statement of Justin Martyr, another second century father, in his *Dialogue with Trypho*: "Having become man, [Jesus Christ] laid open all the mysteries that had been locked up in Scripture by his Resurrection and Ascension."[7] Concurring with Irenaeus and Justin, who practiced typological hermeneutic in the second century, was the perspective of the fourth century allegorical preacher, Hilary, bishop of Poitiers:

Every part of Holy Writ announces through words the coming of Our Lord Jesus Christ, reveals it through facts and establishes it through examples . . . . For it is our Lord who during all the present age, through true and manifest adumbrations, generates, cleanses, sanctifies, chooses, separates, or redeems the Church in the Patriarchs, through Adam's slumber, Noah's flood, Melchizedek's blessing, Abraham's justification, Isaac's birth, and Jacob's bondage.[8]

Over a millennium later, Protestant Reformers, despite their sharp critique of the extremes to which allegorical approaches had "complicated" biblical interpretation by the sixteenth century, would nonetheless concur with the Fathers' insistence that Scripture's whole message centers in Christ.[9]

In Justin and Irenaeus we see an early patristic hermeneutic that stands in fundamental continuity with the New Testament's interpretation of the Old, emphasizing the importance of Old Testament Scriptures' original historical context, as well as giving attention to the texts' complete canonical context—specifically, the fulfillment of

---

6   Hall, *Reading Scripture*, 192. Also cited in fuller context by Greidanus, *Preaching Christ*, 176.

7   Cited in O'Keefe and Reno, *Sanctified Vision*, 24.

8   Hilary of Poitiers, *Treatise on the Mysteries*, I Pref., cited in Hall, *Reading Scripture*, 192.

9   Note, for example, Luther's focus on what "advances" Christ in each text. To Luther, admittedly, this christocentric focus was often a focus on justification by faith alone, an indispensable but not exhaustive description of Christ's work as Savior and Lord. See Greidanus, *Preaching Christ*, 119–26.

Israel's experience in the coming and redemptive work of Jesus the Christ.[10] Both ventured to draw multiple lines of connection between Old Testament shadows and types, on the one hand, and Christ, on the other, even with respect to textual details that seem incidental to the central issue of God's covenantal interactions with his human servants (thus occasionally drifting from sober typology toward more complex "typologizing," en route toward allegory).[11] Irenaeus, for instance, explained categories of animals distinguished in the Levitical dietary laws as symbolizing various groups' responses to the gospel. Clean animals, which part the hoof and chew the cud, symbolize Jewish and Gentile Christian believers, who both meditate on God's word (chew cud) and stand on the Father and the Son (part the hoof). Pagans do neither and are therefore unclean, as are unbelieving Jews, who "chew the cud" (meditate on the law) but do not part the hoof (that is, do not believe in the Son).[12] In these creative connections, the Apostolic Fathers' interpretive strategy anticipated the more full-orbed allegorism to be developed by the School of Alexandria, yet their approach remained grounded, by and large, in a respect for the text's original historical situation as providing decisive and indispensable context for the determination of its meaning.[13]

In one sense, allegory and typology are subcategories of metaphor and points on a continuum. They both affirm that events recounted in biblical historical narrative have symbolic depth beyond their literal "factuality," and both find in this symbolic significance the key to the text's relevance to later readers. Therefore, in the Apostolic Fathers we find christological/ecclesiological/eschatological interpretations of Old Testament history (and other biblical narratives, such as parables) that flow rather fluidly between the categories that would later be sharply distinguished in the polarized hermeneutic debate between Alexandria (led by Clement, Origen, and others) and Antioch (led by Diodore, Theodore of Mopsuestia, John Chrysostom, and others). In the third century, Alexandria (for reasons mentioned below) stressed

---

10   Greidanus, *Preaching Christ*, 73–80.

11   Greidanus, *Preaching Christ*, 97–98.

12   Irenaeus, *Against Heresies*, 5.8.4, summarized in Greidanus, *Preaching Christ*, 79; and in Hall, *Reading*, 139.

13   The Apostolic Fathers, particularly Justin, also grounded their typological interpretation of the revelation of Christ in Old Testament events on the belief that the Son who would become incarnate in the fullness of the times was engaged with Israel as the preexistent Logos.

Scripture's symbolic depth and the decisive role of canonical context as a whole. This school, therefore, justified and magnified the Apostolic Fathers' tendencies to proliferate (or complicate) points of comparison between the details of Old Testament narrative and Christian dogma and church life. In the fourth century, Antioch reacted by reemphasizing the interpretive weight of the text's original life and literary context and the author's intended meaning for his first readers.

Despite the sharpness of their disagreement over layers of symbolism, however, Alexandria and Antioch shared an underlying consensus, already visible in Justin and Irenaeus, which affirmed both the biblical text's historical context and its broader canonical context. Unlike the philosophers' allegorizing of pagan myths and even, to some extent, Philo's allegorizing of the Jewish Scriptures to make them compatible with neo-Platonic thought, the allegorical emphasis of Alexandria did not minimize the "literal" historical reality of the biblical events.[14] (The "literal" level, however, receded in its interpretive and pastoral significance.) Unlike some Jewish, dispensational, and historical critical interpreters, the typological emphasis of Antioch did not restrict an Old Testament text's meaning to its sense in its original context but always sought to keep in view the broader canonical context, as well as the focus and fulfillment of the whole trajectory of redemptive history in Christ.

Clement (ca. 150–215) and Origen (ca. 185–254) led Alexandria into an intentional allegorical hermeneutic out of pastoral, evangelistic, and apologetic motives. Literalist readings of the Old Testament had been employed as arguments to deprive the Old Testament of its legitimacy and authority as Christian Scripture, both by rabbinical interpreters, who objected to the transfer of Israel's privilege to the multiethnic church, and by Christian heretics, such as Marcion and the Gnostics, who sought to eradicate the church's Hebrew heritage.[15] The Alexandrians sought to remove needless offense

---

14   David Dockery, *Biblical Interpretation Then and Now: Contemporary Hermeneutics in the Light of the Early Church* (Grand Rapids: Baker, 1992), 83: "The first of [Clement's] hermeneutic principles, then, included two levels: first, the literal sense must be observed, and then, the allegorical sense must be discovered. Yet, this allegorical interpretation must not discard the primary meaning of the text unless such meaning violated what was previously known of God's character and dignity."

15   Dockery, *Biblical Interpretation*, 55–62, identifies Judaizing Christianity, Gnosticism (including Marcion), and Montanism as the divergent forces against which mainstream patristic interpretation and preaching were directed.

that could be taken to certain biblical texts when read "literally." For example, the brutal vengeance requested in imprecatory psalms and the sexuality of the Song of Songs seemed to work against the ideals of peace and purity that set the church apart from the violent and sensual Roman culture that surrounded it . . . unless a higher, better meaning could be found hidden in such Old Testament texts. Some biblical texts, read literally, seemed unworthy of God, or in direct contradiction to other passages. Harmonization was obviously needed, and symbolism carried to the heights of allegorical detail could often supply this solution.

Origen found exegetical rationale for discerning multiple levels of meaning in Scripture in Paul's statement that "the letter kills, but the Spirit gives life" (2 Cor. 3:6). Heresies arise from paying too much attention to the "letter," the literal or physical meaning, and insufficient attention to the "Spirit"—its symbolic significance.[16] Moreover, Origen argued, by analogy with his tripartite anthropology, that just as human nature consists of body, soul, and spirit, so also each biblical narrative has three levels of meaning: the narration of historical events (body), the moral lessons to be derived from the events (soul), and the theological truths of christology, soteriology, ecclesiology, and eschatology that lie hidden in the events (spirit).[17] These layers are accessible to believers of various maturity levels in the congregation, from the new and immature who need to learn the facts on which the faith is founded, to growing believers who need moral guidance, to those with maturity and insight to probe the deep mysteries of God's Word.

Leading interpreters and theologians associated with the School of Antioch include Diodore of Tarsus (d. ca. 390), Theodore of Mopsuestia (350–428), and John Chrysostom (ca. 349–407).[18] Antioch's exegetes and preachers objected to the multi-layered allegorism articulated and practiced by Origen for two primary reasons. First, although Origen clearly and appropriately affirmed the historical

---

16   Origen, *First Principles*, 4.2.2, cited in Greidanus, *Preaching Christ*, 83. See also Old, *Reading and Preaching*, vol. 1, 309.

17   Old. *Reading and Preaching*, vol. 1, 310; Dockery, *Biblical Interpretation*, 88; Greidanus, *Preaching Christ*, 84–87.

18   Dates of birth (and even, sometimes, of death) are often uncertain for the fathers. Chrysostom's birth date is that proposed by J. N. D. Kelly, *Golden Mouth: The Story of John Chrysostom—Ascetic, Preacher, Bishop* (1995; repr. Grand Rapids: Baker, 1998), 296–98.

reliability of the biblical text in its literal, "bodily" reading, the allegorical method tended to undermine the theological *significance* of the events of redemptive history in preference of presumably deeper mysteries that may be only tangentially connected to the text's meaning as discernible by its original readers. Second, the higher value accorded to moral and "spiritual" senses, which derived their warrant more from the (presumed) spirituality of the preacher-interpreter than from the contextual features of the passage, undermined the clarity of Scripture and the credibility of the church's appeal to it, particularly in disputation with other communities (Jewish, Gnostic, etc.) that made their own appeals, using their own hermeneutic, to the Hebrew Scriptures or the New Testament documents.

In place of allegory, then, Antioch sought the christological dimension of Old Testament history, poetry, legal codes, and other genres through a typological approach that bound the text's symbolic significance tightly to its original historical and literary context. The Antiochenes recognized that many Scriptures, when read "literally" (that is, according to the interpretive expectations that the ancient author presupposed for his original readers in their horizon of experience and understanding), employed metaphor to convey spiritual truths through material analogy. They also recognized as normative the New Testament's interpretation of Old Testament events, persons, and institutions as foreshadowing and now coming to fulfillment in Christ and his church. Their objections to Alexandrian allegorism, however, were that its hermeneutic priorities (a) devalued (without denying) the text's meaning within its original historical and literary context, and (b) cut the text's spiritual significance loose from the constraints of the original context and demonstrable apostolic warrant in the New Testament. Without these controls, the interpreter or preacher is no longer the servant of the Word, subject to Scripture, but a master and manipulator of biblical words and images for his own theological purposes (orthodox though those purposes may be). In words to be echoed by later Reformers, Chrysostom wrote:

> We are not the lords over the rules of interpretation, but must pursue
> scripture's interpretation of itself.... This is everywhere a rule in scripture:
> when it wants to allegorize, it tells the interpretation of the allegory, so
> that the passage will not be interpreted superficially or be met by the

undisciplined desire of those who enjoy allegorization to wander about and be carried in every direction.[19]

The preacher who seeks to serve the Word submits his expository reflection to the restraining discipline of biblical texts' original contexts and to the clear apostolic warrant defined in the New Testament for drawing redemptive-historical parallels between Old Testament types and their christological/eschatological fulfillment. Preachers of the School of Antioch therefore sought to limit their symbolic interpretation of Scripture to meanings for which they could demonstrate clear warrant in the text read in its original historical context, and to trace a historically oriented line of continuity between the promise implicit in the text's original sense and the fulfillment in Christ in the fullness of time.

The process of complication, however, was not significantly curtailed by the fourth and fifth century Antiochenes' objection to allegorical imaginative excess. Also in the fifth century, no less a champion than Augustine of Hippo (354–430) weighed in strongly on the side of allegorical interpretation, and his endorsement, as well as the church's widespread homiletic practice, secured allegorism's influence as the church moved into the Middle Ages. In *De Doctrina Christiana*, for example, Augustine wrote:

> Sometimes not just one meaning but two or more meanings are perceived in the same words of scripture. Even if the writer's meaning is obscure, there is no danger here, provided that it can be shown from other passages of the holy scriptures that each of these interpretations is consistent with the truth. The person examining the divine utterances must of course do his best to arrive at the intention of the writer through whom the Holy Spirit produced that part of scripture; he may reach that meaning or carve out from the words another meaning which does not run counter to the faith, using the evidence of any other passage of the divine utterances. . . . Could God have built into the divine eloquence a more generous or bountiful gift than the possibility of understanding the same words in several ways, all of them deriving confirmation from other no less divinely inspired passages?[20]

---

19   Chrysostom, *Interpretatio in Isaiam* 5.3, cited in Dockery, *Biblical Interpretation*, 117.

20   *De Doctrina Christiana*, 3.27–29, ET *On Christian Teaching*, trans. R. P. H. Green (Oxford: Oxford University Press, 1997), 87.

Thus Augustine, like Origen, commends the value of discerning the meaning intended by the biblical author in the passage's original context; and he argues that other meanings, extraneous to that sense, must also have biblical warrant, of a sort. But the warrant may be found in any text, or any doctrine truly taught in the biblical canon taken as a whole. While acknowledging that Scripture must exercise some sort of control over its own interpretation, the greater weight that Augustine accorded to the theological context of the canon as a whole effectively gave far greater liberty to the imaginative ingenuity of individual interpreters and preachers than Chrysostom and his colleagues associated with Antioch found permissible.

Medieval exegesis and preaching shows the influence of the Alexandrian and Augustinian search for hidden levels of symbolism in the biblical text. Augustine's lesser known contemporary John Cassian (ca. 360–435) not only distinguished literal from figurative levels of meaning but also distinguished three categories of figurative, symbolic, or spiritual meaning: "There are three genera of spiritual *scientia: tropologia, allegoria, anagoge.*"[21] These three layers of spiritual readings, in addition to the text's historical sense, came to constitute the medieval fourfold hermeneutic.[22] Augustine maintained that in addition to affirming the historical events of salvation, biblical narratives were also intended to inform believers' *faith* in the system of Christian doctrine (*allegoria*), their *love* for God and one another (*tropologia*, moral instruction), and their *hope* in the heavenly world to come (*anagogia*).[23] These four categories would dominate biblical interpretation in the West, and particularly its application in preaching, for roughly a millennium.

Meanwhile, in the dissolution of classical civilization as a result of Rome's decline and fall, levels of clerical education declined, at least for pastors serving parishes—in contrast to monastic communities, which preserved ancient learning, both Christian and pagan.

---

21   Greidanus, *Preaching Christ*, 103.

22   F. F. Bruce cites an old jingle which summed up the four senses of a text: *"Littera gesta docet, quid credas allegoria, Moralis quid agas, quo tendas anagogia."* "('The literal sense teaches what actually happened, the allegorical what you are to believe, the moral how you are to behave, the anagogical where you are going.')" "The History of New Testament Study," in I. Howard Marshall, ed., *New Testament Interpretation: Essays on Principles and Methods* (Grand Rapids: Eerdmans, 1977), 28.

23   See Greidanus, *Preaching Christ*, 104, for further explanation and examples. Cf. also Dockery, *Biblical Interpretation*, 145; Bruce, "History," 28–29.

Concurrently, the gospel was spreading to barbarian peoples, such as those of central and northern Europe, who were less oriented toward the written word than ancient Judaism and Hellenism had been. Moreover, the church's practicing shepherds felt an urgent need to give high priority to the inculcation of basic biblical moral order into tribes recently and often only superficially converted from paganism. H. O. Old comments on the pastoral challenges faced by Benedictine preachers as Charlemagne (ca. 742–814) sought to make France a Christian kingdom:

> The speed with which the missionary work was being done and the political and cultural motives for which many accepted baptism meant that great masses of only partially converted people had been received into the Church. Basic Christian doctrines were poorly understood, the Christian life was poorly practiced, and the ways of paganism were not entirely left behind.[24]

This confluence of factors—an increasingly complex hermeneutic, poorly educated preachers, and the urgency of curbing pagan behavioral practices in new believers—tended to deflect homiletic attention away from Christ and his grace, foreshadowed in the Old Testament and unveiled in the apostolic gospel, and toward a stress on moral duty. There were bright spots in medieval preaching, such as the preaching of Columbanus (ca. 543–615) among the Celts[25] and the manual of homiletic resources compiled by Pirmin (ca. 700–753) for missionary monks in Baden and Alsace, in which evangelistic and edifying proclamation is grounded in the history of redemption, with Christ's incarnation, death, and resurrection as the fulfilling climax.[26] Nevertheless, Old, who offers a sympathetic and respectful assessment of medieval preaching, finds it necessary to observe that one

> . . . characteristic of the ministry of the Word during this period is the increasing difficulty preachers had in interpreting Scripture. Medieval preachers tried very hard to take their exegesis seriously, but they faced formidable problems. By the year 500 Jesus and his disciples had become figures of long ago and far away. . . . With the fall of the

---

24   Old, *Reading and Preaching*, vol. 3, 189.
25   Old, *Reading and Preaching*, vol. 3, 114–18.
26   Old, *Reading and Preaching*, vol. 3, 137–41, citing *Dicta abbatis Pirminii de singulis Libris Canonicis Scarapsus.*

Roman Empire and the barbarian invasions, the New Testament—and in fact the whole Bible—was becoming very difficult to understand. It more and more became a book of mysteries that could only be solved by mystical contemplation. . . . True expository preaching was almost impossible. No wonder the conscientious preacher found allegorical exegesis attractive![27]

The loss of access to the original languages and cultural settings of the Scriptures directed medieval preachers away from a passage's original literary and historical contexts as warrants for legitimate interpretation, removing restraints to interpreters' and preachers' associative ingenuity other than the boundary of the "rule of faith" defined by the church's councils and tradition on the basis (it was assumed) of the canonical context of the entire Bible.

Chastening: The Reformation[28]

Protestant Reformers had a keen interest not only in doctrinal reformulation but also in questions of hermeneutics. They recognized that distortions in the church's piety and practice (indulgences, veneration of saints and images, etc.) typically arose from errors in doctrine, that errors in doctrine arose from errors of biblical interpretation, and that specific errors of biblical interpretation were attributable to a hermeneutic method that gave too large a place to ecclesiastical tradition (with its political dimension) in determining what God's Word teaches. The Reformers also saw extremes in another direction: groups and individuals who not only rejected the Roman claim that ecclesiastical officers and traditions had infallible authority to interpret Scripture but who went on to claim for themselves a private, invincible access to the mind of the Spirit. The Spirit, they claimed, revealed to them directly what Bible passages really meant, whatever others might surmise from examining such mundane matters as grammar, vocabulary, historical setting, and relation to other biblical texts on the same subject.

In both extremes—the virtual deification of church tradition as infallible interpreter of Scripture, or the virtual deification of personal experience as infallible interpreter—the main stream of the

---

27   Old, *Reading and Preaching*, vol. 3, xv–xvi.

28   Westminster Confession of Faith (1645), 1.1, 1.9; Second Helvetic Confession (1566), ch. 2.

Reformation recognized the same dangerous tendency to replace the divine authority of the Word with a human authority that insulated itself from the corrective voice of Scripture and therefore enslaved others rather than bringing the liberation that Jesus' truth effects.

Reformation confessions of faith are careful to avoid both the extreme of traditionalism and the extreme of new private revelations in their discussions of the interpretation and authority of Scripture. One of the fuller statements of Reformation hermeneutic principles is found in the Second Helvetic (Swiss) Confession (1566), chapter 2, "Of Interpreting the Holy Scriptures; and of Fathers, Councils, and Traditions":

> *The True Interpretation of Scripture.* The apostle Peter has said that the Holy Scriptures are not of private interpretation (II Peter 1:20), and thus we do not allow all possible interpretations. Nor consequently do we acknowledge as the true or genuine interpretation of the Scriptures what is called the conception of the Roman Church, that is, what the defenders of the Roman Church plainly maintain should be thrust upon all for acceptance. But we hold that interpretation of the Scripture to be orthodox and genuine which is gleaned from the Scriptures themselves (from the nature of the language in which they were written, likewise according to the circumstances in which they were set down, and expounded in the light of like and unlike passages and of many and clearer passages) and which agrees with the rule of faith and love, and contributes much to the glory of God and man's salvation.
>
> *Interpretations of the Holy Fathers.* Wherefore we do not despise the interpretations of the holy Greek and Latin fathers, nor reject their . . . treatises concerning sacred matters as far as they agree with the Scriptures; but we modestly dissent from them when they are found to set down things differing from, or altogether contrary to, the Scriptures. . . .
>
> *Councils.* And in the same order also we place the decrees and canons of councils. Wherefore we do not permit ourselves, in controversies about religion or matters of faith, to urge our case with only the opinions of the fathers or decrees of councils; much less by received customs, or by the large number of those who share the same opinion, or by the prescription of a long time.[29]

Several features of this statement are worth noticing.

---

29   Arthur C. Cochrane, ed. *Reformed Confessions of the 16th Century* (Philadelphia: Westminster, 1966), 226–27.

1) Rejection of extremes. These confessors distance themselves, on the one hand, from "private interpretation," even as they also deny that their rejection of a claim of infallibility for church tradition leaves them open to "all possible interpretations." They suspect and reject interpretations that are allegedly given directly "by the Spirit" to an individual and therefore not open to verification through attention to the language of the text itself. At the same time, they distance themselves, on the other hand, from the claims of infallible ecclesiastical interpretation made by Rome (as well as the traditionalism of Constantinople or Antioch).

2) Interpretation derived from Scriptures themselves. Echoing the declaration of John Chrysostom, these confessors affirm that it is only as the Scriptures are permitted to interpret themselves that we can listen humbly to them, hear the voice of our Lord and Savior calling us to repentance and reformation, and heed his summons to faith and obedience. But what does it mean to say that Scripture must interpret itself, that there is a hermeneutic intrinsic to the written Word, and that this hermeneutic must control our study of the Word? The Swiss confessors offer several specifics.

(a) "The nature of the *language*" (grammatical-linguistic). Reformation hermeneutic is often called "grammatico-historical" because of its focus on the "grammar" (language) of the text and its historical setting (in contrast to patristic and medieval allegory, which often produced "meanings" for biblical texts completely extraneous to the texts' original historical circumstances). Attention to language, of course, is not the same thing as a literalistic overreaction to medieval fourfold allegory, as though the cure for symbolic imagination run wild were to deny symbolism altogether and commit themselves to a prosaic and wooden reading of any and every biblical genre. Rather, as practiced by the Reformers, attention to the language of Scripture entails sensitivity to the varieties of the use of language displayed in Scripture, from texts and genres in which highly symbolic usage is clearly indicated (e.g., Rev. 18 or poetic metaphor in the Psalms) to those in which there is little, if any, symbolic language.

(b) "The *circumstances* in which they were set down." Attention must be given to the *life context*, the historical and cultural situation of the first readers of a biblical book or text. What was their religious experience? What were the issues confronting Israel when a particular prophet spoke, or confronting a church to whom Paul the apostle addressed a letter? Could aspects of the text be illuminated by increasing knowledge about the politics, family structure, education, literature, and religious sects of the time? What was the relationship between the human author (Isaiah, Paul, Peter) and the first readers: warm and loving, strained or estranged? This emphasis on returning *ad fontes*, to the sources read in their original context, was of course part of the fifteenth and sixteenth centuries' much broader cultural rebirth (*renaissance*) of interest in humane letters and ancient classical civilization.

The circumstances of the biblical text also include its place in the history of redemption and revelation.[30] Although this has been more fully explored in more recent times, it would be arrogant to claim that the Reformers and their successors overlooked the significance of the redemptive-historical transition from Old Testament promise to New Testament fulfillment with the coming of Christ.[31] To understand a biblical text, as well as to apply it rightly, we must take account of the fact that it was given to God's people either before or after the coming of the Messiah.

(c) *Like and unlike passages, many and clearer passages.* This principle reminds us that each text of Scripture is to be understood not only in terms of its *life* context but also in terms of its *literary and theological-canonical contexts*, namely the rest of Scripture. Although each text has its own unique contribution to make to the over-all teaching of God's Word, the divine authorship of Scripture and the absolute truthfulness of the divine Author provide the basis for the Reformers' confidence that the message of every text, when it is rightly interpreted, will be found to be compatible with that of every other text. Compare each text with like passages (parallel accounts in the Synoptics) and with unlike passages (Paul's teaching on marriage in Eph. 5 [pro!] and 1 Cor. 7 [con?]; or Galatians and James

---

30   Geerhardus Vos, "The Idea of Biblical Theology as a Science and as a Theological Discipline" (1894), in Richard B. Gaffin, Jr., ed., *Redemptive History and Biblical Interpretation: The Shorter Writings of Geerhardus Vos* (Phillipsburg: Presbyterian and Reformed, 1980), 3–24. G. Vos, *Biblical Theology: Old and New Testaments* (Grand Rapids: Eerdmans, 1948).

31   Note, for example, the redemptive-historical distinctions drawn by the Westminster Confession of Faith (1646) with respect to the various administrations of the covenant of grace (7.5–6) and the applicability of diverse aspects of the Edenic and Mosaic law structures (19.1–5).

on faith and works). If your reading of one text makes it seem to contradict the teaching of another text (or a group of texts), you can be sure that you have misunderstood one or the other or both—or that you have failed to grasp a larger unity in which the texts' teachings ultimately cohere.

(d) *Purposes* "of faith and love, . . . the glory of God and man's salvation." We have noticed Paul's insistence on the personal and practical transformation that Christian preaching is intended to evoke. So also the Swiss confessors emphasize that a criterion for faithful biblical interpretation—interpretation that arises *intrinsically* from the text rather than being imposed *extrinsically* by an interpreters' heritage, experience, or mental ingenuity—can be discerned by the fruit it produces in people's hearts and lives. If our interpretation of a particular text or group of texts does not strengthen trust in Christ and love for him and others, something is amiss. If an interpretation diminishes God's glory and elevates human self-confidence, it has missed the point. "The proof of the pudding is in the eating." "By their fruits you will know them."

3) *Balanced relationship to earlier biblical interpreters.* We should also note that this confession specifically addresses the relationship of contemporary interpreters to those who have gone before us as students of Scripture and teachers of the church. On the one hand, the framers of this confession emphasize that they do not arbitrarily reject the interpretations of the fathers or councils. They recognize, unlike many post-Enlightenment critics, that the Spirit of God has given insight into Scripture to the church's teachers in previous generations, as well as in their own. On the other hand, particularly in response to the use of ecclesiastical tradition by Roman Catholic theologians, these Reformers insist that they will not be convinced of a particular interpretation by an uncritical appeal to fathers, counsels, or customs. In particular, they contend that appealing to the fact that a large number of theologians have adopted a certain interpretation cannot settle the question of what the text means in its linguistic and historical contexts. Nor does an appeal to the antiquity of a custom or interpretation prove that the custom or interpretation accurately reflects the teaching of Scripture. To use either the age or the popularity of a view as the deciding factor in determining the meaning of Scripture is to try to steal the right of Scripture to

interpret Scripture, to usurp God's prerogative to address and reform his church through his Word.

Almost a century later, in the 1640s, the Westminster Assembly's Confession of Faith made similar points, rejecting both human tradition and mystical experience as authorities on a par with Scripture, and affirming (over against the medieval fourfold sense) that each text of Scripture has a single meaning:

> The whole counsel of God concerning things necessary for His own glory, man's salvation, faith and life, is either expressly set down in Scripture, or by good and necessary consequence may be deduced from Scripture: unto which nothing at any time is to be added, whether by new revelations of the Spirit, or traditions of men. (1.6)

> The infallible rule of interpretation of Scripture is the Scripture itself: and therefore, when there is a question about the true and full sense of any Scripture (which is not manifold, but one), it must be searched and known by other places that speak more clearly. (1.9)

Yet, although the Reformers and their Puritan successors drew back from the elaborate fourfold approach to the "full sense" (*sensus plenior*) that had developed during the Middle Ages, they did not break from the church's history of reading Scripture as finding its central theme and hermeneutic key in Christ. That development awaited the Enlightenment.

Rejection: The Enlightenment and Historical-Critical Biblical Theology[32]

With the rise of "historical criticism" in the context of Enlightenment naturalism, the theological foundation for viewing Scripture as a unified divine revelation, progressively disclosed throughout the drama of redemptive history from promise to fulfillment, was undermined. Instead of viewing the Bible as essentially one Book, written through many human authors but unified through the pervasive control of one divine Author, the God of truth, the Scriptures came to be regarded as a collection of diverse human documents that belonged to a unified but evolving religious and historical tradition and trajectory. Because that tradition was itself in constant

---

32   G. W. H. Lampe, "The Reasonableness of Typology," in Lampe and K. J. Woollcombe, *Essays on Typology* (Naperville: Alec R. Allenson, 1957), 16–17.

flux and development, it could not be assumed (as the apostles and earlier Christian generations had) that all the biblical books shared a unified or unifiable understanding of God and his ways with mankind. Johann Salomo Semler's *Treatise on the Free Investigation of the Canon* (1771–1775) drew a sharp distinction between the books that constituted the Christian church's canon and the Word of God itself: "Holy Scripture and the Word of God are clearly to be distinguished, for we know the difference. . . . To Holy Scripture . . . belong Ruth, Esther, the Song of Songs, etc., but not all these books that are called holy belong to the Word of God, which at all times makes men wise unto salvation."[33] Semler went on to insist that morally mature readers were fully justified in passing "judgment in light of their own knowledge both on individual books [such as the Apocalypse] and on certain parts of many books, with reference to their moral and generally beneficial value . . . ."[34]

Not all Enlightenment scholars denied as overtly as Semler did that the biblical books are theologically unified by their ultimate source in the trustworthiness of one divine Author. Rather, some insisted that the question of the divine inspiration of Scripture was really a dogmatic concept established by the church and therefore had to be "set aside" for the purposes of examining more "scientifically" the unique theological perspective of each biblical author and writing. J. P. Gabler, in his inaugural lecture as professor of biblical theology at the University of Altdorf in 1787, said that in order to avoid assuming what needed to be proved, he would "overlook the doctrine of divine inspiration in this initial investigation (where with what authority these men wrote is of no consequence, but only what they thought) and only to employ it when the dogmatic use of biblical concepts enters into consideration."[35]

But of course the interpretation of individual literary texts is dependent, at least in part, on one's understanding of the larger context in which those texts are found. If texts by two different authors seem to be saying contradictory things, we may conclude without much misgiving or hesitation that they in fact disagree with each

---

33   Cited in W. G. Kümmel, *The New Testament: The History of the Investigation of Its Problems* (Nashville: Abingdon, 1970), 63.

34   *Treatise*, cited in Kümmel, *New Testament*, 63–64.

35   J. Ph. Gabler, *On the Proper Distinction between Biblical and Dogmatic Theology and the Proper Determination of the Goals of Each* (Altdorf, 1787), cited in Kümmel, *New Testament*, 99.

other regarding the subject under discussion. If, however, we read two seemingly contradictory texts by the *same* author, we are faced with several possibilities—the author is intellectually inconsistent, or he later changed his mind, or there is an explanation that harmonizes the two texts, perhaps within a broader unity. The issue of authorship influences our hermeneutic expectations and consequently the exegetical energy we invest in understanding the relationship of the texts to each other. Therefore, it is not surprising that once Enlightenment scholars dismissed as exegetically irrelevant the question of a divine Author (in the interests of allowing each biblical book to speak afresh, without dogmatic encumbrances from ecclesiastical tradition), the focus on diversity among the biblical writings prematurely led to conclusions that biblical books were not merely *diverse* in viewpoint and emphasis, but *contradictory* in doctrine.

Historical critics also attacked the historicity of biblical narratives and the scientific credibility of biblical miracles. Once they had set aside the concept of a divine Author of Scripture, nothing stood in the way of their critiquing the biblical authors' statements with regard to Ancient Near Eastern history, human origins, or a whole host of other issues. Conservative scholars responded with carefully researched and carefully argued defenses of Luke as a historian, of the Genesis accounts of Abraham, and so on. Yet, while conservative theologians were caught up in attempts to deflect charges of historical inaccuracy or scientific error that were leveled against Scripture, the Enlightenment shift in hermeneutics—with its intentional "ignore-ance" of the divine Author of Scripture—had even more disastrous implications for the use of the Bible in theology and preaching in general. In particular, the New Testament authors' reading of the Old Testament as a book that predicted, prefigured, and prepared for the coming of Jesus the Messiah could only be dismissed as hopelessly naive, archaic, and biased (from a historical-critical perspective). G. W. H. Lampe comments on the real significance of the shift in attitude toward the Bible that came with the Enlightenment:

> The typological method of interpretation, like the traditional form of the argument from prophetic fulfillment, became, it is hardly too much to say, an historical curiosity, of very little importance or significance for the modern reader. The new emphasis upon the diversity of Scripture and the original independence of its several parts tended to overthrow

the foundations upon which that method rested. This was perhaps the most important, as well as the most profoundly revolutionary, effect of the 'higher criticism.' At the time it seems to have received relatively little direct attention or explicit notice; the impact of modern literary and historical criticism was felt primarily in the field of the 'letter'. The literal truth of historical narratives was being called into question; the dating and ascription of the various books was being drastically revised, and the principal question that was asked concerned the factual reliability of the Biblical records. In the end, however, the most definite and conclusive result of all this critical investigation was the breaking down of the old conception of the unity of Scripture and the consequent discrediting of the typological and prophetical exegesis familiar to so many generations of Christians.[36]

The Enlightenment's argument with apostolic hermeneutic rested not only on a rejection of the divine inspiration of Scripture but also on a repudiation of God's sovereign control of history. By denying the divine Lordship over history, historical criticism undercut the basis for biblical typology. If the events of history happen not according to God's purpose and plan but accidentally and randomly as the result of a blind and unpremeditated process, then it is obviously both arrogant and foolish for a New Testament writer to tell his readers that the sufferings of David prefigured the sufferings of Jesus, that the bronze serpent lifted by Moses in the desert was a preview of the cross, or that there is a connection between Noah's flood and Christian baptism. Of course, human ingenuity can draw all sorts of analogies between individuals and events at different points in history, but the New Testament writers claim more than this. They are not simply saying, "*I see* a similarity between the exodus and Christian salvation, don't you?" They are saying, "*God planned and carried out* the exodus not only to effect rescue for ancient Israel but also to portray for his people *in real history* the significance of the comprehensive liberation that his Messiah would later achieve." They are saying, "What happened to Abraham, to Moses, to David, to Jonah and the prophets happened as it did because God had designed it to be a limited but true reflection (Hebrews calls it a 'shadow') of the future experience and redemptive work of Jesus Christ." It is this implied claim of apostolic hermeneutics that Enlightenment historical critics found incredible. Hence, they challenged the authority of the biblical

---

36   Lampe, " Reasonableness of Typology," Lampe and Woollcombe, *Essays,* 16–17.

texts to interpret the events they narrate for us. Here the issue is not the Bible's historical accuracy. Rather, the question is whether historical events intrinsically "mean" anything at all. Are they not just raw data, brute facts, so that it is left to every interpreter to construct for himself or herself what they might mean? In the perspective of naturalistic historical criticism, then, the biblical interpreter has the right not only to pass judgment on the biblical author's accuracy in narrating facts but also to discard the biblical author's explanation of the facts and to reconstruct his (the interpreter's) own explanation.

The inevitable result of the subjection of the biblical text to the acids of the Enlightenment's denial of divine sovereignty in history and divine authorship of Scripture was a (perceived) fragmentation of the canon's theological unity and harmony. In his highly respected theology of major New Testament authors, Werner Georg Kümmel acknowledges how relatively recent a development this perception of the Bible is:

> Now of course even the insight that the views of the Old and New Testaments do not agree with each other had by no means always been self-evident to Christianity . . . . in the second half of the eighteenth century, in connection with the intellectual movement of the Enlightenment, within Protestant theology the insight began to prevail that the Bible is a book written by men, which, like any product of the human mind, can properly be made understandable only from the times in which it appeared and therefore only with the methods of historical science. . . . One simply could not stop halfway: if the Bible must be historically investigated as the work of human authors in order to understand its actual meaning, then one may not and cannot climb to the assumption that the Old Testament and the New Testament form, each in itself, a conceptual unity, and then one must also heed the differences *within* the two Testaments and also take into consideration a possible development and adulteration of the ideas.[37]

As Kümmel observes, when the assumption is made that interpreting each biblical book in relation to its historical context requires the reduction of Scripture to a collection of merely human writings, not only is the theological harmony between Old and New Testaments called into question but also the conceptual unity of the documents within each Testament can be challenged. Thus, for example,

---

37   Werner Georg Kümmel, *The Theology of the New Testament* (Nashville: Abingdon, 1973), 13–15.

New Testament scholar James D. G. Dunn concludes from his study of the *Unity and Diversity in the New Testament*:

> Our study has also forced us to recognize *a marked degree of diversity* within first-century Christianity. We can no longer doubt that there are many *different expressions of Christianity within* the NT. . . . We must conclude therefore that *there was no single normative form of Christianity in the first century.* When we ask about the Christianity of the New Testament we are not asking about any one entity; rather we encounter different types of Christianity, each of which viewed the others as too extreme in one respect or other—too conservatively Jewish or too influenced by antinomian or gnostic thought and practice, too enthusiastic or tending towards too much institutionalization.[38]

The influence of historical criticism is now so pervasive that even many evangelicals feel a certain degree of bad conscience or discomfort with the typological approach to interpretation that is exemplified in so many New Testament texts. To cite two examples:

(1) While commenting on the parable of the wicked tenant farmers, Robert H. Gundry, a careful evangelical New Testament scholar, observes that an allusion by Jesus or a redactor of this parable to the story of Joseph's suffering at the hands of his brothers "remains uncertain, though still possible, *since New Testament use of the Old Testament often strays from the Old Testament meaning and context.*"[39]

(2) Evangelical scholar Richard Longenecker, author of an influential study on biblical interpretation in first-century Judaism and the New Testament, offers the following defense of sorts for Paul's treatment of Old Testament texts in Galatians 3–4:

> Before we comment directly on [ch. 3] vv. 6–14, however, the obvious must be said: Paul's exegesis of Scripture in these verses (and throughout the rest of chaps. 3 and 4) goes far beyond the rules of historico-grammatical exegesis as followed by biblical scholars today. That is a fact that everyone recognizes, though it is not explained by everyone in the same way. Yet understood in terms of his own presuppositions and inherited exegetical procedures (cf. my *Biblical Exegesis in Apostolic Period*, 19–50, 104–32),

---

38   James D. G. Dunn, *Unity and Diversity in the New Testament: An Inquiry into the Character of Earliest Christianity* (London: SCM, 1977), 372–73. Emphasis original.

39   R. H. Gundry, *Mark: A Commentary on His Apology for the Cross* (Grand Rapids: Eerdmans, 1993), 687. Emphasis added.

Paul's arguments from Scripture are understandable and cogent (cf. Betz, *Galatians*: keeping in mind his inherited exegetical method, "it can be shown that Paul's argument is consistent").[40]

Longenecker's carefully measured historical description could be read as leaving open the possibility that a twenty-first century student of Scripture could share Paul's presuppositions and exegetical procedures; but such a position would put the contemporary exegete or preacher outside the circle of "biblical scholars today" who follow the "rules of historico-grammatical exegesis." The reader is left with the impression that Paul's use of Scripture, while intelligible and persuasive in his time, would be anachronistic today. These expressions are in fact quite conservative and respectful when compared with the scathing criticism that other modern scholars have heaped upon the biblical (Old Testament) interpretation exemplified in the New Testament writings.[41] They are typical of the desire of a number of evangelical interpreters to distance themselves from the apostolic application of biblical texts to Christ and his church.

Clearly, those who hold such a view of the New Testament's handling of Old Testament texts cannot in good conscience adopt the New Testament's hermeneutic method as their own. At most, they might view the apostolic authors' treatment of Old Testament texts as instances of creative, playful intertextual "reader response," hermeneutically legitimate only within a postmodern framework that has abandoned the illusion that texts have definitive meanings. Scholars influenced by Enlightenment naturalism are bound to be suspicious of approaches to biblical interpretation that seek to relate every text to Christ and his work, if the latter dares to allege that a christological fulfillment of an Old Testament passage was in any sense intended by the text's human author (since the possibility of a divine Author must be left out of the picture). Isn't such redemptive-historical interpretation simply a return to the artificial Alexandrian-Medieval allegorism that the Reformers rejected? Can we in good conscience affirm that the original Old Testament audience understood—or should have understood—a christological

---

40   Richard N. Longenecker, *Galatians* (WBC 41; Waco: Word, 1990), 110.

41   S. V. McCasland, "Matthew Twists the Scriptures," and Morna D. Hooker, "Beyond the Things That Are Written? Saint Paul's Use of Scripture," both in G. K. Beale, ed., *The Right Doctrine from the Wrong Texts?* (Grand Rapids: Baker, 1994), 146–52, 279–94.

fulfillment dimension for this text or that? These questions will be considered more fully in the next chapter, which addresses particularly the post-Enlightenment objections that have been raised against apostolic, christocentric hermeneutics.

Recovery: Geerhardus Vos and Reformed Biblical Theology

It was this intellectual situation, in which a so-called "biblical theology" based on the naturalistic presuppositions of the Enlightenment had produced a picture of theological fragmentation of the biblical canon, that Geerhardus Vos (1862–1949) addressed in his 1894 inaugural lecture as professor of biblical theology at Princeton Theological Seminary.[42] Vos acknowledged that his conception of biblical theology differed sharply from the presuppositions and procedures generally associated with the term in critical circles. The infection of Enlightenment biblical theology by the concept of evolution "from the lower and imperfect to the higher and relatively more perfect forms, from impure beginnings through a gradual purification to some ideal end" Vos found altogether contradictory to the objectivity of God's self-revelation in history.[43] He also rejected views that limited revelation to divine acts and relegated the words of Scripture to the category of human interpretation of God's revelatory deeds in history, as well as those who completely subjectivized "revelation" in the human consciousness.[44]

In contrast to other approaches, Vos laid out the agenda that he intended to pursue as he occupied Princeton's newly created chair: "Biblical Theology, rightly defined, is nothing else than *the exhibition of the organic progress of supernatural revelation in its historic continuity and multiformity.*"[45] Vos announced his intention to do greater justice to the historical character of biblical revelation without sacrificing the church's historic confidence in its objectivity and divine authority.[46] God had chosen to tie his self-revelation to the

42   Geerhardus Vos, "The Idea of Biblical Theology as a Science and as a Theological Discipline," in *Redemptive History and Biblical Interpretation: The Shorter Writings of Geerhardus Vos*, Richard B. Gaffin, Jr., ed. (Phillipsburg: P & R, 1980), 3–24.

43   Vos, "Idea," 16.

44   Vos, "Idea," 17–18.

45   Vos, "Idea," 15. Emphasis original.

46   Because of the negative (evolutionary, subjectivist) connotations of the term "biblical theology," Vos preferred to describe the discipline that he was pursuing as "the history of special revelation." Vos, *Biblical Theology*, 23.

outworking of his saving plan in the history of redemption. There-fore, the greater the respect we have for Scripture, the more carefully we will pay attention to the historical mode in which God gave us this, his written Word, and to its resultant structure. Vos rejects the simplistic identification of the diversity of Scripture with its human-ity, as though diversity stood in tension with the divinely given unity of the canon. Rather, the diversity—both diachronic (among vari-ous epochs of redemptive and revelatory activity) and synchronic (among diverse human organs of revelation within a particular ep-och)—expresses God's plan and purpose in revealing himself.

As Vos charted the path for biblical theology in an orthodox Re-formed context, then, the discipline brings together the recognition of the redemptive-historical structure of the Bible with the principle that a text can only be understood properly in terms of its relevant contexts. Each book of the Bible has its place in a particular age and phase of God's redemptive program. The basic distinction is between old covenant and new, promise and fulfillment. But (as Vos would show in his influential volume, *Biblical Theology*) within these two main divisions are sub-categories: patriarchal, Mosaic, and prophetic, as well revelation imparted through John the Baptist, in Jesus' pub-lic ministry, and through the apostles after Jesus' exaltation.[47]

Respect for God's mode of self-disclosure also demands a rec-ognition of God's restraint in the periods of redemptive history prior to the final order, which Christ has inaugurated in his incarnation, ministry, death, resurrection, and exaltation. Although the old cov-enant revelation stands in a line of consistent, organic development with the new, we should expect and do find greater clarity and full-ness in the later revelation that accompanies Christ's accomplish-ment of his redemptive mission. In contrast to well meaning christo-centric preachers earlier in church history, who often tried to make Genesis speak as explicitly of Christ as Matthew's Gospel does, Vos and his Reformed successors insisted that interpreters and preachers must respect the limits of the "horizon" visible from each successive stage of redemptive history.[48] Only after identifying as clearly as we can the text's meaning to its original recipients, with due recogni-tion of the fact that early revelation may offer only an indistinct and general testimony to the Messiah who would come in the fullness of

---

47 Vos, *Biblical Theology*, 28–36ff.
48 Clowney, *Preaching and Biblical Theology*, 87–98.

time, should the interpreter place the text's message in the broader context of the biblical canon as a whole.

Vos's primary calling was that of a biblical exegete and theologian, not a preacher. The slim (and only) volume of his sermons published in 1922 contained just six messages, and a recently enlarged edition contains ten more that later were found in Vos's personal sermon book in the Calvin Theological Seminary archive.[49] As its subtitle shows, these sermons were preached not to ordinary congregants but to the students and faculty of Princeton Theological Seminary, a theologically sophisticated audience. Even for so elite a group of listeners, both the profundity of theological content and the complexity of expression may well have been challenging, as Sinclair Ferguson, the author of the collection's introduction, speculates:

> Such is the character of these sermons that, to a world which is obsessed with 'sound-bites' and in a church which has become unused to concentrated thought, their content and style may seem overwhelming. . . . Every sensitive and thoughtful reader will be struck by the mountain peaks which Vos's mind and vocabulary seemed to be capable of scaling. . . . So remarkable are these sermons that we may even be tempted to ask, 'What group of people—even of theological students—could have taken in the substance of any of these sermons at one hearing?' . . . There is no doubt that if Vos assumed that all of his hearers would be able to follow him he was mistaken; even the supposition that most of his listeners would be able to do so was perhaps too complimentary to theological students. But for those errors of judgement grateful readers of these pages will forgive him.[50]

These observations suggest that Vos's application of his hermeneutic insights in the seminary pulpit may not be the best *homiletic* model for pastors who are charged to proclaim Christ from and in all the Scriptures, not only to ministerial candidates being educated in the disciplines of exegesis and theology but also to ordinary Christians, young and old, spiritually immature and mature, college educated and working class—and to non-Christians, to whom Christ's apostle sought to present the glory of Christ's grace in unveiled, unobstructed clarity.

Vos's hermeneutic insights and methodology have been applied to both biblical interpretation and preaching by a growing entourage of successors in the twentieth and twenty-first centuries, as I

---

49   Geerhardus Vos, *Grace and Glory: Sermons Preached in the Chapel of Princeton Theological Seminary* (Edinburgh: Banner of Truth, 1994), ix.

50   Sinclair Ferguson, "Introduction," in Vos, *Grace and Glory*, x–xii.

suggested in profiling redemptive-historical homiletics in chapter 2. Among the first and most influential to apply Vos's emphasis on the history of redemption to *preaching* was Edmund P. Clowney, late president and professor of practical theology at Westminster Theological Seminary, to whose memory the present volume is dedicated.[51] Clowney made his indebtedness to Vos evident as he closed the first chapter of his first publication on homiletics, *Preaching and Biblical Theology*:

> The preacher who takes up Vos's *Biblical Theology* for the first time enters a rich new world, a world which lifts his heart because he is a preacher. Biblical theology, truly conceived, is a labor of worship. Beside Vos's *Biblical Theology* should be set his little book of sermons, *Grace and Glory*. There we hear a scholar preaching to theological students (the sermons were delivered in Princeton Seminary), but with a burning tenderness and awesome realism that springs from the grace and glory of God's revelation, the historical actualization of his eternal counsel of redemption.[52]

Others who are carrying forward this renaissance of apostolic, Christ-centered, redemptive-historical preaching were mentioned briefly in chapter 2.

Part 2 will present in greater detail the New Testament precedent and principles for proclaiming Christ from the whole Scripture in the twenty-first century, as Peter, Paul, and other apostolic preachers did in the first. Before we engage in this constructive project, however, further attention must be given to answering objections and reservations that have been raised in response to the proposal that apostolic hermeneutic and homiletic practice retains its normativity for Bible students and preachers today.

---

51 As president of Westminster, Dr. Clowney also oversaw the founding of Westminster Seminary California, where he later served as visiting and adjunct professor of practical theology.

52 Clowney, *Preaching and Biblical Theology*, 18–19.

5

Challenges to Apostolic Preaching

As was noted in the introductory chapter, the disparity between the New Testament authors' interpretive handling of Old Testament texts, on the one hand, and exegetical methodologies and criteria that we have inherited from the Reformation and the Enlightenment, on the other, has driven a wedge, in the minds of many, between the apostles' authoritative *doctrinal content* and the *hermeneutic* by which they defended it.[1] Because historical critical approaches developed within the naturalistic worldview of the Enlightenment abandoned allegiance not only to apostolic hermeneutic and homiletic but also to apostolic doctrine, it is not surprising that scholars who deny or "overlook" such doctrines as God's sovereignty in history and the inspiration of Scripture also dismiss the apostles' belief that God designed events in Israel's history to foreshadow the coming Messiah and his mission. We have also seen, however, that evangelical students of Scripture, practicing the Reformation's grammatical-historical interpretive method with a high regard for the Bible's *theological* normativity, have problems with aspects of the New Testament's *hermeneutic* handling of the Old Testament. They feel particular discomfort over sometimes surprising ways in which apostolic authors find ancient Scriptures "fulfilled" in Jesus, his work, and his church. In reading and preaching Scripture, twenty-first century evangelicals have inherited both the

---

1   Although some contributors to the collection edited by Beale, *The Right Doctrine from the Wrong Texts?*, would not affirm that the apostles always articulated "the right doctrine," the debate carried on in that volume focuses largely on the tension felt by evangelicals between allegiance to New Testament theology and unease concerning the New Testament's handling of Old Testament texts.

Reformation's hermeneutic restraint and the Enlightenment's faith in scientific methodology as part of our almost invisible but virtually inevitable mental framework.

Evangelicals are heirs of the Reformation, grateful for the exegetical sobriety that its *sola Scriptura* emphasis introduced as a corrective to the allegorical excesses that preceded it. In reaction against the medieval fourfold hermeneutic, the Reformers and their successors emphasized that each text of Scripture has *one* sense, not many. They also emphasized (in reaction against an otherworldly devaluing of the physical world and the events that occur in it) that the historical character of Scripture must be respected. Events in history have real significance before God, for God has determined to effect redemption in real history. Israel's exodus from Egypt, Jesus' blood, a wooden cross, an empty tomb: these are not allegorical fiction, a secret code behind which the text's "real" meaning hides. Yet, we find the New Testament picking up Old Testament motifs that have concrete, physical overtones (descendants, land, inheritance, Zion, temple, circumcision, sacrifice, washing, creation) and applying these motifs in new (and sometimes non-physical) senses to the experience of Jesus' followers. Of course, the New Testament does not deny the reality of Solomon's temple in history when it describes believers as the temple and house of God. Likewise, the miraculous conception and birth of Isaac in real history is foundational for the ethnically mixed "family" of believers to whom Paul applies the title "seed of Abraham" (Gal. 3:29; 4:21–31). Yet, the haunting question remains: Is this "spiritualizing" of Old Testament concepts merely an apostolic innovation or a strategy derived from intertestamental Judaism (*pesher*), without precedent in the Old Testament itself and without warrant in sober hermeneutics?[2]

Evangelical preachers therefore have a mixed reaction when they consider the case for preaching Christ from every text of Scripture, in Old Testament as well as New. On the one hand, they know that their calling is always and only to "preach Christ," as we saw in chapter 3 (1 Cor. 1:23; Col. 1:28). They acknowledge that the risen Christ could and did instruct his disciples regarding the things written about himself in the Law of Moses, the Prophets, and the Psalms (Luke 24:27, 44–48). They know that all Scripture is profitable for teaching, rebuking, correcting, and training in righteousness

---

2   See chapter 7 in Part 2 for an answer to this question.

(2 Tim. 3:16). Since Christian growth in knowledge and godliness is always growth in *Christ*-likeness, we sense that no Scripture achieves these divinely designed objectives apart from its connection to Jesus, the only mediator between God and humanity. In fact, evangelical pastors know that eternal life itself is knowing the only true God and Jesus Christ, whom he has sent (John 17:3).

On the other hand, they are sometimes uncomfortable with this Christocentric emphasis. They do not want to foist on a text an interpretation that is alien to it, however appealing such an interpretation may be devotionally, homiletically, or theologically. They may have heard or read examples of Christ-centered expositions that made artificial and superficial connections between a passage and Christ's death and resurrection, traveling to the "metropolis" of Scripture not via well marked roads but by jumping hedges and fording ditches, as Spurgeon's Welsh preacher would do. We want to preach Christ, but we also want to preach each biblical text with integrity.

It is also true, whether we realize it or not, living as we do at our place in history, that we cannot avoid altogether being influenced by the mind-set and issues of the Enlightenment and the historical critical tradition. Even if we could expunge from our consciousness all traces of the last three centuries' anti-supernatural bias, if we were simply to ignore historical criticism's objection to biblical typology and the theocentric worldview that drives it, we would fail to fulfill our apostolic calling to *communicate* Christ's gospel in intelligibly to our contemporaries, as Paul engaged the religious and philosophical pluralism of the Greco-Roman world. If we are to preach Christ as the apostles did, we must responsibly engage our contemporaries' (as well as our own) objections to the New Testament's hermeneutic starting point: the affirmation that Jesus Christ is the focal point of Israel's scriptures and the key that unlocks their true and full meaning.[3]

In this chapter we will first face the sources of evangelicals' discomfort with apostolic hermeneutics and homiletics. Second,

---

3   Dan G. McCartney observes that critics have pointed to the failure of New Testament authors to follow widely accepted modern norms of grammatical-historical interpretation as the "skeleton in the closet" of evangelicals' confession of biblical inerrancy. McCartney argues, however, that apostolic hermeneutics, when seen in the context of the entire biblical worldview, is rather "our skeleton key to open all the doors in the inerrant Word of God." "The New Testament's Use of the Old Testament," in Harvie M. Conn, ed., *Inerrancy and Hermeneutic: A Tradition, a Challenge, a Debate* (Grand Rapids: Baker, 1988), 102, 116.

the central issue—the question of context—will be discussed and various evangelical stances toward the New Testament's Christocentric interpretation of the Old Testament will be surveyed. Finally, a biblical-theological and canonical approach to the interpretive contexts of Old and New Testament passages will be proposed as a bridge to Part 2, which will explore the principles and practice of the apostles' reading and preaching of Scripture.

Modern Misgivings about Apostolic Preaching

One of the vivid memories of my childhood is visiting my grandparents, who had immigrated to the United States from Sweden as young adults. I remember the fun of matching wits with my grandparents in a board game we called "Chinese Checkers" and they called "hop shing" (i.e., "hop ching" with a Scandinavian accent). The goal of the game is to move ten marbles from one triangular point of a six-pointed star, across the star's network of triangular paths demarcated by a web of holes, into the opposite corner, jumping over single marbles only and touching down in empty spots all along the way.

Now, in fact our wits were no match for my grandparents at "hop shing." My grandmother was particularly frustrating as a Chinese Checkers' opponent because she could start with a marble in the deepest corner of her "home" point in the star, wave it mysteriously over the board, and put it down in the opposite corner, the goal. Where, we wondered, was the path of single marble, empty space, single marble, empty space, that she had followed? We couldn't see the marble's route, but it is a delicate matter to challenge one's grandma's sportsmanship. Nevertheless, when we (meekly) dared to ask her, she always graciously showed us precisely the route her marble had taken from start to finish. She had seen the pattern so clearly that she didn't need to set the marble down at every jump; but we needed to be shown step by step, jump by jump.

Some readers are probably responding with a similar uncomfortable suspicion to the proposal that twenty-first century preachers should follow the lead of the first century apostles by preaching Christ from all the Scriptures. They may wonder whether the path is really "there" between every text of the Old Testament and the work of the Savior in the New. Is it, perhaps, only the figment of a well-meaning expositor's hyperactive imagination, ingenuity, and creativity? Let us therefore begin by stating frankly some of the reasons that contemporary theologians and preachers, both historical critical and evangelical, harbor suspicions about attempts to interpret every biblical text in relation to Christ and his saving mission. They fall into three general categories: (a) misgivings about biblical unity; (b) misgivings about interpretive accountability; and (c) misgivings about interpretive credibility.

Misgivings about Biblical Unity

Historical Criticism v. the Theological Unity of Scripture. Ancient, Medieval, Reformation, and modern evangelical Christians together confess that the whole Bible, Old Testament and New, is the Word of God written. Implied in this confession is the conviction that the Bible's teaching is unified. We normally expect consistency of viewpoint from a book by one human author, although we grant the possibility that human authors can contradict themselves. With respect to the Bible, because we are dealing with one Divine Author speaking through diverse human authors by his Spirit, and because this Divine Author is the very standard of truth (if he is not true, the concept "truth" has no meaning), we expect consistency of teaching from beginning to end.

Yet, God's network of truth was revealed progressively over many generations, in tandem with phases in his plan to redeem his people. Paul therefore speaks of the great message of God as a "secret" or "mystery," once hidden but now unveiled. This mystery was once "hidden" in the sense that the protagonist, God the Son, had not yet entered history as the incarnate God-Man to accomplish his great redemptive mission. Now, however, the secret is revealed in the apostolic gospel. On the other hand, the mystery was "witnessed to" by the earlier parts of God's Book, the Law and the Prophets (Rom. 3:21; 16:25–26). This means that God's new covenant secret in Christ does not spring forth "out of the blue" onto the stage of history but comes as the fulfillment of ancient divine promises and foreshadowings. As Augustine observed, "The New is in the Old concealed, the Old is in the New revealed."[4]

---

4 The oft-quoted couplet, *Novum Testamentum in Vetere latet, Vetus in Novo patet,* is probably adapted from Augustine, *Quaestiones in Heptateuchum,* bk. 2 *Quaestiones Exodi* (20, 19): " . . . *ad uetus testamentum timorem potius pertinere, sicut ad nouum dilectionem: quamquam et in uetere nouum lateat, et in nouo uetus pateat* (. . . fear pertains to the Old Testament as love does to the New—although

Alongside this conviction regarding the divine origin and resultant theological unity of Scripture is the Bible's witness to the sovereignty of God in the universe and in the course of human affairs.
The God of the Bible is so much the Lord that he can use not only
words (spoken through humans) but also events that transpire in human history (involving uncoerced human decisions and actions) to
reveal himself and his plan to remedy sin's ravages. God's actions in
the past—creation or the exodus, for example—can be seen as his own
announcement (not only in words but also in concrete events) of his
greater actions of creation and deliverance to come. The ancient event
is a "pattern" (*typos*) that points to the coming redemptive event and to
the Redeemer who will accomplish it. The typological interpretation
employed by Jesus and the apostles (and the church down through
the centuries) therefore rests on the Lordship of God over history—to
order it and to intervene in it in deliverance and in judgment.

As we noted in the last chapter, however, modern historical criticism has challenged these life-long convictions of the church: (1) By
denying the divine authorship of Scripture, historical criticism has
destroyed (for those who accept its naturalistic worldview) the theological basis for expecting a unity of teaching or theology within the
Bible: between Old Testament and New, among particular biblical
authors (Paul and James, Jesus and Paul), or even within one author
(some, for example, find Paul at odds with himself with respect to
the role of women in the church and the family). (2) By denying the
divine sovereignty in history, historical criticism has destroyed the
theological foundation for affirming a divinely intended correspondence between Old Testament persons and events and the person,
work, and experience of Jesus and his new covenant church. Thus
typological correspondences drawn by the Old Testament between
Moses and Jesus or David and Jesus, for example, are dismissed (or
admired) as the *imaginative reconstruction* of the various New Testament authors, or as instances of intertextual, "reader response"
playfulness. Such uses of the Old Testament may be of interest in describing a New Testament author's theological perspective, pastoral
priorities, or literary artistry, but such "commentary" by biblical authors of subsequent epochs have no special authority to define what
the Old Testament text itself originally meant.

---

in the Old the New is hidden, and in the New the Old is opened)." *Corpus Christianorum, Series Latina*, vol. 33 (Turnholti: Brepols, 1958), 106.

An analogy illustrates the difference between the classic under-standing of the Bible's unity and the historical critical view. Allusion was made above to Paul's reference to the message of Christ as God's "mystery," previously hidden but now revealed in the incarnation, ministry, death, and exaltation of Jesus. In a modern mystery or de-tective novel, clues embedded in the early chapters must often await explanation at the denouement, when the culprit, his or her motive, and the method of murder are disclosed. In many respects it is only the conclusion that clarifies the significance of the clues and the pat-tern that integrates them coherently, and only the conclusion reveals which earlier details of the narrative were not true clues but "red her-rings," injected by the author to throw the reader "off the scent." The implied contract between writer and readers built into the genre of mystery fiction demands that the author integrate clues, tie up loose ends, and enable readers to dispose of red herrings appropriately by the last sentence on the last page. To fail to do so is an unforgivable breach of contract on the author's part. Therefore, although it would spoil the fun, in principle one should be able to read, for instance, Dorothy Sayers's *Five Red Herrings* or *Nine Tailors* or *Gaudy Night* "backwards," from solution to problem, or at least, having read the novel "forward," one should be able to go back through the story, solution in mind (criminal, motive, means, opportunity), and dis-cern the significance of every clue (and insignificance of each red herring).

Consider, however, another mystery project in which Dorothy Sayers participated. In 1931 the members of the Detection Club in the United Kingdom published their jointly authored mystery, *The Floating Admiral*.[5] The premise of the project, Sayers explained in the introduction, was that members of the club would write chap-ters in succession, each obligated both to take account of previously introduced clues and to propose a plausible (and secret) solution to the crime that would account for all information presented through his or her chapter. G. K. Chesterton wrote the prologue, in which the corpse of Admiral Penistone is found floating in a rowboat on the River Whyn. Thereafter, Agatha Christie, Dorothy Sayers, and their colleagues took turns contributing chapters that advanced the investigation, complicated the mystery, and moved the plot toward

---

5   Agatha Christie and other members of the Detection Club, *The Floating Admiral* (London: Hodder and Stoughton, 1931).

whatever solution each contributor conceived. (The proposed solutions, which are diverse, are published at the end.)

The Floating Admiral illustrates the greatest degree of unity that could be expected of Scripture on the basis of the Enlightenment's rejection of biblical inspiration and divine sovereignty. Of course, the Bible is more diverse in many ways: genre, time span of composition, language, intended readership, and so on. Yet, both the Bible and the *Admiral* are composed by multiple authors belonging to a shared "tradition." In both, these successive authors seek to make sense of a single narrative stream as information is progressively added. At least some (though not all) biblical interpreters working within the historical critical tradition might even grant that Old Testament authors, like the authors of the *Admiral*, wrote with a particular eschatological goal or solution in view. In the absence of a single unifying author, however, it would be ridiculous to read this mystery "backwards," as if Dorothy Sayers's solution, penned after completing her own chapter (roughly in the middle of the mystery), could clarify the meaning of earlier stages of the narrative *as conceived by her predecessors* (or, for that matter, later developments *as conceived by her successors*). In a similar way, once the Enlightenment had made the procedural decision to "overlook" Scripture's divine authorship (in Gabler's terms), no basis remained for reading the apostles' testimony to Jesus at the *end* of the story as though it could reliably reveal the mystery that integrates and makes sense of all prior clues in the biblical tradition. The subtle influence of this shift in understanding revelation and history is that biblical interpreters come to assume that the only approach to interpreting the Old Testament that has integrity is one that stays independent of the New Testament writers and limits its interpretive context to that of the Old Testament author and his readers. The comments by Gundry and Longenecker cited in the previous chapter move in this direction.

Dispensationalism vs. the Unity of God's Plan and People. Another group of interpreters will have reservations about the hermeneutic advocated here for different reasons, which also touch on the unity of Scripture. These are interpreters persuaded of the dispensationalist approach to the history of redemption. Unlike the historical criticism just discussed, dispensationalism is committed to the divine inspiration and inerrancy of Scripture and therefore, ultimately, to its doctrinal unity. Nevertheless, dispensationalists view the Bible from the standpoint of sharp distinctions between God's dealing with ethnic Israel under the Mosaic Covenant before Christ's coming and in a future millennium, on the one hand, and his dealing with the multiethnic church in this period between the comings of Christ.[6]

It is open to question whether the driving force of dispensationalism is its doctrinal system (including, for example, the disjunction between Israel and the church) or its underlying hermeneutic standard, often expressed simply in the motto, "literal where possible"—that is, biblical prophecies in particular should be interpreted "literally" (in terms of physical, observable realities rather than as symbolic of spiritual realities) whenever such an approach produces a "possible" explanation. One laudable motive behind this criterion for defining precisely the meaning of an Old Testament prophecy is the desire to safeguard interpretation from the subjectivity of ancient and medieval allegorism and of modern dialectic and postmodern reader-centered hermeneutics. For this reason, the "literal where possible" hermeneutic will be discussed under the next category of misgivings concerning apostolic preaching. Here it is sufficient to note that the application of this hermeneutic in classical dispensationalism has produced a bifurcated perspective on God's purpose in history and his mode of relating to two distinct peoples, ethnic Israel and the multiethnic church. When New Testament authors apply Israel's titles, privileges, and mission to the new covenant church composed of believers from all nations, dispensationalism finds it necessary to explain that these inspired authors are doing so by way of application, not interpretation, of Old Testament Scriptures.

Misgivings about Interpretive Accountability

As the Protestant Reformers challenged the hermeneutic hegemony of ecclesiastical tradition and hierarchy, they recognized their

---

6   Dispensationalism is a movement in motion and so-called progressive dispensationalists, such as Darrell Bock, Craig Blaising, and Robert Saucy, give greater interpretive weight to the New Testament's affirmations that many Old Testament promises to Israel are now being fulfilled in Christ's multiethnic church. Progressive dispensationalism, therefore, approaches historic premillennialism with a stronger emphasis on the unity of God's redemptive plan and people. See, for example, Craig L. Blaising and Darrell L. Bock, *Progressive Dispensationalism* (Wheaton: Victor, 1993); and Robert L. Saucy, *The Case for Progressive Dispensationalism: The Interface between Dispensational and Non-dispensational Theology* (Grand Rapids: Zondervan, 1993).

responsibility to replace these with a responsible procedure and criterion for discerning valid from invalid readings of Scripture. The history of patristic and medieval commentary and preaching, as well as the mystical extremes of some seventeenth-century movements, revealed the need for a method with a credible check on exegetical ingenuity. This method they articulated as *grammatical-historical* exegesis: attending to the *language* of the text (not only grammar, but also semantics, figures of speech, genre, literary context, and parallels), and to the meaning that the text's original recipients could be expected to understand in their *historical context*. Since God was pleased to speak to his people in history, in their own language, and through human messengers, it is plausible to conclude that his intended meaning is to be identified with the meaning intended by the human author for his original readers in their life setting. This means that historical narrative is to be read as historical narrative, not as covert prophetic prediction of things to come. Moreover, even explicit prophecies of future events should be understood within the "horizon" of experience and understanding accessible to those to whom it was first addressed. As heirs of the Reformation, evangelical preachers today wish to avoid the excesses of some practitioners of the fourfold-level allegorical approach developed from the Alexandrian school, through Augustine, and into the Middle Ages. We have read (and perhaps even heard) elaborately symbolic approaches to every detail of a biblical text, interpretations that reveal far more about the preacher's imaginative ingenuity than about the message of God in that passage.

Dispensationalist interpreters sometimes critique those who read as symbolic or spiritual narrative passages that can be understood "literally."[7] In dispensationalist estimation, the promise of a rebuilt temple in the later chapters of Ezekiel could not possibly be *fulfilled* in

---

7   I have, however, heard dispensational preachers interpret, for example, the seven churches of Revelation as "symbolic" of seven phases of ecclesiastical life in the church age, from the doctrinally vigilant apostolic era (Ephesus) to (what else?) today's church, which is (at least in America) materially rich, spiritually poor, and disgustingly lukewarm (Laodicea). Much in Revelation must be taken symbolically (see my *Triumph of the Lamb*), but nothing in the book suggests that those letters to first-century congregations of Asia Minor are intended to provide a symbolic time line of church history. Ironically, just such *allegorical* interpretation by dispensationalist *"literalists"* gives the symbolic interpretation of apocalyptic prophecy an undeserved bad name!

a "spiritual house" composed of "living stones" (1 Peter 2:5), a "holy temple" and "dwelling place for God by the Spirit" composed of reconciled Jews and Gentiles (Eph. 2:21–22), for Ezekiel's hearers could not be expected to anticipate and appreciate the apostles' later, probably merely *illustrative* use of the temple metaphor. Likewise, the dispensationalist concern to secure interpretive objectivity with respect to prophecy in *words* is accompanied by a rigorously restrictive approach to typological correspondence between Old Testament historical *events and institutions* and the later work of Christ in his church.

In some evangelical circles to speak of the "spiritual" or symbolic fulfillment of certain Old Testament prophecies originally expressed in physical categories appears perilously close to Rudolf Bultmann's "demythologization" of New Testament narrative, in which the gospel accounts of Jesus' healing of blindness, deafness, or other disabilities, as well as his resurrection, were reduced to mere metaphor, drained of their supernatural power and shocking physicality. Just as Origen employed allegory to answer objections from the gospel's cultured despisers in the third century, so Bultmann and his disciples saw themselves as trying to communicate the New Testament's "true" message, stripped of its pre-scientific the mythical clothing, to modern audiences steeped in scientific naturalism. Yet, evangelicals insist that Jesus' *bodily* resurrection and other expressions of New Testament supernaturalism challenge the naturalistic worldview that Bultmann exalted to presuppositional status.[8] They are therefore suspicious that any movement away from "literal" interpretation will prove to be the first step on a slippery slope that will lead to abandoning the historical character of redemption and revelation altogether. If, as various New Testament texts claim, Gentile Christians are now the seed of Abraham, the Messiah's Davidic throne is not in Jerusalem but in heaven, and his earthly reign now manifests itself in individuals' conversion and the gathering of a suffering believing community rather than in political dominion, what is to keep us from going further into ethereal symbolism? Why not replace Jesus' bodily resurrection with a "spiritual" resurrection that consists in the memory and hope living on in the hearts of his disciples? Could not Adam be reduced to Everyman? Might Jonah's ordeal in the fish and preaching to Nineveh be only a parable told

---

8   Rudolf Bultmann, "Is Exegesis without Presuppositions Possible?" in *Existence and Faith,* trans. S. M. Ogden (London: Hodder & Stoughton, 1961), 289–96.

to combat racial prejudice? If historical narratives about Israel, its land, and its political and military enemies are merely "preliminary sketches" tracing the pattern of a coming Masterpiece, where does the movement from the literal to the symbolic, from the concrete and physical to the abstract and "spiritual" end?

Yet, as we will see in chapters 7 and 8, the hermeneutic of Jesus and the apostles rests on the convictions that (1) the redemptive events in Israel's history and Jesus' ministry occurred in time and space, in flesh and blood; and that (2) the redemptive events narrated in the Old Testament had a symbolic depth; and finally that (3) with the coming of Christ physical Old Testament types (patterns) and prophecies are fulfilled in ways that transcend the physical. Because these convictions are united in the biblical motifs of creation and God's sovereignty and providence at work in history, we can see how the apostles could affirm the historical veracity of biblical historical narrative and *at the same time* confess that those *real* historical events were invested by God with symbolic significance that pointed beyond their own time and place in the history of redemption, directing the gaze of God's people forward in history to the coming King.

Even apart from the issue of "literal"/physical versus symbolic/spiritual readings, the question remains, what hermeneutic guidelines can curb the subjectivity of the individual interpreter and hold all readers accountable to generally recognized criteria that ensure the objectivity and validity of our reading of Scripture? As Chrysostom said, our aim is not to be "lords over the rules of interpretation" but to listen to Scripture interpreting itself, and this requires mental self-discipline more than inventiveness.

New intellectual currents arising toward the end of the twentieth century have posed the issue of interpretive accountability even more urgently by focusing attention on *readers'* contribution to a text's meaning from the vantage point of their own experience, place, and perspective. The "fusion of horizons" hermeneutic developed by linguistic philosopher Hans-Georg Gadamer and adopted by New Hermeneutic theologians has tended to relativize the authority of the biblical text by portraying its meaning as in constant evolution through a "dialogue" with the world-view "horizon" of each succeeding generation of readers. New Criticism in literature challenged the older assumption that authorial intention provides a definitive criterion for discerning valid and invalid interpretations. After all, current readers have no direct access to past authors' "intentions" but only indirect reflections of those intentions through the text itself. Moreover, literary texts may say more than their original authors understood at the time of composition, so the preeminence of the author as interpreter of his or her own work has been challenged. Reader-response criticism, couched in the relativism espoused by postmodernist epistemology, has dealt even further damage to the pre-modern and modern assumptions that texts have fixed meanings that can be discerned, to some extent objectively, by recognized exegetical procedures.[9]

In response to such intellectually sophisticated advocacy of principled subjectivism, influential evangelical scholars have embraced the interpretive model of E. D. Hirsch, in which the criterion for valid interpretation of a text can only be the meaning intended by the original author, that is, the understanding that the author expected his first readers to derive from the text within their shared experiential and conceptual horizon.[10] This approach to textual meaning offers an objective criterion for literary interpretation and therefore allows ancient texts to articulate meanings that genuinely challenge the modern and postmodern reader's preunderstanding. It is not, however, without difficulties, even when we are studying a piece of literature that is of merely human origin; and its problems increase when we take into account, in interpreting Scripture, the activity of the Bible's divine Author, who knows exhaustively (even though the human author of a particular Old Testament text may not) how

---

9   See Kevin J. Vanhoozer, *Is There a Meaning in This Text? The Bible, the Reader, and the Morality of Literary Knowledge* (Grand Rapids: Baker, 1998) for a careful analysis of the successive assaults on author, text, and even reader as criteria for accountability in interpretation, as well as a nuanced reaffirmation of the real possibility of discerning a meaning in biblical texts, with due consideration to both the author's original objectives and the text's distinctive features, as well as the experience and perspective that readers bring to their encounter with the text.

10   Walter C. Kaiser, Jr., has consistently advocated the Hirsch model, emphasizing that "validity in interpretation" is to be determined in light of the original author's intended meaning in the biblical text's original historical context. See, for example, Walter C. Kaiser, Jr., *Toward an Exegetical Theology: Biblical Exegesis for Teaching and Preaching* (Grand Rapids: Baker, 1981), 29–34; Walter C. Kaiser, Jr., and Moisés Silva, *An Introduction to Biblical Hermeneutics: The Search for Meaning* (Grand Rapids: Zondervan, 1994), 27–45. See E. D. Hirsch, *Validity in Interpretation* (New Haven: Yale University Press, 1967); and *Aims of Interpretation* (Chicago: University of Chicago, 1976).

particular prophetic words or ancient typological-prophetic events will eventually fit into the larger pattern of the plan of redemption, which culminates in Christ.

It is important to recognize the historical and progressive character of God's revealing activity and therefore to recognize and respect the limits of the theological "horizons" of earlier phases in the history of revelation.[11] In this way, we avoid "reading back into" Old Testament texts the fuller christological disclosure that has come only with the incarnation of the Son of God and his redemptive accomplishment. But if we take seriously that Scripture not only has many human authors writing in many different historical epochs but also one divine Author whose saving purpose spans the epochs, we will not allow recent debates over the competing or complementary interpretive roles of author, text, and reader to lead us too quickly to a solution that promises objectivity at the expense of doubting that the New Testament is justified when it reads Old Testament narratives and prophecies in the light of the subsequent fulfillment of Israel's hopes and longings through the person and work of Christ.[12]

The argument offered in this chapter, and amplified in chapters 7 and 8, invites readers to consider whether the pursuit of objectivity and interpretive accountability by means of hermeneutic criterion, "literal where possible," or the restriction of a biblical text's meaning to the human author's original historical horizon is consistent with the unique character of the Bible as a divine and human word. If these commonsense checks on interpretive innovation preclude aspects of later Scripture's handling of earlier Scripture, they do not deserve the status of a ruling norm, in the light of the apostolic example of biblical interpretation, whether or not they are valid in the reading of other literature.[13] To look at this question another way, the issue is whether we seek interpretive accountability in a general grammatical-historical approach that in recent centuries has seemed intuitively cogent and appropriately self-critical or in an approach that (as well as attending to original linguistic, literary, and historical contexts) also takes the New Testament *literally* when the latter affirms that an Old Testament pattern is "fulfilled" in the redemptive

---

11   See Clowney, *Preaching and Biblical Theology*, 89–98.

12   Clowney, *Preaching and Biblical Theology*, 98–100.

13   A clear and thoughtful discussion by a covenantal interpreter of Scripture of the differences between dispensational and covenantal hermeneutics is Vern S. Poythress, *Understanding Dispensationalists* (Grand Rapids: Zondervan, 1991).

work of Christ. I am arguing that if the New Testament itself affirms a symbolic-typological interpretation of an Old Testament feature (for example, that the multiethnic church "is" the Israel with whom God makes his new covenant), we are on safer ground to follow the New Testament's lead rather than clinging to a different, "literal" reading that might seem, in the abstract, to be more objectively verifiable.

Commendable Humility. Evangelical scholars who affirm the unifying divine authorship of Scripture and even the legitimacy of the christocentric or "christotelic"[14] hermeneutic, when applied by the inspired New Testament authors themselves, may still be reticent to apply the apostolic hermeneutic in cases where the New Testament itself does not provide explicit commentary on, quotation of, or allusion to an Old Testament passage or event. Their argument is that we must humbly recognize the unique authority that Christ delegated to his apostles and other authors of inspired Scripture, by which they could perceive, through special revelation, linkages between God's acts toward Israel and his redemptive work in Christ, though such links are imperceptible to non-inspired interpreters with the resources and procedures available to us. Apostles may do with Old Testament Scriptures what we may not, precisely because the Spirit of Christ spoke through them in unique, non-replicable ways. Lacking their unique authority and insight, it is argued, we must *not* follow their interpretive lead with respect to *other* Old Testament texts.

Thus, for example, when Jesus himself (Matt. 27:46), the evangelists' allusions (27:35), and other New Testament texts (Heb. 2:12) explicitly apply Psalm 22 to Jesus' suffering and subsequent vindication, we know we are on solid ground. But how should we handle Psalm 88, a lament similar to Psalm 22 in theme and tone but only alluded to obliquely, if at all, in the New Testament?[15] Since we have

---

14   Peter Enns, *Inspiration and Incarnation: Evangelicals and the Problem of the Old Testament* (Grand Rapids: Baker, 2005), 154, argues that "christotelic" more accurately conveys a nuanced Christian perception of the Old Testament's witness to Christ, in that it does not so much imply the need "to 'see Christ' in every, or nearly every, Old Testament text" but instead that Christian interpreters read the Old Testament "already knowing that Christ is somehow the *end* [*telos*] to which the Old Testament story is heading" (emphasis original).

15   Editors of the cross references in Nestle-Aland, *et al, Novum Testamentum Graece* (27th edition; Stuttgart: Deutsche Bibelgesellschaft, 1993), suggest an allusion to Ps. 88:8 in Luke 23:49: "And all his acquaintances . . . stood at a distance."

no *indisputable* apostolic commentary on Psalm 88, should humility constrain us to refrain from relating this psalm to the rejection and anguish suffered by the Savior? Should we not humbly acknowledge our limitations and affirm typological connection and christological fulfillment *only* for Old Testament texts that are so treated in the New Testament?

This objection is commendably humble and soberly vigilant against the dangers of *eisegesis*, "reading into" a text our own ideas, though they are foreign to the passage in its original context. At some points the line between typology, parable, and allegory may seem exceedingly fine, and the history of exegesis, particularly in the patristic and medieval periods, provides ample examples of biblical students who started with a sensitivity to biblical symbolism and ended with detailed, multi-layered readings of biblical texts that, despite the best of intentions, vitiated both the clarity and the authority of the Word they sought to expound.

On the other hand, a very different inference from the obvious and humbling fact that we are not inspired apostles is worth considering. Precisely *because* we lack the extraordinary and mysterious operations of the Holy Spirit that produced the New Testament documents, should we not be guided by the hermeneutic method exemplified in their christological and redemptive-historical interpretations when we approach Old Testament texts that they did not explicitly address, rather than turning to a useful, but ultimately subapostolic, methodology?

Misgivings about Interpretive Credibility

This third category of evangelical misgivings about practicing apostolic hermeneutics today is related to the second. Whereas the previous section concerned the relation of apostolic hermeneutics to the Old Testament *text* in its original literary and historical contexts, these objections focus on the relation of apostolic hermeneutics to *our readers and hearers*. Even if the apostles' interpretive approach can be shown to treat the biblical text with integrity in *their first-century venue*, some evangelical exegetes and preachers doubt that our *twenty-first century* hearers will find the New Testament's reading of the Old persuasive. Therefore, it is alleged, apologetic and evangelistic concerns demand a minimalist interpretive strategy that limits itself to the meaning that a text's original recipients could reasonably be expected to grasp within their own historical and intellectual "horizon." Should concerns for the defense of the faith and for the plausibility of our interpretation in the judgment of those whom we seek to persuade preclude our reading and preaching the Old Testament as the apostles did?

Concerns for the Defense of the Faith. Some evangelical preachers worry that in interpreting biblical prophecy, for example, any move beyond literalism and the parameters of the original historical context will render such prophecy useless in Christianity's ongoing struggle against unbelief and false belief systems. They contend that if a prophecy's "fulfillment" takes place in a form that differs significantly from the what the prophecy's first hearers could have understood at their point in history, the "fulfillment" cannot be used to demonstrate God's power to foretell the future and to fulfill his prediction. When the Lord called the King Cyrus of Persia by name as the one who would authorize the temple's reconstruction (Isa. 45:1–7), the subsequent literal fulfillment of this prophecy several centuries later confirmed the Lord's claim to be the only God who can control and therefore foretell the future. Likewise, Micah's prediction that Judah's eternal king will emanate from Bethlehem finds literal, physical fulfillment in Jesus' birth in David's town (Matt. 2:1, 5–6; Luke 2:1–4). Such objective and indisputable[16] correspondences between promise and fulfillment have evidentiary value in making the case for Jesus' messiahship. On the other hand, if Israel and Judah are not regathered to the land of Palestine, and if the temple is not rebuilt and the center of the Davidic kingdom not reestablished in Jerusalem, will not unbelievers mock at and dismiss the Bible? If Christian preachers claim that God's promise to restore David's son to his throne is "fulfilled" in Jesus' heavenly session (as Peter does in Acts 2:30–36), can such a non-literal "fulfillment" serve any persuasive purpose to draw unbelievers to faith? If we follow Paul and allege that God's land promise to Abraham envisioned not just Palestine but "the world" (Rom. 4:13) and that the seed promise is fulfilled in believing Gentiles rather than biological descendents (Rom. 4:18; Gal. 3:28–29; 4:22–31), will not such radical reinterpretation of ancient promises evacuate our preaching of credibility?

---

16   In fact, of course, both the pre-exilic dating of Isaiah 45 and the Evangelists' identification of Bethlehem as Jesus' birthplace have been disputed by critical scholars.

The Gospels' account of John the Baptist presents a poignant instance of this difficulty. John's prophetic ministry had been marked by the Spirit's convicting power, effecting large-scale repentance, and had been widely recognized as a restoration of the ancient gift of prophecy. John had announced that the kingdom of God was about to invade history in the person of the Coming One, who would sift the righteous grain from the wicked chaff, inflicting divine judgment in destruction on the unrepentant (Luke 3:16–17). John had, in fact, witnessed God's identification and acclamation of Jesus as that promised Coming One in the Spirit's dove-like descent. Yet, the eschatological discrimination of righteous from unrighteous and God's vengeance on his enemies seemed not to be high on Jesus' agenda, even when John the forerunner himself was imprisoned. Understandably, John sent his disciples to inquire whether Jesus was the Coming One, after all, "or shall we look for another?" (Luke 7:18–20) Jesus' answer conflated prophetic texts that associate God's eschatological intervention with healing for the disabled, liberation for the imprisoned (such as John?), and good news for the helpless (7:21–23, alluding especially to Isa. 35:5–6; 61:1–2). But Jesus made no mention of imminent judgment on the wicked, the motif that was central to John's expectation and message.

Was John, then, a false prophet? On the contrary! Jesus' benediction, "Blessed is the one who is not offended by me"—not "tripped up (*skandalizō*) by me"—summoned John and his disciples to a persevering faith that is not dissuaded or deflected by the unexpected way in which Jesus was fulfilling John's prophecies. What John needed to learn, as did Jesus' disciples at a later point (Acts 1:6–8), was that God reserves the right to fulfill his promises in his own way, even if his ways should contradict our natural, normal, ordinary, literal reading of those promises. Although Old Testament anticipation (whether in prophetic words or in "types," those "incarnated prophecies" embedded in Israel's concrete historical experience) and New Testament fulfillment are bound together by strands of similarity, the move from promise to fulfillment, from "shadow" to "reality" (in the words of Hebrews) also entails magnification in directions that a rigidly "literal" hermeneutic could not have anticipated. The credibility of Christ's gospel is not best served by subjecting Scripture to an interpretive grid that disqualifies, even in part, Scripture's own methods in interpreting itself. Rather, our hearers must be shown persuasively the logic of apostolic hermeneutics, which are grounded in divine sovereignty over history, divine inspiration of Scripture, and the divine agenda that drives history forward toward the redemption of his people and the ultimate recreation of his cosmos. Blessed are we and our hearers, if we and they do not stumble over the surprising ways that Jesus shows himself to be the long-promised Coming One! Discovering not only *that* but also *how* Jesus fulfills ancient promises and satisfies ancient longings is indeed a God-given blessing, for which a supposedly objective "literal" interpretive matrix is not an adequate substitute.

Concerns for the Plausibility of Our Interpretations. Finally, we must consider the misgivings of those who have reservations about the practice of apostolic hermeneutics today, not because they insist that Old Testament prophecy must be fulfilled "literally" and Old Testament narrative must be read exclusively in its original context but because they find the apostles' interpretive strategies consistent with first-century practices and expectations but less than persuasive in the context of twenty-first century hermeneutic norms. Here the issue is whether our twenty-first century hearers and readers will find our explanation of the Bible convincing if we interpret biblical texts using the methods that we observe in the New Testament documents.

The apostles read Israel's ancient Scriptures as other first century Jews, such as the members of the Qumran community, read Scripture. Each group tended to find Old Testament promises fulfilled in its own time, its own community, and its own leader, and they sometimes did so by means of maneuvers with the biblical text that jar against modern sensibilities.[17] This observation does not necessarily imply a critique of apostolic hermeneutics as though these ancient interpretive methods were intrinsically invalid. Rather, it can be said to demonstrate God's condescension and accommodation to reveal himself in modes wisely adjusted to his human audience in a particular time and place.

On the other hand, the very fitness of apostolic hermeneutic method for its own first century provenance is believed by some to make it inappropriate, implausible, and unpersuasive in our time. This seems to be the implication of Richard Longenecker's and Hans

---

17   Cf. Richard Longenecker, *Biblical Exegesis in the Apostolic Period* (Grand Rapids: Eerdmans, 1975), especially his conclusion, 205–20.

Dieter Betz's comments, cited in the previous chapter, that Paul's exegesis of Scripture in Galatians 3 and 4, when "understood in terms of his own presuppositions and inherited exegetical procedures" is "understandable and cogent," even though it "goes far beyond the rules of historico-grammatical exegesis as followed by biblical scholars today."[18] Likewise, Peter Enns offers samples of biblical interpretation in Second Temple Judaism (Wisdom of Solomon, Book of Biblical Antiquities, Jubilees, Qumran literature) and then profiles "apostolic hermeneutics as a Second Temple phenomenon," with examples of the New Testament authors' interpreting Old Testament passages that originally had reference to Israel's ancient history as finding prospective, eschatological fulfillment in Jesus and his movement (e.g., Hos. 11:1 in Matt. 2:15; Isa. 49:8 in 2 Cor. 6:2; Ps. 95 in Heb. 3).[19] He then poses the dilemma facing evangelical interpreters of Scripture.

1. If we follow the apostles [in their interpretive methods], we may wind up handling the Old Testament in a way that violates some of our interpretive instincts.
2. If we don't follow them, we are either admitting that the New Testament authors were misguided in showing us how Jesus is connected to the Old Testament, or that their hermeneutics is theirs alone and cannot be reproduced today.

This is a *real* dilemma and there is no simple solution.[20]

Enns goes on to propose a solution, which is not simple and which will be engaged below. At this point we merely note the intellectual discomfort that he frankly identifies with the proposal that students and preachers of the Word today should derive their hermeneutic from the ancient apostolic example. Their interpretive methods "worked" for them not because, as Spirit-inspired authors, they could pull off maneuvers forbidden to mere pastors but because they spoke the hermeneutic *lingua franca* of Second Temple Judaism. For that very reason their methods are in principle no more appropriate in our cultural and intellectual context, which has been molded by patristic, Reformation, Enlightenment, and subsequent

---

18 See chapter 4, note 40.
19 Enns, *Inspiration and Incarnation*, 120–51.
20 Enns, *Inspiration and Incarnation*, 156.

hermeneutic debates, than it would be if we were to compose our books or sermons in *Koine* Greek.

The Central Issue: Which Context(s)? Whose Context(s)?

Although the misgivings just profiled raise a host of hermeneutic questions,[21] the significant concerns seem to cluster around one central issue: the role of context in validating our interpretation of biblical literature. We have seen that the Reformation's hermeneutic exemplified in the Second Helvetic Confession highlighted context—the circumstances of the author and first readers, their linguistic context, and the literary-canonical context of "like and unlike" and "many and clearer" biblical passages—as an indispensable factor in discerning the meaning intended by the Holy Spirit as he speaks in Scripture and interprets his own word to us. Beale's collection focuses the debate over the "replicability" of apostolic hermeneutics on the question whether the New Testament authors respected the

---

21   For example, Enns, *Inspiration and Incarnation*, 138–42, calls attention to instances in which NT authors modify the wording of OT texts as they cite them, in order to apply the OT passage more directly to the situation of the Christian community in "these last days" (Heb. 1:2). He cites the changes of preposition (and therefore direction) in Paul's citation of Isa. 59:20 in Rom. 11:26, from "The deliverer will come *to* Zion" to "The deliverer will come *from* Zion," bringing the Gentile mission into view; and the citation of Ps. 95:7–11 in Heb. 3:7–11, in which the Psalm's association of Israel's forty-year wilderness experience with God's *anger* is transformed into the church's wilderness watching of God's *acts of provision*. He could have cited other instances, such as the citation and adaptation of Ps. 68:18 in Eph. 4:8 (cf. 4:11) and the apostolic expansion of Gen. 2:7 in 1 Cor. 15:45. On the latter, see Peter R. Jones, "Paul Confronts Paganism in the Church: A Case Study of First Corinthians 15:45," *JETS* 49 (2006): 699–711. Jones argues that Paul intends his interpolations, as well as the words he has taken from Genesis 2:7, to be understood as God-given Scripture (*houtōs . . . gegraptai*), delivered through himself as the second Moses, now imparting new covenant revelation. As we shall see below, for Paul, "the last apostle," the line of demarcation is sharp and clear between the divinely given *canon* for faith and life, Scripture, and the church's subcanonical reading and preaching of the message of Scripture. In proposing, therefore, that we follow the apostles' hermeneutic lead by interpreting OT passages in the context of Jesus, I am *not* suggesting that we may take the liberty to modify, amplify, or conflate OT passages as they did. While recognizing that in this respect the apostolic writers' practice had affinities with Second Temple Jewish hermeneutics, I believe that in these instances the inspired authors were used by Scripture's primary Author to illumine dimensions of his earlier word through uniquely "canonical" methods that *cannot* be replicated with the same authority by non-inspired readers and preachers of Scripture such as we are.

context of the Old Testament texts that they cited and to which they alluded.[22]

The precise question, however, is: What constitutes the *appropriate* context or contexts for the interpretation of biblical texts? To be appropriately "contextual," must our interpretation of an Old Testament passage, for example, limit its purview only to factors present in the text's immediate context and its immediate extra-literary environment? Attending to the text in its *literary* context involves viewing it in its section and its book, perhaps also in the corpus of works by the same human author, and in light of earlier and contemporary literature (including previously received Scripture) that the readers could be expected to have encountered. The literary context therefore also encompasses other ancient works belonging to the same genre and the tacit interpretive covenant between author and readers that that genre would have entailed: the signals given to readers regarding the way in which the author intends a particular text, within its genre, to convey its meaning. Tremper Longman defines literary genre simply as "a group of texts that bear one or more traits in common with each other," and goes on to show how this collection of shared traits raise certain expectations in readers that either commend or disqualify various strategies for discerning meaning.[23] From this perspective, Antioch's, the Reformers', and the Enlightenment's objections to allegorism can be seen as grounded in disagreement with Origen and his successors over the appropriate generic (genre-related) context in which to read Old or New Testament historical narratives. Should such texts be read primarily as affirming God's specific actions in history or as providing an encoded, symbolic disclosure of suprahistorical truths, as Hellenistic philosophers had been reading ancient myths and as Philo had read Moses?

Including the immediate *extra-literary* environment brings into view the writer's and first recipients' shared historical background, social and cultural venue, the revelatory "horizon" accessible to them

---

22   Beale, *Right Doctrine from Wrong Texts?*, Parts 3, 4, 5, 7. A negative answer to the question is offered in essays by Barnabas Lindars, S. V. McCasland, Richard T. Mead, and Morna D. Hooker (137–63, 279–94). Affirmations (nuanced in various ways) that the NT authors practiced "contextual" exegesis are offered by C. H. Dodd, I. Howard Marshall, David Seccombe, and Beale himself (167–81, 195–276, 387–404).

23   Tremper Longman III, *Literary Approaches to Biblical Interpretation* (Foundations of Contemporary Interpretation, vol. 3. Grand Rapids: Zondervan, 1987), 76ff.

in their redemptive-historical epoch and covenantal context, and the first readers' distinctive need or crisis that provided the occasion for writing. This life setting (*Sitz im Leben*) is accessible to us primarily through clues in the passage itself and its literary context but also through other documents and archaeological artifacts of the period.

It is these "immediate" contexts, the contexts accessible to a biblical document's first readers and hearers (at least to the extent that we can reconstruct them at the distance of many centuries or millennia) that are in view in the debate over whether or not the apostles respected the Old Testament texts' original contexts. It is therefore primarily with respect to these original contexts that Beale defends the New Testament authors against the charge of committing "non-contextual" exegesis.[24] To be precise, however, critics of apostolic hermeneutic object not to the New Testament's *non*-contextual interpretation of the Old, but to its *wrong* contextual interpretation. The charge alleges that apostolic exegesis disregarded what contemporary biblical scholars consider to be the only *legitimate* context for interpretation, the original *Sitz im Leben* and literary-linguistic context setting, and gave preference instead to a different context as though it were more definitive—namely, the ministry, death, resurrection of Jesus and the launch of his Spirit-baptized church through the apostles. Just as they find it illegitimate for Origen to have read biblical historical narratives in the alien generic context of the allegorical methods of his time, so they question the legitimacy—or at least the imitability—of the New Testament authors' reading of Israel's and prophecy in the context of Jesus and his nascent church.

We therefore confront a variety of opinions regarding the propriety of the apostles' interpretation of Old Testament texts, both with respect to the latter's original contexts and with respect to the new redemptive-historical context initiated by the arrival of the Christ. Several of these Enns concisely describes as "options in evangelical scholarship for addressing the odd manner in which the New Testament authors use the Old Testament:

1. To argue, wherever possible, that the New Testament authors, despite appearances, were actually respecting the context of the Old Testament text they are citing. . . .
2. To concede that the New Testament author is not using the Old Testament text in a manner in which it was intended, but

---

24   Beale, *Right Doctrine from the Wrong Texts?*, 387–404.

then to say that the New Testament author himself does not intend to "interpret" the text, but only to "apply" it. . . .

3. To concede, on a variation of option 2, that the New Testament authors were not following the intention of the Old Testament authors, but to explain it as a function of apostolic authority. In other words, since they were inspired, they could do as they pleased. We are not inspired, so we cannot follow their lead.[25]

Option 1 is recognizable in the approach of Beale, following Dodd and elaborating on the latter's suggestive insights with formidable argument and exegetical detail. Although I am uncertain to whom Enns refers in options 2 and 3, both find expression in the hermeneutic writings of Walter Kaiser, to be discussed more fully below. Alongside these options we could put two more:

4. To acknowledge that the New Testament author, although conveying authoritative theological truth by divine revelation, used the Old Testament text in ways plausible for his time and place but no longer persuasive in our intellectual milieu. This is Longenecker's proposal.
5. As a variation of 4, to concede that the New Testament author used the Old Testament text in ways appropriate to his intellectual milieu but not ours, yet to affirm the abiding *hermeneutic* normativity of the New Testament—not in its (Second Temple Jewish) exegetical *method* but in its interpretive *goal*, which was to testify to the death and resurrection of Christ as the eschatological objective toward which Israel's history was aimed in God's redemptive agenda. This is Enns's proposal for "christotelic" and "ecclesiotelic" interpretation—interpretation that sees the entire Old Testament as moving toward the goal of Jesus and his church. It is in essential agreement with the approach earlier articulated by his colleague Dan McCartney.[26]

---

25   Enns, *Inspiration and Incarnation*, 115.
26   Enns, *Inspiration and Incarnation*, 158–60; cf. McCartney, "New Testament's Use" in Conn, *Inerrancy and Hermeneutic*, 107–16, who locates the distinction between Qumran and New Testament in their use of the Old Testament not in exegetical methods but in divergent hermeneutical goals.

Thus, Longenecker affirms the continuing normativity of *what* the apostles taught through appeal to the Old Testament, but not of *how* they employed the Old Testament in the process (at least where their methods diverge from the more recent hermeneutic consensus).[27] Enns and McCartney affirm the abiding normativity both of *what* the apostles taught and of *why* they handled the Old Testament as they did (to testify to Christ as Scripture's goal), but Enns in particular backs off from affirming the ongoing normativity of the *how* of apostolic interpretation.

The distinctions drawn in these last two options are appealing because they promise to permit a rigorously "contextual" exegesis that will have credibility across a broader spectrum of contemporary biblical scholarship, while at the same time enabling the evangelical student and preacher to affirm his solidarity with the apostles' foundational testimony to the centrality of Christ. Yet, a dilemma remains: Is it intellectually consistent to stand with the apostles at their hermeneutic "destination," when we cannot in good conscience walk with them on the path that led them there?[28] Is there another way to approach the disharmony between the commonly received norms and expectations of grammatical-historical exegesis and the apostolic treatment of Old Testament texts that we observe in the New Testament?

---

27   Enns says in critique that in Longenecker's view apostolic interpretive methods remain normative only when they coincide with more recent grammatical-historical expectations: "We all feel an instinctive discomfort with people who interpret the Bible in ways that have no connection with its original context. Still, to limit apostolic authority in the way Longenecker does, it seems to me, amounts to not following the apostles in any meaningful sense. The ultimate standard is still *ours*, not theirs" (*Inspiration and Incarnation*, 158, emphasis original).

28   I can anticipate the rejoinder that the apostles did not "travel through" the Hebrew Scriptures to arrive at Jesus but began with their "destination"—the conviction that Jesus is the long-promised Messiah, who would enter glory through suffering—and *only then* enlisted the ancient Scriptures to bolster a conclusion already reached on other grounds. This viewpoint contains an element of truth (the apostles did find in Jesus the Christ, as McCartney says, the "skeleton key" to unlock previously closed Scripture); but it underestimates the testimony of both the New Testament and church history to the effect that the apostles' preaching of Israel's Scriptures as fulfilled in Jesus *effectively expanded* the early Christian community. Many Jewish people (and Gentiles) *were* brought to the "destination" of faith in Jesus along the path of the apostles' preaching of the Old Testament.

Conclusion: Toward Accountable, Credible Christ-Centered Hermeneutics

With the clarifying perspective of temporal distance, and particularly in the light of the Reformation's chastening and the Enlightenment's sharp criticism of earlier interpretive assumptions and practice, it is not difficult for twenty-first century exegetes and preachers to see the flaws of patristic and medieval allegorism. It is quite obvious to most contemporary students of Scripture, whether historical critical or evangelical, that too often these early Christian teachers ignored or devalued the biblical text's "near" contexts—its original life setting, worldview "horizon," immediate literary context, and genre—and gave hermeneutic priority instead to another, more distant context. Whether or not the Alexandrian Fathers and their successors perceived it, this more distant context included not only the New Testament revelation that completed the biblical canon but also the church's subsequent dogmatic and traditional elaboration, as well as their culture's norms and strategies for the literary interpretation of sacred texts.

It is more difficult for us to recognize that the grammatical-historical hermeneutic that has molded the interpretive instincts of today's biblical scholars and preachers, whether historical critical or evangelical, could also pose the danger of ignoring or devaluing essential contexts for the valid and complete interpretation of biblical passages. Specifically, we need to be self-critical enough to entertain the possibility that our discomfort with apostolic hermeneutics is a signal that grammatical-historical exegesis falls short if it leads us to exclude or ignore the redemptive-historical setting of the fulfillment of God's covenantal relation to his people in Jesus the Messiah, as that setting appears in the documents of the New Testament, which completed the canon of the written Word of God. If the Scriptures are indeed the Word of the Creator who sovereignly directs world history to his intended outcome, and if the Old Testament is eschatologically oriented toward a fulfillment beyond itself, the modern scholar who rejects at the outset the possibility that Jesus' life provides an indispensable context for interpreting the Old Testament is as reductionistic in one direction (excluding the complete canonical context) as Origen and his allegorist successors were in another (devaluing the immediate, original context). In other words, it seems that the adequacy of the grammatical-historical method itself needs to be challenged.[29]

Since the Reformation, the grammatical-historical method has been invoked and implemented as a bulwark against the imposition of alien contexts on the process of interpretation—preeminently against reading biblical texts in the literary context of genres to which they do not properly belong (e.g., allegory) and in the theological context of accumulated ecclesiastical tradition. In this boundary-setting function, grammatical-historical hermeneutics have served a salutary function. More recently, grammatical-historical hermeneutics and the reassertion of authorial intention as definitive of textual meaning have been embraced as alternatives to the quasi-relativity of Gadamer's "fusion of horizons" (the text's and the reader's) model of literary interpretation and the radical subjectivism of postmodern reader-response interpretation.[30] This, too, has been a benefit of the grammatical-historical method. The Bible teaches, and the history of hermeneutics confirms, that sin's noetic effects are such that human interpreters cannot be trusted to submit our thinking to the meanings that Scripture conveys, apart from a norm outside our own experience and perspective to which we are held accountable.[31] The grammatical-historical method's fixation on the text's immediate literary and situational context has rightly demanded that the readers of Scripture recognize the alienness of its message and the challenge it poses to our own assumptions, beliefs and preferences, as well as those of our tradition.

---

29   Both McCartney and Enns acknowledge that the meaning derived from Old Testament texts by a strict application of the grammatical-historical method "does not take us far enough" (McCartney, "New Testament's Use," 115). Likewise, Enns states, "Christian proclamation must move well beyond the bounds of such scientific markers [as Hebrew syntax and ancient Near Eastern context]." (*Inspiration and Incarnation*, 162).

30   See not only the works of Walter Kaiser cited in footnote 10 above, but also Hendrik Krabbendam, "Hermeneutics and Preaching," in Logan, *Preacher and Preaching*, 212–45, who asserts: "The biblical text has only one, single, and unchangeable meaning that is determined by the intent of the author as expressed in the text by means of linguistic symbols. . . . To assign an intended meaning to the divine author different from that of the human writers would violate not only the notion that Scripture is a single uncompounded product, but also the concept of its unimpeded humanity. When God used human writers to produce Scripture as His Word, He therewith adopted voluntarily and by definition the total range of possibilities and limitations inherent to their humanity" (p. 215).

31   For more on the noetic effects of sin, see Dennis E. Johnson, "Spiritual Antithesis, Common Grace, and Practical Theology," *WTJ* 64 (2002): 73–94.

Nevertheless, when any hermeneutic method disqualifies—or seems to disqualify, by pitting an Old Testament text's "original" meaning against its interpretation in the New—the ways that Jesus, the Word of God incarnate, interpreted the Word of God written and taught his apostles to do so, this dissonance is a signal that something is seriously amiss. The question must be asked whether a grammatical-historical hermeneutic that limits a text's valid meaning to that which was potentially visible to its original readers within their own "horizon" of experience and prior revelation is the only or best protection against ancient allegorism or postmodern subjectivism. If we confess that Scripture has an organic unity, should we not expect that the fundamental hermeneutic perspective and approach that Jesus, the apostles, and other inspired New Testament writers apply to so many of the major individuals, events, and institutions of the Old Testament not only point us to the "right texts" to support their "right doctrine," but will also guide our approach to other Old Testament individuals, events, institutions, and texts? If explicit New Testament interpretations of Old Testament texts lead us in the direction of viewing Israel's experience (exodus, trial in the desert, judgment for unbelief, inheritance through Joshua, rescue from enemies through judges and kings, sanctuary, sacrifice, priest, prophet, king, etc.) as patterns pointing to Christ and his church,[32] should not this perspective hold with respect to Old Testament texts not addressed in the New Testament? Or, on the other hand, should we presume that, in texts not explicitly commented on in the New Testament, ancient Israel's experience is related to Christian experience in a way *completely different* from those Old Testament texts that are interpreted in the New? In preaching the bleak Psalm 88, which may not be alluded to at all in the New Testament,[33] should we ignore its place in the genre or "family" of lament psalms that includes Psalm 22, a cry of the suffering heart frequently cited in the New Testament as fulfilled in Christ's cross? The fact that no New Testament text *explicitly* quotes Psalm 88 as "fulfilled" in Jesus' abandonment does not exclude it from membership in the "family" of lament psalms, and I would contend that the whole "family" paints a portrait of undeserved suffering that cries out for a resolution that can be seen finally only in the anguish of the absolutely innocent bearer of others' sins, Jesus.

---

32 This premise will be supported more fully in chapter 7.
33 See the discussion of this psalm in chapter 7.

Three further questions concerning the application of apostolic hermeneutics to Old Testament need to be addressed. First, if the text's original context is no longer regarded as the *single* determinant of the text's valid meaning, have all hermeneutic criteria external to the interpreter, to which our exegesis can be held accountable, been jettisoned? Second, does the inclusion of later New Testament revelation and the whole completed canon of Scripture as interpretive contexts of equal or even greater relevance than text's immediate literary context and life situation tend to "flatten out" the landscape of biblical revelation and obscure its progressive character? Third, how should we evaluate those instances in which the text's meaning in its original context seems incompatible with the meaning attributed to it by later apostolic usage in the broader canonical context?

The answer to the first concern, which is quite valid, is found in the boundary drawn by the Bible's identity as divinely revealed *canon*—that is, a fixed and final *norm* for the church's faith and life throughout its sojourn between the comings of the Christ.[34] Meredith G. Kline has demonstrated that the concept of a canon, a document containing divinely imparted revelation, was intrinsic to God's covenantal relationship to Israel from the time of the exodus and the establishment of the Mosaic covenant at Sinai. The Lord, Israel's great king, rehearsed his record of mighty and merciful deliverance of the Israelites and communicated his expectations of his people as his vassal-servant through a written suzerainty treaty, inscribed by God's finger and preserved for future generations in Israel's sanctuary.[35] The treaty was progressively amplified through the line of prophets who succeeded Moses, sent to press the covenant Lord's lawsuit against his wayward servants.

As Jesus' parable of the wicked tenant farmers shows, he presented himself as the climax of the Lord's messengers, sent to claim the tribute due to Israel's Owner, King, and Protector. He came not

34   The Greek noun, *canōn*, first referred to a reed pole used for measurement (like our yardstick) and was metaphorically employed in other spheres to signify an authoritative criterion or standard by which acceptability was gauged. Thus Paul identifies confidence in the cross of Christ, the defining mark of "new creation," as the *canōn* defining the community on which God's peace and mercy rest (Gal. 6:14–16).

35   See Meredith G. Kline, *The Structure of Biblical Authority* (Grand Rapids: Eerdmans, 1972), building on his earlier study, *Treaty of the Great King: The Covenant Structure of Deuteronomy: Studies and Commentary* (Grand Rapids: Eerdmans, 1963).

merely as a delegated messenger but as the beloved Son who is the heir of God's domain (Mark 12:1–12). The New Testament identifies Jesus as the mediator of the new covenant that transcends the old, transacted through Moses at Sinai, and as the spokesman through whom God has spoken his final, "last days" word (Heb. 1:1–2; 8:6–12). It also includes the foundational role of the apostles as those through whom Jesus the risen Messiah "confirmed" his word to future generations (Heb. 2:3–4; cf. Luke 10:16). The apostles, along with prophets in the apostolic period, function as the new temple's "foundation," with Christ himself as its cornerstone, specifically because "the mystery of Christ, which was not made known to the sons of men in other generations . . . has now been revealed to his holy apostles and prophets by the Spirit" (Eph. 3:4–5; cf. 2:20–21).

Moreover, this apostolic foundation has a fixed shape and clearly defined circumference. As Peter Jones has demonstrated, Paul's self-description as "the last apostle" is neither an "off-handed or circumstantial opinion," much less an expression of false (or even true) modesty. [36] Rather, Paul's description of himself as "last" (*eschatos*) "must therefore mean that the [resurrection] appearance was chronologically the last,"[37] and therefore also that his calling as the apostle sent to the Gentiles brings "the apostolic gospel to completion" and "closes the apostolic circle."[38] Therefore, Jones concludes, "The notion of a unique apostolic ministry limited to the time of the incarnation carries within it the idea of completed revelation as norm or canon for the church.[39]

Unlike both the "fusion of horizons" hermeneutic of Gadamer and the reader-centric hermeneutic of postmodernism, apostolic hermeneutics is founded on the concept of a written canon, the inscripturated divine Word, which was given over a period of centuries but reached its completion in the Spirit-breathed apostolic writings of the New Testament. This canon constitutes the supreme hermeneutic norm, definitive context, and divinely sanctioned "check" on subsequent interpretive activity. Readers and preachers who seek to follow in the apostles' hermeneutic footsteps will gladly see themselves as accountable to offer warrant for their interpretations by

---

36   Peter R. Jones, "1 Corinthians 15:8: Paul the Last Apostle," *Tyndale Bulletin* 36 (1985): 3–34. The words cited are on p. 33.

37   Jones, "1 Corinthians 15:8," 18.

38   Jones, "1 Corinthians 15:8," 28, 30.

39   Jones, "1 Corinthians 15:8," 30.

appeal this authority, both to the *content* of the apostolic gospel and to the hermeneutic by which the apostles proclaimed and defended that gospel.

Rather than fitting Gadamer's model of an ongoing open-ended conversation or negotiation of meaning, therefore, apostolic hermeneutics is circumscribed by the normativity of Scripture's completed canon. In his nuanced and articulate defense of authorial intent and textual content and context in the face of the spiral toward solipsism and subjectivism in recent literary theory, Kevin Vanhoozer argues that to read the Bible contextually *as the Word of God* must include the completed canon as the ultimate context of any particular passage:

> A text must be read in light of its intentional context, that is, against the background that best allows us to answer the question of what the author is doing. For it is in relation to its intentional context that a text yields its maximal sense, its fullest meaning. *If we are reading the Bible as the Word of God, therefore, I suggest that the context that yields this maximal sense is the canon, taken as a unified communicative act.* The books of Scripture, taken individually, may anticipate the whole, but the canon alone is its instantiation.
>
> If God is taken to be the divine author, in other words, then it is the canon as a whole that becomes the communicative act that needs to be described . . . . That Jesus is the referent of the whole relies on, but cannot be reduced to, the intended meaning of the individual books; yet the unity of Scripture emerges only at the canonical level.[40]

It is precisely Scripture's identity as divinely revealed canon, conveyed through human authors yet clearly distinguished from the church's and individuals' (and Qumran's and other Second Temple Jewish communities') uninspired reflection on Scripture as the Word of God, that sets the *authority* of the New Testament's use of Old Testament texts apart from contemporary practices in Second Temple Judaism, even though the two may exhibit formal similarities in exegetical procedures. The boundary between canon and all non-canonical interactions with biblical texts also distinguishes apostolic hermeneutics from more recent literary experiments in intertextuality, as Gary E. Schinttjer has observed:

---

40   Kevin J. Vanhoozer, *Is There a Meaning in This Text? The Bible, the Reader, and the Morality of Literary Knowledge* (Grand Rapids: Zondervan, 1998), 265 (emphasis original).

The canon itself is the ultimate determinative realm of meaning for biblical texts including narratives. The canon defines the universe within which the reader can traverse between narrative worlds. Thus, the narrative multiverse of the scriptures exhibits its interconnectivity within the innerbiblical sphere of the canonical context.[41]

Chapters 7 and 8 attempt to trace more specifically the interpretive parameters that the completed canon of Scripture maps out for our interpretation, the controls to which readers and preachers are accountable.

Secondly, we must address the suspicion that apostolic hermeneutics, by intruding into the interpretation of Old Testament passages the later context of Jesus and his apostles, an interpretive matrix not accessible to the text's first readers, undermines the progressive nature of revelation and "flattens" the rich topography of God's word, which was spoken incrementally over diverse epochs. Walter Kaiser has consistently maintained that it is both theologically and hermeneutically wrong-headed to import the completed canon of Scripture as context into the exegesis of Old Testament texts. In 1981, for example, he wrote:

> ... the whole canon must not be used as the context for every exegesis. ....
> In our chapter on theological analysis we will argue that the Church at large (since the time of the Reformers especially) is in error when she uses the analogy of faith *(analogia fidei) as an exegetical device for extricating meaning from or importing meaning to texts that appeared earlier* than the passage where the teaching is set forth most clearly or perhaps even for the first time. It is a mark of *eis*egesis, not *ex*egesis, to borrow freight that appears chronologically later in the text and to transport it back and unload it on an earlier passage simply because both or all the passages involved share the same canon.[42]

---

41   Gary Edward Schnittjer, "The Narrative Multiverse within the Universe of the Bible: The Question of 'Borderlines' and 'Intertextuality,' " *WTJ* 64 (2002): 231–52. The quotation is from p. 239.

42   Kaiser, *Exegetical Theology*, 82. In the later discussion to which he refers, Kaiser insists that in exegesis the use of the analogy of faith principle must be limited to the use of Scriptures antecedent to the text being interpreted, if theological conclusions are to be "objectively derived from the text," rather than "subjectively imposed on the text by the interpreter (136–37). As a step distinct from and subsequent to exegesis, he allows for consideration of subsequent developments in revelation in "our conclusion or summaries after we have firmly established on exegetical grounds precisely what the passage means" (140).

In 1994, specifically interacting with the "fusion of horizons" hermeneutic of Gadamer and Paul Ricoeur, Kaiser reaffirmed that the analogy of faith principle—the appeal to other biblical texts to clarify the meaning of any passage—must be limited to "antecedent theology."[43] He also affirmed that the "divine-human concursus" involved in the inspiration of Scripture necessitates the conclusion that "to understand the intention of the human author is to understand the intention of the divine author," although he was prepared to grant that "the divinely intended referents" of an Old Testament text were not necessarily "limited to those that the [human] author saw or meant. It was only necessary that the writer have an adequate understanding of what was intended both in the near and the distant future. . . ."[44] Thus, for example, to interpret an Old Testament prophecy that speaks of Israel as referring to or being fulfilled in the multiethnic New Testament church, "unless this identification can be formally located in the Old Testament text itself, . . . would be a case of eisegesis."[45] Even more recently, in 2003 Kaiser continued to maintain that the approach that would "go to the New Testament first to form an understanding of the Bible's teachings and then go backward into the Old Testament, interpreting it in the light of the New Testament," is "wrongheaded historically, logically, and biblically."[46] "The Bible was meant to be read forward, not backward. To read it backward is to end up with a flat Bible. . . ."[47]

These statements, published over a span of more than twenty years, make clear that Kaiser believes that reading the Old Testament through the lens of the New is to do the former a grave injustice, and to compromise the objectivity of one's exegesis. Yet, in *Preaching and Teaching from the Old Testament,* Kaiser also offers the example of a Christ-centered exposition of Leviticus 16:1–34, which highlights in each point of the sermon both the similarities and the differences between the ancient Day of Atonement ceremony and the fulfillment of atonement accomplished by Jesus the sinless high priest through his once-for-all sacrifice of himself.[48] As a Christian preacher, Kaiser

---

43   Kaiser, *Introduction,* 195.
44   Kaiser, *Introduction,* 40–41.
45   Kaiser, *Introduction,* 142–43.
46   Kaiser, *Preaching and Teaching from the Old Testament: A Guide for the Church* (Grand Rapids: Baker, 2003), 26.
47   Kaiser, *Preaching and Teaching,* 51.
48   Kaiser, *Preaching and Teaching,* 146–51.

cannot help but preach Leviticus 16 not only in its ancient Israelite setting but also in light of the priesthood and sacrifice of Christ, the eschatological priest "according to the order of Melchizedek." This is as it should be, for Kaiser recognizes both the divine authorship of the whole biblical canon and the trajectory of the whole history of redemption and revelation, which aims toward Jesus the Christ.[49]

As was suggested by the earlier illustration of a mystery novel by a single author, the New Testament's handling of the Old Testament rather implies that God's redemptive story is one that *must* be read "backward" if we are going to make sense of any part of it.[50] Of course, in the unfolding of God's mystery neither the readers nor the participants in the narrative know the end from the beginning (although they are not kept *wholly* in the dark en route to the denouement). Yet, earlier "clues" are finally placed in their proper context of interpretation, and thus rightly explained, only when the mystery is solved. The Author has sprinkled those clues throughout the story, knowing how each would relate to the finale and inviting the astute reader to anticipate the eventual disclosure of the secret. But each chapter leading up to the last presents puzzling "loose ends" that cannot be tied together coherently until the great Narrator makes all things clear. I suspect that Kaiser's strong disapproval of "reading the Bible backward" is grounded in his belief that to do so invites the illusion that the mystery's reader and its characters understand clearly, at the end of every chapter, the "solution" to be disclosed in the final chapter. But this is a caricature, not an accurate portrayal, of apostolic

---

49   Kaiser, *Preaching and Teaching*, 20–23.

50   Of course God's mystery story is not fiction, but worked out in real history. Interestingly Paul's use of the Greek term *mystērion* corresponds more closely to the sense of "mystery" in a mystery novel (as in the earlier illustration about *The Floating Admiral* and *Five Red Herrings*) than it does to the theologians' typical use of "mystery." In theology a "mystery" is a truth that transcends understanding by human rationality, such as the doctrines of the Trinity (one God, three persons) or the Incarnation (one person with both a divine and a human nature, each maintaining its own characteristics—e.g., the divine nature omniscient, while the human consciousness is both limited and developing in knowledge). Paul's use of *mystērion*, however, has to do with the redemptive accomplishment of Christ, which was kept "secret" in previous generations but now has been revealed in the fullness of time (Eph. 3:2–12). Paul also emphasizes, however, that the "secrecy" of the gospel in former times did not entail a complete absence of clues. In fact, the gospel of Christ was revealed in the law and the prophets (Rom. 16:25–26; cf. 3:21). Rather, Christ and his work were "secret" in the sense that he had not yet entered history as a man to accomplish his redemptive mission.

hermeneutics and homiletics. The apostles were (and their successors should be) profoundly aware of their privileged vantage point in the history of redemption. Jesus himself had told them, "Truly, I say to you, many prophets and righteous people longed to see what you see, and did not see it, and to hear what you hear, and did not hear it" (Matt. 13:17). They therefore told their contemporaries,

> Concerning this salvation, the prophets who prophesied about the grace that was to be yours searched and inquired carefully, inquiring what person or time the Spirit of Christ in them was indicating when he predicted the sufferings of Christ and the subsequent glories. It was revealed to them that they were serving not themselves but you, in the things that have now been announced to you through those who preached the good news to you by the Holy Spirit sent from heaven, things into which angels long to look. (1 Peter 1:10–12)

For this very reason—because they realized that even the prophets themselves could not, in their own time and place, plumb the depth of the promises that the Spirit spoke through them—the apostles refused to leave their listeners and readers in the condition of Israel in the time of Moses, David, or Isaiah. Nor can preachers today leave their hearers (nor biblical scholars their readers) in the place that sleuths such as Peter Wimsey, Jane Marple, Father Brown, or Sherlock Holmes might find themselves at the end of chapter 2 or chapter 3. Precisely *because* we are aware that the Old Testament text, "standing on its own,"[51] leaves so many crucial questions unanswered and "loose ends untied," we *must* follow the apostles' example, within the methodological boundaries established by the apostolic canon, to show our hearers the One who is the End (*telos*) of the Story, and the Solution to all the riddles.

Reading the Bible's story "backward," allowing the light of Jesus to illuminate the shadows that anticipated his saving mission and showed its contours in rough outline before his incarnation, does not "flatten" the topography of biblical revelation precisely because it begins with attention to the text's original context within its book, its

---

51 Kaiser, *Preaching and Teaching*, 27: "The Old Testament can stand on its own, for it has done so both in the pre-Christian and the early Christian centuries." As will be argued in Chapter 6, the preacher to the Hebrews saw in the Old Testament Scriptures themselves various indications that the Old Testament and its institutions could not "stand on their own but testified to a better, more "perfect" order to come.

recipients' life situation, and its redemptive-historical epoch. In fact, as we shall see in chapter 6, practicing apostolic hermeneutics as the author to the Hebrews did actually sensitizes us to the "loose ends," open questions, and unresolved tensions of Old Testament revelation that could be "tied together," focused, and reconciled only in their fulfillment in Christ.

One poignant example is Psalm 89, which opens with an exultant celebration of God's sworn, eternal faithfulness to Israel and to the Davidic dynasty in particular (89:1–37) and then shifts sharply into a minor key of confusion and lament because the Lord has rejected his anointed in wrath (89:38–45). The plaintive question, "How long, O Lord?" and plea, "Remember, O Lord" that close the Psalm (89:46–51) jar against the benediction that follows it as the climax of Book Three of the Psalter: "Blessed be the Lord forever! Amen and Amen" (89:52). How can we bless the Lord, when his covenant faithfulness to David seems utterly forgotten in the devastation of David's sons? It is precisely the psalmist's perplexity and anguish in his own time and place that cries out for the solution to the mystery to which the apostles bear witness: in Jesus' cross David's line would endure, has endured, more abject repudiation that the ancient psalmist had seen; but also in Jesus' resurrection God has "remembered" his faithful covenant with David in a way beyond all prior hopes or expectations.

Psalm 89 presents in microcosm the overarching tension that stands unresolved over the Lord's covenant bond with Israel throughout the Old Testament period. How can God's certain, oath-bound promise to bless Abraham and his seed, and all earth's families through them, come true in view of Israel's persistent waywardness and liability to curse, not blessing? Giving full weight to the incompleteness of Old Testament revelation, apostolic preaching preaches Christ as gracious Lord and faithful Servant in whom this excruciating tension is resolved. Thus Bryan Chapell, for example, affirms that not only those Old Testament texts that are predictive of Christ but also those that are "preparatory," exposing in God's commands and Israel's failures—even the failures of Israel's Patriarchs, kings, and other leaders—the need for one who would keep covenant flawlessly in their place, and ours.[52] In a similar vein, Sidney Greidanus notes that some Old Testament texts and events rightly preach Christ not

---

52   Chapell, *Christ-Centered Preaching*, 283–84.

by their resemblance to the coming Messiah and his saving work, but by *contrast* to his covenant loyalty.[53] Rather than "flattening" the landscape of the history of revelation, apostolic preaching of Christ as the climax and focal point of God's redemptive plan sharpens the contrast between previous shadows and the Sun of righteousness, who has risen with healing in his wings (Mal. 4:2).

Finally, how should we respond when an Old Testament text's meaning in its original literary context and historical setting appears to be at cross-purposes with the way it is employed in the New Testament? In other words, what conclusion should we draw if a text's sense in its "near" contexts cannot be connected, even by way of extension or the drawing out of implications, to the sense attributed to it within the larger canonical context, including, most importantly, the semi-eschatological burst of "fulfillment" revelation associated with the incarnation and redemptive mission in Christ and inscripturated in the canon-completing New Testament?

Here I believe the analogy of playing "hop shing" with my grandmother applies appropriately and helpfully. It illustrates the wisdom of humility, expressed in willingness to second guess our preliminary conclusions concerning the text's immediate "contextual" meaning and its apparent tension with its broader canonical sense. If we share the presuppositions on which apostolic hermeneutics is founded, namely the confidence that the written canon of Scripture, by virtue of its ultimate origin in the veracity, purposefulness, and sovereignty of its divine Author, has an over-arching theological unity that incorporates all its diversities of times and perspectives and that its theological unity is historically driven along a trajectory that leads to Jesus the Christ, we will not dismiss too easily the possibility that the New Testament authors, taught by Jesus himself and guided by his Spirit, have in fact seen lines of connection between Israel's history and Jesus that have thus far escaped our notice. We will ask, What subterranean substructure, presently invisible to me, have they perceived to link ancient promise to present fulfillment in the Messiah? We will conclude that we must dig more deeply to sound the depths of the Bible's unity in the one and only mediator between God and his people, the man Christ Jesus (1 Tim. 2:5). As the exegetical work of Beale and others has illustrated, the discipline to persist in exploring Scripture's unity and diversity, expecting that the paths linking

---

53   Greidanus, *Preaching Christ*, 224–25, 271–76.

the Old Testament's wide diversity to Christ the center exist and can be found, bears a rich harvest of deepening insight into the beauties of the Mystery once hidden, now revealed.

Of course, such apostolic hermeneutics, grounded as it is in the interlocking convictions that God is sovereign in history, is working out in history his one redemptive plan focused in Jesus the incarnate Son, and reveals this one plan with one Voice through Scripture's many human voices and historical eras, will only seem cogent and compelling from within this framework. Evangelicals whose calling is to address the academic guild of biblical scholarship may find little receptivity among colleagues for a claim that first-century fishermen, tax collectors, and one notable rabbi are more reliable guides into the meaning of the collection of Ancient Near Eastern religious texts that Israel revered as Scripture than are the methods and resources for linguistic, literary, and historical research now available. Then again, the guild's suspicions concerning the appropriateness of the New Testament's intertextual engagement with the Old may be, as Lampe suggested, only one symptom of a more comprehensive repudiation of the worldview presented in the Bible. Those called to the academy should count the defense of apostolic hermeneutic as part of their apologetic mission to the guild in which they serve.

Meanwhile, pastors are called to preach Christ boldly and persuasively, from the Law, the Prophets, the Writings, the Gospels, the Acts, the Epistles, and the Apocalypse. We are not apostles, of course. We have not been taught by Jesus on the road to Emmaus or in an upper room in Jerusalem; nor have we been inspired to write Scripture as they were. For these very reasons, a humble recognition of our limitations in contrast to the revelatory insights of the apostles should lead us not to depart from but to follow the apostles' hermeneutical example *particularly* as we interpret those Old Testament texts on which the New Testament writers have not commented. Can we not derive from a careful reflection on the New Testament's interpretation of the Old a *paradigm*, a pattern, a way of viewing the experiences, officials, institutions, and expectations of ancient Israel, a model that discloses the integral wisdom of the vast redemptive plan of God, which reaches its climax in Jesus Christ?

To practice apostolic hermeneutics with integrity and a clear conscience, we need to discern the theological underpinnings, the foundational understanding of the ways of God that provide the basis for the way in which Jesus and the apostles interpreted the Old Testament. The next three chapters are intended to help us probe these foundations, first through an extended canonical example of apostolic preaching (the epistle to the Hebrews) and then through detailed analyses of the apostles' treatment of Israel's Scriptures as the substructure of their proclamation of Christ. Then, in chapters 9 and 10, a series of case studies will apply these perspectives to the challenge of proclaiming Christ from the diverse genres of Old Testament and New Testament literature.

Part 2

The Practice of Apostolic, Christocentric Preaching

6

The Epistle to the Hebrews as an Apostolic Preaching Paradigm

This book contends that the apostolic preachers through whom God gave us the New Testament normatively define not only the content that twenty-first century preachers are to proclaim but also the hermeneutic method by which we interpret the Scriptures and the homiletic method by which we communicate God's message to our contemporaries. One challenge confronting this thesis is the fact that although the New Testament is replete with models of the apostolic *interpretation* of the ancient Scriptures as fulfilled in Jesus, the same cannot be said for apostolic *preaching*, at least to congregations like those to whom most pastors preach each week. This problem is acute because effective preaching is highly contextualized, spoken to a particular audience, with particular characteristics (pre-understandings, problems, relation to the preacher, etc.), at a particular time and place. The more preaching contexts differ from each other, the more caution is called for in deriving normative, transferable principles from one to the other.

The New Testament abounds with examples of the redemptive-historical, Christ-centered *hermeneutic* that the apostles had learned from their risen Lord (Luke 24:27–28, 44–49; Acts 1:3-8). The narrators of the four Gospels and the authors of the Epistles trace the eschatological fulfillment of Old Testament events, institutions, longings, and promises in Jesus and the community that he gathers as his church, Israel come into her own. Jesus is the Creator who breathes life into the new humanity (John 20:22). He is the last Adam, the image of God and covenant servant who obeyed where the first Adam

167

failed (Col. 1:15; Rom. 5:12–21) and who in his bodily resurrection has not only taken up his own life again but also become the One who gives life to others by his Spirit (1 Cor. 15:45). In Jesus' community is safety from final judgment, as Noah's ark bore the faithful through the waters of destruction (1 Peter 3:20–21). He is the seed of Abraham, in whom all earth's nations now receive blessing (Gal. 3:16); and he is the only Son, not spared as the patriarch was permitted to spare Isaac but sacrificed as the long-awaited lamb whose death secures others' life (Rom. 8:32). He is Israel, God's Son called out of Egypt (Matt. 2:15). He is the prophet like Moses (Acts 3:21–23), the royal Son of David (Acts 2:29–36), the sanctuary in which God indwells his people (John 2:19–22), the exile restored on the third day (1 Cor. 15:3–4; Hos. 6:2). The links drawn by the apostles between Old Testament "shadows" and New Testament realities could be multiplied, and have been multiplied.[1]

Much rarer are examples of apostolic *homiletic* in the New Testament, at least samples of preaching that share significant affinities with the venues in which twenty-first century pastors typically preach. The Gospels and Acts do record oral discourses both from Jesus and from his apostles. Nevertheless, differences in audience and (in some cases) redemptive-historical epoch limit the parallels that can be drawn between these discourses and our preaching situation today. Jesus' discourses, for example, were delivered prior to the climax of God's redemptive plan in the cross, resurrection, ascension, and bestowal of the Spirit. For this reason, Geerhardus Vos rightly categorized them as revelation belonging to the penultimate, not the final, phase of the inauguration of the kingdom of God.[2] Although these sermons, conversations, and disputations reliably attest to how Jesus proclaimed the kingdom of God and its consequences for his hearers, Jesus himself indicated that their timing in God's plan restrained the explicitness of his speech even with his disciples (John 16:25). Moreover, as we now interpret Jesus' teaching—whether parables, the Sermon on the Mount, the Upper Room Discourse, or any other—we cannot ignore our interpretive advantage derived from the fact that these discourses now come to us in the canonical

---

1   Leonhart Goppelt, *Typos: The Typological Interpretation of the New Testament in the Old*, trans. D. H. Madvig (Grand Rapids: Eerdmans, 1982), 61–197.

2   Geerhardus Vos, *Biblical Theology: Old and New Testaments* (Grand Rapids: Eerdmans, 1948), 368–69.

context of the entire gospel story, especially the accounts of Jesus' passion and resurrection. To pull these discourses out of this context, as though they could serve as sermon models apart from the cross and resurrection, toward which the Gospels' narrative is driving, would be to misinterpret the discourses and to misapply the lessons that they have to teach us about new covenant preaching. Two examples illustrate this point.

The Sermon on the Mount (Matt. 5–7) is probably Jesus' best-known sermon. As the new and greater Moses, Jesus has ascended the mountain to deliver the stipulations of the new covenant to his disciples (Matt. 5:1).[3] Therefore, although the sermon opens with Beatitudes that invoke and promise God's blessing on those who are humble, repentant, hungry, and merciful (5:2–11), and although forgiveness of sins is mentioned in the Lord's Prayer (6:12), the mood of this sermon is overwhelmingly imperative: "Let your light shine. . . . Avoid anger, lust, divorce, oaths, revenge. . . . Love your enemies. . . . Give and fast secretly. . . ." Matthew has introduced this sermon as an example of the "gospel of the kingdom" that Jesus proclaimed in Galilean synagogues (4:23), but we may well ask, "Where is the *good news* here?" The answer must be that the Sermon on the Mount can be read as good news *only in the context of the whole story* that Matthew has to tell, for in this larger context we see that Jesus came to "fulfill" the Law and the Prophets (5:17) not only in his filling out the implications of God's ancient law but also in the beloved Son's "fulfilling all righteousness" by identifying with sinners in a baptism of repentance (3:15), in his humility as the Servant (12:17–21) and meek entrance into Jerusalem (21:4-5), and preeminently in his sacrifice for sinners (20:28; 26:28). In the context of the cross, Jesus' sermon is good news indeed; apart from it, Jesus' revelation of the law's depth and intensity drives us to despair.

The parable of the prodigal son (or two lost sons, or welcoming father; Luke 15:11–32) evidences more features of the gospel of grace than we see in the Sermon on the Mount. In this story, told by Jesus to justify his friendship with sinners (more accurately, to indict his critics' scorn for sinners), we hear grievous sin portrayed in its ugliness, and undeserved forgiveness extended to the offender. Yet, even in this grace-saturated parable (15:32), the whole gospel story is not told. The injustice about which the older brother complains—that the

---

3   Goppelt, *Typos*, 67–68.

contemptuous rebel is welcomed with honor while his obedient sibling is taken for granted—remains an unresolved problem at the close of the parable. The father's invitation to celebrate the restoration of the lost is a rebuke to the Pharisees' grumbling, of course, but this parable does not disclose the full extent of the father's love. Only when the beloved Son is "numbered with the transgressors" (22:37) and opens paradise to a criminal from the cross (23:42-43) do we glimpse the satisfaction of divine justice and the fullness of divine mercy.

Jesus' discourses often were addressed to opponents or to the uncommitted crowds, as well as to the disciples. These audiences have various relations to the kingdom, from hostility to curiosity to believing commitment (albeit with a weak and confused faith). More significantly, all of the preaching events narrated in the Gospels *preceded* the redemptive-historical watershed of Pentecost. Thus, although we can learn much about Christ-centered homiletics from the preaching of Christ himself, the distance between his earthly ministry and our pastoral and redemptive-historical context requires significant adjustment as we apply those lessons to our post-cross, post-resurrection, and post-Pentecost situation, as we address established Christian congregations.

We might expect that the apostolic preaching in Acts, standing as it does with us on *this* side of the watershed events of redemption—cross, resurrection, outpouring of the Spirit—can serve as a more direct template for our preaching today. It some respects, this is so.[4] Nevertheless, all but one of the sermons in Acts is addressed not to Christian congregations but to Jewish or pagan listeners whose response to Jesus hangs in the balance. The one exception is Paul's farewell discourse to the elders of the church at Ephesus (Acts 20:18–35), but this message is unlike our weekly congregational gatherings in that here Paul addressed a summoned group of church elders on the special occasion of his departure from them, with the expectation that he would not see or minister to them again.

Acts, then, is most instructive for the pastor's responsibility to preach evangelistically to those not yet committed to the faith.

---

4   See especially Roger Wagner, *Tongues Aflame: Learning to Preach from the Apostles* (Fearn: Mentor, 2004) for a thorough and insightful examination of the apostolic sermons in Acts and what they have to teach twenty-first century preachers about boldness, Christ-centeredness, and heart-searching relevance to hearers' real needs. See also Dennis E. Johnson, *The Message of Acts in the History of Redemption* (Phillipsburg: P & R, 1997), 141–65.

Because pastors today must preach the gospel in ways intelligible (as far as lies in us) to unbelievers with a view toward their conversion, the apostolic sermons summarized in Acts have much wisdom to offer. They exhibit the homiletic fruit of Jesus' instruction during the interim between his resurrection and his ascension (Luke 24), and they illustrate how the one gospel can be communicated to diverse audiences, who had various religious backgrounds and degrees of exposure to Scripture. If, however, we are seeking New Testament precedents for the weekly sermons preached *to Christian congregations*, we must look elsewhere than the book of Acts.

The New Testament does offer one paradigm of a sermon preached to a Christian congregation: the epistle to the Hebrews. It, too, has a unique context and audience, and therefore distinctive features (as do all pastorally sensitive sermons), so it would be unwise to treat even Hebrews as a rigid structural template, as though all of its formal features were indispensable to "apostolic preaching" in our contemporary venues. One aspect of Hebrews as a sermon that is worthy of imitation, in fact, is the way its author has contoured his message to the condition and context of the congregation to which it was first "preached" (e.g., Heb. 6:10; 10:32–34; 12:12–17). Honoring and emulating Hebrews' pastoral commitment to audience analysis and adaptation, therefore, may mean that the structure of our sermons diverges from those of Hebrews, so that our preaching may accomplish for our hearers what Hebrews did for its first recipients.

We consider first the rationale for classifying Hebrews, which classically appears as the first of the General Epistles in the New Testament, as a sermon in written form. Then, having surveyed the evidence for the Hebrews' homiletic genre, we will explore the normative guidance it provides for our practice of apostolic preaching.

Hebrews Is a Sermon, a Word of Exhortation

The author (better, preacher) to the Hebrews concludes his document with an appeal to bear with "my word of exhortation" (*tou logou tēs paraklēseōs*) in view of its brevity (Heb. 13:22). "Word of exhortation" is an apt description for this work, which exhorts believers to exhort each other daily to persevere in faith (3:13; 10:25) and calls attention to the "strong encouragement" (*paraklēsis*) that God provides to believers through his unchangeable oath-bound promise (6:18; cf. also 12:5).[5] The expression itself, however, has a more specific meaning in the context of first-century Hellenistic Judaism. As William Lane demonstrates, it is an "idiomatic expression for the homily or edifying discourse that followed the public reading from the designated portions of Scripture in the hellenistic synagogues"—in other words, a sermon expounding and applying the Bible.[6] Lane cites 2 Maccabees 15:8–11, which applies the term "encourage" (*parakaleō*) to Judas' speech, rousing his army to courage by appeal to the Law and the Prophets, and the later Apostolic Constitutions 8.5, which present a liturgy in which a newly consecrated bishop brings "words of exhortation," also called his "teaching," prior to the observance of the Lord's Supper. Lane also suggests that Paul's instruction to Timothy to give attention to "the reading" (of Scripture), "the exhortation" (*tē paraklēsei*), and "the teaching" may well identify liturgical elements and order, with "the exhortation" and "the teaching" flowing from the "reading" as the sermonic instruction that expounds and applies Scripture (1 Tim. 4:13).

The most convincing confirmation of Lane's understanding of "word of exhortation" as sermon is found in Acts 13:15, when, "after the reading from the Law and the Prophets," Paul and Barnabas are invited by synagogue leaders in Antioch: "If you have any *word of exhortation* (Greek: *logos paraklēseōs*, emphasis added) for the people, say it." The "word of exhortation" that Paul brings in response to this invitation is a selective history of Israel from the exodus to the death and resurrection of Jesus, the Savior descended from king David, and it includes exposition of key Old Testament texts in light of their fulfillment in Christ, as well as a concluding application that is both encouraging and sobering (13:16–41). Therefore, both biblical and extrabiblical evidence confirms that "word of exhortation" is a first-century synagogue equivalent for "sermon."[7]

---

5   Twice the author explicitly states that he is "exhorting" (*parakaleō*) his hearers (Heb. 13:19, 22—esv: "urge," "appeal"). He also expresses many of his commands to its hearers as *hortatory subjunctives* (first person plurals, in which the speaker obligates himself along with his hearers) rather than second person imperatives (e.g., 4:1, 11, 14; 6:1; 10:19–25). Second person imperatives are also used, however, to convey the hearers' obligation (e.g., 3:12–13), as is the construction "it is necessary to . . . "(Greek *dei* + infinitive, 2:1—esv: "we must").

6   William Lane, *Hebrews 9–13* (WBC 47B; Waco: Word, 1991), 568; see also his discussion of genre in WBC 47A, lxix–lxxx.

7   Heb. 10:24 refers to the Christian assembly as a "gathering" (dej, *episynagōgē*), and James uses the term *synagōgē* to designate the worship gatherings of the "twelve

Recognizing Hebrews as a sermon, an exposition and application of Scripture reduced to writing because of the preacher's current absence (Heb. 13:19, 23), explains several distinctive features of this New Testament "epistle." This preacher prefers to refer to the mode of God's revelation and his people's reception in oral and aural categories, rather than in terms of writing and reading. The sermon opens with God having *spoken* of old through prophets and now *speaking* in the Son (1:1-2). Since the word of salvation was *spoken* through the Lord and confirmed to the church by the apostles who *heard* him, the recipients of Hebrews must attend to *the things heard* (2:1-4). Since Israel and even Moses trembled at the daunting sound of God's voice speaking on earth at Sinai, how much more must those who hear Christ speaking from heaven attend to his voice with reverence (12:25-29).

When we hear Hebrews as sermon, we grasp the rationale for the preacher's frequent formula for introducing quotations from Scripture, which differs markedly from that used by Paul and other New Testament authors.[8] Paul typically clinches his theological argument by appealing to what "is written" (*gegraptai*, e.g., Rom. 3:4, 10). Both the verb (*graphō*, cognate of *graphē*, "Scripture") and its aspect and voice (perfect passive) emphasize the antiquity and permanence of the Scripture's authority. Hebrews, on the other hand, characteristically introduces Scripture with verbs of speaking (*legō, laleō, martyreō*) in the present tense: "Therefore, as the Holy Spirit says" (Heb. 3:7), "As it is said" (3:15), "as he says also in another place" (5:6), "And the Holy Spirit also bears witness to us" (10:15).[9] Appropriate to the oral genre of the sermon, Hebrews reinforces for

---

tribes of the Dispersion" who worship through Jesus Christ (James 2:2; 1:1)

8   For a brief discussion of the problems with the widely held belief in Pauline authorship of Hebrews, see my notes in the *New Geneva Study Bible* (NKJV; Nashville: Thomas Nelson, 1995), now also published with other versions: *Spirit of the Reformation Study Bible* (NIV; Grand Rapids: Zondervan, 2003); *Reformation Study Bible* (ESV; Orlando: Ligonier Ministries, 2004). A more thorough discussion is found in my audiotaped course (with study guide), *The Epistle to the Hebrews* (Grand Rapids: Institute of Theological Studies, 1999).

9   For other introductory formulae in Hebrews using verbs of oral communication, see Heb. 1:5; *1:6*; *1:7*; 2:6; 2:12; *3:15*; 4:3; 4:4; 4:7; 6:14; *7:17*; 8:8; *9:20*; *10:5*; *10:8*; 10:9; 11:18; 12:5; 12:21; 12:26; 13:5; *13:6*. Italicized references contain verbs in the present tense. By contrast, "it is written" (*gegraptai*) appears in Hebrews only once, in the midst of an Old Testament citation (10:7).

its hearers[10] the reality that God is speaking to them in the present, in the preaching.[11]

The author to the Hebrews exhibits pastoral sensitivity to his congregation's stamina and attention span in hearing his sermon read aloud, twice indicating that he is abbreviating what could have been a much longer and more detailed discussion. He begins to list and describe the furniture in the ancient tabernacle, but declines to delve more deeply into the significance of each piece, noting instead, "Of these things we cannot now speak in detail" (9:5). Later he traces in some detail the heritage of ancient people of faith from Abel to Joshua; but when he reaches the period of the judges, he trims his discourse to a list of names and tersely mentioned exploits of faith, introduced by, "And what more shall I say? For time would fail me to tell of Gideon . . ." (11:32). These abbreviations keep his whole sermon within reasonable bounds, a fact that he can use to motivate his hearers to pay attention to the end, "for I have written to you briefly" (13:22).[12]

When Hebrews is viewed as a first-century Hellenistic Jewish "word of exhortation," addressed to Jews who followed Jesus as the Messiah, an important feature of the structure of this sermon comes into view. In the characteristic structure of a Pauline epistle, a section devoted to historical and theological foundations (doctrinal exposition, clarification, and argumentation) precedes a clear transition to ethical application (e.g., Rom. 12:1; Gal. 5:1; Eph. 4:1;

---

10   The average member of any first century congregation would experience all Scripture, whether Old Testament law or an apostolic epistle, by hearing it read aloud in the congregation (a practice alluded to in Rev. 1:3, which pronounces a blessing on the one reader and his many hearers when they keep what is written in this book).

11   Lane (*Hebrews 1–8*, lxxiv–lxxv) also calls attention to the author's use of verbs of speech (in contrast to writing, except at Heb. 13:22 in the postscript) in referring to his own communication with the congregation, as a way of reducing the sense of distance between himself and his hearers (Heb. 2:5; 5:11; 6:9; 9:5; 11:32).

12   My unscientific "experiment" in testing the author's claim that he had written "briefly" indicated that the epistle/sermon can be read aloud in Greek, even by one who is not fluent in *spoken* Hellenistic Greek (as few are in the twenty-first century), in roughly 50 minutes to an hour—apparently, a *brief* sermon by first century standards! A quick and unscientific survey of sermons by John Piper and Tim Keller shows that 45-50 minutes is not unusual for one of Dr. Piper's sermons, and 35-40 minutes is average for Dr. Keller, with an occasional sermon lasting 44 minutes. Thus, even by modern standards, Hebrews is not unusually long for a sermon preached by a gifted preacher.

Col. 2:6; 1 Thess. 4:1). In Hebrews, on the other hand, hortatory application of each theological motif is embedded in its theological discussion, so application is dispersed throughout the sermon. Although various proposals have been made as to the boundaries and interrelationships of the main movements, I find this six-point outline persuasive.

1. Jesus is superior to *the angels* as an agent of revelation (1:4–2:18).
2. Jesus is superior to *Moses* as an agent of revelation (3:1–4:13).
3. Jesus is superior to *Aaron* as the priest who perfects worshippers forever (4:14–7:28).
4. Jesus is superior to the *old covenant sacrifices* as the one who cleanses consciences forever (8:1–10:31).
5. Jesus is superior to the *patriarchs*, bringing believers into the promised inheritance that the fathers greeted from afar (10:32–12:17).
6. Jesus is superior to *Moses* as the mediator of worship, bringing believers into the heavenly assembly on Mount Zion (12:18–29).

The pervasive thesis of Hebrews is the *superiority of Jesus* to the revelatory and redemptive institutions ordained by God for Israel in the Law of Moses.[13] The unity of each movement is maintained through the exposition of a single Old Testament text that anchors the movement's "case" for the superiority of Jesus, as we will see.

The six "movements" are grouped thematically into three couplets. The first couplet argues Jesus' superiority to God's ancient modes of revelation, the means through whom he spoke "long ago," namely, the angels and Moses, through whom the law was given at

---

13 Thirteen of the nineteen uses of "better" (*kreittōn*, also spelled *kreissōn*, comparative degree of the adjective *kalos*, "good") in the New Testament appear in Hebrews (1:4; 6:9; 7:7, 19, 22; 8:6 (twice); 9:23; 10:34; 11:16, 35, 40; 12:24). With the possible exception of Heb. 6:9, all contrast the superiority of Jesus and the new covenant (or Melchizedek, Jesus' precursor, 7:7) to the agents and institutions of the old covenant. Other terminology of comparison is used to affirm that Jesus has received a "more excellent" (*diaphorōteros*, comparative degree of *diaphoros*) name and priesthood (1:4; 8:6); and that Jesus the Son is worthy of "more" (*pleiōn*, comparative of *polys*) glory and honor than Moses the servant (3:3).

Sinai (along with lesser prophets). The second couplet shows that Jesus' priestly office and sacrificial offering surpass those of the Aaronic-Levitical order. The third couplet focuses on the destination of believers' earthly pilgrimage, affirming the superiority of the inheritance and sanctuary into which Jesus leads those who trust in him. Thus the flow of thought through the sermon as a whole moves from revelation, through reconciliation, to rest.

In each of the six "movements" in the sermon, the exegetical and theological argument is constructed to provide grounds for a hortatory section that urges the hearers to respond appropriately to the privilege that is now theirs in Jesus. We could aptly say that there is a hortatory "bottom line" for each step in the sermon's theological argument.

1. Because the salvation spoken in the Son is better than the law spoken through angels, do not refuse to hear the "last days word" spoken through Christ. (2:1–4)
2. Because Jesus the faithful Son deserves greater honor than Moses the faithful servant, do not harden your hearts toward God's good news, as Israel did in the desert. (3:7–4:13)
3. Because Jesus' high priesthood excels that of Aaron in perfection and permanence but sluggish hearing will not apprehend it, do not have dull ears but press on to the perfection that Jesus has accomplished for you. (5:11–6:12)
4. Because Jesus' once-for-all sacrifice of himself cleanses your conscience, not your flesh, and opens access to the heavenly sanctuary, not merely its earthly replica, draw near to God through faith in Christ's flesh. (10:19–31)
5. Because Jesus as forerunner has entered the inheritance for which Old Testament believers longed and now sits at God's right hand, run your race persistently, your gaze fixed on him. (12:1–17)
6. Because Jesus mediates a new covenant on joyful heavenly Zion, not terrifying earthly Sinai, do not disregard him as he speaks from heaven, but offer acceptable worship through him. (12:25–29)

These hortatory sections are not interruptions to the pristine flow of the theological discussion, although some commentators have spoken of them in this way.[14] Rather, they are the very point of the theological and exegetical argument that Hebrews builds, boulder by massive boulder, for the superiority of Jesus and the salvific order that his sacrifice has ushered in. They are the *destination* of Hebrews' rich exposition of Old Testament Scriptures.[15]

The skillful and pastoral interweaving of theological discussion and exhortation, of doctrine and application, illustrates two truths about apostolic preaching that are often ignored in the polarized atmosphere of contemporary preaching. On the one hand, truly apostolic preaching is not ethical imperative ungrounded in theological indicative. It is not psychological manipulation, moralistic harangue based on guilt, or pragmatic life coaching, untethered to the truth of Christ's redemptive accomplishment on behalf of believers. When the apostolic preacher directs his hearers in God's name as to their way of life, that direction flows naturally and inevitably out of Christ's redeeming work on their behalf. Apostolic preaching is profoundly practical *because* it is profoundly theological. Transformed convictions transform attitudes and behavior.

On the other hand, apostolic preaching is not merely literary analysis or theological contemplation that stops short of changing the values, affections, allegiance, and behavior of its hearers. Some preachers, reacting against moralistic preaching that reduces Scripture's message to instructions for living and enamored by the Christ-focused interconnections between Old Testament and New, seem to think that they have accomplished their mission when they have

---

14 Raymond Brown, *The Message of Hebrews: Christ Above All* (The Bible Speaks Today; Downers Grove: InterVarsity, 1982): "This *parenthesis* [2:1–4] deals with the gospel of God. It is the logical outcome of the author's insistence on the superiority of Christ. . . . In this *parenthesis* the writer reminds us of the Christian revelation in the gospel. . . ." Regarding 5:11ff., Brown comments (p. 103): "So [the author] *digresses* to discuss three closely related spiritual problems confronting some of his readers" (emphasis added).

15 Richard B. Gaffin, Jr. "A Sabbath Rest Still Awaits the People of God," in Richard C. Gamble and Charles G. Dennison, edd. *Pressing toward the Mark: Essays Commemorating Fifty Years of the Orthodox Presbyterian Church* (Philadelphia: Committee for the Historian, Orthodox Presbyterian Church, 1986), 35: "It is misleading to view Hebrews basically as an apologetic-polemic treatment of the person and work of Christ and the superiority of the new covenant to the old, to which various imperatives have been appended in a secondary fashion. . . . Hebrews does provide profound and extensive teaching, especially in the areas of Christology and soteriology, but it does that only 'in solution' with application, only as the parenetic element is pervasive and shapes the course of the argument as a whole."

established their text's location in the grand sweep of redemptive history. The preacher to the Hebrews, however, did not assume that he had discharged his duty to his first-century congregation when he had made a convincing case from Old Testament Scriptures that Jesus surpasses prophets, Moses, Aaron, tabernacle and sacrifices, Canaan, and Sinai. He did not assume that the Holy Spirit would mystically disclose to his hearers the response they should make to the majestic truths unfolded in his theological discourse. Rather, he saw himself as the pastoral means by which the Spirit would shepherd Christ's sheep, showing them from the great truths of divine grace the shape of their grateful response in persistent faith. He summoned them not only to persevering trust in Jesus but also to mutual encouragement (Heb. 3:12–13; 10:24–25; 12:12–16), peace and sexual purity (12:14–17; 13:4), hospitality, generosity, and contentment (13:2, 5–6), hopeful endurance of suffering (12:3–11), and other concrete actions flowing from faith.

Hebrews Expounds How the *Old Testament* Preaches Christ

The preacher to the Hebrews was addressing a Jewish Christian congregation that had endured imprisonment, public humiliation, and forfeiture of property as followers of Jesus (Heb. 10:32–34) and was currently suffering ostracism from the rest of the Jewish community (13:12–13), with the prospect of more violent measures on the horizon (12:4). Under external pressures that forced an inevitable choice between two avenues of access to God—temple ceremony or faith in Jesus—some members were entertaining second thoughts regarding their allegiance to Jesus and the reliance on unseen, untouchable realities that faith in him required.

With consummate pastoral wisdom, the author-preacher makes his case for holding fast confidence in Christ by persuasive appeal to Israel's ancient Scriptures, in which he and his hearers hear the Holy Spirit speaking. One scholar has identified Hebrews as "a homiletic midrash [interpretation] on Psalm 110,"[16] and the pervasive presence of quotation and allusion to this psalm, particularly verses 1 and 4, throughout the sermon supports this identification. The prologue climaxes with the Son taking his seat at the right hand of the Majesty, and

---

16   George Wesley Buchanan, *To the Hebrews* (AB 36; Garden City: Doubleday, 1972), xix.

its claim is reinforced by the citation of Psalm 110:1 as the climactic Scripture of the opening series of citations that set the Son apart from the angels (Heb. 1:1, 13). That Christ, like Aaron, was appointed priest directly by God is confirmed in the citation of Psalm 110:4 in Hebrews 5:6: "You are a priest forever, after the order of Melchizedek." Yet, the Son's priesthood surpasses Aaron's in its permanence, grounded in the Son's eternal life and the Father's unbreakable oath, both found in Psalm 110:4 (Heb. 6:20; 7:11–28). The Son's priestly service also transcends Aaron's in that (again, fulfilling Ps. 110:1) it is offered in the heavenly sanctuary (in which the Son sits at the Majesty's right hand, 8:1) rather than the earthly tent-replica, and because his posture (seated) signifies the completeness and therefore completion of his sacrificial offering for atonement of sins (10:12). The Son's seated posture at God's right hand in heaven promises ultimate victory and rest to those who run the race of faith with endurance (12:2).

On the other hand, although repeated reference to Psalm 110 unifies the sermon as whole, each of the six movements is grounded in a distinctive Old Testament passage,[17] which is shown to testify to the incompleteness of the ancient institutions ordained by God in anticipation of the perfection now brought by Jesus. The Scriptures at the core of each movement in the sermon's argument are

1. Psalm 8:4–6 (Heb. 2:6–8, with interpretation in vv. 8–9): The Son, shown by seven Scriptures to be superior to the angels, became briefly lower than the angels but is now crowned with glory and honor.
2. Psalm 95:7–11 (Heb. 3:7–11, 15; 4:3, 5, 7; with interpretation throughout Heb. 3–4): Promised a better rest than Canaan, pilgrims who hear the voice of the Son—superior to Moses the servant—must not harden their hearts but meet and mix gospel words with confident trust.

---

17 The structuring role of key Old Testament passages in Hebrews was first pointed out to me in an unpublished essay, "The Structural Function of the Major Old Testament Quotations in the Epistle to the Hebrews," by Allen Mawhinney (although Mawhinney identifies *four* major sections and Old Testament texts, whereas I see six). Subsequently, R. T. France has published "The Writer of Hebrews as a Biblical Expositor," *Tyndale Bulletin* 47 (1996): 245–76 (although France identifies *seven* major sections and Old Testament texts, treating the exposition of Prov. 3:11–12 in Heb. 12:4–13 as a distinct unit rather than as a further development of the exposition of Hab. 2:3–4, as I believe).

3. Psalm 110:1, 4 (Heb. 5:6; 7:17, 21; with interpretation in 5:10; 6:20; 7:1–8:2): Christ, like Aaron, was appointed priest by God; but Christ, unlike Aaron, maintains his priestly office forever by the power of his indestructible life and the authority of the Father's oath.

4. Jeremiah 31:31–34 (Heb. 8:8–12; 10:16–17; with interpretation in 8:6–7, 13; 9:1, 11–22; 10:14–15, 18; and elsewhere): Jesus is mediator of the new covenant, superior to Sinai, because his once-for-all sacrifice of himself brings conscience-cleansing forgiveness, so that God remembers our sins no more.

5. Habakkuk 2:2–4 (Heb. 10:37–38; with interpretation in 10:39; 11:1–2, 4–6): Because Jesus, the promised Coming One, will bring those who live by faith into the better, heavenly country and God-built city, for which our fathers in faith looked and longed, we, too, must persist in faith and not draw back.

6. Exodus 19:16–23 (Heb. 12:18–21, 26–27; Deut. 4:11; cf. Hag. 2:6): Jesus, the mediator of a new covenant, welcomes you not to a terrifying and touchable mountain on earth but to the joyful heavenly Jerusalem, the city of the living God.

Although space does not permit a full exploration of the hermeneutic principles exhibited in Hebrews' handling of the Old Testament, several features of the preacher's interpretive approach should be mentioned.[18] This preacher calls his hearers' attention to passages in Israel's Scriptures in which God promises a superior redemptive arrangement, thereby implying that the then-current arrangement was inadequate and therefore temporary. God's oath to appoint a priest in the order of Melchizedek, spoken in Psalm 110, as Levitical priests carried on their ministry, implied the imperfection and eventual replacement of the latter:

> Now if perfection had been attainable through the Levitical priesthood (for under it the people received the law), what further need would there have been for another priest to arise after the order of Melchizedek, rather than one named after the order of Aaron? (Heb. 7:11)

---

18   For fuller discussions, see Graham Hughes, *Hebrews and Hermeneutics: The Epistle to the Hebrews as a New Testament Example of Biblical Interpretation*, SNTS Monograph Series, 36 (Cambridge: Cambridge University Press, 1979); and France, "Writer of Hebrews."

The promise of a new covenant issued through Jeremiah implied that the old covenant delivered at Sinai was faulty (more precisely, the "fault" lay in the Israelites): "For if that first covenant had been faultless, there would have been no occasion to look for a second" (8:7). God's very announcement of a coming new covenant rendered the Mosaic covenant obsolete, aging, and ready to vanish (8:13). Likewise, although Scripture records that God gave Israel "rest" from enemies both in the days of Joshua (Josh. 21:44–45) and again in David's and Solomon's time (2 Sam. 7:1; 1 Kings 8:56), our preacher finds in the still future prospect of entering God's rest, spoken long after Joshua's conquest of the land, a tacit signal that the "rest" achieved through Joshua (occupancy of Canaan) should not be confused with "God's rest," which is promised to people of faith (Heb. 4:7–10). Even the restricted access into the holiest chamber of the tabernacle was the Holy Spirit's way of indicating that, as long as that earthly tent functioned as the meeting place of God and his people, the way into his very presence had not yet been disclosed (9:8).

Secondly, the preacher to the Hebrews finds in the plurality and repetition that characterized features of the "old covenant" implicit signals that those institutions were less than perfect and less than permanent. The genealogical criterion of priestly succession built into the Aaronic-Levitical system was necessary because death prevented each successive generation from maintaining their ministries: "The former priests were many in number, because they were prevented by death from continuing in office" (Heb. 7:23). What is needed is a priest who needs no successor, who lives forever to intercede for his brothers, and just such a priest is promised in Psalm 110:4 (Heb. 7:24–25; cf. vs. 16). The Mosaic requirement that sacrifices be offered daily (10:11) and annually (9:25–26) implicitly acknowledged that those sacrifices, rather than cleansing consciences and effecting forgiveness, were only recurrent reminders of sin (10:1–4). By contrast, Christ's sacrifice of himself once for all brought about all that is needed to effect cleansing of conscience and forgiveness of sins (10:10, 12–14). Likewise, God's ancient speech through prophets came over centuries in many installments and modes; it was true but incomplete revelation that looked forward to "these last days," in which he would speak his last, best word in a Son who radiates his own glory (1:1–3).

Thirdly, underlying the contrast between God's speaking "long ago" and his last days speech in the Son is the preacher's conviction that God is moving purposefully in both revelation and redemption through history from the "shadow of good things to come" to those good realities themselves (10:1; cf. 9:11), now inaugurated in the incarnation, suffering, exaltation, and heavenly priestly ministry of Jesus the Son.[19] "Christ has appeared once for all *at the end of the ages* to put away sin" (9:26). The purposeful movement from God's good provisions for Israel to his better provisions in Jesus' incarnation, humiliation, and exaltation summons the congregation to see themselves as latter days Israel, freed from slavery to the fear of death (2:15) yet still threatened in the desert as they move toward promised rest (3:16–4:11).

Our preacher sometimes finds the two ages, with their attendant characteristics, set in direct contrast in a single Old Testament text. Jeremiah 31:31–34, for example, sets the promised new covenant, characterized by internalization of God's law, expansion of intimate knowledge of God, and forgiveness of sins, in contrast to the covenant that God made with the fathers after the exodus from Egypt. More subtle, but reflective of the preacher's redemptive-historical sensitivity, is the contrast that he draws in his exposition of Psalm 40:6–8 between Mosaic animal sacrifices and the offering of Jesus' body once for all (Heb. 10:5–7). Picking up key words from the Psalm citation in Hebrews 10:8–10, he extricates the elements that the psalmist had

---

19   Hebrews' approach to the typological links between promise and fulfillment is somewhat more complex than the structure evident in other New Testament writers. Like them, Hebrews sees Old Testament persons, institutions, and events as patterns (outlines) pre-embedded by God in Israel's history, now fulfilled (filled in) by reality in Christ. The rest that Joshua gave prefigured God's real rest, to be entered through faith in Jesus; Melchizedek's description in Genesis 14 and Psalm 110 is the template for Jesus' eternal, superior priesthood. But Hebrews adds the further perspective that the Old Testament types or templates were themselves "antitypes" or copies of already-existing eternal, heavenly realities. Moses' tabernacle was constructed to copy the heavenly original, shown to him on Sinai (Heb. 8:5–6; 9:11, 23–24). Melchizedek was so apt a template for Christ's eternal, royal priesthood because Melchizedek himself was "made like the Son of God" (7:3—esv: "resembling"), that same Son who in the last days entered human history, lowered himself beneath angels, and shared his children's flesh and blood to set them free. For discussions of Hebrews' unique approach to typology, see Geerhardus Vos, *The Teaching of the Epistle to the Hebrews* (1956; repr. Phillipsburg: P & R, 1972), 55–65; and Richard M. Davidson, *Typology in Scripture: A Study of Hermeneutical typos Structures* (Berrien Springs: Andrews University Press, 1981), 336–96.

set in antithetical parallelism (e.g., in 10:5, "sacrifices and offerings" v. "a body . . . prepared for me") and collects synonymous terms into a two-age template:

> Old: "You have *neither desired* nor *taken pleasure* in *sacrifices* and *offerings* and *burnt offerings* and *sin offerings*." (italicized words reflective of Greek terms derived from the Psalm)

> New: "*Behold, I have come to do your will* . . . . And by that *will* we have been sanctified through the offering of the *body* of Jesus Christ once for all."

The temporally successive order of these two means of atonement is made explicit in verse 9b: "He abolishes the first in order to establish the second." Our preacher's reading of Scripture is nuanced: he has not forgotten that the animal sacrifices, though now pronounced undesirable to God, were originally "offered according to the law" that God had given. Since Christ's entry into the world to assume the body prepared for him to offer according to God's will, however, those once divinely sanctioned shadows have been dispelled by the reality of the once-for-all sacrifice that *thoroughly* sanctifies.

As Christ's coming and cross turn world history from "promise" to "fulfillment," the consequences of hearers' response to God's voice are magnified, both for good and for ill. On the one hand, if animals' blood effected external, ceremonial cleansing, "how much more" will the blood of Christ cleanse guilty consciences, qualifying believers to enter God's presence confidently (9:13–14). On the other hand, "how much worse punishment" do those deserve who now spurn God's greater gift in his Son (10:28–29; cf. 2:2–3; 12:25)! This moment in redemptive history places before Hebrews' hearers unprecedented mercy and, should they spurn the eschatological mercy provided in Jesus, unprecedented vengeance.[20]

Hebrews Preaches Christ and His Redemptive Work

Although a full exposition of Hebrews' proclamation of Jesus' person and redemptive work cannot be attempted here, tracing its

---

20   This form of argument "from less to greater" is well known in Western logic and rhetoric as *a fortiori* reasoning. In Jewish rabbinical biblical interpretation and theological reasoning it was called *qal v'homer* ("light and heavy"). See Richard Longenecker, *Biblical Exegesis in the Apostolic Period* (Grand Rapids: Eerdmans, 1975), 34.

main contours will provide essential categories to guide our own proclamation of the Bible's multifaceted testimony to Christ, the guarantor of the new and better covenant (Heb. 7:22; 8:6) and the only mediator between God and humanity (1 Tim. 2:5). First, we will survey Hebrews' testimony to both the deity and the humanity of Christ, noting ways in which the sermon relates the union of these two natures in one person to Jesus' role as Lord of the covenant and as Servant of the covenant. Second, we note the ways in which Christ fulfills the three primary offices of covenantal mediation in the Old Testament: the prophet, the priest, and the king. This attention to Christ's roles in the covenant is appropriate not only because the covenant is a distinctive emphasis of Hebrews,[21] but also because it equips us to examine other texts throughout Scripture from the standpoint of the promises and obligations that bind God to his own in covenant and of Jesus' fulfillment of those promises on God's behalf and those obligations on our behalf.

Divine and Human, Lord and Servant

The sermon opens with a prologue that contrasts the Son first to prophets and then to angels (Heb. 1:4). The purpose of the Son-angels contrast becomes evident when the preacher concludes a series of seven Scripture citations establishing the Son's superiority and turns to the sermon's first word of exhortation (2:1–4). The "message declared by angels" is the law delivered to Moses on Mount Sinai, where the Lord descended amid his heavenly entourage of attendants and spiritual messengers to ratify his covenant with Israel (Gal. 3:19; Acts 7:53). The preacher's reasoning is that the dignity of the messenger dictates the significance of the message and the consequences

---

21   Of the thirty-three appearances of the Greek word *diathēkē* (covenant) in the New Testament, seventeen—slightly over half—appear in Hebrews. Of these uses, fourteen appear in the exposition of Jeremiah 31:31–34 in chapters 8–10, while the other three either anticipate (Heb. 7:22) or refer back to that discussion (12:24; 13:20). Moreover, the longest continuous citation of an Old Testament text in the New Testament is the citation in Hebrews 8:8–12 of Jeremiah 31:31–34, the most explicit Old Testament promise of a new covenant to succeed God's covenant with Israel at Sinai and a text to which other New Testament references to "covenant" allude (e.g., Luke 22:20; 1 Cor. 11:25; 2 Cor. 3:6, 14). For a fuller discussion of the covenant theology of Hebrews, see Geerhardus Vos, "Hebrews, Epistle of the *Diatheke*," *Princeton Theological Review* 13 (1915): 587–632 and 14 (1916): 1–61; now reprinted in Geerhardus Vos, *Redemptive History and Biblical Interpretation*, ed. Richard B. Gaffin, Jr. (Phillipsburg: P & R, 1980), 161–233.

(for good or ill) of one's response to the message. God signaled the sanctity of his law by speaking it through angels, but now a message of salvation has been announced by an even more exalted spokesman, "the Lord" (Heb. 2:3).

The title "Lord" (*kyrios*) appeared in the sixth (and longest) of the seven Old Testament citations leading up to this exhortation. Whereas the series opened with texts showing the Son's superiority to angels (1:5, citing Ps. 2:7 and 2 Sam. 7:14; cf. also Heb. 1:6 "the firstborn" and 1:8 "the Son"), in the later Scripture citations the Son is not only accorded divine titles (1:8 "O God"; 1:10 "Lord") but also credited with the divine task of creation and the divine attribute of immutability (1:10–12, citing Ps. 102:25–27). The latter truth—the fact that, whereas earth's foundations will perish and the heavens will wear out, "you are the same, and your years will have no end" (Heb. 1:12)—becomes a recurring motif in Hebrews' proclamation of Christ. Most explicit is the echo of Psalm 102:27 in the epistolary conclusion that the preacher has appended to his sermon, in which the hearers are reassured that even though one generation of beloved leaders has passed from the scene, "Jesus Christ is *the same* yesterday and today and forever" (Heb. 13:8). The fragile mutability of human shepherds should not shake the confidence of those under the care of "the great shepherd of the sheep" (13:20), who is the unchanging guardian of his people. The eternal, "indestructible life" of Jesus, attested by God's oath-bound decree, "You are a priest *forever*" (7:16–17), is integral to his priestly representation of believers before God's throne of grace. As one who is eternally, immutably God the creator, Jesus our high priest "lives forever to make intercession" for those who approach God through him (7:25 dej). His presence as their high priest in the heavenly Most Holy Place is "a sure and steadfast anchor of the soul" (6:19). The hearers' anxiety in the face of changing circumstances meets its answer in the Lord who remains forever "the same" and who promises to believers an unshakable kingdom that will withstand even the final "shaking" and dissolution of the present heavens and earth (12:26–28).

The divine changelessness of Jesus as covenant guardian of his people is great comfort to people unsettled by transient circumstances, but they (and we) must not underestimate his majesty. As the Creator who laid earth's foundations and stretched the heavens with his hands, whose "word of power" upholds the universe (1:2–3), the Son is worthy of highest honor as the divine "builder" of all things (3:3–4). Jesus the Son is also the divine judge whose thunderous voice will "shake" the present sin-infected cosmic order. More than that, his voice now thunders from heaven (not just on earthly Sinai), and he must not be ignored (12:25)! He is terrifyingly "other" than sin-stained humanity, "separated from sinners" (7:26); and even Moses rightly trembled in terror as the prospect of approaching him (12:18–21). Indeed, "*our* God" (not just ancient Israel's God) "is a consuming fire" (12:29), and the Son whom God acclaims as "God" in Psalm 45 wields a scepter of uprightness in his kingdom, loving righteousness and hating wickedness (Heb. 1:8–9). The spurning of heightened grace and privilege incurs heightened judgment: "How much worse punishment, do you think, will be deserved by the one who has spurned the Son of God . . . ?" (10:29; cf. 6:6). Jesus the Son is divine Lord of the covenant, constant in faithfulness and majestic in holiness.

Hebrews also affirms in the strongest possible terms the Son's full identification with his human brothers and sisters in all things except sin. "Since therefore the children [given him by God][22] share in flesh and blood, he himself *likewise* partook of *the same things*, that through death he might destroy the one who has the power of death, that is, the devil" (2:14). "He had to be made like his brothers *in every respect*, so that he might become a merciful and faithful high priest" (2:17). "We do not have a high priest who is unable to sympathize with our weaknesses, but one who *in every respect* has been tempted as we are, yet without sin" (4:15). In graphic terms that match the pathos of the Gospel portraits of Christ's anguish in Gethsemane, the preacher recalls that "Jesus offered up prayers and supplications, with loud cries and tears, to him who was able to save him from death, and he was heard because of his reverence" (5:7). As the preacher and his hearers well know, Jesus was "heard" not by being spared the cross but by being "brought again from the dead" (13:20) in the joy that lay beyond the cross and its shame (12:2).

His genuine and complete humanity qualifies Jesus to be the covenant Servant who secures the bond between the faithful, holy God and his unfaithful, unholy people. The preacher invokes a

---

22   The preacher has just cited Isa. 8:18, apparently interpreting it as a "window" on the pre-creation "pact of salvation" (*pactum salutis*) or covenant of redemption among the persons of the Trinity, to which Jesus alludes in prayer in John 17:6, 24; cf. Rev. 13:8; 17:8.

creation Psalm, which marveled at God's care for his tiny human creature: "You made him for a little while lower than the angels; you have crowned him with glory and honor, putting everything in subjection under his feet" (Heb. 2:7–8, citing Ps. 8:5–6). His introduction applies the Psalm to "those who are to inherit salvation" (Heb. 1:14), the salvation that was declared first by the Lord and then attested by his apostles (2:3). To them, not to angels, God subjected the world to come. "It is not angels that he [Jesus] helps, but he helps the offspring of Abraham" (2:16). Yet, Hebrews does not hear in this Psalm a lament for paradise lost, a nostalgic look back to idyllic order before the fall. Rather, this Psalm is a forward-looking promise of human dominion in "the world to come"—an orderly subjection of all things under man's feet that "we do *not yet* see" (2:8). We do, however, see One who, though infinitely superior to the angels, became for a little while lower than the angels (in this context, by submission to the angelic-mediated law received by Moses, 2:2), and who is now crowned with glory and honor (2:9). We see Jesus, whom Paul called the second and last Adam (1 Cor. 15:45–47; cf. vv. 20–22; Rom. 5:12–21), the One who was perfectly faithful where Adam failed. Christ came into the world to assume the body prepared for him, with the words of Psalm 40 on his lips, "Behold, I have come to do your will, O God, as it is written of me in the scroll of the book" (Heb. 10:7). In fact, the divine will that the Son was committed to fulfill was not only the keeping of the commands that Adam and Israel had failed to keep, it was "that will" that mandated "the offering of the body of Jesus Christ once for all" to sanctify sinners by faith (10:10).

Thus, Jesus was the obedient Servant not only in his sinless submission to divine commands but also in his sacrifice for others' sins. He maintained covenant faithfulness in our place, obeying where Adam rebelled and succeeding where Adam failed, thereby leading his people as forerunner into the inheritance that awaits the righteous. "Although he was a son, he learned obedience through what he suffered. And being made perfect, he became the source of eternal salvation to all who obey him" (5:8–9).[23] Jesus is also the faithful covenant Servant who suffers covenant curse in our place, cleansing

---

23 Hebrews' strong affirmations of Jesus' sinlessness (4:15; 7:26–27) preclude interpreting "learning obedience" or "being made perfect" as implying prior defect in Jesus. The preacher means that Jesus' priestly consecration ("perfection"—see note 25 below) was via the path of obedience that endured every (escalating) test with fidelity.

our conscience (2:9; 10:5–10). The sacrificial blood used to ratify covenants symbolized the penalty justly due to violators of covenant commitments. When Israel, having sworn allegiance to the Lord and been sprinkled with the blood that signified covenant curse, subsequently transgressed the covenant, its own blood was forfeit. But Christ's death provides redemption from the transgressions committed under the first covenant, so that those called to faith "may receive the promised eternal inheritance" (9:15–22).

Hebrews also brings into view a third fruit of Jesus' faithfulness as covenant Servant. Not only does his sacrifice remove the covenant curse from believers and his positive obedience warrant our entrance into the heavenly country and city for which the patriarchs looked and longed in hope, but also his redemptive work produces a people who are, themselves, being transformed subjectively toward holiness. The blessings of the new covenant are not only forensic, setting us right in terms of the legal outcomes of fidelity or rebellion toward the Lord of the covenant. They are also dynamic and transformative. In the new covenant, God said, he would put his laws in his peoples' minds and write them on their hearts (8:10; 10:16), and the preacher has seen in his congregation the fruit of this inscribing process: they have responded to God's good Word, falling like life-giving rainfall from heaven (cf. Isa. 55:10–11), by bearing a useful crop—"your work and the love that you showed for his sake in serving the saints" (Heb. 6:7–10). They have "done the will of God," enduring suffering and identifying with those who suffered for Jesus' sake (10:32–36). Likewise, for the future, the preacher expects to see in his hearers a grateful response to grace: reverent worship, acceptable to God, in thanks for the unshakable kingdom he has given (12:28); brotherly love, hospitality to strangers, marital purity and material contentment (13:1–6); generous deeds (13:16) and submission to leaders (13:17). The Son leads many sons to glory not only by obeying and suffering in their place as Servant of the covenant (though these are primary) but also by sanctifying many sons in the process of leading them to glory (2:10–12). His identification with those whom he is not ashamed to call brothers is not only legal but also vital, including the subjective, progressive transformation of their motives, values, words, and deeds. As Paul would say it, these siblings of Jesus are "predestined to be conformed to the image of his Son, in order that he might be the firstborn among many brothers" (Rom. 8:29).

Prophet, Priest, King

Another helpful perspective, to be developed more fully in chapter 8, is to examine the mediatorial work of Christ from the perspective of the distinctive offices and officers God used to establish and maintain his covenant and reign over Israel. Classic Protestant catechisms (Heidelberg and Westminster) have found the offices of prophet, priest, and king—with their respective privileges and responsibilities—a helpful template for appreciating the comprehensiveness of Christ's redemptive achievement. Hebrews certainly exemplifies the usefulness of this threefold paradigm for capturing the richness of Jesus' mission.

The sermon opens with the Son's prophetic role as spokesman for God, delivering new revelation that qualitatively transcends that delivered through the ancient prophets (Heb. 1:1–4). The congregation must attend to what they have heard, for its content is the "salvation" that was first spoken through the Lord (2:1–3). They must "consider Jesus, the apostle and high priest of our confession" (3:1). This text is unique in attributing the title "apostle" to Jesus, although in the fourth gospel Jesus repeatedly speaks of having been "sent" (*apostellō*) by the Father (e.g., John 6:57; 7:29; 8:42; 17:3, 8, 18, 21, 23, 25). The preacher may prefer the title "apostle," rather than "prophet," to designate Jesus the eschatological spokesman of God because he has already applied the latter title to messengers belonging to the old era, prior to "these last days" (Heb. 1:2). The first-century Hebrew Christians to whom this sermon was addressed needed to hear the voice of God in the voice of his Son, to hear the God of truth define their situation according to the pattern of Israel in the wilderness, liberated from past slavery but not yet beyond the reach of the hardening effects of "the deceitfulness of sin" (3:13). They needed to open their ears and hearts to the divine Speaker who warned them from heaven (12:25) through leaders "who spoke the word of God to you" (13:7 NIV). Thus the sermon appropriately opens, in its first two movements, with a focus on the prophetic and revelatory office of the Son of God.

The heart of the sermon unveils the priestly office and work of Christ. This motif, in fact, is the "main point" (*kephalaion*) of all that the preacher is saying.[24] It is introduced as early as the prologue,

---

24 *Kephalaion* appears in the New Testament also at Acts 22:28, where it designates a sum of money paid to procure Roman citizenship (cf. also Lev. 5:24 LXX

which speaks of the Son's having made purification for sins as the precursor to his heavenly enthronement (1:3), and the title "high priest" is first applied to Jesus in 2:17 to explain the redemptive purpose for the Son's temporary subordination to angels. Although Jesus' priesthood pervades the entire sermon, in the third and fourth movements Christ's priestly office (4:14–7:28) and his priestly ministry (8:1–10:31) take center stage.

Jesus' priestly office resembles Aaron's in that both were authorized by direct divine appointment (5:4–6) and both entailed sympathetic identification with weak brothers for whom they interceded (2:17–18; 4:14–5:3, 7–10). Yet, Christ's high priesthood supersedes Aaron's because Christ was installed in office *permanently* by God's immutable oath and his own endless life (7:15–25). The mediatorial superiority of Jesus' priestly office according to the order of Melchizedek is demonstrated exegetically by the priestly benediction that Melchizedek pronounced upon the patriarch Abraham and by the Lord's tithe that Abraham (and his descendants Levi and Aaron in him) presented to Melchizedek (Gen. 14:17–20).

Jesus' priestly ministry focuses on his atoning sacrifice and his intercession before God's throne on behalf of his brothers, effecting the forgiveness of their sins and "perfecting" them, qualifying them to approach God and to worship him acceptably.[25] Christ's priestly work surpasses Aaron's in several respects: (1) Its venue is heaven itself, the true and original sanctuary of God, rather than the earthly tabernacle (or temple), which was copied after the pattern shown to Moses on the mountain (Heb. 8:1–6; 9:11). (2) His sacrifice—not of goats, bulls, or calves, but of himself—is eternally effective to cleanse the conscience, not merely the flesh, and is therefore "once for all," in contrast to the constantly repeated daily and yearly sacrifices offered

---

[6:5 MT]; Num. 5:7 LXX). The term is also used in the LXX to refer to a census or inventory (Num. 4:2; 31:26, 29). Its use in extrabiblical Greek in the sense that it bears in Heb. 8:1, namely "summary, most important theme," is well documented (BD, *ad loc*). Lane translates it "crowning affirmation" in Heb. 8:1, on the grounds that the foregoing argument has led to the new, climactic affirmation that "Christ exercises his priestly ministry in the heavenly sanctuary (8:2)." *Hebrews 1–8*, 200.

25 "Perfection" (*teleioō, teleiōsis*) in Hebrews is influenced by the LXX usage of this term to translate the Hebrew expression for priestly consecration, "fill the hand" (*mille' yod*, Ex. 29:9, 22, 26, 27, 29, etc.; Lev. 8:33; 16:32; 21:10; Num. 3:3). The sinless Son himself was "perfected" when he was installed permanently in his priestly office (Heb. 5:9–10; 7:28), and his sacrifice now "perfects" worshipers, so that we may draw near to God (7:19).

by Aaron's priestly order (9:13–14; 10:5–14). (3) His intercession for his brothers is ceaseless, since he lives forever and retains his priestly ministry forever (7:23–25). Consequently, he has entered the heavenly sanctuary not merely as a *representative* of others, who remain forever banned from God's holy presence (as was so in the old sanctuary, 9:7–8), but also as his brothers' *forerunner* (6:20), through whose sacrifice they, too, may enter God's sanctuary, boldly drawing near to God through the conscience-purifying blood of Jesus (10:19–22; cf. 4:14–16). Those whom the Son sanctifies become priests, fit to offer worship pleasing to God, confessing his name and serving his people (12:28; 13:15–16). Christ's priestly office and ministry show that we need not only revelation to hear the voice of God (the prophet's role) but also reconciliation: forgiveness, cleansing, and intimate access to the presence of God (the priest's role).[26]

Although Christ's fulfillment of the king's responsibilities—just rule and strong defense of his people—is less central to this sermon than is his priesthood, royal themes appear repeatedly. The Son's authority to rule is implied in the prologue when he is described as "the heir of all things" (1:2), particularly as we soon hear the preacher demonstrating Jesus' identity as Son through citations from a royal psalm (1:5, citing Ps. 2:7) and a royal promise to David (Heb. 1:5, citing 2 Sam. 7:14). The Son's kingly glory is evident in Psalm 45:6–7 (cited in Heb. 1:8–9), for the Son whom God calls "O God" sits on an eternal throne, wields a righteous scepter, and upholds justice toward the upright and the wicked. Psalm 110:1 (cited in Heb. 1:13) not only speaks of the Son's royal throne at God's right hand but also promises utter submission of all his enemies under his feet. Like ancient Melchizedek, whose position as king of Salem is interpreted as "king of peace" and whose name means "king of righteousness," Jesus combines in himself and his mission the kingly and the priestly roles (Heb. 7:1–2).

Human beings are destined for dominion, when the world to come will be subjected under their feet (2:5–8). Although that

---

26   As we will see in chapter 8, in Israel priests also had a significant "prophetic" role in teaching the Torah on an ongoing basis and a "royal" role in conferring with elders and judges to apply the principles of Scripture with wisdom and justice. Nevertheless, the priestly emphasis in Hebrews, as in the Reformed catechisms that employ Israel's three theocratic offices as paradigms for understanding the fullness of Christ's redemptive work, is on the priest's reconciling mission through sacrifice and intercession.

universal submission to man as God's vicegerent is "not yet" visible, it already can be glimpsed by those who see Jesus, who presently is "crowned with glory and honor" (2:9). Even his substitutionary death is sometimes portrayed in terms more reminiscent of a king's military combat than of a priest's sacrificial offering: " . . . that through death he might *destroy* the one who has the power of death, that is, the devil, and *deliver* all those who through fear of death were subject to lifelong slavery" (2:14–15). Not only do we need to *hear* God's Word through his greatest and final Spokesman and receive *cleansing* to approach God in worship, we also need to be *ruled and defended* by the King whose throne is eternal, whose scepter is upright, and whose might is displayed in his death for sin's captives and his return from death as the great shepherd of the sheep (13:20).

In chapter 8 we will explore more deeply the fruitfulness of these categories for discerning the thematic strands that anchor Scripture's widely diverse passages to their center point in Christ.

Hebrews Addresses the Needs of a *Specific Audience*

One final feature of apostolic preaching that Hebrews illustrates (as do the sermons reported in Acts) is the preacher's attention to the situation and spiritual needs of his hearers. This feature shows that Hebrews' classification among the general (or catholic) epistles is doubly misleading. We have already seen that, with respect to genre, Hebrew is more a sermon than an epistle. Nor is it really "general," at least not in the sense that James or 1 Peter, addressed to churches dispersed over broad geographical areas, are (James 1:1; 1 Peter 1:1). Hebrews has as local a destination and original readership, as does 1 Corinthians, although at the distance of two millennia we cannot be certain about the locale of the congregation that first received Hebrews.[27]

The preacher of Hebrews sees no conflict between making his sermon uncompromisingly Christ-centered as to content and strategically hearer-contoured as to communication and application. As he engages his hearers' past and present circumstances and the challenges confronting their faith, he does not simply acquiesce to their diagnosis of their dilemma. Rather, he authoritatively guides them

---

27   The closing greeting from "those who come from (*apo*) Italy" (Heb. 13:24; cf. Acts 18:2) sounds like a greeting sent by expatriates back to their home region, and Lane cites other evidence in support of an Italian (perhaps specifically Roman) destination (*Hebrews 1–8*, lviii–lx).

in the reinterpretation of their experience according to the God-given categories of redemptive history. In this way, the particularity of their trials (and their blessings) does not evaporate into ageless abstractions but instead is placed into the illumining context of God's great history-long agenda to gather his kingdom of priests into his heavenly sanctuary.

Although good sermons are configured to communicate with a specific audience, they often speak meaningfully to others as well, even those far removed from their original setting. This is because much of what is significant about human beings is not those peculiarities of background, culture, and experience that distinguish us from others but the characteristics that we share in common as bearers of the divine image, inhabitants of God's universe, and fallen rebels against the Creator. A full analysis of the contexts that color our hearers' reception of the preached word therefore demands that we consider several concentric "horizons" of shared human experience. The preacher to the Hebrews alludes to these various horizons in the course of his sermon.

At the broadest level, the preacher is conscious of the circumstances that his audience shares with all people. They live in the universe created by Christ (Heb. 1:2, 10–12), but this universe is destined for ultimate destruction (1:10–12; 12:27). They are created in God's image to rule over their fellow creatures under the Creator's supreme authority (2:6–8), yet they are sinful and therefore subject to the frustration of their royal calling (2:8), to suffering, and finally to death (2:14–15).

A narrower horizon is the one that the Hebrew Christians share with the people of God's covenant of past generations, the "fathers" to whom God spoke by prophets (1:1), Israel in the wilderness (3:7–4:13), and the ancient saints who awaited by faith the promised "perfection" that finally arrived in Christ (11:39–40). Like ancient Israel, the Hebrew Christians belonged to a community in which God's saving power was at work (3:16; 2:3–4; 6:4–6) and God's voice was heard (3:7; 4:1–2; 12:25), promising entrance into God's rest, the heavenly homeland and lasting city (4:1; 6:12–18; 11:10, 14–16; 13:14). Also like Israel, however, the Hebrew Christians faced an ordeal of wilderness testing, in which external adversity and internal misgivings opposed the preacher's exhortation to hold fast their confession to the end (3:12–4:3, 11–13; 12:12–17).

Drawing the circle yet more tightly, the Hebrews who first heard this sermon shared a common framework of experience with other believers (including you and me) who belong to the new covenant inaugurated by Jesus. Unlike ancient Israel, they and we live in "these last days" of God's superior speech in the Son (1:1–2). They and we live in "the time of reformation" in which previous restrictions of access to God's presence have been removed, so that through Christ we all may and must approach God's throne of grace with confidence (9:9–10; 4:14–16; 10:19–25). Such heightened mercies and privileges entail heightened accountability. As a result, those who spurn the expanded display of God's grace in his Son will receive even more devastating penalties than those imposed under the old covenant (2:1–4; 10:28–31; 12:25). While insisting that in the Old Testament Scriptures "the Holy Spirit bears witness to us" (10:15) in our present situation (3:7), the preacher never lets his hearers forget their privileged moment in God's redemptive plan, standing on this "last days" side of the threshold between promise and fulfillment. Nor does he let us forget that the abundance of grace now displayed in the sacrifice of Christ makes faith all the more incumbent on those who hear the gospel.

Finally, the preacher refers to elements of that narrowest horizon of experience and understanding, which set that congregation apart from all others. Knowing the reverence with which they rightly regard Israel's Scriptures, and perhaps anticipating counter-arguments from Scripture that have shaken their faith (cf. 7:13–14), he carefully builds his case from Scripture, appealing specifically to the Greek translation (Septuagint) most widely used in the Dispersion. He recalls their past history of having heard the gospel through the apostles, who heard the Lord himself (2:3–4). Despite his dire warnings against apostasy, he nourishes a confidence that their faith will prove its genuineness in endurance because in the past they have served their fellow-saints (5:11–14) and joyfully endured public ridicule, imprisonment, and loss of property for their faith (10:32–34). Before them lies a choice. Either they will stay loyal to Jesus and bear his reproach "outside the camp," excluded from synagogue and temple (13:10–14); or they will falter in faithlessness, shrinking back and falling short of the promised inheritance (3:16–18; 10:35–36, 39). The preacher alludes to the prospect of more violent persecution in their future (12:4), assuring them that Christ's death sets them free

from the slavish fear of death (2:14–15) and commending to them
the exemplary faith of ancient saints who endured martyrdom in
expectation of a "better resurrection" (11:27, 33–38). In the midst of
these stresses, the congregation has experienced a transition from
their first "generation" of leaders, whose faith is to be remembered
and imitated (13:7), and their present leaders, whose authority and
responsibility the preacher feels the need to bolster with his personal
endorsement (13:17).

More alarming to the preacher than his congregation's external
pressures are the internal, spiritual deficiencies that he finds among
them. Their hearing of God's voice has grown dull, sluggish (5:11–14;
6:12). Their resolution in pursuing the path of pilgrimage toward the
inheritance is flagging, aptly described in the prophetic imagery of
drooping hands, weak knees, and disabled feet (12:12; cf. Isa. 35:3–4).
Doubting and discouraging words infect congregational conversations—a "root of bitterness" that threatens to defile many (Heb. 12:15;
cf. Deut. 29:18). As a result, some stand in real danger of "throwing
away your confidence" and "drawing back" (Heb. 10:35, 39, dej), "falling away from the living God" in unbelief, hardened by sin's deceitfulness (3:13). Their misgivings may arise from the contrast between the
challenge of walking by faith in the unseen glory and priestly ministry
of Jesus, on the one hand, and the all-too-visible sacrificial pageantry
of the Temple that still stood in Jerusalem, on the other (10:2, 11).
They hesitated between two quite different answers to the question of
the legitimate means of access to God and atonement from God, each
of which appealed to Israel's ancient Scriptures. One offered a variety
of visible reassurances: a majestic sanctuary, a priesthood legitimated
by genealogy, and the shed blood of slain animals. The other, presented so persuasively by our preacher, argues that those visible features
of the ancient system are signals of its mutability and impermanence
(1:10–12). Those who long for lasting security need a hope anchored
in heaven itself (6:19), an ever-living priest who never needs replacement (7:24) serving in an eternal sanctuary not constructed by human hands (8:2; 9:11), a once-for-all sacrifice that needs no repetition
(10:11–14), and a future city founded by God himself and therefore
sure to last, unlike Jerusalem and its Temple, which would soon lie in
ruins (11:10; 13:14).

In view of the dominant danger of apostasy, the preacher's
exhortation repeatedly returns to the theme of holding fast one's

confession and confidence in Jesus (3:6, 14; 4:14; 10:23, 35–36). He even enlists his hearers' experience of the broader Hellenistic culture, appealing to the analogy of athletic competition in which runners strip off excess weight and run the marathon with endurance, minds ever fixed on the finish line (12:1–2).[28] Knowing that this endurance cannot be an individualistic achievement, he repeatedly urges his hearers to hold together as a community through mutual encouragement, especially of the weak and wavering (3:12–13; 10:24–25; 12:12–15; 13:1–3). Knowing, moreover, that even the community of faith cannot supply the strength to endure, the preacher urges that them to avail themselves of the access now opened by Jesus, drawing near to God "that we may receive mercy and find grace to help in time of need" (4:16; cf. 10:19–22).

The preacher also gives attention to his hearers' situation in a variety of other concrete exhortations that address diverse areas of life: peacemaking and sexual purity (12:14, 16–17; 13:4), brotherly love and generous hospitality (13:1–2, 16), compassionate identification with the suffering (13:3), and contentment grounded in the assurance of God's constant presence and provision (13:5–6). These are not simply generic commands; they are specific applications of the call to persevering faith designed to fit the hearers' circumstances and spiritual needs.

Conclusion

The epistle to the Hebrews, our one New Testament example of apostolic preaching addressed to an established congregation, illustrates the integration of Christ-centered biblical interpretation with hearer-contoured communication and application. Its exhortation to enduring faith, expressed in the sacrifices of good deeds and generosity, is grounded in exposition of Scripture and persuasive demonstration that the Old Testament bears testimony to a new and better covenant, established by a Mediator superior even to Moses, the faithful servant. This preacher's blunt warnings and hard-hitting admonitions never wander into moralism because his "word of exhortation" is

---

28   Although his argument is almost exclusively grounded in biblical interpretation and allusion (somewhat unlike Paul, who refers more frequently to Greco-Roman cultural institutions and practices), the preacher to the Hebrews uses not only this "extra-biblical" analogy from Greek athletics but also nautical metaphors of a boat losing its moorings (2:1) and, by contrast, dropping anchor (6:19).

grounded in divine grace, which has reached its "last days" expression in the incarnation, suffering, and resurrection of Jesus the Son, whereby he assumes the office of eternal high priest on behalf of his people. His elaboration of Jesus' mediatorial roles as both Lord and Servant of the covenant, and as the prophet, priest, and king who unites God to his people in truth, reconciliation, and righteousness suggest categories of thought that point the way for our imitation of the apostles in proclaiming Christ to our contemporaries in the twenty-first century. These motifs and their homiletic usefulness will be developed in chapter 8, and then applied to various genres of Old Testament and New Testament texts in chapters 9 and 10.

7

Theological Foundations of Apostolic Preaching

As we observe the insightful and sometimes striking ways in which the preacher to the Hebrews "teases" out of the Old Testament its testimony to the coming Christ, we are prompted to seek the deep, foundational convictions regarding God's ways with his people that undergird his reading of the Scriptures. The connections that he draws between promise and fulfillment, though they are the fruit of that mysterious work of the Holy Spirit on biblical authors that we call "inspiration" (2 Tim. 3:16; 2 Peter 1:21), are not the product of ineffable bursts of mystical vision, nor is their rationale utterly inaccessible to us, if we have patience and humility to listen carefully.

In order to read and preach the Bible as Peter and Paul and the preacher to the Hebrews did, what we need is not a foolproof step-by-step procedure to follow; rather, it is a *way of viewing* the Scripture and its witness to what God has done, is doing, and will do to redeem and recreate his people and his kingdom. (Later, however, such a procedure will be offered as a means of training ourselves in this "way of viewing.") The God who creates, reigns, redeems, and judges in history, and who speaks in Scripture, abounds in surprising ingenuity, but he is also a wise planner who works by pattern and gives human beings, created in his image and recreated in the image of the Son, glimpses into the patterns of his planning. Long before he sent his Son to bring rescue in "the fullness of time" (Gal. 4:4), he sovereignly designed events, institutions, and individual leaders to provide foretastes of the feast, whetting Israel's appetite for the coming Savior and salvation. Israel's historical experiences of bless-ing and judgment, weal and woe, also prepared a rich symbolic "vo-cabulary," embedded in the dust and blood of real history: concepts and categories pre-designed to articulate the sufficiency and com-plexity of Jesus' saving work.

How, then, can the eyes of our hearts be trained to perceive the patterns that God prepared as promises and previews (even prelimi-nary installments) of Christ and his redemptive achievement? At the risk of mixing metaphors, it could be said that our eyes adjust to the patterns as we *discern the foundations* of the biblical authors' un-derstanding of God's unified plan and purpose for history. In archi-tectural construction, the foundation fulfills its indispensable func-tion, stabilizing the superstructure and setting its parameters, even though the foundation itself remains out of sight, driven deep into the earth. Those with an eye for architecture, however, can discern important features of the foundation by viewing the structure that rests on it. So, also, careful students of the Bible can see behind and beneath its authors' specific interpretations of earlier Scriptures (the visible building) a foundational framework for God's entire redemp-tive and re-creative enterprise.

In this chapter we will take "soundings" into the foundation by way of two lines of exegetical investigation. First, we will survey the New Testament's typological interpretations of the Old Testament, grouped successively into five general categories, moving from those that are explicit and obvious to those that are more subtle and im-plicit. Think of these as geological strata, from those most visible on the surface of the biblical text (and therefore least controversial) to deeper lines of connection between Scripture's diverse texts and Christ, on which there is greater disagreement. Second, we will step back into the Old Testament to observe the foundations already laid for apostolic, Christ-centered hermeneutics in the interpretation of earlier events and passages by later Old Testament texts.

Strata of Typological Correspondence Identified by the New Testament

Old Testament texts that are interpreted by New Testament authors as fulfilled in Jesus can be grouped into five categories. In the first two categories, the links drawn between the Old Testament text and its New Testament fulfillment are so overt that there is little debate over whether the reference is intentional on the part of the New Testament authors.[1] The next two categories include Old Testament texts, events, institutions, or persons to which allusion by New Testament authors is less explicit but still made sufficiently clear by verbal echoes or other linguistic and literary conventions. The last category brings together Old Testament passages and events for which no particular New Testament text can be cited as providing even implicit typological interpretation. The interpretation of Old Testament texts in this final category, according to more general and more deeply embedded patterns of covenantal and redemptive correspondence, will be our focus of attention in chapter 8.

Typos Texts

The first category consists of those Old Testament persons, events, and institutions to which the Greek term *typos* ("imprint, copy, pattern, archetype, model") or one of its cognates is applied in the New Testament. The Greek term *typos* itself can be applied to a variety of patterns or templates that give shape to copies: for example, the imprint of nails creating wounds in hands (John 20:25), a moral or spiritual example (Phil. 3:17; 1 Thess. 1:7; 2 Thess. 3:9; 1 Tim. 4:12; Titus 2:7), or a system of teaching (Rom. 6:17).[2]

In a few New Testament texts, however, this word-group is employed to articulate a specific relationship between a pattern and its replica, in which persons or events in the history of Israel were designed by God to prefigure Christ and his redemptive work. The key factors in this specialized use of *typos* and its cognates are a strong similarity between the earlier type and its later replica-fulfillment, the historical movement from promise to fulfillment, and therefore, with the similarity, a magnification or "heightening" in the historical

---

1   Of course, for scholars who question the divine origin and normativity of the New Testament books, as we saw in chapter 4, the obvious intention of a New Testament author to cite an Old Testament precedent as fulfilled in Jesus does not settle the question of the meaning of the Old Testament text in its original context. See, for example, S. V. McCasland, "Matthew Twists the Scriptures," in G. K. Beale, ed. *The Right Doctrine from the Wrong Texts?* (Grand Rapids: Baker, 1994), 146–52. Likewise, as we saw in quotations in chapter 4, evangelical scholars such as Longenecker and Gundry accept the theological authority of the New Testament, but not its hermeneutic normativity, and therefore assert that a New Testament author's intention still need not control our interpretation of an Old Testament text that he enlists to expound Christ and his work.

2   See Davidson, *Typology in Scripture,* 147–81.

move from type to antitype. Leonhart Goppelt summarizes the foundational conviction underlying those New Testament passages in which typological interpretation of the Old Testament is explicit:

> These passages declare that there is something here which corresponds to the substance of the Old Testament parallels and yet is *greater*. This something greater is what constitutes a genuine typological heightening. . . . The things that are compared are related to each other in redemptive history; therefore, this is not the same as the parallels that are observed in the history of religions. The relationship in redemptive history is taken for granted by the evangelists and the rest of the New Testament because they are convinced that there is a continuity between Old Testament history and Jesus Christ in the sense of promise and fulfillment. . . . Type and antitype are interrelated as prophecy and fulfillment in the Gospels also, and this is a genuine typological relationship.[3]

The Old Testament type functions in the sphere of historical events and persons in a way similar to Old Testament prophecy delivered in words. Goppelt comments further on the combination of continuity and discontinuity that links Old Testament type with its New Testament counterpart:

> Each typology includes typological correspondence and heightening. Accordingly, every typology presupposes that the God of the OT is the Father of Jesus Christ and that Jesus of Nazareth is the Christ, the one who fulfills OT redemptive history. . . . The NT values the OT as a true, though merely provisional, redemptive history which in its literal meaning originated from God.
>
> . . . Persons, events, and institutions are interpreted only insofar as they express some aspect of man's relationship to God. Consequently, typology does not deal with inherent or external features in the events and accounts in the OT. Because Christ alone is the fulfillment of this relationship to God, another principle is always added that arises from the subject matter. This principle specifies that all typology proceeds through Christ and exists in him.[4]

The *correspondence* between an Old Testament type and its New Testament fulfillment makes the type a credible and intelligible

---

3 Leonhart Goppelt, *Typos: The Typological Interpretation of the Old Testament in the New* (trans. D. H. Madvig; 1939; ET Grand Rapids: Eerdmans, 1982), 199 (emphasis original).
4 Goppelt, *Typos*, 202.

anticipation of its fulfillment in Christ. The *heightening* or "something greater" dimension is called for because Israel's condition under the Mosaic law (and, before Sinai, the redemption experienced by Adam, Noah, and the patriarchs) had built into it unresolved tensions and unfulfilled longings that could only be satisfied when the Messiah himself arrived in "the last days." There is continuity between type and antitype because Old Testament redemptive events, persons, and institutions truly reveal some aspect of God's new-creation reversal of sin and its woeful consequences, a process of reversal and renewal that reaches its climax only in Christ and his work. There is also discontinuity because every Old Testament type is marred by human sin or impaired by creaturely limitation. Even faithful kings failed. Pious priests died. Animal sacrifices had to be repeated again and again. Psalmists protested their undeserved mistreatment at the hands of the wicked, even in words fit to describe the utter devotion of the Messiah to come, "Zeal for your house has consumed me, and the reproaches of those who reproach you have fallen on me" (Ps. 69:9; see John 2:17). Yet, the same singer also confessed, "O God, you know my folly; the wrongs I have done are not hidden from you" (Ps. 69:5). Zealous as he was, David was not *the* flawless representative that God's people needed. One higher, purer, and "better" (as Hebrews reminds us) was needed.

In the following significant New Testament texts, then, apostolic interpreters explicitly instruct us to view various features of Old Testament history and religious institutions as "types." The Old Testament person, event, or institution is a "pattern" or template that anticipates and prefigures the work of Christ, and therefore both interprets and is interpreted by its christological fulfillment.[5]

Romans 5:14. Adam was a *typos* of the Coming One. This first example vividly illustrates the similarity and dissimilarity between type and fulfillment that characterizes biblical typology. The similarity between Adam and Christ is that each acts as a covenantal representative whose response to God's authority affects all those whom he represents. Adam acts, many are affected; Christ acts, many are affected. The dissimilarity lies in the fact that Adam's and Christ's responses to the divine will are polar opposites, and therefore the

---

5 These "hermeneutical *typos* passages" were the focus of Richard Davidson's dissertation, *Typology in Scripture*, which ably exegetes these texts and draws out their implications for our understanding of the relationship of Old Testament to New.

effects on those represented are likewise diametrically opposed to each other. Because Adam disobeyed, all for whom he acted were constituted sinners, condemned to death. Because Christ obeyed, all for whom he acted are constituted righteous, vindicated in life (5:15–21). Two further observations derived from this explicitly typological text are instructive.

First, Paul traces the same typological correspondence between Adam and Christ in 1 Corinthians 15 (especially vv. 20–21, 45–49), but without the use of *typos* or its cognates. This suggests that the apostles read the Old Testament Scriptures typologically not only when they explicitly used *typos* terminology but also when they traced the pattern of correspondence-with-heightening in other ways. The apostle expected his Corinthian readers to recognize the validity of the parallel he drew between Adam and Christ as covenantal representatives even before he applied the *typos* label to Adam in his later epistle to Rome.

Second, the contrast between type and antitype, which Goppelt describes in such terms as "intensification" or "heightening," sometimes is to be seen in the *failure* of the type to fulfill a covenantal responsibility that type and antitype share. Christ, the antitype, proved faithful where Adam failed. Adam disobeyed on behalf of his own, bringing condemnation and death; Christ obeyed on behalf of his own, bringing justification and life.[6] Adam's failure as *typos* of the Coming One suggests that when dealing with Old Testament individuals whose office or covenantal role is inherently typological, our interpretation must pinpoint not only what makes their role similar to Christ but also what makes their fulfillment of that role *unlike* Christ's perfect and complete fulfillment.

1 Corinthians 10:6, 11. Israel's trials in the wilderness occurred "typologically" (*typikōs*). Some scholars have understood Paul's use

---

6   Similarly, Israel failed the test of faith during forty years in the desert; Christ sustained the test of faith during his forty days in the desert. David, though sometimes a champion of trust in his God (confronting Goliath), also miscarried justice toward loyal servants and dependents (Uriah, Mephibosheth). In his failures, David betrayed his calling as ruler and protector of God's people. But Israel awaited a branch from Jesse's stump who would not judge by surface appearance but in truth (Isa. 11:1–5). Thus, even in his sin, David the anointed did not cease to be a type of Jesus the Messiah, but David's falls showed dramatically that David himself was not the goal of Israel's hopes. David was only a fragmentary and flawed reflection of the perfect King to come, Jesus the Son of David.

of *typos*-language here to indicate nothing more than a moral example or a negative lesson from past history, without any predictive connection between the situation of the wilderness generation and that of the New Testament church. *Typos* is sometimes used in this sense, as we have seen. Here, however, Paul's use of Israel's wilderness experience to warn the Corinthian church against idolatry and sensuality presupposes a relationship between ancient Israel and the church that is more than mere analogy.[7]

Three lines of evidence demonstrate that Paul views Israel's desert experience as a history-embedded foreshadowing of the church's privilege and trial in the new covenant. First, the apostle bluntly affirms that the rock from which Israel drank miraculous water "was Christ" (vs. 4). Biblical language commonly expresses symbolism using a simple verb of identification: "The Lord *is* my shepherd," "I *am* the true vine," "This bread *is* my body." In other words, Scripture often uses metaphor (implicit comparison) rather than simile (explicit comparison using "like" or "as"). The wilderness rock, when struck with the judgment blow of the rod of God, supplied life-giving water to God's thirsty people (Ex. 17:1–7). Such provision and privilege, however, did not make the members of the covenant community immune to judgment when they later engaged in idolatry and sexual sin. The rock's role as source of the water of life for Israel prefigured Christ's provision of the life-giving Spirit to his church, but simply being numbered among the members of the New Testament church does not insulate a person from divine judgment if the individual commits infidelity by engaging in idolatrous worship.[8]

Second, Paul describes Israel's exodus blessings in terms that cannot fail to bring to Christians' minds the sacraments of the new covenant: baptism and the Lord's Supper. All Israel was "baptized into Moses" in the cloud and the crossing of the Red Sea and they ate the same "spiritual food" and drank the same "spiritual drink" (1 Cor. 10:2–4). Paul interprets Israel's passage through the Red Sea as a preview of the church's initiation sign, baptism-identification with Christ (even as Israel was identified

---

7   Thus Davidson rightly categorizes this passage among the "hermeneutical *typos* passages" that are the focus of his study. *Typology in Scripture*, 182, 193–297.

8   Recall the similar warning drawn from Israel's hardness of heart in the wilderness in Hebrews 3–4.

with Moses, the typological covenant mediator/redeemer) by passing through the waters of death and emerging into a new life of liberty (cf. Rom. 6:4; Col. 2:12; 1 Peter 3:21).[9] Similarly, the daily gift of manna and miraculous water from the rock are interpreted typologically and sacramentally as "spiritual" food and drink, respectively. The manna and the water are called "spiritual" not to deny their material properties or ability to sustain physical life but because, like their physical New Testament counterparts, the bread and wine of the Lord's Supper, they signify the grace and power of the Spirit of Christ to nourish life before the face of God. Paul is assuming the typological correspondence already disclosed in Jesus' "bread of life" discourse (John 6).

Third, and most important, is Paul's explicit designation of the redemptive-historical "location" of his Corinthian brothers and sisters. Israel's desert trials and failures were inscripturated "for our instruction, on whom the end of the ages has come" (1 Cor. 10: 11). Paul makes explicit the eschatological dimension implicit in biblical typology. His point is not simply that history repeats itself or that ethical lessons can be learned by observing others' actions and their consequences in like circumstances in the past. Rather, Paul insists that God's purpose in the experiences of Israel's wilderness generation and the recording of those experiences in Scripture concerned *not* (primarily) ancient Israel but the new people of God, composed of believing Jews and Gentiles, who lived in first-century Corinth (and all other such audiences who live "at the end of the ages"). God's inscripturation of the books of Moses was not only intended to address Israel's needs but was also directed primarily toward the needs of a future generation, specifically the eschatological generation who has now witnessed the appearance of the Messiah, in whom God's promises are fulfilled. Other New Testament passages state that promises spoken by Old Testament prophets pertained not to their own contemporaries but to those who would witness Messiah's coming at the consummation of the ages (see Heb. 3:5; John 5:45–47; and especially 1 Peter 1:12, cited below). Here Paul shows us that it was not only *spoken* Old Testament prophecy but also *"incarnate"* Old Testament prophecy (as we could call typology, in light of the link drawn by Goppelt)

---

9   See M. G. Kline, *By Oath Consigned: A Reinterpretation of the Covenant Signs of Circumcision and Baptism* (Grand Rapids: Eerdmans, 1968).

that was addressed primarily to future generations who would be blessed to live in the age inaugurated by the coming of King Jesus and his reign of grace.

1 Peter 3:21. Baptismal water is an "antitype," a fulfillment of the floodwaters that brought salvation with judgment in Noah's time. According to Peter, the ancient floodwaters that destroyed the disobedient also were a means used by God to save Noah and his family. As they (few though they were) entered the ark, they were saved "through water." So, water also has a role in the salvation now revealed to Peter's readers through the sufferings of Christ and the following glories, of which the prophets spoke long ago. In fact, earlier in his epistle Peter paralleled Paul's thought in 1 Corinthians 10, asserting that the ancient prophets' words served not themselves nor their own generation but Peter's contemporaries, who live in "the last times" when Christ has been manifested to suffer and be glorified (see 1 Peter 1:10–12, 19–20). Thus the waters that bore Noah and his family safely through judgment in the ark have their *antitypon* in the waters of baptism. Peter insists, however, that baptism is to be understood not merely in terms of an external rite of physical cleansing but in terms of the unseen spiritual reality to which it points: an appeal to God for a good conscience, for the heart-cleansing efficacy of the blood of Christ (3:21; cf. 1:2).

Typos Terminology in Hebrews. The typology of Hebrews in relation to the earthly tabernacle differs from the Pauline and Petrine examples above. Paul and Peter draw the connection between type (promise) and antitype (fulfillment) strictly historically or "horizontally" (as Davidson says) from past to future.[10] Type precedes and implicitly prophesies its antitype. In Hebrews, however, typology proceeds on a vertical as well as a horizontal plane. The earthly tabernacle is the antitype, the replica copied from a heavenly template (*typos*) that, being eternal, antedates the tabernacle on earth (Heb. 8:5; 9:24). In another sense, however, Hebrews also exhibits the historical or "horizontal" axis, teaching that the earthly tabernacle and its sacrificial atonement rituals pointed *forward* in history to "good things to come" (10:1), that is, the atoning sacrifice of Christ and his eschatological priestly mediation, now taking place in the heavenly

---

10   Davidson, *Typology in Scripture*, 193–335.

original, after which the earthly tent was copied. Hebrews therefore introduces a *dual* typological perspective, both "horizontal" (tabernacle pointing forward to Christ's priestly work) and "vertical" (tabernacle copied after the pattern of the eternal heavenly sanctuary of God).[11]

To sum up, in texts that explicitly apply *typos* terminology with redemptive-historical and eschatological connotations to Old Testament persons and events, the apostolic authors of the New Testament teach us to understand Adam in his role as covenant representative of all humanity, the salvation of Noah amid world judgment, Israel's exodus liberation and wilderness wanderings, and the tent of God in the midst of Israel's camp as prophecies embedded in history and inscribed on the pages of Scripture for the sake of those who would witness the fulfillment of these "incarnate promises" in the fullness of time, through the last Adam, the Son greater than Moses the servant, the Lord of glory himself.

Old Testament Quotations Applied to Christ

Into this second category fall Old Testament passages that are explicitly cited in the New Testament as reaching their fulfillment in Jesus and his saving work, often introducing the Old Testament citation with a formula such as "this was to fulfill," or "this fulfilled." Although the New Testament authors do not apply *typos* terminology in citing these Old Testament texts, few would doubt that they intended their readers to see in the Old Testament persons, events, or institutions referred to divinely designed foreshadowings of the Messiah.

If we were to maintain a sharp distinction between prophecy spoken in words and typology as prophecy embedded in historical experience, we would need to exclude from this category texts typically considered to be messianic "prophecies," such as the future-oriented prediction that Israel's ruler would come from Bethlehem (Mic. 5:2, cited in Matt. 2:6–7). On the other hand, because of the close connection between promise through word (prophecy) and promise through event (typology), we should not draw too sharp a line between verbal prophecy and embodied prophecy. Old Testament texts may both refer (even retrospectively) to an

---

11   Davidson, *Typology In Scripture*, 336–88. Geerhardus Vos, *The Teaching of the Epistle to the Hebrews* (1956; repr. Phillipsburg: P & R, n.d.), 55–65.

Old Testament event (type) and find fulfillment (prospectively) in a New Testament event (antitype). Matthew's application of Hosea 11:1, "Out of Egypt I called my son," to the sojourn of Joseph and Mary with the child Jesus in Egypt is often cited as an egregious example of the irresponsible absurdity of apostolic hermeneutics (Matt. 2:15).[12] Hosea plainly spoke not prospectively of the Messiah but retrospectively of the exodus, say Matthew's critics. In one sense they are right: Hosea's text does indeed look back to the exodus. But Matthew's critics ignore (or simply reject) a more foundational conviction to which Matthew is leading his readers: Jesus is the true Israel, delivered from infant death, brought out of Egypt, tested in the wilderness, and finally exalted as Son of Man, invested with all authority as representative head of the eschatological "saints of the Most High" (Dan. 7:13–14 is echoed in the Great Commission, Matt. 28:18–20). By affirming that Hosea's words are "fulfilled" in the young Jesus' return from Egypt with his parents, Matthew is not claiming that Hosea's words fit Jesus *instead of* Israel but that they fit Jesus *because he is Israel's fulfillment.*

Similarly, the Davidic lament of Psalm 22:1, "My God, my God, why have you forsaken me?" belonged on Jesus' lips (Matt. 27:46) not because the sufferings portrayed in the psalm had no referent in David's own experience but because David himself—in his experience of undeserved affliction and his hope of ultimate vindication—was a type of his greater messianic son, Jesus. Precisely because David was the anointed king, his words expressive of *his own* sufferings appropriately apply to the suffering of his Son, the eschatological Anointed One. In fact, the psalmists' description both of their own innocence and of the severity of their own sufferings find "heightened" fulfillment in Christ, so that what had been hyperbolic and symbolic description in the Old Testament setting sometimes receives an even more "literal" fulfillment in Jesus: "For my clothing they cast lots" (John 19:24, citing Ps. 22:18); "You will not abandon my soul to Hades, or let your Holy One see corruption" (Acts 2:27, citing Ps. 16:10).

Among individuals, institutions, and events that are identified by apostolic authors and preachers as "fulfilled" in Christ through explicit citation and commentary on Old Testament passages are the creation of Adam (1 Cor. 15:45, citing Gen. 2:7), the union of

---

12   McCasland, "Matthew Twists the Scriptures," in Beale, ed., *Right Doctrine.*

Adam and Eve (Eph. 5:31, citing Gen. 2:24), the Passover lamb (John 19:36, citing Ex. 12:46), David's endurance of betrayal by an intimate (John 13:18, citing Ps. 41:10; cf. Acts 1:20), of senseless hostility (John 15:25, citing Ps. 35:19), and of gambling over his garments (John 19:24, citing Ps. 22:18), Israel's proverbial wisdom passed from generation to generation (Matt. 13:35, citing Ps. 78:2), Israel's deafness to the prophets' words (Matt. 13:14–15, citing Isa. 6:9–10), and the grief of Judah's exile (Matt. 2:18, citing Jer. 31:15). Space constraints preclude analyzing these and other quotations in relation to their Old Testament contexts and referents, on the one hand, and in relation to their New Testament application to interpret the significance of Christ and his redemptive reign on the other. Even so brief a sampling suggests, however, an increasingly rich and complex texture of interconnections between Israel's history and Jesus' fulfillment of that history.[13] The *typos* texts sketched a broad outline and clearly marked several points of connection between Old Testament history and New Testament fulfillment: Adam and his temptation in the Garden, salvation and judgment in the Flood, Israel's exodus and trial in the desert. Now in Old Testament passages quoted as "fulfilled" in Christ more details of the portrait are being added.

Unmistakable Allusions to Old Testament Events, Applied to Christ

This category differs only slightly from the preceding one in terms of the explicit clarity with which the New Testament authors link Old Testament types to Christ. Whereas previously the focus was on direct quotations, sometimes introduced with a fulfillment formula, in the third category belong Old Testament events, persons, or individuals identified as typological of Christ and his church not by means of a direct citation but through unmistakable and undeniable

---

13   To build consensus incrementally rather than seeming to overreach the evidence, I have refrained from mentioning the many quotations of the servant songs of Isaiah (not only the frequently cited Isaiah 53 but also Isaiah 42, 49, 50, and 61) and their interpretation as finding fulfillment in Jesus. A case could be made for interpreting these passages as applicable in the first place to the experience of the prophet himself and then as fulfilled in Jesus, of whose fidelity, sufferings, and vindication Isaiah himself was a *typos*. However, since the church has often read these texts *exclusively* as messianic prediction, without any reference to the experience of the Old Testament messenger, I am content to leave the question of the referent or referents to which these Isaianic passages refer unresolved at this point.

allusions. One example is Jesus' comparison of his impending death to the lifting up of the bronze serpent by Moses (John 3:14–15, alluding to Num. 21:4–9). What at first glance seems to be a simple analogy—"as Moses lifted up . . . so must the Son of Man be lifted up"—shows itself, when read in the context of John's gospel, to be a profound disclosure of redemptive-historical correspondence between the mediatorial work of Moses and the superior mediatorial work of Christ (cf. John 1:17–18; 6:31–51; etc.). Thus a strange incident that might have seemed to involve primitive magic in which cure came only by staring at an image of the judgment itself (in the paradoxical words of poet-composer Michael Card, "the symbol of their suffering was now the focus of their faith"),[14] is shown to prefigure the Son's absorption of sin's venom when "lifted up" under curse on the cross.

In this category belongs much of the biblical exposition in the sermon to the Hebrews, although, as we have seen, Hebrews is so laced with actual Old Testament quotations, with commentary— Palms 95, 110, 40; Genesis 14 (details of Abraham's encounter with Melchizedek); Exodus 19 (terror at Sinai); etc.—that the distinction between this third category and the second seems largely irrelevant to that inspired preacher's hermeneutic.

The Gospel according to Luke incrementally builds a "case" for recognizing the typological significance of the prophetic ministries of Elijah and Elisha through a series of intertextual allusions concentrated primarily in one section (Luke 7–9). The resurrection of the widow's son at Nain climaxes in the simple sentence, "Jesus gave him to his mother" (7:15), an exact echo of the conclusion of the account of the resurrection of the widow's son at Zarephath through Elijah (1 Kings 17:23 LXX). In the transfiguration, Elijah appears with Moses to discuss with Jesus his impending "exodus" (Luke 9:30–31). The request of James and John for permission to call fire from heaven to destroy an inhospitable Samaritan town recalls the fire from heaven that destroyed troops sent from Samaria's king to take Elijah into custody (2 Kings 1:9–12). Jesus' refusal to allow a would-be disciple to bid farewell to his family, couched in the metaphor of plowing, calls to mind—and contrasts with—Elijah's permission to Elisha when he called him from the plow (Luke 9:61–62; 1 Kings 19:19–21).

---

14   Michael Card, "Lift Up the Suffering Symbol" (1989), recorded on *The Ancient Faith* (Nashville: Myrrh, 1989).

Readers have been prepared to recognize these quite evident echoes of the Elijah-Elisha narratives by Jesus' earlier recollection in Nazareth that Elijah and Elisha were sent to serve Gentiles (Sidonian widow, Naaman the Syrian), thus disclosing the pattern that explains why his own Jewish neighbors were dismissing his authority (Luke 4:25–27).[15]

A few examples from John's Gospel further illustrate the typological links that fall into this category of clear and unmistakable allusion. Jesus' body is the temple that the son of David will rebuild after its destruction in judgment (John 2; 2 Sam. 7:13; cf. Zech. 4:6–14). As Israel observed the Passover to commemorate the exodus that initiated both liberty and trial in the wilderness, Jesus identifies himself as the heaven-sent bread to which manna pointed (John 6). In the context of the Feast of Tabernacles, a reenactment of the desert wanderings, Jesus announces that he is the fulfillment both of the rock that gave living water and of the fiery cloud that gave light to Israel's camp (John 7:37–39; 8:12; Ex. 17:1–7; 13:21–22). Jesus is the Good Shepherd, which David's sons failed to be (John 10; Jer. 23:1–8; Ezek. 34). Jesus is the true vine, which Israel failed to be (John 15:1–17; Isa. 5:1–7; Ps. 80:8–19).

Examples of such widely recognized allusions to Old Testament persons, events, and institutions throughout the New Testament's testimony to Jesus could be multiplied and have been well documented elsewhere.[16] What has been cited is sufficient to establish that, even without employing *typos* terminology or direct Old Testament quotations, the apostolic authors of the New Testament have articulated

---

15   These widely recognized allusions also raise the question whether other allusions, more thematic than linguistic, link Jesus' ministry to that of Israel's prophets of reform, Elijah and Elisha. For instance, Mark and Matthew record Jesus' traveling to the region of Tyre granting the insistent pleas of a woman from Syrian Phoenicia (the region of ancient Zarephath) on behalf of her daughter (Mark 7:24–30; Matt. 15:21–28). The exorcism of a boy concludes with the refrain, "Jesus . . . gave him back to his father" (Luke 9:42). Jesus' feeding of five thousand from five loaves and two fish, with leftovers, reproduces and magnifies Elisha's multiplication of twenty loaves to feed one hundred, with leftovers (Luke 9:10–17; 2 Kings 4:42–44). Might Jesus' mercy to a Roman centurion, a Gentile military officer of extraordinary faith, find its typological counterpart in the cleansing of Naaman, the Gentile military officer of extraordinary faith (Luke 7:1–10; 2 Kings 5)?

16   Goppelt, *Typos*, 61–197; Patrick Fairbairn, *The Typology of Scripture: Viewed in Connection with the Whole Series of Divine Dispensations* (1900; repr. Grand Rapids: Baker, 1975); Paul S. Minear, *Images of the Church in the New Testament* (Philadelphia: Westminster, 1960).

with unmistakable clarity, through linguistic and thematic allusion, an even wider panorama of typological correspondence between the "incarnated" promises embedded in Israel's experience and the incarnate Fulfiller of all God's promises, Jesus the Messiah.

Subtle and Debatable Allusions to Old Testament Events, Persons, and Institutions

With this category we enter a region of greater ambiguity and controversy, calling for increased caution in proposing typological connections and reaching the interpretive conclusions that we intend to preach. In these cases, a parallel between type and fulfillment is not explicitly identified by *typos* terminology, quotation, or undeniable allusion. The lines of connection are subtler, and typically several elements of correspondence are combined to direct the reader to the Old Testament text in view. When individual allusions are subtle rather than overtly stated, these multiple strands of connection between Old Testament pattern and New Testament fulfillment can encourage our confidence that the parallel is in fact embedded in the text of Scripture and not simply imported into it by our own imagination.

One indispensable link, as Goppelt observed in the statement quoted above, must be a shared *thematic* affinity between Old Testament type and New Testament fulfillment in addressing "some aspect of *man's relationship to God*."[17] As we will explore more fully in the next chapter, the patterns of correspondence that God's redemptive plan embedded in Israel's history are *covenantal*, focused on the bond of loyalty by which he binds his creaturely servants to himself as their Lord, Rescuer, Defender, and Commander. Interpretive weight should not be placed on exterior details of an Old Testament narrative, for instance, unless the text itself points to their symbolic or covenantal significance.

On the other hand, a secondary and supportive indicator of typological significance can be the New Testament author's specific semantic choices. The appearance of words or constructions that are atypical of the New Testament author or rare in biblical Greek may signal intentional literary dependence of a New Testament text on a particular Old Testament account. For example, the Greek verb *nosphizomai* ("keep for oneself, embezzle") occurs in biblical Greek

---

17   Goppelt, *Typos*, 202 (emphasis added).

only in the account of Achan's sin at Jericho (Josh. 7:1 LXX) and twice in the New Testament (Acts 5:2; Titus 2:10). Acts 5 narrates the deceptive sin of Ananias and Sapphira and their resultant death for presuming to lie to the Holy Spirit. The lexical peculiarity of the verb selection, in combination with the situational and thematic similarities (Achan and Ananias commit deceit regarding wealth devoted to the Lord, are exposed through divine revelation, and are punished by death), constitutes credible (though not undeniable) grounds for inferring that Scripture's divine and human authors intend us to discern a typological parallel between the purification of ancient Israel through the death of Achan and the purification of the new Israel through the death of Ananias and Sapphira.

Similarly, the coincidence of radiant divine glory and an overshadowing (*episkiazō*) cloud (*nephelē*) with the presence of Moses links the Mount of Transfiguration with the Lord's initial indwelling of the tabernacle (Ex. 40:35 LXX; Matt. 17:5; Mark 9:7; Luke 9:34). The verb "overshadow" (*episkiazō*) in fact appears only three times elsewhere in the Greek Old Testament (Ps. 90:4 [91:4 in ESV]; 139:8 [140:7 in ESV]]; Prov. 18:11), and twice elsewhere in the New Testament (Luke 1:35; Acts 5:15). Peter's proposal to build three tabernacles (*skēnas*), misguided though it was, reinforces the Evangelists' implication that Jesus must be understood as fulfilling the tabernacle, and the tabernacle as anticipating Jesus. This typological link probably even illumines one of the other New Testament instances of *episkiazō*, the mysterious metaphor by which the angel Gabriel responds to Mary's confusion regarding her conception of the promised Messiah in her virginity: "The Holy Spirit will come upon you, and the power of the Most High will overshadow you" (Luke 1:35).

If the appearance of "overshadow" in Luke 1:35 were considered in isolation from its usage in the transfiguration account (9:34) and the broader New Testament motif of the fulfillment of the sanctuary (tabernacle and temple) in Jesus,[18] the claim that Moses' tabernacle and Mary's womb are typologically connected by God himself might well deserve skeptical dismissal. Yet, Gabriel's words do not appear in isolation but in the context of a gospel that paints an intricate fabric of promise-fulfillment patterns to establish Jesus as the unifying focal point of God's entire redemptive agenda for Israel and the nations. Read in the light of the earlier, more explicit categories

---

18   E.g., John 1:14; 2:19–21; 1 Peter 2; etc.

that we have surveyed, these texts, too, fit the framework of apostolic typological-christological-eschatological interpretation of the Old Testament and add texture to the portrait of the coming King that emerges from the Scriptures of promise.

Nevertheless, the lessons learned from patristic and medieval allegorism underscore the wisdom of drawing lines of typological connection cautiously and self-critically, particularly in interpreting texts that fall in this category and the next (in which apparent allusions are dubious and multiple strands are not visible). To be responsible to the Bible's divine Author and credible to our hearers, our identification of typological similarities (as well as contrasts between type and antitype) must be warranted by evidence in the text of Scripture, not merely the product of our own hyperactive imaginations. Literary or linguistic correspondences, as well as thematic resonance and broader contextual factors, are important evidence demonstrating a divinely intended connection between Old Testament persons, events, or institutions and an aspect of New Testament fulfillment, which is centered in Christ and encompasses his church.[19]

General Old Testament Patterns Fulfilled in Christ and His Work

To this category belong those Old Testament passages where we see no direct and convincing linguistic and thematic ground to warrant drawing a typological link between an Old Testament person, event, or institution and the New Testament redemption accomplished by Christ. To recall Spurgeon's illustration, the Hebrew Scriptures in particular abound with texts that give the impression (in the words of the young minister to his Welsh mentor) that "Christ was not in the text." Many Proverbs, for example, seem designed merely to hone relational skills, self-discipline, and other dimensions of pragmatic wisdom, rather than to proclaim "Christ and him crucified." Similar impressions might be taken from blocks of civil legislation in the books of Moses, or prophetic oracles that target Israel's aggressive Ancient Near Eastern neighbors.

Even figures who play a prominent role in redemptive history may not be related to Jesus by way of an explicit quotation or a clear or probable allusion in a particular New Testament passage. Joseph, for example, was instrumental in preserving the covenant line from

---

19   See note 26 in chapter 1, which describes and illustrates the feature of "intertextual allusion" in Scripture.

starvation during drought and famine, and his undeserved suffering was integral to his role as savior. Yet, the only Old Testament quotation pertaining to Joseph in the New Testament concerns Jacob's blessing of Joseph's two sons (Heb. 11:21). Although there is a probable allusion to one of Joseph's dreams in Revelation 12:1, its purpose in John's vision is not to draw a parallel between the ancient patriarch and the messianic child of the heavenly woman. Must we, then, conclude that without a concrete New Testament proof text we are left without apostolic warrant for seeing in Israel's salvation through Joseph's suffering and exaltation any foreshadowing of the final Savior through suffering?

In fact, we do have warrant for seeing Joseph's ordeal and its beneficial outcome, at least in broad outline, as foreshadowing the suffering of Jesus and the rescue that flows from it. Joseph is a key figure in the covenantal history traced by Stephen in Acts 7. First in Joseph, then in Moses, then in the prophets generally, and finally, climactically, in the Righteous One himself,[20] a repeated pattern appears: Although God's people consistently reject the leaders and spokesmen sent by God, he patiently preserves their lives through the very deliverers whom they have spurned. Without invoking *typos*-terminology, Stephen traced a pattern (*typos*) embedded in redemptive history, which had reached its climactic expression in the eschatological appearance of the Righteous Servant, Jesus.

To take another example, I have suggested that David's articulation of lament in Psalm 22 referred, metaphorically and hyperbolically, to his own suffering as anticipatory of the intensified sufferings awaiting the Messiah. We can say this with confidence on the basis of the New Testament's citation of and allusions to Psalm 22. What shall we say of other psalms of lament? Can the apostolic interpretation of explicitly messianic-typological psalms provide the key to the interpretation of other psalms of the same genre? Psalm 88, for instance, sounds depths of despair tragically similar to Psalm 22 ("O Lord, why do you cast my soul away? Why do you hide your face from me?" Ps. 88:14) but without Psalm 22's final ascent from suffering to celebration. It is possible that Luke alludes to Psalm 88:8 ("You have caused my companions to shun me") as he describes Jesus' acquaintances standing at a distance from his cross (Luke 23:49), but by itself

---

20 "Righteous One" is a title of the suffering Servant of the Lord in Isa. 53:11, a text frequently applied to Jesus in the New Testament.

that slight literary thread might seem to some too fragile to tie this bleak psalm to Christ's crucifixion. If, on the other hand, the representative samples of apostolic hermeneutics recorded for us in the New Testament are intended not only to teach us doctrine and the interpretation of isolated Old Testament texts but also to acclimate our minds to *a way of viewing* all of God's dealings with humanity, the patriarchs and Israel in the period of promise, we have good reason to believe that the New Testament interpretation of Psalm 22 teaches us to read the *whole genre of lament psalms* as revelatory of the anguish and abandonment of the ultimately Innocent Sufferer.

The performance of *every* covenantal mediator and participant—patriarch, prophet, priest, judge, king, husband, father, son, parents, children, servant—ultimately is to be interpreted in light of the ways it reflects (or falls short of reflecting) the perfect covenant obedience to be offered by Jesus as the Servant of God and the rescue to be accomplished by Jesus as the Lord of his people—in sum, the consummate mediation that would be achieved by Jesus the Son of God and brother of his people. Judges' failings and kings' injustices demonstrated to Israel the need for a coming king who would render justice with absolute equity and divine omniscience (Isa. 11:1–5). Priests' pollution and mortality showed Israel the need for a coming priest who would represent the people before the presence of God in unblemished moral purity and permanence. Prophets' sufferings in bringing the message of God reflected for Israel the sufferings of the faithful eschatological Word, but even the prophets on occasion display misgivings and a faltering of faith in the message entrusted to them by God. Thus the mixed behavior of covenantal leaders makes each, by virtue of his office, in one way or another, typological of the Coming Deliverer, in whom the roles of prophet, priest, and king would be perfectly fulfilled.

When preparing to preach a passage from which, at first glance, Jesus seems to be "absent," we do well to step back and view the text in the light of the broad themes of Scripture and God's covenant bond with his servant people—motifs such as Lord and servant, or theocratic offices of prophet, priest, and king. The next chapter proposes creational and covenantal frameworks that emerge from Scripture itself to help preachers discover how such passages relate to the Bible's central motif, the redemptive plan of God that centers on Christ's incarnation, obedience, suffering, resurrection, and on-going presence with his people by the Spirit.

Our brief survey of the varying degrees of explicit clarity in the New Testament's Christocentric handling of Old Testament events, institutions, and individuals has acknowledged that it is easier in some Old Testament terrain than in others to follow the interpretive path that the apostles have blazed (through Jesus' instruction and the Spirit's inspiration). Nevertheless, as we have moved from the most overt to the more subtle and suggestive, we have glimpsed a pervasive matrix even in events, texts, and genres that seemed at first to have little demonstrable connection to Christ, the focal point of the apostolic gospel. The next step in acclimating our eyes to this Christocentric pattern is to observe that the way of reading Scripture that the apostles learned from their Master was not a novelty but had precedent in the way that the Old Testament interpreted its own redemptive events and sacramental institutions.

Old Testament Foundations of New Testament Hermeneutics

When we inquire how the apostles and other New Testament authors learned this Christ-centered, redemptive-historical, semi-eschatological[21] way of reading Israel's Scriptures, several plausible

---

21   Apostolic hermeneutics is "*semi*-eschatological" because it expresses the conviction that the last days of judgment and redemption promised in the Old Testament Scriptures have dawned in the incarnation, life, death, resurrection, and exaltation of Jesus (including his bestowal of the eschatological gift of the Spirit), but that God's patient plan for the establishment and expansion of his kingdom of grace among all nations necessitates a delay of the *consummation* of prophetic hope until Jesus' Parousia from heaven. Theological students sometimes refer to this with the shorthand expression "already-and-not-yet." This is handy jargon for seminary lunchroom discussions, but apostolic preachers called to proclaim good news to the nations will need to find translation equivalents (with illustrations) to make this profound reality intelligible to broader audiences. The generation that remembers World War II, for example, would grasp the distinction between "D-Day" (June 6, 1944), the war's decisive turning point, when allied forces began to retake the European continent from Nazi Germany in the costly landing at Normandy, on the one hand, and "VE-Day" (May 8, 1945) and "VJ-Day" (August 15, 1945), on the other, when the final victory over the Axis powers had been achieved. See Oscar Cullman, *Christ and Time: The Primitive Christian Conception of Time and History*, trans F. V. Filson (Rev. ed. Philadelphia: Westminster, 1964), 141–42. Younger generations of listeners will need comparable analogies of triumphs decisively secured but not yet consummated.

answers can be given. First, as we have seen, the canonical Evangelists themselves trace the apostles' insights into Christ's fulfillment of Scripture to the instruction of Jesus himself, both prior to his suffering and especially after his resurrection (John 5; Luke 22:37; 24:25–27, 44–47). This dominical origin of apostolic hermeneutic is the decisive determinant of its authority for those who trust and follow Jesus. Second, parallels have been drawn between the interpretive methods employed in the New Testament's treatment of the Old Testament and the hermeneutic principles and strategies operative in various groups in Second Temple Judaism contemporaneous with the ministry of Jesus and the apostles.[22]

Of course, neither Jesus (who demonstrated noticeable hermeneutic authority and independence from tradition, Mark 1:27; Matt. 5:17–48) nor his Pharisaic, Sadducean, and Qumranic contemporaries within Judaism created a hermeneutic system and strategy *ex nihilo*.[23] Not only did the rabbis appeal to the tradition of the ancients in support of their reading of Scripture; so also Jesus and his apostles insisted that the truths that *they* were drawing out of the Scriptures could have been (and, by God's grace, were) discovered by astute, believing readers of the Old Testament *during the Old Testament period*. It is, as we have seen, implicit in the hermeneutic of Hebrews that the ancient Scriptures themselves contained clues of their eventual obsolescence, signals that the events and institutions to which they bore witness contained a preview of a greater redemption to come. Other New Testament texts teach this even more directly. "Your father Abraham rejoiced that he would see my day. *He saw it* and was glad" (John 8:56). "Isaiah said these things because *he saw his [Jesus'] glory* and spoke of him" (John 12:41). To be sure, Peter states that the prophets inquired into "what person or time the Spirit of Christ in them was indicating when he predicted the

---

22   Longenecker, *Biblical Exegesis in the Apostolic Period*; Enns, *Inspiration and Incarnation*, 120–51.

23   On the other hand, Jesus' hearers found his teaching "new" because he brought it with an authority unparalleled in rabbinic interpretation of the Torah (Mark 1:27; Matt. 7:28–29). His sharp contrast between what had been said in the long succession of Jewish tradition and his own interpretation of God's commands, prefaced by the bold, "But I say," set Jesus apart from Israel's teachers of the law. See Ernst Käseman, "The Problem of the Historical Jesus," in *Essays on New Testament Themes*, trans. W. J. Montague, Studies in Biblical Theology 41 (London: SCM, 1964), 37; Jacob Neusner, *A Rabbi Talks with Jesus: An Intermillennial, Interfaith Exchange* (New York: Doublday, 1994), 29–32.

sufferings of Christ and the subsequent glories" (1 Peter 1:11). But in response to their inquiry, God revealed to prophets (1:12) that their prophetic ministry was not for themselves but for those to whom Peter was writing, who live in "the last times" in which Christ has been manifested (1:20).[24] Although the full disclosure of God's mystery of salvation came only with the historical life, death, and resurrection of Jesus Christ, the New Testament suggests that those living prior to Christ's coming could and did have sufficient revelation to rest their reliance on the coming Redeemer.

Therefore, we should not conclude that it would have been impossible for faithful Israelites in Old Testament times to have discovered in their Scriptures the implications that the apostles later drew out of them. In fact, the theological foundations and roots of New Testament typological hermeneutics can be traced back into the Old Testament itself. Three features of apostolic hermeneutics in particular have precedents in the Old Testament's self-hermeneutic. The Old Testament (1) invests physical events and institutions with symbolic spiritual significance, (2) portrays future redemptive events in imagery drawn from past deeds of God in creation and salvation, and (3) testifies to the incompleteness of the redemption accessible through its own institutions, directing the longings of the people of God forward to a future salvation and Savior.

The Old Testament Invests Events and Institutions in the Physical and Visible Experience of God's People with Symbolic Significance

As far back as the Garden of Eden, the Tree of Knowledge of Good and Evil symbolized a spiritual issue. Eating from it would bring death but not because the fruit was physically poisonous. Indeed, its fruit was "good for food" (Gen. 3:6). Nor was the death that resulted on "the day" (2:17) that Adam and Eve ate the fruit the physical death of their bodies (although that would inevitably come). Rather, the act of eating from the tree constituted a spiritual decision that Eve and her husband made regarding the criterion by which they would "know" good and evil. The issue was whether their moral judgment and behavior would be controlled by what God

---

24 Perhaps Peter is thinking specifically of the scene at the end of Daniel, when the prophet confesses his lack of understanding and is instructed that his words are sealed until their fulfillment at the time of the end (Dan. 12:8–13).

had said (2:16–17; 3:1, 3) or by their "independent" (really, Satan/serpent-influenced) perception of what is good and desirable (3:6). Their autonomy itself and consequent alienation from the Creator who is life's source and sustainer, symbolized in their expulsion from the Garden, was the death that ensued immediately. As the Lord later indicted Israel, using another vivid metaphor, "they have forsaken me, the fountain of living waters, and hewed out cisterns for themselves, broken cisterns that can hold no water" (Jer. 2:13). Thus from the beginning of the Torah, Moses invites his readers to recognize a spiritual depth to events in the physical world.

Further examples could be multiplied, but a few are sufficient to establish the point. The earthly, physical tabernacle that was erected after Israel's exodus from Egyptian slavery is a copy of a heavenly original, shown to Moses on Mount Sinai (Ex. 25:9, 40; see Heb. 8:5). The recognition of an unseen heavenly original standing behind and validating the earthly sanctuary was implied by Solomon at the dedication of the temple, when he distinguished the "house" on earth that he had built from the Lord's dwelling place in heaven, from which the Lord would hear and answer prayers directed toward the earthly temple:

> But will God indeed dwell on the earth? Behold, heaven and the highest heaven cannot contain you; how much less this house that I have built! Yet have regard to the prayer of your servant and to his plea, O LORD my God, . . . that your eyes may be open night and day toward this house, the place of which you have said, "My name shall be there . . . ." And listen to the plea of your servant and of your people Israel, when they pray toward this place. And listen in heaven your dwelling place, and when you hear, forgive. (1 Kings 8:27–30; see also Isa. 66:1–2)

Similarly, Old Testament texts show the animals slain at the sanctuary as atoning sacrifices pointed beyond themselves. The sacrifice of animals was clearly commanded by God in Leviticus. Yet, the Old Testament Scriptures themselves warned that the death of animals would not remove the guilt of the obstinate and rebellious heart (Ps. 40:6-8; 50:7–15; 51:16–17; Isa. 1:11–17; Mic. 6:6-8). "To obey is better than sacrifice, and to listen than the fat of rams," the prophet Samuel told the guilty but defensive King Saul (1 Sam. 15:22). David, Saul's successor, recognized that slain animals could not purge his own guilt: "For you will not delight in sacrifice, or I would give it; you will not be pleased with a burnt offering. The sacrifices of God are a broken spirit; a broken and contrite heart, O God, you will not despise" (Ps. 51:16–17; see Ps. 40:6–8). Moreover, the Old Testament prophetic scriptures spoke of a coming Servant whose sufferings on behalf of the guilty people are compared to the slaying of a sacrificial lamb (Isa. 53).

The olive oil poured over the heads of kings (1 Sam. 10:1, 6, 9–10; 16:13) and priests (Ex. 30:22–33; Lev. 8:12; Ps. 133:2) and prophets (1 Kings 19:16) pointed to endowment with the Spirit of God. The Spirit imparts to kings the wisdom to rule justly (Isa. 11:1–5), to priests the holiness to serve before God (Zech. 3–4), and to prophets the words to speak on God's behalf (Isa. 61:1–2).

Circumcision, the bloody cutting of the foreskin from the male organ, symbolized removal of rebellion and unresponsiveness from the hearts of the Israelites (Deut. 10:16). Circumcision of flesh only was useless when "all the house of Israel is uncircumcised in heart" (Jer. 9:25–26). The Israelites were accountable for the uncircumcised uncleanness of their hearts, but their final hope lay in the promise that the Lord would, in the end, circumcise the hearts of his people and their children (Deut. 30:6).

Old Testament texts also interpret other aspects of the physical rituals of cleansing in terms of their symbolic depth and the spiritual reality to which they point. The "sprinkling with water" ceremony by which defiled people received cultic cleansing to rejoin the worshiping community in the sanctuary pointed to a washing that would be more than skin deep: God's Spirit will replace hearts of stone with hearts of flesh, tender to hear and obey the word of the Lord (Ezek. 36:26–29). Likewise, the hyssop branch used to sprinkle the cleansing blood of atonement (Ex. 12:22; Lev. 14:4–7) points to the cleansing of the conscience within (Ps. 51:7).

Prophetic promise typically employs imagery from Israel's experience of the physical world in order to speak vividly of Israel's spiritual needs and hopes. Physical disability or weakness portrays spiritual timidity: "Strengthen the weak hands, and make firm the feeble knees. Say to those who have an anxious heart, 'Be strong; fear not! Behold, your God will come with vengeance, with the recompense of God. He will come and save you' " (Isa. 35:3–4). The following verses promise the opening of blind eyes and deaf ears, the liberation of mute tongues, and the leaping of the lame like a deer (Isa. 35:5–6). This promise was fulfilled in the physical miracles of Jesus (Luke 7:22–23), but those miracles themselves were *signs*, pointing to deeper and more comprehensive healing. Thus Jesus moves from the healing of a man born *physically* blind to discuss the blindness of people who think they see (John 9). A biblical precedent for this interplay between physical blindness and the more serious spiritual blindness it symbolizes can be seen in Isaiah 42:6–7, 16–20: The Servant is to restore the blind eyes of God's servant-people, turning darkness into light before them in a new exodus-pilgrimage through the desert. But why does God say that *his own servant* is blind (42:19)? "He sees many things but does not observe them; his ears are open, but he does not hear" (42:20). Israel's real disability is not physical but spiritual, not a physical glaucoma but a spiritual inattentiveness and unbelief.[25]

Moses had announced that if Israel kept covenant loyalty with their God, he would send abundant rainfall to nourish the crops of the field (Deut. 28:12). Conversely, if they proved unfaithful, among the curses that would fall upon them would be drought and resulting famine (Deut. 28:22–24). Israel proved unfaithful, and the curse was executed in their physical experience (1 Kings 17:1; etc.). But the prophets also use the imagery of rain to speak of even greater blessings that will fall from heaven (Isa. 44:3–5): "For I will pour water on the thirsty land, and streams on the dry ground." What does this promise mean? The following line explains: "I will pour my Spirit upon your offspring, and my blessing on your descendants." Then Isaiah returns to the image: "They shall spring up among the grass like willows by flowing streams." The meaning? They will confess the Lord's name, saying, "I am the LORD's."

In other words, the Old Testament itself suggests that the visible, external (socio-political-military-agricultural) experience of Israel and its leaders was not only the result of Israel's covenantal-spiritual relationship with the Lord but also a visible reflection of that covenantal-spiritual relationship. Covenant curses and covenant blessings in Israel's exterior experience were signs pointing

---

25   Another example of the interplay of physical miracle and the spiritual reality to which it points as a "sign" (*sēmeion*): The time is *coming*, says Jesus, when all who are in the graves will come out in response to the voice of the Son of Man (John 5:28–29), but the time *has already arrived* when "the dead" (who have not yet *physically* expired and been buried) hear his voice and come to life (5:24–25). The physical resurrection of Lazarus is therefore a sign (12:17–18) that pointed to the reality that the believer will live, even if he dies (11:25–26).

to the invisible, "interior" relationship of the covenant people with their God, either as recipients of the joys of communion with God through trusting obedience or as those deprived of the life-giving favor of God through their stubborn infidelity.[26]

The Old Testament Prophets Promise the Coming Redemption in Imagery Drawn from God's Past Deeds of Creation and Salvation

In the works of the latter prophets (Isaiah, Jeremiah, Ezekiel, the Twelve Minor Prophets), God rebukes his people for their past and present unfaithfulness and speaks of judgment to come but he also promises their renewal and restoration through his coming to them in power and grace in the future. Often this future salvation is portrayed in imagery and language derived from God's mighty deeds in the past. In other words, the Old Testament prophets themselves treat earlier redemptive acts of God as *typological*, as providing a pattern or paradigm by which the believing remnant in Israel can grasp and cling to God's promise that he will intervene in salvation in the future.

The coming salvation will be a new creation: "For behold, I *create* new heavens and a new earth, and the former things shall not be remembered or come into mind. But be glad and rejoice forever in that which I *create*; for behold, I *create* Jerusalem to be a joy, and her people to be a gladness" (Isa. 65:17–18 [emphasis added]; see 66:22). This prophetic promise is the source of the New Testament authors' anticipations of a new heavens and earth, purged of sin and its curse (2 Peter 3:13; Rev. 21:1); but the apostles also announce that this new creation has begun, former things dissolved and new things initiated, whenever and wherever anyone is in Christ (2 Cor. 5:17).

The coming salvation will be a new exodus: "Therefore, behold, I will allure her, and bring her into the wilderness, and speak tenderly to her. And there I will give her her vineyards and make the Valley of Achor[27] a door of hope. And there she shall answer as in the days of her youth, as at the time when she came out of the land

---

26 For further discussion of the symbolic depth of Old Testament events and institutions, see Clowney, *Preaching Christ in All of Scripture*, 20–30.

27 *Achor* means trouble. According to Joshua 7:26, the valley was so named at the beginning of the conquest of the land under Joshua, when Achan's theft of treasures from Jericho that were to be wholly "devoted" to the Lord in destruction "troubled" Israel by introducing defilement into the camp.

of Egypt" (Hos. 2:14–15). E. Earle Ellis has noted: "Exodus 'typology' was not original with Paul or even the early Church. The concept arises in the OT prophets who 'came to shape their anticipation of the great eschatological salvation through the Messiah according to the pattern of the historical exodus under Moses'. "[28] But the future exodus and covenant-making, while in one sense replicating the ancient pilgrimage from Egypt via Mount Sinai to Canaan, also would transcend the old pattern:

> Behold, the days are coming, declares the LORD, when I will make a new covenant with the house of Israel and the house of Judah, not like the covenant that I made with their fathers on the day when I took them by the hand to bring them out of the land of Egypt, my covenant that they broke, though I was their husband, declares the LORD. But this is the covenant that I will make with the house of Israel after those days, declares the LORD: I will put my law within them, and I will write it on their hearts. And I will be their God, and they shall be my people. And no longer shall each one teach his neighbor and each his brother, saying, 'Know the LORD,' for they shall all know me, from the least of them to the greatest, declares the LORD. For I will forgive their iniquity, and I will remember their sin no more. (Jer. 31:31–33)

The preacher to the Hebrews has shown us the fulfillment of this promise—and therefore of the covenant pattern set at Sinai in the similar yet superior covenant of which Jesus is now mediator and guarantor (Heb. 7:22; 8:6–13). Jesus himself pointed the way to this identification by incorporating Jeremiah's prophecy into the covenant ratification meal he instituted: "This cup that is poured out for you is the new covenant in my blood" (Luke 22:20 par.).

The prophets also foresee that the coming salvation will revive the kingship of God over his glad subjects, under the scepter (shepherd's staff) of a new David:

> For thus says the Lord God: Behold, I, I myself will search for my sheep and will seek them out. As a shepherd seeks out his flock when he is among his sheep that have been scattered, so will I seek out my sheep, and I will rescue them from all places where they have been scattered on a day of clouds and thick darkness. And I will bring them out from the peoples

---

28   E. Earle Ellis, *Paul's Use of the Old Testament* (Edinburgh: Oliver and Boyd, 1957), 131, citing also H. Sahlin, "The New Exodus of Salvation According to St. Paul," in *The Root of the Vine*, A. Fridrichsen, ed. (London, 1953), 81.

and gather them from the countries, and will bring them into their own land. And I will feed them on the mountains of Israel, by the ravines, and in all the inhabited places of the country. . . . And I will set up over them one shepherd, my servant David, and he shall feed them: he shall feed them and be their shepherd. And I, the LORD, will be their God, and my servant David shall be prince among them. I am the LORD; I have spoken. (Ezek. 34:11–13, 23–24)

When Jesus identifies himself as the true and Good Shepherd, whose voice the sheep recognize and follow and who lays his life on the line (unlike hired help who care not for the sheep but their wage or thieves who ravage and exploit the flock), he is employing imagery already deeply ingrained in the fabric of Scripture generally (Gen. 48:15; 49:24; Ps. 23; 77:20; 78:52; 80:1; 95:7) and prophetic expectation in particular (Isa. 40:11; Jer. 23:1–8; Mic. 5:4; 7:14; Zech. 11; 13:7).

The coming salvation will include the building of the City of God as a new temple, a sanctuary-spring from which life-giving water flows, supplying trees that bear fruit year-round and leaves that impart healing (Ezek. 40–47; esp. 47:1–12). The entire city—even its most mundane utensils—will be purged from all that defiles, as only the sanctuary had been under the old covenant: "And on that day there shall be inscribed on the bells of the horses, 'Holy to the LORD.' And the pots in the house of the LORD shall be as the bowls before the altar. And every pot in Jerusalem and Judah shall be holy to the LORD of hosts, so that all who sacrifice may come and take of them and boil the meat of the sacrifice in them. And there shall no longer be a trader in the house of the LORD of hosts on that day" (Zech. 14:20–21).

The prophets thus show the close kinship between biblical typology and biblical prophecy. The awesome events that God enacted in the past (creation, exodus, covenant-making at Sinai), theocratic leaders (David) and institutions (temple) all are interpreted by the prophets as "types," as templates or patterns pointing toward eschatological salvation and the eschatological Savior to come. These types, of course, are anchored in real history. It is for this very reason that looking back to them also encourages Israel to look forward to the antitype that fulfills and transcends them. Since the God who speaks the Old Testament Scriptures is the Lord of history, he can and does design historical persons, offices, institutions, and events to function as "incarnate prophecies" of the full redemption to come.

What God said in the *words* of the prophets as they pointed Israel's faith toward the future in the imagery of the past and present, God had also said through his design of the *events* of the history of Adam, Noah, Abraham and the patriarchs, Moses, Israel, and David.

The Old Testament Testifies to the Incompleteness of the Redemption Accessible through Its Own Institutions, Directing the Longings of the People of God Forward to a Qualitatively Superior Future Salvation and Savior

The biblical understanding of history is not cyclical but linear. Thus the element of resemblance or similarity that is highlighted when the New Testament interprets an Old Testament event, person, or institution as a *typos*—a preview pattern of Christ and his redemptive work—is not based on the perspective of the common cliché, "History repeats itself." Rather, history has direction. It is moving toward a specific goal, the triumph of God and the universal acknowledgement of the kingship of God. One assumption on which apostolic hermeneutics is based, therefore, is that the Old Testament Scriptures and the institutions established in response to God's instruction in the Law and the Prophets are incomplete, leaving loose ends that could only be tied together through an eschatological intervention of God in an era that lay in the future from the standpoint of the ancient prophets and their contemporaries.

As we saw in the previous chapter, one of the key emphases of the epistle to the Hebrews is that Old Testament Scriptures contained divinely intended, semi-latent signals that something "better" than the then current (pre-Messiah) situation awaited the people of God. Hebrews argues that the promise of a new covenant in Jeremiah 31 implies the need for a better bond that transcends the law and secures eternal forgiveness (Heb. 8:7–13). This prophecy implied the first covenant made at Sinai was not faultless, for if it had been "there would have been no occasion to look for a second" (8:7). In promising a "new" covenant, God implicitly declared the Sinaitic covenant old and obsolete, on its way to expiration (8:13). Likewise, the preacher to the Hebrews points out that the warning of Psalm 95 against hardness of heart that excludes the unfaithful from God's rest was spoken by David (Heb. 4:7–8) long after Joshua's day, when Israel enjoyed rest on every side (Josh. 21:43–45). This warning therefore implies that those dwelling in the land and even enjoying rest from surrounding enemies may fail to enter into the fullness of blessing signified by the promise of "God's rest" (cf. also 2 Sam. 7:1, which applies the language of Joshua 23 to David). The land bestowed through Joshua was no more than a faint shadow of the secure inheritance for which the patriarchs and their children in faith looked and longed: a heavenly country (Heb. 11:16), an enduring city (11:10, 16; 13:14), a kingdom that cannot be shaken (12:28). So also the promise of a royal priest in the order of Melchizedek in Psalm 110 is God's way of indicating the insufficiency of the Levitical order of priests, even while those priests still ministered in the temple (Heb. 7:11–19). The law that mandated priestly succession based on genealogical descent had the weakness of death built into it. But in Psalm 110, God prophetically consecrates a priest who will hold his office and perform his atoning and intercessory service forever.

The prophetic pictures that portray the coming age of salvation via the *typoi* of early redemptive events characterize the future not merely as a replication of earlier patterns but as a "correspondence with heightening" (as Goppelt rightly observed). The "heightening" that the prophets predict implies some inadequacy in the covenantal structures by which Israel related to her Lord. In Ezekiel 34, for example, the promise is indeed that "David" will again shepherd the flock of God. But because the human shepherds of Israel (including David's royal dynasty as well as the Aaronic priesthood) have failed to defend and rule God's sheep in justice, *the Lord himself* intends to come and search out his lost sheep and bind the wounded (Ezek. 34:11–22). Will the Lord be Israel's true shepherd? Yes. Will the Branch descended from David be Israel's true shepherd? Also yes—and the Branch raised up to David will bear the name, The LORD Our Righteousness (Jer. 23:5–6). The eschatological shepherd of Israel would correspond to the pattern set by David, for he was the norm of whole-souled commitment by which all his successors would be judged (see 1 Kings 14:8; 15:3, 11; etc.). Yet, the final Shepherd of Israel will be greater than a son of David, even greater than David himself: "I will gather the remnant of my flock" (Jer. 23:3).

Thus within the Old Testament itself, we find the hope and promise of a coming redemption that not only fits the pattern of earlier divine deeds in history (creation, exodus, conquest) but also transcends the old patterns and institutions ordained by God for that promise period in which the prophets preached and wrote. To come in the future is a covenant that cannot be broken by Israel's sin, a divine rest that transcends peace in Palestine, an eternal priest to replace Aaron's stained and mortal sons, and an act of atoning obedience that will render sacrificial animals obsolete. The transitory nature of the Old Testament order and institutions is implied in the prophets' promise of a greater salvation to come.

The inadequacy of the Old Testament order also is indicated by the "loose ends," the unresolved tensions that plagued Israel's experience under the law. The promises of God, on the one hand, and the situation confronting Israel, on the other, were often in sharp contradiction, and the conflict cried out for resolution. Consider, for example, Psalm 89. The first section of the psalm (vv. 1–37) celebrates the eternity of God's covenant with David and the inviolability of the divine promises on which the Davidic royal dynasty was resting: "My steadfast love I will keep for him forever, and my covenant will stand firm for him. I will establish his offspring forever and his throne as the days of the heavens" (vv. 28–29). Here the psalmist stands squarely on the promise that God spoke to David in 2 Samuel 7:15–16: ". . . my steadfast love will not depart from [your son], as I took it away from Saul. . . . And your house and your kingdom shall be made sure forever before me. Your throne shall be established forever." Then, at verse 38 the tone suddenly changes: "You are full of wrath against your anointed. You have renounced the covenant with your servant; you have defiled his crown in the dust" (vv. 38–39). The descendant of David is dethroned, covered with shame and disgrace. In anguish the psalmist cries out, "How long, O LORD?" (vs. 46). The promise of God stands in unresolved tension with the experience of the exile, yet the psalmist's response is not cynicism or despair. Rather, he looks to the future and cries out longingly for the reversal of "David's" dishonor, a reversal that must eventually come from the God who keeps his promises.

A similar tension exists with respect to the priesthood. In Numbers 25:11–13, in recognition of the zeal of Aaron's son Phineas for the holiness of Israel when it was threatened by Moabite seduction, the Lord promised a covenant of eternal priesthood to Phineas and his descendants. Yet, as we have seen, the Old Testament also contains the motif of another category of priesthood established by God, a royal priesthood patterned after the ancient king-priest Melchizedek, whom Abraham acknowledged as a mediator by offering the Lord's tithe and receiving the Lord's blessing (Heb. 7:1–10, commenting on

Gen. 14:18–20). In Psalm 110:1–4 we find the promise that *this* king, seated at God's right hand, will serve as priest forever, his eternal tenure in office secured by an oath from God himself. Who holds the eternal priesthood: the successive generations of Phineas' descendents or the single successor to Melchizedek, the priest-king who lives forever? How can this tension *within the Old Testament Scriptures themselves* be resolved?

Other "loose ends" in the Old Testament could be cited. First, Israel in the north and then Judah in the south were carried off into exile, expelled from the Lord's land for breach of his covenant. Yet, the Lord preserved a remnant of Judah, returned them to his land, and resettled them there. From the ruins of Solomon's temple, another was built, though not as splendid as its predecessor. The restoration from exile did demonstrate God's faithfulness and power to keep his promises. But the remnant returned not to the glories of the kingdom of David and Solomon (much less to an Edenic paradise restored) but to a situation of weakness, fragile peace, and spiritual ennui. Those who returned from exile had been chastened and purged from the most overt expressions of pagan idolatries but still lay in the grip of self-centeredness and acquisitive materialism (Hag. 1:1–11). Could the return from exile to a city and land in shambles, still subject to alien oppressors, be the "new exodus" and "new creation" promised in the prophets? Must there not be more?

These intolerable tensions arise from the fact that life and blessing in covenant communion with God is, on the one hand, *absolutely secured* by God's promise, and yet it is, on the other, certainly *contingent* on the submissive obedience of God's servant-people and their leaders. How, indeed, can God's richest, greatest promises come true for his people, if those blessings are to any degree contingent on the faithful obedience of the human covenant servant (whether Israel/Judah or the king)? As the books of Samuel-Kings show so clearly, sons of David who resemble their ancestor in whole-souled commitment were few and far between. Worse yet, as 2 Samuel demonstrates too clearly, David himself was far from a *perfect* prototype of just and holy leadership. The "man after God's heart" (Acts 13:22) also abused his power and position to gratify his desires, cover his guilt, and exploit his loyal subjects. In order for the richest blessing promised by the Lord to come to his people, we needed the arrival of a covenant Servant characterized by a purity of devotion to God unparalleled by *anyone* in Israel's previous history, even God's friend Abraham, Moses who saw the face of God, and David the model king. The unresolved tensions within the Old Testament cried out for resolution in the coming of the Lord and the coming of a Servant unstained by the infidelities that had always polluted Israel and her leaders.

The Hermeneutic Implications of Old Testament Typology

As we view these three features of Old Testament revelation— the symbolic depth of Old Testament events and institutions, the prophetic portrayal of future redemption in patterns (*typoi*) set by God's previous deeds, and the embedded signals of incompleteness—we discover that the connecting threads that come to expression in apostolic hermeneutics have been woven into the fabric of Scripture from its very beginning. This discovery, in turn, can help us to avoid two of the serious missteps that have plagued preachers throughout church history as they sought to draw lines of relevance from the biblical text to their contemporary hearers. As we have seen in Paul's theology of preaching, both the covenantal character of Scripture and its purpose to address hearers' deepest needs for reconciliation with God and re-creation in his image demand that preachers show the relevance of the Bible to their listeners. Too often, as we saw in chapter 4, the line of relevance has been drawn, either unconsciously or with creative intentionality, either by way of allegorism or by way of moralism. How does the pattern of connection between the biblical text and our contemporary hearers that we have seen exemplified in Hebrews and now see emerging more generally from both Old Testament prophetic and New Testament apostolic hermeneutics differ from allegorism and from moralism?

Students and readers who have benefited from Edmund P. Clowney's insights into Christ-centered, redemptive-historical preaching will recognize Figure 1, which appears in slightly different forms in his homiletic publications.[29]

---

29   Edmund P. Clowney, "Preaching Christ from All the Scriptures," in Logan, *The Preacher and Preaching*, 179; Clowney, *Preaching Christ in All of Scripture*, 32. This figure is taken from the latter work, with permission of Crossway Books. Clowney credits Richard Craven for the suggestion to add the "allegory" and "moralism" arrows to the figure.

Figure 1 "maps" several "roads" (think of each arrow as a road) by which preachers may try to transport the message of an Old Testament event or institution in its original historical and literary con-

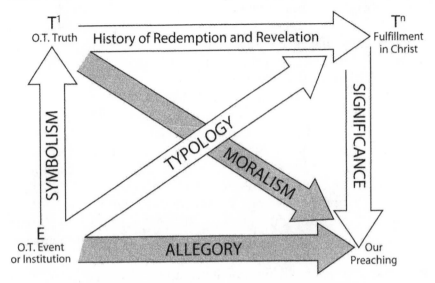

Figure 1: Redemptive-Historical Hermeneutical "Map"

text (= E in the lower left corner of the rectangle) and the spiritual needs of our twenty-first century listeners (= "Our Preaching" in the lower right corner). Most preachers instinctively recognize that we must make this trip, transporting our precious cargo, if we are to avoid turning our sermons on Old Testament narrative into lectures on Ancient Near Eastern history. But only one of the road networks mapped above retraces the route by which the apostles expounded the Scriptures, exposing their pervasive witness to the Christ. The others are "short cuts" that seem to do a plausible job of connecting ancient text with modern hearers, but they bypass the crucial intersection in Jesus (upper right), and so impoverish the message that is finally delivered.

Allegory

Allegory is based on a recognition that Old Testament events must be read in light of the symbolic depth of Israel's redemptive history. As we saw in chapter 4, in its more reflective patristic expressions, its ancient practitioners saw themselves as reproducing apostolic hermeneutics (such as Paul's "allegory" of Hagar and Sarah in Galatians 4) and saw allegorizing as a cogent method for interpreting texts in which biblical characters receive implicit or explicit divine approval for actions that violate other moral norms in Scripture (e.g., Abraham's sacrifice of Isaac). In one sense, then, the allegorical hermeneutic could be credited with resisting a rigid moralism that turns every Old Testament character or event into a positive or negative illustration of ethical behavior.

On the other hand, as the shaded arrow at the bottom of the rectangle implies, allegory draws direct symbolic connections between the historical details of an Old Testament event and our hearers' experience or theology, with little or no regard for the event's symbolic depth and redemptive significance *in its own place in redemptive history*. The event is treated as a disembodied and dehistoricized picture of a theological truth, and the question is often ignored whether the original readers—at their point prior to Christ's coming—could even possibly have glimpsed in the event the meaning that the Christian interpreter now attributes to it. The result is a symbolic reading of Old Testament narratives that largely disregards the historical "shaping" of special revelation as recorded in Scripture and cuts the interpreter's imagination free from the "control" of the Bible's original contexts, both historical and theological. The allegorical interpreter prematurely draws too direct a line between the ancient text and his Christian hearers, without first asking the question of the spiritual and covenantal significance to its ancient participants and original recipients (T^1 = truth to the first power). As a result, the meaning (or layers of meaning) that he symbolically derives from the text, even when it articulates doctrines related to Christ and his saving work, fails to disclose how Christ fulfills the redemptive significance of the original Old Testament event, replacing the imperfect with perfection and historical foreshadowings with reality (T^n = truth to the ultimate power). T^n unquestionably surpasses T^1 by far; the exponents imply that fulfillment in Christ transcends the covenantal, redemptive, and spiritual efficacy of Old Testament event, persons, and instructions not merely quantitatively but qualitatively. But there are important lines of real continuity between Adam's, Abraham's, and Israel's experience of deliverance and communion with their covenant God and the fullness of rescue and intimacy achieved for us by Jesus. To ignore these in preference for symbolic links of one's own imagination is to devalue God's progressive outworking of redemption and revelation in history, as well as to undercut the credibility of the relevance one is seeking to draw between the ancient text and one's listeners.

Moralism

Moralism has been defined in various ways. Occasionally, any summons to concrete behavioral change in a sermon has been dismissed and condemned as "moralism," even though the New Testament epistles and the teaching of Jesus are full of such ethical instructions. More credible is the definition of moralism as the homiletic practice of issuing ethical demands without grounding them in the gospel or showing how they are integral to a grateful response to the redemptive work of God in Christ. The result of such moralistic preaching is that hearers come away with the impression that God's favor towards them rests to some degree on their (always imperfect) performance of obedience and love, rather than wholly on the perfect obedience and vicarious suffering of Jesus Christ. This moralistic subtext may not be the intent of the preacher, whose doctrine of salvation may be orthodox. It may rather be the indirect result of omission, perhaps based on the assumption that eventually Christians no longer need to be reminded that Christian living (both its power—union with Christ—and its motive—grateful love, secure in the Father's favor) flows from the grace revealed in the gospel. Nevertheless his hearers may come away with a heavy sense that God's approval must be achieved by strenuous effort.

The subset of moralism represented in Dr. Clowney's diagram is sometimes called "exemplarism," which treats Old Testament events and individuals primarily as examples, either positive or negative, of the life of covenant faithfulness. Exemplaristic preaching seems to be imitating apostolic models when it urges Christian listeners to avoid negative examples such as Israel's unbelief in the wilderness (Heb. 3–4; 1 Cor. 10) and to emulate positive examples such as the champions who acted on their faith (Heb. 11). At its best, then, moralistic preaching does ask about the covenantal (spiritual, ethical) dynamics and symbolic depth at work in the Old Testament event and text in its original context. In this respect its interpretation respects the integrity of redemptive history and places the preacher's interpretation under the legitimate constraints of the historical and literary contexts in which the text appears within the unfolding of progressive revelation and the canon of Scripture. Drawing the shaded diagonal line ("Moralism") directly from the symbolic/spiritual/ covenantal significance of the Old Testament event in its original context ("T¹") to our current ethical issues ("Our Preaching") does, at least, take seriously the spiritual and symbolic significance of the original event in its Old Testament setting.

The great weakness of moralistic, exemplaristic preaching is its tendency to enlist Old Testament examples in order to lay ethical obligations on hearers without showing how Christ kept covenant faithfulness where the negative examples failed, and how Christ's perfect righteousness fulfills even the best obedience offered by the Old Testament's most positive examples. By "cutting the corner" and bypassing the text's "fulfillment in Christ" (Tⁿ in the upper right corner of the rectangle) in a desire to show the text's relevance to hearers' daily struggles and relationships, moralism excises from the biblical narratives the source of their life-changing power, which is their testimony to the saving mercy of God in the obedience and sacrifice of Jesus. When Christ and his all-fulfilling role as Lord and Servant of the covenant are left out of the "equation," the narratives of Noah, Jacob, Joseph, Samson, David, and Nehemiah are subtly transformed from gospel into law: "Do this and live"; "Imitate X and live."[30] The law, however, as "holy and righteous and good" as it is as a divine standard (Rom. 7:12), is weakened by our fallen, sinful nature and cannot impart the life and spiritual strength needed for us to obey its commands or emulate its positive exemplars (Rom. 8:3; Gal. 3:21; 2 Cor. 3:6–9). What, then, sets apostolic, redemptive-historical typology apart from allegory on the one hand and moralism on the other?

Redemptive-Historical Typology

Old Testament events, offices, and institutions (E) are invested by God with spiritual significance as integral steps in his history-long project to reverse sin and its effects, bringing his redeemed people into the new creation in which he will be glorified not only for his majesty, holiness, justice, power, and wisdom, but also for his amazing grace. Like the New Testament sacraments of baptism and the Lord's Supper, these Old Testament events, offices, and institutions

---

30   Chapell, *Christ-Centered Preaching*, 289–93, warns against "The Deadly Be's": "Be Like" Messages, "Be Good Messages," and "Be Disciplined" messages.

point beyond themselves, symbolizing the comprehensive, eschatological salvation that is God's purpose for history and that has been inaugurated by Christ in his first coming and that will be consummated by Christ in his second coming. As we have seen, even in the Old Testament the prophets revealed the symbolic depth of events (exodus), offices (king), and institutions (sanctuary, sacrifices). They called the hopes of God's people forward to a greater, deeper, more lasting salvation, inheritance, worship, etc., than that experienced by Israel in the period of promise.

Old Testament types were like the sacraments in another respect: they were seals as well as signs or symbols. That is to say, they were not merely pictures by which God revealed to the patriarchs and Israelites salvific blessings reserved completely for those privileged to live in the aftermath of the Messiah's redemptive achievement. Rather, those ancient events and institutions (including "sacraments" such as Noah's rainbow, Israel's feasts, and the sanctuary with its sacrifices) were actually means of grace by which God elicited and strengthened faith in the coming Messiah, thereby applying to Old Testament believers in advance the benefits of the redemption that Christ would accomplish "in the fullness of time" through his death, resurrection, and ascension. Thus God "preached the gospel beforehand" to Abraham, who believed (Gal. 3:8). God had bypassed Abraham's sins in anticipation of Christ's propitiating sacrifice, by which God is now, at last, shown to be just (Abraham's sins have not gone unpunished) and yet also the justifier of the believer in Jesus (Rom. 3:26). Although Paul confessed his personal history as one who acted "ignorantly in unbelief" (1 Tim. 1:13), he also could speak as a representative of ancient Israel, distinguishing "we [Jews] who were the first to hope in Christ" from the Gentiles who were subsequently included through the gospel (Eph. 1:12).

As we shall see more fully in the next chapter, following the apostles' hermeneutic and homiletic footsteps demands disciplined and patient attention to all the relevant contexts of any biblical text. To understand how any Old Testament event (or office or officer or institution) preaches Christ and finds its fulfillment in him, we first must grasp *its symbolic depth in its own place in redemptive history* (the "symbolism" vertical arrow from E to T^1 [truth to the first power]). The Passover lamb's blood declared that the exodus was not simply the political liberation of an oppressed people from a wicked and tyrannical empire: Israel's sons were as liable to death at the hands of God's angel of wrath as were the sons of Egypt! Without a substitute's blood smeared on the doorframe of Israelite houses, their firstborn were under the divine death sentence, no less than those of their oppressors. The ram supplied by God as substitute for Isaac provides prior context, and the interpretation of animal sacrifices offered in the tabernacle within the Pentateuch itself points the way to the symbolic depth of this ritual. Later Scripture corrects Israel's failure to recognize the depth to which the slain animals pointed (Ps. 40:6–8; 50:7–15; 51:16–17), and prophets pointed to a Servant who would justify many by bearing their sin and guilt as a silent lamb (Isa. 53).

Then we need to consider how the event's (office's/officer's, institution's) original symbolic depth (the aspect of redemption to which it pointed in shadow-form) finds final and complete fulfillment in Christ (the "history of redemption and revelation" horizontal arrow from T^1 to T^n [Truth to the "nth" power]). Every redemptive, salvific experience of Old Testament saints fell short of the fullness of salvation brought by Christ and was dependent, ultimately, on his redeeming work. The exodus was a marvelous demonstration of the Lord's faithfulness, power, and mercy to Israel for the patriarchs' sake, but many of those who experienced it dropped in the desert through unbelief (Heb. 3–4). David was a man after God's own heart, but he committed adultery and murder. When his external enemies had been put down (2 Sam. 7:1), soon his own sin gave rise to more dangerous enemies within his own house (2 Sam. 12:11). Paul's "mystery revealed" language (Rom. 16; Eph. 3; Col. 1; etc.) shows that the earlier chapters in the story can only be interpreted rightly in light of the story's climax. Unless we place the "clues" that are strewn along the way in the light of the resolution of the mystery at the end, we will misread the clues. Therefore, having identified the spiritual significance of the event in its own place in redemptive history, we do not move immediately from Joseph's spiritual trials (for example) to ours. Instead we let the history of revelation guide our line of sight from Joseph to Jesus (the horizontal arrow across the top of the rectangle). The "typology" diagonal is drawn with confidence and credibility when we have walked deeply into the event's symbolic meaning in its own epoch, and then walk forward along the trajectory of history to the fulfilled meaning of the event in Christ. We are following the hermeneutic path that the apostles learned from Jesus, neither bypassing the meaning of the event in its own historical context nor ignoring the fact that the event and its immediate historical context are threads woven into a larger tapestry, the pattern of which is seen finally and fully in Jesus.

Finally, having viewed the text through the lens of the fulfillment of its redemptive, symbolic depth in Christ, we must identify and articulate how its message applies to ourselves and our twenty-first century listeners (the "significance" vertical arrow from T^n "Fulfillment in Christ" to "Our Preaching"). Although we have acknowledged that "redemptive-historical preaching" has sometimes gotten (and perhaps sometimes deserved) a reputation for avoiding any application more specific than "rejoice in what Christ has accomplished for you and in your heaven-centered life in him," in fact the apostles' proclamation of Christ as the fulfillment of all God's promises provides abundant direction for the grateful outworking of this good news in personal discipline, family life, church life, and public life in the marketplace—and, if necessary, in a prison, like Paul.

Christians are united to Christ by faith, both *representatively* and *vitally*. Our representative union with the Savior entails the objective gospel truths that he obeyed God's law *for* us, suffered the law's curse *for* us, and was raised and vindicated *for* us. Therefore we have obeyed, been condemned, and been vindicated in him, our covenant head. Our vital union with Christ entails the subjectively applied gospel truth that he imparts his resurrection life to us by the Holy Spirit, initially and invincibly drawing us out of death and into the life of the new creation and subsequently producing covenant faithfulness—the fruit of the Spirit—*in* us.[31] The typological interpretation of the Old Testament that is shown in the apostolic writings of the New Testament does not stop when the "typology" diagonal has been drawn from the Old Testament event to its infinite fulfillment in Christ. Christ's saving work is not only forensic, outside us (justification, adoption) but also dynamic, within us (new creation: regeneration, sanctification)—and the two strands will converge in glorification. On that day, when our lowly bodies are transformed to

---

31 Goldsworthy, *Preaching the Whole Bible*, 92–94, helpfully summarizes the relation of the gospel to Christian believers: "The Gospel as the work of Christ FOR us. . . . The fruit of the Gospel as the work of Christ IN us. . . . The consummation of the Gospel as the Work of Christ WITH us."

be like Jesus' glorious body (Phil. 3:21), our resurrection not only will be the public demonstration that God has declared us righteous and adopted us as his children through faith in Christ (Rom. 5:17–18; 8:23), it also will complete the project of subjective vivification and conformity to Christ's holiness that the Spirit began in our regeneration (Rom. 8:10–11, 29–30; 1 John 3:2–3). So redemptive-historical preaching, as the apostles practiced it, addresses not only what Christ has done *for us* as the faithful covenant Servant but also what Christ is doing *in us* to make us into faithful covenant servants. We draw the "significance" arrow from who we are in Christ to how we are to express this new identity, the gift of his grace, in living—from "Fulfillment in Christ" to "Our Preaching."

Conclusion

Seeing Christ throughout the Scriptures demands a patient and humbling process of listening as the apostles point out to us the interwoven patterns (or, if your prefer Spurgeon's metaphor, the interlocking highway system) that make the Bible's diverse documents, belonging to diverse genres and ages, cohere around a central theme: God's redemptive, restorative, recreative agenda for world history. Our survey in this chapter has moved from the most explicit and least controversial Old Testament typological interpretations that the New Testament authors offer to more subtle intertextual allusions and thematic links that tie the events, leaders, and institutions in ancient Israel, on the one hand, to the person and work of Jesus the Christ for and in his new community, on the other. We also have observed the roots of apostolic hermeneutic and homiletic in the Old Testament's interpretation of itself, further enriching our perception of the texture interwoven into the pages of Scripture and the ages of redemptive history. In the next chapter, our discussion turns from observing the patterns of apostolic hermeneutic and homiletic to questions of how to implement apostolic proclamation today. We will see how two pervasive biblical motifs—creation and covenant—function both as bridges and as guardrails—linking the wide diversity of both Old and New Testament Scriptures to their central hub and at the same time providing reassuring restraint for all whose aim is to proclaim not their own ingenuity but God's pure Word and witness to his Son.

8

Preaching Christ, Head of the New Creation and Mediator of the New Covenant

If, in fact, God's design to redeem his creation and the special revelation that accompanies its outworking (now preserved for us in Scripture) are constructed on a substructure, a divinely designed foundation that links anticipation and fulfillment, foreshadow and reality, in a pattern of correspondence with intensification, simply recognizing that so marvelous a tapestry exists does not in itself settle the question of validity in interpretation.[1] We need a "map" of the foundation that will serve us in two ways: first, to protect us from missteps in guiding our hearers from Scripture's diverse texts to Jesus and, in Jesus, to ourselves; and second, to demonstrate to others a persuasive warrant for the route that we invite them to walk with us.

As we surveyed the ebbs and flows of Christ-centered preaching in the church's history, we saw sharp disagreements among those who were confident that they perceived the Christ-focused pattern embedded in redemptive history and Scripture. In part as a result of such conflicts, the enterprise of reading and preaching every Scripture as witness to Christ was subjected to much needed chastening by the Reformation's insistence on Scripture's single sense and, subsequently, came under hostile attack through the Enlightenment's

---

1 E. D. Hirsch, *Validity in Interpretation* (New Haven: Yale University Press, 1967), critiques the dialectical hermeneutics of Hans Georg Gadamer, *Truth and Method* (1960; ET New York: Seabury, 1975), as well as later reader-response theories of interpretation, arguing that a text's meaning can be reasonably and responsibly inferred as that intended by a text's original author and must be accorded preeminence.

challenges to divine sovereignty in history and divine authorship of Scripture. Much of the debate between Alexandria and Antioch, between allegorical and typological approaches to Christ-centered reading and preaching of Scripture, concerned the question of which contexts illumine and validate one's interpretation of a biblical text. Similarly, the conflict between the consensus of the church's historical hermeneutic (whether patristic allegorical or typological, medieval fourfold or Reformation single sense) and modern historical criticism focuses on the simple but profound question whether later revelation—specifically, the New Testament's witness to Jesus as the Christ—constitutes a legitimate context that warrants or validates interpretations of earlier revelation.

The life context (*Sitz im Leben*) of a text's original recipients constitutes the occasion of its composition, which in turn shapes the purpose that the author sought to achieve through his writing. This life context also typically sets the parameters of the cognitive "horizon" within which the first recipients would have interpreted the text as it came to them. Although various historical and documentary resources can be useful in the effort to reconstruct the original recipients' life context, it can be inferred most reliably from signals in the text itself and its close literary contexts. Although it must be confessed that some ancient interpreters (and some modern preachers[2]) have been guilty of "non-contextual"[3] readings of biblical texts, neglect of the text's meaning in its original context cannot be charged against recent advocates of redemptive-historical preaching. Clowney, for example, insists that the text first be read in the context of its original situation and epoch in the history of revelation: "The first step is to relate the text to its immediate theological horizon. This is to carry the principle of contextual interpretation to the total setting of the revelation of the period. It is a step which homiletical hermeneutics cannot afford

---

2   See Greidanus' critique of Charles Spurgeon's disregard of OT texts' original contexts in his effort, even by means of allegory, to lead his hearers to Christ (*Preaching Christ from the Old Testament*, 158–62).

3   G. K. Beale *Right Doctrine*, 387–404, defends the NT writers from the charge of "noncontextual exegesis," that is, interpretation that disregards an OT text's original historical and literary contexts. In another sense, however, Jewish and Christian allegorists (Philo, sometimes Origen, and the latter's Alexandrian, medieval, and modern successors) were not so much guilty of *non*-contextual interpretation as of exegesis that gave *other* contexts (e.g., subsequent church dogma and tradition) preemptive preference over the original contexts in the validation of interpretation.

to overlook."[4] Greidanus, likewise, in laying out "the Christocentric method" of redemptive-historical interpretation and proclamation, insists: "First, understand the passage in its own historical context."[5]

Redemptive-historical homileticians, such as Clowney, Goldsworthy, and Greidanus, would go on to insist, however, that apostolic precedent warrants our reading and preaching ancient Old Testament texts not only in their original contexts but also within the flow of the history of revelation, and especially in light of the climax of that history in Jesus the Christ. To "preach the whole Bible as Christian Scripture" (Goldsworthy) means to take the context of the whole canon into account as we proclaim any text—not only the Scriptures already extant when a particular passage was given, but also those given in subsequent epochs of redemptive history. Here, as we have seen, historical-critical and even evangelical biblical scholars demur for various reasons: a denial of divine sovereignty over history or divine inspiration of Scripture, a literary theory that restricts a text's "meaning" to that which could be discerned in its original literary and historical contexts, or a desire to maintain credibility by shunning the imaginative extremes of the church's pre-critical reading of Scripture.

In my estimation, none of these objections to the apostolic way of seeing Scripture can withstand the cumulative evidence provided by the signals surveyed in the previous chapter, from the explicitly identified types to the subtler "advance echoes"[6] that NT authors find in Old Testament events, persons, and passages. The pattern that emerges from these points of correspondence affirms the reality of God's interventions in the history of Israel—hence the importance of attention to the text's original historical and literary contexts—and

---

4 Clowney, *Preaching and Biblical Theology*, 88.

5 Greidanus, *Preaching Christ from the Old Testament*, 228. He goes on to describe this first step as including literary, historical, and theocentric interpretation (229–30).

6 This vivid metaphor for Old Testament types is derived from Philip Yancey, *The Bible Jesus Read* (Grand Rapids: Zondervan, 1999), 199. Yancey credits as the source of this picture C. S. Lewis's essay, "The Weight of Glory," in which Lewis portrays the experiences that intimate that we are created for another world, which he elsewhere calls Joy, Longing, or *Sehnsucht*, as "the scent of a flower we have not found, the echo of a tune we have not heard, news from a country we have never visited." (C. S. Lewis, *The Weight of Glory and Other Addresses* (1949; repr. Grand Rapids: Eerdmans, 1965), 5. Like the biblical image of "shadow" (Heb. 10:1), the "advance echo" metaphor implies that historically earlier revelation is dependent on subsequent revelation for both its meaning and its soteric effectiveness.

the orientation of those past interventions toward the apex of God's redemptive intervention, the incarnation, ministry, death, and resurrection of the Son.

Still, the question remains, does Scripture itself—from Genesis to Revelation—disclose motifs that both warrant and control our practice of Christ-centered hermeneutics and homiletics in the "school" of the apostles (and, ultimately, of the risen Lord)? Two motifs that seem to undergird the whole redemptive agenda unveiled in Scripture are the themes of new creation and new covenant. Both appear on the opening pages of Genesis, as well as in the closing pages of Revelation. Each contains a variety of sub-themes that suggest a web or network of connections that can help us trace warranted, credible links not only between diverse Old Testament protagonists and events and Jesus but also between diverse Old Testament literary genres and Jesus. The motifs of new creation and new covenant also point the way toward appropriate (heart-searching, grace-grounded, behavior-transforming, and specific) application of each text's unique message.

The Bible's Theology of History and Contextual Interpretation

As we have seen, the Second Helvetic Confession (ch. 2) identifies *purpose* and *context* as two key elements in biblical interpretation (as in the interpretation of any literature). Literature is written for a purpose: to inform, persuade, motivate, inspire, comfort, entertain, elicit emotion, instill hope, effect reconciliation, or in some other way to summon to action or evoke response. It is especially evident that the Bible is written to effect change, to instill in people the wisdom that leads to salvation by teaching, rebuking, correcting, and training in righteousness (2 Tim. 3:15–17). As Paul writes to the Colossians, the word of truth bears fruit and grows as God imparts, through that gospel, the spiritual understanding and wisdom that enables those who believe it to "walk in a manner worthy of the Lord" and pleasing to him as they bear fruit and grow (Col. 1:5–6, 9–10).

The purposes of Scripture are not unrelated to each other; they are complementary reflections of God's manifold wisdom. The diversity and unity of Scripture disclose the marvelously diverse and unified plan of God for the whole history of the cosmos. Paul speaks of this purpose of God in Ephesians 1: "And he made known to us the mystery of his will according to his good pleasure, which he purposed in Christ, to be put into effect when the times will have reached their fulfillment—to bring all things in heaven and on earth together under one head, even Christ" (vv. 9–10 NIV). Here is an over-arching statement of the biblical theology of history. History is under God's control, and is in fact the working out of his purpose (see vs. 11). His purpose is the unification of all things under the sovereignty of Christ. As Peter T. O'Brien has observed, these "all things" include both "things in heaven" (namely, spiritual principalities and powers that are in rebellion against God's righteous reign, Eph. 6:10; cf. 1:21; 3:10) and "things on earth" (especially Jews and Gentiles, who stand in need of reconciliation through Christ's blood, 2:11–22; cf. 1:11–13).[7] "Both Ephesians and the companion Letter to the Colossians presuppose that the unity and harmony of the cosmos have suffered a considerable dislocation, even a rupture, requiring reconciliation or restoration to harmony."[8] Although in Ephesians Paul envisions the summing up and unification (*anakephalaioō*) of "the fragmented and alienated elements of the universe" in Christ as awaiting future consummation, in Colossians he stresses that the reconciliation already has begun in the death of Christ.[9] Yet, in writing to the Ephesians, Paul implies that the reunification of the shattered universe has begun with Christ's atoning work on the cross when he affirms in Ephesians 3:10 that the church, now composed of reconciled Jewish and Gentile believers, exhibits God's manifold wisdom to spiritual powers in heaven, bearing witness that demonic forces of evil have been decisively defeated at the cross and "now await their final overthrow."[10]

At the most general level we are therefore justified in concluding that no event of history is adequately interpreted apart from its relation to this cosmic agenda of God, centered in the eschatological Lordship of Christ. This is even more obvious with respect to the events of redemptive history recorded in Scripture, and thus we can also recognize—still at a very general, abstract level—that no text of Scripture is adequately understood, explained, or applied unless it is somehow related to God's cosmic plan.

God's plan to bring everything under Christ's headship has the particular shape that it does because human sin has introduced

---

7   Peter T. O'Brien, *The Letter to the Ephesians* (Grand Rapids: Eerdmans, 1999), 112–13.

8   O'Brien, *Ephesians*, 114

9   O'Brien, *Ephesians*, 112, 114.

10   O'Brien, *Ephesians*, 247.

rebellion, disruption, opposition, decay, and death into history. The presence of these ugly realities is acknowledged in Ephesians 1: for those chosen by God to be holy and blameless in his sight, adopted as his sons, bringing praise to his glory, there must be "redemption through the blood" of God's Beloved One, "the forgiveness of tresspasses" (vs. 7). Therefore, we could rightly describe the cosmic plan of God for history, revealed in Scripture, as an agenda for erasing sin and its effects—and in fact through grace carrying us (and creation with us) *even higher and deeper* into knowing and glorifying him than would have been possible in an unfallen world. God through Christ is in the process of reversing the effects of the fall into sin and producing a "new creation" in which relationships between God and humans, humans and one another, and humanity and the rest of the created order are right, harmonious, and delightful. He is in the process of establishing an everlasting kingdom of "righteousness and peace and joy in the Holy Spirit" (Rom. 14:17), a kingdom of love for God and love for one another (Matt. 22:37-40). Covenant is the dominant biblical structure for *relationship*—between God as Lord and his people as servant, but also among his people as fellow servants of the covenant Lord.[11] Therefore, the relational and corporate dimensions of the new creation objective that God pursues throughout history are well captured in the "new covenant" promise of Jeremiah 31:31–34, and we have seen how central this theme is to the whole theology of history laid out in the epistle to the Hebrews.

The Bible is the instrument of the Holy Spirit to announce and to apply what God has done to reverse sin's dire results, for it is through this Word, God's personal communication to his people, that the Spirit liberates us from self-trust and creature-worship so

---

11   Others have argued that "kingdom" is the dominant biblical context for relationship, and that God's reign over his people has been structured from the beginning in a series of covenantal administrations. See, for example, Meredith G. Kline, *Kingdom Prologue: Genesis Foundations for a Covenantal Worldview* (Eugene, OR: Wipf and Stock, 2006); Graeme Goldsworthy, *Gospel and Kingdom*, in *The Goldsworthy Trilogy* (Carlisle, UK: Paternoster, 2000), 51–122. For many people today, however, "kingdom" has overtones limited to the political sphere. God's relationship to his people, while it certainly is a relationship of a sovereign to his subjects, is more complex than the analogy of human political arrangements can capture. Scripture's own imagery implies as much in supplementing the concept of a political treaty-covenant with the family metaphors of the bond between husband and wife, and the combination of authority and gentle compassion that characterizes a father's relationship to his children.

that we trust and serve the Creator who alone deserves our absolute allegiance. So our interpretation of any particular text ultimately needs to consider how that text contributes to this comprehensive, redemptive "new creation/new covenant" purpose of God for world history, and of course also to the comprehensive purpose that he intends his Word to fulfill in the application of Christ's saving achievement to particular individuals and congregations.

We must consider the relationship of our particular text to other portions of Scripture, its place and meaning in relation to its relevant contexts, which are not only the paragraphs that precede and follow it, the biblical book of which it is a part, and other biblical books prior to or at the same point in redemptive history, but also subsequent passages that lie further along on its trajectory toward the consummation of new creation and new covenant. Preachers who recognize the divine authorship of Scripture and divine sovereignty over history realize that these relationships cannot be random, accidental, or arbitrary; rather, they must reflect the manifold wisdom of God as they disclose the marvelously diverse and unified plan of God for history. Thus our interpretation of Scripture and our proclamation of its message not only should examine each text in its immediate historical and literary contexts but also relate it to the comprehensive redemptive purpose of God and therefore to the structure of the rest of Scripture: How does *this specific text* fit into the "big picture," and what is its distinctive contribution to the "big picture"?

The Grand Drama: Creation, Fall, Redemption, Consummation

Scripture opens with the creation of a universe that is pronounced "very good" by its Creator (Gen. 1:31), once he has formed the crown of his creation, man: created in God's image, created male and female, exercising delegated authority over the rest of creation. Sadly, the Bible soon records the forfeiture of the Creator's good gifts by Adam and Eve through their belief in the lie and their enacted declaration of independence from their Creator. The creature's treachery, however, cannot thwart the Creator's good and wise purpose. God persistently intervenes in human history and eventually invades history in person through the Son's incarnation, death, and resurrection as the second and last Adam. The Son's entrance to accomplish the Father's redemptive will (Heb. 10:5–10) marks the dawn of the "last days," the birth of a new creation that eventually will be consummated in a "new heavens and a new earth in which righteousness dwells" (2 Peter 3:13; cf. Rev. 21:1, 4). Hence the "big picture" overview of global history can be summed up in four words: creation, fall, redemption, and consummation. In other words, paradise prepared, paradise lost, paradise reopened, and paradise regained.

Creation: The Divine Image Bestowed

Although the Bible affirms the goodness and value of the whole created universe, including plant and animal organisms subordinated to humanity, the Genesis record concentrates on the creation of man, male and female, "in the image of God," emphasizing the pivotal role occupied by our human race in the plan of God and the authority structure of his created order. The curse pronounced not only on the first man and woman but also on the ground for Adam's sake (Gen. 3:17) implies his role as a covenant representative whose decision and action brings consequences (potentially benevolent, but actually destructive) on all his subjects throughout his whole kingdom. These implications of Adam's covenantal role are made explicit by the apostle Paul, who traces both humanity's guilt and our death to Adam's disobedience (Rom. 5:12–21; 1 Cor. 15:21–22).

Paul echoes the original creation account to portray the transformation according to the divine image that is now being experienced by those who are in Christ: renewal in knowledge (Col. 3:10) and in righteousness and holiness of the truth (Eph. 4:24). These elements are taken up by the Reformed catechisms as providing clues to the content of humanity's original innocence as the bearers of God's image, an innocence that was lost in our fall into sin. The Westminster Shorter Catechism, for instance, explains that "God created man male and female, after his own image, in *knowledge, righteousness, and holiness*, with dominion over the creatures."[12] The Heidelberg Catechism, having spoken of human depravity and spiritual impotence, asks, "Did God create people so wicked and perverse?" and answers, "No. God created them good in his own image, that is, in *true righteousness and holiness*, so that they might truly *know* God their creator, *love* him with all their heart, and *live with him* in eternal happiness for his praise and glory."[13] Thus from Paul's implication that those who undergo new creation in the image of God will

---

12   WSC 10 (emphasis added).
13   Heidelberg Catechism Q/Ans. 6 (Lord's Day 3), emphasis added.

be increasingly characterized by right knowing (truth), right ruling (righteous and loving exercise of authority), and right relationship (holiness in God's presence), the implication is drawn that these virtues were constitutive of humanity's original innocence and were lost through Adam's disobedience. (In another sense, as will be observed below, human beings continue to bear, or to be,[14] God's image even after the fall into sin.)

Genesis is sparse in its description of conditions prior to sin's entrance into human experience, but there are clues to justify the inference drawn by the Reformed catechisms. Righteousness in the exercise of authority is implied in the mandate given to the first couple to "fill the earth and subdue it and have dominion over the fish of the sea and over the birds of the heavens and over every living thing that moves on the earth" (Gen. 1:28). Moreover, the restriction placed on humanity's authority to rule—the prohibition of the Tree of the Knowledge of Good and Evil—entails a requirement to exercise authority righteously, in submission to the Creator by whose delegation Adam and Eve have received dominion.[15]

The tree and the test focused on the issue of knowledge: its source and it criterion. As the temptation account will show, God's prohibition of a single tree in the Garden called Adam and Eve to trust God as their source of knowledge, above his deceptive rival and even their own senses, which perceived the tree not as posing the threat of death (as God had said, 2:17) but as "good for food . . . a delight to the eyes . . . and to be desired to make one wise" (3:6). Prior to that tragic act of epistemological independence, however, we see evidence of Adam's true knowledge, reflective of his Creator,

---

14   See D. J. A. Clines, "The Image of God in Man," *Tyndale Bulletin* 19 (1968): 53–103, who argues that the Hebrew grammar in Gen. 1:26 should be read, "Let us make man *to be* our image," that is, to function as the visible representation of God and thus to symbolize his dominion over his earthly realm. On Clines's reading, then, humanity's creation *as* (rather than "in") image of God is to be explained not in terms of specific ways in which human nature resembles the Creator's nature (intelligence, volition, etc.) but in the functional role of "exercising dominion" over other creatures. Nevertheless, "after our likeness," probably placed in synonymous parallelism with "in/as our image," implies resemblance to God as well as rule on behalf of God.

15   Kline, *Kingdom Prologue*, 29: "Man is made with the glory of an official dominion that is holy, righteous, and true in its ethical character, a dominion that has promise ultimately of a perfected manifestation in the luminosity of human glorification."

in his naming of the animals (2:19–20) and in the words by which he identifies the companion provided for him (2:23). As God exerted his authority and expressed his truth, creating and defining his creatures through his spoken words, so Adam exhibited intelligence and exercised his delegated authority through his words.

Later in redemptive history, holiness would characterize the tabernacle and temple, sanctuaries that were consecrated and set apart as the place of meeting between the Lord and his people. Because the Lord himself is supremely holy (Isa. 6), set apart from his creatures in his infinite majesty and purity, access into his presence demanded holiness, as was dramatically demonstrated in the plethora of ceremonial regulations guarding the sanctuary from defilement, and those who were defiled from the consuming holiness of God. Eden itself was a sanctuary, and Adam was to be the guardian of its holiness.[16] "The LORD God took the man and put him in the garden of Eden to work it and keep it" (Gen. 2:15). The verb "keep" (*shamar*) will appear again in Genesis 3:24, when God places cherubim with a flaming sword at the Garden's entrance to "guard" (*shamar*) the way to the Tree of Life. When the original guardian of the holiness of God's meeting place failed and God's presence caused him terror rather than delight (3:8), cherubim were stationed to forbid the fallen priest-protector entrance into the presence of the holy King.[17]

Fall: The Divine Image Defaced

The temptation itself constituted a challenge to and a violation of truth, authority, and relationship (Gen. 3:1–6). The Evil One, speaking through the serpent, invited God's vice-regents to establish themselves as independent authorities, usurping the right of God to define good from evil. He contradicted God's declaration of truth, denying the death sanction that God had threatened for disobedience (3:4). The tempter promised a knowledge that would make creatures "like" their Creator not as image bearers but as equals (3:5). Consequently, Eve set aside the way of knowing by hearing and heeding the voice of her Maker and sought knowledge instead from the tongue

---

16   Kline, *Kingdom Prologue*, 31–32

17   In Solomon's temple, two massive statues of cherubim, each approximately eighteen feet high and eighteen feet from outstretched wing tip to wing tip, guarded the entrance from the holy chamber into the Most Holy Place. Past these guardians only the high priest, only once yearly on the Day of Atonement, could pass (1 Kings 6:23–28).

of the deceiver and her own perception (3:6). Satan even assaulted Adam's and Eve's relationship with God by planting in their minds suspicion of God's motives in forbidding the Tree of the Knowledge of Good and Evil (3:5).

The effects of the fall likewise can be viewed in terms of the damage done to truth, authority, and relationships (3:7–24). The guilty man and woman, having exchanged God's truth for a lie but now confronted with the reality of their sin by the presence of their holy Creator, sought to evade the truth of their own accountability, shifting blame to others (3:12–13). Nevertheless, God exerted his authority in the form of curses on the man, the woman, the serpent (3:14–19). Among the curses is that the earth henceforth would resist man's authority (bearing thistles in response to wearying labor), just as man had tried to cut himself loose from God's authority. God also demonstrates his authority by excluding them from the Garden. The broken relationship between the human couple and God is indicated in their flight from the coming Lord, showing that their guilty consciences sensed their alienation from him (3:8). This breach is judicially confirmed in his decree that they be excluded from the Garden of God (3:22–23). Other relationships also fell apart, of course: husband and wife hide from one another even before they hide from God, ashamed of their nakedness (3:7). Husband turns on wife in a futile attempt to deflect the searching gaze of the Holy One (3:12). Marriage becomes a power struggle rather than an intimate collaboration (3:16).[18] The soil itself turns hostile to man's labors (3:17). Adam and Eve are expelled to a wilderness existence, clouded by confusion and deceit, oppressed by futility, injustice, and the abuse of authority by humanity, polluted and banned from the Father's holy home, for which they were created, as terrifying fiery guardians now block their access to the Tree of Life.

Thus the fall into sin distorted humanity's knowledge of God's truth, our exercise of God's authority, and our relationship with God. Sinful people still must be protected and honored as bearers of the

---

18 The meaning of "Your desire shall be for your husband, and he shall rule over you" has been much debated, but the use of the same verbs, "desire" (*teshuqah*) and "rule" (*mashal*) in God's warning to Cain about the enemy about to ambush him imply that conflict and power struggle are in view: "Sin is crouching at the door. Its desire (*t^eshuqah*) is for you, but you must rule (*mashal*) over it" (Gen. 4:7). See Susan T. Foh, *Women and the Word of God: A Response to Biblical Feminism* (Phillipsburg: P & R, 1979), 67–69.

divine image. Therefore, the wanton destruction of human life warrants the judicial taking of the murderous aggressor's life: "Whoever
sheds the blood of man, by man shall his blood be shed, for God
made man in his own image" (9:6). Even contemptuous speech toward others is condemned as a violation of their identity as bearers
of God's image: "With [the tongue] we bless our Lord and Father, and
with it we curse people who are made in the likeness of God" (James
3:9). Fallen humans still think and know God, but apart from God's
gracious Spirit, they suppress this knowledge, fleeing down the laby-
rinthine paths of their own minds. Fallen humans still "subdue" the
earth and maintain societal structures of authority, but apart from
God's gracious Spirit we resist other human authorities and God's authority and resent the "unfairness" of a world insubordinate to our
preferences. Fallen humans still are in relationship with each other
and even with the Creator whose holiness we have offended, but apart
from God's gracious Spirit, the relationships among us are soured by
self-centeredness and our relationship with the Creator can only be
one of alienation, since our self-inflicted pollution is repugnant to his
purity.

Redemption: New Creation Begun and
the Divine Image Restored

As implied by the apostle in Colossians 3:10 and Ephesians 4:24,
one fruitful way of viewing God's history-long redemptive project
is in terms of the new creation of the human race in the image of
God. Christ, the image of God and the last Adam, is (not surprisingly) the pivot point of this new creation. In Christ, God has accomplished the decisive reversal of the fall and its toxic by-products.
A new Adam has faced and obediently endured temptation, not in a
garden-sanctuary but in a hostile desert-exile, "with the wild animals"
(Mark 1:13). Throughout his life on earth, he lived "by every word
that comes from the mouth of God," unlike Adam and (later) Israel
(Matt. 4:4), thereby submitting both his will and his knowledge to his
Father. "Concerning that day and hour no one knows, not even the
angels of heaven, nor the Son, but the Father only" (Matt. 24:36). His
exercise of authority was righteous, not self-serving, but intent always
and only on accomplishing "the will of him who sent me" (John 4:34;
5:30). He was announced by God's angel and confessed even by demons as the Holy One of God (Luke 1:35; Mark 1:24). Obviously, his

relationship with the Father is uniquely intimate (Matt. 11:27; John 17:22–23), and of him God says, "This is my beloved Son, with whom I am well pleased" (Matt. 3:17).

Through their union with Christ believers experience a progressive reversal of the fall in the new creation, and it is this subjective renewal, initiated and now in process, to which Paul refers in Colossians 3:10 and Ephesians 4:24. Jesus, the Light of the World, exposes our guilt, but he also cleanses it through his sacrifice. Consequently, those who are drawn to the Father through Jesus no longer need to flee God's truth, distort God's truth, or evade or suppress God's truth. After the image of their Creator, they are "created in righteousness and holiness *of the truth*" (Eph. 4:23 NASB) and "renewed in *knowledge*" (Col. 3:10).

Similarly, our redemption and restoration constitute a return to "rightness" with respect to God's *authority* and our authority. We are renewed "in *righteousness*," set free from the ancient curse but also liberated in will from the enslaving dominion of sin and set free to obey the living God. Although we do "not yet" see all other creatures subdued under the feet of the new humanity, the heirs of salvation, the crowning of Jesus with glory and honor carries with it the assurance that his brothers are being led with him and by him to glory (Heb. 2:8–10; cf. 1:14). The Son of Man exercised his universal authority in an unexpected way, not demanding service but serving others (Mark 10:44–45). So also those being renewed in his image share his authority and must exercise it both justly and humbly.

Finally, the new creation involves a restoration of holiness in *relationship to God*: "renewed in *holiness*," that is, the purity that makes us fit to stand in God's presence, to glorify and enjoy him forever. Salvation accomplished by Christ and applied by the Spirit is more than forensic justification, more than the forgiveness of sins and vindication on the ground of Jesus' righteousness. It also includes objective reconciliation, erasing the alienation that kept us at a distance from God and others, the creation of a community and family characterized by trust, integrity, intimacy, and love. And it includes subjective sanctification in inner and outer life, producing in us minds confirmed to God's truth and desires obedient to God's authority. Ultimately, it even includes the reversal of the physical outworking of sin at Christ's return and in our resurrection and the formation of the new heavens and earth, as we will see below.

Because these three aspects of our original identity as image of God—*knowledge* of the truth, *righteousness* in exercising authority, *holiness* in relationship—have been distorted and defiled by our fall into sin, they provide useful categories for our analysis of the various occasions that lie behind the different texts of Scripture. Bryan Chapell has defined a biblical text's Fallen Condition Focus as "*the mutual human condition that contemporary believers share with those to or about whom the text was written that requires the grace of the passage for God's people to glorify and enjoy him.*" More concretely, it is the spiritual need of the original recipients that "required the writing of this text." [19] Their need may be intrinsic, that is, their own sin or unbelief may need to be confronted and corrected in and by the text; or it may be extrinsic, at least in part: false teaching, persecution for the faith, injustice, or other forms of suffering. Or it may be a combination of internal and external "fallenness" factors, such as we noted in the first recipients of the "sermon" to the Hebrews. Analyzing the needs of Scripture's first recipients in terms of the three aspects of the divine image and sin's distortion of knowledge, authority, and relationship will help preachers recognize the relation of the passage's *telos* to God's history-long "new creation" project. Did Israel need to hear Isaiah 40 because she was deceived and deceptive (instead of embracing true knowledge), willfully disobedient (instead of righteous), or defiled and alienated (instead of holy, with access to God's presence)? (Of course, Israel's need and the divine remedy presented in the text may be a complex that combines more than one aspect of humanity's fallenness and distortion of the image of God.) Viewing the text through these perspectives on the image of God (bestowed, distorted, and restored) also enables the preacher to discern and demonstrate the relevance of the text to the needs of his contemporary hearers, who, like ancient Israelites or first-century Galatians, are created in God's image and need to be created anew into the image of Christ, both individually and communally.

These three aspects of our identity as the creaturely image of God roughly correspond to three categories of mediatorial leaders who functioned in Israel: prophets, kings, and priests.[20] Prophets

19   Chapell, *Christ-Centered Preaching*, 50-51.
20   Meredith G. Kline, *Images of the Spirit* (Grand Rapids: Baker, 1980), analyzes man's creation in the image of God in terms of kingly (pp. 27–28ff.), priestly (pp. 35–56), and prophetic (pp. 57–96) roles with greater detail and exegetical support than are offered in this chapter.

spoke God's *truth*, summoning his people and their established leaders (priests, kings, and elders) to face reality as God defines it. Kings and judges were responsible to reflect God's *authority*, his right to order his servants' lives according to his perfect justice. Priests entered into God's holy presence, bringing sacrifices to remove pollution and effect reconciliation—to reestablish a *relationship* of intimacy and blessing between the Lord and his wayward servants.[21] The New Testament's witness to Jesus as the apex of covenantal mediation affirms his fulfillment of each of these offices: prophet (Acts 3:22; cf. Heb. 1:1–2; John 1:1), king (Acts 2:30–36), and priest (Heb. 7). Reformation catechisms wisely followed the New Testament's lead, summarizing the redemptive work of Jesus Christ under these three categories.[22] We will reflect more on the work of Christ as prophet, priest, and king after we have considered another pervasive biblical perspective on God's redemptive purpose, the inauguration, breach, restoration, and consummation of God's *covenant*.

Consummation: New Creation Completed and the Divine Image Perfected[23]

The realization that the "last days" foretold by Israel's prophets had dawned with the incarnation, ministry, death, and exaltation of God's Son as Messiah did not lead the apostles to conclude that God's history-long campaign to recapture his own kingdom and to eradicate his enemies had reached its ultimate objective. Although it was widely expected in Second Temple Judaism that Messiah's appearance would precipitate cataclysmic "birth pangs" and the last judgment and final separation of the righteous from the wicked, Jesus' parables, especially the tares sown among wheat and the servants entrusted with minas, told a different story (Matt. 13:24–30, 36–43; Luke 19:11–27). Even when the Messiah had been vindicated by resurrection and had bestowed the eschatological gift of the Spirit on his community, the long-suffering God would still delay the day of final sifting, prolonging rebels' opportunity to repent (2 Peter 3:9). That

---

21 The priests' ministry also included communication of God's truth, inasmuch as they were the custodians and teachers of the law of God given to Moses (Deut. 31:9–13; Mal. 2:4–7).

22 E.g., Heidelberg Catechism, 31; WSC 23–26; WLC 42–45.

23 I am thankful to my colleague David VanDrunen for suggesting, in response to an earlier draft of this chapter, that this fourth category, consummation, is needed to complete the biblical story.

delay also entails, however, believers' ongoing struggle against their own sin and suffering in the midst of a sin-cursed world. Although in a real and significant sense those in Christ have entered the new creation and "put on" the new Adam in his righteousness, holiness, and truth (2 Cor. 5:17; Eph. 4:24), they cannot and do not claim to have reached sinless perfection (Phil. 3:12–13; 1 John 1:8–10). Nor are they immune to the sufferings common to the present sin-cursed order. In fact, their identity as members of Christ's new creation order now exposes them to intensified, and even violent, opposition from the enemies of their King.

Christians' present experience of the regenerating and sanctifying Spirit of God, who vivifies the whole new creation order, only serves to whet their appetite for the complete re-creation, yet to come: "And not only the creation, but we ourselves, who have the firstfruits of the Spirit, groan inwardly as we wait eagerly for adoption as sons, the redemption of our bodies" (Rom. 8:23). Achievement of the purpose of *perfection*, of which Paul wrote in Colossians 1:28, still awaits the day of *presentation*, when the exalted Christ returns from heaven bodily and in overwhelming glory. Only then will history witness "the . . . restoration of all things" (Acts 3:21 nasb), and those who have tasted the firstfruits will be satisfied with the fullness of the Spirit's new creation transformation: "Beloved, we are God's children now, and what we will be has not yet appeared; but we know that when he appears we shall be like him, because we shall see him as he is. And everyone who thus hopes in him purifies himself as he is pure" (1 John 3:2–3). The future hope of consummate purity as those completely recreated into the image of Christ spurs on Christians' present pursuit of holiness in their semi-eschatological present (see also Col. 3:1–4). Likewise, the prospect that the radiant return of their King will end their suffering and sorrow fortifies their perseverance under present afflictions: "Our citizenship is in heaven, and from it we await a Savior, the Lord Jesus Christ, who will transform our lowly body to be like his glorious body, by the power that enables him even to subject all things to himself" (Phil. 3:20–21).

The certain hope of becoming fully conformed to the image of the beloved Son (Rom. 8:29) therefore "spills back" into believers' present both to motivate and to empower their growth in imitation of Christ by grace, through faith. Their incremental progress by Christ's Word and Spirit only serves to stir their longing for the sight of One who is the supreme image of God, for only in the presence of his glory will they reflect without any distortion whatsoever the Creator's true knowledge, righteous authority, and holy intimacy. The book of Revelation portrays history's consummation as a new heavens and earth, cured of the curse once for all, which will be home to a human community that has been transformed to *know* God and each other truly, having kept the trustworthy words of God (Rev. 22:6–9; cf. 20:4), to reign *righteously* with the Lamb (22:5; cf. 3:21; 5:10), and to see God's face and worship in *holiness* (22:4; cf. 3:4–5; 7:9–17).

Covenant: Lord and Servant

Although the term "covenant" (*berith*) is not used in Genesis to designate the original commitment that bound the newly created Adam to his creator,[24] the essential features of later biblical covenants between God the covenant Lord and his people as his servant are visible in Genesis 1–2. Characteristically, divine-human covenants in Scripture are formal, legal, oath-bound commitments to maintain loyalty that are secured by a sanctioning curse, in the event that loyalty should be breached. In later covenants, the curse sanction often was symbolized in the ratification ceremony by the blood or carcasses of sacrificial animals (Gen. 15:7–21; Jer. 34:15–20; Ex. 24:6–8). Although no bloodshed is entailed in the covenantal commitment that God demands of Adam prior to the fall, the Lord of the covenant clearly identifies the curse sanction that should have secured Adam's persistent loyalty (Gen. 2:17). Later biblical references to Adam as a covenant breaker (Hos. 6:7) and one whose guilt- and death-inflicting disobedience parallels Christ's righteousness- and life-bestowing obedience (Rom. 5; 1 Cor. 15) confirm identifying the Lord-servant relationship between God and unfallen Adam as a covenant.[25]

Space does not permit a thorough survey of the unfolding history of biblical covenants. This has been provided well by others,[26] and at this point our interest in the covenantal structure of Scripture focuses on the roles of the Lord and servant in the covenant relationship. Reformed confessions have good warrant, I believe, for

---

24   *Berith* first appears in connection with God's commitment to Noah, Gen. 6:18.

25   See M. G. Kline, *Kingdom Prologue*, 1–4, 10–14; O. Palmer Robertson, *Christ of the Covenants*, 67–87.

26   Vos, *Biblical Theology*; Kline, *Kingdom Prologue*, especially for covenants leading up to God's call to Abraham; Robertson, *Christ of the Covenants*.

distinguishing God's covenantal arrangement with unfallen Adam as a "covenant of works," in which the avoidance of curse and implied reception of blessing were directly contingent on Adam's personal unswerving obedience, from God's later covenants, all of which are administrations of an overarching "covenant of grace" which God has established with his sinful people. In each expression of the covenant of grace, God has bound himself to bestow blessing on people who have broken his covenant and violated his commands, on the basis of a Surrogate's covenant keeping, which God graciously imputes to them despite their infidelity.[27] The typological link that Paul draws between Adam and Christ in Romans 5 presupposes that each exercises the office of a covenantal representative whose fidelity or failure in covenantal commitments effects the blessing or cursing of those on whose behalf he acts. Of course, the apostle cannot leave the impression that performance of the covenant heads of the old humanity and the new humanity are merely parallel structures, even though they share the common feature of covenantal representation: "But the free gift is *not like* the trespass. For if many died through one man's trespass, *much more* have the grace of God and the free gift by the grace of that one man Jesus Christ abounded for many" (Rom. 5:15, emphasis added). Christ excels Adam not only because he obeyed where Adam rebelled, but also because the vindication and blessing of eschatological life that Jesus' fidelity justly deserves are bestowed on believers as a free gift of grace.

The covenantal structure is built into God's relationship with his human creatures from creation and finds various expressions in subsequent redemptive history. In view of this pervasive structure, readers and preachers of Scripture do well to approach every text with special attention to the information it yields concerning the parties, obligations, and consequences of the covenant. The first post-fall covenant, brief as it is, brings into view the participation of both parties to the covenant, Lord and servant, in undoing the damage done through Adam's failure. Genesis 3:15, the proto-evangelium, is the earliest announcement in history of God's plan to reverse sin and its consequences and to restore humankind and creation to our original purpose. Because God has determined that the plan would be *revealed* and clarified in progressive stages corresponding to its *implementation* in progressive stages down through

---

27 WCF, ch. 7. WLC 20.

history, this first announcement of the gospel is understandably general: "I will put enmity between you [Satan/the serpent] and the woman, and between your offspring and her offspring; he shall bruise your head, and you shall bruise his heel." Entailed in this terse curse on the Evil One is the truth that the bringing of redemption to mankind is God's work—and it is man's. We see God's initiative: "I will put enmity between [the serpent] and the woman." But we also see a crucial role for the woman's seed, who will *through his own suffering* crush the Evil One. In subsequent covenants with Noah, Abraham, Isaac, Jacob, Moses, Levi, David, and finally the new covenant promised in Jeremiah 31 and secured by Jesus, the spotlight falls sometimes on the role of the Lord, sometimes on the role of the servant, and sometimes on their mutual commitments.

The two-sided activity alluded to in the primeval redemptive promise of Genesis 3:15 provides a useful paradigm for us as we seek to relate every Scripture to the cosmic renewal to which God has set his hand. Redemption and renewal come to this sin-sick world only by God's initiative, but at the same time redemption and renewal does not come apart from the costly faithfulness of the woman's Seed. This two-sidedness is embodied in the institution of covenant, which structures God's relationship with his people down through the Old Testament (old covenant) ages and on into the New. Biblical covenants are treaties that express a committed relationship of love and loyalty (gratitude, exclusive allegiance, obligation) between God as sovereign and his chosen people as servant. Genesis 3:15 is the redemptive covenant in miniature. The initiative for restoring the bond of love and loyalty is taken by the Lord of the Covenant. The very concept of "new creation" implies, as the Bible often repeats, that the initiative for reversing the fall cannot lie with fallen humanity. We are responsible and therefore guilty but also utterly incapable of undoing the damage we have done. Nevertheless, from another perspective, the restoration of human beings to covenant blessedness is contingent, finally, on the fidelity of a human Servant of the Covenant. The new creation cannot come apart from *a man's* defeat of Satan (Gen. 3:15). The man first created to be God's image had failed. Israel, the son and servant of God would fail. Israel's prophets, kings, and priests would all fall short. Still, one who is the image of God must be the head of the new humanity.

We will be helped in practicing apostolic hermeneutics if we keep in mind the two-sided relationship that was disrupted by sin and that must be reestablished by costly, faithful initiative *from both sides*: the covenant Lord must extend grace to rebellious servants; a covenant Servant must offer himself up in unblemished covenant faithfulness and in so doing bear the covenant curse in place of the rebels. The "indicatives" and the "imperatives" of Scripture—law and gospel—ultimately find their meeting point in Jesus Christ, the God-man. He is the center point of Scripture's "indicative" gospel proclamation of the gracious initiative of God to rescue, redeem, and renew. He also is the ultimate Covenant Servant, the embodiment of obedience to the law imperatives of God, and as the Seed of the Woman he not only offers perfect obedience *for* us throughout *his* earthly life (even obedient to death, the death of the cross) but also effects growing obedience *in* us throughout *our* earthly lives.

The Lord and the Servant Who Is Prophet, Priest and King

Combining our reflection on redemption as our restoration to true knowledge, righteous authority, and holy relationship with our reflection on the reality that redemption is both the work of God the Covenant Lord and the work of the faithful man, the Covenant Servant, we will find this matrix of categories helpful as we reflect on the diverse themes of Scripture and seek to find their unifying center in the person and work of the Messiah.

With respect to God's *truth*, Christ comes as the Lord of the Covenant, the spokesman for the Father, the prophet like Moses, the Word in flesh, and the Truth who defines truth. From the perspective of his role as the Servant of the Covenant, Christ is the Israel who lives in the desert by every word that proceeds from God's mouth, who can speak the Word because his ear is always humbly open to the Father's instruction (Isa. 50:4–9, alluded to in Luke 9:51; cf. Matt. 26:67).

With respect to God's *authority*, Christ is the King, the champion who rescues us from Satan's domain, the Commander whose royal law gives true liberty. But Christ has this authority and wields it rightly not only because he is God the Son eternally, the Lord of the Covenant, but also because, as Messiah and Servant of the Lord, he is rightly related to the Father's authority in unswerving obedience.

With respect to our *relationship* to God, Christ is the Holy One from whose pure presence demons recoil. But he also is the Holy

One who lives among sin-stained humans and restores us to intimacy with God.[28] More than that, he is the Lamb of God, whom God provides to atone for sin, and he is the holy brother-priest who cares for us with compassion and cleanses our consciences so that we may serve in God's presence acceptably. He is the ever-living priest who intercedes for his kinfolk without interruption.

We can add more detail to our "map" of the covenantal texture of the Bible by remembering that Jesus not only is Lord and servant of the covenant but Lord and servant in one person. He is the mediator of the new covenant (and of all preceding expressions of the covenant of grace, from Genesis 3:15 on) as the divine Sovereign who fulfills all the promises by which he has committed himself to his people and as the human Servant who fulfills all the obligations imposed by the Lord. As we read the Old Testament in particular and observe prophetic, royal, and priestly figures functioning (well or poorly) as intermediaries of the Lord's truth, authority, and holiness to the people of God, we must keep in mind how each office and officer illumines the complex and comprehensive sufficiency of Christ as the "one mediator between God and men" (1 Tim. 2:5).

The distinctive role of each of these offices suggests a cluster of features that need to be viewed together. *Prophets*, for example, are messengers from God who (in vision) are caught up into his divine council and so qualified to declare his will and word to his people. Miraculous signs are particularly associated with the prophetic office (Moses, Elijah, Elisha) inasmuch as these signs both attest and illustrate the message they bring from the Lord. Israel's prophets pressed the Lord's claims upon his unfaithful people and suffered rejection in delivering their Sovereign's ultimatums and his tender appeals. In his parable of the wicked vinedressers, Jesus employs imagery from Isaiah's "song of the vineyard" (Isa. 5:1–7) to portray Israel's sordid record of rejecting and mistreating the prophets sent by God to file his lawsuit against his traitorous servant people, who had failed to grant to their Lord the tribute due to him (cf. 2 Chron. 36:15–16). At

---

28   In our context of highly charged emotional piety and New Age spirituality, "intimacy with God" often can be conceived as unmediated, direct, subjective, mystical, and virtually impervious to articulation in intelligible words and concepts. In Scripture, on the other hand, sinful humans can approach the holy God only through mediation, and our access to our Creator and knowledge of him is conveyed through his Word, by which he reveals himself, person to person, to us as those created in his image to hear him, adore him, and gladly serve him.

the climax of the parable, Jesus identifies himself as the "beloved son" who brings to a finale the succession of servant messengers whom God had sent to claim his vineyard's fruit (Mark. 12:1–8).

Kings are defenders and judges. The warrior theme is therefore related to the king's role, as also is the theme of wisdom (Solomon) that qualifies the king to render just verdicts. Jesus' teaching in parables (Hebrew: *meshalim*) is thus a royal activity, corresponding to Solomon's proverbs (*meshalim*, 1 Kings 4:32; Prov. 1:1, 6; see Ps. 78:2, cited in Matt. 13:35). Jesus' *meshalim* also stand in the tradition of prophetic visions granted to Ezekiel and others (see Ezek. 17:2ff.), communicating eschatological realities in visual forms.[29] Jesus also is the royal champion who defends his people and disarms their enemies—paradoxically through the apparent weakness of his cross (Col. 2:14–15; Heb. 2:14–16).

Priests serve the Lord in his sanctuary, offering sacrifices that remove covenant curse and alienation, thereby effecting reconciliation and enabling guilty Israel to approach her holy Lord. As those who stand in the presence of the Holy One, the priests must be characterized by holiness, symbolized externally by freedom from blemish and isolation from cultic contamination (contact with death, menstrual blood, etc.). Their role also includes instruction in the law, the holiness code that sets Israel apart from the pagan nations who are her neighbors. They and the regulations they administer signify the sharp demarcation of that purity that can stand in intimate relation to the living God in contrast to the defilement that is common in the sin-stained world: separation of diet, clothing, planting, plowing, Sabbath vs. work days, and so on. As we have seen in chapter 6, the sermon to the Hebrews abundantly interprets Jesus' fulfillment of the priests' role not only in sacrifice and intercession but also in the consecration of God's worshipers with a cleansing that reaches to the depths of the conscience.

Figure 2 will help us visualize the roles filled by the parties of the covenant (Lord and Servant) and by the covenantal mediators (prophets, kings, and priests) and supremely *full*-filled by the eschatological Mediator, Jesus Christ:

---

29   The refrain with which Jesus summoned his listeners to invest effort to extract meaning from the metaphor in his parable, "He who has ears to hear, let him hear" (Mark 4:9) is echoed, interestingly, in the New Testament's highly symbolic book of apocalyptic prophecy (Rev. 2:7, 11, 17, 29; 3:6, 13, 22).

Dimension of Image of God	TRUE KNOWLEDGE	RIGHTEOUS AUTHORITY	HOLY RELATIONSHIP
Parties to the Covenant			
LORD	Speaks truly, Illumines hearts	Rules justly, Defends, judges	Consecrates, Receives worship
MEDIATORS	Prophet: Hears, delivers the Word to God's people	King: Executes the Word, judges wisely & justly, defends God's people	Priest: Teaches the Word, atones and prays for God's people
SERVANT	Hears and trusts God's Word	Obeys God's Word	Pursues purity & peace in reconciled relation to God & God's people

Figure 2: Covenant Parties, Mediators, and the Image of God

Christ comes both as the faithful and gracious covenant Lord and as the trusting, obedient covenant Servant. Moreover, he comes to bear the covenant curse earned by the rebellious servants of the covenant. But he does even more: he comes to rescue us, rebellious and unfaithful covenant servants, not only from the covenant curse but also from the dominion of sin, that we might be liberated for covenant faith and faithfulness. Jesus unites us to himself in his obedience, death, and resurrection not only representatively but also Spiritually—that is, by the gift of his Holy Spirit he summons us out of death and into life through the gospel and continues to apply to believers the transforming effects of his sacrifice and risen life. Incrementally and progressively, the Spirit of the risen Christ is actually creating faithful covenant servants out of former covenant breakers! God's gracious redemptive initiative, announced in Scripture's indicatives, creates the context for our grateful, faithful response to Scripture's imperatives. Therefore, finally, we can see that interpreting and preaching every text of Scripture in terms of its connection to the substructure of new creation and new covenant in Christ opens the way for heart-searching, grace-driven, life-transforming application of Scripture to the lives of our contemporaries.

Preaching Christ to Effect New Creation Transformation

When our preaching connects each biblical text to Scripture's over arching context of God's mighty and merciful work in history to reverse the effects of sin and bring the created order to its glorious consummation (new creation) and to reestablish a bond of loyalty between himself and redeemed humanity (new covenant), our application of the text to twenty-first century hearers will display an apostolic relevance that is neither faddish nor "timeless." The faddish approach confuses relevance with superficial timeliness in the form of up-to-date allusions to current events or cultural trends, or with efforts to "translate" biblical concepts into categories more amenable or intelligible to the modern and postmodern mind-set. For example, as we noted in chapter 2 some preachers who seek to reach secularized, unchurched, biblically illiterate populations recast archaic biblical notions such as "sin" into therapeutic or legal categories, reducing it either to a medical disability or to a violation of specific regulations. Preachers whose concept of relevance is faddish may contextualize their sermons by seasoning them throughout with allusions to entertainment media or political controversies.

At the opposite extreme are preachers who, often intentionally reacting against faddish relevance, seek to produce timeless messages that pertain to the universal human condition and in doing so make no reference (at least overtly) to their listeners' specific life context. Theoretically, such messages could be preached to any congregation anywhere in any era, with merely linguistic translation. Illustrations, if they are used, are drawn from Scripture itself or, if necessary, from features that are presumed to be common to general human experience.

Apostolic preaching as we hear it in the New Testament, however, is neither faddish nor timeless. On the one hand, the apostles lifted their hearers' sights from the immediate and ephemeral aspects of their lives and cultures, showing them instead the cosmic context of their lives, that is, God's majestic deeds of creation and redemption and his worthiness of their devotion and trust. Whether speaking to Jewish audiences (Acts 13:16–41) or to Gentiles (Acts 17:22–31) or to Christian believers (Hebrews), apostolic preachers challenged their audiences' temporal and cultural parochialism, disclosing their place in the panorama of God's global, history-spanning redemptive agenda.

On the other hand, the apostles were not reticent to contextualize their message to their audiences, citing Old Testament Scriptures in synagogues and pagan poets among the philosophers of Athens. The preacher to the Hebrews, as we have seen, recalled a specific congregation's history of suffering faith as well as pointedly diagnosing the present spiritual peril in which some of its members stood. Paul summoned his Corinthian brothers and sisters to single-minded devotion to God and his Christ in a context in which there were many "so-called gods in heaven and on earth—as indeed there are many 'gods' and many 'lords' " (1 Cor. 8:5). The rhetoric of his epistles leveraged principles and illustration drawn from Roman law, Greek athletics, Jewish worship, farming, marriage, warfare, and commerce to persuade minds and move hearts toward the Christ whom he proclaimed.[30] Because they preached in the era in which God's good news burst forth to all nationalities, including pagans never exposed to Israel's treasure, the oracles of God (Rom. 3:2), the apostolic preachers did not limit their illustrative repertoire to events and images found in previous Scriptures (although these have pride of place by virtue of their authority as the revelation that pointed ahead to the Christ). Moreover, apostolic preaching had so many lines of connection with its hearers' daily lives precisely because they knew that it was in this mundane context that the Spirit of God was at work, quietly injecting the "earnest" of new creation life into the decaying structures of the old creation.[31]

The specificity of the apostles' address to their hearers in their own situation demands of twenty-first century preachers the discipline to probe and understand that ancient context with all the resources and investigative skills at our disposal. Its model of preaching that is timely without being faddish, incarnate and yet transcendent, sets the standard for twenty-first century preachers. As technological advances in communication and transportation and increasing economic interdependence shrink the world, and as Western culture itself, once saturated and contoured by Christian faith, becomes both secularized and spiritualized in pagan directions, twenty-first century preachers serve Christ's gospel and church in venues that resemble more and more closely the semi-globalized religious pluralism that the apostles addressed in the first century.[32]

---

30   David J. Williams, *Paul's Metaphors: Their Context and Character* (Peabody: Hendrikson, 1999).

31   Paul's references to the Holy Spirit as the "earnest" (*arrabōn*, also rendered "pledge, guarantee, down payment)" of our inheritance implies that his present sanctifying operation in believers' lives is not only a confirmation that the inheritance will come but also the first installment (in the present) of that future inheritance (2 Cor. 1:22; 5:5; Eph. 1:14).

32   David W. Henderson, *Culture Shift: Communicating God's Truth to Our Changing World* (Grand Rapids: Baker, 1998); Robert L. Wilken, *Remembering the*

Discerning the new creation and new covenant motifs woven into the fabric of the Bible and tying its every text to Jesus will make the preacher's application of God's word apostolic in two important respects. (1) It builds exhortations to behave as those renewed in the image of God on the sole foundation of divine grace. (2) It shows our hearers the specific texture that new creation takes in the lives of those who belong to Jesus as we focus on the dimensions of the divine image (truth, authority, relationship) and our callings in the world as prophets, kings, and priests in union with Christ.

Apostolic application builds exhortations on grace. A perennial and pivotal issue in preaching, counseling, and pastoral care generally is how to motivate believers to pursue holiness and obedience to the Lord, without compromising the freeness of God's grace. We know from Paul's refutations to Judaizers in his epistles to Galatia, Rome, and Philippi that in their ears Paul's gospel sounded like an invitation to sheer license and lawlessness, undercutting motivation to obey with assurance of gracious forgiveness (e.g., Rom. 6:1). The fear of judgment for disobedience and the hope of reward for well doing should and sometimes do motivate compliance to God's commands. God's covenant of creation with upright Adam was established on the sanction announced by the Sovereign that disobedience would bring death. Likewise, as Israel entered the Promised Land, the Mosaic law announced a "works principle" under which the Israelites' tenure in the land would be contingent on their loyalty to the Lord and his covenant.

Yet, human history and Israelite history dramatically demonstrated that even God's "holy and righteous and good" law (Rom. 7:12), with its promised rewards and threatened penalties, was nevertheless "weakened by the flesh" (8:3) and unable to give life to those dead in sin (Gal. 3:21). Consequently, contrary to legalists' expectations, attempts to motivate obedience through making God's favor (and favors) contingent on human performance actually work against the law's central objectives, love of God and neighbor, by encouraging self-trust, judgmental competition, and legalistic pride (on the one hand) or instilling self-condemnation, unrelenting guilt, and hopelessness (on the other). As Luther noted, as long as he

---

Christian Past (Grand Rapids: Eerdmans, 1995); Peter Jones, *Spirit Wars: Pagan Revival in Christian America* (Mulkiteo, Washington: Winepress, 1997).

understood "the righteousness of God" as nothing more than that perfect justice by which God judges sinful humans (such as Luther), the term fanned to flame his *resentment* against the Judge whose standard was so unattainable.

Apostolic preaching, however, reverses the order that makes sense to human wisdom. Instead of motivating obedience by offering God's favor as contingent on human performance, the apostles spoke for a God who had *begun* the process of new creation by extending unmerited mercy and who thereby evokes from renewed people a grateful love and eager desire to obey. On the basis of the obedient life and vicarious death of Jesus, the last Adam and faithful Servant of the Lord, God initiates a new creation and inaugurates a new covenant, graciously granting not only forgiveness and right standing for Jesus' sake but also mighty personal transformation by his Spirit of grace.

We observed in chapter 6 that Hebrews speaks of Jesus' fulfillment of the Servant's side of the covenant in three specific ways: (1) He maintains flawless loyalty to the Lord and fulfills every command and requirement, thereby achieving the blessedness promised by the Lord for himself and those he represents. He is like them in every way "yet without sin" (Heb. 4:15; cf. 7:26). (2) He endures on their behalf the curse that the covenant pronounced on its violators. The "will" of God that he performs is the offering of his body once for all to "perfect" others (10:5–10). (3) He inscribes the Lord's law in their hearts (8:10) so that by grace they, though still dull of hearing (6:12) and needing strong encouragement (6:18), can do the will of God (10:36) and offer sacrifices that please God (13:15–16). All three of these dimensions of Jesus' covenant keeping benefit us as gifts of sheer grace. The first two constitute the ground of the forensic act that Paul calls justification, with its double imputation of our sin to Jesus and of his obedience to us. The preacher to the Hebrews, employing the terminology of priestly consecration, expresses the same truth when he assures his hearers that Jesus has "perfected" them once for all (10:14), even though his sermon makes clear that they are not yet subjectively free from sin. Jesus' obedience and sacrifice are objective acts that occur "outside us"—a truth that Luther found so comforting.

What preachers must see and help their hearers to see is that the third act of covenantal faithfulness, the sovereign transformation of our hearts, though it is subjective rather than objective, is *no less gracious* than are his once-for-all obedience, death, and resurrection on our behalf. Because sanctification also entails our responsibility as well as God's sovereign initiative, it is easy to forget that sanctification, no less than justification, is by grace alone and through faith alone.[33] The Westminster Shorter Catechism captured apostolic, gospel truth when it echoed Paul's new creation language to define sanctification as "the work of *God's free grace*, whereby *we are renewed* in the whole man *after the image of God*, and *are enabled* more and more to die unto sin, and live unto righteousness."[34] Both the attribution of sanctification to the work of God's *grace* and the passive verbs "are renewed" and "are enabled" highlight the wholly gracious character of the process by which we grow in holiness by the almighty and all-merciful Spirit of Christ. Union with Christ is comprehensive, and salvation in Christ leaves no aspect of sin and its damages unchallenged or unchanged. Those justified by faith in the Son are recipients of the Spirit of the Son, the Spirit of holiness, who (through our feeble efforts at faith and obedience) is at work to conform us to the image of the Son in purity and love.

From the time of sin's primeval invasion of human experience, in God's covenantal relations with his people, their response consistently flowed from and responded to the priority of his grace. This is illustrated graphically in the order of the covenant treaty form itself. Employing the literary conventions of Ancient Near Eastern international treaties (which his providence had prepared), God inscripturated his covenant with Israel in order to emphasize that he was not only superior but also supremely merciful and mighty in drawing Israel to himself.[35] Ancient Near Eastern treaties opened with identification of the contracting parties and a historical prologue narrating the suzerain's previous benevolence toward the vassal, after which exclusive loyalty was enjoined and specific stipulations and consequences listed. So also, the Lord's covenant with Israel opens not with regulations but with a rehearsal of his past mercies, whether we think of the brief prologue to the Ten Commandments ("I am the

---

33   See Johnson, "*Simul iustus et peccator*" in Clark, ed., *Covenant, Justification and Pastoral Ministry*; Neil H. Williams, *The Theology of Sonship* (Jenkintown, PA: World Harvest Mission, 2002).

34   Westminster Shorter Catechism, Ans. 35 (emphasis added).

35   See Meredith G. Kline, *Treaty of the Great King: The Covenant Structure of Deuteronomy: Studies and Commentary* (Grand Rapids: Eerdmans, 1963), 13–26.

LORD your God, who brought you out of the land of Egypt, out of the house of slavery," Ex. 20:2) or of Moses' rehearsal of God's sustaining faithfulness in the wilderness before issuing the "second law" (Deut. 1–4)[36] or of the entire pre-patriarchal and patriarchal narrative that fills Genesis as a prelude to the covenant-making at Sinai. The foundational priority of divine grace is likewise expressed in the explanation of the commandments that Israelite parents were to give their children:

> When your son asks you in time to come, "What is the meaning of the testimonies and the statutes and the rules that the LORD our God has commanded you?" then you shall say to your son, "We were Pharaoh's slaves in Egypt. And the LORD brought us out of Egypt with a mighty hand. And the LORD showed signs and wonders, great and grievous, against Egypt and against Pharaoh and all his household, before our eyes. And he brought us out from there, that he might bring us in and give us the land that he swore to give to our fathers. And the LORD commanded us to do all these statutes, to fear the LORD our God, for our good always, that he might preserve us alive, as we are this day." (Deut. 6:20–24)

Since the grace of the exodus set the context for the stipulations that Israel was to observe as the Lord's servant, how much more should Christian preachers expound those many biblical texts that shine the spotlight on the responsibilities of God's covenant servants (whether commandments, wisdom maxims, or narratives that profile faithful or unfaithful responses to the Lord of the covenant) by calling attention to God's gracious provision of Jesus, the Servant who kept covenant commandments and bore covenant curse in our place! But our exposition of imperative texts does not stop with what Christ has done for us; it also extends to what Christ, by his Word and Spirit, is doing in us. In the context of his achievement of our redemption, the Spirit's gracious, persistent application of redemption in our sanctification is good news as well.

Apostolic application displays the texture of renewal in the image of God. We will also be helped in relating any text to the Scripture's central purpose as we sensitize ourselves to the categories of truth (knowledge), authority (righteousness) and relationship (holiness)—themes that sum up the pre-fall perfections of Adam and Eve,

---

36 Kline, *Treaty*, 52–61.

as originally created in the image of God. These categories quite comprehensively capture the dimensions of human life that were damaged by sin and therefore provide a more textured matrix as we seek to discern a text's Fallen Condition Focus, both in its original historical context and in its relevance to twenty-first century hearers who encounter the same spiritual challenges, though often in quite different garb. As Paul points out, these mark the contours of the divine image into which we are to be renewed by the grace of Christ (Eph. 4:24; Col. 3:10). Related to these themes are the mediatorial roles and offices that God ordained to reestablish rightness in these dimensions: truth (prophet), authority (king), relationship (priest). These theocratic officers who served Israel during the age of promise serve as windows on the redemptive and renewing mission of Jesus, the final Prophet, King, and Priest. The Heidelberg Catechism also wisely invokes the distinctive roles associated with these offices to map out the calling of every believer by virtue of our union with Christ. After explaining Jesus' title "Christ" in terms of his having been anointed "to be our chief prophet . . . our only high priest . . . and our eternal king," the Catechism asks, "But why are you called a Christian?" and answers, "Because by faith I am a member of Christ and so I share in his anointing. I am anointed to confess his name, to present myself to him as a living sacrifice of thanks, to strive with a good conscience against sin and the devil in this life, and afterward to reign with Christ over all creation for all eternity."[37] The parallelism of the answers signals that the same threefold anointed office preeminently received by Jesus is received derivatively by those who trust Jesus through our union with him. We are prophets called to confess his name, priests who offer ourselves in worship, and kings who war against evil now in expectation of rule with Christ hereafter.

Further reflection on the attributes necessary to the performance of each office suggests an even more textured framework by which we can discern the relation of diverse biblical texts and genres to God's new creation project in Christ and therefore also its relation to the transformation that we and our hearers need from the Spirit of God, the Lord and Giver of life. As emissaries of the God of truth, prophets not only must speak truth but also be trustworthy themselves. Certainly, apostles and other ministers of the Word must always be aware of their high accountability as stewards of God's

---

37   Heidelberg Catechism, Lord's Day 12 (Q/A 31, 32).

mysteries and trustees of God's deposit to maintain its purity un-adulterated and to convey it undiminished (1 Cor. 4:1–2; 2 Cor. 2:17; 1 Tim. 6:20; 2 Tim. 1:14; 2:2). The Heidelberg Catechism rightly infers, moreover, that all Christians have a prophetic role in articulating (as well as believing) God's word, confessing Christ's name (Col. 3:16; Heb. 13:15).

The mediatorial calling of priests, while it included instruction in the Word of God and even participation in judicial decisions, was distinctive in its association with the sanctuary and its rituals. Many detailed regulations pertaining to sacrificial procedure and cleansing ritual focused attention on the consuming purity of God and the corresponding whole-souled consecration that he demanded of the people in whose midst he dwelt in tabernacle and temple. Complementary to this concentration on holiness was the priests' calling to compassion. The preacher to the Hebrews observes, "Every high priest is selected from among men and is appointed to represent them in matters related to God, to offer gifts and sacrifices for sins. He is able to deal gently with those who are ignorant and are going astray, since he himself is subject to weakness" (Heb. 5:1–2 NIV). In this gentle empathy with the weak, Aaronic priests were only faint shadows of the supremely sympathetic high priest, Jesus (4:15); yet both they (before his sacrifice) and we (after it) are called to exhibit his gentle compassion toward the frail and the failing.

Kings were anointed to defend and to rule. Israel sinfully sought a king in order to be like the other nations, but their understanding of the king's task was correct: "to lead us and to go out before us and fight our battles" (1 Sam. 8:20 NIV). At first they had such a champion in Saul (1 Sam. 11), and later David succeeded him in this role—single-handedly defeating the Philistine Goliath even before his coronation (but after his anointing, 1 Sam. 16–17). Christ is the champion who disarmed his people's ultimate enemy; he is the woman's Seed who struck the serpent's head as his own heel was struck (Gen. 3:15). Yet, the Heidelberg Catechism is also correct to imply that spiritual warfare still rages and assert that each person united to Christ participates in the royal role of combating Satan's evil empire (Eph. 6:10–20). Wisdom and justice, as well as courage and strength, are attributes essential to the responsibility of rule. David's last words were an oracle of an ideal king: "When one rules justly over men, ruling in the fear of God, he dawns on them like the morning light, like the sun shining forth on a cloudless morning, like rain that makes grass to sprout from the earth" (2 Sam. 23:3–4). Neither David nor his successors fully fit that portrait, yet God promised just such a ruler from the stump of Jesse, David's father:

> And the Spirit of the LORD shall rest upon him, the Spirit of wisdom and understanding, the Spirit of counsel and might, the Spirit of knowledge and the fear of the LORD. And his delight shall be in the fear of the LORD. He shall not judge by what his eyes see, or decide disputes by what his ears hear, but with righteousness he shall judge the poor, and decide with equity for the meek of the earth; and he shall strike the earth with the rod of his mouth, and with the breath of his lips he shall kill the wicked. Righteousness shall be the belt of his waist, and faithfulness the belt of his loins. (Isa. 11:2–5)

Jesus is the wise, just, and mighty ruler *par excellence*. Nevertheless, just as the first human couple in the Garden received royal authority to exercise dominion over the created order, so also, even now, despite sin and its adverse consequences, those who share Christ's royal anointing are called to exert influence in the culture, the state, and the workplace in ways consistent with the King's justice and wisdom (Eph. 6:5–9; 1 Peter 2:13–21). The close association of Israel's wisdom tradition with Solomon, the preeminent sage, suggests the connection that links Proverbs, Job, Ecclesiastes, and the Song of Songs into God's new creation project, our renewal in the divine image in its royal dimensions and the restoration of orderly peace with justice and mercy in the earth. Ultimately, of course, the destruction of the last enemy and emergence of the peaceable kingdom in its fullness, the new heavens and earth, awaits the return of the King. Yet, his kingdom has begun, and its grace enables its grateful subjects and vice-regents to display the King's wisdom and justice even in a decomposing world.

Conclusion

Our exploration of the new creation and new covenant themes has not produced a rigid sermon template, or even a set of orderly exegetical steps guaranteed to link every biblical text to Christ and, through him, to our hearers in a way that will be self-evidently appropriate to everyone. Frankly, I would be suspicious of a method that made such promises, and I suspect you would be, too. The Bible commends prayerful meditation on the Word and promises that patient reflection eventually bears fruit in deepened insight into the matchless treasures of God's wisdom. Although such slow disciplines frustrate those accustomed to lightning-quick search software and enamored of foolproof checklists, they are nevertheless the means by which the Lord Jesus not only discloses the good news he wants preached but also conforms, attunes, and subdues his messenger to that message of sovereign justice and grace. There are processes and practices, strategies of reading and study that can guide and guard our reflection on a biblical passage in its grand canonical context (see Appendix A: "From Text to Sermon"). But the process offers no guarantees. Rather, it is a means of *cultivating a way of seeing* Scripture and the pattern woven through it, and *a way of hearing* the Christ who speaks and is spoken of throughout the Bible. The final two chapters offer samples of the ways in which reading various texts of God's Word in the context of God's new creation and new covenant trajectories can open our eyes and ears to each Scripture's testimony to Christ, so that we discover how it reveals his person and work as the last Adam and head of the new humanity and as the covenant mediator who is both Lord and servant.

9
Preaching the Promises: Apostolic Preaching of Old Testament Literary Genres

I t is time to put our theoretical discussion to practical tests. However appealing or pious it sounds to assert that twenty-first century preachers should emulate the apostles' hermeneutics and homiletics, and however persuasive the argument supporting this assertion, the question remains, Can it be done? Is it possible, with the guidance provided by our apostolic exemplars, to proclaim Old Testament texts—not only those on which New Testament authors have commented but also those on which they are silent—in such a way that our hearers are led to Jesus as the climax toward whom every Scripture drives, and to do so with integrity, accountability, and credibility?

A small but growing body of resources is providing an affirmative answer to this question. Edmund P. Clowney's *The Unfolding Mystery* is an exegetically profound but homiletically accessible study of the Old Testament's witness to the coming Christ in its narratives of creation and the fall, the patriarchs, Moses and the exodus, and Kings David and Solomon, and in the latter prophets' predictions of a coming day of redemption and judgment. His more recent *Preaching Christ in All of Scripture* brings together some of the most insightful and powerful Christ-centered sermons from throughout his long and widely recognized ministry to Christ's church. [1] The second half of Graeme Goldsworthy's *Preaching the Whole Bible as Christian Scripture* addresses the application of biblical theology to preaching the various genres of the Old and New Testaments, blending theoretical and procedural guidance with examples that point the way toward

---

1   See chapter 2, footnote 43.

preaching.[2] Sidney Greidanus's *The Modern Preacher and the Ancient Text* likewise gives detailed attention to various biblical genres. Both *Modern Preacher*, which interacts extensively with a wide range of critical biblical scholarship as well as diverse homileticians, and Greidanus's later *Preaching Christ from the Old Testament* provide helpful guidance on the move from the interpretation of the text to the communication of its message through the structuring of the sermon, attention to its relevance to one's hearers, and other homiletic issues.[3] S. G. De Graaf's four-volume *Promise and Deliverance*, though originating in his training of Sunday school and Christian day school teachers, exhibits the fruit of his own pulpit ministry in the Netherlands and provides preachers with a stimulating "sounding board" for their own biblical-theological reflection on the historical narratives of redemption in the Old Testament (volumes 1 and 2) and the Gospels and Acts (volumes 3 and 4).[4] In the introductory chapter mention was made of P & R Publishing's *The Gospel According to the Old Testament* series, with volumes by Raymond Dillard on Elijah and Elisha, by Iain Duguid on Abraham, Isaac, and Jacob, by Tremper Longman on worship in Israel's temple, and by Bryan Estelle on Jonah.[5] Some of these volumes, in fact, had their origin in sermon series preached to contemporary congregations. More recently, P & R Publishing has launched the Reformed Expository Commentary with volumes by Philip Graham Ryken on Galatians and 1 Timothy, Iain M. Duguid on Esther and Ruth, Richard D. Phillips on Hebrews and Zechariah, and Daniel M. Doriani on James.[6] This series intends to expound both Old and New Testament books from a redemptive-historical and Christ-centered perspective.[7]

Nevertheless, Old Testament passages are so diverse in genre, subject matter, purpose, and temporal setting that even more detailed

---

2 See chapter 2, footnote 45.

3 Again, see chapter 2, footnote 45.

4 See chapter 2, footnote 45.

5 See chapter 1, footnotes 15, 16, 17; see also Bryan D. Estelle, *Salvation through Judgment and Mercy: The Gospel according to Jonah* (Phillipsburg: P & R, 2005).

6 Philip Graham Ryken, *Galatians* (Phillipsburg: P & R, 2005); Philip Graham Ryken, *1 Timothy* (Phillipsburg: P & R, 2007); Iain M. Duguid, *Esther and Ruth* (Phillipsburg: P & R, 2005); Richard D. Phillips, *Hebrews* (Phillipsburg: P & R, 2006); Richard D. Phillips, *Zechariah* (Phillipsburg: P & R, 2007); Daniel M. Doriani, *James* (Phillipsburg: P & R, 2007).

7 "Series Introduction" by series editors Richard D. Phillips and Philip Graham Ryken, in Duguid, *Esther and Ruth*, viii.

reflection, direction, and guidance by means of example are needed, especially for the biblical-theological reading and preaching of
challenging genres such as legal material, wisdom literature, and the
covenant lawsuit pressed by the prophets. Our hope and intention is
that such can be offered to preachers in the near future.[8] This chapter
and the next attempt the more modest goal of whetting readers' appetites to follow the apostles' lead in preaching Christ from Old Testament (chapter 9) and New Testament texts (chapter 10) in a way
that exhibits the unity and triumph of "God's great plan,"[9] the glory
of his grace, and the faith-filled, grateful, and faithful response that
his redemptive achievement elicits in his covenant servants.

After a brief overview of our interpretive method, in this chapter
we will sample the application of apostolic hermeneutics-homiletics
to the proclamation of Old Testament texts belonging to five genres:
historical narrative, law, wisdom, song, and prophetic vision.

Interpreting Scripture in Two Horizons

The Appendix "From Text to Sermon" traces in detail the processes to be followed and questions to be answered as preachers and
teachers of Scripture move "From Text to Sermon."[10] Those catalogues
of interpretive "steps"[11] can be grouped in two general categories: the

---

8   The Westminster Seminary California Master of Divinity homiletics curriculum builds on foundational courses on the theory and practice of apostolic
Christ-centered preaching with a practicum focused specifically on narrative texts
(historical narrative, parable) and one concentrating on non-narrative genres (law,
wisdom, prophetic vision, epistolary discourse, paraenesis, etc.). Members of the
practical theology and biblical studies faculty have discussed producing additional
works to guide preachers as they attempt to handle the rich variety of God's Word
with integrity.

9   Derke P. Bergsma, *Redemption: The Triumph of God's Great Plan* (Lansing,
Illinois: Redeemer Books, 1989).

10   "From Text to Sermon" is addressed most directly to those who have had
opportunity to study in depth the original languages of Scripture and the theory
and practice of biblical interpretation. Pastors and teachers of the Word who have
not had this privilege will need to adapt its steps to the level of their resources and
theological education as they seek to expound the Scriptures' witness to Christ as
faithful stewards of the Holy Spirit's gifts.

11   As the introductions to these appendices acknowledge, in actual practice
the art and discipline of biblical interpretation do not follow a rigid progression
of sequential steps but instead entail an interplay of focused lexical and historical
research and syntactic analysis with more wide-ranging meditation on the text's
contribution to larger covenantal and theological motifs.

text's "close" contexts (immediate literary setting, including previous and contemporaneous revelation as well as genre, and life situation, including general historical and cultural background and first recipients' need: the text's occasion) and its completed canonical context (subsequent covenant history and revelation, especially climaxing in Jesus' mediation of the new covenant).[12] Consideration of our hearers' life-situation and the conceptual "horizon" within which they will receive (or misperceive) the text's message is also a crucial component of apostolic preaching, as the epistle to the Hebrews and the sermons in Acts demonstrate by example.[13] But it is the text's message and purpose, defined and circumscribed by its close and canonical contexts, that provide the diagnostic template that enables our hearers to interpret their experience and assumptions within the categories of God's covenantal self-revelation in Scripture.

The Text in Its Close Contexts. All the linguistic, literary, and historical disciplines must be engaged in our attempt to read the passage, as accurately as we can, within its own original "horizon." We must identify words' semantic fields and the limitations imposed on each word's specific sense by the syntax, qualifiers, synonyms, antonyms, and other features in the passage. And we need to consider the degree and role of metaphor, parallelism, compositional structure (e.g., chiasm) and other literary conventions apropos to the genre.

The text must be read in light of all that can be learned about the historical situation and experience of the first recipients, as well as their broader cultural and religious environment. Each passage is an answer to questions that lie behind and beyond it, a solution to its readers' needs, problems, and crises. What were those questions and problems? What, moreover, could and did the author expect them to understand and believe—or at least hold them accountable for knowing and believing—in light of their previous exposure to God's

---

12 See Clowney, *Preaching and Biblical Theology*, pp. 89–100.

13 Although demurring from H. G. Gadamer's hermeneutic in which a later reader's understanding of an ancient text entails a "fusion" of the text's original conceptual "horizon" and the interpretive "horizon" that the reader brings to the text (as well as subsequent postmodern reader-response hermeneutic, which replaces even Gadamer's metaphor of interpretation as dialogue between text and reader to negotiate new meaning with the hegemony of the reader in determining a text's meaning), I do believe that the homiletic practice of the apostles and of their best successors throughout church history exhibits careful attention to the hearers' presuppositions and previous exposure to God's revelation.

self-disclosure in the created order, in his covenantal dealings with Israel, and in Scriptures already in their possession?

Hermeneutics textbooks and exegetical handbooks typically give detailed attention to the resources and skills required to interpret a biblical text in its "close contexts," historically, linguistically, and literarily.[14] We need not duplicate such discussions here.

The Text in Its Canonical Context. The complementary disciplines of systematic theology and biblical theology bring different perspectives to the task of reading each biblical passage "in the light of like and unlike passages, and many and clearer passages" (as the Second Helvetic Confession described using Scripture to interpret Scripture). Systematic theology approaches the Old and New Testaments as the completed canon of Scripture and poses topical or thematic questions to the canon as a whole: As we read each biblical text in its relevant contexts, what does the aggregate of all the passages that address the theme disclose to us about the holiness of God, the image of God in man, justification, the church, or any other topic? Biblical theology gives attention to the historical, and therefore progressive, process by which God gave Scripture, focusing attention on the interpretation of each text, first within the context of its own position in redemptive history and then on the relationship of its content to what precedes and follows it in the unfolding of God's self-disclosure and saving agenda through the ages.[15]

Both systematic theology and biblical theology are essential to our study of Scripture for preaching. One contribution of systematic theology, including the historic creeds and confessions of the church, is to safeguard our interpretation of a particular text, lest we misread

---

14   See, for example, Douglas Stuart, *Old Testament Exegesis: A Handbook for Students and Pastors,* 3rd ed. (Louisville: Westminster John Knox, 2001); and Gordon Fee, *New Testament Exegesis: A Handbook for Students and Pastors,* 3rd ed. (Louisville: Westminster John Knox, 2001).

15   Vos therefore rightly categorized biblical theology as a subdiscipline of exegetical theology, broadening consideration of "relevant context" from the close contexts of the document in which a text appears and the immediate circumstance that occasioned it to bring into view also the broader revelatory flow in which the text appears. *Biblical Theology,* 12–13. See also John Murray, "Systematic Theology (Second Article)," and Richard B. Gaffin, Jr. "Systematic Theology and Biblical Theology," in John H. Skilton, ed., *The New Testament Student and Theology. The New Testament Student,* vol. 3 (Phillipsburg: P & R, 1976), 18–50. Murray's essay originally appeared in *WTJ* 26 (1963–4): 33–46; and Gaffin's appeared in *WTJ* 38 (1976): 281–99.

(and preach) its message in such a way as to bring it into direct contradiction with the pervasive teaching of the Bible in many other texts. Knowing, for example, that the absentee landowner in Jesus' parable of the wicked vinedressers in some sense represents God, by reading the parable with detailed allegorical precision, we might infer from the landowner's expectation, "They will respect my son" (Mark 12:6), that Jesus' impending death was unforeseen by God—a conclusion that can be dismissed immediately as absurd not only in the light of the Bible's revelation of God's omniscience generally but also in light of the Old Testament's predictions of Christ's death specifically.

Biblical theology in particular focuses its spotlight on the implications of the apostolic testimony that the salvation long promised through prophets to Israel now has been accomplished in the incarnation, obedience, suffering, and resurrection of the Messiah Jesus. It teaches us to place each Old Testament text into the context of a historical trajectory that points from the shamed and banished Adam and Eve at history's dawn to the second Adam at history's crux. Several disciplines and resources can equip us to read each Old Testament text in the context of the historical outworking of redemption and the progressive unfolding of special revelation that accompanies God's saving acts and agenda. The following steps are helpful in discerning the intertextual links between New Testament texts and their sources in the Old Testament:

Become familiar with the Septuagint (LXX). The Greek translation of the Old Testament was commonly used by the apostles and the churches they founded, particularly among the Jewish Dispersion and the Gentiles. As we will see in chapter 10, when New Testament writers wish to signal a typological connection between an Old Testament text and the fulfillment in Christ, they often do so by way of specific linguistic allusion to the Greek vocabulary and phrasing of the LXX. A concordance to the LXX is a valuable guide to surveying the use of a particular Greek word in the Old Testament most familiar to the apostles' first readers.[16]

16 Electronic search programs such as BibleWorks permit rapid word-searches in the most widely used edition of the LXX (edited by A. Rahlfs, et al; published by Würtembergische Bibelanstalt Stuttgart). Book lovers will prefer either the terse concordance edited by George Morrish, *A Concordance to the Septuagint* (Grand Rapids: Zondervan, 1976), which lists reference numbers only and lacks citation to

Check reliable cross references. A Bible with well-selected cross-references gives access to parallels between Old Testament and New (normally linguistic, but sometimes topical) that other biblical scholars have discerned. A wise and thorough selection of cross references can be found in the *New Geneva Study Bible* (NKJV), the *Reformation Study Bible* (ESV), the *Jerusalem Bible*, the *New American Standard Bible* (Updated), *Novum Testamentum Graece* (edited by E. and E. Nestle, and subsequently by K. and B. Aland), and the *Greek New Testament* (edited by K. Aland, et al, and published by the United Bible Societies). Both of these Greek New Testaments contain appendices listing in Old Testament order the citations and allusions[17] to Old Testament passages that the editors have identified discerned in New Testament texts.

Reflect on how the passage fits into the general patterns of divine-human covenantal relations. Explicit quotations or unmistakable

---

the apocryphal books; or the large concordance edited by Edwin Hatch and Henry A. Redpath, *et al, A Concordance of the Septuagint and Other Early Greek Versions of the Old Testament* (Graz: Akademische Druk- u. Verlangsanstalt, 1957), which includes the context (phrase) in which the word appears.

17   The criteria for distinguishing an allusion to an Old Testament text from a quotation cannot necessarily be defined or applied with precision. Robert H. Gundry opens his discussion of the use of the Old Testament in Matthew's Gospel with the observation, "The distinction between formal and allusive quotation is not always easily made. I have tried to judge by whether the quoted words flow from and into the context (allusive) or stand apart (formal)." *The Use of the Old Testament in St. Matthew's Gospel with Special Reference to Messianic Hope*, Supplement to *Novum Testamentum*, 18 (Leiden: E. J. Brill, 1975), 9. Ancient written Greek lacked the conventions for visually marking the direct citation of words from a source, such as quotation marks or indentation of a block quotation. The *hoti recitativum* was used to introduce both direct discourse (e.g., Mark 2:12; including quotation, Rom. 3:10) and indirect discourse (Acts 9:22; including the paraphrase of a source, Gal. 4:22). Introductory formulas such as "it is written" (*gegraptai*, Rom. 4:17) or "saying" (*legōn*, Heb. 2:6) often introduce a direct quotation that "stands apart" (Gundry's criterion for formal quotation), but even the presence of such a formula is not a sure indication that the New Testament author is quoting rather than paraphrasing (e.g., Gal. 4:22 cited above: "it is written that . . ."). Intertextual allusion is even more subtle, exhibiting a range of explicitness from undeniable to the subtle and therefore questionable. The discussion in ch. 7 above (pp. 199–217) on the range of explicitness in the New Testament's identification of typological correspondence between Old Testament events and institutions and their fulfillment in Jesus applies to the identification of Old Testament allusions in the New Testament.

allusions to an Old Testament text, institution, event, or person in the New Testament are the most reliable guides to our understanding how such features were intended by God to prefigure or anticipate the climactic redemptive work of Jesus Christ. Because of the occasional character of the New Testament, however, we should not conclude prematurely that Old Testament texts that are not explicitly interpreted typologically by a New Testament writer cannot be read in the context of Christ's climactic work as Lord and Servant of the covenant, and as prophet, priest and king. Rather, we must seek to relate particular texts to the broader structures and institutions that provide the framework for God's relation to his people throughout the history of redemption. This requires a more comprehensive hermeneutic perspective.

The book of Esther, for example, is never quoted in the New Testament, and only three verbal allusions to Esther have been identified in the New Testament. None of these allusions is applied to Christ or his redemptive work for his people.[18] Nevertheless, the dramatic confrontation, announced in Genesis 3:15 between the seed of the woman (exemplified in Mordecai, Esther, and the threatened Jewish subjects of Persia) and the seed of the serpent (exemplified in Haman, their politically powerful enemy) could hardly be sharper than in this historical narrative. Moreover, the Lord's promise to grant Abraham innumerable seed and to bless all nations in him (a promise that ultimately would be fulfilled in Jesus) seems jeopardized by Haman's plot to secure a royal edict authorizing the genocide of the Jews. Esther's willingness, in response to her uncle's strong exhortation, to place her own life at risk for the sake of rescuing her people foreshadows the readiness of Christ to lay down his life for his people. For a fuller exposition of Esther in the context of redemptive history and its consummation in Jesus, see Iain M. Duguid, *Esther and Ruth* (Phillipsburg: P & R, 2005).

Recognize the Continuity and Discontinuity in Biblical Covenants. We have noted that God built into the Old Testament institutions,

---

18   Rev. 4:5 alludes to the LXX reading of Esther 1:1 in its description of God's throne. Luke 10:13 echoes Esther 4:3 (and other OT texts such as Jonah 3:6) in associating abject repentance with "sackcloth and ashes." Mark 6:23 reports Herod Antipas' promise to give Salome "up to half my kingdom," even as the Persian king Ahasuerus promised Queen Esther (Esth. 5:3, 6; 7:2). "Loci citati vel allegati" ("Index of [OT] citations or allusions") in *Novum Testamentum Graece,* 27th ed.

leaders, and events various limitations and defects (for which the covenant servants, not the covenant Lord, were culpable). He did so to make clear that in none of these Old Testament events or agents of salvation had the final Savior arrived. Thus along with lines of similarity we also observe elements of discontinuity between the Old Testament type and its New Testament fulfillment. The prophet Jonah was "resurrected" from the depths of the sea to preach to the Gentiles. But Jonah had been brought into the depths by his own rebellion, and his "resurrection" was not *literally* from the dead. Jesus voluntarily descended into the grave for others' sins, and he returned to life from real, physical death. This tension of continuity and discontinuity between the revelation of God (in word and deed) in Old Testament promise and his revelation now in New Testament fulfillment has important implications for our proclamation of several Old Testament genres.

With respect to the law, Reformed confessions such as the Westminster Confession (19) distinguish three categories of regulation contained in the covenant treaty delivered to Moses for Israel on Mount Sinai: moral law, ceremonial laws, and judicial laws. [19] There is biblical warrant for this threefold distinction: The "ten words" are given special prominence in the Pentateuch as containing the heart of the covenant bond between the Lord and his people. From these commands (as well as the two great commandments, Deut. 6:4–5; Lev. 19:18) the New Testament writers regularly draw examples of behaviors still binding on Christian believers (Rom. 13:9–10; Gal. 5:14; James 2:8–11). Although every attempt at self-justification through law-keeping by fallen humans will fail miserably, those who have been justified through faith in Christ alone have received the Spirit whose fruit consists in growing, free congruence with this moral law, which discloses the perfect love and purity of their Father, in whose image they are being recreated (Gal. 5:22–23; Rom. 8:4). The "ceremonial laws" pertain to the earthly sanctuary, including the annual feasts, the sacrificial system, and the laws of ritual purity demanded of priests and of the whole people as a "holy nation." The New Testament consistently views these laws as institutional "types"— prophecies embedded in the physical life of Israel to point *inward*

---

19   For a thorough and reflective interpretation of the legal sections of the Pentateuch in relation to their fulfillment in Christ, see Vern S. Poythress, *The Shadow of Christ in the Law of Moses*.

to spiritual pollution and cleansing and to point *forward* in history to the climactic once-for-all sacrifice of Christ, which has cleansed not merely the flesh but the conscience (Heb. 9:9–10, 13–14). The Messiah now declares that non-kosher food no longer defiles people, making them unfit for God's presence (Mark 7; Acts 10–11). Christ is the reality to whom the Passover lamb and the unleavened bread pointed (1 Cor. 5:6–8), as he is the reality to whom meat and drink offerings, feasts, New Moon celebrations and Sabbaths all bore witness (Col. 2:16–17). With the coming of Christ, these shadows find their fullest meaning and, having accomplished their prophetic mission, relinquish their claim on the people of God.

The place of the judicial laws in light of the coming of the reality in Christ is more controversial.[20] The Westminster Confession treats these laws as one aspect of the typological nature of the Old Testament people of God, and therefore affirms their expiration at the transition of the new covenant, when the covenant community was transformed from the Israelite "body politic" into the multiethnic church (WCF 19.4). For example, Leviticus 20:11 required that Israel put to death a man who had sexual relations with his father's wife. The apostle Paul, addressing the same situation in 1 Corinthians 5:1–13, instructs the church to exercise ecclesiastical excommunication, not physical execution. This formal expulsion of the unrepentant sinner is a sobering and severe sanction, since it is "to deliver this man to Satan." Yet, excommunication also envisions the possibility that God's mercy will soften the offender's hardened heart through the church's discipline, to the end "that his spirit may be saved in the day of the Lord" (vs. 5). By closing his discussion with a citation from another text from the Mosaic law dealing with penalties for sexual sins ("Purge the evil person from among you," Deut. 22:22, 24), Paul identifies the church as the fulfillment of Israel and the spiritual discipline by which the church protects its communal purity as the fulfillment of the penal sanctions by which Israel was to maintain its corporate holiness. In the books of Moses, the same formula, "Purge the evil person from your midst," is applied to the execution of Israelite idolaters (Deut. 17:7), malicious false witnesses

---

20   The so-called "judicial" or "civil" laws given to Israel through Moses appear throughout the books of Exodus, Leviticus, Numbers, and Deuteronomy, often intermingled with ceremonial regulations. The main concentrations of the Mosaic judicial laws are in Exodus 21–23; Leviticus 18–20, 24-25; Deuteronomy 18–25.

(19:19), and defiant and abusive youths (21:18–21), as well as those found guilty of various sexual sins. In each of these cases, the formula reinforces that the rationale for so severe a punishment is not an abstract principle of justice among the nations at large, but rather the preservation of Israel's purity as God's covenant people. The procedures of church discipline specified by Jesus (Matt. 18:15–20) and his apostles (1 Cor. 5:1–13; 1 Tim. 5:20–25; etc.) are the means by which God now calls his new covenant people to protect its purity.

The same conviction that the community regulations originally given to Israel find their richer fulfillment in the new covenant church undergirds Paul's transformation of a stipulation requiring humane treatment of domestic animals (Deut. 25:4) into a mandate for the equitable compensation of the church's teachers and shepherds (1 Cor. 9:8-12; 1 Tim. 5:17-18). Paul's reasoning seems to coincide with the "how much more" perspective that we have observed in Hebrews: if the Lord protected oxen's rights to fair compensation as they threshed Israel's grain, how much more does he expect his redeemed people to supply the material needs of those who plant in their hearts the life-giving seed of the gospel!

Yet, the Confession also recognizes that these laws, inasmuch as they are concrete applications of the culture-transcending moral law of God to the communal life of his covenant people, also embody a "general equity" of abiding obligation on all human beings as created in the divine image. Western Christians' thirst for a divine blueprint for political, legal, and societal issues is intense, particularly as they observe with dismay the surrounding culture's dissolution into a morass of self-seeking individualism and sensuality. But the Confession recognizes that the "judicial laws" delivered on Sinai must be related differently to modern societies and governments than they were to Israel, the holy people and kingdom of God. The reality corresponding to ancient Israel today, according to the New Testament, is not the United States, the modern state of Israel, or any other nation-state, but the international church of Christ (1 Peter 2:9–10), whose purity as a community is enforced and protected not by physical sanctions but by the Word and church discipline.

Church discipline here and now is flawed and fallible, of course. Therefore, the New Testament also points us to the final antitype of the Mosaic sanctions by which Israel's purity was guarded and restored:

For if we go on sinning deliberately after receiving the knowledge of the truth, there no longer remains a sacrifice for sins, but a fearful expectation of judgment. . . . Anyone who has set aside the law of Moses dies without mercy on the evidence of two or three witnesses. How much worse punishment, do you think, will be deserved by the one who has spurned the Son of God, and has profaned the blood of the covenant by which he was sanctified, and has outraged the Spirit of grace? (Heb. 10:26–29)

In the light of these New Testament commentaries on the Mosaic penalties and sanctions, we should follow the apostles' lead in viewing the Mosaic judicial laws' primary purpose, now that Christ has come, to be one of clarifying the character of holy living that the church is called to pursue presently, in gratitude for the gracious redemption we have received through Christ, as well as portraying the ultimate, consummative separation of the holy from the profane when the King returns to winnow chaff from grain and to separate tares from wheat.[21] As applications of God's culture-transcending moral law specifically adapted to Israel's unique identity as the Lord's covenant people in its typological geopolitical form, the judicial laws also bear witness to a "general equity" that God's character and his authority as Creator enjoin not only on his covenant people but also on humanity in general.[22] They may therefore also have secondary usefulness, when their distinctive covenantal context is first taken into account, as God's law is applied in its "civil" use, to restrain violence and other evil in society.[23]

---

21   For a more detailed development of this approach, see Dennis E. Johnson, "The Epistle to the Hebrews and the Mosaic Penal Sanctions," in W. S. Barker and W. R. Godfrey, eds., *Theonomy: A Reformed Critique* (Grand Rapids: Zondervan, 1990), 171–92.

22   For example, standing before the Jewish Sanhedrin, Paul acknowledges his obligation to adhere to Exodus 22:28: "You shall not speak evil of a ruler of your people" (Acts 23:5), even though the high priest had unjustly ordered that Paul be struck for speaking truth. Even outside such a covenantal venue, the Apostle insists that believers in Jesus show due respect to governing authorities as appointees of God (Rom. 13:1–7; cf. 1 Peter 2:13–17). Likewise, James indicts the rich who delay payment of the day laborers in their fields, in violation of Leviticus 19:13: "The wages of a hired servant shall not remain with you all night until morning" (James 5:4). Such exploitation of the powerless poor is a failure to love one's neighbor as oneself (Lev. 19:18) and a subtle form of theft.

23   On the civil use of the law, see John Calvin, *Institutes of the Christian Religion*, 2.7.10; Louis Berkhof, *Systematic Theology* (Edinburgh: Banner of Truth, 1958), 614.

Likewise, God's promise of a homeland as inheritance for Abraham and his seed finds a fulfillment far beyond the bounds of ancient Canaan, both in its geographical extent[24] and in its invincible security. Hebrews' commentaries on the failure of Joshua's conquest to usher in God's rest (Heb. 4:8) and the heavenly property promised to the patriarchs (11:10–16) demonstrated that the final and greater Joshua will usher his pilgrim people into an inheritance that no sin of theirs can ever jeopardize nor enemy threaten. In contrast to the earthly Jerusalem that once was destroyed by Babylon and would soon be razed again by Rome, the preacher to the Hebrews assures his hearers that their inheritance consists in a coming city that *endures* (13:14), a kingdom that will outlast even the ultimate, eschatological "shaking," when the thunder of God's voice puts the present heaven and earth to flight (12:26–28). Likewise, Peter assures suffering Christians, now homeless aliens even in the towns of their birth, that they have an inheritance in heaven, beyond the reach of decay and defilement, and that they themselves are protected in their pilgrimage to this destination by the invincible power of God (1 Peter 1:1–5).[25]

With these guidelines in mind, let us survey texts from five Old Testament genres, ears attuned to hear them as Jesus taught his apostles to listen for the "advance echoes" of his person and mission as mediator of the new covenant, the bond for which all earlier covenants prepared and to which they witnessed.

Historical Narrative: "Falsely Accused" (2 Samuel 16:5–14)

This text opens with the reminder that David is king, but this is far from David's finest hour in office. The king and those loyal

---

24   In Romans 4:13, Paul paraphrases the land promise to Abraham and his offspring: "that he would be heir of the *world.*" The apostle apparently selects *kosmos* for its global (at least, and potentially universe-wide) connotation in preference over *ge*, used in the ancient accounts of the Abrahamic covenant (e.g., Gen. 12:1; 13:15 LXX). Since *ge* can refer to a bounded "land," although it does sometimes encompass the whole "earth" (Gen. 1:1 LXX), Paul makes explicit that God's promise of a homeland to Abraham the believer and his children by faith, whether circumcised or not, is *world*-wide, not confined to even the widest borders of the "land" once occupied by Israel.

25   On the motif of God's glory resting on his sanctuary, which is identified with his suffering, pilgrim people, see Dennis E. Johnson, "Fire in God's House: Imagery from Malachi 3 in Peter's Theology of Suffering (1 Pet. 4:12–19)," *JETS* 29 (1986): 285–94.

to him are fleeing in exile from his capital, threatened by the king's own son, Absalom. Moreover, Absalom's revolt is the outworking of God's judgment, pronounced through the prophet Nathan, on the king who abused his power by stealing the wife of his soldier Uriah and then conspiring to cover his sin by orchestrating Uriah's death to appear as a casualty of war:

> Why have you despised the word of the LORD, to do what is evil in his sight? You have struck down Uriah the Hittite with the sword and have taken his wife to be your wife and have killed him with the sword of the Ammonites. Now therefore the sword shall never depart from your house, because you have despised me and have taken the wife of Uriah the Hittite to be your wife. Thus says the LORD, "Behold I will raise up evil against you out of your own house. And I will take your wives before your eyes and give them to your neighbor, and he shall lie with your wives in the sight of this sun. For you did it secretly, but I will do this thing before all Israel and before the sun" (2 Sam. 12:9–12).

David now flees his son's sword because he himself had despised the Lord and his word, abusively using his royal power to commit adultery and murder and shedding the blood of a trustworthy and trusting servant, who had distinguished himself in self-denying devotion to David's cause.

Not surprisingly, the editors of *Novum Testamentum Graece* and the United Bible Societies' *Greek New Testament* find no quotation of or allusion to this text in the New Testament.[26] If David is an image of his greater Son to come, he must be a negative image—at least in the broader context of this shameful period of his reign. How, then, can such a passage proclaim Christ, and what response to the King to come should it elicit from us and our hearers?

The close literary context of the narrative of Shimei's cursing and David's patient response traces David's descent under God's judgment, followed by his resurrection to the throne by God's mercy. In the spiral of descent as the king flees his own capital, he encounters Ziba the servant of Mephibosheth (16:1–4) and then Shimei a kinsman of Saul (16:5–14). After Absalom's defeat and death, as the king returns to Jerusalem he meets Shimei (19:16–23), and then Ziba (19:17)

---

26 The *New Geneva Study Bible* does cite as thematic cross-references: Rom. 9:20 in relation to the rhetorical question in 2 Sam. 16:10. Also, Rom. 8:28; Heb. 12:10–11 are linked with 2 Sam. 16:12 by the theme that God uses evil to produce good ends.

and Mephibosheth (19:24–30). Both Shimei and Mephibosheth have a connection with Saul, since Mephibosheth is the son of Saul's son Jonathan. In fact, David has begun to look troublingly like his predecessor on the throne, having mistreated the loyal Uriah as Saul would have eliminated David himself, were it not for God's purpose and the loyal friendship of Jonathan. The breach between David and his son Absalom in some ways seems to repeat the alienation between Saul and Jonathan, although the bitter and defiant Absalom is unworthy to be compared with the upright Jonathan.

As we read the king's interchange with Ziba just preceding our text (16:1–4), readers have no way to tell whether the servant's evil report about his master's royal aspirations (now that David is in flight) are true. Neither, however, does David at that point. Yet, in direct conflict with the Mosaic commands that forbid Israel's judges from condemning anyone on the basis of the testimony of a single witness (Deut. 19:15–21; cf. 17:6; Num. 35:30), as Israel's chief justice David is quick to countenance Ziba's evil report concerning Mephibosheth and to dispossess the latter of his paternal inheritance and all means of support. In good times, David had exalted Jonathan's only surviving son, the disabled Mephibosheth, as one of his own sons for Jonathan's sake, but now how easily a king on the run forgets his covenantal allegiance to the fast friend who risked his own life to protect David's! Moreover, the sequel that follows the defeat of Absalom's revolt reveals how grievously David has betrayed Jonathan's loyalty in his treatment of Mephibosheth (19:17, 24–30). As the king returns to his capital with Ziba in his entourage, Mephibosheth, whose appearance bears witness to his mourning throughout the king's exile, meets him. Mephibosheth accuses his servant of having betrayed him and preyed on his disability, thwarting his desire to leave Jerusalem with the king's company. Either unwilling to acknowledge the injustice of his earlier snap judgment against Mephibosheth or else lacking the wisdom to sort out the truth amid the exchange of accusations, David simply orders the division of Mephibosheth's property between the master and the servant. Yet, the truth of the matter is shown in Mephibosheth's response: in his joy over the king's restoration, he is willing to forfeit his whole inheritance to his treacherous servant. David's son and successor Solomon, a wiser judge than his father, confronted with a similar "she said, she said" dilemma, knew that the truth-telling mother would forfeit her child rather than let him be divided (1 Kings 3:16–28); but David does nothing more to vindicate the loyal Mephibosheth (a true son of his loyal father Jonathan) or to punish the false witness Ziba.

Even the first readers of 2 Samuel could be expected to assess David's conduct as king not only in light of the previous Mosaic revelation but also in light of the oracle that provides a bridge between the books of Samuel and Kings. David's "last words" describe the perfect king who rules in the fear of God and therefore judges justly (2 Sam. 23:3–4). They go on to affirm, based on God's everlasting covenant with David's house, the king's hope that God will fulfill his longing for such a ruler. In the subsequent history of Israel and Judah given in the books of Kings, monarchs would be compared either to the standard of David's faithfulness (e.g., 1 Kings 15:3, 11) or to the evil precedent set by Jeroboam son of Nebat (1 Kings 15:26, 34; 16:19, 26, 31). Thus 1 and 2 Kings show that the dynasty of the sons of David still contains, rarely, individual kings who exhibit to some degree the faithfulness to the Lord that is requisite in the ruler of God's people. Nevertheless, the sordid events of 2 Samuel 11–19 (recalled once more in the mention of Uriah as the last of David's mighty men, 2 Sam. 23:39), not to speak of the royal arrogance that prompted the census that closes 2 Samuel, reinforce the point that David, though a "man after God's heart" and the standard for his successors, fails to fit the profile of the righteous ruler portrayed in his prophetic last words (2 Sam. 23:1–7). The redemption of God's people awaits the arrival of the perfect Redeemer and final Son of David, an anointed shoot from Jesse's stump who "shall not judge by what his eyes see, or decide disputes by what his ears hear, but with righteousness he shall judge the poor, and decide with equity for the meek of the earth" (Isa. 11:3–4).

Yet, it would seem that in our passage the exiled king's patient, passive response to undeserved cursing by Saul's kinsman provides a fleeting glimpse, even in this, David's darkest hour, of the long-suffering of a truly innocent King, who refused to retaliate when his subjects heaped abuse and false accusation on him. Then again, the complexity of the issues surrounding Shimei's charge (which is simultaneously false, and yet also true) illustrate the accuracy of Goppelt's observation that the relation between type and its fulfillment is characterized both by correspondence and by heightening: David is both like and unlike the coming Messiah, whose subjects will curse and kill him.

The narrative is structured around three agents who are, more precisely, primarily speakers. First, the readers' attention is drawn to Shimei and his foolish and futile attempt to execute the fleeing king, hurling stones with his curses, charging David with shedding the blood of Saul's house (2 Sam. 16:5–8). Second, we hear the readiness of Abishai, David's cousin and military officer, to slice off Shimei's cursing, cursed head (vs. 9). Finally, we hear David's complex rebuke to the loyal Abishai, acknowledging divine justice and expressing hope for divine mercy (vv. 10–12). The conclusion narrates Shimei's persistent, unresisted abuse and the resultant wear and tear on the king and his company. A sermon on this text could well be structured around these three speakers/participants, reflecting both the narrative tension in the account and the theological progression to the climax in the speech of David.

1. Shimei, Saul's cursing kinsman, the insolent subject who lies about his king (as you have done).
2. Abishai, David's killing kinsman, the loyal soldier who would defend his king for the wrong reason, in the wrong way (as you have done).
3. David the king, falsely and truly accused.

Yet, the text's morally mottled portrait of David cries out for resolution in the coming King, whom David would foresee as sunrise on a cloudless morning in his final oracle (2 Sam. 23:4). To preach this text in the context of 2 Samuel and the completed canon, we must add a fourth point or movement in our message:

4. Jesus the King, falsely accused, condemned and punished for the charge that was true of David (and of you).

How would each of these motifs be developed?

Shimei's cursing of the king, evaluated in the context of the Mosaic law, was no mere exercise of freedom of expression or civil disobedience. It was a pointed violation of the authority of God himself, the Great King, who had replaced Saul with David, anointing the latter with his Spirit and giving Israel deliverance through this son of Jesse. The Lord's covenant had closely linked the dignity of God and the honor of his royal delegates: "You shall not revile God, nor curse a ruler of your people" (Ex. 22:28). Even if Shimei's charges against David were true, they would not justify his verbal and physical assault on the Lord's anointed. His resistance to God's appointed leader contrasts sharply with David's patient response when King Saul pursued him (1 Sam. 24:6) and to the apostle Paul's repentant submission when rebuked for (inadvertently) cursing Israel's high priest (Acts 23:5). Shimei, however, stands in a long line of rebels who showed that they resent God's authority by their rejection of the leaders whom God designates: Joseph's brothers, the Israelite who rejected Moses, nations who conspire against the Lord and his Christ in Psalm 2, and finally the leaders and people of Jerusalem who demanded Jesus' execution (cf. also Luke 19:14; 20:14–18). Our hearers need to see themselves in Shimei, to see the resistant rebel in themselves: "Do you resent the fact that God calls you to submit to Jesus as Lord? Oh, you may not curse him, but do you bridle at the way his commands curtail your independence and interrupt your comfort and convenience?"

Shimei's sin not only violated God's authority but also violated God's truth. From whatever source Shimei formed the opinion that David was to be blamed for blood in Saul's house, the readers of the books of Samuel know better. David had sworn covenant love to Jonathan and his descendants (1 Sam. 20) and had twice spared Saul's life when given the opportunity, even though Saul had repeated tried to kill David (1 Sam. 24). The Lord had used Philistine suspicion to keep David out of the conflict in which Saul and Jonathan died (1 Sam. 29–30), and David subsequently ordered the execution of the man who boasted that he had killed Saul (2 Sam. 1:1–16). David had repudiated Joab's cowardly murder of Abner, after that great general had changed allegiance from Saul's son Ishbosheth to David (2 Sam. 3:28–29). For this murder, David pronounced a curse on Joab (Abishai's brother) and his descendants. Finally, David repudiated the assassins of Saul's son Ishbosheth and ordered that they be executed (2 Sam. 4). If there is one thing that David cannot justly be accused of, it is shedding blood in the house of Saul![27] Yet, Shimei seems so certain that he knows truth that he need not bother to learn

---

27   David later allowed the Gibeonites to avenge harm that they had received from Saul, for which the Lord had imposed a famine on Israel, by hanging seven of Saul's descendents (2 Sam. 21:1–14). Even that account, however, closes with David's showing respect for the remains of Saul, Jonathan, and the seven executed Saulites.

the facts. As a self-appointed judge, jury, and executioner, he pronounces his baseless verdict and attempts to stone the king whom he accuses of murder. In his arrogant and foolish rush to judgment Shimei keeps company with the king he curses, who had just condemned a close friend's loyal son to destitution, and with the king's zealous defender, Abishai.

Abishai, David's kinsman and loyal soldier, at first seems in the right in his eagerness to defend the Lord's anointed and to avenge the indignity done to the Lord in the dishonoring of his deputy. Admittedly, Abishai is eager to repay Shimei's insult with insult. The rebel who labels his king a "man of blood" is himself a "dead dog," impotent and despicable.[28] It is also possible that family solidarity and pride are mingled with his more worthy motives. Yet, Abishai stands solidly with the king of God's choosing, zealously loyal to the Lord's anointed. Is not his zeal for the king an expression of zeal for God himself? Does not David himself say, "Do I not hate those who hate you, O Lord? And do I not loathe those who rise up against you? I hate them with complete hatred; I count them my enemies" (Ps. 139:21–22)? Therefore, given a nod from his cousin the king, Abishai would be across the ravine, his sword flashing from its scabbard, and Shimei's acid rain of insults, stones, and soil would stop in an instant. If our hearers can see themselves in Abishai, outraged at the contempt shown to God and his Christ in our time and culture, they will be primed for the shock of the king's reply.

Instead of permission or commendation, however, the king issues a sharp rebuke to his would-be defender. David's "What have I to do with you, you sons of Zeruiah?" classes Abishai with his bloodthirsty brother Joab and places them both at arm's length. The Hebrew expression is stronger than its English equivalent sounds. It means not merely, "Do I know you?" but "What do you have against me?" or "Why are you stirring up trouble for me?" (Cf. Judg. 11:12). Believing himself to be the king's loyal ally, Abishai had become David's enemy. Centuries later James and John, incensed at a Samaritan village that refused hospitality to their Master, would seek Jesus' permission to call fire from heaven, as Elijah had done, to incinerate the inhospitable; but they would receive his terse rebuke (Luke 9:51–56; cf. 2 Kings 1:9–12). Peter, in misguided allegiance, would rebuke Jesus' prediction

---

28   When Mephibosheth is first honored by David for Jonathan's sake, he uses the same metaphor to describe his disability and insignificance (2 Sam. 9:8).

of the cross, only to be rebuffed by Jesus' harsh, "Get behind me, Satan!" (Matt. 16:21–23). And Peter would nonetheless wield his sword, Abishai-like (though without asking permission), severing the ear of the high priest's servant in one last, futile effort to avert the suffering of his king (John 18:10–11). All of these loyalists thought they were defending the honor of the king, when he suddenly turned on them as though they were enemies. How had their zeal gotten so far off track? The answer lies in the words of David, the Lord's anointed, both his confession of guilt and his hope of grace.

David reveals the complexity of the issues in his rebuke to Abishai. Although the readers of 1 and 2 Samuel know that Shimei has borne false witness by accusing David of shedding blood in Saul's house, at a deeper level Shimei's lies are truer than even he had imagined. David's present trouble is not because he is guilty of shedding blood in the house of Saul, who had threatened David's life more than once. Rather, David was even guiltier than Shimei suspected, for David had treacherously conspired to shed the innocent blood of a loyal servant. Although Shimei's cursing violates God's prohibition in Exodus 22 and reveals a heart that (as subsequent events will show) remains hard, though repeatedly spared much-deserved judgment (2 Sam. 19:18–23; 1 Kings 2:8–9, 36–46), David twice insists that the Lord "told" Shimei to pronounce his curses (2 Sam. 16:10, 11). Although Shimei is not issuing the curses of the covenant as a submissive prophet of God but from evil motives, David hears in his words the verdict of the Lord who is sovereign over his enemies.

David also confesses that God is just, for his poignant "My own son seeks my life" (16:11) inserts into the narrative the occasion of the king's exile, the covenant curse pronounced by the faithful prophet Nathan upon the monarch who defiled his office by adultery and murder. Having resisted the temptation to kill Saul, who had pursued him as an enemy, David betrayed the trust of his loyal soldier, first taking Uriah's wife and then, to cover his infidelity, conspiring to take Uriah's life. The sword introduced into David's house by his own sin had already destroyed his children through incestuous rape and fratricide, and Absalom's armed revolt would end in the violent death of another beloved son of the king. David is a "man of blood" far worse than Shimei imagines and richly deserves the exile he now suffers!

The uncertain history of the writing of the books (originally book) of Samuel complicates our identification of the situation and need of its first recipients. Some evangelical scholars have maintained that the material in Samuel was collected in essentially its present form soon after the division of the northern and southern kingdoms.[29] Others believe that the books of Samuel and Kings, as least in their final forms, were addressed to Judah's exiles in Babylon.[30] Whether the earlier or the later date is adopted, the original readers of this passage could have seen their own experience in microcosm in the exile of King David from his capital. The tenth-century schism that tore most of Israel from the hands of David's grandson Rehoboam is ominously foreshadowed in our text, as is Judah's later, sixth-century expulsion from the Lord's land. Such banishments also echo the exclusion of Adam and Eve from the Garden of God and access to the Tree of Life, and in that justly imposed exile all our twenty-first century hearers share.

In addition to acknowledging God's justice in this exile, David confesses hope that the undeserved mercy of God may reverse his fortunes. Turning around Shimei's curse, "The Lord has *returned* to you all the blood of the house of Saul" (16:8 dej), David hopes that despite his guilt "Perhaps the Lord will see my trouble and the Lord will *return* to me good in place of his [Shimei's] curses" (16:12 dej). How could David—the king who committed two capital crimes, adultery and murder, against a loyal Gentile soldier before whom the Lord's Anointed should have shone like a light to the nations—hope for good from the God of justice? He could do so in part because he had already received mercy beyond expectation or imagination. When confronted by the prophet Nathan, David humbly repented and heard the sweet assurance: "The LORD also has put away your sin; you shall not die" (2 Sam. 12:13). Horrific temporal consequences would flow from David's wicked acts, beginning with the death of his and Bathsheba's newborn son; but God's grace would shield David from eternal wrath and condemnation. It may be too much to speak of that infant receiving the death that David deserved (as a natural descendent of Adam, this child, too, stood guilty of his

29   Edward J. Young, *An Introduction to the Old Testament* (Grand Rapids: Eerdmans, 1964), 177–78; R. K. Harrison, *Introduction to the Old Testament* (Grand Rapids: Eerdmans, 1969), 709.

30   E.g., Raymond Dillard and Tremper Longman III, *An Introduction to the Old Testament* (Grand Rapids: Zondervan, 1994), 136, 145–46; Barry L. Bandstra, *Reading the Old Testament: An Introduction to the Hebrew Bible* (Belmont, California: Wadsworth, 1995), 251.

first father's rebellion). He seems to be merely a bystander caught in the cross-fire of David's destructive self-centeredness. Eventually, however, another Son of David would come, God the Son incarnate, the Holy One from his mother's womb, exempt from Adam's guilt and sin, and worthy to offer himself to atone for adulterers, murderers, and other sinners. As one who had "utterly scorned the LORD" (2 Sam. 12:14) and yet received forgiveness, David bore patiently the contempt of Shimei and refused to sanction the latter's richly deserved execution.

The unresolved complexity of the issues surrounding David's insulted dignity and his deserved indictment cries out for resolution in *Jesus the King*, history's one true Innocent, who was falsely accused, condemned and punished for the charge that was true of David and the accusations that truly indict us. Jesus silently endured false accusation and undeserved torture and execution. "He committed no sin, neither was deceit found in his mouth. When he was reviled, he did not revile in return; when he suffered, he did not threaten, but continued entrusting himself to him who judges justly" (1 Peter 2:22–23). Instead of lashing back in self-defense, Jesus awaited the vindication of resurrection morning.

Moreover, Jesus endured injustice not merely to set an example of patience, but also and primarily to embody God's astonishing mercy toward us and our hearers, who are justly accused. Shimei's ultimate violent end (1 Kings 2:36–46), when he abandoned the safety of his city of refuge, the king's city, shows that the unrepentant rebel and slanderer will not endure forever with impunity. But Jesus' patience in suffering and power in resurrection remind us that the remedy to injustice is not our own self-righteous vigilante crusade against false accusers (James 1:20) but the grace of the cross in the present and the certainly of God's holy judgment in the future. God's forgiving grace in Christ becomes the foundation and fountain of transforming grace, which enables us to follow the King's footsteps in our own patient, non-retaliatory response to injustice and ill-treatment (1 Peter 2:19; 4:19).

Law: "The Grace Behind God's Commands" (Deuteronomy 6:20–25)

This text concludes a chapter that often is quoted in the New Testament. This frequency of quotation is not surprising inasmuch as Deuteronomy 6:4–5 contains the *Shema'*, that confession of the Lord's uniqueness and unity that became the touchstone of Israel's faith, along with the concomitant command of exclusive, exhaustive allegiance, the first great commandment: "Hear, O Israel: The LORD our God, the LORD is one. You shall love the LORD your God with all your heart and with all your soul and with all your might" (Deut. 6:4–5; cf. Mark 12:29–30 par.; Rom. 3:30; 1 Cor. 8:4; James 2:19). Proceeding from that confession and exclusive commitment are injunctions to teach the Lord's commands to Israel's children everywhere and all the time (Deut. 6:7–9), reinforced by sober warnings that when Israel enters the land they must not forget the Lord, embrace his rivals, or put him to the test as they had in the wilderness (6:10–19). The text before us, verses 20 through 25, elaborates on the themes of instructing the children, keeping faith with the Lord, and retaining possession of the land of promise. This passage, however, is not quoted in the New Testament and may be alluded to only by a very general thematic connection.[31] How, then, can this passage proclaim Christ?

Deuteronomy presents a series of discourses, delivered by Moses on the plains of Moab, to prepare Israel for the imminent conquest of the Promised Land under Joshua's leadership. The discourses are appropriately forward looking, and they anticipate not only the adjustment of the legal stipulations of the Lord's covenant to settled life in the land but also the spiritual trial that coexistence with Canaan's pagan residents will pose for the Lord's people and the adverse consequences that would follow Israel's fall. Yet, Israel's apostasy and the Lord's covenant curse are not Moses' last word. Beyond the devastation of the land and the destruction and dispersion of Abraham's children, Moses glimpses a day of repentance and forgiveness of regathering and restoration: "And the LORD your God will circumcise your heart and the heart of your offspring, so that you will love the LORD your God with all your heart and with all your soul, that you may live" (Deut. 30:6).

---

31 The *Novum Testamentum Graece* index lists no quotations or allusions to Deuteronomy 6:20–25 in the New Testament, nor does the *Jerusalem Bible* cite New Testament texts as cross-references to this passage. The editors of *Greek New Testament* discern a general allusion to its theme in Paul's instruction to fathers to raise their children in the discipline and instruction of the Lord (Eph. 6:4). The *New Geneva Study Bible* lists as a cross-reference to the statement that keeping the commandments "will be righteousness for us" Paul's mention of the righteousness based on law described by Moses (Rom. 10:3, 5).

Our passage's close context reveals that this future conversation between with Israel's inquisitive children and their parents recapitulates the function of the early chapters of Deuteronomy, which is to place Israel's covenantal responsibilities in the context of the redemption that Israel already had received in the exodus. M. G. Kline has shown how this "second law" (the meaning of the book's Greek title *Deuteronomion* in the LXX) is structured as an Ancient Near Eastern treaty, with a preamble (1:1–5), a historical prologue (1:6–4:49), stipulations (5:1–26:19), sanctions (27:1–30:20), and provisions for dynastic disposition (31:1–34:12).[32] The function of a treaty's historical prologue was to set the context that would motivate the vassal, on whom the covenant was being imposed, to maintain exclusive loyalty to the suzerain who had rescued, defended, and shown other acts of kindness to the vassal in the past. So also, the prologue section of Deuteronomy rehearses the Lord's gracious provision and strong protection of Israel throughout the wilderness wanderings, despite his people's unbelief and stubborn rebellion, leading up to a recital of the Ten Commandments delivered on Mount Horeb amid terrifying displays of the Lord's holiness and might. So also, Israelite fathers are expected to explain the significance of the detailed commandments delivered at Horeb by telling their sons the story of the exodus from Egypt and the conquest of the Promised Land (6:20–23). The meaning of the commandments is to be sought, first of all, in the Lord's prior acts of redemption on his people's behalf.

Moving out from the immediate documentary context of Deuteronomy into the first four books of Moses and the subsequent narrative of Joshua, we see that the father-son conversation envisioned here belongs to a fourfold collection of similar interrogations. The annual observance of Passover would evoke the younger generation's curiosity, giving parents the opportunity to explain its rationale: "It is the sacrifice of the LORD's Passover, for he passed over the houses of the people of Israel in Egypt, when he struck the Egyptians but spared our houses" (Ex. 12:27). Likewise, the consecration and redemption of Israel's firstborn would again evoke the question, "What does this mean?" To this the answer must be given:

By a strong hand the LORD brought us out of Egypt, from the house of slavery. For when Pharaoh stubbornly refused to let us go, the LORD

---

32   M. G. Kline, *Treaty of the Great King*, 48–49.

killed all the firstborn in the land of Egypt, both the firstborn of man and the firstborn of animals. Therefore I sacrifice to the LORD all the males that first open the womb, but all the firstborn of my sons I redeem. (Ex. 13:14–15)

Israel's firstborn sons, no less than those of their Egyptian oppressors, were liable to the death that had been inflicted by God's messenger of judgment, yet redemption had been provided Israel's firstborn through the blood of the Passover lamb. This redemption was commemorated in every generation, giving repeated occasion to rehearse and remember both the exodus from slavery and the deliverance from death that had preceded it. In a Passover season some forty years after the exodus, another monument to God's power and grace toward Israel would be erected on the Jordan's west bank, a pile of twelve boulders from the midst of the riverbed, where priests bearing the ark of God's covenant stood as the Lord restrained the Jordan's floodwaters for his people to pass into his land. This memorial, too, would evoke future generations' questions, to be answered with a rehearsal of the Lord's mighty deeds: ". . . you shall tell them that the waters of the Jordan were cut off before the ark of the covenant of the LORD. . . . You shall let your children know, 'Israel passed over this Jordan on dry ground' " (Josh. 4:7, 22). Thus the association of Deuteronomy 6:20–25 with other texts that summon Israelite parents to rehearse the Lord's redemptive acts to future generations further reinforces the gracious context of the commandments. Children must be told the story: the Lord had not only spared Israel's firstborn from the angel of his wrath, freed Israel from slavery, and given Israel a land to call home, he also had given a law to lead them into life under his blessing.

A sermon on this text should highlight the passage's emphasis on the grace and power of the covenant Lord as standing before and behind his commandments and explaining their meaning. Thus this text unveils the implicit logic that unites the earlier Shema' ("The Lord our God is one") with the immediately subsequent instruction to teach the Lord's commands to Israel's children everywhere and all the time (Deut. 6:4–8). The outline might look like this.

1. The commandments mean that, when we were slaves, the Lord graciously set us free. (vv. 21–22)

2. The commandments mean that, when we were homeless aliens, the Lord graciously brought us home. (vs. 23)
3. The commandments mean that the Lord even gives us grace to respond to his grace. (vv. 24–25)

The sermon follows the text's redemptive-historical structure, grounding the summons to obedience first in the exodus, then in the conquest of the land, and finally in the promise of future, ongoing blessing in the land for those who maintain covenant faithfulness to the Lord. These motifs furthermore address the deep needs of fallen humanity for liberation to replace our bondage, security to replace our rootless wandering, and single-minded devotion to replace our wayward and fleeting loyalties. In its full canonical context, this text also should be preached in light of the New Testament's portrayal of the life of the church, existing between the two comings of Christ, according to the pattern of Israel's pilgrimage from initial redemption (the exodus) to final rest from threatening enemies (entry into the land, e.g., Heb. 3–4, 1 Cor. 10).

By grounding the rationale of the law's commands, first of all, in the prior event of Israel's exodus from Egypt—first the Red Sea, then Sinai—Moses underscores that for fallen people to enjoy the blessing of God, his sheer grace must precede their obedient response (Deut. 6:20–22). In fact, Moses proceeds almost immediately to underscore the point that the rationale for Israel's deliverance from Egyptian bondage does not lie in her qualifications.

> It was not because you were more in number than any other people that the LORD set his love on you and chose you, for you were the fewest of all peoples, but it is because the LORD loves you and is keeping the oath that he swore to your fathers, that the LORD has brought you out with a mighty hand and redeemed you from the house of slavery, from the hand of Pharaoh king of Egypt. Know therefore that the LORD your God is God, the faithful God who keeps covenant and steadfast love with those who love him and keep his commandments, to a thousand generations, and repays to their face those who hate him, by destroying them. (Deut. 7:7–10)

Israel's smallness and weakness magnify the mercy and faithful love of the Lord who has delivered them from slavery, while at the same time precluding any self-righteousness or self-congratulation on the part of the covenant servant.

On the other hand, it also is true to say that Israel, though small and stubborn, is receiving the land through obedience. Moses has already drawn a connection between obedience and conquest of the Promised Land in Deuteronomy 4:1: "And now, O Israel, listen to the statutes and the rules that I am teaching you, and do them, that you may live, and go in and take possession of the land that the LORD, the God of your fathers, is giving you." Israel is to hear and to do the Lord's commands "that" the promised consequences might follow, namely life and possession of the land. Israel's reception of the relative and temporal/temporary possession of life and land as a reward for relative fidelity to the law of the Lord foreshadows a covenantal principle of reciprocity that the apostle Paul will articulate in its eschatologized, absolutized form: "The one who does [God's commands] shall live by them" (Gal. 3:12). But the apostle knows, as one once considered "blameless" under the law but now gladly trusting in a righteousness not his own (Phil. 3:6–9), that the radical covenant obedience that entitles one to expect the radical covenant blessing of life in the age to come is beyond the reach of Adam's fallen children.

Yet, the Pentateuch also shows us that Israel is entering the land not only by grace but also by obedience in another sense: the Lord's oath to Abraham was in recognition of Abraham's loyalty to the Lord and his covenant. His heirs' eventual reception of the Promised Land will be, in a sense, the Lord's reward for Abraham's fidelity both in the rescue of Lot (Gen. 15:1) and in his willingness to sacrifice his "only" son Isaac (22:16–18; 26:2–5). M. G. Kline comments concerning Genesis 26:

> Here the significance of Abraham's works cannot be limited to their role in validation of his own faith. His faithful performance of his covenantal duty is here clearly indicated to sustain a causal relationship to the blessing of Isaac and Israel. It had a meritorious character that procured a reward enjoyed by others.[33]

Israel, then, would take possession of the land through obedience— the obedience of another. Kline elaborates, "Within this typological structure Abraham emerges as an appointed sign of his promised

---

33   M. G. Kline, *Kingdom Prologue: Genesis Foundations for a Covenantal Worldview* (Overland Park, KS: Two Age Press, 2000), 324–25. This edition is cited as *Kingdom Prologue* (2000) below.

messianic seed, the Servant of the Lord, whose fulfillment of his covenantal mission was the meritorious ground of the inheritance of the antitypical, eschatological kingdom by the true, elect Israel of all nations."[34]

Believers in Jesus, who have experienced the greater exodus, of which Israel's departure from Egypt was only a faint shadow, should hear this text in the light of the "how much more" logic of Hebrews: delivered from a crueler tyrant and a more unbreakable bondage, we have all the more reason to respond to the greater grace now granted us in Jesus, mediator of the new and better covenant. By the perfect obedience and covenant loyalty of one greater than Abraham, to whose "day" Abraham rejoiced to look, we are ushered into a far greater inheritance than Canaan, an inheritance that is "imperishable, undefiled, and unfading, kept in heaven for you" (1 Peter 1:4). The Israelites were "baptized into Moses in the cloud and in the sea" (1 Cor. 10:2); we have been baptized into Jesus in his death and resurrection. They watched as Pharaoh's pursuing forces were destroyed by the Lord's floodwaters; our Champion assumed our flesh and blood "that through his death he might destroy the one who has the power of death, that is, the devil, and deliver all those who through fear of death were subject to lifelong slavery" (Heb. 2:14–15). Israelite children must hear repeatedly the logic of grace-evoked obedience, which comes to its fullest fruition in the gospel of Christ. The typical structure of several Pauline epistles makes this clear: the indicative of the glorious redemptive work of Jesus (Rom. 1–11; Eph. 1–3; Col. 1:1–2:5) precedes, motivates, and empowers the imperatives that define the response of the redeemed (Rom. 12–15; Eph. 4–6; Col. 2:6–4:6). Viewed from the perspective of the order of the application of redemption, justification grounded solely in God's grace and Christ's obedience for us precedes sanctification, and the assurance it provides propels grateful hearts to gladly obey their Redeemer's commands.

Secondly, Israelite parents are to explain the Lord's commands in relation to the gift of the land that Abraham's seed would soon begin to enjoy (Deut. 6:23). After centuries of alien sojourning, cruel bondage, and wandering pilgrimage, Israel was at last about to take possession of the homeland promised to Abraham when God first called him to leave his Mesopotamian home (Gen. 12:1–3; 15:7–21).

---

34 Kline, *Kingdom Prologue* (2000), 325.

Again, Moses emphasizes that this provision of a home for this homeless people has nothing to do with their worthiness or qualification.

> Do not say in your heart, after the Lord your God has thrust them out before you, "It is because of my righteousness that the Lord has brought me in to possess this land. . . ." Not because of your righteousness or the uprightness of your heart are you going in to possess their land, but because of the wickedness of these nations the Lord your God is driving them out from before you, and that he may confirm the word that the Lord swore to your fathers, to Abraham, to Isaac, and to Jacob.

> Know, therefore, that the Lord your God is not giving you this good land to possess because of your righteousness, for you are a stubborn people. Remember and do not forget how you provoked the Lord your God to wrath in the wilderness. (Deut. 9:4–7)

Just as the grace of liberation directs all glory to God and none to his weak people, so also the grace of inheritance will magnify the Lord even as it humbles his stubborn and unworthy people. The Lord's oath to the patriarchs, mentioned in verse 23 of our text, should be traced back to the Lord's oath on his own immutable life to secure his promise after providing a substitute for Abraham's "only" and beloved son Isaac on Mount Moriah (Gen. 22:16). To this same oath, Moses had appealed to beg mercy for Israel in the aftermath of their spiritual adultery with the golden calf (Ex. 32:11–13). Nothing but the Lord's loyal love to a disloyal people could explain Israel's entrance into the homeland that he so amply furnished for them (cf. 6:10–11; 8:7–10).

Yet, within Deuteronomy itself, foreboding and prophetic previews of Israel's subsequent history make clear that the conquest soon to be led by Joshua does not mark the destination of Israel's long pilgrimage but only a way station along the road to God's rest. The summary that speaks of rest from surrounding enemies at the conclusion of Joshua's military campaigns notwithstanding (Josh. 21:43–22:6), the preacher to the Hebrews is right to infer that the rest conferred through Joshua fell short of "God's rest," promised in Psalm 95 (Heb. 4:8). Even in Deuteronomy 6, Moses warns Israel against following the gods of their pagan neighbors in the land (Deut. 6:14), and he subsequently amplifies his warning by noting that the very abundance of the land may ensnare their hearts to forget the Lord, trust themselves, and serve other gods (8:11–20). It is no mere coincidence that Deuteronomy's sanctions section as a covenant treaty is weighted heavily toward curses for disloyalty (28:15–68), rather than blessings for obedience (28:1–14), for Israel's future will be marred by capitulation to the insidious idolatry of their neighbors in Canaan. Even in the Lord's land, Israel's hearts would be restless, their faith and faithfulness constantly under attack and often overcome.

The New Testament portrays Christians' present pilgrimage as a similar admixture of security and threat. On the one hand, through our union with Christ our representative and head we have already entered our heavenly inheritance and taken our seat there with our greater Joshua, who has accomplished the conquest (Eph. 2:6). Our life is hidden, even now, with Christ in God (Col. 3:1–4). On the other hand, believers endure intense trials as "elect exiles of the dispersion" who have not yet entered the "inheritance that is imperishable, undefiled, and unfading, kept in heaven for you" but must take courage from the promise that they "by God's power are being guarded through faith for a salvation ready to be revealed in the last time" (1 Peter 1:1, 4–5). The better hope of a heavenly country and a yet-future city with foundations set by God himself (Heb. 11:10, 16; 13:14) provides all the motive we should need to embrace wholeheartedly God's commands for our good; yet Deuteronomy and later Scriptures show us that nothing less than the guarding power of God through faith will secure our hearts in persevering, faith-filled obedience.

In the text's third motif Israelite fathers are to turn their sons' thoughts toward the future (Deut. 6:24–25). To the graces of liberation and inheritance, the Lord has added, at Sinai, the grace of direction in life and to life. The law is indeed a good gift, "holy and righteous and good" (Rom. 7:12). Any who keep its commands shall live by them (Lev. 18:5), for indeed Moses would conclude his discourses on the plains of Moab:

> Take to heart all the words by which I am warning you today, that you may command them to your children, that they may be careful to do all the words of this law. For it is no empty word for you, but your very life, and by this word you shall live long in the land that you are going over the Jordan to possess. (Deut. 32:46–47)

Continuing and increasing blessing would come not by mere external compliance with regulations but by the inner devotion that is summed up in the phrase, "to fear the LORD our God" (cf. 5:29;

31:12–13). Repeatedly in Deuteronomy, the summons to fear the Lord is coordinated with the summons to love the Lord exclusively and wholeheartedly, and obedience to his commands is traced to this deeply grateful response to his grace and trust in his promises of greater good to come:

> And now, Israel, what does the LORD your God require of you, but to fear the LORD your God, to walk in all his ways, to love him, to serve the LORD your God with all your heart and with all your soul, and to keep the commandments and statutes of the LORD, which I am commanding you today for your good? (Deut. 10:12–13)

Nevertheless, the sobering reality of Israel's (and our own) proclivity to respond to amazing grace with thoughtless infidelity casts a stark shadow over the prospect of so stubborn a people fearing, loving, and serving the Lord. What is needed is a circumcision of the heart itself (Deut. 10:16), for nothing less than so radical a surgery can cure our proneness to forget the Lord's grace, resist the Lord's authority, and wander after the Lord's rival. As Moses peers down through the coming years, past the centuries of Israel's treachery and the Lord's forbearance, past the eventual infliction of covenant curses in Israel's destruction and dispersion, he catches sight of this coming grace, the grace that circumcises hardened, defiled hearts and imparts the grace to meet grace with deep gratitude and eager obedience.

> When all these things come upon you, the blessing and the curse, which I have set before you, and you call them to mind among all the nations where the LORD your God has driven you . . . the LORD your God will bring you into the land that your fathers possessed. . . . And the LORD your God will circumcise your heart and the heart of your offspring, so that you will love the LORD your God with all your heart and with all your soul, that you may live. (Deut. 30:1, 5–6)

The apostles declare that the future day of heart-circumcision performed by the Lord himself has come not only for Israel but for all Abraham's faith-children as well. Those once "dead in your tresspasses and the uncircumcision of your flesh," Paul now assures Gentile believers in Jesus, "In him also you were circumcised with a circumcision made without hands, by putting off the body of the flesh, by the circumcision of Christ, having been buried with him in baptism, in which you were also raised with him through faith in the powerful working of God" (Col. 2:11–13; cf. Rom. 2:25–29). In addition to the grace of liberation from sin, death, and Satan in our past and the grace of a sovereignly secured homeland in our future, in the present we receive the grace of Holy Spirit-wrought love for the Lord who freed us, guards us, and will welcome us home. How much more, then, must parents of the new Israel impart to their children the meaning of his commands as testimonies to the grace that lies behind his law for all who belong by faith to Jesus the true Israel.

Wisdom: "The Disaster of Affluence" (Proverbs 15:27)

Wisdom literature poses special challenges for Christ-centered preaching. We have heard the apostle Paul declare that "all the treasures of wisdom and knowledge" lie hidden in Jesus the Messiah, the image of the invisible God (Col. 2:3; 1:15). The apostle has even claimed that Christ is our God-given wisdom especially, paradoxically, through the "folly" of his cross (1 Cor. 1:18–31). We also have heard Jesus himself speak the wisdom of the kingdom in proverbial form (Matt. 13:35, citing Ps. 78:2). Yet, much of Israel's wisdom literature seems to reflect general human experience, rather than being integral to the drama of redemptive history and the particularity of the Lord's covenant with Israel, and many couplets in the Proverbs seem simply to be pragmatic maxims for making one's way in an imperfect world or superfluous truisms that none would question.

Moreover, a deep tension runs through the Bible's wisdom literature. One strand of Israel's wisdom tradition exudes confidence that, because a just God rules an orderly universe, diligence and integrity are bound to bring prosperity, while evil and sloth spell disaster: "The LORD does not let the righteous go hungry, but he thwarts the craving of the wicked. A slack hand causes poverty, but the hand of the diligent makes rich" (Prov. 10:3–4). Another strand (Job, Ecclesiastes, Psalms 37, 73, etc.) runs "across the grain" of this confidence, wrestling painfully with the disillusioning discovery that often no correlation can be seen between one's character and one's lot in life.

We may wonder, therefore, whether Christ can be preached from *all* the Proverbs, for instance. G. F. Handel has helped us see Christ in Job's startling burst of confidence, "For I know that my Redeemer lives,

and at the last he will stand upon the earth. And after my skin has been
thus destroyed, yet in my flesh I shall see God" (Job 19:25–26); but can
Jesus also be heard in Job's confused laments?

Several attributes of the wisdom literature set a framework for
perceiving its connection to Scripture's over-arching covenant and
redemptive plot line. First, Israel's wisdom is grounded in the blessings and curses of God's covenant with Israel (Deut. 28). As Thomas
Long has observed,

> . . . proverbs make sense only when seen as the foreground for which
> the whole fabric of the covenant relationship between God and the
> community serves as backdrop. Proverbs are spoken into a culture in
> which the religious character of life permeates every relationship, every
> corner of society. . . . To listen to a proverb without at the same time
> hearing its covenantal background is to pry a gem from its setting.[35]

The prologue to Proverbs portrays the competition of wisdom and folly
as a covenantal conflict, a rivalry between two women whose houses
occupy the city's highest point, the site of a temple (Prov. 9:3, 14):

> In the Ancient Near East, only one person had the right to dwell on
> the highest point in the city, the god of that city. . . . The reader is thus
> confronted with a decision. Both women are calling him to come to them
> to dine, to share intimacy, and unpacking the metaphor, to worship them.
> Will it be Wisdom or Folly? Will it be Yahweh or Baal?[36]

Secondly, even when Proverbs incorporates insights derived
from reflective observation of human experience and resembling
the wisdom of surrounding Ancient Near Eastern cultures, an even
broader covenantal context is presupposed. Although God's redemptive covenant posed the wisdom-or-folly, life-or-death alternative for
Israel in a particularly pointed way, it is also true that through Adam
the whole created order and all humanity, though not sharing in
Israel's covenant, are covenantally related to the Creator whose will
defines justice and whose omniscience and authority set the norm
for wisdom. There is therefore reason to anticipate that eventually

---

35   Thomas G. Long, *Preaching and the Literary Forms of the Bible* (Philadelphia: Fortress, 1989), 58–59.

36   Raymond B. Dillard and Tremper Longman III, *An Introduction to the Old
Testament* (Grand Rapids: Zondervan, 1994), 243. See also Tremper Longman III,
How to Read Proverbs (Downers Grove: InterVarsity, 2002), 33–34.

faithfulness on those created in God's image will further their well-being, while resistance to God's order will bring woe. The sages who speak in Proverbs observe, not only in Israel but elsewhere, the principle that on the whole wise and righteous behavior yields benefits, while shortsighted folly yields poverty and punishment in the end.

Yet, the human race in general, like Israel in particular, is in violation of our covenantal obligation and thus under the Lord's curse, a curse that touches not only particular covenant breakers but also those in their sphere of influence and the created world itself. In fact, the pervasive reality of sin in the world means that even those who, by the grace of God, have been restored to covenantal faithfulness nevertheless are not immune the effects of humanity's fallenness. Why does the righteous Job suffer? Has the God who rules the universe forgotten his justice and his promises to those who serve him? The pious psalmist likewise comes close to stumbling over the Lord's mysterious ways in permitting those who defy him to prosper nonetheless (Ps. 73). Occasionally, but rarely, such questions are resolved in part within the earthly lifetime of God's faithful servants, as in the restoration of family and fortune to Job. At least as often, however, the incongruity that the faithful feel between God's character and power, on the one hand, and the misery of his servants or the comfort of his enemies, on the other, cries out for resolution that must lie beyond the bounds of life "under the sun."

Thirdly, there are connecting strands between wisdom literature's generalizations and the concrete, divine-human drama played out in Scripture's narrative of redemptive history. Despite their appearance as timeless truths, proverbs are in fact the sage's terse, reflective distillations of dramatic human stories. Thomas Long cites Paul Ricoeur's wise insight, "Without being a narrative, the proverb implies a story," commenting further that each proverb actually presupposes "a set of stories. The proverb calls forth a series of everyday vignettes which are varied on the surface but bundled together by a deep harmony discerned through the proverb itself."[37] Since human life is lived in fidelity to God's covenant or in breach of it, the drama behind a biblical proverb must ultimately be linked to the Bible's grand narrative that reaches its climax in the Sage greater than Solomon. As we will see below, the accounts of Achan, Judah, and (by contrast) Naboth illumine Proverbs 15:27 from various angles.

---

37   Long, *Preaching and the Literary Forms*, 57.

How, then, should we preach Christ from Proverbs 15:27: "Whoever is greedy for unjust gain troubles his own household, but he who hates bribes will live"? The editors of the Greek testaments and English versions find in the New Testament neither citation of nor allusion to this terse couplet (seven Hebrew words). In what comprehensive, covenantal context should we view its warning and its promise? How does it relate to Jesus the Wisdom of God?

We begin by noting how this proverb applies the cosmic clash of covenantal claims between the Lord and his rivals to a specific competitor who vies with God for our trust and loyalty. Here the false god who demands allegiance and promises blessing in return is named "profit" (vs. 27a, *betza'*; ESV: "unjust gain") and "gifts" (vs. 27b, *mattanōt*; ESV: "bribes"). Neither term is intrinsically pejorative (see below), but in this context both refer to money magnified to divine status as a covenant lord. As Wisdom incarnate would sagely observe: "No servant can serve two masters, for either he will hate the one and love the other, or he will be devoted to the one and despise the other. You cannot serve God and money" (Luke 16:13). Here we see, in one slice of daily life, the two divergent roads that Proverbs constantly maps out to their destinations: the road of wise righteousness that leads to life, and the road of foolish evil that leads to destruction.[38]

Human experience abounds with illustration and confirmation of the proverb's cautionary first line. From the myth of King Midas' golden touch to modern horror stories of acquisitive, avaricious, opportunistic, amoral executives clawing their way to the top, no matter whom they trample and what laws they break, the motif is clear: grasping greed spells trouble not only for the ambitious corporate climber but also for his or her family.[39] Shattered marriages are left as the upwardly mobile "mover and shaker" trades the wife of his youth for a younger model—a coworker, perhaps—to enhance his image at corporate social events. Even when the marriage inexplicably survives, the wounds suffered by children "orphaned" by their parents' career aspirations fester. We might say, "*Of course* greed is foolish

---

38   The antitheses in the couplets surrounding our text, Prov. 15:25–26, 28–29 (perhaps also vs. 24), contrast the house of the proud to the boundaries of the widow, wicked thoughts and gracious words, the righteous heart and the wicked mouth, the Lord's distance from the wicked and his attention to the righteous.

39   See, e.g., Tom Wolfe, *The Bonfire of the Vanities* (New York: Farrar, Straus, and Giroux, 1987).

and self-defeating, and honesty is the best policy! Who needs to be told this?" It is simply too obvious that "those who desire to be rich fall into temptation, into a snare, into many senseless and harmful desires that plunge people into ruin and destruction" (1 Tim. 6:9).[40]

Yet, snares entrap because their danger is invisible to their prey. It is not transparent to everyone that the quest for money and what it can buy is bound to trouble one's family. Few who pursue financial security and affluence at any price, whatever the toll to their dependents and their own character, set out to harm those closest to them. It may not be apparent that the greedy over-achiever's family is suffering from his insatiable thirst for "the good life." Proverbs even observes frankly that in this life the one-to-one match between moral compromise and family disaster is sometimes far from visible. "A man's gift (*mattan*) makes room for him and brings him before the great" (Prov. 18:16). "A gift (*mattan*) in secret averts anger, and a concealed bribe, strong wrath" (21:14). A strategic "investment" may be a stepping stone to advancement.

Nor does it always seem true to say that the person who is too upright (some would say, too uptight) to take a bribe will enjoy "life," as this proverb promises, more than the person who can be purchased when the price is right. Sometimes, sadly, it is the person of unimpeachable integrity, the unbribable judge or the investigator who cannot be intimidated, who is gunned down on the street rather than living long to savor truth's hard-won victory.

The deferral of the consequences of allegiance to the Lord (life) or to his rival (trouble) in God's patient providence makes this proverb's obvious truth seem counterintuitive to many people, who consequently disbelieve both its warning and its promise. They might even justify their quest of wealth as fulfilling their obligation to provide for one's family. After all, the Bible condemns those who fail to provide for their own households as deniers of the faith, "worse than an unbeliever" (1 Tim. 5:8). Proverbs elsewhere commends the vigorous, strategic pursuit of profit and paints contemptuous portraits of the

---

40   The expression "greedy for unjust gain" in Prov. 15:27 echoes the same Hebrew expression in 1:11–19, which describes the folly of thugs who conspire to assassinate the innocent and steal his property but in so doing ensnare their own lives: "For in vain is a net spread in the sight of any bird, but these men lie in wait for their own blood; they set an ambush for their own lives. Such are the ways of everyone who is greedy for unjust gain; it takes away the life of its possessors" (1:17–19).

poverty that sloth brings: "I passed by the field of a sluggard . . . it was all overgrown with thorns; the ground was covered with nettles, and its stone wall was broken down. . . . A little sleep, a little slumber, a little folding of the hands to rest, and poverty will come upon you like a robber, and want like an armed man" (Prov. 24:30–34). Why, then, does this proverb sound so negative about the pursuit of wealth?

This proverb diagnoses the distortion of a God-given responsibility into a God-denying drive. It shows us duty run amok into idolatry. Although the Hebrew noun *betza'* ("profit, gain") by itself can rarely refer to profits achieved by morally neutral means (e.g., Job 22:3; Mic. 4:13; Mal. 3:14), the construction *botza' betza'* "he who makes his cut" = "he who makes (or pursues) a profit" customarily has the pejorative connotation expressed in the ESV's "greedy for unjust gain" (Ps. 10:3; Prov. 1:19; cf. 28:16; Jer. 6:13; 8:10; Ezek. 22:12–13, 27; etc.). The contrast drawn in the second line confirms the morally negative connotation of "profit," illustrating concretely one type of ill-gotten gain that brings ruin both to individuals and to their families. If the righteous person "hates bribes," the greedy man must love them. As a judge, a decision-maker, a businessman, a teacher—yes, even as a pastor—the profit-seeker has put his integrity for sale to the highest bidder (Eccl. 7:7).

Of course, profitable vocations are not, in and of themselves, a route to illicit gain. This proverb, however, probes the deep motives of our hearts, demanding that we face honestly the source to which we look for ultimate security. Divided loyalties are derived from misplaced and short-sighted trust, and the ground of one's trust places its indelible imprint on one's character. Can one whose conscience can be bought off in the marketplace for the right price be trusted, in the end, to keep wedding vows or baptismal vows in the home, or to lay his life on the line for his wife and children?

Yet, the divergent roads of wisdom and folly can only be assessed accurately in the perspective of their ultimate destinations, which (as was noted above) lie beyond the horizon of this present evil age. Far from being a naïve caricature of real life, in which good is immediately rewarded and evil immediately punished,[41] Proverbs

---

41 My colleague Bryan Estelle has pointed out that Proverbs inhabits a world in which the innocent are ambushed and the wicked successfully distort justice (Prov. 1:11; 6:17; 13:23; 17:23, 26; 18:5). Therefore Proverbs at least occasionally looks beyond death for the redressing of injustice (10:7; 12:7; 11:7; 12:28).

calls its readers to a far-sighted wisdom that looks beyond short-term profit or loss, beyond the "here and now," to ultimate outcomes, both regarding "trouble" and regarding "life." Far from conveying the mundane, moralistic pragmatism articulated by Job's "comforters," Proverbs articulates an eschatology: the individual maxim's expectation that things will go right for the righteous and go ill for the iniquitous finds only erratic and temporary fulfillment in the present.

The biblical stories of Achan, Judah, Naboth, and, climactically, Jesus dramatize both the truth encapsulated in Proverbs 15:27 and the tension between that truth and our present experience, this side of the Last Day. In Hebrew, the Proverb begins with the (participial) verbal form, "Troubler" (ʿōkēr). This verb had given its name to a valley (or ravine) near Jericho that had witnessed the first instance of infidelity and consequent curse after Israel's entrance into the Promised Land. There Achan *and his whole household* were destroyed by stoning because he would not keep his hands off the Lord's property, the plunder of Jericho devoted to destruction before Israel's Holy Champion (Josh. 7:22–26). Before their execution, Joshua pronounced an exchange of "trouble" (ʿakar): as Achan had "troubled" Israel, so the Lord was about to "trouble" Achan. The valley was known henceforth as the "Valley of Trouble," the Valley of Achor. In the genealogy of 1 Chron. 2:7, Achan is even named *Akar*, the ʿōkēr of Israel, that is, "Trouble, Israel's Troubler." Achan the troubler trusted the robe, silver, and gold he could see and seize more than he trusted the word of the Lord, the Lord who saw his heart from the start.[42]

Earlier in redemptive history, Jacob's son Judah provides another sobering example of greed's capacity to trouble one's house. Thrust into leadership by the foolish and wicked acts of his older brothers Reuben (Gen. 35:22), Levi, and Simeon (34:25–31),[43] Judah proposed to his brothers a more profitable plan for disposing of Joseph, their father's favorite, than leaving him to die of thirst in

42   We have also noted in ch. 7 [p. 212–13] the lines of connection drawn lexically (*nosphizomai*) and thematically (hidden theft from the Lord, punished by execution) between the sin of Achan in Joshua 7 and the sin of Ananias and Sapphira in Acts 5. Although the offense of Ananias and his wife Sapphira are described as lying to the Lord and putting him to the test, their unwillingness to release the whole profit from their land sale in this case evidenced not only contempt for the Spirit's holiness and omniscience but also a lingering trust in finances for security.

43   Jacob rebukes the crafty revenge of Simeon and Levi on their sister's rapist: "You have brought trouble (ʿacar) on me by making me stink to the inhabitants of the land" (Gen. 34:30).

a pit: "What profit (*betza'*) is it if we kill our brother and conceal his blood? Come, let us sell him to the Ishmaelites. . . ." (Gen. 37:26–27). Judah's eye for profit troubled his household not only through his father's inconsolable grief (vv. 34–35) but also in Simeon's subsequent imprisonment in Egypt and the threatened captivity of Benjamin as well—a disaster that would kill Jacob with grief. This final trouble finally forced from Judah's lips the confession, "God has found out the guilt of your servants" (44:16).

On the other hand, consider the pious Naboth, who would not accept a gift in exchange for abandoning his family's ancestral vineyard to the avarice of King Ahab (1 Kings 21:2–3). Here is the righteous man envisioned in the second line of our proverb, one who hates bribes and holds his ancestors' covenantal allotment in the land of promise so sacred that neither the promise of a better vineyard elsewhere nor the offer of money could sway him. Surely, Naboth should live long and prosper, if this proverb holds true. Yet, his hatred of the king's bribe brought him not long life but false accusation and undeserved execution—legalized murder (vv. 9–14). Naboth's tragedy only makes sense and conveys hope in the perspective of Hebrews 11, as a further instance of those ancient people of faith who lost property, wandered homeless, and lost life itself, all in the hope of a better inheritance, a heavenly homeland, a far better resurrection than the extension of a few more years on this sin-cursed earth.

Our biggest problem with Proverbs 15:27, however, is not that the threat of trouble in its first line does not always fall immediately on the avaricious, nor that the promise of life in its second line seems postponed indefinitely for the incorruptible. Our biggest problem is that, one way or another, whether or not we have crossed the line into legally chargeable theft, fraud, or embezzlement, we have all earned for ourselves and our families the trouble of verse 27a. We have not turned aside in repulsion every bribe, every offer to trade a piece of our integrity for some comfort, influence, or false sense of security. Can anyone really say, looking back over his or her life, "My integrity is priceless, pure—never compromised, never traded away even for a moment in response to money, power, intimidation, pleasure, fear, or desire"?[44] Who, then, can deliver us from the "trouble"

---

44   It is true that Scripture speaks of certain individuals as "blameless" or "upright" (Gen. 6:9; Job 1:1; Luke 1:6; Phil 3:6). Nevertheless, the narrative contexts of such statements make clear that these individuals, although their integrity and

we deserve and can impart the life that we do not deserve? Who can transform the "Valley of Achor (Trouble) [into] a door of hope" (Hos. 2:14–15)?

These questions can be answered only in the one true hater of bribes, Jesus Christ. Once in all of history, there was a judge, a king, a defender, a protector of his family who could not be bought or corrupted because he loved the Lord his God with all his heart, soul, mind, and strength. Neither the tempter's encouragement to satisfy his hunger by a self-centered exercise of messianic power, turning stones to bread, nor the tempter's promise to give him "all the kingdoms of the world and their glory" could deflect Jesus from his purpose to live by every word that proceeds from God's mouth and to "worship the Lord your God, and serve him only" (Matt. 4:1–11 NIV). Although he was the Son of Man, to whom dominion would be given, so that all peoples and nations would serve him (Dan. 7:14), nevertheless he came not to be served, but to serve and to give his life as a ransom for many (Matt. 20:28).

Although he rejected and hated the devil's bribes in the desert and every other compromise, he did not live a life free of trouble, nor did he inherit the eschatological "life" that was rightly his in return for his covenant faithfulness, without first passing through the Valley of Achor, through death itself under the curse of God. Jesus' "Trouble Valley" was a hill called Skull (Golgotha) outside Jerusalem. As dusk settled on Jerusalem that first "Good Friday," this proverb seemed to have been stood on its head. A mere thirty pieces of silver had suborned one of Jesus' closest associates to arrange a quiet arrest, out of sight of the crowds: Judas sold his integrity cheaply (Matt. 26:14–16; cf. John 12:6). False witnesses, eerily echoing those who provided

---

piety stood out from those of their contemporaries, were by no means free from sin and guilt: Noah's faith in constructing the ark would be followed by drunkenness after the flood (Gen. 9:20–21). Job acknowledges his need for the "watcher of mankind" to pardon his transgression (Job 7:20–21) and finally shuts his mouth in shame and fear when God challenges his right to critique divine providence and wisdom (Job 40:3-5; 42:1-6). The upright priest Zechariah spends nine months in silence for failing to believe God's promise (Luke 1:18–20). Saul the Pharisee was simultaneously "blameless" as to righteousness under the law and a persecutor of the church, the worst of sinners, in desperate need of divine mercy (Phil. 3:6; 1 Tim. 1:12–16; see 1 Cor. 15:9). From the perspective of God's utter holiness and heart-searching omniscience, there is no exception to the verdict, "None is righteous, no, not one; no one understands; no one seeks for God" (Rom. 3:10–11)—except Jesus.

the pretext for Naboth's execution, had perjured themselves to give the authorities grounds to condemn the troublesome teacher against whom no actual sin could be alleged (Matt. 26:59–66; cf. John 8:46). The Prince of Life hung lifeless on a Roman cross.

Within three days, however, wisdom literature's eschatological hope broke into the midst of history, and this proverb's threat and promise received resounding, world-changing confirmation. Judas, who had sold his soul for silver, hung lifeless—"troubled" to death by his own hand; he left no legacy for his own house—only a "field of blood" for aliens (Matt. 27:3–10; Acts 1:18–20). Infinitely more important, the Holy One who could not be bought could not be held by death's cords or pangs (Acts 2:24–32). Jesus, the supreme display of divine integrity in human nature, took up his life again in resurrection power, and in so doing carried his whole "household"—all who hold fast our confidence in him (Heb. 3:6)—with himself into the life of the coming age.

Not only did Jesus fulfill for us the covenant's demand of exclusive loyalty to the Lord, he also grants the Spirit of holiness to transform his forgiven family into the image of his own unimpeachable integrity. Secured in the Father's favor by the Son's atonement and the Spirit's presence, we are no longer up for sale to the highest bidder but instead stand amazed by the grace by which we have been "bought with a price" (1 Cor. 6:20; 7:23) and redeemed from an empty way of life not with perishable silver or gold, but with the infinitely more precious blood of Christ, the lamb without blemish (1 Peter 1:17–19). Jesus has the integrity that we lack, and he gives it freely to all who humbly confess how compromised they are. He gives the wisdom we need to resist immediate pressures to sell ourselves cheaply, and by his grace we can lead our families out of the Valley of Trouble and into life, by the power of his Holy Spirit.

Our meditation on Proverbs 15:27 in the light of wisdom literature's role in the redemptive history, then, yields a sermon that places the threat and promise of the proverb in a context that is both eschatological and ultimately Christ-centered and grace-revealing. This sermon could be structured like this:

1. The Wisdom of the Proverb: The god whom you trust, seek, and serve spells the difference between trouble and life.
   a. When money is your god, it and you will destroy those you hold dear.

b. When the Lord is your God, he gives life to you and those you hold dear.

2. Our First Problem with the Proverb: Is it really true?
   a. Its threat and promise do not seem to come true, consistently, here and now.
   b. But its threat and promise will ring true in the end.

3. Our Second Problem with the Proverb: It is really true!
   a. We have troubled our household by grasping money at all costs, and have no right to claim the "life" promised to those who cannot be bribed or bought.
   b. But Jesus, who could not be bought, bought life for us by bearing the trouble we deserve.
   c. Because Jesus bore our trouble and gives life to his household, you can and must trust him alone as the God whose promise and presence sets you free from the love of money.

The sermon's first movement will expound the proverb itself, drawing in other passages in the wisdom literature and illustrating its sober warning from the life of Achan (and perhaps Judah). The second movement places this proverb's wisdom in the context of the ambiguities of divine providence in this age of the restraint of God's just wrath. The third leads from the proverb's function as "law"— covenant prohibition and demand, enforced by sanctions of curse and blessing—to the gospel of grace in Christ, the wise covenant keeper, who alone can speak comfort and hope to those whose consciences are pierced by the law's indictment. A fitting Scripture to clinch the application is Hebrews 13:5–6, which sets the Lord's gracious presence over against money's hollow promises of protection: "Keep your life free from love of money, and be content with what you have, for he has said, 'I will never leave you nor forsake you.' So we can confidently say, 'The Lord is my helper; I will not fear; what can man do to me?'"

Song: "The Mystery and Misery of the Downcast Soul" (Psalms 42 and 43)

Israel's psalmists sing with a wide array of voices, both individual and corporate. They respond to a broad spectrum of experience, from worship to exile, from rejection to deliverance; and they convey a range of emotions, from confused desperation to exultant praise and thanksgiving. Some Psalms selectively rehearse the historical ebbs and flows of God's covenant with Israel, highlighting his faithfulness or Israel's failure or both together (e.g., Pss. 78, 105, 106). Some memorably transmit God-given wisdom from generation to generation (e.g., Pss. 1, 119). Some look forward with longing to the consummation of the covenant in the just destruction of the godless and the gracious vindication of the oppressed, who cling in hope to God's promises (Ps. 72).[45]

Israel's Psalter is closely identified with its corporate worship as the community in covenant with the Lord, and therefore with Israel's theocratic leaders—especially priestly and royal officers. Almost half of the Psalms are attributed to David, who speaks in them not merely as poet but as the Lord's anointed king and suffering servant, as well as a forgiven sinner (e.g., Pss. 32 and 51).[46] Others are attributed to Levitical families such as Asaph and his descendents, who were appointed to be temple musicians (1 Chron. 6:39; 16:4–6; 25:1), and the sons of Korah, who survived their notoriously rebellious ancestor (Num. 16:28–33; 26:10–11) to become gatekeepers of the Lord's sanctuary (1 Chron. 9:19; 26:1, 19; cf. 2 Chron. 20:19).[47] Psalm 72 is attributed to Solomon, and Psalm 90 is attributed to "Moses, the man of God."

Biblical scholars have typically identified certain psalms as "messianic" because of their focus on the king's office and future orientation, and because such psalms are explicitly (and in some case

---

45   Helpful brief introductions to the interpretation of the psalms include Tremper Longman III, *How to Read the Psalms* (Downers Grove: InterVarsity, 1988) and Mark D. Futato, *Transformed by Praise: The Purpose and Message of the Psalms* (Phillipsburg: P & R, 2002).

46   Scholars debate, however, the antiquity, reliability, and meaning of the Psalm superscriptions in the Massoretic text. Peter C. Craigie, *Psalms 1–50* (WBC 18; Waco: Word, 1983), 31–35, helpfully surveys the questions pertaining not only to the superscriptions' antiquity but also to the significance of the prepositional prefix, l^e, traditionally translated "by" as an ascription of authorship but also capable of other interpretations, such as "for," "to," or "with reference to."

47   In the Hebrew text, Psalm 42 is ascribed to the sons of Korah, and Psalm 43 lacks a superscription. The LXX insertion of a superscription, "A Psalm of David," over Psalm 43, whatever its origin, is untenable, since the linguistic unity of Psalms 42 and 43 argues strongly not only for a single author but also for these psalms' original unity as a single song.

repeatedly) cited in the New Testament as having found their fulfillment in the suffering and exaltation of Jesus the Christ (e.g., Pss. 2,
22, 45, 110). Clowney has contended provocatively, however, that all
150 psalms should be viewed as messianic and read in the light of
Jesus' fulfillment of the psalmists' varied experiences of suffering and
vindication, inasmuch as David and his fellow Israelite poets composed their prayers and praises under the inspiration of the Spirit of
Christ and in relation to their typological theocratic offices.[48]

Psalms 42 and 43 are not among those typically considered to
be messianic. Instead, they are treated, quite appropriately, as a bru-
tally honest portrayal of the struggle with spiritual depression that
sincere believers may undergo.[49] Yet, the psalmist's soul-struggle has
a specific cause and can only be treated with a specific remedy. His
unquenched thirst is for God's presence, and it is specifically related to his distance from God's sanctuary and his inability to access
the Lord's holy hill. The superscription of Psalm 42, associating it
with the gatekeeping Levitical clan descended from Korah, should
be understood as applicable also to Psalm 43 (see note 47 and the
discussion of these psalms' unity below). The author's intimate and
privileged association with the temple in Jerusalem adds poignancy
to his recollection of past joys in the midst of a crowd of fellow worshipers at the sanctuary (Ps. 42:4), even as it intensifies his anguished
longing in his present, distant exile from the house of God (vv. 1–2,
5; 43:3). How should we hear Jesus the Savior singing in these twin
psalms? How should we preach them as fulfilled in him?

The editors of the standard editions of the Greek New Testament (Nestle-Aland and United Bible Societies) find allusions to
these psalms in the Gospels' descriptions of Jesus' state of mind as he
looked toward the cross. In John 12:27, for example, Jesus prefaces
an announcement of his impending "hour" of exaltation through
suffering: "Now is my soul troubled (*hē psychē mou tetaraktai*). And
what shall I say? 'Father, save me (*sōson me*) from this hour'? But for
this purpose I have come to this hour." Although Jesus' words, "my
soul is troubled" and "save me," more closely echo Psalm 6:4–5 LXX,[50]
there may also be a more distant allusion to the refrain of Psalms 42

48   In addition to his other works of biblical theology already cited, see also Edmund P. Clowney, "The Singing Savior," *Moody Monthly*, July-August 1979, 40–43.
49   See D. Martyn Lloyd-Jones, *Spiritual Depression: Its Causes and Cure*
(Grand Rapids: Eerdmans, 1965), 9–21.
50   Psalm 6:4–5 LXX reads, in part, *hē psychē mou etarachthē . . . Sōson me.*

and 43, "my soul . . . why are you in turmoil" (*psychē . . . hina ti syntarasseis me*). A clearer allusion is evident in Mark 14:34 (par. Matt. 26:38), in which Jesus at Gethsemane appeals to his closest associates to remain with him and awake as he wrestles with the prospect of his coming suffering: "My soul is very sorrowful, even to death" (*perilypos estin hē psychē heōs thanatou*). The adjective "(very) sorrowful" (*perilypos*) appears twice elsewhere in the Greek Old Testament and twice elsewhere in the New Testament, but only in Psalms 42–43 and these Gospel narratives of Gethsemane is it found in association with "soul" (*psychē*). Cross references in English versions and study Bibles do not add to the selection of explicit literary connections between these twin psalms and the New Testament's proclamation of Jesus. The allusive connection between these psalms' refrain and Jesus' anguish of soul at the prospect of the cross is sufficient not only to identify these psalms with other songs of lament but also to point the way toward preaching Christ. But there is more.

When we probe more deeply the literary and thematic unity of these twin psalms, we discover that Psalms 42 and 43 show the marks of having originally been a single song, in which the psalmist cried out in lament toward God while giving himself a bracing pep talk to elicit hopeful patience in his own downcast heart. Their most obvious tie is the threefold question and exhortation addressed by the poet to himself, "Why are you cast down, O my soul, and why are you in turmoil within me? Hope in God; for I shall again praise him, my salvation and my God" (42:5, 11; 43:5). This refrain marks off and closes the three strophes of the original song, 42:1–5, 42:6–11, and 43:1–5. Equally clear is the parallel in the questions addressed to God in 42:9 and 43:2:

I say to God, my rock:	"For you are the God in whom I take refuge;
"Why have you forgotten me?	why have you rejected me?
Why do I go mourning	Why do I go about mourning
because of the oppression of the enemy?"	because of the oppression of the enemy?"

Moreover, the first (42:1–5) and third (43:1–5) strophes contain explicit references to God's sanctuary, the "house of God" (42:4), his dwelling on his holy hill (43:3), from which the psalmist is presently far removed, as the second strophe (42:6–11) implies, in the distant north at the Jordan's headwaters on Mount Hermon.

As the psalmist looks back in longing toward past experiences of joyful worship amid the congregation, the pain of his present deprivation from the meeting place of the Lord with his people is acute: his soul thirsts for God, his only bread is his own tears, he is drowning under the Lord's crushing ocean breakers, and his bones are shattered. The repeated taunts of mockers, "Where is your God?" (42:3, 10) compound his anguish; but his most intense pain arises from his sense of abandonment by God himself, reflected in the perplexed question that he repeats to God, his rock and refuge, "Why have *you* forgotten me, rejected me?" The enemies' oppression and mockery are like crushing of his bones (42:10), but what threatens to extinguish his life are *the Lord's* floodwaters, those waves and breakers whose voice echoes in the waterfalls crashing down from Hermon's snowcapped peak (42:6–7). As both absence and excess of water is lethal, so the psalmist finds himself at death's door both by drought (Deut. 28:24; 1 Kings 17:1; Ps. 22:15) and by the floodwaters of the deep (Gen. 7:11–24; Jonah 2:3–7). Korah's son ransacks the resources of redemptive history to apply images of destruction and deprivation to his own experience of banishment as a son of Adam, expelled both from Eden and its Tree of Life and from the Lord's later sanctuary on his holy hill in Jerusalem.

Nevertheless, in his refrain the psalmist calls his heart to look forward to a future day in which he will "again" praise God for his salvation, again participating in the procession of worshipers gathering at the Lord's dwelling place. This hope is sustained not only by memories of bygone worship celebrations (Ps. 42:4) but also by a confidence that even in the present, as he languishes in exile from the temple, simultaneously parched by God's absence (42:1–2) and drowned by God's presence in judgment (42:7), the Lord's steadfast love, or covenant loyalty (Hebrew: *chesed*), and song are with him (42:8). Such hope prompts the prayer at the core of the third strophe, the climax toward which this song drives:

> Send out your light and your truth;
> Let them lead me;

Let them cause me to come[51] to your holy hill
And to your dwelling!
Then I will come[52] to the altar of God,
To God my exceeding joy. . . . (Ps. 43:3-4 dej)

God's light (*'or*) was associated with the tabernacle and the temple through the cloud of glory that overshadowed and filled these sanctuaries with radiance (Ex. 40:34–38; cf. 13:21–22; 1 Kings 8:10–11; 1 Tim. 6:16; Rev. 15:8). Likewise, God's truth (*'emet*) found its home in the law of God, the covenant treaty tablets deposited in the ark of the presence, in the temple's holiest inner chamber (Ps. 119:142, 151, 160). "I bow down toward your holy temple and give thanks to your name for your steadfast love (*chesed*) and your faithfulness (*'emet*) . . ." (Ps. 138:2). Thus God's radiant presence and his faithful word are poetically portrayed as emissaries to be sent north (so Korah's son prays) on a sortie to rescue and retrieve the psalmist, whose life languishes on the brink of expiration for lack of refreshing, reviving communion with God, his rock and refuge. When God's light and truth, sent out from the divine presence, recover the psalmist from his place of exile and cause him to come to God's holy hill, he will indeed come to God's altar to offer songs and sacrifices of praise (Ps. 43:4).

When we view this song of lament and hope from the perspective of the prayer of Psalm 43:3, it becomes not only the song of the downcast soul generally, and not only the song of the troubled and banished Messiah specifically, but also a prayer for the incarnation of God's light and truth, to be sent forth from the heavenly sanctuary to rescue and retrieve exiles by becoming the rejected exile, experiencing the ultimate thirst for God (John 19:28) and floodwaters of judgment (Luke 12:50) on our behalf. Jesus, after all, is the light of God sent into the world to pierce and conquer its darkness (John 1:9; 3:19–21; 8:12). He is the way, the truth, and the life, the only avenue by which we can come to God (John 14:6). And Jesus did so by taking the psalm's lament onto his lips and taking into his own soul an infinitely greater turmoil, a more excruciating unquenched thirst for his Father's face and favor, than Korah's son could have borne or had

---

51   The Hebrew verb rendered "bring" by the ESV is *bo'*, "come," used here in the *hif'il*, "cause to come."

52   The Hebrew verb rendered "go" by the ESV is, again, *bo'*, this time in the qal, "I shall come."

to bear. "For Christ also suffered once for sins, the righteous for the unrighteous, that he might *bring us to God*, being put to death in the flesh but made alive in the Spirit" (1 Peter 3:18).[53]

How, then, might one preach both this psalm's probing portrayal of human perplexity and depression and its testimony to God's remedy for the downcast soul? Certainly, the graphic imagery of the psalm itself in its portrayal of an ancient Levite's lament and longing for God's presence must be explored, since it not only illumines the psalm's message in its ancient context but also provides vivid, imaginative links to the experience of our listeners today. The questions posed by the psalmist's adversaries ("Where is your God?") and by the psalmist, both to himself ("What are you cast down, O my soul?") and to his God "Why have you rejected me?"), drive the psalm's diagnosis deeper, beyond circumstantial setbacks to the source of the problem: the perplexing absence of God. Finally, the ultimate answer to the psalmist's confusion and distress can be proclaimed as the fulfillment of the future-focused hope reiterated in the refrain, a fulfillment that provides the surprising yet perfectly appropriate answer to the prayer, "Send out your light and your truth; let them lead me; let them bring me to your holy hill and to your dwelling!" The sermon could be entitled "The Misery and Mystery of the Downcast Soul" and be structured as follows:

1. The *Misery* of the Downcast Soul: External trials and internal troubles can send *even people who love God* into a tailspin of despair, from bad to worse to worst.
   a. BAD—*External circumstances* can and do drive our souls down. (Exile on Hermon far from the temple, Ps. 42:6–7)
   b. WORSE—*Unsympathetic companions* compound the pain of our depression. (42:3, 10; cf. Job)
   c. WORST—*God's apparent absence* leads us to death's door. (42:1–2)

2. The *Mystery* of the Downcast Soul: Our distress is compounded when we cannot understand our own reactions or God's inaction.

---

53   The wording is ESV, but I have capitalized "Spirit," convinced that the reference is not to Jesus' human spirit (as ESV implies) but to the resurrection life imparted by God's Holy Spirit on the third day, as similar New Testament texts containing the "flesh/Spirit" contrast show (1 Tim. 3:16; Rom. 1:3–4; 8:9–11; etc.). The NIV has "made alive by the Spirit."

a. Often we cannot understand *our own inner disquiet.* (42:5, 11; 43:5)

b. Often we cannot understand *our God's apparent indiffer-ence.* (42:9; 43:2)

3. *Grace* to Lift the Downcast Soul: God has sent his Light and Truth to lift the sorrows from our downcast souls and bring us rejoicing into his presence.

a. We have *the strongest reason* to argue against despair and affirm God's faithfulness: We have *seen* what the psalmist could only long for and pray for, the apex of God's past and present faithfulness in sending Jesus, his Light and Truth (John 8:12; 14:6), to endure our exile (Mark 14:34) and to usher us into his holy home. (Ps. 43:3–4)

b. Therefore, we must *argue* with our confused and down-cast souls, putting our present troubles and internal tur-moil into the context of God's *past* and *future* faithful-ness. (42:4–5, 11; 43:5)

c. We also must *affirm* by faith our Lord's *present* faithful-ness, despite appearances. (42:8) For Jesus' sake, *nothing* in all creation can separate us—ever—from his covenant love and loyalty. (Rom. 8:35–39)

The flow of the sermon connects immediately with the hearers' experience of inexplicable sadness and depression, portraying its intensity honestly and graphically, even as it "locates" the psalm as specifically as possible in the concrete circumstances of an Old Testament son of Korah who found himself deprived of access to the sanctuary and presence of God, his only source of satisfaction, delight, and life itself. Thus the sermon follows the psalm's lead in plumbing the deep sources of depression and despair in our alienation from God and our human race's expulsion from Eden. Finally, the sermon points our sight forward along the trajectory of the psalmist's expectant prayer for rescue by the Lord's light and truth and restoration to the Lord's dwelling, bringing into view the Light and Truth who endured unspeakable turmoil of soul in order to usher his own into God's Most Holy Place (Heb. 10:19–22).[54]

---

54 The Heidelberg Catechism summarizes the biblical testimony to Jesus' in-ternal anguish well in its explanations of the confession in the Apostles' Creed that Christ "suffered" and "he descended into hell" (even if the Catechism's interpreta-

Prophecy: "Immanuel in Flood and Fire" (Isaiah 43:1–7)

Because Hebrew prophecy includes a variety of literary genres or subgenres—including historical narrative,[55] covenant lawsuit, doom oracle, apocalyptic vision, and more—a single example of interpretation of a prophetic text is insufficient as a guide to the application of apostolic hermeneutics to this diverse family of texts. Prophecy is commonly associated with predictions of future events, and indeed anticipations of future interventions by God in judgment and deliverance, both proximate and more distant, are abundant in the Latter Prophets (roughly, Isaiah through Malachi in the canonical order followed by English versions). God also sent his prophets, however, to diagnose his people's (and sometimes the pagan nations') spiritual treachery and to summon them to deep repentance. To revive their flagging hopes, he painted vivid landscapes, in colors drawn from creation, exodus, and the glory days of David and Solomon, in which his oppressed people could glimpse a new world to come, ultimately purged of sin and curse. Although space prevents our sampling every flavor of the spiritual feast found in the prophets' testimony to the coming Lord, Savior and Judge, a small taste may whet readers', preachers', and their hearers' appetites for more.

The broader literary context of Isaiah 43:1–7 is the Lord's announcement to King Hezekiah through Isaiah the prophet that Babylon, the nation to whose envoys Hezekiah had proudly and foolishly displayed his royal treasures, would carry both those treasures and the king's heirs off into exile (39:5–8). That sobering prediction of Judah's exile is the dark backdrop against which God then instructs his spokesman, "Comfort, comfort my people, says your God. Speak tenderly to Jerusalem, and cry to her that her warfare is

---

tion of the latter differs from the intention of the Fathers who inserted it): " . . . during his whole life on earth, but especially at the end, Christ sustained in body and soul the anger of God against the sin of the whole world . . ." (Ans. 37). " . . . Christ my Lord, by suffering unspeakable anguish, pain, and terror of soul, especially on the cross but also earlier, has delivered me from the anguish and torment of hell" (Ans. 44).

55 The Old Testament books that modern versions, following the LXX, typically group together as "historical" books (Joshua, Judges, Samuel, Kings) are categorized in the Hebrew canon as "former prophets," in distinction from the latter prophets (Isaiah, Jeremiah, Ezekiel, the Twelve [Minor Prophets]). The narrative of Israel's life with God is thus told not as a dispassionate rehearsal of facts but as a covenantal commentary preserved and preached by messengers commissioned and sent by the Lord of the covenant to press his claims upon his servant people.

ended, that her iniquity is pardoned, that she has received from the
LORD's hand double for all her sins" (40:1–2). Despite Hezekiah's
folly and the wickedness of so many of his royal predecessors and
successors, the exile would not be the last chapter in the story of
God's covenant with Israel and of his covenant with David, Israel's
king. Redemption from captivity and restoration to the Lord's land
are promised, despite the unworthiness not only of Judah's royal
house but of the people as a whole. Immediately preceding our text,
God rebukes all Israel for their deafness and blindness (42:18–20;
cf. 6:9–10). Although Israel was called into covenant as the Lord's
servant to witness his saving works and bear his message to the nations, Israel has failed to take to heart the wonders they have seen.
Consequently, the curses of the covenant are to fall on Jacob. He is
plundered by pagan looters and consumed in battle by the fire of
the Lord's wrath (42:24–25).

   Into this bleak scene of a smoldering battlefield the Lord speaks
the comfort of our text. The boundaries of the passage are marked by
reminders that the Lord had "created" (*bara'*) and "formed" (*yatzar*)
his people (43:1, 7)—a literary *inclusio* that looks back both to the
creation of the universe and the human race (Gen. 1:1, 27; 2:3, 7) and
to the creation of Israel as the Lord's people through the waters of the
sea and the fiery pillar of God's presence in their midst. The repetition of key terms throughout the text also suggests a more complex
chiastic structure within the opening and closing *inclusio*, as Figure
3 illustrates.

   The vocabulary of creation, drawn from Genesis 1 and 2, describes the Lord's sovereign intervention in *irresistible power* at the
exodus to fulfill his promise to Abraham by redeeming his seed from
slavery and forming them by his covenant at Sinai (A, A'; Isa. 43:1, 7).
The twice-spoken prohibition, "Fear not" (B, B'; vv. 1, 5) is grounded in two truths: (1) the Lord's *particular grace* to Israel, calling his
people by their name and by his name (B.1, B.1'; vv. 1, 7), and (2)
the Lord's *presence* with Israel (B.2, B.2'; vv. 2, 5). As a result, Israel
can anticipate that neither floodwater nor flame, portraying the ordeal of the exile, will destroy them (vs. 2); and that their seed will
return from dispersion at the end of the earth (vv. 5–6). Whereas the
previous chapter lamented the plunder and captivity from which no
one would rescue God's wayward people and none would command
their captors to send them back (42:22), now the Lord promises that

he will command east and west, north and south, to relinquish his
sons and daughters and send them home.

```
         ¹ But now thus says the LORD,
A   he who created you, O Jacob,
         he who formed you, O Israel:
B              "Fear not,
                   for I have redeemed you; (see C, C')
B.1            I have called you by [your] name, you are mine.
B.2                ² When you pass through the waters, with you [am I];
                   and through the rivers, they shall not overwhelm you;
                   when you walk through fire you shall not be burned,
                   and the flame shall not consume you.
                       ³ For I am the LORD your God,
                       the Holy One of Israel, your Savior.
C                          I give [as your ransom] Egypt,
                           Cush and Seba in exchange for you.
D                              ⁴ Because you are precious in my eyes,
                                  and [glorified], and I love you,
C'                         I give men in [exchange] for you,
                           peoples in exchange for your life.
B'         ⁵ Fear not,
B.2'           for with you [am I];
               from the east I will bring your offspring,
               and from the west I will gather you.
               ⁶ I will say to the north, Give up,
               and to the south, Do not withhold;
               bring my sons from afar
               and my daughters from the end of the earth,
B.1'               ⁷ everyone who is called by my name,
A'  whom I created for my glory,
       whom I formed and made."⁵⁶
```

Figure 3: Chiastic Structure in Isaiah 43:1–7

At the heart of the passage, the pivotal point of the chiasm (D; vs. 4), the Lord affirms the value, glory, and love that he has lavished on his people, demonstrating how greatly and graciously he treasures them by sacrificing many, mighty nations as ransom in exchange for Israel's life (C, C'; vv. 3–4). (The sheer graciousness of this redemptive exchange is underscored by the fact that two chapters earlier

---

56 Brackets indicate modifications to ESV, to reflect Hebrew word order and repetition of key vocabulary (e.g., ESV renders the verb *kabad* "honored" in vs. 4, but translates the cognate noun *kabōd* as "glory" in vs. 7).

the prohibition, "Fear not," had been addressed to "you *worm* Jacob," emphasizing Israel's weakness and unworthiness in themselves [41:14].) Although flood and fire and expulsion from the Promised Land await the Lord's blind, deaf, unfaithful people, his power as Creator, his mercy as Redeemer, and his personal presence with them through the ordeal to come provide strong grounds for clinging confidently and fearlessly to his promises.

It is not surprising that an eighteenth-century hymn writer found in this prophetic passage a wealth of powerful metaphors for God's promise of power, mercy, and presence in the midst of believers' trials.

> How firm a foundation, ye saints of the Lord,
> Is laid for your faith in his excellent Word! . . .
> "Fear not, I am with thee, O be not dismayed;
> I, I am thy God, and will still give thee aid; . . .
> When through the deep waters I call thee to go,
> The rivers of woe shall not thee overflow;
> For I will be with thee thy troubles to bless,
> And sanctify to thee thy deepest distress.
> When through fiery trials thy pathway shall lie,
> My grace all sufficient shall be thy supply;
> The flame shall not hurt thee; I only design
> Thy dross to consume and thy gold to refine. . . .
> The soul that on Jesus hath leaned for repose,
> I will not, I will not desert to his foes;
> That soul, though all hell should endeavor to shake,
> I'll never, no, never, no, never forsake."[57]

Such treasures from an earlier age show that the heartbeat of apostolic preaching, the centrality of Christ in all of Scripture, can be heard down through the centuries. How should our preaching enable our hearers to hear Isaiah's testimony to Jesus—or, more accurately, the Spirit of Christ's testimony through Isaiah—in this text?

An appropriate starting point is the need that evoked these words of comfort. Judah's impending exile (actually to come several centuries after Hezekiah's folly and Isaiah's prophecy) would be a bitter recapitulation of our first parents' expulsion from the Garden.

---

57   The author's identity is uncertain. The hymn apparently first appeared in John Rippon, ed., *A Selection of Hymns from the Best Authors, intended to be an Appendix to Dr. Watts's Psalms and Hymns* (London, 1787).

Violators of God's covenant cannot remain in God's holy presence or retain residence in God's holy inheritance, whether the sanctuary is Eden or Canaan. Covenant curse is aptly portrayed by floodwater, as Noah's contemporaries, Pharaoh's forces, and the wayward prophet Jonah could attest. Likewise, biblical history often illustrates the destruction of God's enemies by his consuming fire: Sodom, Nadab and Abihu, and Israelite troops sent to arrest Elijah. The apostle Peter reminds us that whereas the prediluvian world was destroyed by water, the present world is reserved for destruction by fire (2 Peter 3:5–7; cf. Ps. 66:12). Perhaps Moses' announcement that Israel's infidelity would incur the Lord's curse of "fever, inflammation and fiery heat," as well as drought, blight and mildew (Deut. 28:22), is reflected in the description of the exile that immediately precedes our text: "So he poured on him the heat of his anger and the might of battle; it set him on fire all around, but he did not understand; it burned him up, but he did not take it to heart" (Isa. 42:25). The sobering reality is that we, like ancient Judah, deserve destruction by flood and by flame. Even the worst of traumas people experience in this life are faint echoes of the destruction that is our due in the strict justice of God.

Yet, our text is a word of comfort, a proclamation of unimaginably good news. In it the God whom we have offended promises not only preservation through water and fire and eventual repatriation in his good land but also *his presence* with his failing people as they—as we—stumble through the consequences of Adam's sin and our own. To our amazement the Holy God who banishes his defiled people from his holy land *travels with them* into exile, as the chariot-throne seen by Ezekiel made dramatically clear (Ezek. 1). In our text the Lord echoes his earlier promise and sign to the unbelieving King Ahaz, "Behold, the virgin shall conceive and bear a son, and shall call his name Immanuel" (Isa. 7:14; cf. Matt. 1:23). The son given *to us*, the child born to reign forever on David's throne, is named "Wonderful Counselor, *Mighty God*, Everlasting Father, Prince of Peace" (Isa. 9:6–7).

The God who created (*bara'*), formed (*yatzar*), and made (*'asah*) the universe as a whole and humanity in particular as his image-bearers (all three verbs in Isa. 43:7 are applied to the creation of man in Gen. 1:26–27; 2:7) had created his people anew by the redemption of the exodus. Yet, the creation/redemption that launched Israel's life as the people whom God called by name, and by his name, was not *the* new creation that the first creation implicitly promised and anticipated. If Moses' meeting with the Lord on Sinai had been *the* new creation, Israel would not be facing exile in Isaiah's day and thereafter. In one sense it could be said that in the exodus the Lord had given mighty Egypt as a ransom in place of tiny Israel, for by the death of Egypt's firstborn and the drowning of Egypt's charioteers in the sea's waters, a slave nation walked to freedom. But of course neither Egypt nor its north African neighbors and kin, Cush and Seba,[58] could take Israel's place, could provide "cover" or "an atoning ransom"[59] from the fiery wrath of Israel's jealous sovereign. The psalmist rightly recognized that no fallen human could "ransom" the life of another (Ps. 49:8), much less one sinful nation for another. Here is where an apostolic reading and preaching of Isaiah 43 must look beyond both the exodus and Judah's return from exile to the climactic exchange of a Ransom,[60] the ultimate demonstration that those whom God calls by name are precious in his sight, honored, and beloved by him.[61] Of course, the prophet himself foresaw this ransom, as he would later attest:

> Behold, my servant . . . his appearance was so marred, beyond human semblance. . . . Surely he has borne our griefs and carried our sorrows; yet we esteemed him stricken, smitten by God, and afflicted. But he was wounded for our transgressions; he was crushed for our iniquities; upon him was the chastisement that brought us peace. . . . All we like sheep have gone astray; we have turned every one to his own way; and the LORD has laid on him the iniquity of us all. . . . He bore the sin of many, and makes intercession for the transgressors. (Isa. 52:13–14; 53:4–6, 12)

In a confluence of fulfillment and demonstration of grace beyond our expectation, the promised Immanuel, "God with us," came to

---

58   See Gen. 10:6–7.
59   The Hebrew term translated "ransom" in ESV is *kōpher*, which characteristically signifies either a substitutionary sacrifice or payment releasing liability to death, or the atonement transaction itself. See, e.g., Ex. 21:30; 29:33; 30:12; Lev. 23:28; Num. 35:31–32; Deut. 21:8.
60   The LXX counterpart of *kopher* in Isa. 43:3, *allagma*, does not appear in the New Testament, so it provides no direct literary link between this text and the Scriptures of fulfillment. A cognate appears in the compound verb "reconcile," *katallassō*, in such texts as Rom. 5:10–11; 2 Cor. 5:18–20. See *apokatallassō* (also "reconcile") in Eph. 2:16; Col. 1:20. The Greek noun behind the ESV "ransom" in Matt. 20:28 and Mark 10:45 is *lytron*.
61   Jesus, the good shepherd, not only calls his sheep by name (John 10:3) but also lays down his life for his sheep (vv. 11–14).

walk with his people—rather, to walk *for* his people, *instead of* his people—through floodwaters and flaming fires of judgment. He said as much: "I came to cast fire on the earth, and would that it were already kindled! I have a baptism to be baptized with, and how great is my distress until it is accomplished!" (Luke 12:49–50). Both the fire that Jesus was to kindle and the baptism that he was to undergo were his death as a ransom for others, so it is no surprise that he felt intense distress. But he would be the final Jonah, emerging from the deeps in resurrection life and witness as the climactic sign from God (Matt. 12:39–41).

The final Ransom, therefore, infinitely surpassed Isaiah's Ancient Near Eastern geopolitical illustration, thereby proving to our fearful and untrusting hearts the true height, depth, length, and breadth of God's love: "For God so loved the world, that he gave *his only Son*" (John 3:16). "For if while we were enemies we were reconciled to God by the death of *his Son*, much more, now that we are reconciled, shall we be saved by his life" (Rom. 5:10). "He who did not spare *his own Son* but gave him up for us all, how will he not also with him graciously give us all things?" (Rom. 8:32). And the apostle goes on to draw the inevitable conclusion that no threat or hostile force, present or future, anywhere in creation, can separate us from the love of God in that Son, Christ Jesus our Lord (vv. 35–39).

As the Ransom surpasses its Old Testament shadow, so also does the regathering from dispersion. Actually, Isaiah's words hinted at this: exiles transported to Babylon would return from the east, but the Lord promises to address all four poles of the compass, commanding the whole earth to release Israel's descendants, who are his own sons and daughters, and restore them to his presence. The Lord's command to north and south to "bring my sons from afar and my daughters *from the end of the earth*" (Isa. 43:6) anticipates Isaiah's later prophecy, in which God assures his Servant that his restorative mission will not be limited to Israel's scattered remnant: "I will make you as a light for the nations, that my salvation may reach to *the end of the earth*" (Isa. 49:6).[62] Isaiah himself could foresee the eschatological gathering of the Lord's sons and daughters not only from

---

62   The Hebrew construction *qetzēh haʾaretz* appears in Isa. 43:5 and 49:6, although the LXX translates it differently in 43:6 (*akrōn tēs gēs*) and in 49:6 (*eschatou tēs gēs*). On the latter, see Dennis E. Johnson, The *Message of Acts in the History of Redemption* (Phillipsburg: P & R, 1997), 32–52, and Johnson, "Jesus against the Idols: The Use of Isaianic Servant Songs in the Missiology of Acts," *WTJ* 52 (1990): 343–53.

Israel's dispersion but from all the nations, fulfilling God's promises to Abraham both to multiply his seed to innumerable dimensions and to bless all nations through him. It is fitting, therefore, that Paul weaves terms from our text into other ancient Scriptures to summon Gentile Christians, in light of their new identity, to make a clean break with the pagan idolatry of their past.

> I will make my dwelling among them and walk among them, and I will be their God, and they shall be my people. Therefore go out from their midst, and be separate from them, says the Lord, and touch no unclean thing; then I will welcome you, and I will be a father to you, and you shall be *sons and daughters to me*, says the Lord Almighty. (2 Cor. 6:16–18)

A sermon on Isaiah 43:1–7, therefore, could be structured to compare and contrast the situation in which Isaiah's ancient audience—namely, Israel confronting the exile—would have understood God's words of comfort, on the one hand, and, on the other, the redemptive-historical context in which we have now seen the infinitely fuller expression of God's love—namely, the incarnation of Immanuel. These comparisons and contrasts could be paired with each other under a narrative sequence that moves from the initial threat or danger, to the Divine Deliverer's assurance of his power, mercy, and presence, to the resolution of the problem (which confirms the Lord's affirmation of his love and might on behalf of those he calls by name). Through this narrative structure our hearers' experience of the text's comfort and reassurance could, in a sense, follow the footsteps of ancient Israel's encounter with the prophecy, even as our new covenant hearers are also led to marvel at the fuller disclosure of God's power and grace that we are privileged to witness in Jesus, the virgin's son who is "God with us." The outline would be:

1. Israel and we have reason to fear, for our blindness to God's glory and deafness to his Word have exposed us to the floodwaters and flames of his holy justice.
   a. Israel, like Adam, turned a deaf ear to God's word of warning and would be punished with the exile to Babylon—expulsion from God's sanctuary and exposure to God's flood and flame.
   b. You, like Adam, have turned a deaf ear to God's word of

warning and deserve to be punished with extreme expulsion from God's sanctuary and extreme exposure to
God's flood and flame of ultimate, eternal judgment.

2. Israel and we have reason *not* to fear, for the God whom we
have offended is our faithful Creator, our loving Redeemer, and
our constant Companion—even in the flood and the flames.
   a. God commands guilty Israel *not* to fear, but to trust his
   promise that his commitment as Israel's Creator and Redeemer (in the exodus and at Sinai) is unbreakable, and
   his presence with Israel (even through exile) is constant.
   b. God commands us, who are equally guilty, *not* to fear,
   but to trust his promise that his commitment as our
   Creator and Redeemer is unbreakable, and his presence
   with us is constant.

3. Israel and we have watched God make good his profession
of constant love and his promise to redeem us at great price,
bestowing glory on us far beyond what we deserve.
   a. Israel would see the Lord accompany his exiles and return their remnant through the edict of King Cyrus of
   Persia, whose name the Lord calls centuries beforehand
   (cf. Isa. 45:1–7).
   b. We have seen God-With-Us, Jesus Christ, go through
   the flood and flame of divine justice as our ransom on
   the Cross and rise again to bring God's sons and daughters from the end of the earth.

Conclusion

The contemporary preacher who would follow the apostles'
footsteps, as they were led by Jesus, along the various paths of the
Old Testament's witness to the coming Christ faces a daunting but
rewarding task. Our illustrative treatments of representative texts
and genres have shown that a conscientious, Christ-focused reading
of the Old Testament demands rigorous attention to each passage's
original literary and historical contexts. This honors God's purpose
to reveal himself and his redemptive agenda in the events of real history, in the life struggles of real people, whom he called, sovereignly
and graciously, as a people in covenant with himself. At the same
time, God intended Israel's experience to be incomplete, anticipatory

of, and preparatory for the climactic accomplishment of redemption through the incarnation, obedience, suffering, and resurrection of the divine Son, Jesus, the Messiah. To read and preach any Old Testament text in its appropriate contexts, therefore, means not only to ascertain (as clearly as we can) how its first hearers should have understood it but also to place that meaning in the context of the divinely designed flow of redemptive history and saving revelation that was always moving believers' hearts toward Christ. Standing, as we do, on this side of the watershed constituted by Jesus' death, resurrection, ascension, and bestowal of the Spirit, we hear the ancient history, law, wisdom, song, and prophecy that God spoke to his waiting people in a new and major key, with a fuller orchestration than was possible until the beloved Son arrived on this sin-sick earth to be and enact the Father's resounding "Yes" to all the ancient promises (2 Cor. 1:19–20). Our task as preachers to proclaim, explain, and apply the Old Testament in its integrity as God's witness to his Son is challenging, but it is also a high privilege, refreshing our own souls and bringing salvation to our hearers, by the grace of God's Spirit.

10

Preaching the Promise Keeper: Apostolic Preaching of New Testament Literary Genres

It might seem that a chapter on how to preach the texts and genres of the New Testament would be superfluous in a book advocating the practice of apostolic preaching today. After all, are not the New Testament books *themselves* the preeminent and normative exemplars of apostolic preaching? Have they not been our guide and norm in the preceding chapters, showing us how to discern the Old Testament's diverse and unified witness to Jesus, the Christ? Should we not be able to assume that any sermon that expounds a New Testament text will *inevitably* be apostolic—Christ-centered, attentive to redemptive history, grace-driven, missiologically articulated—simply because the text itself exhibits these virtues?

It is, of course, true that we have been looking to the New Testament as the canonical revelation of the way of reading Israel's Scripture that the apostles learned from Jesus himself, exhibited in their preaching, and conveyed to their successors. Yet, it is also sadly true that preachers have taught and proclaimed New Testament texts in various ways that diverge from the texts' original, apostolic meaning and purpose. After all, any New Testament text that we might preach is a piece of a broader context (at least an entire "book"), and ignoring that context by taking a sentence, paragraph, or chapter in isolation from its context can lead to our preaching a message that falls short of, or even contradicts, the text's meaning when it is viewed in the context of the entire document in which it appears. The danger is particularly acute when a text is expounded and applied without reference to the central themes of the apostolic gospel concerning Jesus' redemptive mission. Two examples illustrate the problem.

In Matthew 19:16–22 (Mark 10:17–22; Luke 18:18–23), Jesus is approached by a young man who asks, "What good deed must I do to have eternal life?" Jesus' answer is, "If you would enter life, keep the commandments," and then he recites several of the Ten Commandments and the command to love one's neighbor as oneself. When the man claims to have kept all God's commands and inquires what he still lacks, Jesus then seems to add just one more command, which will enable this observant law keeper to reach his goal of obtaining eternal life through his own achievement: "If you would be perfect, go, sell what you possess and give to the poor." Clearly, such a text, if extracted and isolated from the gospel in which it is embedded, seems to warrant or even demand a sermon that promises salvation through one's own law-keeping and sacrificial generosity, apart from faith and apart from the cross, to which (as Matthew's broader context reiterates) Jesus was inexorably traveling when this conversation occurred (Matt. 16:21; 17:22; 20:17–19; cf. 20:28; 26:28). On the other hand, when we read this exchange within the flow of the entire gospel, and particularly in light of the climax toward which Matthew's narrative drives, we come away with a different impression of Jesus' purpose in pointing first to God's commands and then to the grip that the young man's property had on his heart. This reading is confirmed by Jesus' affirmation in the immediate sequel that the liberation of the rich from the tyranny of their riches, though impossible with man, is well within the power of God, to whom "all things are possible" (Matt. 19:26).

The second example comes from the apostle Paul's epistle to the Romans. In Romans 2:6–11, taken in isolation from the larger argument of the epistle as a whole, Paul seems to espouse the same soteriology that might have been inferred from Jesus' remarks to the rich young man. In this chiastically arranged paragraph, not only does the apostle affirm that God "will render to each one according to his works" (vs. 6) and conclude that "God shows no partiality" (vs. 11), but he also illustrates this principle both with respect to those who do good (vv. 7, 10) and with respect to those who do evil (vv. 8–9). If this paragraph is abstracted from its immediate setting and rhetorical function as a component of Paul's allegation that God's self-revelation in majesty and justice indicts all humanity, pagan

Gentile and observant Jew alike, for ingratitude and ungodliness (cf. 1:18; 3:9–20), it could be marshaled as evidence supporting a soteriology that moves Jesus' obedient covenant-keeping and vicarious curse-bearing to the periphery and in its stead places the individual's performance at center stage: "glory and honor and peace for *everyone who does good*, the Jew first and also the Greek" (2:10). Such a preaching of Romans 2:6–11, however, would turn it *against* Paul's major thesis: that the gospel, which reveals a righteousness of God "through faith in Jesus Christ for all who believe" *apart from* the law and our law-keeping, is the power of God for salvation (1:16–17; 3:21–22). It is not *apostolic* preaching to take a string of apostolic words out of their context in the apostolic gospel—the good news that turns hearers' trust away from themselves and toward the once-and-for-all achievement of God's Son.

Moreover, the New Testament is intended to be read in the context of the Old Testament, the rich foundation that God laid to draw his ancient people's hearts toward the coming Messiah and to illumine their minds about the significance of his redemptive mission. Our listeners today are, on the whole, so illiterate with respect to the Old Testament that they will fail to "hear" the New Testament in this canonical context, and therefore fail to apprehend much of the New Testament's multidimensional disclosure of Jesus' person and work, unless we preachers show them. We need to paint the redemptive-historical backdrop against which the "drama" of the climax of salvation is played out in the work of Jesus, the mediator of the new covenant. The variations among the sermons of Acts show that the apostles exercised pastoral wisdom in gauging the depth of redemptive-historical texture that would be appropriate in addressing non-Christian audiences, whether biblically informed Jews, proselytes and God-fearers, or pagan Gentiles unacquainted with the Old Testament Scriptures. Nevertheless, the substructure of God's plan for history and the consciousness that this plan had reached its decisive moment with the arrival of Jesus the Messiah permeates all the messages (see, for instance, Acts 17:30–31). As for our calling to preach to the church gathered in worship, we have seen that the epistle to the Hebrews, the prototypical canonical sermon to a Christian congregation, as well as the other New Testament epistles, displays how fully the apostles led their believing hearers into the rich discoveries that Jesus had opened to them in the days between his resurrection and his ascension (Luke 24).

Yet, it is quite possible, again, to fail to imitate the apostles even in preaching the apostles' own words. How many sermons have been preached on the parable of the prodigal son (Luke 15:11–32) without a hint of the prophets' portrayal of Ephraim as the Lord's wayward son, for whom the Father longs (Jer. 31:9, 18–20; cf. Hos. 11:1–8)? (Could the Pharisees who so disapproved of Jesus' welcome to the unworthy have so completely forgotten their own Scriptures' testimony to God's paternal compassion toward his undeserving son?) Has our preaching "unpacked" for our hearers the dramatic exodus overtones—both deliverance from death and liberation from slavery—embedded in Paul's term "redemption" in Ephesians 1:7, "In him we have redemption through his blood"? It is probably not as grievous an omission to preach Christ from a New Testament text while failing to display the Old Testament shadows and hopes that God has now fulfilled as it is to preach an Old Testament text without reference to the Messiah, who is the destination toward which Israel's ancient Scriptures move. Nevertheless, no conscientious preacher wants to deprive his hearers of the assurance derived from seeing the beautiful unity of the Scriptures, from promise to fulfillment. Nor does he wish to obscure from their view the vividness of rich biblical motifs such as creation, covenant, holiness, sanctuary, inheritance, the divine warrior king, atonement, and vindication, all of which have their roots deep in the Old Testament Scriptures and their fruit in the mission of the Son, to whom the New Testament Scriptures testify.

This models presented in this chapter show how representative genres of the apostolic New Testament Scriptures can be preached in an apostolic way: (1) gospel narrative, (2) parable, (3) doctrinal discourse and (4) ethical application in the Epistles, (5) wisdom literature, and (6) the prophetic-apocalyptic visions of the book of Revelation. The New Testament contains other genres, of course: Jesus' discourses to the crowds and to his disciples, the sermons of Acts, songs of praise, and primitive confessions of faith. My hope is that these six samples will point the way and whet readers' appetites to explore and proclaim the riches of new covenant revelation as the Spirit's testimony to the Son, grounded in the ancient Scriptures, displaying God's life-transforming grace, and addressing all peoples with Christ's summons, "Turn to me and be saved, all the ends of the earth! For I am God, and there is no other. . . . To me every knee shall bow, every tongue shall swear allegiance" (Isa. 45:22–23; cf. Phil. 2:10–11).

Gospel Narrative: "The Scorned Servant King" (Luke 9:51–56)[1]

This text is about respect: who deserves it and what should happen when people disrespect the supremely respectable One. The passage narrates Jesus' rejection by a Samaritan village, the zeal of James and John to avenge the slight to their Master's dignity, and his rebuke—not of the inhospitable Samaritans, but of his own loyal partisans. At first glance, the reaction of James and John seems excessively vengeful, and, of course, Jesus' rebuke shows that their particular proposal to defend Jesus' dignity was misguided. Yet, the sons of Zebedee had a truer apprehension of the honor that Jesus deserves than do many of their later critics, and they had biblical precedent for their fiery solution to the Samaritans' disrespect. Still, their eagerness to see justice fall from heaven betrays their blindness to the shadow of the cross that looms over Jesus' every step.

The significance of this text as a watershed in Luke's gospel is signaled by the accumulation of theologically significant terms in verse 51. Jesus' trek to Jerusalem begins as "the days of his assumption were being fulfilled" (dej). In Luke-Acts, Jesus' assumption (*analēmpsis*)—that is, his being "taken up" (*anelēmphthē*) into heaven—marks the completion of his resurrection appearances to the Eleven and draws the boundary between the earthly and the heavenly phases of his messianic activity (Acts 1:2, 11, 22; see also 1 Tim. 3:16). Jesus had already informed his followers that an ordeal of rejection, suffering, and death stood between him and that glorious exaltation (Luke 9:21–22, 44–45); yet Luke points his readers beyond those coming traumas to the glories that would follow them. The verb "fulfilled" (*sumplērōthēnai*) and its cognate noun appear rarely in biblical Greek and are charged by these rare appearances with eschatological significance, marking the climax of a promised and long anticipated event of salvation.[2] Finally, the comment that Jesus "set his face" (ESV) alludes

---

1 For further examples of the application of apostolic hermeneutics to New Testament narratives, see Dennis E. Johnson, *The Message of Acts in the History of Redemption* (Phillipsburg: P & R, 1997); and Dennis E. Johnson, *Let's Study Acts* (Edinburgh: Banner of Truth, 2003).

2 In addition to our text, the verb appears in Acts 2:1, marking the "fulfilling" of the day of Pentecost, on which Jesus' promise of the outpouring of the Spirit

to the resolution of the suffering Servant who, at the prospect of injury and contempt from those who would strike his back, yank out his beard, and spit in his face for God's sake, nevertheless affirmed, "I have set my face like a flint, and I know that I shall not be put to shame" (Isa. 50:6–7). A momentous pilgrimage, leading ultimately to enthronement at God's right hand in heaven, was beginning.

The refusal of hospitality to Jesus and his companions by the residents of a Samaritan village was more than a breach of ancient etiquette. The reason for their rejection, "because his face was set toward Jerusalem," points to the deep-seated religious animosity between Jews and Samaritans and to their long-standing debate over the proper venue for worship (see John 4:20). It is quite conceivable that the motive behind the Samaritans' rebuff lay in this ethnic-religious dispute, rather than being targeted specifically at Jesus. Nevertheless, James and John, elsewhere called "sons of thunder" (Mark 3:17), construed the closed Samaritan doors as a personal affront to Jesus himself and stood ready to avenge the insult by invoking fire to fall from heaven to incinerate the uppity Samaritan half-breeds.[3] In our age of terrorism and religious *jihad,* the eagerness of Zebedee's sons to enlist God's firepower to destroy their enemies seems shocking, and we are relieved to read that Jesus rebuked his would-be defenders.[4] After all, our contemporaries see themselves as superior to those benighted eras in which people actually believed that religious convictions were important enough to fight over.

James and John deserved Jesus' rebuke, of course, but not necessarily for the reasons that many moderns might suppose. Assessed

---

would occur. It is used non-metaphorically in Luke 8:23 to describe the filling of the disciples' boat by storm waters. In 2 Chron. 36:21 the cognate noun *sumplērōsis* designates the fulfillment or completion of the prophesied seventy years of exile, during which the land received its Sabbaths (see also 1 Esdr. 1:55; Dan. 9:2 [Theodotian]). One major LXX manuscript has *sumplēroō* also in Jer. 25:12, which likewise predicts the completion-fulfillment of the seventy years of Judah's exile.

3   The bizarre syncretism that characterized Samaritan religion—devotion to the books of Moses mixed with pagan elements—arose, in part, from the religious compromises of the northern kingdom of Israel (such as worship at the high places and rival shrines to the Jerusalem temple) and in part from the ethnic relocation and resulting religious mergers that accompanied Assyria's conquest and domination (see 2 Kings 17:24–41).

4   The situation—the anointed king's rebuke of loyalists who sought to defend his honor with violence—exhibits parallels with David's rebuke of Abishai in 2 Sam. 16:5–14, discussed above in chap. 9.

in the context of Luke's gospel and ancient Scripture, the Samaritans' refusal to welcome Jesus, whatever its historical roots, *should* be seen as deserving instant incineration by fire from on high. In this respect, James and John drew proper conclusions from Jesus' own self-disclosure.

The preceding context in Luke's gospel underscored the majesty of Jesus and his worthiness to be welcomed and worshiped—particularly in the transfiguration to which James, and John, with Peter, had been eyewitnesses (Luke 9:28–36). Both his radiant appearance and the heavenly voice identifying him as the elect Son (echoing Ps. 2:7; Isa. 42:1) justify the brothers' conviction that Jesus' glory is so great that he cannot be scorned with impunity. Jesus is the supreme and final prophet promised by Moses, whose words must be "heard" (Deut. 18:15).

Subtler allusions to Old Testament texts reinforce the motif of Jesus' greatness. A more wooden translation that Jesus "sent *messengers* ahead of him . . . to *make preparations*" (Luke 9:52) would be: "He sent *'angels' before his face* . . . to *prepare*." Although the English word "angel" refers specifically to superhuman spiritual servants of God, "ministering spirits" (Heb. 1:14), the Greek word behind it includes both human and superhuman "messengers." Luke's choice of words echoes two Old Testament texts. First, the Lord assured Moses and the Israelites, "And behold I am *sending* my *angel before your face*, in order that he might guard you in the way, so that he might lead you into the land that I *prepared* for you" (Ex. 23:20 LXX [dej]). Jesus is the fulfillment of Israel, the faithful servant of the Lord that the Israelite nation failed to be. He endured his forty-day trials in the wilderness with perfect faithfulness, whereas Israel failed miserably in its forty-year trials in the wilderness. Jesus is the rightful heir of the Promised Land; and yet, although he is traveling through his own land on his way to his ancestor David's capital, Jerusalem, he has endured rejection not only from Samaritans but also from his own Nazarene neighbors (Luke 4:28–29) and from "his own people," who likewise "did not receive him" (John 1:11). Second, the wording of Luke 9:52 even more closely repeats the wording and content of Malachi 3:1: "Behold, I am *sending* my *angel*, and he will 'see to' the way *before my face*, and suddenly he will come to his own temple— the Lord whom you seek, even the angel of the covenant, whom you desire" (LXX; dej). Here the "face" before which the angel prepares a royal road belongs to the Lord himself. The implication of this allusion is that Jesus is not only Israel, the faithful covenant servant; he also is God, the glorious covenant Lord.

Another collection of Old Testament allusions in Luke explains the specific form of judgment that Zebedee's sons desire for the defiant Samaritans: the prophetic witness of Elijah to the northern kingdom of Israel (Samaria's antecedent). Elijah had recently appeared with Moses on the Mount of Transfiguration to speak with Jesus concerning his impending exodus (Luke 9:30–31). Earlier in Luke's gospel, Jesus had explained the skepticism of his Nazarene neighbors by referring to God's sending Elijah to bring saving sustenance to a Gentile widow in pagan Zarephath, instead of any widow in Israel (4:25–27). Having raised from death a widow's son in the Galilean village of Nain, Jesus "gave him to his mother" (7:15): the evangelist replicates exactly the wording of 1 Kings 17:23 (LXX), linking the resurrection with that of the widow's son in Zarephath through Elijah the prophet. Finally, the evangelist's selection of "being taken up" (*analēmpsis*) to refer to Jesus' impending exaltation, in such close literary proximity to Elijah's appearance at the Transfiguration, is probably intended to call to mind the prophet's being "taken up" (*anelēmphthē*, 2 Kings 2:11 LXX) to heaven in a fiery chariot before the eyes of his successor Elijah.

Since these and other connections portray Jesus as continuing and fulfilling the prophetic ministry of Elijah, the conclusion drawn by James and John made sense. When Israel's King Ahaziah sent soldiers to summon Elijah to Samaria, his royal capital, two platoons of fifty were destroyed by fire from heaven because their commanders presumed to assert Ahaziah's authority over God's prophet (2 Kings 1:9–12).[5] If trying to impose a demand from a corrupt king on God's servant warranted destruction by fire, James and John had reason to infer that Samaritan rejection of the one whom God had acclaimed as his chosen Son deserved no less. If God punished the contempt that military officers showed his prophet long ago, surely God would be equally jealous to defend the dignity of his beloved, chosen Son!

The brothers also had reason to view the Samaritans' rejection of Jesus' *forerunners* as a refusal to receive *Jesus himself* and therefore finally as an act of defiance toward his divine Father. Treatment of

---

5 A third platoon survived when its commander appealed to the prophet meekly (2 Kings 1:13–15).

those who bear Jesus' name constitutes treatment of Jesus and of the Father who sent him, and the context of his passage makes clear: "Whoever receives this child in my name receives me, and whoever receives me receives him who sent me" (Luke 9:48). "The one who hears you hears me, and the one who rejects you rejects me, and the one who rejects me rejects him who sent me" (10:16). When expounding this text to contemporary Americans, who are allergic to authority and immunized to awe, the preacher should not rush too quickly to Jesus' rebuke but first help hearers appreciate the logic and appropriateness of the brothers' zeal for Jesus' honor.

Nevertheless, Jesus rebuked the sons of Zebedee, bypassed the village, and moved on to another. Where had their Christ-centered zeal gone wrong? Both the context and the allusion to Isaiah 50:7, which we noted above, provide the answer. Jesus' pilgrimage to Jerusalem would reach its destination in glorification as the King whose enemies ultimately would be destroyed (Luke 19:14, 27). But in Luke 9:51, as repeatedly in this chapter, that path to *glory* is clearly marked as the path of *suffering and death* (9:22, 44). Hereafter, whenever Luke marks the miles on this long road by the mention of "Jerusalem" (13:22, 33–34; 17:11; 18:31; 19:11, 28), the shadow of suffering looms over Jesus. It is for this reason that Jesus must "set his face to go to Jerusalem": because that face would be beaten, bruised, and bloodied, spat upon, scorned, and pierced by thorns. The scene foreseen by Isaiah would be played out in brutal, ugly reality (22:63–65; Mark 14:65).

Moreover, that brutal treatment would be instigated not by despised Samaritans but by the leaders of Israel, God's own people. It is not surprising (though inexcusable) that Samaritans would refuse to open their homes to a Jewish rabbi and his followers who were travelling to Jerusalem and its temple, which showed their shrine on Mt. Gerazim to be illegitimate. What is shocking is how violently the covenant people themselves repudiated their long-awaited Rescuer and Ruler. "He came to his own, and his own people did not receive him" (John 1:11). The Samaritan village that forfeited its opportunity to welcome Jesus experienced real judgment when "the Savior of the world" (as other Samaritans acclaimed him, John 4:42) passed it by and turned to other towns. In fact, Jesus had told the disciples to shake the dust of unwelcoming towns off their feet as a testimony against those towns (Luke 9:5). Even worse wrath awaited Jerusalem, whose true King wept in lament because that city "did not know the time of your visitation" (Luke 19:44).

The obedient Listener (Isa. 50:4–5) steeled himself for the rejection and torture that he foresaw (as the later Servant Song shows), in order to bear the punishment due others, so that the stripes on his beaten back might bring them healing and his right standing before the righteous Judge might be theirs as well (Isa. 53:4–6, 11; see Luke 22:37; Acts 8:32–35). In their impatient zeal to see God's fire fall immediately in holy vengeance, James and John revealed the naïveté concerning their own liability to divine judgment (and thus their own need for the Servant's substitutionary suffering) that often characterizes us and our listeners. Having experienced the privileged glimpse of Jesus' glory on the mountain, they considered it quite appropriate that they would occupy the thrones of honor in his coming kingdom. After all, they were prepared to drink his cup and undergo his baptism—or so they thought (Mark 10:35–40). They knew their own hearts as little as Simon Peter knew his (Luke 22:31–34)—as little as we, too often, know ours. What they could not see was that they, too, deserved the lightning bolt from heaven, the contempt, dishonor, beating, and tortured death that awaited their Master in Jerusalem—the Master whom they would cravenly abandon to his enemies.

Despite dishonor from Samaritans, violent rejection by Jewish leaders, and abandonment by his own friends, Jesus moved resolutely to Jerusalem to die for defiant rebels, rather than execute them. For this reason, his amazing grace moves us to honor him in ways that mere duty never could. We who glimpse, even partially, the wrath we deserve and the mercy that bore it for us adore the Lord's faithful Servant not merely because we must but because we cannot help but worship One who so loved us and gave himself for us. For disrespectful Samaritans and failing disciples alike, grace has the last word, for immediately after the indictment of "his own people" who refused their King welcome comes the promise: "But to all who did receive him, who believed in his name, he gave the right to become children of God" (John 1:12).

A sermon on this text should expose our contemporaries' numbness to God's holiness and to the honor that Jesus deserves by focusing first on what James and John got right, and then, addressing what they got wrong, by pointing our hearers to Jesus' redemptive purpose in setting his face toward Jerusalem, there to suffer heaven's fiery judgment in the place of inhospitable rebels such as the Samaritans, Zebedee's sons, and ourselves.

1. What James and John got right: Jesus is the glorious Son of God who deserves our highest respect.
   a. Jesus is the Chosen Son, whose bright glory overpowered James and John on the Mount of Transfiguration (Luke 9:29, 35).
   b. Jesus is the true Israel, protected by the Father's angels until he returns to his heavenly home (9:52; Ex. 23:20).
   c. Jesus is the Lord himself, who sends his angels before his face to prepare his royal road (Luke 9:52: Mal. 3:1).
   d. Therefore, James and John knew how Jesus (and his messengers) must be honored: as the divine Father who sent him (Luke 9:48; 10:16).
   e. And James and John knew what contempt for Jesus deserves: fire from heaven (2 Kings 1:10, 12).

2. What James and John got wrong: at that point Jesus was going to Jerusalem not to rule in justice but to suffer in mercy.
   a. He "set his face" toward Jerusalem, to endure the sufferings of the Lord's obedient Servant (Isa. 50:4–10).
   b. Jesus' mission was not to destroy disrespectful rebels but to endure the fiery ordeal that they (we) deserve.
   c. So Jesus' presence by his Spirit now confronts us with the urgent opportunity to welcome him in humble faith, or we shall face his wrath to come.

Parable: "A Strategist in Crisis" (Luke 16:1–13)

Jesus' parables are extensions of Israel's wisdom tradition, as the citation of Psalm 78:2 in Matthew 13:34–35 shows: "This was to fulfill what was spoken by the prophet: 'I will open my mouth in parables; I will utter what has been hidden since the foundation of the world.'" The Greek *parabolē*, "parable," represents the Hebrew word *mashal*, often translated "proverb." The thread that unites Jesus' fictional narratives with the terse couplets in the Hebrew Scriptures is the element of analogy or comparison, which makes concrete, everyday experience an apt source of illustration for spiritual instruction.

Jesus' parables, however, are not mere illustrations of timeless moral or spiritual realities. They are part and parcel of his proclamation of the coming of the long-awaited kingdom of God in his own person and thus of the arrival of the great watershed moment in God's plan to redeem his people and to inaugurate his new covenant with them. Herman N. Ridderbos has called attention to the programmatic role of the Parable of the Sower, not only as the opening story in the synoptics' parable collections (Mark 4:1–9; Matt. 13:1–9; Luke 8:4–8) but also as the key that unlocks the meaning of the others: "Do you not understand this parable? How then will you understand all the parables?" (Mark 4:13). Ridderbos observes that this parable reveals a truth more profound than the obvious point that differing soils symbolize various responses to the seed of the Word: what initially would have surprised Jesus' hearers is that the herald of the kingdom is portrayed as a Sower spreading vulnerable seed rather than as a Reaper ushering in final judgment.[6] The two-phase inbreaking of the kingdom—first in a form that effects salvation but is subject to resistance, and then finally in invincible and overpowering glory and justice—likewise finds expression in such parables as the wheat and tares, the mustard seed, the wedding banquet and its rude invitees, the wise and foolish virgins, and the ten minas.

In fact, Jesus' parables sometimes send mixed messages about the timing of the coming kingdom. He speaks the parable of the wedding banquet in response to a fellow dinner guest's pious-sounding beatitude that seemed to envision a distant future age, "Blessed is everyone who will eat bread in the kingdom of God!" (Luke 14:15). On the contrary, Jesus' story underscores that the feast of the kingdom is now ready and its host is issuing his urgent invitations in the present: those who make excuse now will never enjoy his table fellowship or taste his banquet. On the other hand, when many who accompanied his approach to Jerusalem "supposed that the kingdom of God was to appear immediately" (19:11), he told the story of the ten minas to disabuse them of that expectation and to prepare them for faithful stewardship during his absence. In one sense, the kingdom feast is spread and its invitation must be responded to immediately; in another sense, the kingdom will arrive in consummation form only after a prolonged period of the king's absence, during which obedient

---

6   Herman N. Ridderbos, *The Coming of the Kingdom* (Philadelphia: Presbyterian & Reformed, 1962), 129–34.

servants must invest his gifts, although defiant subjects oppose his reign (19:13–14).

Jesus' parables show the kingdom of God to be surprising not only in its double arrival (first in grace and weakness, finally in justice and power) but also in its reversal of received wisdom and conventional expectations. Jesus' stories are subversive. In them the younger son who shamed his father's name and squandered his father's wealth is feted upon his return in rags, while his obedient, hard-working brother sulks outside. The tax collector who has sold out his own people to Gentile oppressors leaves the temple right with God, whereas the scrupulously obedient Pharisee does not. Invited guests forego a wedding feast to pursue other interests while disabled outcasts take their places at the groom's table. Farm workers who put in one hour of work receive equal pay with those who labored for twelve, through the heat of the day, as their employer insists that his right to show lavish generosity to some does no injustice to others.

The parable of the dishonest steward or manager (Luke 16:1–9) shows Jesus the storyteller at his most provocative. Commentators have observed its challenges.[7] Leon Morris characterized is as "notoriously one of the most difficult of all the parables to interpret."[8] I. Howard Marshall observed, "Few passages in the Gospel can have given rise to so many different interpretations. . . ."[9] Robert Stein concurred: "Few passages of Scripture have caused as much confusion. . . ."[10] In the story, the steward compounds a history of financial mismanagement with a clever parting strategy to defraud his master of vast amounts of "accounts receivable." Yet, this all-too-common story of malfeasance and dishonesty takes a bizarre twist when the defrauded master actually *commends* the manager for shrewdness, rather than flying into a rage over his losses. Then the narrative turns stranger still when *Jesus himself* holds up the white-collar criminal as an example to be imitated! What does this strange story reveal about the kingdom and the messianic king who had come to inaugurate it? How should such a parable be preached?

---

7   See, in addition to those cited below, Alan R. Odiam, "The Parable of the Shrewd Manager: Luke 16:1–13," *Mid-America Theological Journal* 21 (1997): 69–86.

8   Leon Morris, *The Gospel according to St. Luke: An Introduction and Commentary* (TNTC; Grand Rapids: Eerdmans, 1974), 245.

9   I. Howard Marshall, *Commentary on Luke* (NIGTC; Grand Rapids: Eerdmans, 1978), 614.

10   Robert H. Stein, *Luke* (NAC; Nashville: Broadman, 1992), 411.

Factors in the cultural and literary contexts of the third gospel illumine the significance of Jesus' story and should be noted. The position of trust occupied by stewards in affluent households of various ancient cultures would have been well understood by Jesus' hearers and Luke's original readers. It is well illustrated in Joseph's authority as the chief slave in Potiphar's house: "Because of me my master has no concern about anything in the house, and he has put everything that he has in my charge. He is not greater in this house than I am, nor has he kept back anything from me except . . . his wife" (Gen. 39:8–9). Such authority, when wielded by a man of less integrity than Joseph, provided opportunity both for incompetence and for corruption.[11] In Greco-Roman cultures, stewards, although ordinarily slaves, wielded extraordinary authority over their fellow-servants and enjoyed significant flexibility in the management of their masters' resources, with the understanding that their records of accounts must be ready for audit on demand and that malfeasance would be severely punished.[12] Jesus has already introduced a surprising twist in this parable by having the steward envision a future in which he has been turned out of his master's household and employ altogether, rather than being subjected against his will to hard manual labor in the master's fields.

The parable's placement within Luke's gospel sets it in the context of Jesus' disputes with Pharisees. This story follows those of the lost sheep, coin, and son; and it is linked with the last of these by the comment that the manager, like the wayward son, had "wasted" (*diaskorpizō*) the possessions of one who was his superior and benefactor (Luke 15:13; 16:1).[13] This linguistic connection reinforces the situational similarities between the stories: both the son and the steward are cast into a crisis of survival by their own mismanagement of another's property, and both devise a plan to address the crisis. Jesus spoke the parable of the lost son in defense of his table fellowship with tax collectors and other notorious sinners, which

---

11   The steward is not actually called "unjust" or "dishonest" (*tēs adikias*) until after he has cut the deals with each of his master's debtors, so it is possible that Jesus portrays his "wasting" of his master's possessions as resulting from imprudence or undisciplined spending.

12   Paul Veyne, ed. *A History of Private Life*. Vol. 1: *From Pagan Rome to Byzantium*, trans. Arthur Goldhammer (Cambridge, Massachusetts: Belknap Press/ Harvard University Press, 1987), 144–46.

13   Other uses of *diaskorpizō* in the NT refer to the scattering of persons (or sheep symbolizing persons)—Matt. 26:31; Mark 14:27; Luke 1:51; John 11:52; Acts 5:37.

had been criticized by the Pharisees and scribes (15:1–2). Following the parable of the unjust steward, Jesus clarifies the sort of shrewdness that befits "the sons of light," who are heirs of God's kingdom, by issuing warnings against devotion to money (16:10–13). These cautions situate the parable within the larger context of Jesus' teachings about wealth and its seductive power in Luke's gospel, such as his parables of the rich fool (12:13–21) and of the rich man and the beggar Lazarus (16:19–31). Jesus concludes his clarifying remarks on our parable with the pronouncement that one cannot be a loyal servant of God *and* mammon—a statement that evoked ridicule from the money-loving Pharisees (16:14–15). Thus references to the Pharisees' resistance to Jesus and his message envelope the two parables of wastrels in crisis in an *inclusio*.

The soon-to-be-unemployed chief financial officer and chief operations officer has a cunning plan to cushion his landing after the crash of his career: he will use his master's money, which he still controls, as he prepares the financial records for a final audit—to "befriend" those who owe his master payment for products already received. They may not hire him as their manager or accountant (would anyone?), but he expects that at least one of the beneficiaries of his last-minute "generosity" will repay him with a grateful welcome and comfortable living, sparing him the toil of field labor and the shame of begging.

Each preacher will need to weigh the interpretive options that have been proposed to soften the scandal of Jesus' commendation of the manager's desperate solution, which appears to be manifestly dishonest. Commentators have suggested that his reduction of debts owed to his master, including the production of new documentation, merely eliminated the interest on the outstanding balances—thus bringing the master's practice into conformity with the prohibition of the Mosaic law against charging usury of a fellow-Israelite. Others have proposed that the new, lower figures cited by the manager reflected his deduction of his own extortionary "cut" of the original transactions.

Yet, Jesus emphasizes that the manager dealt with each debtor "one by one" and instructed each to write the reduced amount "quickly," suggesting that Jesus is portraying the manager's action as deceptive and the exchange of documentation as having been transacted behind his master's back. In fact, it seems that it has been a desire to exonerate Jesus from the charge of recommending shady dealings, rather than evidence in the text itself, that has compelled Bible students to find some honest (or semi-honest) explanation for the actions of the *dishonest* steward (as Jesus plainly labels him: "the steward of unrighteousness," *ton oikonomon tēs adikias*). Just as Jesus would dare to compare the prayers of the saints addressed to God with the petition of a helpless widow addressed to a "judge of unrighteousness" (*kritēs tēs adikias*)—not to cast God as an unjust judge or unwilling defender but to emphasize by contrast his eagerness to bring justice for his elect (18:1–8)—so also Jesus shocks his hearers and Luke's readers to attention by holding up *something* about the behavior of an unsavory, self-seeking, white-collar criminal as worthy of his master's commendation *and* of believers' emulation. The question that this wisdom text challenges us to ponder is, What is that commendable "something" hidden amid the corruption?

The answer lies in the expression "for his shrewdness" (ESV; literally, "because he acted shrewdly"). Although our English adverb "shrewdly" often carries connotations of cleverness, cunning, or calculating craftiness, its Greek counterpart, *phronimōs* and the adjective from which it is derived need not imply deception or even self-interest. Earlier in the third gospel Jesus had summoned his disciples to prove themselves to be faithful and wise (*phronimos*) stewards, who are not lulled by their master's delay into lack of vigilance or abuse of their authority but who stand ever ready for his appearance (Luke 12:42–48; see Matt. 24:45–51). Likewise, in the parable of ten virgins awaiting the bridegroom, the five who gave prudent forethought to the need of oil for their lamps are commended as wise (*phronimos*, Matt. 25:2, 4, 8, 9).[14] The quality that elicits the master's praise and the Lord Jesus' implied approval is the manager's prudence, foresight, and strategic response to an impending crisis.

Jesus' commentary in Luke 16:8 places both the defrauded master's commendation of the manager and the manager's strategic

---

14   *Phronimos* also appears in Jesus' exhortation to be "shrewd as serpents (*opheis*)" (Gen. 3:1 LXX uses the superlative form of the adjective, *phronimōtatos*, "shrewdest" to describe the serpent [*ophis*]) but "innocent as doves" (Matt. 10:16). Moreover, Paul's uses of the adjective are negative, in warnings against or ironic rebukes of thinking oneself wiser than one actually is (Rom. 11:25; 12:16; 1 Cor. 4:10; 10:15; 2 Cor. 11:19). Nevertheless, although the Greek adjective has negative overtones in some NT passages, its positive reference to *prudent forethought and strategic planning* for the future comes to the fore in Luke 16, as in Luke 12 and Matthew 24–25.

maneuver into perspective: "For the sons of this age (ESV margin, Greek *aiōn*) are more shrewd (*phronimos*) in dealing with their own generation than the sons of light." The master, a profit-driven man of the world, could only admire the cleverness of his steward, both in planning for his future and in covering the tracks of his financial shenanigans. What Jesus expects of his followers as sons of the light, however, is a strategic investment of the resources that they manage for God in view of a future horizon that transcends this age: "And I tell you, make friends for yourselves by means of unrighteous wealth (*tou mamōna tēs adikias*), so that when it fails they may receive you into the eternal dwellings" (16:9). Like the manager in the parable, the sons of light have temporary custody of resources that properly belong to their Master. Like the manager, they should use these resources to secure their future welcome by "friends" who can give them shelter when the riches of the present age will be worthless. Who are these friends?

Ultimately, of course, only God himself has authority to welcome people into his eternal dwelling (or "tent", Greek *skēnē*), just as only the aggrieved father could welcome the prodigal home (Luke 15:20–24). A vision granted to John would reveal the international multitude of those whose robes had been whitened in the blood of the Lamb: "And he who sits on the throne will shelter them" (Greek: 'cast a tent over them,' *skēnōsei ep' autous*; Rev. 7:15).[15] In another sense, however, there are others whom the sons of light can befriend through liberality with their Master's money. Jesus advised his dinner host on one occasion, "When you give a feast, invite the poor, the crippled, the lame, the blind, and you will be blessed, because they cannot repay you. You will be repaid at the resurrection of the just" (Luke 14:13–14).[16] This "repayment" will come because Jesus counts liberal hospitality and acts of compassion extended to those who bear his name as gifts given to himself and to the Father who sent him (Matt. 10:40–42; Luke 10:16).

Herein lies the paradox of this parable's relationship with the reality it represents. Our Master, unlike the master in the parable, does

---

15   Elsewhere in the NT *skēnē* is typically applied to the tabernacle (Acts 7:44; Heb. 8:5; 9:2ff., 11; 13:10), its heavenly archetype (Heb. 8:2; Rev. 13:6; 15:5; 21:3), or to other religious shrines (Matt. 17:4; Mark 9:5; Luke 9:33; Acts 7:43), as well as to tents in which nomadic pilgrims dwell (Heb. 11:9).

16   Compare Prov. 19:17: "Whoever is generous to the poor lends to the LORD, and he will repay him for his deed."

not grudgingly congratulate a shrewd servant for a clever maneuver. Our Master is actually delighted when his servants, the sons of light, treat his debtors—the poor who cannot repay—with lavish generosity. Having received his lavish generosity when he completely canceled our debt (Luke 7:41–50), how can we fail to love him lavishly and to love others for his sake? That is precisely what our Master wants his servants to do, for such reckless extravagance in our stewardship of his goods is the hallmark of kingdom faithfulness. For sons of the light, shrewdness is not self-seeking deception but God-fearing faithfulness in little things, and such "kingdom shrewdness" will receive its reward as stewards are transformed into heirs (Luke 16:10–13). Jesus' later parable of ten servants entrusted with minas elaborates on the approach to management that he commends as faithful: not fearful, frugal caution but risky enterprise and daring investment of the Master's resources in the Master's interests (19:11–27). The resources that we often mistakenly consider our own are his after all, and our parting with them will not impoverish him but instead will increase his profit in the lives of the needy and the outcast touched by his grace—in friends made for his kingdom.[17] Those who know that a heavenly homeland awaits them can keep a loose grip on the stuff of this age, knowing that "here we have no lasting city, but we seek the city that is to come" (Heb. 13:14; cf. 11:9–10, 13–16).

Through this strange story, Jesus urges his followers to act shrewdly and strategically in handling material wealth, in view of the facts that their grip on it is only temporary and an "audit" of our stewardship is coming soon. As "sons of light," however, we are to see shrewd investment of our Master's money in radically different terms from the dishonest and self-serving strategies practiced by the "sons of this world." We do not need to go behind our Master's back to extend forgiveness to his debtors, for such liberal generosity is precisely the response on our part that delights the Lord and receives his commendation as a reflection of his own amazing grace.

A sermon on this challenging and complex parable and the explanatory comments that follow it must address the story's interpretive difficulties while retaining the "shock value" of Jesus' daring commendation of a crooked manager's exemplary (in one sense)

---

17   To explain and defend the lavish, unself-conscious love of the woman who wept as she anointed his feet, Jesus told a brief parable that portrayed divine grace as completely canceling debts beyond our capacity to repay (Luke 7:41–50).

strategic planning. Moreover, the preacher needs to draw his hearers into this story, so that they will discover the crisis in their own situation and embrace the shrewd and faithful handling of money that God's kingdom demands. Quite obviously, the focus of attention in Jesus' parable and subsequent commentary is not on the graciousness of the inbreaking of God's kingdom but on the kingdom's exposure of human guilt and the need to take immediate and strategic measures to avoid impending devastation. Nevertheless, the joining of this story with that of the lost son, which invites its hearers to join the celebration of the Father's mercy to the undeserving, and its place in the narrative of Jesus' relentless movement toward Jerusalem, where suffering awaits him as the Lord's chosen Servant, embed this text in the atmosphere of grace. The sermon could be structured like this.

1. The manager's crisis and ours: We have mismanaged God's goods and stand exposed by his audit (Luke 16:1–2).
   a. The manager, like the lost son, faced a desperate future for having mismanaged the wealth of another (16:1; 15:13–16).
   b. The biblical motif of stewardship teaches that everything we think we have is actually God's property, entrusted to us to manage as he pleases.

2. The manager's shrewd strategy and the master's praise: Make friends for the future at the master's expense (16:3–8).
   a. The manager's shrewd strategy defrauds his master of his possessions in order to secure a future (16:3–7).
   b. The manager and his master, men of this age, are shrewd and strategic . . . within a short-sighted horizon (16:8).

3. The shrewd strategy of grace: Extend openhanded generosity at the Master's expense in the confident hope of your eternal home (16:9–13).
   a. Our Master promises us welcome to his heavenly dwelling, changing us from slaves and stewards into sons and heirs (16:9–12).
   b. To cling to the Master's goods as though they were our own is to serve a rival master (money), to be owned by our possessions (16:13).

c.   Therefore, we can please our Master with the faithful management that gives his goods away to those who need his grace (14:14; 19:16–27).

Epistolary Doctrine: "Jesus the Wall-Demolisher" (Ephesians 2:11–18)

Both of our examples from Paul's epistles—one an "indicative" text that teaches doctrine, the other an "imperative" text that directs motives and behavior—are drawn from the epistle to the Ephesians. While Paul's letters often exhibit this indicative/imperative structure (e.g., Rom. 1–11, 12–16; Gal. 1–4, 5–6; Col. 1:1–2:5, 2:6–4:6), Ephesians is an especially clear example of the interplay between the apostle's gospel foundation (Eph. 1–3) and the ethical outworking of Christ's redemptive and new creation achievement (Eph. 4–6). This epistle, which has been described aptly as the "quintessence of Paulinism,"[18] contains some of the apostle's most eloquent elaborations of God's sovereign grace in Christ and of the character of the people of God (the church, body, and bride of Christ) in the new covenant era. Because it is addressed to a Gentile readership, and because it connects the reconciling death and resurrection life of Jesus to the inclusion of the Gentiles in his one church, the message of this epistle is especially appropriate for our listeners, who typically are predominantly Gentile in descent and identity.

The doctrinal "half" of Ephesians (the transition from indicative to imperative falls at 4:1, preceded by 66 verses and followed by 89) is enveloped not only in *doxology* (1:3–14; 3:20–21) but also in *prayer* (1:15–19; 3:14–19). In fact, Paul's opening report of the thrust of his prayers for the Ephesians[19] merges into our text, as his thoughts move from (a) his petition that God would enable his readers to know, among other things, the surpassing greatness of his *power* (*dynamis*) toward believers *exerted* (*energeia*) according

---

18   F. F. Bruce, *Paul: Apostle of the Heart Set Free* (Grand Rapids: Eerdmans, 1977), 424.

19   The absence of the words "in Ephesus" (*en Ephesō*) in a very early papyrus and several ancient and reliable vellum manuscripts, together with the implications that Paul's knowledge of his hearers was by reports heard from others rather than personal recollection of his ministry in their midst have suggested to various scholars that this may have been a circular letter intended for churches in various cities of Asia, including Ephesus. I am inclined in favor of this hypothesis, but refer to the recipients as "Ephesians" for simplicity.

to the *might* (*kratos*) of his *strength* (*ischys*, 1:19) to (b) his exposition of Christ's resurrection and exaltation as the supreme *exercise* (*energeō*) of that power (1:20–23) to (c) his reminders of the effect of Christ's mighty saving work in his readers' experience, first as *resurrection* that overcomes spiritual death (2:1–10) and then as *reconciliation* that overcomes alienation and grants access to God the Father through the Son in the Spirit (2:11–22). It appears that the apostle's meditative "digression" on the power of God would have returned to prayer at 3:1, which opens with "for this reason" (*toutou charin*) but then turns onto another contemplative byway (Paul's Gentile mission) before returning, with a resumptive "for this reason" (*toutou charin*) at 3:14, to a further report of Paul's prayer for the Gentiles, a petition that is bursting with power and strength terminology (*dynamis, krataioō, exischyō*, 3:14–19). Finally, the language of *power* spills over into the brief doxology that immediately precedes the epistle's transition to exhortation:

> Now to him who is able (*tō dynamenō*) to do far more abundantly than all we ask or think, according to the power (*tēn dynamin*) at work (*energoumenēn*) within us, to him be glory in the church and in Christ Jesus throughout all generations, forever and ever. Amen." (Eph. 3:20–21)

By God's power in Christ, Gentiles, once dead in sin and alienated from God and his community, have been raised from death and reconciled, constituted God's dwelling in the Spirit (2:20–21), and filled with all the fullness of God (3:19) to be the holy assembly in which God's glory is displayed "throughout all generations, forever and ever" (3:21).

Thus the thematic structure of Ephesians 1:3–3:21 could be visualized like this.

A   *Doxology* to the Triune God for glorious grace to Jews and Gentiles in Christ (1:3–14).

  B   *Prayer* for believers' *knowledge* of God-given hope, inheritance, *power* (1:15–23).

    C   *Elaboration* of God's grace and power for believers in *resurrection* (2:1–10).

C'   *Elaboration* of God's grace and power for Gentile believers in *reconciliation*, granting access through the Christ in the Spirit (2:11–22).

B'   Return to *prayer* for Gentile believers . . . almost (3:1).

C"   Further *elaboration* of God's grace and power for Gentile believers in *reconciliation*, constituting us God's *temple-dwelling* in the Spirit (3:2–13).

B"   Return to *prayer* for believers' *power* to *know* the *fullness* of God's indwelling presence through the Christ in the Spirit (3:14–19).

A'   Return to *doxology* to the triune God for his *power* and the display of his *glorious presence* in the Christ and the church (3:20–21).

From the majestic opening doxology (Eph. 1:3–14), Paul has in view the sharp religious and covenantal division between Israel and the pagan nations, which had characterized the period of redemptive promise. In this paean of praise to the triune God's mercies in electing love and adoption, redemptive suffering, and sealing presence, the apostle's many references to the beneficiaries of grace as "us" and "we" seem to include both Jewish and Gentile believers, until we reach verses 12–14, where a distinction is introduced between "we who previously hoped in the Messiah" (dej) and "you also," who came to faith in the gospel of "your" salvation and were sealed by the Holy Spirit of promise. The contrast is between the ancient covenant people, Israel, nourished on the promise of a coming Redeemer, and the pagan nations that had been excluded from God's covenant and his promise. The doxology's final destination is the replacement of the "we/you" separation by a fully inclusive use of "we" as descriptive of the whole church, now unified by grace in the new epoch that has begun with Christ's coming and his bestowal of the Spirit, the down payment of "our" inheritance (vs. 14).

The Jew/Gentile distinction that characterized the era of promise reappears in the retrospectives on his readers' past condition (dead in sin, alienated from God) and in the elaborations on God's powerful and gracious intervention in Christ to raise the dead and to reconcile his enemies. In Ephesians 2:1–2, the apostle diagnoses his Gentile readers' previous spiritual death in willful disobedience: "*you were dead . . . you* once walked." Then his dire diagnosis immediately includes God's covenant people as well, for whom Paul confesses, "*we all* once lived in the passions of our flesh . . . and were by nature children of wrath, like the rest of mankind" (2:3).

Even more explicitly, the text that we are considering (2:11–18) opens with a sobering catalogue of the disqualifications that had excluded Gentiles from God's covenant, communion, and community: uncircumcision, separation from Messiah, alienation from the commonwealth of Israel, strangers to the covenants of the promise, hopeless and godless in the world (2:11–12). This ancient rift had separated humanity into two camps at least from the time that God called Abram *out from* the nations, in order to make his seed a blessing *to* the nations.[20]

Now, however, Paul announces the inauguration of a new creation in which the old dividing wall has been broken down through the sacrifice of Christ. This new creation motif links the apostle's complementary elaborations on God's grace to the Gentiles in Ephesians 2. First, by means of their union with Christ in his resurrection, both Gentile and Jewish believers have been made God's workmanship, "created (*ktizō*) in Christ Jesus for good works" (2:10). Then, by means of their union with himself in his sacrificial death, Christ has "created (*ktizō*) one new man in place of the two" (2:15)—that is, in place of Gentile and Jew in their separate and alienated identities. As Paul affirms elsewhere, in the sphere of this new creation, produced by Christ's death under our curse and resurrection for our vindication, the barriers that isolate groups in the old humanity have been removed: "For neither circumcision counts for anything, nor uncircumcision, but a new creation" (Gal. 6:15; cf. 3:28; Col. 3:10–11). As we shall see, in the imperative section of Ephesians, Paul enjoins attitudes and behaviors appropriate both to the ethical newness and to the interpersonal unity of this creation of the "one new man (*hena kainon anthrōpon*)," echoing the terminology of 2:15 as he motivates holy, truth-formed living by reminding his readers that they have been clothed with "the new self (*ton kainon anthrōpon*), created (*ktisthenta*, participle of *ktizō*) after the likeness of God" (4:24).

The agent of the reconciliation, who has transformed Gentiles from aliens into "members of the household of God" (2:19) with

---

20   In fact, the division is even older, and can be seen in Gen. 4—in the divergent paths of the "seed of the Serpent" (exemplified in Cain and Lamech) and the "seed of the woman" (exemplified in Abel, Seth, and Noah).

access to the Father (2:18), is Christ himself, whom Paul identifies strikingly as "our peace" (2:14; cf. Isa. 9:6). The apostle sees Christ's peacemaking and peace-proclaiming mission foreshadowed in Isaiah's prophecies, which predicted a time when the Lord would heal and restore Israel, saying to his people, "Peace, peace, to the far and to the near" (Isa. 57:19). Paul also alludes to and applies to Jesus the promise of an eschatological messenger with beautiful feet, who would proclaim good news of peace and salvation in the arrival of the reign of God (Isa. 52:7).[21] Of course, Jesus never physically set his beautiful feet on Ephesian streets. As the risen Lord, however, he did indeed come to those "far off" Gentiles through his sovereign Spirit and his commissioned spokesmen who, united to him by faith, were participants both in his resurrection life and in his evangelistic mission to the nations.[22]

The focal point of Jesus' peacemaking is his sacrificial death, to which Paul refers repeatedly in our text: "the blood of Christ" (Eph. 2:13), "his flesh" (vs. 14), "one body" (vs. 16), and "the cross" (vs. 16). The "wall" that had to be destroyed to make the two (Jew and Gentile) one was "the law of commandments and ordinances" (2:15)—that is, the Mosaic law as a covenant treaty that circumscribed the boundaries between Israel as God's people and the pagan nations that stood outside Israel's intimate and privileged access to the Creator.[23] The

---

21   Although some versions (e.g., NIV) have pluralized the peace-preacher with beautiful feet in Isa. 52:7 to "*those* who bring good news," both the Hebrew text and the LXX speak of a single individual, supporting Paul's christological usage of this text (see Acts 10:36).

22   For this reason in Rom. 10:15 Paul himself can pluralize the reference in another allusion to Isa. 52:7, describing preachers sent by Christ to announce good news; and he calls believers generally to strap the gospel of peace onto their own feet to arm themselves for spiritual warfare (Eph. 6:15).

23   When Paul pictures the "law of commandments" as a "dividing wall of hostility" that has been broken down through the death of Christ in Ephesians 2:14–15, he is referring to the preparatory function of the ceremonial law (including circumcision, sacred calendar, kosher diet, and other regulations pertaining to distinctions between clean and unclean, such as in farming, clothing, etc.) as setting Israel visibly apart from the Gentile nations as God's covenant people. Under the new covenant, God's "one new man," the church, is still called to holiness, but it is manifested in spiritual integrity rather than physical observances (1 Cor. 5:6–8; Heb. 9:9–14; see Westminster Confession of Faith 19.3). In Colossians 2:13–15, Paul uses a different but related metaphor to describe the effect of Christ's death on our relationship to the law: until Jesus bore the curse of the law for us (see Gal. 3:13), the law functioned as "the record of debt that stood against

wall or fence imagery is drawn from the Old Testament (e.g., Isa. 5:5; Ps. 80:12), but Paul may well have been thinking of a concrete expression of the Gentiles' exclusion. Signs posted on the balustrade separating the Court of the Gentiles from the inner courts of the Jerusalem temple warned: "No man of another race is to enter within the fence and enclosure around the Temple. Whoever is caught will have only himself to thank for the death which follows."[24] Ironically, the confinement from which Paul wrote this epistle began when he was falsely accused of bringing an uncircumcised Gentile Ephesian into the Temple's forbidden area (Acts 21:27–29). Nevertheless, despite Israel's privileged placement within the covenantal territory defined by the law's boundaries, even as "those near" the Jews were themselves "children of wrath, like the rest" and therefore stood as much in need of Christ's reconciling sacrifice as did the Gentiles "far away."[25] The hostility between Jew and Gentile was itself symptomatic of their common solidarity in sin, and thus of their desperate need for a new solidarity in the grace of the Messiah. Therefore, although the paragraph began with an emphasis specifically on the *Gentiles'* alienation, its argument moves to the conclusion that it is only as Jews and Gentiles are united in one undivided body—Jesus' physical body, suffering representatively for his own of every race—that Jew

---

us with its legal demands." Now, however, the law's demands for our punishment have been nailed to the cross, and we are accounted as having been punished once for all for our transgressions of the law because we are "in Christ" (and, as Paul adds elsewhere, we are accounted as righteous in Christ, credited with his perfect law keeping, 2 Cor. 5:21; Phil. 3:9). On the other hand, as an abiding reflection of God's holy and loving character (and therefore as an abiding obligation on all his human image-bearers), the moral law of God maintains its validity for believers as a norm for our grateful obedience in response to his grace. Therefore Paul, who opposes introducing any aspect of law-keeping into our reception of God's justification in Christ, readily affirms that the Holy Spirit who unites us to Christ by faith produces in us the fruit of love for God and neighbor that the law enjoins (Rom. 13:8–10; Gal. 5:13–14, 22–23).

24   Cited in Andrew T. Lincoln, *Ephesians* (WBC 42; Waco: Word, 1990), 141. Josephus describes these warning signs (Antiquities 15.11.5; Jewish Wars 5.5.2), and two have been recovered by archaeologists and are preserved in museums in Istanbul and Jerusalem, according to F. F. Bruce, *The Epistles to the Colossians, to Philemon, and to the Ephesians*, NICNT (Grand Rapids: Eerdmans, 1984), 297.

25   Note the echo of Isa. 57:19 in the report of Christ's commission to Paul in a vision in the temple: "Go, for I will send you *far away* to the Gentiles" (Acts 22:21). On rabbinic precedents for Paul's interpretation of Isa. 57:19 as promising peace to Israel, the people close to the Lord (Ps. 148:14), and to the Gentiles "far away," see Marcus Barth, *Ephesians 1–3* (AB 34; Garden City: Doubleday, 1974), 276.

and Gentile alike are reconciled to the God whom they all had offended (Eph. 2:14–16).

Just as in past ages the Gentiles' alienation from Israel's God had
had the practical consequence of barring their access to Israel's worshiping community, so now Paul concludes his glad announcement
of peace by articulating explicitly the reversal of that exclusion, as a
result of Jesus' reconciling work: "For through him we both have access in one Spirit to the Father" (2:18).[26] The noun "access" (*prosagōgē*)
appears only three times in the New Testament, all in Paul's letters
(2:18; 3:12; Rom. 5:2), and not at all in the LXX. Its cognate verb,
"bring" (*prosagō*), however, frequently describes the action of worshipers who approach the Lord's sanctuary with gifts and sacrifices in
hand (e.g., Lev. 1:2, 3, 10; 3:1, 3, 7, etc.). This Old Testament context,
in combination with the context of Ephesians, which speaks first of
the destruction of the wall that had excluded the Gentiles (Eph. 2:14–
15) and then of the construction of Gentiles with Jews to become the
Lord's new sanctuary, supports the conclusion that *prosagōgē* refers to
"unhindered access to the sanctuary as the place of God's presence."[27]
Through Jesus, believing Gentiles now join believing Jews as priests
welcomed to approach God with adoration and in prayer.

When preaching this text, the pastor will want to point his hearers forward from its marvelous gospel indicatives concerning Christ's
reconciling grace to the imperatives later in the epistle, which direct
our response to the Peacemaker's mercy. Three responses in particular arise from the text.

1) Recollection. Paul begins the paragraph with the command,
"Remember that at one time you Gentiles in the flesh . . . were . . .

---

26   Although a case could be made for preaching Eph. 2:11–22 as a single unit,
beginning with the Gentiles' exclusion from God's presence and concluding with
their inclusion as integral components of God's new temple, this text's richness of
content also warrants subdividing this passage into two preaching portions, with
the first concluding in the climactic statement that through Christ both Jew and
Gentile now "have access in one Spirit to the Father" (2:18). Eph. 2:19–21 sums
up the movement from alienation to intimate access that was traced in the verses
11–18, but it also presses the theme further by introducing the architectural motif
of the temple, with its foundation and cornerstone, and its process of construction—ample material for a second sermon!

27   Lincoln, *Ephesians*, 149. Barth, *Ephesians 1–3*, 312, comments on vs. 18:
" . . . worship is the tangible result of peace, the sign of its presence, its confirmation and attestation."

separated from Christ, alienated . . . strangers . . . having no hope and without God in the world" (2:11-22). Scripture repeatedly identifies forgetfulness as a lethal spiritual danger. In his farewell discourses on the plains of Moab, preserved in Deuteronomy, Moses commanded Israel to remember the Lord's faithful provision throughout their forty years in the wilderness (Deut. 8:2), warning them, "Take care lest you forget the LORD your God by not keeping his command-ments" (8:11). The very blessings of the Promised Land would tempt the Israelites to complacency, self-reliance, and forgetfulness of the Lord their God, who had rescued them from Egypt, the house of slavery, sustained their lives through the terrifying wasteland and its threats, and brought them into his good land (8:12-20).

Likewise, 2 Peter, a "farewell discourse" intended to prepare the new covenant church for life beyond the apostles' lifetime, empha-sizes the importance of remembrance and the dangers of forgetful-ness: "I intend always to remind you . . . to stir you up by way of re-minder . . . so that after my departure you may be able at any time to recall these things" (1:12-15; see also 3:1-2). By contrast, the church member who does not exhibit growth in the attributes of godliness and love that are the Holy Spirit's fruit "is blind, having forgotten that he was cleansed from his former sins" (1:9).

Paul's exhortation to his Gentile readers to recall their previous alienation and exclusion as the context in which Jesus accomplished his peace-creating and peace-proclaiming mission reinforces the im-pact of his magnification of divine grace in the preceding paragraph (Eph. 2:1-10). The apostle knows well that his call to "maintain the unity of the Spirit in the bond of peace," through humility, gentle-ness, patience and forbearance (4:1-3), can be heeded only by those who are gripped with a lively awareness of the mercy and welcome they have received from God through Christ. Remembering our past and God's grace fuels grateful love and glad obedience.

2) Unity. Our text celebrates the "one new man" created by Christ as he reconciled both Jew and Gentile "in one body" to God and grant-ed them both access "in one Spirit." The apostle will repeat each of these terms as he summons his readers to conduct befitting their call-ing from God, to maintain the unity of the Spirit in the bond of peace (4:3-4, 24). In chapter 2, of course, Paul emphasizes that the unity of this new humanity is wholly God's work in Christ, a new creation which only the Creator could bring about (2:15). In chapter 4, Paul exhorts his readers that they must "no longer walk as the Gentiles do" (note the retrospective emphasis) but instead live the truth that they have learned in Jesus, that they have "put on" the new man, who is "created after the likeness of God in true righteousness and holiness" (4:17–24).[28] The Greek infinitives "to put off . . . to be renewed . . . to put on" might have imperatival force as commands: "you *must* put off . . . be renewed . . . put on." But it is also possible that their significance is indicative ("you *have* put off . . . *are being* renewed . . . *have* put on") as the theological and motivational ground for the commands that surround them. Paul's use of the same or similar verbs as participles in the parallel passage, Colossians 3:9–11, rightly translated in the ESV, "seeing that . . . *you have put on* the new self [better: 'man'] which *is being renewed* . . . ," favors reading both these "put off/put on" passages as declaring the transition from old humanity to new, from first Adam to last Adam, which occurred at conversion and which now grounds the exhortations to a new pattern of living. Note also the emphasis on unity in Colossians 3:10–11, where the new man, bearing the image of his creator, is one in whom "there is not Greek and Jew, circumcised and uncircumcised, barbarian, Scythian, slave, free; but Christ is all, and in all." The deepest divide in the old creation was the rift between Israel and the nations, for this division was rooted in God's covenant with Israel. Once that wall fell in the death of the last Adam, who reconciled both "near" enemies and "far" enemies to God through his sacrifice, no other barrier can be allowed to keep at arm's length from each other those who embrace Christ as their peace.

3) Prayer. The "storyline" of our text, which moves from the Gentiles' alienation from God and exclusion from his people to their access to God along with his ancient people through Christ, must evoke our prayer and worship as the preeminent privileges bestowed by Jesus' peacemaking work. Here again the apostle lays the indicative foundation for the imperatives with which he will close the epistle:

---

28   Many English versions, including the ESV, unfortunately render *ton kainon anthrōpon* in 4:24 as "the new *self*," thereby obscuring Paul's recapitulation of the term that he had introduced in 2:15 (*hena kainon anthrōpon*, "one new man") to allude to the apostle's "second Adam" Christology. The "new man" that believers have "put on" is Christ himself (cf. Rom. 13:12–14), whose new life, purity, and unity replace the death, defilement, and division that were Adam's bitter legacy (cf. 1 Cor. 15:47–49).

> Take up the whole armor of God . . . praying at all times in the Spirit, with all prayer and supplication . . . for all the saints, and also for me, that words may be given me in opening my mouth boldly to proclaim the mystery of the gospel, for which I am an ambassador in chains, that I may declare it boldly, as I ought to speak. (Eph. 6:13, 18–20)

The reversal effected by Christ's work of new creation is astonishing. Once, when Paul considered his Israelite lineage and circumcision as profit credited to his account (Phil. 3:4–6), he himself would have dismissed and excluded those whom he labeled "the uncircumcision." Now, however, the former Pharisee himself seeks priestly intercession not only for other saints but also on his own behalf from once "far off" Gentiles, who enjoy access to the Father through Christ and in his one Spirit. Our text opens new vistas on prayer, enabling us to see it not as the onerous or mundane duty that too many Christians feel it to be but as a priestly calling of unimaginable privilege.

How, then, might this rich text be preached? The structure of the text, which sets the recipients' past history of alienation in contrast to their present privilege as reconciled both to Israel and to Israel's God, suggests a sermon constructed to reflect the passage's two movements. To do justice to the passage's epistolary context, and especially to Paul's return to the "one new man" motif in the hortatory section of the epistle, a concluding application drawn from Ephesians 4 and 6 flows from the exposition of the reconciling grace of Christ.

1. Remember that you were God's enemies, excluded from his people (Eph. 2:11–12).
   a. Do not forget your shameful, helpless past, a constant stimulus to humility and safeguard against complacent pride.
   b. Your physical uncircumcision signaled alienation and exclusion:
      i.   From Messiah, Israel's promised redeemer-king.
      ii. From Israel's community.
      iii. From Israel's covenants with God.
      iv. From hope and from God himself.
2. Marvel that you, the once-excluded enemies, have been reconciled and included through Christ. (2:13–18).
   a. Christ the peacemaker brought you into God's people. (2:13–15)

       i.   By his death, Christ demolished the wall between Jew and Gentile, between the included and the excluded (2:14).

      ii.   By his resurrection, Christ created Jew and Gentile together into "one new man," in which our old differences no longer divide (2:15).

   b. Christ the peacemaker brings you into God's presence. (2:13, 16–18)

       i.   By his death, Christ demolished the wall between guilty humanity and the holy God, for Jew and Gentile alike need to be reconciled to the Creator (2:16; see also vs. 3).

      ii.   In his resurrection life, Christ now preaches peace to people far and near, bringing both together to the Father through the Spirit (2:17–18).

3. As outsiders now included by grace, keep the unity of the one new man that Christ created—through humility, gentleness, patience and love, exercising your priestly privilege of prayer for all the saints (4:1–6, 20–24; 6:18–20).

Quite possibly, a majority of our listeners are ethnically Gentile, as Paul's first readers were. Yet, in contrast to Paul's original addressees, those raised in Christian homes and churches may also think of themselves more as "insiders" than as "outsiders." Since the apostle asserts that both those "near" and those "far off" stood in need of Christ's reconciling sacrifice and are granted access to the Father only through him, *all differences* among listeners' lineage, culture, and religious heritage are nullified, in view of their prior "solidarity" in alienation from their Creator and their present solidarity as recipients of his wall-dismantling mercy. The whole spectrum of humanity, at whatever proximity to or distance from the community of God's covenant, needs the reconciling grace of Jesus the Peacemaker.

Epistolary Exhortation: "Body-Building Words, Actions, and Attitudes" (Ephesians 4:25–5:2)

This passage bristles with imperatives, both commands and prohibitions. Surely, those who identify "practical" preaching with an abundance of concrete directives and instructions about what hearers must do or refrain from doing will find this text eminently "practical." These verses contain thirteen verb forms in the imperative mood—eleven positive commands and two prohibitions. Yet, these statistics fail to reflect the fact that no fewer than six evil reactions (bitterness, wrath, anger, clamor, slander, malice) are banned by the single verb, "be put away" in Ephesians 4:31, while three opposite virtues (kind, tenderhearted, forgiving) are enjoined by the single verb "be" in the next verse. No one can read a text like this without recognizing that the apostle was deeply concerned to see specific, dramatic behavioral change in the lives of believers.

Perhaps less obvious and yet equally undeniable is the observation that the text's exhortations are interwoven with and grounded in the theological truths—gospel truths—expounded elsewhere in the epistle, which appear throughout as the motivations for adherence to the apostolic injunctions. Why must believers speak truth to each other? "We are members of one another"—an allusion to the metaphor of the church as body (4:4, 16; 5:30; cf. 2:15; Rom. 12:4–5; 1 Cor. 12:12ff.). Why must anger not be permitted to fester? Because such bitterness gives a foothold to the devil, who wages war against the church (Eph. 6:10–12). Our speech is to "build up" (*pros oikodomēn*) because the risen Christ is erecting his church to become a dwelling of God in the Spirit (2:20–22) and the body's various members are engaged in the construction (*eis oikodomēn*) by speaking truth in love (4:15–16). Our speaking is to "give grace" (*charis*) to hearers, just as God has shown amazing grace to the speakers (1:6, 7; 2:5, 7, 8; 3:2, 7, 8; 4:7). Hostile words and bitter attitudes that grieve the Holy Spirit are banned, for he is the seal that secures the church as God's property for the day of redemption (1:13–14). Those forgiven by God (1:7) must be quick to forgive. Those beloved and adopted by God (1:5; 2:4) must imitate their loving Father. Those redeemed by the fragrant sacrifice of Christ's love (5:25; cf. Gal. 1:4; 2:20) must themselves "walk in love."

This interweaving of gospel indicatives with ethical imperatives is precisely what we would expect in view of the discussion that immediately precedes this passage. In Ephesians 4:17–24, the apostle looked back to his readers' past in Gentile ignorance, alienation, and self-destructive sensuality, echoing the earlier retrospective that we considered above (2:11–12). Now, however, he insists that their "walk" (an ancient biblical metaphor for a pattern of behavior[29]) must no longer be controlled by their prior pagan darkness and dissolution (4:17) but by "the way you learned Christ . . . as the truth is in Jesus" (4:20–21). As we saw above, this new creation truth entails believers' dissociation from the old man (Adam) and his legacy of deceit and corruption, and their incorporation into the new man (Christ) in a vital union that entails renewal into the divine image in holiness and in truth (4:22–24). Our text, then, goes on to specify what this exchange entails in concrete terms: the "walk" appropriate to those clothed by grace with the new man is to be evident in believers' speech, acquisition of wealth, response to interpersonal conflict, and (beyond our text) in our sexual purity, personal integrity, self-control (5:3–21), and self-sacrificing submission in marriage and in other relationships (5:21–6:10).

The exhortations of Ephesians 4:25–5:2 must be preached not only in light of the grace-saturated theological context of the epistle itself but also in light of the numerous Old Testament texts that appear in quotation or allusion in these verses. Elsewhere in his epistles, Paul asserts directly that the new pattern of life evoked and empowered by Holy Spirit wrought faith in the gospel is really, after all, simply the fulfillment of the core requirement of the ancient law imparted to Israel at Sinai:

> Owe no one anything, except to love each other, for the one who loves another has fulfilled the law. The commandments, "You shall not commit adultery, You shall not murder, You shall not steal, You shall not covet," and any other commandment, are summed up in this word: "You shall love your neighbor as yourself." Love does no wrong to a neighbor; therefore love is the fulfilling of the law. (Rom. 13:8–10)[30]

In Ephesians 4, he makes the point more subtly, embedding the language of Old Testament ethical texts outside the Mosaic law into his injunctions to the new Israel of God, while simultaneously placing the covenant Lord's expectations of his servants in the

---

29   See, e.g., Gen. 5:24; 6:9; 17:1; Ps. 1:1; 15:2; etc. In Ephesians, see 2:2, 10; 4:1, 17; 5:2, 8, 15; and elsewhere in Paul, see Rom. 6:4; 8:4; 13:13; 14:15; 1 Cor. 3:3; 7:17; 2 Cor. 4:2; 5:7; 10:2–3; 12:18; Phil. 3:17–18; Col. 1:10; 2:6; 3:7; 4:5; 1 Thess. 2:12; 4:1, 12; 2 Thess. 3:6, 11.

30   See also Gal. 5:14; 1 Tim. 1:8–11; Matt. 22:36–40.

intensified context of the redemption and new creation that are now inaugurated in Jesus.

Thus in Eph. 4:25, Paul cites the prophetic directive of the Lord of hosts through Zechariah, "Speak truth, each with his neighbor" (Zech. 8:16 dej), a command that expands and deepens the Decalogue's prohibition of false testimony against a neighbor (Ex. 20:16) to venues beyond the courtroom.[31] Yet, Paul does more. He invokes a new reality created by the reconciling "new creation" work of Jesus, which provides even stronger motivation to heed the Law's and the Prophet's summons to truth-telling: because believers of every race belong to one body, "we are members of one another." Deception among members of Christ's church is as dangerous to its health as a breakdown of the central nervous system would be in its physical analogue. Similarly, in "Be angry and do not sin" (Eph. 4:26) the apostle quotes Psalm 4:4, which advises patience to those who suffer undeserved contempt (cf. Ps. 4:2). Then Paul appends to the psalmist's counsel both a caution against persistent resentment and a reminder that another, fiercer enemy than the human occasion of one's anger stands ready to seize every opportunity to destroy the church's unity: "give no opportunity to the devil" (Eph. 4:27).

In verse 30, Paul alludes to Isaiah 63:10, which indicted Israel for having rebelled "and grieved his Holy Spirit," despite the Lord's deliverance from Egyptian slavery and his care and provision for his people in the wilderness: "Where is he who put in the midst of them his Holy Spirit, who caused his glorious arm to go at the right hand of Moses, who divided the waters before them to make for himself an everlasting name . . . ?" (vv. 11–12). As he employs this biblical language, Paul has in view particularly the divisive attitudes and words that he is about to name: bitterness, wrath, anger, clamor (or "shouting" Greek *krauge*), slander, malice. These particularly grieve the Spirit because his mission is to unite the body of Christ (Eph. 4:3–4) and to secure the body's safety as the "seal" (*sphragis*) that

---

31   Paul's wording, including "his neighbor" (*tou plesion autou*), reflects the LXX, which in turn reflects the Hebrew original (*re`ehu*). Zech. 8:16 includes the speaking of truth in legal settings, since it continues: "render in your gates judgments that are true and make for peace." But the breadth and depth of the prophet's explanation of the command is also evident in the vs. 17: "do not devise evil in your hearts against one another, and love no false oath, for all these things I hate, declares the LORD."

signals both protection and possession by the Lord until "the day of redemption" (see Eph. 1:13–14; 2 Cor. 1:22; cf. Rev. 7:2–8).[32]

Finally, the apostle's exhortation to unifying love among its members reaches its climactic motivation in his appeal to the love of Christ, who "gave himself up for us, a *fragrant offering* and sacrifice to God" (Eph. 5:2). From the early chapters of Genesis, the expression "fragrant offering" (in older versions, "sweet savor"; LXX *osmē euōdias*) is used anthropomorphically to convey the Lord's pleasure in sacrifices offered according to his will and consequently his readiness to turn his wrath away from those who worship him through such sacrifices.[33] The apostle can also apply this imagery to the Philippian Christians' generous contribution to relieve his financial need (Phil. 4:18), even as elsewhere he calls believers to present their bodies as living sacrifices, well pleasing to God (Rom. 12:1; cf. 15:16). Yet, Paul's entire theology of sin and salvation makes it clear that any act of service or worship offered by human beings must derive its "pleasant aroma" before God from our union by grace through faith with the well-pleasing Son who loved us and gave himself for us, whose sacrifice in our stead has deflected God's holy wrath from us once and for all. The threads of Old Testament terminology and imagery that run through the tapestry of Paul's application of the gospel to ordinary human relationships and interactions cast new light on ancient Scriptures, even as they also deepen our understanding of the high calling to which new covenant believers, Jews and Gentiles together, have been called (Eph. 4:1).

One challenge that a text such as this poses for the preacher is the variety of ethical behaviors addressed in it. On the surface, it would seem that the apostle's thought meanders from deceitful speech (vs. 25) to anger (vv. 26–27) to theft (vs. 28) to corrupting speech (vs. 29), back to anger and its vengeful expressions (vv. 30–31), and finally to the positive motifs of forgiveness (4:32–5:1) and love (5:2). This

---

32   The Song of Moses foretells Israel's defeat at the hands of pagan oppressors, but also the Lord's eventual retribution toward the enemies and vindication of his people. These future events, according to the LXX's wording, are "sealed up (*sphragizō*) in my treasuries. In the day of vindication (*en hēmera ekdikēseōs*) I will repay" (Deut. 32:34). Despite verbal echoes, it is questionable whether an allusion to this text is intended in Paul's "sealed for the day of redemption."

33   Gen. 8:21 (Noah's sacrifice after the flood), Ex. 29:18, 25, 41 (sacrifices at the priests' consecration), and in the instructions regarding burnt offerings, grain offerings, peace offerings, sin offerings, and sacrifices at festivals in Leviticus (e.g., 1:9ff; 2:2ff; 3:5ff; 4:31), and Numbers (e.g., ch. 15, 28, and 29).

thematic diversity, in combination with the text's theological richness (due to the grace-grounded motives and Old Testament allusions interspersed throughout, as we have seen), provides a strong argument for expounding this text in several sermons rather than one.

On the other hand, it is possible to surrender prematurely to the apparent disunity of a passage of Scripture and in so doing to fail to perceive deeper, unifying factors that disclose the structure of a biblical author's reasoning. In the case of Ephesians 4:25-5:2, it would be appropriate to expound it in several (perhaps as many as five or six) discrete sermons. There is also value, however, in proclaiming it "whole" as articulating the behavioral and interpersonal implications of the church's unity as the body of Christ, who is the representative head of the new humanity. The deeper bond that unites the text's diverse commands and prohibitions becomes visible in the apostle's recurring references to speech, both of which are reinforced by allusions to Paul's metaphor of the church as body and temple (vs. 25 "members", vs. 29 "building up"). Likewise, at two points the apostle forbids emotions and behaviors associated with interpersonal conflict (vv. 26–27, 31). He reinforces his second ban by reference to the grief that such divisiveness brings to God's Holy Spirit (vs. 30); and over against attitudes that aggravate alienation, Paul commends the attributes of kindness, compassion, and forgiving forbearance that reflect the grace that God has shown to believers in Christ (vs. 32). Even the injunction to the thief to cease stealing and to engage in useful labor instead, which at first glance seems out of place in a paragraph apparently concerned primarily with speaking and conflict, is linked linguistically with its context: the purpose of the (former) thief's new commitment to "work with his own hands the good (*to agathon*, dej)" is not merely to provide for his own needs honestly rather than dishonestly but to enable him to give to "anyone in need (*chreia*)" (4:28). Likewise, corrupt speech must be replaced by that which is "good (*agathos*) for building up the need (*tēs chreias*, dej)" (4:29). Moreover, this lexical link suggests a deeper thematic continuity: both in speech and in action, the new creation grace of God in Christ must shift one's focus from individual desires and rights to the needs of others and our responsibility for their well-being, "for we are members one of another" (4:25).

Finally, 5:1–2 not only has close ties to 4:25–32 in the repetition of "be" (or "become," *ginesthe*) and the inferential conjunction "therefore" (*oun*), it also sums up more generally the contrast between the "walk" that befits these Christians' new calling "in love" (4:1–2) and their previous "walk" of self-indulgent self-deception among the Gentiles (4:17–19). The concentration of the vocabulary of love in these last two verses ("beloved," *agapētos*; "in love," *agapē*; "loved," *agapaō*) and the reference to Christ's sacrifice as the epitome of divine love therefore gather up all the concrete instructions that precede this conclusion under a single command, "Walk in love," while calling to mind the only fountain from which such selfless love can flow, the good news of the "great love with which he loved us" in Christ, "even when we were dead in our trespasses" (2:4–5).

The sermon's theme, then, would be that our new identity as members of Christ's body calls us to exhibit the love of the Father and the Son in our relations with fellow members through true and kind communication, ready forgiveness, and open-handed generosity. Its outline could look like this.

1. Christ's new-creation grace must control the *words* you say and how you say them (4:25–27, 29–31).
   a. Because you are members of each other in Christ's one body, choose words that convey *truth* to your neighbor (4:25).
   b. Because you share in the *building* of the body, choose words that *meet needs and give grace*, rather than wounding the Holy Spirit through words used as weapons to assault other members (4:26–27, 29–31; see Isa. 63:10).

2. Christ's new-creation grace must transform the *actions* you perform to gain and use wealth (Eph. 4:28).
   a. The thieving *taker* must become a useful *worker* (his motives transformed from a focus on his *rights* to his *responsibilities*).
   b. The thieving *taker* must become a graceful *giver* (his motives transformed from a focus on his own *desires* to *others' needs*).

3. Christ's new-creation grace must control the *attitudes* of your heart, especially *your response to injuries* inflicted by others (4:26–27, 4:32–5:2).

a. With prompt, peacemaking responses that do not let grievances fester (4:26; Ps. 4:4).
b. With discerning recognition of your real Enemy (Eph. 4:27; see 2:2; 6:10–20).
c. With a forgiving grace that characterizes children forgiven and beloved by the Father through Christ, the "sweet savor" sacrifice (4:31–5:2).

This text exhibits an uncomfortable specificity that will not let preachers or their hearers "take cover" in vague or sentimental words about "the tie that binds our hearts in Christian love."[34] Paul shows us that Christian love—the real thing—meddles with our speech patterns, financial priorities, and habits of the heart. At the same time, the apostle does not confuse "practicality" in preaching with a moralistic catalogue of duties or steps toward improvement, abstracted from the gospel motives that draw God's beloved children forward into their identity as those who bear the image of the Son, who loved us and gave himself for us. Our preaching of such ethical passages must reflect the texts' heart-searching specificity as well as their heart-inflaming appeal to divine grace.

Wisdom: "Born from the Father of Lights" (James 1:12–18)

The epistle of James is a genuinely catholic epistle—that is, an epistle addressed not to a congregation or group of congregations in a single city or region but to "the twelve tribes in the Dispersion," to Jewish-Christian congregations scattered throughout the Roman Empire and beyond (James 1:1). The geographical breadth of its audience helps to explain why the epistle's many ethical directives are concrete without being limited to a distinctively local situation. This blend of specificity with general applicability also is attributable, however, to the strong influences of the Hebrew wisdom and prophetic traditions.

James is indebted, with respect to content and to form, to the canonical Wisdom books of the Old Testament, the Wisdom literature of intertestamental Judaism (especially the Wisdom of Jesus

---

34 I suspect (and confess) that the words of John Fawcett's eighteenth century hymn are more often emotionally sung than sacrificially lived: "We share our mutual woes, our mutual burdens bear, and often for each other flows the sympathizing tear."

PREACHING THE PROMISE KEEPER

Ben Sirach), and, in distinctive ways, to the wisdom teaching of Jesus that is preserved for us in the Synoptic Gospels.[35] Not only does James extol heavenly wisdom at the heart of his epistle (3:13–18) and direct his readers to ask God (in unwavering faith) for the wisdom they need (1:5–8), he also alludes repeatedly to canonical and intertestamental Jewish Wisdom texts. As a God-given sage, he places before his readers the choice between two "ways," one leading to life and the other to death—roads characterized in various ways: faith vs. doubt (1:6), doing the Word vs. only hearing it or professing it (1:22–26; 2:14–26), showing respect and mercy to the poor vs. favoritism (2:1–13), heavenly vs. demonic wisdom (3:13–18), and humility vs. pride (4:6–10; cf. 1:9–11). Embracing and embellishing[36] the use of analogy by Israel's ancient sages and by Jesus in his parables, James dramatically paints parallels between the physical creation, on the one hand, and spiritual and ethical insights, on the other:

> The stream of illustrative examples on the tongue in James 3:3–12 is breath-taking: bits in horses' mouths, great ships and little rudders, sparks and forest fires, the taming of animals, fresh and salt water springs, and fruit trees, all in just ten verses. The reader also encounters dead bodies (2:26), waves and wind (1:6), mist vapors (4:14), mirrors (1:23), fading flowers (1:10), and patient farmers (5:7–8).[37]

James knows that true wisdom, the gift of God, is counter-intuitive to the assumptions of fallen human hearts, which cannot imagine a deity who calls trials a joyful blessing, declares the lowly to be exalted, and chooses the poor to be rich in faith and heirs of his kingdom (1:2, 9–12; 2:5; cf. 4:6). He therefore employs the sage's proven poetic/pedagogical strategy of comparing unexpected spiritual truths to familiar objects and everyday experience.

---

35   Richard Bauckham, *James: The Wisdom of James, Disciple of Jesus the Sage* (New York: Routledge, 1999), 97–107; Dan G. McCartney, "The Wisdom of James the Just," *Southern Baptist Journal of Theology* 4.3 (Fall 2000): 52–64.

36   Bauckham, *James*, 76, cites Sir. 21:15a as expressing the blend of respectful preservation and creative elaboration that characterizes the relationship of Jewish sages, including James, to the Wisdom traditions that they inherited: "If an intelligent person hears a wise word, he praises it and adds to it."

37   McCartney, 53, summarizing E. Baasland, "Der Jakobusbrief als Neutestamentliche Weisheitsschrift," *Studia Theologica* 36 (1982): 123–24.

Furthermore, his use of terse aphorisms chained together through link words aids both memory and meditation.[38] Thus, for instance, in the opening verses: (1) "Greetings" and "joy" are cognates (*chairein, chara*) in 1:1–2; (2) "steadfastness" (*hypomonē*) links verses 3 and 4; (3) "lack" (*leipō*) links verses 4 and 5; (4) "ask" (*aiteō*) links verses 5 and 6; and "trial" / "tempt" (*peirasmos, peirazō*) in different but related senses, as the English glosses indicate, links verses 12 and 13. James's words are to be retained in the mind and turned over, again and again, in reflective contemplation.

Yet, it would be painting with too broad a brush to categorize James's epistle only as one more contribution to the body of Israel's Wisdom tradition. For one thing, James sometimes sounds more like a fiery prophet than like a reflective observer of the way life works "under the sun." His sharp warning to presumptuous entrepreneurs (4:13–17) and even harsher words to the exploitive rich (5:1–6) have been characterized as conforming "to the pattern of the prophetic oracle of doom."[39] Since James turns sharply from his condemnation of "you rich" to his comfort of his "brothers," it could well be that just as Israel's prophets sometimes "addressed" words of judgment to Israel's unlistening oppressors (e.g., Isa. 14:29–32 to Philistia; 23:1–12 to Tyre; Nah. 2:1–13 to Nineveh; cf. Isa. 14:4–20, Judah's taunt to the corpse of Babylon's king) so James is speaking as a prophet against the church's wealthy persecutors (cf. James 2:6–7), both to console those suffering injustice at their hands and to caution those tempted to envy and imitate their persecutors.[40]

---

38   In addition to brief aphorisms, the epistle also contains extended discourses on such themes as the evils of social partiality (2:1–13), the necessity of appropriate action to express living faith (2:14–26), and the dangerous capacities of the unbridled tongue (3:1–12). This stylistic feature also has precedents in OT Wisdom, for instance in the discourses extolling Wisdom (Prov. 8) and contrasting Wisdom and Folly (Prov. 9) that precede the collections of individual Proverbs and the acrostic discourse on the woman of virtue that concludes the book (Prov. 31:10–31).

39   Bo Reicke, *The Epistles of James, Peter, and Jude* (AB 37; Garden City, NY: Doubleday, 1964), 50.

40   The literary device of addressing an unhearing (often impersonal, imaginary, or absent) audience is *apostrophe*, as in the famous "Apostrophe to the Ocean" by George Gordon, Lord Byron: "Roll on, thou deep and dark blue ocean roll. . . ." Without using the literary term, Reicke, *James, Peter, and Jude*, 52, suggests that James may not have expected his doom oracle to reach the ears of its affluent and indifferent objects but instead spoke with such fervor to comfort and caution his economically disadvantaged "brothers," who are the epistle's intended and imme-

The epistle of James is more than a piece of Jewish Wisdom literature for a second, more significant reason: the pervasive influence of Jesus and his gospel on the wisdom that James offers his readers.[41] Admittedly, the name of Jesus appears only twice in James (1:1; 2:1),[42] and it has been suggested that these were inserted to give a thin Christian veneer to a Wisdom collection that is otherwise wholly unrelated to Jesus and his movement. There is no explicit mention at all of the central gospel events: the cross and the resurrection. It is well known that Luther dismissed James as an "epistle of straw," not exactly *excluding* it from his German New Testament but demoting it to *de facto* deutero-canonical status (along with Hebrews, Jude and Revelation).[43] Others, at later points, have apparently concurred with Luther's judgment: Adolf Jülicher (1894) called James "the least Christian book of the New Testament," and James Dunn described it as "the most Jewish, the most undistinctively Christian document in the New Testament."[44]

Despite these negative opinions, there are good reasons for discerning features woven deeply into this epistle (not merely attached as a surface veneer) that mark it as a *new* covenant, *Christ*-centered expression of canonical Wisdom. This is not to minimize its continuity with Old Testament Wisdom literature, which is, after all, what

---

diate audience. Note also James B. Adamson, *James: The Man and his Message* (Grand Rapids: Eerdmans, 1989), 56: "The rich here denounced need not be taken to be present in the listening congregation any more than the nations and people are present in Isa. 34:1. James is here using the common OT method of comforting the afflicted by predicting—in effect, promising—the fall of their enemies and oppressors. . . ."

41 As his subtitle indicates, Bauckham's *James: The Wisdom of James, Disciple of Jesus the Sage* offers a detailed argument for James's dependence on and development of the teaching of Jesus. See also, more briefly, Adamson, *James*, 169–94.

42 On the other hand, I would contend that "the good *name* that *was called over you*" (James 2:7, dej) refers to the invocation of Jesus' name (Acts 2:38) or the name of the triune God (Matt. 28:19) in baptism. The OT background of this phrase lies in Amos 9:12 LXX, cited in James's speech at the apostolic council called to discern the status of uncircumcised Gentiles in the church (Acts 15:17) and, further back, in the placing of the Lord's name on his people in benediction (Num. 6:23–27).

43 See, for example, a reproduction of the contents page to Luther's "September Bible" in J. A. Roberts and A. B. du Toit, *Guide to the New Testament*, vol. 1, trans. D. Roy Briggs (2nd ed.; Pretoria: N. G. Kerkboekhandel Transvaal, 1985), 164 (with comment by Roberts and du Toit, pp. 163, 259–62).

44 Both cited in Bauckham, *James*, 107–8.

we should expect in view of the New Testament's claims that Jesus is the fulfillment of all God's promises and of Israel's proper hopes and longings. Biblical wisdom, whether in Old Testament or New, is not merely the product of abstract reflection on generic patterns of "life under the sun." Although many parallels can be drawn between the insights of Israel's sages and those of their pagan counterparts in the Ancient Near East, Israel's wisdom was always couched in a covenantal context that presupposed the Lord's previous intervention on his people's behalf, his present reign, and the promise of his future coming to make all things right (Prov. 1:7).[45]

Because the Lord who has bound Israel to himself in holy covenant is the sovereign of the entire universe, Old Testament Wisdom literature wrestles with a paradox. On the one hand, Proverbs characteristically assumes that faithfulness, prudence, and diligence bring beatitude, while evil, folly, and sloth lead to misery. On the other hand, Ecclesiastes, Job, and certain Psalms (37; 73) confront the perplexing reality that the righteous do not always prosper, nor rebels consistently suffer, in the present. Ultimately, this tension could only be resolved eschatologically: as long as the Lord of the covenant withholds his just wrath against those who defy his authority and defile his creation, covenant keepers will suffer, covenant breakers will survive and even thrive, and the orderly universe presupposed in Proverbs will seem to be wishful thinking. Hence Israel's Wisdom cries out for the final coming of the Lord of the covenant in righteousness, as promised in the Torah (Deut. 32) and predicted by the prophets.

Since James addresses Israel's dispersed tribes as a "servant of the Lord Jesus, *the Messiah*" (James 1:1 dej), his lessons in wise living are predicated on the truth that the coming of the Messiah in his redemptive mission has now highlighted elements of Old Testament Wisdom ethics. The redemptive-historical moment in which James and his readers stand—namely, the inauguration of God's kingdom and the end of the age through Jesus' words and deeds—adds vivid color to the patterns traced by Israel's ancient sages. Since James addresses those among the dispersed twelve tribes who confess faith in "our Lord Jesus Christ, the Lord of glory" (2:1), he presupposes

---

45 Recall the covenantal-religious antithesis underlying the metaphorical portrayal of wisdom and folly in Prov. 9 as two women, each inviting the naïve into her home on the high point of the city, discussed in the previous chapter.

that they have glimpsed history's consummation at history's mid-point, namely at Jesus' crucifixion and resurrection. At the cross, the supremely innocent Covenant Keeper endured utterly undeserved suffering. Jesus was, in a preeminent sense, "the righteous person" who did not resist when condemned and murdered by the world's powerful (5:6; cf. Isa. 53:7, 11). Yet, Jesus' empty tomb attests the Judge's vindicating verdict on his behalf. Because Jesus, who lowered himself, has been highly exalted (*tapeinoō, hyperypsoō*, Phil. 2:8–9), James can assure the "lowly brother" that he, too, will be exalted (*tapeinos, hypsos*, James 1:9).[46]

This eschatological intensification of Wisdom, effected by Messiah's arrival, sets the teaching of James (along with that of Jesus, his mentor and master) apart from Old Testament Wisdom literature in several ways:[47]

First, James offers the comforting assurance that present suffering is temporary and can be endured in light of the certainty *and proximity* of coming justice. Suffering Christian brothers must be patient "until the coming of the Lord" (James 5:7). For the wealthy oppressors of the poor that coming will be "a day of slaughter"[48] for which they have been fattening themselves in selfish and ruthless acquisitiveness (5:5), but for their victims it is the day of long-awaited harvest (5:7). Moreover, it is a day that is not remote but near in God's redemptive agenda for history: "the coming of the Lord is at hand. . . . The Judge is standing at the door," ready to break into history in climactic vengeance upon the unrighteous (5:8–9; see Matt. 24:33; Rev. 3:20; Luke 12:36). The prospect of the Lord's coming offers comfort and encouragement not only because it will bring the wicked to justice but also because it will bring to suffering believers the reward of their faithful endurance under trials—"the crown of life, which God has promised to those who love him" (James 1:12; cf. 2 Tim. 4:7–8).

Second, James paints in vivid colors both the law's severity and its sweetness. Bauckham identifies, among the new emphases that set the teaching of Jesus the sage (and of James, his disciple) apart from predecessors, the feature that Jesus' and James's "ethical

---

46   See Matt. 11:29, in which Jesus, echoing Wisdom's summons to come, shoulder her yoke, and learn, describes himself as gentle and "lowly" (*tapeinos*).

47   See also McCartney, "Wisdom of James," 57–61; Bauckham, *James*, 97–107.

48   James draws this expression from Jeremiah's lament over the prosperity of the wicked (Jer. 12:1–4).

demands are more radical than the Torah as conventionally interpreted" in Second Temple Judaism.[49] Wisdom knows that appearances can be deceiving, and that people are not always what they
seem to be on the surface. For this reason, James cautions his readers
against self-deception (James 1:16, 22), against hollow claims to piety (1:26) and faith (2:14–26) that are unsubstantiated by behavioral
transformation, against contradictory, destructive uses of the tongue
(3:1–12), and against a counterfeit and demonic "wisdom" that is
fueled by pride and strife, rather than bearing the pure and peaceful
fruit of righteousness (3:13–18). God's law is an apt diagnostic tool
for distinguishing true faith, piety, and wisdom from false. Rather
than rushing to speak our own words in anger, we must quickly hear
and meekly receive the word uttered by God (1:19–21). Rather than
hearing only and promptly forgetting the word we have heard and
its disclosure of our own spiritual condition, we must gaze so persistently into the perfect law, as into a mirror that exposes every defect,
that we become the word's "doers," and so receive the blessing of its
Author (1:22–25). This perfect law indeed demands perfection, for
"whoever keeps the whole law but fails in one point has become accountable for all of it" (2:10). One who speaks against or judges his
brother has abandoned his proper place as a doer of the law and has
become instead the law's judge, usurping the role of God himself,
the "one lawgiver and judge, he who is able to save and to destroy"
(4:11–12). James has learned from Jesus' teaching in the Sermon on
the Mount and elsewhere that God's law is deep and wide, piercing
to the deepest motives of the heart that give rise to our actions in
every relationship and sphere of life. The law is, on the one hand,
simple and unified, demanding love preeminently to God, and then
to one's neighbor as oneself (James 1:25; 2:5, 8; see Matt. 22:34–40;
Gal. 5:14). It is also extensive and intrusive into every sphere of life,
indicting careless words, indifference toward the needy, contempt
for the poor, self-confident planning, self-centered quarrels and
prayers—in short, any and every omission of the righteousness that
it enjoins: "Whoever knows the right thing to do and fails to do it,
for him it is sin" (4:17). The law is so comprehensive and pierces
so deeply that our only hope is divine grace extended to humbled
hearts: "God opposes the proud, but gives grace to the humble" (4:6,
citing Prov. 3:34).

---

49   Bauckham, *James*, 97.

Within the context of grace, then, James can characterize this severe law not only as the perfect law (James 1:25) and the royal law (2:8) but also twice as the "law of *liberty*" (1:25; 2:12), the law that does not enslave but that sets its hearers and doers free. As the logic that links James 2:12 and 2:13 implies, to be judged by the law of liberty is to be judged according to the expectation that recipients of divine mercy will show mercy to others—and conversely, that a merciless condemnation of others excludes the self-appointed judge from God's mercy, which "triumphs over judgment" (a concise summary of Jesus' parable of the unforgiving servant, Matt. 18:21–35). The law is so perfect and the human heart so wayward, that a serious encounter with the law must replace self-confident boasting with a humble appeal for God's mercy and grace. In this respect the law in all its conscience-searching precision does, after all, bring liberty.

Third, James teaches that God's sovereign, saving intervention is reversing the conventions and assumed value system of ordinary human society. God has exalted the poor and abased the rich (although daily experience may not yet show it, James 1:9–11; 4:6–10). This social upheaval was glimpsed in the Old Testament, as in Hannah's song of celebration when her shame was removed by the birth of her son Samuel (1 Sam. 2:7–8). But the reversal theme reaches even higher, semi-eschatological expression in the song of Mary, Messiah's mother (Luke 1:52–53), and it is concretely demonstrated in Jesus' ministry of mercy to powerless and despised outcasts. James's paradoxical announcement that God chose the *poor* to be *rich* in faith and *heirs* of his kingdom (James 2:5) not only echoes Jesus' beatitude (Luke 6:20) but also demonstrates that divine grace, not human qualification, is the determining factor in the bestowal of the kingdom's eschatological benefits (cf. 1 Cor. 1:26–31). Because God's sovereign grace contradicts fallen humanity's assumptions about the source of personal value, James indicts those who curry the favor of the rich and demean the poor because these hypocrites have violated Scripture's "royal law" of love and therefore have violated *every* commandment in the entire law (James 2:8–13). The only hope for such spiritual "adulteresses"[50] is the undeserved mercy and grace of God,

---

50   James addresses his entire readership with the plural feminine noun "adulteresses" (*moichalides*, rendered "You adulterous people" by the ESV) to invoke the OT metaphor of Israel as the Lord's adulterous wife. See Raymond C. Ortlund, Jr., *God's Unfaithful Wife: A Biblical Theology of Spiritual Adultery*, New Studies in Bible Theology (Downers Grove: InterVarsity, 2003).

received through humbling themselves before the Lord in the hope that he would exalt the humble (4:10) through "faith in our Lord Jesus Christ, the Lord of glory" (2:1).

Finally, the motifs of eschatological fulfillment and divine grace meet in James 1:18, the climax of the text on which our sample sermon on New Testament wisdom is based: "Of [the Father's] own will he brought us forth by the word of truth, that we should be a kind of firstfruits of his creatures." This is a striking and profound theological statement that stands out in the midst of James's practical counsel for living with wisdom and integrity.

1) James articulates *God's sovereign grace* in the lives of believers through the imagery of *birth and begetting*, emphasizing our passivity and utter dependence in the reception of life and salvation, just has Jesus had done by means of the same metaphor in conversation with Nicodemus, "the teacher of Israel" (John 3:3–8). The sovereignty, and therefore the completely merciful and unmerited nature, of God's grace is further signaled in the mention of God's will (*bouleutheis* is a verbal form, an aorist passive particle, "having willed/determined/resolved").

2) The role of *faith* in the process is implied in the mention of *"the word of truth"* as the means by which this spiritual birthing has occurred (see 1 Peter 1:3, 23). This word, "implanted" as seed is sown in soil, is the means by which believers receive salvation, when the word is welcomed in meek receptivity (see Matt. 13:1–9, 18–23; cf. also Col. 1:5–6; Heb. 6:4–8; 1 Cor. 3:6–7; Acts 6:7).

3) The *cosmic and eschatological ramifications* of the new birth experienced by individuals are implied in the striking metaphor "a kind of firstfruits (*aparchē*) of his creatures" (James 1:18). James has just invited remembrance of the original creation by referring to God as "the Father of lights" (1:17, sun, moon, and stars, Gen. 1:14–19; Ps. 136:7). But the orientation of the phrase as a whole is not toward the past but toward the future. In ancient Israel's agricultural and cultic cycle, the "firstfruits" were the initial sheaves of grain that were considered the best portion of the harvest and were therefore to be presented to the Lord. Israel was to offer the firstfruits of the first harvest after entering the Promised Land (Ex. 23:19; Deut. 26:1–11) and annually at the Feast of Firstfruits (Lev. 23:9–14), thereby providing for the Aaronic priests through the firstfruits of grain, wine,

and oil (Num. 18:11–13; Deut. 18:4–5). The firstfruits metaphor is applied to persons in the Old Testament (Pss. 78:51; 105:36) and even more frequently in the New Testament. Christ is the firstfruits of the final resurrection harvest (1 Cor. 15:23). The Holy Spirit is the firstfruits of our adoption, the redemption (again, resurrection) of our bodies (Rom. 8:23). Individuals who are the first converts to Christ in various regions are the "firstfruits" of those areas (Rom. 16:5; 1 Cor. 16:15; 2 Thess. 2:13). Finally, John hears the martyrs portrayed as firstfruits of a general harvest to come (Rev. 14:4; cf. vv. 14–16). When James applies to those whom the Father of lights has "brought forth" through the word of truth the description "firstfruits of his creatures," he is suggesting that the new life that they have received by God's gracious purpose is the first installment of a cosmic "regeneration" that will ultimately encompass and transform the entire created order (Matt. 19:28;[51] Rom. 8:18–25).

This profound complex of theological motifs (distinctively *new covenant* motifs), which at first seems unexpected in the context of James's down-to-earth wisdom, nevertheless fits seamlessly into the fabric of his advice and admonition. The redemptive-historical perspective of James 1:18, expressed in everyday metaphors of childbirth and farming ("firstfruits"), is consistent with Wisdom's parabolic pedagogical strategy and James's literary style. It also provides a fitting conclusion to the discussion of trials (leading to proven fidelity, leading finally to joyful blessedness), which began in James 1:2 and resumed in 1:12,[52] and therefore serves as a constant subtext for the first main section of the epistle (1:2–18).

---

51   The Greek term *palingenesia*, used in Matt. 19:28 to refer to the cosmic renewal of the entire created order at the consummation of history, means "rebirth" or "regeneration," although some recent versions obscure the birth metaphor: "the renewal of all things" (NIV), "the new world" (ESV).

52   Repetition of the terms "trial" (*peirasmos*) and "test" (*dokimion/dokimos*) from James 1:2 in vs. 12 signals an explicit return to (and conclusion of) the theme of the joy (*chara*, vs. 2) or blessedness (*makarios*, vs. 12) to be found in the unpleasant experience of diverse trials. The paradoxical encouragement to the "lowly brother" to boast in his exaltation (vs. 9), which almost immediately precedes the recapitulation of "trial" terminology, expresses the joy of trial in slightly different terms and with specific application to the economically and socially disadvantaged. Since the exaltation of the lowly is not yet visible (cf. 5:7–11, where James returns to the theme of endurance), 1:9 also expresses the *eschatological perspective* enjoined in vv. 2–3 (where the *joy* is explained in terms of a testing that proves

Although the subsections in this opening discussion of trials and the joys to which they lead are rather loosely joined (more by lexical links, as we noted above, than by tightly structured arguments), there are good reasons for treating James 1:12–18 as a single preaching text. Verses 13–16[53] and verses 17–18 are tied to each other not only by the birth metaphor, "bring forth" (*apokueō*), which concludes each paragraph (vv. 15, 18), but more importantly by the antithesis that is expressed, climactically, in the birth imagery.

1. Temptation—that is, invitation to evil—cannot be attributed to God, the untempting and untemptable One, but must be traced to the sinner's own self-deceiving desire, which conceives and gives birth to sin, which in turn "brings forth" death (1:13–16).
2. On the other hand, every good and perfect gift descends from above, from the faithful, light-filled (shadow-free) Father who once created the heaven's great lights and who now graciously "brings forth" children through the word of truth, to be the first installment of his new creation (1:17–18).

The unity of verses 13–18 is found, then, in the way these two paragraphs give negative and positive answers to the question, "What in our experience should we attribute directly to God?"[54] Verses 13–16 answer negatively, "Not temptation or enticement to doubt and disobedience, which gives birth to sin, which gives birth to death—all these spring from fallen humans' corrupt desires." Verses 17–18

---

faith genuine through endurance that ends in perfection) and in vs. 12 (where the *blessedness* is represented by the crown of life, to be graciously granted when the testing process is sustained).

53 The warning against being deceived in vs. 16 is associated by different scholars either with the preceding discussion (of temptation's origin in one's own desires) or with that which follows (affirming that God gives only good gifts). Most also note that vs. 16 can appropriately be seen as a bridge that applies in both directions. See, e.g., Ralph P. Martin, *James* (WBC 48; Waco: Word, 1988), 31, 37, who sees vs. 16 both as a conclusion to the preceding prohibition against attributing temptation to God and as a transition to the positive exposition of God's immutable goodness and generosity.

54 Sophie Laws, *A Commentary on the Epistle of James* (HNTC; San Francisco: Harper & Row, 1980), 66: "The general theme of this section [1:12–18] is of what may or may not be said to come from God, in terms of future reward or destiny, present experience, and formative past events."

answer positively, "Every good and perfect gift, changeless purity and faithfulness, the birth that springs from his gracious will and truthful word, and (by implication) eventually a new heavens and earth—all these come from God, the Father of lights and of his children chosen by grace."

It might be questioned, however, whether James 1:12 is should be closely linked with the paragraphs that follow it. As was noted above, in the Greek original a lexical linking is clearly visible between "trial" (*peirasmos*) in verse 12 and "tempted" (*peiraz*) in verse 13, but in the former (as in verse 2) the term, although connoting difficulty and adversity, does not carry the negative moral or ethical overtones that we associate with "temptation" and that James clearly has in view in verse 13 when he denies that God can be tempted "with evil" or that God tempts anyone else in this seductive sense. It might appear, then, that James uses the cognate noun and verb in successive verses not to suggest thematic continuity between them but merely as a formal literary device. On the other hand, Israel's Wisdom is known to use linguistic repetition in successive statements to create an apparent contradiction that brings to light complexities and nuances that could not be seen apart from the tension created by the paradoxical form of expression. For example,

> Answer not a fool according to his folly,
>   lest you be like him yourself.
> Answer a fool according to his folly,
>   lest he be wise in his own eyes. (Prov. 26:4–5)

The prohibition and the command are in direct contradiction to one another formally; yet the second line of each couplet, by identifying the undesirable result of violating either the prohibition or the command, invite the wise reader to contemplate the differing senses in which answering a fool "according to his folly" may or may not be prudent, either for oneself or for the fool. Similarly, James 1:12–14 invites the reader to view "trial" from two perspectives. On the one hand, Wisdom recognizes that "trials" such as difficult circumstances that challenge faith and demand endurance are by no means outside God's control. If they were, James could offer no assurance that encountering trials could be an occasion of joy (1:2) or that enduring trials and so receiving blessedness is even a possibility (1:12). On the other hand, Wisdom knows well the proclivity of the sinful human heart to shift blame and seek excuses for one's own shameful desires—as, for instance, in Adam's desperate attempt at self-defense in answer to God's interrogation: "The woman whom you gave to be with me, she gave me fruit of the tree, and I ate" (Gen. 3:12; cf. Prov. 19:3). Therefore, when the same adverse circumstances or trials are viewed as invitations to disobey or disbelieve God, James asserts in the strongest possible terms that God is neither temptable (vulnerable to any invitation to contradict his own holiness and truth) nor the source of any such temptation. Recognizing the danger of self-deception (James 1:16) that finds expression in the words "I am being tempted by God" (vs. 13), James the sage teaches us to recognize God's sovereignty over and good purpose in our trials, even as he warns us against foolish and wicked efforts to evade our own responsibility. The apparently mixed signals about "trials" articulated in verses 12 and 13 are what biblical wisdom is all about: probing behind surface appearances, pondering paradoxes, catching the nuances, viewing experience from contrasting and complementary perspectives in order to respond faithfully to life's challenges.

As we prepare to preach this text, the rich Old Testament background and New Testament parallels of such phrases as "Blessed is the man . . ." (Ps. 1:1; 32:1; 34:8; Prov. 8:34; Isa. 56:2), "crown" (Prov. 1:9; 4:9; 16:31; 1 Cor. 9:25; 2 Tim. 4:8; 1 Peter 5:4) or "crown of life" (Rev. 2:10), and "those who love [God]" (Ex. 20:6; Deut. 5:10; Ps. 145:20) should be explored. These themes should be introduced strategically in the sermon to help hearers appreciate the richness of these concepts in the context of God's covenant with his people, whetting their spiritual appetites for the blessing promised in James 1:12.

Moreover, faithfully preaching the message of this text will require balanced attention both to its encouragement to endurance in the face of trial and to its warning against the self-deceiving temptation to shirk responsibility by blaming God for one's fall into sin. Divine grace permeates the passage in subtle ways, particularly in "God has promised" (vs. 12) and "every good *gift* and every perfect *gift* is from above" (vs. 17).[55] This reference to good gifts from above

---

55 James uses different words, both translated "gifts" in the ESV: *dosis* and *dōrēma*. Most commentators consider these words synonymous and their use together to add emphasis (confirming the ESV's translational decision). Martin, *James*, 38, observes: "If the two terms are not synonyms, the distinction may be drawn that *dosis* is the act of giving, *dorema* is the gift itself." Thus he translates: "All good giving and every perfect bounty. . . ."

reminds readers of James's assurance that those who lack wisdom can ask "God, who *gives* generously to all without reproach, and it will be *given* him" (1:5),[56] even as it anticipates his later portrayal of wisdom that "comes down from above" (3:15, 17–18). Grace shines even more brightly in the climax: "Of his own will he brought us forth" (1:18). James will soon assert more explicitly that God's will in election overturns human scales of value and worth: "Listen, my beloved brothers, has not God chosen those who are poor in the world to be rich in faith and heirs of the kingdom, which he has promised to those who love him?" (2:5) Yet, even before our text, James has hinted at the surprising character of sovereign grace by speaking of the exaltation of the lowly and the humiliation of the rich (1:9–11).

The preacher must call attention not only to these intimations of God's grace but also to James's searching exposure of our need for such grace. His sobering diagnosis of the source of the sordid cycle of temptation, desire, sin, and death precludes all blame shifting, for he demands that we face the harsh reality that our stumbles and falls into disbelief and disobedience cannot be attributed to external circumstances ordained by God's providence but arise from the wayward wants of our fallen human hearts (1:13–15). He will later trace the tongue's incendiary destruction and poisonous venom to its source, the corrupt heart, just as Jesus had done: "Can a fig tree, my brothers, bear olives, or a grapevine produce figs? Neither can a salt pond yield fresh water" (3:12; cf. Matt. 7:15–20; 12:33–37; 15:11, 18–20). Since the source of corruption lies deeper than circumstances, or even learned patterns of behavior and speech, a radical prescription is needed. Without a remedy that reaches to the root and transforms our inmost desires, the blessing and crown promised to those who love God and are proven true by trial must remain a distant and unattainable prize. That remedy is a new creation, which touches individual hearts with the power that effects new birth and will, in the end, embrace the whole created order (James 1:18; cf. 2 Cor. 5:17; Gal. 6:15; Col. 3:9–11).[57]

---

56   Both verbs translated "gives" and "will be given" are forms of *didōmi*, cognate of the verbal nouns in 1:17.

57   Martin, *James*, 40, comments: "Whenever men and women yield under *peirasmoi* and succumb to the fateful nemesis of the sorry train of desire-sin-death they are doomed. But God's new order breaks the entail, and thanks to his sovereign will to save and by means of his word he offers new life to those who confess

The focus of this text is unquestionably on the subjective dimension of our need and God's saving work, on the application of redemption in the renewal complex that includes, in traditional theological terms, regeneration and sanctification. Can the preacher also say anything in relation to this text about the *objective* accomplishment of redemption by Jesus Christ in *history*? I believe so, when this text is read, as biblical Wisdom Literature must be read, in the larger context of God's covenant. The beatitude that opens this text, like that which opens Psalm 1, refers first of all to a single individual, and with precise accuracy applies only to him. No other person has flawlessly endured the trial and loved God unreservedly, so no one else stands fully qualified to receive the promised crown of life. If, as I suggested above, a faint echo of Isaiah 53 can be heard in James 5:6, we have grounds for associating the "righteous person" who does not resist his murderers with the despised Servant of the Lord. What applies to Jesus—both his righteousness and his suffering—preeminently and perfectly also applies, derivatively and imperfectly, to those who are united to him by faith, including James's suffering readers. The same holds true for the promise of James 1:12: in the strictest sense, only Jesus "in every respect has been tempted (*peirazō*) as we are, yet without sin" (Heb. 4:15), just as only Jesus is the blessed man who delights in the Lord's law day and night (Ps. 1:2) and loves God unreservedly and his neighbor as himself (Matt. 22:37–39). In this sense the promised crown of life belongs to Jesus alone as the one who has "stood the test" and loved the Father through the fires of trial. Because Jesus did so, we who are his by faith likewise have a share, derivatively and by his grace, in his blessing, his crown of life.

A sermon that delivers this text's message of heart-searching warning and heart-stirring encouragement might be structured like this:

1. The Promise: God promises eternal life to those who cling to him in stubborn love throughout our trials (James 1:12).
   a. You can expect that life in the present will be full of endurance-demanding "trial."
   b. God promises the crowning reward of eternal life to the one who passes the trial by loving him persistently.
   c. But can you pass the test?

---

him in baptism and so enter the eschatological community where the powers of evil are broken."

2. The Problem: Doubting and defying God comes naturally to our desire-driven hearts, which reproduce a ceaseless cycle of desire, sin, and death (vv. 13–16).
   a. Our desire-driven hearts twist trials, which should be joyful paths to blessing, into temptations to doubt and disobey God.
   b. Our defensive hearts try to turn the blame for our doubt and disobedience back on the holy God who is never temptable, and never tempts.
   c. Our deadened hearts compulsively reproduce successive generations of defiling desires, disobedience, and death.

3. The Rescue: God graciously chose to release us from sin's grim cycle, beginning his new creation by giving us birth through his word of truth (vv. 17–18, 12).
   a. God is the pure and constant giver of *every* good gift (vs. 17).
   b. God's greatest gift is his gracious purpose to give birth to us by the word, setting us free from the old creation's desire/sin/death syndrome (vs. 18).
   c. God's great gift of new birth comes to us through Jesus, the blessed man who for love of his Father endured trial and deserves the crown of life (vs. 12).

Prophetic Vision: "Our Accuser Is Disbarred" (Revelation 12:1–18)

The Revelation to John is entitled in the inspired text itself, "The revelation of Jesus Christ" (Rev. 1:1), and this self-description should control our preaching of every text in the book.[58] As pastors preach through this carefully structured collection of prophetic visions, they must repeatedly ask, "How does this vision, this song of praise, this interpretive comment from John the seer, reveal Jesus Christ?" In some visions the answer is obvious. The first of several cycles of seven opens when John sees "one like a son of man," who had died but now lives forever, in the midst of lampstands that stand for his churches on earth (in the Roman province of Asia, specifically), and this son of man directs John to write letters to each of the seven churches (1:9–20). The second cycle is preceded by a scene in

---

58   Likewise, Rev. 19:10d, "For the testimony of Jesus is the spirit of prophecy," also should control our preaching of every text in the book.

heaven in which a Lamb, who has triumphed by being slain, receives from God a sealed scroll amid escalating songs of worship sung by ever-expanding choirs (4:1–5:14). Subsequently, John sees the child of the woman snatched from the claws of his nemesis, the ancient Serpent, and exalted to God's throne (12:1–6); he sees the warrior Word of God, who is Lord of lords and King of kings, wreaking righteous wrath on his enemies (19:11–21); and he sees the Lamb as the bridegroom of his church and the luminary who floods his holy city with radiant beauty (19:7; 21:2–4, 9–10, 22–23; 22:1–4). Even where Jesus the Lamb is not directly in John's line of vision, his power and presence permeate the book, for he is the one worthy to open the scroll (5:6–10), revealing and executing God's purposes for history until the consummation when the kingdom of this world will have fully "become the kingdom of our Lord and of his Christ, and he shall reign forever and ever" (11:15). He is not only the central figure about whom Revelation speaks, he is also the supreme messenger who speaks in Revelation, since the title goes on to affirm that God "gave him" this revelation "to show to his servants the things that must soon take place" (1:1).

Sadly, much popular discussion of the book of Revelation today shows more interest in what it may reveal about political events in our time than in what it reveals about Jesus, whom the book itself identifies from the outset as its central subject. Moreover, underestimating the evidence in the opening paragraph that these visions deliver their message in symbolism ("to show . . . made it known[59] . . . all that he saw," 1:1–2), these popular reading strategies purport to offer "literal" interpretations that link the visions to specific political and military incidents. Ignoring the most natural temporal significance of "things that must soon take place" (1:1) and "the time is near" (1:3), these approaches tend to remove the fulfillment of John's visions to a point thousands of years from the struggles of the seven first-century churches to whom Jesus addressed his Revelation.

Here I do not have the space to present and defend a different hermeneutic approach toward Revelation than that which fuels best sellers today, but I have done so elsewhere.[60] There I have offered a

---

59   The ESV's "made it known" represents the Greek verb *sēmainō*, a cognate of the noun *sēmeion*, "sign," which appears in Rev. 12:1, 3; 15:1.

60   Dennis E. Johnson, *Triumph of the Lamb: A Commentary on Revelation* (Phillipsburg: P & R, 2001).

way of interpreting this strange and wonderful New Testament book that finds warrant in the features of the book itself, based on the following conclusions. (1) We should expect the meaning of Revelation's visions to be intelligible to its first-century addressees, members of seven churches located in western Asia Minor, and the content of the visions to concern matters that impinged on their struggle of faith and faithfulness. (2) Revelation delivers its message predominantly in visual symbolism, which demands a sober correlation of the symbols to their intended referents. (3) The Old Testament—both its prophetic visions and its redemptive history—provides an indispensable key to the symbolism in Revelation. (4) Revelation is structured according to the ancient biblical literary convention of recapitulation, in which several perspectives on significant events emphasize the events' importance and illumine different aspects of their meaning.[61] Therefore, the order of Revelation's visions do not necessarily reflect the order of the events or epochs that they represent. (5) Revelation is addressed to churches under attack from external persecutors, internal deceivers, and invisible spiritual opponents. Its purpose is not to fuel eschatological debate among Christians living in comfort and safety but to fortify believers engaged in battle and to awaken those who are unaware of the conflict in which all are enlisted, wittingly or not.[62]

---

61   E.g., the two narratives of creation in Gen. 1–2; Joseph's two dreams in Gen. 37:5–10; Pharaoh's two dreams in 41:1–7, 17–32; and Nebuchadnezzar's and Daniel's complementary visions concerning the arrival of God's kingdom during the regime of a fourth pagan empire in Dan. 2:31–45 and 7:1–28.

62   My understanding of the genre and historical referents of the visions in the book of Revelation has changed over the years from semi-literal futurist/premillennial, to primarily symbolic semi-preterist/postmillennial, to primarily symbolic recapitulationist/amillennial. Thus I believe that the letters to churches in Revelation 2–3 describe the current conditions in congregations located in the seven named cities of western Asia Minor when John received his visions on Patmos and that the visions of Revelation 4–22 primarily concern events still future from the standpoint of those first-century churches but not necessarily future to us in the twenty-first century. The chronological order of the events and conflicts symbolized in the visions is not necessarily reflected in the order of the visions themselves (since, for example, our text in Revelation 12 recapitulates the history of the conflict between Christ and Satan that began before the churches of Asia were planted: in the Garden of Eden, in the incarnation and birth of Christ, in his suffering and exaltation). I believe that Revelation was written in the last decade of the first century, during the reign of the Emperor Domitian, as reported in early Christian tradition, and that its vision of the trampling of the temple and the holy

Here my purpose is to offer a sample of how these perspectives inform the preaching of a central text—actually *the* central text—in the Revelation of Jesus Christ, delivered to John. Revelation 12 falls at the midpoint of the book as a whole, and it comes after a vision sequence that has brought John's readers to the very end of history. John had been told that when the seventh angel sounded his trumpet, the delay of God's justice would be over and "the mystery of God would be fulfilled" (10:6–7). John had heard the blast of the seventh trumpet and the announcement that the time had come "for the dead to be judged, and for rewarding [God's] servants . . . , and for destroying the destroyers of the earth" (11:18).

In our text, at the very center of the book, John's vision returns to historical events that predate not only the consummation of history but also John's captivity on Patmos and the founding of the churches of Asia. Here, John peers into the heart of the war that has been waged down through history, the conflict between the dragon, "that ancient serpent, who is called the devil and Satan" (12:9), and a child, the Seed of the woman promised in Genesis 3:15. This cosmic conflict, which spans history but has passed its turning point in the birth, death, and exaltation of the Messiah, is the deepest explanation for the specific threats from false teachers, complacent self-confidence, and violent persecutors that confront the churches of Asia (Rev. 2–3). This conflict explains why human history is littered with bloody battles, famines, plagues, the rubble of civilizations ripped apart by rising empires or collapsing from corruption from within (Rev. 6–11). Throughout history, Satan has been trying to destroy the people of God and to prevent the arrival of the divine-human Savior promised by God at the dawn of history; but, as John's visions show, at the crucial moment Satan's attempt to destroy Christ failed miserably. Therefore the dragon is taking out his frustration on the people who belong to Jesus, thrashing around like a wounded and desperate beast "because he knows that his time is short!" (12:12)

The two visions recorded in Revelation 12 (the first in vv. 1–6, the second in vv. 7–17) could well be preached in separate sermons. Certainly the richness of their imagery and allusiveness to the Old

---

city looks back to Jerusalem's fall in 70 A.D. as a metaphor for the ongoing persecution of the church as the true temple and holy city until the return of Christ. For a full defense of these conclusions, readers are invited to examine *Triumph of the Lamb*.

Testament can be exhibited more adequately in two messages than in one. On the other hand, our listeners should be shown that these two visions provide complementary perspectives on the same conflict, like different camera angles on the same sports contest. The clearest signal that the two visions of Revelation 12 concern the same conflict is found in the descriptions of the aftermath of the battle in verse 6 and verses 13–17. In both, the heavenly woman flees into the wilderness, to a refuge of safety and provision, and the dragon tries unsuccessfully to destroy her there. Prior to this, in both visions of the battle itself the dragon is thwarted in its purpose—in the first vision, to consume the woman's child (vv. 4–5), in the second, to retain its place in heaven as accuser of the brothers (vv. 9–12)—but it is not yet destroyed. The unity of the visions and their complementary perspectives on the significance of the dragon's defeat, first for Jesus, the son of the woman, and then for those who rely on "the blood of the Lamb" and maintain his testimony (vs. 11), need to be demonstrated, whether the text is preached in one sermon or two.

Old Testament history and prophetic symbolism provide the key to unlock the identities of the protagonists in the first vision. The woman is called a "great sign" and appears "in heaven." Both descriptions direct reader and hearers to view her as symbolic. She is clothed with the sun, stands on the moon, and is crowned with twelve stars. This symbolism, which alludes to Joseph's dream (Gen. 37:9–10), portrays the woman as the people of God, as Jacob's family was in Joseph's day. This identification is further confirmed when her son is further described as "a male child," alluding to Isaiah 66:7, which in the LXX portrays Zion as a women who gives birth to a "male child" even before her labor pains begin.[63] This pregnant mother is a picture of Israel, the bride of God, about to give birth to the anointed King. The messianic identity of her son is indicated by the prediction that he "is to rule all the nations with a rod of iron," which is virtually a quotation of the Lord's promise to his Anointed, his Son, in Psalm 2:8. Even before there was an Israel, however, in the Garden of Eden God cursed the serpent with the prospect that the woman's seed would bruise the serpent's head, as it bruised its conqueror's heel (Gen. 3:15). Allusion to this more ancient scriptural background is found not only

---

63   Rev. 12:5 reads in Greek "she bore a son (*huion*) a male child (*arsen*), who will rule all the nations with an iron rod." It would be redundant to describe a "son" as "male," unless the intent were to invoke the allusion to Isa. 66:7.

in the description of the dragon as "that ancient serpent" (Rev. 12:9) but also in the description of the woman's other children as "the rest of her offspring" or "seed" (*sperma*, vs. 17). Since the woman lives on after her child is caught up to God's throne and the dragon continues to pursue her and her other children, she seems to symbolize the whole people of God, in the Old Testament and the New.

Clearly her Son is Jesus the Messiah, threatened at birth by the jealous violence of Herod the Great; tempted in the wilderness, by the words of his disciple Simon Peter, and in the garden of Gethsemane; and finally executed on a Roman cross. Yet, his death was not the destruction that the dragon desired to achieve. Therefore, in the first vision the Son's death is subsumed in his ascent "to God and to his throne," although his sacrifice has been a focal point of John's testimony to Jesus to this point (1:5-7, 18; 5:6-10; 7:14) and will be acclaimed as the source of the saints' victory over their accuser in the second vision (12:11).

The dragon, like the woman, is called a "sign." It is not to be understood as a reptile, natural or mythical. Its seven heads and ten horns symbolize power and perhaps cunning (cf. Dan. 7:8), as does the power of its tail to sweep one third of the stars from the sky. In the second, complementary vision, it will be identified as "that ancient serpent, who is called the devil and Satan" (Rev. 12:9; cf. 20:2, where the same fourfold description reappears). The first vision highlights the unevenness of the conflict, which pits a woman in labor and her newborn infant against so forceful a foe. Yet, in an instant, it seems, her child is caught up to God, to share his throne (cf. 3:21), and the woman flees to a refuge in the wilderness prepared for her by God.[64] The first vision thus closes with the triumphant ascent of the Messiah, the decisive defeat of the dragon in its intent to destroy the

---

64   The duration of her sojourn in the wilderness is measured in 12:6 as 1,260 days, and in vs. 14 as "a time, and times, and half a time." If, as seems likely, the "times" in vs. 14 stand for years and Daniel 7:25 is alluded to, these are roughly equivalent time periods: 3 ½ years of twelve 30-day (on average) months work out to 1,260 days, or 42 months (Rev. 11:1-2; 13:5-7). See Johnson, *Triumph*, 171–72, 182–83. The interrelationships of these time period designations would be quite complex to explain in the context of a sermon, however; and in my judgment it is best reserved for a more interactive teaching venue. In preaching I would simply note that the days, months, and "times" in symbolic visions need not be taken as "literal" time designations, and that the ascension of the woman's Son (or, in the second vision, the expulsion of the Accuser from heaven) inaugurates the period of her wilderness sojourn.

Messiah, and the ongoing survival of the people of God, like Israel after the exodus, protected and provided for by God but in a wilderness wasteland, not yet having entered the promised inheritance.

The second vision (12:7–17), which is significantly longer, provides commentary and elaboration on the first, especially with respect to its implications for the embattled churches to which the Revelation is addressed. Again the scene is heaven: John's visions take the seer and his readers behind the veil of historical events to perceive the events' deeper significance. Michael, commander of the angels loyal to God, was introduced in the book of Daniel as the guardian angel and champion of Israel, the people of God (Dan. 10:13, 21). Two armies are arrayed against each other, but, as in the first vision, the conflict is quickly concluded: the dragon "was defeated and there was no longer any place for them in heaven. And the great dragon was thrown down . . . and his angels were thrown down with him" (Rev. 12:8–9). Since the immediate sequel to the dragon's expulsion is its pursuit of the woman and her flight into the wilderness (vs. 13–14), the first vision guides us to interpret the expulsion of the dragon and its angelic allies as referring not to a primeval rebellion that antedated the fall of humanity but to the victory and ascent of the woman's child. This interpretation is confirmed by Jesus in the Gospels, when he affirms the successful ministry of seventy-two disciples: "I saw Satan fall like lightning from heaven. Behold, I have given you authority to tread on serpents and scorpions, and over all the power of the enemy" (Luke 10:18–19; cf. 11:14–22).

Moreover, the defeat and downfall of Satan is the subject of special commentary offered by a loud voice in heaven.

> Now the salvation and the power and the kingdom of our God and the authority of his Christ have come, for the accuser of our brothers has been thrown down, who accuses them day and night before our God. And they have conquered him by the blood of the Lamb and by the word of their testimony, for they loved not their lives even unto death. (Rev. 12:10–11)

This commentary not only interprets the meaning of the symbolic warfare waged between Michael and the dragon but also reveals the significance of the conflict for the churches to which Revelation is addressed: Our prosecutor before God's righteous tribunal has been thrown out of court. Our accuser has been disbarred and can no longer press his case against us before God's bar of justice in heaven.[65]

"The accuser ... who accuses"[66] is essentially a Greek paraphrase of the significance of the Hebrew "the *satan*," the adversary (at law, e.g., Ps. 109:6; or in battle, 1 Sam. 29:4; 1 Kings 11:14, 23, 25). The expulsion of Satan the accuser from heaven spells the end of the prosecutorial role that he was seen to fulfill in the opening chapters of Job and, of particular relevance to Revelation 12, in a vision granted to the prophet Zechariah (Zech. 3). In Zechariah's vision Joshua, Israel's post-exilic high priest, is seen standing before the angel of the Lord clothed in filthy robes and turban, with Satan[67] standing at his right hand to accuse him. Joshua's dirty clothes show that the accuser's charges are true: this man is unfit to intercede for God's people in God's sanctuary. But the Lord[68] rebukes Satan the accuser, commands that Joshua be clothed with spotless robe and turban, and then declares Joshua and his priestly colleagues to be a sign of things to come, when "I will bring my Servant the Branch ... and I will remove the iniquity of this land in a single day" (3:8–9).

The heavenly voice of Revelation 12 declares that this day of purification has come. The accuser of the brothers has been cast down, disbarred, deprived of standing to bring charges against God's elect (cf. Rom. 8:31–34), and the voice also makes clear the means by which the adversary's charges are silenced once for all: "They have conquered him by the blood of the Lamb and by the word of their testimony" (Rev. 12:11). In Revelation 5, John heard that the Lion of Judah had conquered and was therefore authorized to receive and open the mysterious scroll, but he saw a Lamb who was extolled for having been slain "and by your blood you ransomed people for God

---

65 Paul makes the same point in Colossians 2:13–15, where he describes the way that God has decisively answered and removed "the record of debt that stood against us with its legal demands" by nailing it to the cross, and he immediately connects Christ's victory on Calvary with the heavenly sphere by asserting that by his sacrifice Jesus "disarmed the rulers and authorities and put them to open shame." Our accuser is indeed "disarmed," unable any longer to bring accusations against us who have suffered the law's curse in Christ's cursed death on our behalf!

66 Greek: *ho katēgōr ... ho katēgorōn*.

67 The Hebrew is *hassatan*, translated by the Greek as *ho diabolos*. Rev. 12:9 and 20:2, as we have seen, contain both the Greek and the Hebrew titles.

68 As in the account of Moses' call at the burning bush (Ex. 3:2–7, 13–15), the angel of the Lord (*mal'ak YHWH*) and the Lord (*YHWH*) act and speak interchangeably in Zechariah's vision of the defense and purification of Joshua.

from every tribe and language and people and nation" (5:9). Now John learns that the Lamb's triumph through sacrificial death also is the triumph of all who seek cleansing through his blood, holding fast their testimony of trust even to the death.[69] The defeat of the Satan, the accuser, took place in an act of utter weakness, the cross of Christ, "the weakness and foolishness of God," scorned by Greeks as nonsense and by Jews as powerless (1 Cor. 1:18–25). This act of weakness, the Lamb slain on behalf of the guilty, is so strong that it has expelled the accuser from God's heavenly court!

Both visions show that in the aftermath of the decisive battle, the dragon, though decisively defeated in the cross and exaltation of Christ, is not yet destroyed, nor is the enemy inactive. In fact, the rage of the dragon is inflamed by its defeat and its knowledge that its time is short (Rev. 12:12). Therefore in the battle's sequel John sees the dragon pouring a river of water out of its mouth to try to drown the church (vs. 15).[70] In Revelation's visions what proceeds from the mouth represents the power of words, either bringing righteous judgment (1:16; 19:15) or spreading lethal deceit (16:13–14; cf. 13:14; 19:19–20; 20:1–3, 7–8). Here, this flood portrays false teaching, by which "the deceiver of the whole world" (12:9) still seeks to mislead not only his own deluded adherents but also the servants of Christ (2:20). When the strategy of deception fails, the dragon wages war against the woman's offspring, the church's members, in more violent ways. The second vision of the dragon's defeat and its ongoing, though frustrated, resistance merges into the succeeding scene as the dragon stands on the sand of the sea, from which emerges the beast that blasphemously arrogates to itself divine adulation and wages war against the saints (13:1–10).

These twin visions of the watershed battle in the cosmic conflict of the ages unveil[71] in vivid, visual images the hidden realities

---

69   The Greek verb *nikaō*, variously translated "overcome," "triumph," or "conquer," is frequent in Revelation, usually referring to the victory of Christ (3:21; 5:5; 17:14) or to those who trust him and hold fast to the testimony of Jesus (2:7, 11, 17, 26; 3:5, 12, 21; 15:2). Twice, however, the beast is said to "conquer" Jesus' witnesses and saints (11:7; 13:7)—that is, to silence their testimony by violent martyrdom. Yet, the affirmation of Rev. 12:11 is that the martyrs have, in holding fast their testimony to the death, actually conquered the dragon that stands behind the beast in its brutal attempts to threaten, intimidate, and exterminate them.

70   See the D-Day–VE-Day example in chapter 7.

71   The Greek term *apokalypsis* ("revelation," 1:1) is etymologically derived from the taking away (*apo*) of a veil (*kalymma*). Contemporary usage is a more

that explain the challenges confronting the congregations that hold to the word of God and the testimony of Jesus. On the one hand we participate in the Lamb's victory over our accuser, won through the blood that Jesus shed to redeem people from every nation and language. Satan, the adversary, is powerless to bring *any* charge against God's elect, for whom Christ died and for whom he now intercedes at God's right hand (Rom. 8:33–34). On the other hand, precisely because the dragon was decisively defeated at the cross, because "his time is short" and his efforts to destroy the seed of the woman (both the Son and his church) are thwarted by God, this enemy redoubles his efforts to devastate the people of God through violence (the beast, 13:1–10), false teaching (the false prophet, 13:11–18), and seductive affluence (the harlot, 17:1–18). The situations of the seven Asian churches diagnosed by Jesus in his letters to them (Rev. 2–3) exemplify some of the concrete ways in which the dragon's multipronged insurgency may be manifested in the first century or in the twenty-first.

A sermon on the complementary visions of the Child's/Lamb's victory over the dragon should emphasize first of all that Christ's cross, resurrection, and ascension were not simply his personal triumph over Satan. Because believers are united to Jesus in his suffering and his exaltation, his victorious defeat of the accuser was our triumph as well. By the blood of the Lamb and the word of our testimony—a testimony of trust that steels believers' hearts even in the teeth of a martyr's death—we have conquered the accuser. He can no longer accuse because our sin and guilt have been borne by Jesus, punished in Jesus; and Jesus' righteousness is now imputed to us, his spotless purity and impeccable loyalty covering us like snow white robes (7:14).

The sermon should also strike a sobering note, reflecting the visions' realistic acknowledgement that the church, mother and bride of the Messiah, is still in the wilderness, protected and provided for by her God but not yet secured from her enemy's every physical and spiritual assault. Today, in some parts of the world, the persecuted church, like the first century churches in Smyrna, Pergamum, and Philadelphia, needs this text's comfort and encouragement to hold fast to the testimony of Jesus, even at the cost of death. Elsewhere,

---

reliable indicator of a word's meaning than is etymology, but in this case the word's derivation is instructive.

outwardly safe and comfortable churches, like those in Thyatira, Sardis, and Laodicea, need to hear and heed Revelation's warnings that the dragon has other weapons in his arsenal besides violence. False teaching, self-confidence, and compromise with the culture's earthbound values are as lethal and paralyzing to the church's vitality as is the cowardice that cringes from intimidating aggression. The sermon could be structured like this:

1. *The Serpent and the Son*: The age old conflict between the Serpent and the woman's seed reached its climax suddenly in Christ's incarnation and exaltation (12:1–5).
   a. The *combatants* make the contest seem imbalanced in the Dragon's favor (12:1–4).
      i. *The woman* writhing in labor symbolizes the struggling people of God (Immanuel's mother, Israel, and Eve), through whose Seed salvation would come (Gen. 3:15; 37:9–11; Isa. 7:14; 66:7–8).
      ii. *Her child* is the Christ against whom the nations rage but appointed by God to rule them with an iron rod (Rev. 12:5; Ps. 2:7–8).
      iii. *The dragon* is the ancient serpent Satan, full of cunning and power, who deceives the whole earth (Rev. 12:3–4, 9; Gen. 3:1).
   b. The *conflict* yields a sudden, surprising triumph for the Son (Rev. 12:5).
      i. The child born in weakness now rules on God's throne.
      ii. Where is the battle itself? John has already heard it: the Lion's triumph is his redemptive death as the Lamb (5:5, 9; 12:11).
   c. But how does Jesus' victory affect us? (Point 2 . . .)

2. *The Satan and the Saints*: The victory of Christ means the victory of his brothers and sisters, for our accuser is disbarred and expelled from God's court (12:7–12).
   a. In the "video replay" of the battle, the *combatants* are more evenly matched (12:7).
      i. Michael, the captain of God's angelic army, is the guardian and champion of Israel in the unseen realm (Dan. 10:13, 21).

     ii.   The dragon and its armies lack strength, and so cannot retain their place in heaven (Job 1:6ff.; Eph. 6:12).

  b. The *conflict* yields a sudden, surprising victory for the saints over their accuser (Rev. 12:8–12).

     i.   We are guilty: the adversary's (the *satan's*) charges were true (Zech. 3:1, 3; contrast Job 1–2).

     ii.   Yet the Branch removed our iniquity in a single day (Zech. 3:2, 4–9).

     iii.   Our accuser is deprived of charges against us and disbarred from heaven (Rev. 12:8–10; John 12:31; Luke 10:18–19).

     iv.   "Our brothers" (not Michael and his army!) have conquered the accuser through the blood of the Lamb and our testimony of trust in him (Rev. 12:11).

  c. Why, if the accuser is defeated, do we still face spiritual dangers and physical trials? (Point 3 . . .)

3. *The Dragon and the Woman*: Because the devil has been decisively defeated but not destroyed, he furiously (but futilely) attacks Christ's church and its members through lies and violence (12:6, 13–17).

  a. Messiah's mother (God's covenant people, old and new) flees to a safe place in the wilderness, nourished there like Israel and Elijah, but not "home" (12:6, 13–14; Ex. 19:4; 1 Kings 17:2–6).

  b. The deceiver of the world (Rev. 12:9), the "father of lies" (John 8:44) tries but fails to drown Christ's church with deceptive words (Rev. 12:15–17).

  c. The "murderer from the beginning" (John 8:44) summons the beast from the sea's chaos to wage war on the saints, "conquering" them by killing his faithful witnesses (Rev. 12:17–13:1, 5–7; cf. 11:7).

  d. Because the Lamb's triumph over the accuser belongs to you, hold fast in faith to "the testimony of Jesus," resisting Satan's deceitful words and murderous threats.

Conclusion

Even our brief exploration of these few representative New Testament texts has illustrated and demonstrated, I believe, the rich texture of the apostolic writers' interpretation of the Old Testament in the light of Jesus the Messiah and their elaboration of Jesus' person and saving mission in the light of those ancient Scriptures. Their interpretive activity naturally flowed in both directions, since they spoke from and for a God so sovereign that he designed pre-patriarchal, patriarchal, and Israelite history and institutions both to foreshadow Christ's climactic redemptive work and to mediate retrospectively its benefits by evoking and sustaining faith in God's promises. The "shadows" given in old covenant revelation demonstrated the need for the coming Redeemer, and they defined the categories by which his work could be understood, evoking in Israel's faithful both longing and hope for the Lord's coming in judgment and mercy.

Yet, the shadows remained shadows, dark shapes and profiles cast back from the future by the bright light of things to come (Heb. 10:1). For this reason, the apostles preached as those profoundly aware of their privilege to stand where they did in the unfolding drama of redemptive history, among those "on whom the end of the ages has come" (1 Cor. 10:11), whose eyes saw sights and whose ears heard words that many prophets and kings had longed to see and hear (Luke 10:24). They knew that they had been entrusted with the key to unlock the interpretive conundrum that confused the treasurer of Ethiopia as he wrestled with the prophecy of Isaiah, and that this key was Jesus himself, the Lord's faithful and suffering Servant (Acts 8:32–35).

More than that, they knew that they had been entrusted with the message of life for the world, for this Servant, chosen by the Father and anointed with the Spirit, was the preacher who would gently "proclaim justice to the Gentiles . . . and in his name the Gentiles will hope" (Matt. 12:18–21, citing Isa. 42:1–3). For this reason, as we have seen, they strove to proclaim the good news foretold in Israel's Scriptures in languages intelligible to the nations and peoples of the entire world.

This, too, is our mission, as we follow in the apostles' footsteps. Both the content of our message and the method of our mission must be conformed to the pattern of sound words that the Spirit of the risen Christ breathed out in their writings as the divine canon for Christ's church. We are called to proclaim Christ, the faithful covenant keeper and sacrificial covenant curse bearer on our behalf; Christ, the last Adam, seed of Abraham, and son of David; Christ, mediator of the new exodus and bestower of the new inheritance; Christ, in whom "all the promises of God find their Yes" (2 Cor. 1:20) and on whose absolute supremacy God's single "plan for the fullness of time" is focused (Eph. 1:10). In proclaiming Christ as the apostles did, we magnify the justice and holiness of God, calling rebels, who yet bear his image, to turn away from their self-serving and their self-justifying idolatries and to cast themselves on the mercies of the Creator-King whom they have spurned. In proclaiming Christ, we magnify the astonishing grace and mercy of God, who, when we were enemies, reconciled us to himself by the death of his Son (Rom. 5:10). In proclaiming Christ, we are privileged to participate in the gathering and construction of God's new temple, united and vivified by connection with Jesus the Living Stone (1 Peter 2:4–6), and in the spread of the knowledge of the glory of the Lord until it fills the earth as the waters cover the sea (Hab. 2:14). As we proclaim Christ, who is our peace, amazingly through us *he himself is preaching* peace to those far and those near, creating one new humanity that bears his image and radiates his beauty in knowledge, righteousness, and holiness of the truth (Eph. 2:13–18; 4:24). Surely so high and humbling a calling must stir us with the zeal and discipline to study the Bible with Peter and Paul, at the feet of Jesus, and then to rise and broadcast its message among the nations, so that by the mercy of God and the strength of his Spirit our ministry of the Word of life might both reflect and extend their apostolic witness to Jesus Christ, the Son of God and the Savior of his church.

To them God chose to make known
how great among the Gentiles are the riches of the glory of this
mystery,
which is Christ in you, the hope of glory.
Him we proclaim,
warning everyone and teaching everyone with all wisdom,
that we may present everyone mature in Christ.
Colossians 1:27–28

Appendix A

From Text to Sermon—A Step-by-Step Guide to Biblical Interpretation in Sermon Preparation[1]

In the actual practice of sermon preparation, you will discover that the process does not fall into two discrete and easily separable steps—first interpreting what the text means and then deciding how to communicate its meaning in preaching. From the outset, you will be asking the Lord for insight into how to communicate the message of the text, and all the way along you will be learning more about its meaning. Sometimes in writing the sermon outline or in selecting illustrations or in further meditation on the text, you will find that the text's heart-searching message suddenly "snaps" into clearer focus for you. Nevertheless, it is wise to distinguish the discipline of interpretation from the discipline of communication, lest eager preachers get preoccupied with ideas that seem to have great homiletical power but are not central to the text's meaning. This outline gives a detailed step-by-step "how to" of the interpretation process, complementing and applying the hermeneutical principles and exegetical procedures that are typically taught in courses on Old and New Testament biblical interpretation. Appendix B contains two

---

1 Based on, but greatly expanded from, O. Palmer Robertson, "Procedure for a Biblical-Theological Exposition of an O.T. Text" (unpublished class handout, Westminster Theological Seminary, ca. 1971; 1 pg.) and V. S. Poythress, "Procedure for a Biblical-Theological Exposition of a New Testament Text" (unpublished class handout, Westminster Theological Seminary, ca. 1978; 2 pp.). Thanks to Dr. Robertson and Dr. Poythress for their permission and encouragement to include the material that has been assimilated and adapted from their unpublished "Procedure" sheets in this appendix.

sermons, one on an Old Testament text and one on a New Testament text, which serve as examples of the homiletic "fruit" that this step-by-step approach can yield.

1. Select the text and become acquainted with it.
   a. Pray for the humility, insight, and courage to understand the text and to apply it to yourself and to others.
   b. Select the passage. If you have opportunity to preach regularly or often to the same congregation (or even if you preach only occasionally and to different groups), I recommend that you make it a practice generally to preach through a biblical book (*lectio continua*) or at least a major section of a book (the Abraham narrative in Genesis; the David narrative in 1 and 2 Samuel; selected Psalms; the servant songs in Isaiah 40–66; etc.).
   c. Define the limits of the passage: a complete, self-contained unit of thought (usually a "paragraph," but the size of a "preaching text" varies widely depending on the genre, the relative attention to detailed exposition or general thematic overview, etc.).
   d. Covenant before God to *listen* carefully and with obedient faith to the message of that text (James 1:22–25).
   e. Read the passage in the context of the biblical book in which it appears. Pay attention to:
      i. Clues to the *life context* and spiritual need of the original readers (their situation and need, which provided the occasion for the text's composition, have direct bearing on the text's purpose).
      ii. *Themes* of your text *interwoven elsewhere* in the book (broader literary-theological context).
      iii. Indicators of the *genre* of the book as a whole (narrative, epistle, poetry, prophetic/ apocalyptic, etc.), and the genre of your passage within the whole (parable, miracle narrative, doctrinal discourse, ethical instruction, etc.).
      iv. The *texts that immediately precede and follow* your text (narrower literary-theological context).

2. Exegete the text in its original setting.

a. Translate from the Greek, Hebrew, or Aramaic, identifying the form and meaning of each word. Consult reference tools: the standard Hebrew-English and Greek-English lexica,[2] grammars, and/or search software such as BibleWorks, Gramcord, Logos, etc. Does the semantic range of some words open the possibility of different meanings in the context of your passage?[3] A survey of usage/meaning may be called for (using concordance or search software).

b. Make a decision on any textual variants, using the apparatus in *Biblia Hebraica Stuttgartensia*; Nestle-Aland, *Novum Testamentum Graece* (preferred) or *Greek New Testament* (United Bible Societies).

c. Learn as much as you can about the original life context of the passage: human author, audience, circumstances.
    i. Begin inductively from the book itself (1.e. above).
    ii. Consult an OT or NT introduction or the introductory material on "occasion" or "audience" in one or several commentaries.
    iii. Identify the occasion that elicited the text—the problem, error, need, or difficulty confronting the original recipients—the Fallen Condition Focus (Bryan Chapell). Identifying the occasion is crucial

---

2 OT Hebrew: Brown, Driver, and Briggs, *Hebrew and English Lexicon* (Oxford: Oxford University Press, 1995); Köhler, Baumgartner and Richardson, *Hebrew and Aramaic Lexicon* (Leiden: Brill, 1999); or Holladay, *Concise Hebrew and Aramaic Lexicon* (Grand Rapids, Eerdmans, 1972). NT Greek: Bauer and Danker, *Greek-English Lexicon*, 3rd ed. (Chicago: University of Chicago, 2000), or Johannes P. Louw and Eugene A. Nida, eds., *Greek-English Lexicon of the New Testament Based on Semantic Domains*, 2nd ed., 2 vols. (New York: United Bible Societies, 1989).

3 Although "semantic range" is used in more technical senses in linguistics, in biblical studies "semantic range" generally describes the spectrum of meanings or connotations that a particular word conveys, or the functions that it performs, depending on its relations to other words in a particular context. In English, for instance, the noun "house" can refer to a physical building ("he built his house on sand"), a family (perhaps with servants) inhabiting a domicile ("as for me and my house"), a dynasty ("the house of David"), a legislative body ("House of Representatives"), and so on. Because a single word can convey quite different semantic content depending on the other words with which it is connected in a text, Loew and Nida have structured their *Greek-English Lexicon of the New Testament Based on Semantic Domains* not by Greek words listed in alphabetical order but by categories of meaning.

to discerning the text's purpose in the lives of its original recipients and, by extension, in the lives of our hearers.

   d. Analyze the structure of the passage.

      i. Identify main "movements" of thought through syntactic/structural and conceptual evidence

      ii. Analyze the relationship between the main "movements": Temporal sequence? Logical inference? Antithesis? Supplementation? etc.

      iii. Identify the subordinate and supportive concepts, and analyze how they relate to the main thoughts.

      iv. Make the structure "visual" through a conventional outline, or through a "sentence flow" in which subordination is signaled through indentation.[4]

   e. Attempt a provisional theme statement, purpose statement, and outline of the text.

      i. Theme statement: In one sentence, what is the passage "about," and what does it affirm about its topic? As you step back from the many lexical and grammatical details in the passage, what overarching theme and purpose stand out from the text as a whole?

      ii. Purpose statement: What is the passage *intended to accomplish* in the hearts and lives of its hearers? What problem or threat was it written to remedy? What error or sin does it "argue against"? What response was it intended to elicit?

      iii. Outline: By what "thought route" (narration, persuasion, poetic symbol, etc.) does the text lead its original readers or hearers from their present condition toward the purpose, the intended response? What are the major steps in the text's movement from "occasion" to "outcome"?

3. Determine and examine the text's interrelationships with other passages in the canonical content.

   a. Pick two to five (fewer or more, as the text requires) key words and trace their use:

      i. By the same human author.

---

4 See Gordon Fee, *New Testament Exegesis: A Handbook for Students and Pastors*, 3rd. ed. (Louisville: Westminster John Knox, 2002).

ii. By other OT or NT writers.

iii. In the LXX (which is often the linguistic link between the Hebrew OT and the apostolic writings of
the NT).

iv. Choose words that:

    (1) Are central to the passage's main theme, or

    (2) Have a broad semantic field and are capable of
changing the meaning of the text, depending
on which meaning of the word is "operative"
here (*parakaleō* as "comfort" or as "exhort"?), or

    (3) Seem unusual for this author (In the NT the
use of a Greek word that is atypical for the human author may signal intentional allusion
to the LXX text of an OT passage—e.g., *nosphizomai* in Acts 5:2 echoes Josh. 7:1).

v. Check your conclusions regarding the words' meanings and associations by consulting one or more
theological dictionaries.[5]

vi. Use cross references to locate passages most similar
or most contrasting to your text (in the same human author, NT, OT). Well-selected cross references
are found in the *American Standard Version* (1901),
*Novum Testamentum Graece, Jerusalem Bible, New
Geneva Study Bible* (NKJV; also adapted to the NIV as
Spirit of the Reformation Study Bible, and to the ESV
as *Reformation Study Bible*).

b. Examine OT or NT quotations or allusions in their own
original settings, and in their usage by later OT or NT
authors.

c. Consider broader conceptual interrelationships, particularly in terms of the canonical context of the first
readers (How much of the Bible did they have?), then in
terms of the completed canon.

---

5   E.g., Kittel-Friedrich, *Theological Dictionary of the New Testament*; Colin
Brown, *New International Dictionary of New Testament Theology*; X. Léon-Dufour,
Dictionary of the New Testament; L. Ryken, J. Wilhoit, and T. Longman III, *Diction-
ary of Biblical Imagery*; T. D. Alexander, B. S. Rosner, D. A. Carson, and G. Gold-
sworthy, *New Dictionary of Biblical Theology*; W. VanGemeren, *New International
Dictionary of Old Testament Theology and Exegesis*.

    d. Reevaluate your provisional outline and theme and purpose statements (2.e.) in the light of the passage's place in the history of revelation and its literary and theological interrelationships with the rest of Scripture.

4. Consult other interpreters.[6]

    a. Preferably do this after you have wrestled seriously with the text yourself—but also you must not neglect this step! You are not an infallible interpreter, so you need the "iron" of other Bible scholars' work to sharpen your "iron."

    b. Exegetical commentaries:

        i. "Classical" (pre-Enlightenment): T. Oden, ed., *Ancient Christian Commentary on Scripture*; Calvin; Luther; Puritans (many republished by Banner of Truth); etc.

        ii. Post-Enlightenment historical criticism (series: International Critical Commentary, Harper's New and Old Testament Commentaries, Anchor Bible, Hermeneia, etc.).

        iii. Post-Enlightenment conservative/evangelical (series: New International Commentary on the Old Testament, New International Commentary on the New Testament, New International Greek Testament Commentary, Word Biblical Commentary, Evangelical Commentary on the New Testament, New American Commentary, Reformed Expository Commentary).

    c. Specialized studies (monographs, journal articles)— Note, for example, "The Gospel According to the OT" series from P & R[7]; and the "New Studies in Biblical

---

6 These are listed not in order of importance but instead as moving from narrower contexts (book, human author, and redemptive-historical epoch) to the broader canonical context (doctrinal system of Scripture as a whole).

7 R. Dillard, *Faith in the Face of Apostasy: the Gospel According to Elijah*; I. Duguid, *Living in the Gap Between Promise and Reality: the Gospel According to Abraham*; Duguid, *Living in the Grip of Relentless Grace: the Gospel According to Isaac and Jacob*; Bryan Estelle, *Salvation Through Judgment and Mercy: the Gospel According to Jonah*; Tremper Longman III, *Immanuel in our Place: Seeing Christ in Israel's Worship*.

Theology" series from InterVarsity[8]; as well as Vern S.
Poythress, *The Shadow of Christ in the Law of Moses*;
D. E. Johnson, *The Message of Acts in the History of Re-
demption*; etc.

   d. Biblical theologies (G. Vos, W. VanGemeren, D. Guthrie,
L. Morris, G. Ladd).

   e. Creeds, confessions, and catechisms. These summarize
the consensus reached by the church's leaders and teachers in various traditions and eras regarding the central
teachings of Scripture and their interrelationships. They
are a strong antidote to the modern and postmodern
tendencies to read the Scriptures individualistically, a
salutary and humbling reminder that you are not the first
or wisest person to interpret Scripture, and a safeguard
against intriguing but dangerous heretical tangents.

   f. Systematic theologies. Typically the work of individual
theologians, these usually have the strength of providing
fuller explanation and integration of biblical motifs than
do the church's confessions and catechisms.

   g. Fellow students, pastors, elders, etc.

5. "Marinate" your thoughts and insights through prayer,
brainstorming, and meditative reflection.

   a. How does this passage preach Christ?

      i. Is the emphasis on God's redemptive initiative, the
human response required, or both?

      ii. If God's saving work is central, how does the book
elsewhere point us to the appropriate response(s) on
our part?

      iii. If our response is central, how does the book reveal
its source in the saving grace of God?

   b. Consider both the continuity and the "distance" between the original readers' situation and ours.

      i. Are we in the *same redemptive-historical epoch* (be-
tween the accomplishment of redemption in Jesus'
death, resurrection, ascension and outpouring of
the Spirit, on the one hand, and the consummation

---

8   E.g., G. K. Beale, *The Temple and the Church's Mission: A Biblical Theology of
the Temple*; R. C. Ortlund, Jr. *God's Unfaithful Wife: A Biblical Theology of Spiritual
Adultery.*

of redemption in Jesus' parousia and the new heavens and earth, on the other), or did the original recipients live in an earlier epoch? Even within the new covenant era, the differences between the inauguration of the kingdom during Jesus' earthly ministry and the aftermath of his passion and exaltation should be considered. Likewise, in the post-Pentecost epoch there may be distinctions between the age of the apostles, when new covenant revelation was being given, and the subsequent era of the ongoing construction of the church on the foundation of that completed New Testament canon.

ii. If the first readers lived in a previous epoch of redemptive history, how does that affect the text's normativity for us?

(1) Shadows/types given to Israel are now fulfilled in Christ and dispelled, whether sacrificial, ceremonial, or civil/judicial.

(2) Our "how much more" privilege increases our spiritual accountability.

iii. Have socio-cultural factors changed? How will these affect your hearers' understanding of the text's message? How will they affect application? What "bridges" or analogies has God's providence "built into" our culture to facilitate your hearers' understanding the message?

iv. How does the text's occasion, initial problem, Fallen Condition Focus manifest itself in your situation and that of your hearers? E.g., what does "meat offered to idols" represent in a Western culture where butcher shops are not subsidiaries of idol temples?

v. Draw appropriate connections between the text's message and purpose in its original context and your hearers' experience and situation today (especially, of course, in the continuity of God's saving work in Christ).

c. Apply the text first to yourself: How must you respond to this part of God's Word in your thoughts, motives, attitudes, speech, and behavior?

d. What idolatrous habits of the heart does this text expose through its proclamation of law and gospel? How does it expose our tendency to "play God" by being *our own lawgiver* rather than submitting to God's holy law (self-indulgent antinomianism)? How does it expose our tendency to "play God" by being *our own savior* rather than submitting to God's grace in Christ (self-righteous legalism)?

e. How might this text be misunderstood and misused because of the "blind spots" we have absorbed from *our cultural legacy and generational biases*? How can these misunderstandings be counteracted in your proclamation?

f. In these questions you are "turning the corner" toward communication.

    i. *Initial preaching outline.* Reexamine your earlier theme statement, purpose statement, and outline of the text's structure (main points, sub-points), and rework them into a structure appropriate for preaching.

        (1) Express each point and subpoint in complete sentences. An outline in which each point/subpoint is expressed as a "topic" (a word or brief phrase) can help hearers recognize and remember the message's "milestones." But a topical outline may not enable you to discern whether you know what you are going to say about each topical point. Sentence outlines force you not only to list topics but also to articulate the assertions that you will make about the topics, the reasoning and evidence that you will use to support the assertions, and the interrelationship between topics that will give your sermon coherence and climax.

        (2) Make sure that your order of presentation helps hearers "track" coherently from what they know to what they don't know. Often the order of the text and its flow of thought can provide the structure for your order of presentation in the sermon. Letting your sermon follow the flow of the text whenever possible enables your

listeners to "find their bearings" as you preach, and to see that the message does in fact arise from the text of the Word of God. Sometimes, however, you may need to modify the order of your presentation from the order of the text, introducing a theme that occurs late in the text or in the surrounding context, either before or after, in order to help your hearers "get on the same page" with the understanding shared by the biblical author and his original hearers.

(3) Sometimes, if your hearers think they already know what the text has to say, your introduction should push them "off balance," magnifying "cognitive disequilibrium" and evoking in them a recognition that the text has depths they have not explored and a desire for deeper understanding.

(4) Strategically examine your abundance of material from your listeners' point of view. How much of this text's rich detail do your hearers need in order to hear the unique message of this particular text clearly? Which details (though fascinating to you) could be deleted, lest your hearers be overwhelmed with data and the main point obscured? Prune ruthlessly! Having dug up so many gems in your research, you may find it painful to leave any back in the study rather than carrying them all to the pulpit. But remember that your purpose is not merely to "dump data" into information receptacles; it is to speak God's Word in such a way that the glory and grace of Christ changes hearts and lives by his Spirit's sovereign power. (You can always save unused material for another sermon or other use.)

(5) Fill in by using illustrations and explanations, both to aid understanding and to impress vividly the message of the text, stealing past the "watchful dragons" of over-familiarity and

religious sentimentality (C. S. Lewis) to help your hearers feel the text's force full-strength.

(6) Anticipate and answer your hearers' likely misunderstandings, objections, and general confusion.

ii. *Manuscript.* From a clear and tight outline, write (word-process) *in full* what you intend to say. This discipline forces you to discover whether your exposition and application of the text unfolds as a consistent whole, or whether there are gaps in your reasoning or presentation that will distract or frustrate your hearers. Writing out your manuscript also forces you to work at communicating in fresh, vivid, concrete language rather than lapsing into clichés. Read the manuscript aloud to a friend, to discover places that your written English "doesn't work" as spoken English, and then revise.

iii. *Final Preaching Outline.* Condense the written manuscript into a tight outline, perhaps with carefully (but naturally) crafted wording embedded at crucial points (introduction, conclusion, complex theological or interpretive clarifications). Preach from this tight outline *rather than from a full manuscript.* Unless you are a *very* experienced speaker, reading a manuscript always breaks eye contact and thus, to some extent, the interpersonal connection between speaker and hearers. When you speak from an outline, you won't recall and recapture every literary "gem" that you worked and reworked in your written version, but what is lost in literary polish will be compensated for in warm, eye-to-eye, direct address to your hearers.

g. Pray.

i. For your hearers, that God's Spirit will open their hearts to welcome his Word in faith and obedience.

ii. For yourself, that God will give you the grace to forget your "image" and instead get wrapped up in delivering his message as a faithful steward.

h. Preach Christ!

Appendix B
Sample Sermons in the Trajectory of Apostolic, Christ-Centered Preaching

The discussions of Old Testament and New Testament texts in chapters 9 and 10 offer many hints of the ways in which the reading of the Scriptures in light of their focus on Jesus the Christ would bear fruit in preaching. Readers may still wonder, however, what the end product would be when a pastor has tried to follow the route "From Text to Sermon" laid out in Appendix A. Here are two sample sermons, one from the Old Testament and one from the New, that serve to illustrate how I have tried to apply the principles and methods that have been presented in this book. Both of the texts below are closer to full manuscripts than the notes from which I typically preach, but they retain here and there features that reflect the character of preaching as oral communication (rather than polished literary art).

There cannot be a single "template" to which every redemptive-historical, Christ-centered, audience-adapted sermon conforms. Variation in the character and gifts of the preacher, in the maturity and needs of the congregation, and in the distinctive features of a particular occasion will yield great variety in the sermon's form and tone, in the balance of textual exposition, contemporary illustration, and focused application, and in other features. But these messages will give a taste of what preaching in the trajectory of the apostles' proclamation of Christ might sound like.

Milestones, Memory Stones
Joshua 4

This sermon was preached to New Life Presbyterian Church in Escondido, California, the congregation whom I serve as an associate pastor, on the next-to-last day of 2001. I know this congregation well, and they know me, inasmuch as our family has belonged to New Life since 1982, and I served as its interim pastor for twenty months in 1999–2001. Our celebration of the incarnation of Christ had occurred in the preceding week. Television news retrospectives over 2001 were full of the horrifying images of the fiery destruction of the World Trade Towers in New York City, which had occurred on September 11, less than four months before. Security at airports remained extremely tight. At the same time, New Life was experiencing God's refreshing blessing through the ministry of our newly installed pastor, Ted Hamilton, who had begun his ministry among us by leading a specially called gathering for prayer on September 11. This sermon was not an installment of a lectio continua series, but rather a single message preached as our pastor and his family enjoyed a brief, well-earned vacation. (Scripture quotations are from the New International Version, which we use in our services at New Life.)

The end of a year always calls us to look backward and to look forward. As we celebrate the birth of Christ, we hear ancient promises that God made through Israelite prophets—"to us a child is born, to us a son is given"—and we hear the angel's message to the shepherds, good news about something new in human history: a Savior, who is Christ the Lord, is born in Bethlehem—the opening of a new era in the world's story, turning the plot from despair into hope.

And then we come to New Year's Day, just a week after Christmas, and our whole society looks back over the past year as well as looking ahead to 2002. This year, especially, we look back on a fatal Tuesday in September, scarred by a catastrophe beyond anything we would have imagined or believed, if some psychic had predicted it on January 1, 2001.

Perhaps, as you look back over the year, you see personal or family triumphs or sorrows that will forever mark the closing year as a turning point in your life. Perhaps, as you try to peer ahead into 2002, you see threats looming on the horizon—illness, unemployment, grief. Or you have expectations of great joy—a birth, a graduation, a wedding.

New Year's Day is a good time to look back and to look ahead. That's why January is named after Janus, the Roman god with two faces—one looking backward and one looking forward, one looking inward and one looking outward.

But, too often, we miss the opportunity to look inward that this milestone in our time provides us. We Americans are doers, not meditators. Our own instincts and our culture encourage us to go to great lengths to avoid introspection—to fill the milestones of our lives with entertainment, diversions, and distractions, rather than using them as opportunities to remember, reflect, and refocus our hearts on things of lasting significance.

Did you have some "down time," some quiet time, over the Christmas holidays, amid good food and gift exchanges and family gatherings, to pause and ponder what God has done and what difference it makes as you move past the milestone that divides 2001 from 2002? If not, it's not too late!

Now that some of the "dust is settling" from Christmas celebrations, perhaps today or tomorrow (between parades and bowl games), you can find the time—better, make the time—to be still, step back a few steps, and get perspective on your life—to look back and to look ahead.

If you are a Christian, you have good reason to look back in thankfulness (no matter how many troubles you have faced since last Christmas), and you have good reason to look ahead in hope (no matter how many threats loom on your horizon).

If you are not a Christian, you, too, have much to be thankful to God for (whether you feel it or not this morning), and you can have a future worth remembering and celebrating. This text from the ancient book of Joshua, which may sound strange at first reading, shows us how we can connect with the God who has both our past and our future, our joys and our sorrows, in his strong hand.

In fact, as we heard at the end of this passage, the Lord God did what he did for Israel at the Jordan and insisted that Israel remember it "so that *all the peoples* of the earth might know that the hand of the Lord is powerful" (vs. 24). Do you know this? I mean, does your heart deeply believe it, when circumstances seem to say the opposite?

When we discover this truth and surrender control of our lives to this strong God, we find him turning the milestones of our lives into memory stones—reminders of his faithfulness and love—which move us to gratitude and confidence.

The Bible takes very seriously the fact that we live our lives *through time*—not a half-hour sitcom but an epic drama that stretches over hours and days and years. And the God who gave us the Bible knows very well that our memories grow hazy over time. So God constantly embeds in the lives of his people—in our environment of time and space—memorials, monuments, objects (like the rainbow), and observances (like the Lord's Supper) to jog our memory.

In his *New Life Lines* article for December, Ted mentioned the original "Ebenezer"—not Ebenezer Scrooge but the "Stone of Help" that Samuel set up to remind the people of Israel how the Lord had helped them defeat their enemies the Philistines. His reflections there got me thinking about Joshua's pile of twelve "Ebenezers" at an earlier point in history. Long before Joshua, Jacob set up a stone at Bethel ("house of God"), marking the place that God came down and made amazing promises (Gen. 28).

Israel's crossing of the Jordan occurred centuries before the birth of Jesus, after the Israelites had wandered forty years in the Sinai desert, and virtually the whole generation to escape from Egypt under Moses had died. This historical narrative of the pile of memory stones on the Jordan's west bank shows us three factors that go into God's plan to turn our milestones into memory stones of his faithfulness, mercy and power:

1. An event worth remembering,
2. People who forget,
3. A monument that keeps on reminding.

1. An Event Worth Remembering (vv. 1, 6–7, 21–24)

I have in my hand a "memory stone" to remind me of a great event of salvation in our family's life: a sheered-off wheel bolt, with lug nut still attached. I picked it up from the shoulder by the fast lane on Interstate 15, one Christmas Eve many years ago. Our family had been driving north to enjoy family Christmas at my brother's and sister-in-law's home near L.A., when suddenly our hubcap popped off, and the car felt as if it had a flat tire. I pulled from the fast lane into the wide center median on a stretch north of Lake Elsinore and checked the tires. We didn't have a flat—all four were inflated just fine—but no bolts, no lug nuts were holding the right rear tire to the drum and axle. When the tow truck driver from Corona came to our rescue, he said that the last time he saw that happen to a car, the tire had lodged in the wheel well and flipped the whole car on its roof. "You were lucky," he said. "Well, God was looking out for us," I replied.

That is an event worth remembering, and I keep this fragment of bolt and lug nut in my dresser drawer and pull it out from time to time is to remind me how the Lord Jesus kept our car from flipping and actually got us to our family celebration of his birth only a few hours late. That bolt looks like junk, I admit. Anybody who didn't know what had actually happened that afternoon on I-15 would have thrown it away years ago. But our family knows that it actually happened—to us. As ugly and insignificant as that piece of metal is, it is a beautiful reminder of the power and care of our God.

But the piles of stones on Jordan's west bank and in its riverbed commemorated an *even more wonderful act of God*—in fact, a whole series of miraculous events by which the Lord brought a people who had been slaves into a land that they could call home, put down roots, raise families.

This conquest is actually the third memorable event that Israelite children were going to ask about in the generations to come.

The first was the *exodus* from slavery to the Egyptians. The exodus was commemorated annually in the Passover Feast, which was to be observed on the fourteenth day of the first month—just four days after this Jordan crossing! (Josh. 4:19; 5:10). In fact, according to the Law, the very evening of their crossing over to the Jordan's west bank, every Israelite household was to designate a lamb to be slaughtered four days later, when its blood was to be spread on the door frame of their house (or tent) and its meat roasted and eaten with unleavened bread and bitter herbs. And the Lord told them to anticipate that this strange and solemn meal each year would raise questions in their children's minds and mouths:

> "When you enter the land that the Lord will give you as he promised, observe this ceremony. And when your children ask you, 'What does this ceremony mean to you?' then tell them, 'It is the Passover sacrifice to the LORD, who passed over the houses of the Israelites in Egypt and spared our homes when he struck down the Egyptians.' " (Ex. 12:25–27)

The exodus was also to be recounted in answer to children's questions concerning the redemption of Israel's firstborn sons. Whereas the firstborn offspring of animals were to be sacrificed at the sanctuary, the Israelites' sons were bought back from that penalty of death, in remembrance of the night when the Lord spared his people's firstborn but slew those of their pagan slave masters:

> "In days to come, when your son asks you, 'What does this mean?' say to him, 'With a mighty hand the LORD brought us out of Egypt, out of the land of slavery. When Pharaoh stubbornly refused to let us go, the LORD killed every firstborn in Egypt, both man and animal. This is why I sacrifice to the LORD the first male offspring of every womb and redeem each of my firstborn sons.' And it will be like a sign on your hand and a symbol on your forehead that the LORD brought us out of Egypt with his mighty hand." (Ex. 13:14–16)

The second great event that would be remembered through the questions of Israel's children was *the giving of the Law at Mount Sinai*:

> In the future, when your son asks you, "What is the meaning of the stipulations, decrees and laws the LORD our God has commanded you?" tell him: "We were slaves of Pharaoh in Egypt, but the LORD brought us out of Egypt with a mighty hand.... He brought us out from there to bring us in and give us the land that he promised on oath to our forefathers. The LORD commanded us to obey all these decrees and to fear the LORD our God, so that we might always prosper and be kept alive, as is the case today." (Deut. 6:20–24)

The Law itself was a stimulus to recall and recite the liberating power of the Lord, setting his people free from enslavement to human masters.

So the Passover (the sacrifice in place of every firstborn child) and the commands of the Law themselves were designed to raise questions so that kids' incredible curiosity would give parents the opening, and the reminder, to teach them that the Lord had spared them from death, *set them free* from slavery, and that in his Law he had shown how to use their freedom to experience full life and joy.

And now the pile of stones by the Jordan would provide another "teaching moment" for parents. "Every time you ford the river here and your kids ask how those rocks got stacked up like that, tell them how the Lord himself acted to bring Israel into the homeland he promised—a place of security to grow crops and raise children."

And it must have been the Lord! The "first month" here is the month Nisan in the spring, at the end of the rainy season, when the Jordan is so full it overflows its banks. In fact, in Joshua 3:15 it is pointed out that the Jordan was a flood stage, and after Israel had crossed the dry riverbed and the priests carrying the ark stepped onto the West Bank, the Jordan again was so full that it overflowed its banks (4:18). It might be possible to ford the Jordan in September, after summer's drought, but to cross it on dry ground in March or April would take an act of God himself!

And yet, that astonishing and memorable event pales in significance when compared with another event later in history. The Israelites had been freed from slavery to the Egyptians, but too many of them were still enslaved to the fears and desires of their own stubborn hearts. They had life-giving direction in God's commands, but they did not trust him enough to obey him. They had entered the homeland that he had promised, but because of their own unfaithfulness, they themselves would not enjoy peace and security there, and their children would eventually be evicted from the land—carried off into captivity by pagan powers.

We who trust Jesus Christ have been set free in an even greater *exodus*, have been bound to God in a greater *covenant* than Sinai's Law, and have tasted a greater *homeland* than Canaan.

Political and economic slavery, as miserable as it is, is not the worst form of bondage. We all know people who are "free to do what they want" (and Americans are thankful for such freedom), yet those same people are hemmed in, driven by lusts or fears or habits that they cannot break out of. The whole Bible points to the coming of Jesus the Messiah, who would set us free from the slaveries of our hearts—the paralysis and blindness that keeps us chained in patterns that ruin our lives and the lives of others. He came to lead us in a greater exodus, to establish a greater covenant than the Law that God gave to Moses on Mt. Sinai, and finally to bring us into a more secure homeland than the one that Joshua was leading Israel into. But more of that in a few moments!

2. People Who Forget

God is a realist. He designed us to live through time, and he knows that our memories tend to dim with age. In fact, that is not only true of individuals, but it is also true across the generations:

if we don't teach our children what our parents taught us, and what we have learned since, we have no reason to expect that they will somehow learn it on their own! My grandfather was a carpenter and building contractor. My father inspected houses under construction and does beautiful woodworking. As I've struggled with wood a little, I wish I had worked alongside him on his Saturday projects more than I did. I'm sure he would have been happy to have me watching at his elbow, but I didn't ask, and he didn't force me to listen and look and learn, and skills that produced masterpieces of craftsmanship have been virtually dissipated in two generations. The danger of forgetfulness is even more real in spiritual matters for several reasons, which the Lord anticipated as he was leading Israel into the land that he promised them.

First, we face distractions from *enemies* (vv. 12–13). Now, there are many things that make us forget the great things that the Lord has done. One of them is implied quite clearly in this text: Israel was going into the land of promise, the path opened by the Lord himself, but there were enemies ahead. Verses 12–13 remind us that this triumphal entry into the land was just a prelude to conflict: the two and a half tribes crossed over armed . . . "40,000 armed for battle . . . for war."

When God has done something remarkable for us—as he did for our family on Interstate 15 that Christmas Eve—why is it that we don't "get the message" and trust his good plan from there on out. Within a week of our amazing "rescue" north of Lake Elsinore, I was lamenting to my mom on the phone that the repair shop in Corona could not get the rest of the bolts out of the brake drum, and the repair costs might break our budget, to which my mom told her son (who was supposed to be the teacher of theology and trainer of pastors): "Now, Dennis, the Lord has these things in control, you know." (Ouch! That was supposed to be my line!)

What are the "enemies" that threaten to distract your memory and attention from the Lord's many tokens of love and demonstrations of power in your life? Sickness? Financial fears? Interpersonal friction?

We are also distracted by *prosperity* (Deut. 8:10–14, 17). Israel faced—and we face—an even more dangerous enemy than our enemies: our *success*. When the conquest that was about to begin had been concluded at the end of Joshua's life, then Israel was *really* in danger of forgetting, really in need of this pile of stones to jog their memories.

Moses had already warned that our memories can grow sluggish not because of our enemies but *because of our pleasures.*

> When you have eaten and are satisfied, praise the LORD your God for the good land he has given you. Be careful that you *do not forget the LORD your God*, failing to observe his commands, his laws and his decrees that I am giving you this day. Otherwise, when you eat and are satisfied, when you build fine houses and settle down, and when your herds and flocks grow large and your silver and gold increase and all you have is multiplied, then *your heart will become proud and you will forget the LORD your God*, who brought you out of Egypt, out of the land of slavery. He led you through the vast and dreadful desert. . . . You may say to yourself, "My power and the strength of my hands have produced this wealth for me." (Deut. 8:10–14, 17)

And Joshua knew that this would happen to the people of his generation. At the end of his life, he built another monument—a single stone at Shechem that, as Joshua put it, had listened to God's promises to them and to their promises to be loyal to the Lord forever. Joshua told them bluntly,

> "You are not able to serve the LORD. He is a holy God; he is a jealous God. He will not forgive your rebellion and your sins. If you forsake the LORD and serve foreign gods, he will turn and bring disaster on you and make an end of you . . . This stone will be a witness against us. It has heard all the words the LORD has said to us. It will be a witness against you if you are untrue to your God." (Josh. 24:19–27)

Has the answer to your prayers ever caused you to forget the God who answered you? You work hard for a grade or a promotion, and finally it comes. Who gets the credit? People admire your children. Who gets the glory? You prayed and pled with God for a good outcome to a crisis. Do you thank and praise him with equal vigor when he says, "Yes"?

It would be easy for us to stand back in shock at the Israelites' forgetfulness and to say to ourselves, "If *we* had walked as toddlers through the Red Sea at our parents' side, eaten manna for forty years, drunk water springing from dry rocks, and walked across the dry riverbed of the Jordan in flood season, surely *we* would not forget, surely *we* would not fail to pass the good news down to *our* children!" Oh, really? Why, precisely, do you think the Lord Jesus commanded us to observe his Supper regularly and frequently?

3. A Monument that Goes On Reminding

This monument of mute stones actually bore eloquent testimony to the grace and power of our God. The stones said, first of all, "The Lord is your Rescuer and Rest-Giver."

Joshua actually built two pillars of twelve stones each: one on the west bank (4:20), with the boulders carried by the muscle men representing Israel's twelve tribes, and the other in the riverbed itself (4:9). (The NIV translates vs. 9 as if the narrator is looking ahead to vs. 20, but the Hebrew says, "Joshua set up twelve stones in the midst of the Jordan, at the spot where the priests who carried the ark stood.")

Both piles were *set apart as holy* by the feet of the priests who carried the ark of the Lord (4:5), which is also called the ark of the covenant of the Lord (4:7) and the ark of the testimony (4:16). This "ark" is a wooden box, plated with gold. Inside were mementos of God's love and commitment to Israel, including the stone tablets of the Law given to Moses at Sinai and a jar of the manna bread by which he had fed them for forty years in the desert. On the top of the ark were golden statues of two majestic, winged cherubim, awesome attendants of God in his heavenly court. And between the cherubim, under their outstretched wings . . . *nothing*—only an empty golden throne. The Creator of the universe, who in condescending grace stooped down to become the God of Israel, *could not be pictured*: he is bigger and more mysterious than his creatures in every way.

Yet, the ark did represent the Lord's throne in the midst of his people—the holiest symbol of the commitment of the Lord to be with his weak, unworthy people.

> Why was it, O sea, that you fled,
>   O Jordan, that you turned back? . . .
> Tremble, O earth, at the presence of the LORD,
>   at the presence of the God of Jacob! (Ps. 114:5, 7)

Every time a Jewish father and his son, a Jewish mother and her daughter, walked past Gilgal and the child asked, "What's with this pile of rocks?" they were reminded that they lived in the land of promise not because they were so strong or clever in battle but because the Lord himself had erased the obstruction, had dried up the barrier that stood between his people and their homeland. God himself stopped the flooding flow of the Jordan.

Secondly, the stones bore witness to the means by which God rescues and gives rest to those who rely on him. The stones said, "The Lord rescues and gives you rest *through the blood of atonement.*"

Look again at the top of the ark of the covenant and the throne between the cherubim. Do you see the stains that cover the gold plating? For the last forty years the ark had been seen by the Israelites only at a distance, when the Lord gave Israel marching orders and the priests carried it out of the tent of meeting to lead the march through the desert. Between those times, the only person to see the ark was the high priest on the Day of Atonement, and even he could see it only through the heavy smoke of incense that filled the holiest chamber of the tent. His job, on that terrifying and momentous day each fall, was to sprinkle blood on the throne—the atonement cover, some versions translate it, or the "mercy seat," as the KJV puts it.

Those blood drops dried there; no one could actually touch the ark to wipe them off, or he would die instantly. So now the ark has forty years of spilt blood on the point that most closely pictures God's presence with people.

Why was it so crucial that twelve stones be taken from under the ark and another twelve piled up in the riverbed where the ark had stood? Because Israel was to remember that their safe entrance into the homeland that God promised—their triumph over the threatening waters of judgment—came through the blood of a flawless Substitute, who covered their sins from the holy sight of God, and washed away their guilt.

But the blood of animals, no matter how physically perfect and unblemished they were, could not really remove our human guilt. The ark itself, in fact, would eventually be lost, and the temple that replaced the Tent of Meeting would eventually be destroyed.

They were all pointing ahead to a new champion—a better Joshua (for Joshua is the Jewish way to say Jesus: "The Lord saves"). He would shed his blood, though he was innocent and perfect, upright and pure. The blood-stained ark and the piles of stones that commemorated its victory over the river waters were pointing ahead to the cross of Jesus on a hill outside Jerusalem. That ark and those stones were saying to one generation after another not only that the Lord is the champion who can defeat our enemies but also that he would win the final victory through the blood of suffering, because our greatest enemy is not something or someone outside us but our own stubborn and foolish hearts—leading to our own guilt and shame.

And we have a better memorial, a more eloquent monument of remembrance, than the stack of stones beside the Jordan or the stack of stones that showed its top out of the river's water in the dry season: we have the Lord's Supper, established by Jesus himself, less than twenty-four hours before he would give himself in our place. As we enter a new year, 2002, next Sunday, we will return to that monument that reminds us, over and over, that the living God became one of us to shed his own human blood to conquer our greatest enemy and bring us home to himself.

So how should we respond? Our text makes that plain in verses 14 and 24.

4. **The reminders that God builds into our lives call us to fear and to testify: to *fear the Lord and our great Joshua* and to *let the peoples of the earth know* how powerful he is.**

A. *To Fear*

That day the Lord exalted Joshua, so the people revered (feared, were in awe of) Joshua all the days of his life. (Josh. 4:14)

He did this . . . so that you might always fear the Lord your God. (Josh. 4:24)

Fear is never a pleasant feeling—what we fear makes us feel small, insecure, vulnerable, not in control. So it's natural for us to assume that all fear is bad and to try to avoid it at all costs. We shield ourselves from fear by cynicism and sarcasm and the distractions and diversions that we try to pack into our empty hours—even, or especially, at holidays—so we can avoid thinking about who we are as God, who sees the heart, sees us.

Some kinds of fear certainly are bad, or perhaps I should say, there are some things and people who don't deserve the fear we lavish on them.

But there are some things—some persons—worth fearing. God himself, for instance, as verse 24 says: it's actually healthy and realistic to realize that in his awesome presence we *are* small, vulnerable, not in control. If we have no fear of God, such numbness is a symptom not of well-being but of impending death (like feeling warm just before you freeze to death!).

And here Joshua is grouped with God as one worthy of the people's fear, just as Moses had been. Neither of them had earned this by their own power or piety—they were just men—but both were given the privilege of providing a preview of the ultimate Joshua, Jesus, who is God himself. Respecting our leaders, honoring our elders, treasuring our pastor—these are appropriate implications of a healthy fear of the Lord himself—an awestruck discovery of his majesty, might, and mercy, not only at the Jordan but also in Christ's cross and empty tomb.

B. To Testify

> He did this so that *all the peoples of the earth might know* that the hand of the Lord is powerful. (Josh. 4:24)

The Lord loved Israel, but his love is not limited to Israel. Actually, he had chosen Abraham centuries before, specifically so that through Abraham's descendants—and especially the one descendant Jesus—*all the nations of the earth* could taste the Lord's kindness and power. His love is a restless, overflowing love that keeps reaching out to people who have tried to live their lives without him—to their own frustration and misery.

And he is still doing that today. If you are a Christian, remember that Jesus, your champion, embeds milestones of his power and grace into your life, not only to keep you remembering who he is and what he's done but also to move you to share the news with others. Turn your life's milestones not only into memory stones for yourself and your children but also into stones of witness to the world's peoples, with whom you rub shoulders every day.

If you are not a Christian, and always assumed that faith in Jesus was fine for others but that God was as uninterested in you as you have been in him, Joshua's memory stones—and even more so, the cross of Christ, which Christians remember every time we partake of the Lord's Supper—tell you good news: You are wrong! The Lord who created the universe and you doesn't bottle up his grace in a single nation or a single kind of people ("religious people," who naturally gravitate toward prayer and preaching and rituals). No, he wants all kinds of people to know his power and love—more than that, to experience it by surrendering your independence and trusting in his promises.

Begin your new year by believing in Jesus, and every New Year's Day from here on will be a monument to an event worth remembering for all eternity: when the new Joshua, Jesus Christ, brought you out of the desert of your self-reliance and into his family to join the heirs of his heavenly homeland.

An Ever-Living, Never-Leaving Leader
Hebrews 13:5–14

In God's providence, I have been invited to preach to several churches in southern California soon after the pastor of each congregation had been called to another pulpit. In each of these situations, the reassurance that the author (preacher) to the Hebrews brought to a first-century church that had undergone significant changes in leadership, as well as other unsettling changes, conveyed comfort and hope to contemporary Christian communities who were facing similar transitions. Biblical texts cited at various points in the sermon were commented on more fully than this manuscript suggests, but I decided to leave this "manuscript" more in the "bullet point," semi-outline form that I actually use in the pulpit. Again, Scripture citations are from the NIV.

Change is an unchanging reality in our lives. We cannot count how many times we have heard the thought in the last months: "Since September 11, 2001, our world has changed forever." Or, "Our sense of security will never be the same again." Change shakes us out of our comfort zone and brings us face to face with the truth that we don't know as much as we thought we did about what to expect from the future or how to respond to changing situations.

This is true not only of traumatic world changes, such as the destruction of the World Trade Towers and the mounting of the war on terrorism, but also of the everyday changes of life.

Many changes are exciting: baby's first steps, first words, first school day (though that can be scary, too), first romance, driver's license, graduation, marriage, first real job, birth of children, and on it goes. Other changes are not so welcome: first broken heart, losing a job, a cross-country move away from friends and family, economic recession, grown children leaving home for college or career, life-threatening illness, the death of a loved one.

I still remember the nightmares during the summer before I entered high school—and that was a *long* time ago! I had never been in a school where students went from classroom to classroom for different subjects, and I would dream that I couldn't remember my locker number or my locker combination, or I would end up in algebra when I was supposed to be in English or history. In elementary school, I had missed most field trips because my stomach was so upset with the stress of any change in routine!

Your congregation recently experienced the sad change of bidding farewell to your pastor as he accepted a call to pastor another church. In times of leadership transition, it is very natural for us to wonder, "What's to become of our congregation now? What will the new pastor be like? How can we get through the transition?"

Now you may thrive on change and get bored with the same old thing, but all kinds of change—pleasant and painful—brings certain levels of *stress*. Psychologists have even given point rankings to the stress caused by different kinds of change: wedding, birth of a baby, moving, starting or losing a job, divorce, life-threatening disease, etc. If we rack up enough change-stress points, they say, whether the changes are happy or traumatic, our emotional equilibrium starts to go into "melt-down."

That was what was happening to the Hebrew Christians who originally received this letter in the first century. They had already experienced the change *from temple-centered worship to Jesus-centered worship.* They had grown up in Judaism, centered in its temple in Jerusalem—the one special place on earth where, in keeping with his promise through Moses, God had placed his name (Deut. 12). That worship was carried out through things you could see and touch. You knew that there had been a sacrifice for sins because you had brought a sheep or a calf and watched the priest slaughter it. You had seen the beauty of the priests' robes, smelled the incense offered on the altar, marveled at the great stones and the gold plating of the temple's architecture.

But now they were virtually locked out of the temple because they were following Jesus—that's what verses 12–13 are referring to: "Jesus suffered outside the city gate to make you holy through his blood, so now you must gladly go to him outside the camp, bearing the disgrace he bore." The leaders of Judaism rejected him, so now you must be willing to be treated as outsiders—disgraced and excluded because you are trusting in him.

But what did that mean for their worship? No golden altar, no majestic temple, no priests with rich vestments, no shed blood to tell them that their sins had been covered. Now they meet in homes, and their faith is fed not on what they see and touch but on the *Word of God*, which their pastors and elders have taught them (vs. 7). Apart from the water of baptism and the bread and wine of the Lord's Supper, their faith was to feed and grow strong not on visible, touchable things, but through what they heard—the good news about Jesus Christ, the final sacrifice and the forever priest who prays for his people at God's right hand in heaven.

They had also experienced change with respect to *family and friendships*. The disgrace no doubt also impacted relationships with family members who had not become Christians. If the leaders of the Jewish community were shutting out Jewish people, such as the first readers of this letter, because they had come to believe that Jesus is the Messiah, it is no surprise that their parents or siblings—or even husband or wife—who did not trust in Jesus would keep them at arms' length, too.

In 11:24–26 we read that Moses chose the disgrace of Christ as of greater value than the treasures of Egypt, which would have been his as the adopted son of Pharaoh's daughter. He identified with the Israelite slaves and threw away the perks of privilege, the security he could have had as a prince of Egypt, because "he was looking ahead to his reward"—he trusted God's promises about a better inheritance to come and in the process lost the perks of the royal family and former friends.

Maybe you have experienced this "disgrace" if you are the only Christian in your family—the tension and strained relationships, maybe even the accusation that you have become disloyal to your family and your heritage by coming to trust in Jesus Christ.

The stress, pain, and pressures produced by their "change of allegiance" from the temple to Jesus had almost reached the breaking point. But actually, they needed to understand that they had not really changed allegiances, whatever the leaders of Judaism might say. The truth was that God had designed the temple and all its rituals to point his people forward to Christ; the sacrificial animals were "shadows of the good things to come" (10:1).

Still, they were tempted to turn back to the old ways—the ways you could see and touch—for getting near to God in order to find a sense of security in the midst of their changing world, and that is the reason this letter was written: to assure them (and us) that we have a more secure source of security in Jesus—more secure than anything the visible, touchable temple, or anything else in this visible, touchable world, can offer.

On top of these other changes, the congregation that first received this letter was facing changes in *leadership* from one generation of pastors to the next. We pick up the clue to this transition as we compare Hebrews 13:7 and 17:

> *Remember* your leaders who *spoke* the word of God to you. (vs. 7)
>
> *Obey* your leaders and *submit to their authority.* They keep watch over you as men who must give an account. (vs. 17)

The first generation is gone. They no longer speak the word to these Christians, but they are not to be forgotten. The next generation is on the job, keeping watch. But apparently they are not receiving the cooperation and respect from the congregation that their office and responsibility deserve. Maybe people are comparing "the good old days" with Pastor X with the fact that the present pastor and elders don't "do things the way we have always done them." For whatever reason, this change of leadership is part of the mix that has thrown these Christians for a loop.

So God shows them and us in this text how we should *not* respond to change and how we *should.* We will *not* handle life's changes well if we:

1. Retreat from change by clinging to the past.
2. Try to insulate ourselves from change through money.

Instead, we need to *focus our thoughts and rest our hearts on Jesus,* our ever-living, never-leaving leader. Let's examine more deeply first the wrong ways and then the only right way to respond to change.

1. **Resist the tempting responses that *cannot really help* us cope with change.**

Retreating from change by clinging to the past is the first useless response to change that the author to the Hebrews exposes.

> It is good for our hearts to be strengthened by grace, not by ceremonial foods, which are of no value to those who eat them. We have an altar from which those who minister at the tabernacle have no right to eat. (Heb. 13:9–10)

The ceremonial foods are the meat of sacrificed animals, especially the "peace offering," which Israelite worshipers would eat in the temple courtyard after the best parts were consumed by fire on the altar of burnt offering. So this is one more reference to the temptation that the author to the Hebrews has been concerned about through the whole letter: "Don't go back into the shadows of Old Testament worship," to a touchable sanctuary and Levitical priests who die and have to be replaced and animal sacrifices that have to be repeated over and over, because the blood of bulls and goats cannot really cleanse anyone's conscience, cannot wash away our guilt before God."

Back in chapters 3–4, God warned the Hebrew Christians not to be like the wilderness generation of Israel after the exodus, who immediately wanted to run back to Egypt when the going got tough in the desert and their faith in God's promises wavered. How soon they forgot the miseries of Egyptian slavery—the sweat and the whip and the aching muscles from building Pharaoh's great cities as his slave labor force! "We remember the fish we ate in Egypt at no cost— and cucumbers, melons, leeks, onions, and garlic." (Num. 14:1ff). Ah, Egypt—the good old days!

When are your "good old days," your "wonder years," the time that lives in your memory as a time without problems when everything went right? High school? College? Our hazy memory can sometime paint a rosy glow around the past and airbrush away the sorrows, but the truth is that since Adam and Eve rebelled against God in the Garden of Eden, there never have been any true "good old days" in the history of our fallen, sin-cursed human race. The only really good days lie in the future, as vs. 14 shows us: "for here we do not have an enduring city, but we are seeking the one to come." When the Hebrew Christians first received this letter, Jerusalem would soon lie in ruins, its glorious temple dismantled stone by stone by the Roman armies commanded by General Titus.

So don't look back to the past, and don't simply cling to its traditions: there is no security from the threatening changes of the present to be found back there!

Trying to *insulate ourselves from change through money* (or other forms of power) is equally misguided and destined for frustration.

> Keep your lives free from the love of money and be content with what you have, because God has said,
>> "Never will I leave you;
>>> never will I forsake you."
>
> So we say with confidence,
>> "The Lord is my helper. I will not be afraid.
>>> What can man do to me?" (Heb. 13:5–6)

People love money for many reasons: the pleasures it can buy, the popularity it can rent (for a while). But here God warns against loving money as a *source of security*—because money cannot say to you what God does: "Never will I leave you, never will I forsake you."

In the midst of rapid, life-shaking changes, we look around for something to shield us from the winds and waves of uncertainty that beat on our hearts. It's tempting to think that money can be that shield: it can buy a club for the car's steering wheel or a car alarm that keeps your neighbors awake at midnight, a home in a gated community, a bodyguard. With enough money in the right places, you may not have to fear a stock market crash; you might even be able to buy a treatment for cancer that brings a cure. But it cannot last forever.

One of Jesus' parables (Luke 12:13–21) illustrates this vividly. A farmer's land bears bumper crops—no place to store so much grain. "I'll build bigger barns, then say to myself, 'Relax and celebrate! You have savings to keep you secure for years to come. Eat, drink, party!' But God said, 'Fool! Tonight I'm calling in your loan—your life.' " That night he suffered a massive heart attack from too much cholesterol, and he was gone.

Other people replace the idol of money with other idols: friendship or romance, for example. F. Scott Fitzgerald, American novelist and playwright of the twentieth century, once observed: "It is in the thirties that we want friends. In the forties we know they won't save us any more than love did." And he was dead at forty-four. Don't look to *friends* or *love* for salvation, for safety; don't look to *money*. Is there nowhere to look, then?

2. Build your trust—rest your restless heart—on Jesus, the ever living, never-leaving Leader.

A. Jesus Is an Ever-Living Leader.

Jesus Christ is the same yesterday and today and forever. (Heb. 13:8)

Notice that this immediately follows the reminder about the church's leaders who have passed from the scene. They are gone, but Jesus is not.

*1. Jesus is the same **yesterday**.*

Jesus is the same *yesterday* . . . when he *created the universe*:

[God says to his Son]:
 "In the beginning, O Lord, you laid the foundations of the earth,
  and the heavens are the work of your hands.
 They will perish, but you remain;
  they will all wear out like a garment . . . .
 But you remain *the same*,
  and your years will never end." (1:10–12; cf. Ps. 102)

Jesus is the same *yesterday* . . . when he *endured temptation on earth*:

We have a high priest who can sympathize with our weaknesses because he was tempted in every way as we are tempted, yet without sin (cf. Heb. 4:14–16). He remembers what it is like to face threatening change!

Jesus is the same *yesterday* . . . when he *gave his life* to cleanse our guilt *and rose again* to be our eternal Protector and Priest:

The God of peace brought up from the dead the great Shepherd of the sheep, our Lord Jesus, through the blood of the eternal covenant (Heb. 13:20–21). He shed his blood to make an unbreakable bond between us and the Father; he rose again to be our Shepherd who always guards us.

*2. Jesus is the same **today**.*

Jesus is the same *today* . . . as he constantly *prays* for us:

"He is able to save completely and forever those who come to God through him, because he always lives to intercede for them" (Heb. 7:25). Night and day, year in and year out.

Your former pastor still prays for you, as he did when he shepherded many of you. But Jesus' prayers are more constant, more compassionate, wiser, and more effective.

Jesus is the same *today* . . . as he *preaches* to us:

Today, if you hear his voice, do not harden your hearts. (Heb. 4:7)

"See to it that you do not refuse him who speaks. If [the Israelites with Moses] did not escape when they refused him who warned them on earth [at Sinai], how much less will we, if we turn away from him who warns from heaven?" (Heb. 12:25). Through our pastors and teachers and leaders, the Lord Jesus is speaking to us from heaven in his Word, calling us to persevere in our faith and promising the presence and power of his Holy Spirit to give us strength to last.

3. Jesus is the same **forever**.

Jesus leads us into the future: the enduring city to come (Heb. 13:14) is the heavenly Jerusalem, the city of the living God, where Jesus stands at the center as mediator of the new covenant (Heb. 12:22–24).

Because Jesus is the pioneer and perfecter of our faith, change is not our enemy but our servant, carrying us toward the finish line where Jesus stands, having victoriously finished his race, and he has secured *our* victory as well (12:1–3). With his encouragement, we can take hope for the future and keep running.

But it would not be much comfort to know that Jesus lives forever and never changes—always "the same"—if we could not get close enough to him so that his eternal strength would anchor and stabilize us when change pushes us off balance. We also need him to be, as he promises to be . . .

B. Jesus Is a Never-Leaving Leader.

"Never will I leave you,
    never will I forsake you." (Heb. 13:5)

Here we hear his promise to be with us, no matter what—he will never leave us. Hebrews is echoing the promise that God made to people of faith in earlier generations, in troubled times:

Genesis 28:15: To Jacob on the run, fearing for his life from his own brother, God speaks at Bethel: "I am with you and will watch over you wherever you go . . . I will not leave you until I have done what I have promised you."

Joshua 1:5: To Joshua, with a country to conquer: "As I was with Moses, so I will be with you; I will never leave you nor forsake you."

Matthew 28:20: To the apostles, with a world to win with the gospel: "I am with you always, to the very end of the age."

How fitting that Matthew's gospel should end with this tremendous promise on the lips of Jesus, since it opened with the amazing prophetic promise of Isaiah, "The virgin will be with child and will give birth to a son, and they will call him Immanuel"—which means, 'God with us' " (Matt. 1:23; see Isa. 7:14). Jesus' birth of the Virgin Mary was God's making good on that ancient promise, "Never will I leave you, never will I forsake you. I will be God with you, through thick and thin, forever and ever."

And Jesus' presence with is not merely a matter of his commiserating with us in helplessness, holding our hand, and wishing with us that things were different. No, Jesus' presence is powerful, able to steel us to endure suffering with courage and hope, to face danger fearlessly, to respond to aggression with love.

The Lord is my helper; I will not be afraid. (Heb. 13:6)

These words, from Psalm 118:6–7, are not sweet sentimentality written from a comfortable armchair. The author of Psalm 118 has been pushed back by enemies—about to fall as they hound him to death, but in the midst of troubles he takes refuge in the assurance that the Lord is with him as his helper!

How much more we, who have seen "God With Us" walk the earth, Jesus, we who have his promised Holy Spirit living in us, should respond to change not with fear but with calm confidence that our Savior is an ever-present help in troubled times.

3. With your faith fixed firmly in Jesus, you can grow when human leaders change.

The bottom line for each of you, and for your congregation together as you move into a period of change in leadership and perhaps a heightened sense of uncertainty about what the future holds for you, is found in verse 7:

> Remember your leaders, who spoke the word of God to you. Consider the outcome of their way of life and imitate their faith. (Heb. 13:7)

When your new pastor arrives, he won't be quite like the pastor whom you have grown to love and trust, who has moved to another assignment in Christ's kingdom. He may not be as witty or clever, or as intellectually stimulating, or as gentle and nurturing, or as athletic, or as sharp a dresser, or as stirring a speaker, or as charismatic a leader. Or, for that matter, you may discover over time that his gifts and his personality are actually more to your liking than the one who preceded him. But notice what God's Word says that we are to focus upon and to remember about our pastoral leaders: they "spoke the word of God to you" and by faith they lived the word they spoke.

A. *Remember the real source of your past leaders' effectiveness: the Word of God.*

God used your pastor for good and spiritual growth in your lives not because of his humor, culture, friendliness, education, classy wardrobe, or good looks. God used him to bring you his life-giving message, the good news of Jesus. He "spoke the word of God to you"—and *that word is still with you.* Even as you may have a succession of different preachers in this pulpit over the coming months, you can and should expect that through them Jesus, "the great Shepherd of the sheep" (Heb. 13:20), will continue to speak his word to you, so that as his sheep you can hear his voice "Today" (Heb. 4:7; John 10:1–5) and hold fast to his promises.

B. *Reproduce their faith-formed example. "Consider the outcome of their way of life and imitate their faith."*

What we miss about faithful pastors when they move on is the ways in which Christ has reflected his own glory and grace to us through their living faith. Now, don't forget that! Remember it, but not just to reminisce about your former pastor or to resent God for calling him elsewhere or to compare the next pastor to your memories of the last pastor. Remember it in order to imitate the faith and the fruits of faith that you have seen in him.

And notice that here the Lord directs us to look *through* our leaders' "way of life" to their faith. He does not just say, "Do as they do, behave as they behave, try to imitate their acts of kindness, their integrity, their zeal and commitment to the cause of Christ." No, he says, "Imitate their *faith*," because it is only faith—the trust that looks outside of ourselves and rests in who Jesus is and what he has done for us—that unites us to Jesus through the power of his Holy Spirit. It is by cultivating and deepening our trust in Jesus that we can happily turn away from the past, or money, or anything else in this creation as the source of our security in times of change and say confidently, "The Lord is my helper; I will not be afraid. What can man do to me?" So as you remember your pastor, who has spoken the Word of God to you, and as you await the next shepherd that Jesus the Great Shepherd has been preparing for you, your memories of the care that you have received should trigger in your hearts a longing to grow in faith. And this longing, in turn, should stir you to nurture your faith, as Hebrews calls us to do in chapter 12, verse 2: "Let us fix our eyes on Jesus, the author and perfecter of our faith, who for the joy set before him endured the cross, scorning its shame, and sat down at the right hand of the throne of God."

Bibliography

Adams, Jay E. *Audience Adaptations in the Sermons and Speeches of Paul*. Phillipsburg: P & R, 1976.

Adams, Jay. *Preaching with Purpose: The Urgent Task of Homiletics*. Grand Rapids: Zondervan, 1982.

Adamson, James B. *James: The Man and his Message*. Grand Rapids: Eerdmans, 1989.

Alexander, T. Desmond, Brian S. Rosner, D. A. Carson, and Graeme Goldsworthy. *New Dictionary of Biblical Theology*. Downers Grove: InterVarsity, 2000.

Augustine. *On Christian Teaching*. Trans. R. P. H. Green. Oxford: Oxford University Press, 1997.

Augustine, *Quaestiones in Heptateuchum, bk. 2 Quaestiones Exodi (20, 19)* in *Corpus Christianorum, Series Latina.*, Vol. 33. Turnholti: Brepols, 1958.

Bandstra, Barry L. *Reading the Old Testament: An Introduction to the Hebrew Bible*. Belmont, California: Wadsworth, 1995.

Barker, W. S., and W. R. Godfrey, eds. *Theonomy: A Reformed Critique*. Grand Rapids: Zondervan, 1990.

Barth, Marcus. *Ephesians 1–3*. AB 34. Garden City: Doubleday, 1974.

Bauckham, Richard. *James: The Wisdom of James, Disciple of Jesus the Sage*. New York: Routledge, 1999.

Bauer, Walter, W. Arndt, and Frederick W. Danker, eds. *A Greek-English Lexicon of the New Testament and Other Early Christian Literature*. 3rd ed. Chicago: University of Chicago, 2000.

Beale, G. K. "The Old Testament Background of Paul's Reference to 'the Fruit of the Spirit' in Galatians 5:22," *Bulletin for Biblical Research* 15 (2005): 1–38.

Beale, G. K., ed. *The Right Doctrine from the Wrong Texts? Essays on the Use of the Old Testament in the New*. Grand Rapids: Baker, 1994.

Beale, G. K., *The Temple and the Church's Mission: A Biblical Theology of the Dwelling Place of God*. Downers Grove: InterVarsity, 2004.

Bergsma, Derke P. *Redemption: The Triumph of God's Great Plan*. Lansing, IL: Redeemer Books, 1989.

Blaising, Craig L., and Darrell L. Bock. *Progressive Dispensationalism*. Wheaton: Victor, 1993.

Bridges, Jerry. *The Discipline of Grace: God's Role and Our Role in the Pursuit of Holiness*. Colorado Springs: NavPress, 1994.

Brooks, Phillips. *Lectures on Preaching delivered before the Divinity School of Yale College, 1877*. New York: E. P. Dutton, 1894.

Brown, Colin, ed. *The New International Dictionary of New Testament Theology*. 3 vols. Grand Rapids: Zondervan, 1975–78.

Brown, Francis, S. R. Driver, C. A. Briggs, Edward Robinson, (based on W. Gesenius), eds. *A Hebrew and English Lexicon of the Old Testament*. 1907. Repr. Oxford: Clarendon Press, 1978.

Brown, Raymond. *The Message of Hebrews: Christ Above All*. The Bible Speaks Today. Downers Grove: InterVarsity, 1982.

Bruce, F. F. *Paul: Apostle of the Heart Set Free*. Grand Rapids: Eerdmans, 1977.

Bruce, F. F. *The Epistles to the Colossians, to Philemon, and to the Ephesians*. NICNT. Grand Rapids: Eerdmans, 1984.

Buchanan, George Wesley. *To the Hebrews*. AB 36. Garden City: Doubleday, 1972.

Bultmann, Rudolf. *Existence and Faith*. Trans. S. M. Ogden. London: Hodder & Stoughton, 1961.

Calvin, John. *Institutes of the Christian Religion*. 2 vols. Trans. F. L. Battles, ed. J. T. McNeill. Philadelphia: Westminster, 1960.

Card, Michael. *The Ancient Faith*. Audiorecording. Nashville: Myrrh, 1989.

Chapell, Bryan. *Christ-Centered Preaching: Redeeming the Expository Sermon*. 2nd ed. Grand Rapids: Baker, 2005.

Christie, Agatha, *et al. The Floating Admiral*. London: Hodder and Stoughton, 1931.

Clark, R. Scott, ed. *Covenant, Justification and Pastoral Ministry: Essays by the Faculty of Westminster Seminary California*. Phillipsburg: P & R, 2007.

Clines, D. J. A. "The Image of God in Man," *Tyndale Bulletin* 19 (1968): 53–103.

Clowney, Edmund P. *The Church*. Contours of Contemporary Theology. Downers Grove: InterVarsity, 1995.

Clowney, Edmund P. "The Final Temple" *WTJ* 35 (1973): 156–89.

Clowney, Edmund P. *Preaching and Biblical Theology*. London: Tyndale, 1962.

Clowney, Edmund P. *Preaching Christ in All of Scripture*. Wheaton: Crossway, 2003.

Clowney, Edmund P. "The Singing Savior," *Moody Monthly*, July-August 1979, 40–43.

Clowney, Edmund P. *The Unfolding Mystery: Discovering Christ in the Old Testament*. Phillipsburg: P & R, 1988.

Conn, Harvie M., ed. *Inerrancy and Hermeneutic: A Tradition, a Challenge, a Debate*. Grand Rapids: Baker, 1988.

Craigie, Peter C. *Psalms 1–50*. WBC 18. Waco: Word, 1983.

Davidson, Richard M. *Typology in Scripture: A Study of Hermeneutical Typos Structures*. Berrien Springs: Andrews University Press, 1981.

de Graaf, S. G. *Promise and Deliverance*. 4 volumes. Trans. H. E. Runner and E. W. Runner. St. Catherine's, Ontario: Paideia, 1977–1981.

DeRidder, Richard R., and Leonard J. Hofman. *Manual of Christian Reformed Church Government*. 1994 revision. Grand Rapids: CRC Publications, 1994.

Dillard, Raymond B. *Faith in the Face of Apostasy: The Gospel According to Elijah and Elisha*. Phillipsburg: P & R, 1999.

Dillard, Raymond B., and Tremper Longman III. *An Introduction to the Old Testament*. Grand Rapids: Zondervan, 1994.

Dockery, David. *Biblical Interpretation Then and Now: Contemporary Hermeneutics in the Light of the Early Church*. Grand Rapids: Baker, 1992.

Dodd, C. H. *According to the Scriptures: The Sub-Structure of New Testament Theology*. London: Nisbet, 1952.

Doriani, Daniel M. *James*. Reformed Expository Commentary. Phillipsburg: P & R, 2007.

Duguid, Iain M. *Esther and Ruth*. Reformed Expository Commentary. Phillipsburg: P & R, 2005.

Duguid, Iain M. *Living in the Gap Between Promise and Reality: The Gospel according to Abraham.* Phillipsburg: P & R, 1999.

Duguid, Iain M. *Living in the Grip of Relentless Grace: The Gospel According to Isaac and Jacob.* Phillipsburg: P & R, 2002.

Dunn, James D. G. *Unity and Diversity in the New Testament: An Inquiry into the Character of Earliest Christianity.* London: SCM, 1977.

Ellis, E. Earle. *Paul's Use of the Old Testament.* Edinburgh: Oliver and Boyd, 1957.

Enns, Peter. *Inspiration and Incarnation: Evangelicals and the Problem of the Old Testament.* Grand Rapids: Baker, 2005.

Estelle, Bryan D. *Salvation Through Judgment and Mercy: The Gospel According to Jonah.* Phillipsburg: P & R, 2005.

Fairbairn, Patrick. *Pastoral Theology: A Treatise on the Office and Duties of the Christian Pastor.* 1875. Repr. Audubon, NJ: Old Paths Publications, 1992.

Fairbairn, Patrick. *The Typology of Scripture: Viewed in Connection with the Whole Series of Divine Dispensations.* 1900. Repr. Grand Rapids: Baker, 1975.

Fee, Gordon. *New Testament Exegesis: A Handbook for Students and Pastors.* 3rd ed. Louisville: Westminster John Knox, 2001.

Fish, Henry C. *Power in the Pulpit.* 1862 article in *British and Foreign Evangelical Review.* Repr. London: Banner of Truth, n.d.

Foh, Susan T. *Women and the Word of God: A Response to Biblical Feminism.* Phillipsburg: P & R, 1979.

Frame, John M. *The Doctrine of the Knowledge of God.* Phillipsburg: P & R, 1987.

France, R. T. *Jesus and the Old Testament: His Application of Old Testament Passages to Himself and His Mission.* Downers Grove: InterVarsity, 1971.

France, R. T. *Matthew: Evangelist and Teacher.* Grand Rapids: Zondervan, 1989.

France, R. T. "The Writer of Hebrews as a Biblical Expositor," *Tyndale Bulletin* 47 (1996): 245–76.

Gadamer, Hans-Georg. *Truth and Method.* 1960. ET New York: Seabury, 1975.

Futato, Mark D. *Transformed by Praise: The Purpose and Message of the Psalms.* Phillipsburg: P & R, 2002.

Gaffin, Richard B., Jr. "Systematic Theology and Biblical Theology," *WTJ* 38 (1976): 281–99.

Gale, Herbert M. *The Use of Analogy in the Letters of Paul*. Philadelphia: Westminster, 1964.

Gamble, Richard C., and Charles G. Dennison, eds. *Pressing toward the Mark: Essays Commemorating Fifty Years of the Orthodox Presbyterian Church*. Philadelphia: Committee for the Historian, Orthodox Presbyterian Church, 1986.

Goldsworthy, Graeme. *According to Plan: The Unfolding Revelation of God in the Bible*. Leicester: InterVarsity, 1991.

Goldsworthy, Graeme. *The Goldsworthy Trilogy: Gospel and Kingdom, Gospel in Revelation, Gospel and Wisdom*. Exeter: Paternoster, 2000.

Goldsworthy, Graeme. *Preaching the Whole Bible as Christian Scripture: The Application of Bible Theology to Expository Preaching*. Grand Rapids: Eerdmans, 2000.

Goppelt, Leonhart. *Typos: The Typological Interpretation of the New Testament in the Old*. Trans. D. H. Madvig. ET Grand Rapids: Eerdmans, 1982.

Greidanus, Sidney. *The Modern Preacher and the Ancient Text: Interpreting and Preaching Biblical Literature*. Grand Rapids: Eerdmans, 1988.

Greidanus, Sidney. *Preaching Christ from the Old Testament: A Contemporary Hermeneutical Method*. Grand Rapids: Eerdmans, 1999.

Greidanus, Sidney. *Sola Scriptura: Problems and Principles in Preaching Historical Texts*. Toronto: Wedge, 1970.

Gundry, R. H. *Mark: A Commentary on His Apology for the Cross*. Grand Rapids: Eerdmans, 1993.

Hall, Christopher. *Reading Scripture with the Church Fathers*. Downers Grove: InterVarsity, 1998.

Hall, David W., and Joseph H. Hall, eds. *Paradigms in Polity: Classic Readings in Reformed and Presbyterian Church Polity*. Grand Rapids: Eerdmans, 1994.

Harrison, R. K. *Introduction to the Old Testament*. Grand Rapids: Eerdmans, 1969.

Hatch, Edwin, Henry A. Redpath, et al. *A Concordance of the Septuagint and Other Early Greek Versions of the Old Testament*. Graz: Akademische Druk- u. Verlangsanstalt, 1957.

Heidelberg Catechism (1563).

Henderson, David W. *Culture Shift: Communicating God's Truth to Our Changing World*. Grand Rapids: Baker, 1998.

Hirsch, E. D. *Validity in Interpretation.* New Haven: Yale University Press, 1967.

Hirsch, E. D. *Aims of Interpretation.* Chicago: University of Chicago, 1976.

Holladay, William L. *A Concise Hebrew and Aramaic Lexicon of the Old Testament, Based upon the Lexical Work of Ludwig Köhler and Walter Baumgartner.* Grand Rapids: Eerdmans, 1971.

Holwerda, B. *The History of Redemption in the Preaching of the Gospel.* Orange City: Mid-America Reformed Seminary, n.d. Also available online: http://www.spindleworks.com/library/holwerda/holwerda.htm.

Hughes, Graham. *Hebrews and Hermeneutics: The Epistle to the Hebrews as a New Testament Example of Biblical Interpretation.* SNTS Monograph series, 36. Cambridge: Cambridge University Press, 1979.

Hughes, John J. "Hebrews ix 15ff. and Galatians iii 15ff. A Study in Covenant Practice and Procedure," *Novum Testamentum* 21 (1979): 27-96.

Hybels, Lynne and Bill. *Rediscovering Church: The Story and Vision of Willow Creek Community Church.* Grand Rapids: Zondervan, 1995.

Johnson, Dennis E. *The Epistle to the Hebrews.* Audiotapes with study guide. Grand Rapids: Institute of Theological Studies, 1999.

Johnson, Dennis E. "Fire in God's House: Imagery from Malachi 3 in Peter's Theology of Suffering (1 Pet. 4:12–19)," *JETS* 29 (1986): 285–94.

Johnson, Dennis E. "Jesus against the Idols: The Use of Isaianic Servant Songs in the Missiology of Acts," *WTJ* 52 (1990): 343–53.

Johnson, Dennis E. *Let's Study Acts.* Edinburgh: Banner of Truth, 2003.

Johnson, Dennis E. *The Message of Acts in the History of Redemption.* Phillipsburg: P & R, 1997.

Johnson, Dennis E. "Spiritual Antithesis, Common Grace, and Practical Theology," *WTJ* 64 (2002): 73-94.

Johnson, Dennis E. *Triumph of the Lamb: A Commentary on Revelation.* Phillipsburg: P & R, 2001.

Johnson, S. Lewis. *The Old Testament in the New: An Argument for Biblical Inspiration.* Grand Rapids: Zondervan, 1980.

Jones, Peter R. "1 Corinthians 15:8: Paul the Last Apostle," *Tyndale Bulletin* 36 (1985): 3–34.

Jones, Peter R. "Paul Confronts Paganism in the Church: A Case Study of First Corinthians 15:45," *JETS* 49 (2006): 699–711.

Jones, Peter R. *Spirit Wars: Pagan Revival in Christian America*. Mulkiteo, Washington: Winepress, 1997.

Kaiser, Walter C., Jr. *Preaching and Teaching from the Old Testament: A Guide for the Church*. Grand Rapids: Baker, 2003.

Kaiser, Walter C., Jr. *Toward an Exegetical Theology: Biblical Exegesis for Teaching and Preaching*. Grand Rapids: Baker, 1981.

Kaiser, Walter C., Jr., and Moisés Silva, *An Introduction to Biblical Hermeneutics: The Search for Meaning*. Grand Rapids: Zondervan, 1994.

Keller, Timothy. "The Centrality of the Gospel". Available online at: http://www.redeemer2.com/resources/papers/centrality.pdf.

Keller, Timothy. Email to Dennis Johnson, July 13, 1999.

Keller, Timothy. "The Missional Church" (June 2001). Available online at: http://www.redeemer2.com/resources/papers/missional.pdf.

Keller, Timothy. "A Model for Preaching," parts 1, 2, 3, *The Journal of Biblical Counseling* 12.3 (Spring 1994): 36–42; 13.1 (Fall 1994): 39–48; 13.2 (Winter 1995): 51–60.

Kelly, J. N. D. *Golden Mouth: The Story of John Chrysostom—Ascetic, Preacher, Bishop*. 1995; repr. Grand Rapids: Baker, 1998.

Kittel, Gerhard, and Gerhard Friedrich, eds. *Theological Dictionary of the New Testament*. Trans. and ed. Geofffrey W. Bromiley. 10 vols. Grand Rapids: Eerdmans, 1964–1976.

Kline, M. G. *By Oath Consigned: A Reinterpretation of the Covenant Signs of Circumcision and Baptism*. Grand Rapids: Eerdmans, 1968.

Kline, Meredith G. *Glory in our Midst: A Biblical-Theological Reading of Zechariah's Night Visions*. Overland Park, Kansas: Two Age Press, 2001.

Kline, Meredith G. *Images of the Spirit*. Grand Rapids: Baker, 1980.

Kline, Meredith G. *Kingdom Prologue*. South Hamilton, Massachusetts: self published, 1991. [*Kingdom Prologue*]

Kline, Meredith G. *Kingdom Prologue: Genesis Foundations for a Covenantal Worldview*. Overland Park, KS: Two Age Press, 2000. [*Kingdom Prologue (2000)*]

Kline, Meredith G. *The Structure of Biblical Authority*. Grand Rapids: Eerdmans, 1972.

Kline, Meredith G. *Treaty of the Great King: The Covenant Structure of Deuteronomy: Studies and Commentary*. Grand Rapids: Eerdmans, 1963.

Köhler, Ludwig, Walter Baumgartner, J. J. Stamm, and M. E. J. and Richardson, *The Hebrew and Aramaic Lexicon of the Old Testament*. Leiden: Brill, 2001.

Kuiper, R. B. *The Glorious Body of Christ: A Scriptural Appreciation of the One Holy Church*. London: Banner of Truth, 1966.

Kümmel, Werner Georg. *The New Testament: The History of the Investigation of Its Problems*. Nashville: Abingdon, 1970.

Kümmel, Werner Georg. *The Theology of the New Testament*. Nashville: Abingdon, 1973.

Lampe, G. W. H., and K. J. Woollcombe. *Essays on Typology*. Studies in Biblical Theology. Naperville: Alec R. Allenson, 1957.

Lane, William. *Hebrews 1–8* and *Hebrews 9–13*. WBC 47A, 47B. Waco: Word, 1991.

LaRondelle, Hans K. *The Israel of God in Prophecy: Principles of Prophetic Interpretation*. Berrien Springs: Andrews University Press, 1983.

Laws, Sophie. *A Commentary on the Epistle of James*. HNTC. San Francisco: Harper & Row, 1980.

Léon-Dufour, Xavier, ed. *Dictionary of the New Testament*. Trans. P. Joseph Cahill. New York: Seabury, 1973.

Lewis, C. S. *The Weight of Glory and Other Addresses*. 1949. Repr. Grand Rapids: Eerdmans, 1965.

Lincoln, Andrew T. *Ephesians*. WBC 42. Waco: Word, 1990.

Lloyd-Jones, D. Martyn. *Spiritual Depression: Its Causes and Cure*. Grand Rapids: Eerdmans, 1965.

Logan, Samuel T. Jr., ed. *The Preacher and Preaching: Reviving the Art in the Twentieth Century*. Phillipsburg: P & R, 1986.

Long, Thomas G. *Preaching and the Literary Forms of the Bible*. Philadelphia: Fortress, 1989.

Longenecker, Richard N. *Biblical Exegesis in the Apostolic Period*. Grand Rapids: Eerdmans, 1975.

Longenecker, Richard N. "Can We Reproduce the Exegesis of the New Testament?" *Tyndale Bulletin* 21 (1970): 3–38.

Longenecker, Richard N. *Galatians*. WBC 41. Waco: Word, 1990.

Longman, Tremper III, and Daniel G. Reid. *God is a Warrior*. Grand Rapids: Zondervan, 1995.

Longman, Tremper III. *How to Read Genesis*. Downers Grove: Inter-Varsity, 2005.

Longman, Tremper III. *How to Read Proverbs*. Downers Grove: InterVarsity, 2002.

Longman, Tremper III. *How to Read the Psalms*. Downers Grove: InterVarsity, 1988.

Longman, Tremper III. *Immanuel in Our Place: Seeing Christ in Israel's Worship*. Phillipsburg: P & R, 2001.

Longman, Tremper III., *Literary Approaches to Biblical Interpretation*. Foundations of Contemporary Interpretation, vol. 3. Grand Rapids: Zondervan, 1987.

Louw, Johannes P., and Eugene A. Nida, eds. *A Greek-English Lexicon of the New Testament: Based on Semantic Domains*. 2nd ed. 2 vols. New York: United Bible Societies, 1988.

Marshall, I. Howard. *The Gospel of Luke: A Commentary on the Greek Text*. NIGTC. Grand Rapids: Eerdmans, 1978.

Marshall, I. Howard., ed. *New Testament Interpretation: Essays on Principles and Methods*. Grand Rapids: Eerdmans, 1977.

Martin, Ralph P. *James*. WBC 48. Waco: Word, 1988.

Mawhinney, Allen. "The Structural Function of the Major Old Testament Quotations in the Epistle to the Hebrews" [unpublished paper].

McCartney, Dan G. "The Wisdom of James the Just," *Southern Baptist Journal of Theology* 4.3 (Fall 2000): 52–64.

McCartney, Dan, and Charles Clayton. *Let the Reader Understand: A Guide to Interpreting and Applying the Bible*. Wheaton: Victor, 1994.

McLaren, Brian D. *A Generous Orthodoxy: Why I am a Missional, Evangelical, Post/Protestant, Liberal/Conservative, Mystical/Poetic, Biblical, Charismatic/Contemplative, Fundamentalist/Calvinist, Anabaptist/Anglican, Methodist, Catholic, Green, Incarnational, Depressed-Yet-Hopeful, Emergent, Unfinished Christian*. Grand Rapids: Zondervan, 2004.

McGavran, Donald. *Understanding Church Growth*. Grand Rapid: Eerdmans, 1970.

Miller, Calvin. *Marketplace Preaching: How to Return the Sermon to Where It Belongs*. Grand Rapids: Baker, 1995.

Miller, C. John. *Outgrowing the Ingrown Church*. Grand Rapids: Zondervan, 1986.

Minear, Paul S. *Images of the Church in the New Testament*. Philadelphia: Westminster, 1960.

Morris, Leon. *The Gospel according to St. Luke: An Introduction and Commentary*. TNTC. Grand Rapids: Eerdmans, 1974.

Morrish, George. *A Concordance to the Septuagint*. Grand Rapids: Zondervan, 1976.

Murray, John. "Systematic Theology (Second Article)," *WTJ* 26 (1963–4): 33–46.

Murren, Doug. *Baby Boomerang: Catching the Boomer Generation as They Return to Church*. Ventura: Regal, 1990.

Nestle, Eberhard, Erwin Nestle, Kurt and Barbara Aland, *et al, Novum Testamentum Graece*. 27th ed. Stuttgart: Deutsche Bibelgesellschaft, 1993.

Newbigin, Lesslie. *Foolishness to the Greeks: The Gospel and Western Culture*. Grand Rapids: Eerdmans, 1986.

Noll, Mark A. *The Scandal of the Evangelical Mind*. Grand Rapids: Eerdmans, 1994.

O'Brien, Peter T. *Colossians, Philemon*. WBC 44. Waco: Word, 1982.

O'Brien, Peter T. *The Letter to the Ephesians*. Grand Rapids: Eerdmans, 1999.

Oden, Thomas C., gen. ed. *Ancient Christian Commentary on Scripture*. Downers Grove: InterVarsity, 1998—.

O'Keefe, John J., and R. R. Reno. *Sanctified Vision: An Introduction to Early Christian Interpretation of the Bible*. Baltimore: Johns Hopkins University Press, 2005.

Old, Hughes Oliphant. *The Reading and Preaching of the Scriptures in the Worship of the Christian Church*. Vols. 1–6. Grand Rapids: Eerdmans, 1998–2007.

Ortlund, Raymond C., Jr. *God's Unfaithful Wife: A Biblical Theology of Spiritual Adultery*. New Studies in Bible Theology. Downers Grove: InterVarsity, 2003.

Phillips, Richard D. *Hebrews*. Reformed Expository Commentary. Phillipsburg: P & R, 2006.

Phillips, Richard D. *Zechariah*. Reformed Expository Commentary. Phillipsburg: P & R, 2007.

Powlison, David. "Idols of the Heart and Vanity Fair," *Journal of Biblical Counseling* 13.2 (Winter 1995): 35–50.

Poythress, Vern S. *God-Centered Biblical Interpretation*. Phillipsburg: P & R, 1999.

Poythress, Vern S. "Procedure for a Biblical-Theological Exposition of a New Testament Text." Unpublished class handout. Westminster Theological Seminary, ca. 1978.

Poythress, Vern S. *The Shadow of Christ in the Law of Moses*. Phillipsburg: P & R, 1995.

Poythress, Vern S. *Understanding Dispensationalists*. Grand Rapids: Zondervan, 1991.

Pratt, Richard L., gen. ed. *Spirit of the Reformation Study Bible*. Grand Rapids: Zondervan, 2003.

Pritchard, G. A. *Willow Creek Seeker Services: Evaluating a New Way of Doing Church*. Grand Rapids: Baker, 1996.

Rahlfs, Alfred, *et al*, eds. *Septuaginta*. Stuttgart: Würteembergische Bibelanstalt, 1935, 1979.

Reicke, Bo. *The Epistles of James, Peter, and Jude*. AB 37. Garden City, NY: Doubleday, 1964.

Ridderbos, Herman. *The Coming of the Kingdom*. Philadelphia: Presbyterian & Reformed, 1962.

Ridderbos, Herman. *Paul: An Outline of his Theology*. Trans. John R. de Witt. Grand Rapids: Eerdmans, 1975.

Roberts, J. A., and A. B. du Toit, *Guide to the New Testament*. Vol. 1. Trans. D. Roy Briggs. 2nd ed. Pretoria: N. G. Kerkboekhandel Transvaal, 1985.

Robertson, O. Palmer. *The Christ of the Covenants*. Phillipsburg: P & R, 1980.

Robertson, O. Palmer. *The Christ of the Prophets*. Phillipsburg: P & R, 2004.

Robertson, O. Palmer. "Procedure for a Biblical-Theological Exposition of an O.T. Text." Unpublished class handout. Westminster Theological Seminary, ca. 1971.

Ryken, Leland, James C. Wilhoit, and Tremper Longman III, eds. *Dictionary of Biblical Imagery*. Downers Grove: InterVarsity, 1998.

Ryken, Philip Graham. *Galatians*. Reformed Expository Commentary. Phillipsburg: P & R, 2005.

Ryken, Philip Graham. *1 Timothy*. Reformed Expository Commentary. Phillipsburg: P & R, 2007.

Saucy, Robert L. *The Case for Progressive Dispensationalism: The Interface between Dispensational and Non-dispensational Theology*. Grand Rapids: Zondervan, 1993.

Schnittjer, Gary Edward. "The Narrative Multiverse within the Universe of the Bible: The Question of 'Borderlines' and 'Intertextuality,' " *WTJ* 64 (2002): 231–52.

Second Helvetic Confession (1566).

Silva, Moisés. *Has the Church Misread the Bible? The History of Interpretation in the Light of Current Issues.* Foundations of Contemporary Interpretation, vol. 1. Grand Rapids: Zondervan, 1987.

Skilton, John H., ed. *The New Testament Student and Theology.* The New Testament Student, vol. 3. Phillipsburg: P & R, 1976.

Sproul, R. C., gen. ed. *New Geneva Study Bible.* Nashville: Thomas Nelson, 1995.

Sproul, R. C., gen. ed. *Reformation Study Bible.* Orlando: Ligonier Ministries, 2004.

Spurgeon, Charles H. "Christ Precious to Believers" (March 13, 1859). Accessed online: http://www.spurgeon.org/sermons/0242.htm.

Stein, Robert H. *Luke.* NAC. Nashville: Broadman, 1992.

Stuart, Douglas. *Old Testament Exegesis: A Handbook for Students and Pastors,* 3rd ed. Louisville: Westminster John Knox, 2001.

Swanson, Scott A. "Can We Reproduce the Exegesis of the New Testament? Why Are We Still Asking?" *Trinity Journal* 17 (1996): 67–76. Accessed online: http.//www.bible-researcher.com/swanson.html.

Taylor, Barbara Brown. *Speaking of Sin: The Lost Language of Salvation.* Cambridge, Massachusetts: Cowley, 2000.

Trimp, C. *Preaching and the History of Salvation: Continuing an Unfinished Discussion.* Trans. N. D. Kloosterman. Scarsdale, NY: Westminster Book Service, 1996.

United Reformed Churches of North America. Church Order. 2nd ed. Available online: http://www.covenant-urc.org/urcna/co.html.

VanGemeren, Willem, ed. *New International Dictionary of Old Testament Theology and Exegesis.* Grand Rapids: Zondervan, 1997.

VanGemeren, Willem. *The Progress of Redemption: The Story of Salvation from Creation to New Jerusalem* (Grand Rapids: Baker, 1988).

Vanhoozer, Kevin J. *Is There a Meaning in This Text? The Bible, the Reader, and the Morality of Literary Knowledge.* Grand Rapids: Zondervan, 1998.

Van't Veer, M. B. "Christological Preaching of Historical Materials of the Old Testament," Parts 1 and 2. Available online at http://

www.spindleworks.com/library/veer/veer.html, and http://
www.spindleworks.com/library/veer/veer2.html.

Veyne, Paul, ed. *A History of Private Life*. Vol. 1. *From Pagan Rome to Byzantium*. Trans. Arthur Goldhammer. Cambridge, Massachusetts: Belknap Press/Harvard University Press, 1987.

Vos, Geerhardus. *Biblical Theology: Old and New Testaments*. Grand Rapids: Eerdmans, 1948.

Vos, Geerhardus. *The Eschatology of the Old Testament*. Edited by James T. Dennison, Jr. Phillipsburg: P & R, 2001.

Vos, Geerhardus. *Grace and Glory: Sermons Preached in the Chapel of Princeton Theological Seminary*. Edinburgh: Banner of Truth, 1994.

Vos, Geerhardus. *The Pauline Eschatology*. Princeton: Princeton University Press, 1930.

Vos, Geerhardus. *Redemptive History and Biblical Interpretation: The Shorter Writings of Geerhardus Vos*. Edited by R. B. Gaffin, Jr., Phillipsburg: P & R, 1980.

Vos, Geerhardus. *The Self-Disclosure of Jesus: The Modern Debate about the Messianic Consciousness*. Phillipsburg: P & R, 1953.

Vos, Geerhardus. *The Teaching of Jesus concerning the Kingdom of God and the Church*. New York: American Tract Society, 1903.

Vos, Geerhardus. *The Teaching of the Epistle to the Hebrews*. 1956; repr. Phillipsburg: P & R, 1972.

Wagner, Roger. *Tongues Aflame: Learning to Preach from the Apostles*. Fearn: Mentor, 2004.

Wells, David F., ed. *Reformed Theology in America: A History of its Modern Development*. Grand Rapids: Eerdmans, 1985.

Westminster Confession of Faith, Larger and Shorter Catechisms (1646).

Whitefield, George. *Select Sermons of George Whitefield*. London: Banner of Truth, 1958.

Webster, Douglas D. *Selling Jesus: What's Wrong with Marketing the Church*. Downers Grove: InterVarsity, 1992.

Wilken, Robert L. *Remembering the Christian Past*. Grand Rapids: Eerdmans, 1995.

Williams, David J. *Paul's Metaphors: Their Context and Character*. Peabody, Massachusetts: Hendrickson, 1999.

Williams, Neil H. *The Theology of Sonship*. Jenkintown: World Harvest Mission, 2002.

Willimon, William H. *Peculiar Speech: Preaching to the Baptized*. Grand Rapids: Eerdmans, 1992.

Wolfe, Tom. *The Bonfire of the Vanities*. New York: Farrar, Straus, and
    Giroux, 1987.
Wright, Christopher J. H. *Knowing Jesus through the Old Testament*.
    Downers Grove: InterVarsity, 1992.
Yancey, Philip. *The Bible Jesus Read*. Grand Rapids: Zondervan, 1999.
Young, Edward J. *An Introduction to the Old Testament*. Grand Rap-
    ids: Eerdmans, 1964.

Index of Scripture

37:26–27—310
37:34–35—310
39:4—94
39:8–9—344
41:1–7—384n61
41:17–32—384n61
41:40–45—94
44:16—310
48:15—225
49:24—225

Exodus
3:2–7—389n68
3:13–15—389n68
6:10–11—300
8:7–10—181, 300
12:22—221
12:25–27—413
12:27—295
12:46—209
13:14–15—296
13:14–16—414
13:21–22—211, 318
17:1–7—204, 211
19—210
19:4—393
19:16–23—180
20:2—267
20:6—379
20:16—363
21–23—281n20
21:30—326n59
22—291
22:28—289
23:19—375
23:20—337, 341
24:6–8—255
25:9—220
25:40—220

29:9—190n25
29:18—364n33
29:22—190n25
29:25—364n33
29:26—190n25
29:27—190n25
29:29—190n25
29:33—326n59
29:41—364n33
30:12—326n59
30:22–33—221
32:11–13—300
35:30–35—84
40:34–35—77
40:34–38—318
40:35—213

Leviticus
1:2—356
1:3—356
1:9ff.—364n33
1:10—356
2:2ff.—364n33
3:1—356
3:3—356
3:5ff.—364n33
3:7—356
4:31—364n33
5:24—189n24
8:12—221
8:33—190n25
14:4–7—221
16—159
16:1–34—158
16:32—190n25
18–20—281n20
18:5—301
19:13—283n22
19:18—280, 283n22

20:11—281
21:10—190n25
23:9–14—375
23:28—326n59
24–25—281n20

Numbers
3:3—190n25
4:2—190n24
5:7—190n24
6:23–27—370n42
14:1ff.—426
15—364n33
16:28–33—314
18:11–13—376
21:4–9—210
25:11–13—228
26:10–11—314
28—364n33
29—364n33
31:26—190n24
31:29—190n24
35:30—286
35:31–32—326n59

Deuteronomy
1–4—267
1:1–5—155, 179,
  284, 295, 301,
  322, 369
1:6–4:49—295
1:9—72, 84, 92, 210,
  290, 318, 338,
  357, 368, 372,
  374, 379–80, 382
1:12–15—357, 377
3:1–2—341, 352,
  357, 392–93
4:1—298

13:15—269
13:15-16—191,
  265, 269
13:16—172, 188,
  196, 262
13:17—160, 188,
  195, 425
13:19—173, 172n5
13:20—184n21,
  185-86, 192,
  428, 431
13:20-21—428
13:22—41,
  171, 172n5,
  174n11, 174
13:23—173
13:24—192n27
15:8-11—172

James
1:1—173n7, 192,
  367, 370-71
1:1-2—368, 369, 378
1:2—376, 376n52
1:2-3—376n52
1:2-18—193, 376
1:3—369
1:4—369
1:5—380, 369
1:5-8—191, 368, 375
1:6—368, 369
1:9—376n52,
  372, 374
1:9-11—368,
  374, 380
1:10—368
1:12—367, 369,
  372, 376, 376n52,
  377-79, 381, 382

1:12-14—378
1:12-18—367, 377
1:13—369, 378, 379
1:13-15—380
1:13-16—377
1:13-18—377
1:15—377
1:16—373, 379
1:17—210, 312, 375,
  377, 379, 382
1:17-18—210,
  377, 382
1:18—375-76,
  377, 380, 382
1:19-21—351, 373
1:20—293
1:22—373
1:22-25—364,
  373, 398
1:22-26—364, 368
1:23—368
1:25—373-74
1:26—373
2:1—370, 371, 375
2:1-13—368-69,
  369n38
2:2—173n7
2:5—368, 373,
  374, 380
2:6-7—369
2:7—370n42
2:8—373, 374
2:8-11—280
2:8-13—374
2:10—373
2:12—140, 205, 374
2:13—374
2:14-26—368,
  369n38, 373

2:19—294
2:26—368
3:1-12—341, 352,
  369n38, 373, 392
3:3-12—368
3:9—250
3:12—380
3:13-18—368, 373
3:15—380
3:17-18—380
4:6—368, 373
4:6-10—211,
  368, 374
4:10—89, 375
4:11-12—373
4:13-17—176,
  193, 369
4:17—373
5:1-6—369
5:4—283n22
5:5—372
5:6—372, 381
5:7—372
5:7-8—368, 372
5:7-11—376n52
5:8-9—372
5:10—53
5:17-18—53

1 Peter
1:1—192, 284, 301
1:1-5—284, 301
1:2—206
1:3—375
1:4—299
1:10-12—80,
  160, 206
1:11—219
1:12—205, 219

Index of Personal Names and Titles

Index of Subjects

Recommended Resources for
Preaching Christ from All the Scriptures

Chapell, Bryan. *Christ-Centered Preaching: Redeeming the Expository Sermon*, 2nd ed. Grand Rapids: Baker, 2005.

Clowney, Edmund P. *Preaching and Biblical Theology*. Grand Rapids: Eerdmans, 1961. Reprint, Phillipsburg: P&R Publishing, 2002.

Clowney, Edmund P. *Preaching Christ in All of Scripture*. Wheaton: Crossway, 2003.

Clowney, Edmund P. *The Unfolding Mystery: Discovering Christ in the Old Testament*. Colorado Springs: NavPress, 1988. Reprint, Phillipsburg: P&R Publishing, 1991.

Clowney, Edmund P. *How Jesus Transforms the Ten Commandments*. Phillipsburg: P&R Publishing, 2007.

Drew, Charles D. *The Ancient Love Song: Finding Christ in the Old Testament*. Phillipsburg: P&R Publishing, 2000.

Graeme Goldsworthy. *According to Plan: The Unfolding Revelation of God in The Bible*. Downers Grove: InterVarsity, 1991.

Goldsworthy, Graeme. *Preaching the Whole Bible as Christian Scripture: The Application of Bible Theology to Expository Preaching*. Grand Rapids: Eerdmans, 2000.

Johnson, Dennis E. *The Message of Acts in the History of Redemption*. Phillipsburg: P&R Publishing, 1997.

Johnson, Dennis E. *Triumph of the Lamb: A Commentary on Revelation*. Phillipsburg: P&R Publishing, 2001.

Kline, Meredith G. *Glory in Our Midst: A Biblical-theological Reading of Zechariah's Night Visions*. Overland Park, Kansas: Two Age Press, 2001.

Kline, Meredith G. *Images of the Spirit*. Eugene, Oregon: Wipf & Stock, 1999.

Kline, Meredith G. *Kingdom Prologue: Genesis Foundations for a Covenantal Worldview*. Eugene, Oregon: Wipf & Stock, 2006.

Logan, Samuel T. Jr., ed. *The Preacher and Preaching: Reviving the Art*. Phillipsburg: P&R Publishing, 1986.

Poythress, Vern S. *The Shadow of Christ in the Law of Moses*. Phillipsburg: P&R Publishing, 1991.

Pratt, Richard L. Jr. *He Gave Us Stories*. Brentwood, TN: Wolgemuth & Hyatt, 1990. Reprint, Phillipsburg: P&R Publishing, 1993.

Ridderbos, Herman. *Coming of the Kingdom*. Trans. H. de Jongste, ed. Raymond O. Zorn. Philadelphia: Presbyterian and Reformed Publishing Company, 1962.

Ridderbos, Herman. *Paul: An Outline of His Theology*. Tr. John R. de Witt. Grand Rapids: Eerdmans, 1975.

Robertson, O. Palmer. *The Christ of the Covenants*. Phillipsburg: P&R Publishing, 1980.

Robertson, O. Palmer. *The Christ of the Prophets*. Phillipsburg: P&R Publishing, 2004.

Vos, Geerhardus. *Biblical Theology: Old and New Testaments*. Edinburgh: Banner of Truth, 1996.

Vos, Geerhardus. *Eschatology of the Old Testament*. James T. Dennison Jr., ed. Phillipsburg: P&R Publishing, 2001.

Vos, Geerhardus. *Pauline Eschatology*. Phillipsburg: P&R Publishing, 2001.

Vos, Geerhardus. *Redemptive History and Biblical Interpretation*. Richard B. Gaffin Jr., ed. Phillipsburg: P&R Publishing, 2001.

Vos, Geerhardus. *The Teaching of Jesus concerning the Kingdom of God and the Church*. 1903. Repr. Eugene: Wipf & Stock, 1999.

Vos, Geerhardus. *The Teaching of the Epistle to the Hebrews*. 1956; repr. Eugene: Wipf & Stock, 1999.

The Gospel According to the Old Testament

Boda, Mark J. *After God's Own Heart: The Gospel According to David*. The Gospel According to the Old Testament. Phillipsburg: P&R Publishing, 2007.

Dillard, Raymond B. *Faith in the Face of Apostasy: The Gospel According to Elijah & Elisha*. The Gospel According to the Old Testament. Phillipsburg: P&R Publishing, 1999.

Duguid, Iain M. *Living in the Gap Between Promise and Reality: The Gospel According to Abraham*. The Gospel According to the Old Testament. Phillipsburg: P&R Publishing, 1999.

Duguid, Iain M. *Living in the Grip of Relentless Grace: The Gospel According to Isaac & Jacob*. The Gospel According to the Old Testament. Phillipsburg: P&R Publishing, 2002.

Estelle, Bryan D. *Salvation Through Judgment and Mercy: The Gospel According to Jonah*. The Gospel According to the Old Testament. Phillipsburg: P&R Publishing, 2005.

Jackson, David R. *Crying Out for Vindication: The Gospel According to Job*. The Gospel According to the Old Testament. Phillipsburg: P&R Publishing, 2007.

Longman, Tremper III. *Immanuel in Our Place: Seeing Christ in Israel's Worship*. The Gospel According to the Old Testament. Phillipsburg: P&R Publishing, 2001.

Schwab, George M. *Hope in the Midst of a Hostile World: The Gospel According to Daniel*. The Gospel According to the Old Testament. Phillipsburg: P&R Publishing, 2006.

Reformed Expository Commentary Series

Doriani, Daniel M. *James*. Reformed Expository Commentary. Phillipsburg: P&R Publishing, 2007.

Duguid, Iain M. *Esther and Ruth*. Reformed Expository Commentary. Phillipsburg: P&R Publishing, 2005.

Phillips, Richard D. *Hebrews*. Reformed Expository Commentary. Phillipsburg: P&R Publishing, 2006.

Phillips, Richard D. *Zechariah*. Reformed Expository Commentary. Phillipsburg: P&R Publishing, 2007.

Ryken, Philip Graham. *1 Timothy*. Reformed Expository Commentary. Phillipsburg: P&R Publishing, 2007.

Ryken, Philip Graham. *Galatians*. Reformed Expository Commentary. Phillipsburg: P&R Publishing, 2005.

Dennis E. Johnson (ThM, Westminster Theological Seminary; PhD, Fuller Theological Seminary) is professor of practical theology at Westminster Seminary California. He is also an ordained minister in the Presbyterian Church in America, author of *The Message of Acts in the History of Redemption,* and a contributor to numerous books and theological journals.